Fiction and Drama
in Eastern and
Southeastern Europe

Evolution and Experiment
in the Postwar Period

Proceedings of the 1978 UCLA Conference

edited by
Henrik Birnbaum and Thomas Eekman

Slavica Publishers, Inc.
1980

For a list of some other Slavica books, see the last pages of this one; for a complete catalog with prices and ordering information, write to:
Slavica Publishers, Inc.
P.O. Box 14388
Columbus, Ohio 43214

ISBN: 0-89357-064-8.

Typography by Brevis Press, Cheshire, Connecticut 06410.

Printed in the United States of America.

CONTENTS

PREFACE

All twenty-nine papers published in this volume were originally written for presentation and discussion at an international conference concerned with tradition and innovation as manifested in prose writing and theater in East Central Europe, the Soviet Union, and the Balkans since the Second World War. The conference, the sixth in a series of similar scholarly endeavors, was organized by the UCLA Center for Russian and East European Studies and was held on the premises of the UCLA campus and at the University of California Conference Center at Lake Arrowhead, 30 March through 2 April, 1978. Three papers presented at the conference (by Professors Olga R. Hughes, UC Berkeley; Alexander Stephan, UCLA; and Joseph Škvorecký, University of Toronto) are not included here as they were committed for publication elsewhere or will appear in a different context for other reasons. Some of the scholars originally invited to the conference were unable to attend; in one instance, an initial acceptance was subsequently canceled. This circumstance, among others, accounts for a certain imbalance in coverage and assessment reflected in the contributions of the present volume. Two papers, those of Professors Głowiński and Winner, were not actually presented at the conference, but the editors (who also acted as the organizers of the conference) asked and received the authors' permission to include them in the volume as submitted, that is, without the benefit of discussion and possible modification.

In preparing this volume for publication the editors did not strive for uniformity in spelling, transliteration, bibliographical references, etc. Instead, a maximum of internal consistency in matters of style and format was attempted within each contribution. Arrangements were made to have papers presented in other languages translated into English.

When conceiving the conference whose results are presented here, the organizers, convinced of the significance of relevant postwar phenomena and developments in Eastern and Southeastern Europe, hoped for a balanced, many-sided treatment. It lies in the nature of the subject matter that this goal could only be achieved to a limited extent and with some substantial qualifications. Available expertise was somewhat unevenly distributed and some points of view are therefore less well represented than was intended.

Most of the twenty-nine papers included — twenty-five, to be exact — address some specific issue, often (in eighteen cases) as found in the writings of one particular author or even in one single work; moreover, in one instance, the set of literary phenomena and problems discussed is viewed through the prism of the creative interpretation not of a man of letters but of a film and theater director — Andrzej Wajda. Four papers offer broad surveys of and commentaries on the relevant literary output in various countries — Poland, Yugoslavia (in Serbo-Croatian and Slovene), Romania, and Soviet Lithuania — rather than focusing on any particular theme, writer, or piece. Only one paper approaches Eastern and Southeastern Europe as a whole (tracing a Western influence), and one gives a comparison between writers on the Soviet Russian and Czech literary scene. The vast majority of contributions remain within the confines of the literature of one country and usually also one language: nine deal with postwar fiction and/or drama in Russian (or, exceptionally, the contemporary reception of prewar Russian) prose writing, four with Polish literature, four with one or several of the literatures of Yugoslavia, three with writing in Czech, two with German (as represented by work produced in the German Democratic Republic), two with Romanian, and one each with Hungarian, Bulgarian, and Lithuanian literature. The editors are aware, of course, that several countries and languages are not represented at all in this volume: Ukrainian, Belorussian, Slovak, Macedonian, Sorbian, as well as Albanian, Estonian, Latvian, and Yiddish, to mention the obvious. And clearly, not all literatures discussed here are necessarily represented by their most significant or typical works. Major gaps and omissions were thus unavoidable.

Despite these imponderables, the volume offers a broad panorama of some of the most interesting aspects of prose and drama writing in the eastern half of Europe during more than three decades. That there is a certain emphasis on the experimental, avant-garde authors and their work (approximately twelve contributions deal with some form of modernism) is understandable: this is the direction in which many of the creative and inventive minds among the writers went in the fifties and sixties. At the same time, however, realism continued to be a vigorous trend, but in new shapes, settings, and styles, expanding its shores almost infinitely. The contemporary East-Central and East European writers are torn between a single social philosophy that imposes itself forcefully and often inexorably, and a variety of other philosophies. Sartre, Honegger, and Bloch are some of the important influences that eclipsed Nietzsche, Bergson, Freud, and others who had made their impact on previous generations. The writers either comply with the demand of the prevailing socio-political order and ideology, or they try cautiously to find a *modus vivendi*, preserving a maximum of their integrity. Some flatly oppose the system and can express themselves only during a rare liberal spell, or after leaving their country. Whatever the writers' attitudes, virtually all of them attempt in one way or another to incorporate new themes, moods, values, and techniques in their work. This is true both of the older authors with an established position in prewar literature (such as Andrić, Brecht, Gombrowicz, Eliade, Pasternak) and of those belonging to one of the postwar generations who "move forward," but whose "backward glances" — ties with some aspect of the past — are often more than obvious. In several papers it has been demonstrated how closely even the avant-gardists were related to prewar tendencies and personalities, to the surrealists and futurists, Kafka and Witkie-wicz, but also to Gogol' or the romantic poets.

Just as the prose and stage works discussed offer a wide variety of literary creativity — from rational and logical to absurdist and schizophrenic — so the methods and approaches of the various contributors are diverse, too. There can hardly be any doubt that the Russian Formalists, the Prague School, Jakobson, Bakhtin, and Lotman have decidedly influenced and channeled the thinking, methodology, and even terminology of contemporary literary schol-arship. And this precisely is evinced in the present volume.

The editors feel that, all obvious qualifications and imposed limitations notwithstanding, the papers gathered here offer something novel and signifi-cant, attesting to the richness, liveliness, and diversity of today's literary creativity in Central, Eastern, and Southeastern Europe. They are particu-larly gratified that the proceedings of this conference can appear as the first volume in the newly launched series *UCLA Slavic Studies,* published under the auspices of the UCLA Department of Slavic Languages and Literatures.

Los Angeles, December 1978   Henrik Birnbaum
                                                  Thomas Eekman

ACKNOWLEDGMENTS

The conference and resulting publication were made possible by generous support received from several sources. A grant from the James B. Duke Endowment Fund (administered by the Dean of the College of Letters and Science, UCLA) helped defray initial organizational costs as well as travel and subsistence expenses for out-of-town American and Canadian participants of the conference; it also provided a subsidy toward publishing the conference proceedings. Travel and local expenses incurred by attending foreign scholars were offset by grants received from the International Board of Research and Exchanges (IREX) and the American Council of Learned Societies (ACLS). The UCLA Center for Russian and East European Studies, in addition to recommending the use of Duke funds for this purpose, absorbed further expenses by making some of its highly qualified staff, notably, Dr. Dorothy Disterheft and Ms. Elise Kroll, available to assist in editorial work and local arrangements. Last but not least, Slavica Publishers, Inc., headed by Professor Charles E. Gribble, kindly agreed to the swift production of this volume. The conference organizers and editors wish to take this opportunity to express their sincere thanks to the above mentioned organizations and persons.

H. B.   T. E.

Michel Aucouturier

WRITER AND TEXT IN THE WORKS OF ABRAM TERC
(An ontology of writing and a poetics of prose)

Written several years apart, Abram Terc's two long stories (*povesti*), *Sud idët* (*The Trial Begins*, 1956) and *Ljubimov* (*The Makepeace Experiment*, 1962–63) show a certain progression. The first, in spite of "expressionist" traits perhaps reminiscent of Zamjatin, depends, as a whole, on a realistic esthetic: the events described stay within the bounds of the believable. The second, on the contrary, belongs entirely to the realm of the fantastic tale or allegorical fable (one thinks of Saltykov-Ščedrin and his "Istorija odnogo goroda"). But in spite of this difference of genre, they have in common one basic trait, which appears as Terc's poetical signature, his "Apelles' mark": the presence of a narrator, and his complex and ambiguous relationship with the work's subject-matter.

Sud idët is the story of several failures: that of the prosecutor Globov, the stalinist for whom communism is a religious faith, and who finds within his immediate family symptoms of the moral and political disorder he is sworn to suppress; that of his son Serëža, arrested and convicted for wanting to return to the original principles of the revolution; that of the brilliant, but cynical lawyer Karlinskij, who does not believe in communism, and unsuccessfully tries to avoid the anguish of existence and the obsession of death through the pursuit of a woman, Globov's wife, Marina.

These failures coincide chronologically with the death of Stalin, which gives them their common meaning. They express the spiritual vacuum caused by the death of a god, personifying the absolute goal of communism. The essay "Čto takoe socialističeskij realizm?" ("On Socialist Realism"), written at about the same time, draws from this situation a new literary program. It was not without reason interpreted as a testimony of the deep impact of Stalin's death upon the Soviet intelligentsia. But the characters of the story, absorbed in their own personal dramas, are not conscious of this larger and deeper meaning. One of the functions of the narrator is to actualize it in its metaphysical and religious intensity. And he does so in his capacity as a WRITER, through the experience of WRITING.

Actually, in relation to the events and the characters of the story, the narrator takes an ambiguous stance and plays a double role. Arrested and sent to a hard labor camp alongside the young "trotskyite" Serëža and the Jewish doctor Rabinovič (condemned for performing abortions), he is IN the story and accordingly plays the traditional role of the witness, verifying the authenticity of events. But he is also OUTSIDE the story, as its AUTHOR (i.e. its CREATOR, responsible for its existence), who trembles in taking up his pen and pays with a sentence of forced labor for the criminal act the story itself represents. This role of responsible author has the effect of superimposing and even substituting the reality of the written text for that of the events to which it refers, and the existential theme of writing for the ideological and political themes connected with the subject. The death of a god and the crumbling of a religion are experienced through the anguish of writing.

One of the passages in which the narrator interrupts the story to make his own voice heard is precisely devoted to this theme. He refers to the graffiti that adorn the walls of public restrooms. Not the men's — they only know how to write obscenities. But those of women, who

> ... write words of love and indignation... Those to whom they are addressed will never know of them. They are not written to be read, but cast at random into space, to the four corners of the world, and only God or some chance eccentric will ever gather up these prayers and incantations . . .
> I wish I could believe in words as do these women, and, sitting in my room no bigger than a cabin, at dead of night while everyone is asleep, write short, simple words, without ulterior motive and with no address.[1]

"Words without ulterior motive and with no address": writing appears, through this metaphor, as a vital need for self-expression, as irrepressible, disinterested and pathetic as that which moves people to graffiti the walls of public toilets.

The image of the bottle in the sea, of the distress signal tossed haphazardly towards an unknown, improbable recipient, also appears in *Gololedica* (*The Icicle*, 1961) and *Pxenc* (*Pkhenttz*, 1957). It can certainly be explained by the situation of the "underground" writer condemned to loneliness, secrecy and fear by a police state — such was Sinjavskij's situation when he wrote his *Fantastic Stories*. But this "historical" situation is but a developer of the peremptory, vital, irrepressible compulsion to write, associated with the feeling of an essential unlawfulness of writing.

Similarly, one can read *Grafomany* (*The Graphomaniacs,* 1960) as simple social satire denouncing a specific phenomenon of Soviet society, since graphomania as a "social ill" is tied up with a censorship that lets everyone believe he is a great writer suffering for his opinions. But the character of the graphomaniac has a deeper and more universal meaning. He is to the writer what writing is to literature. For literature is a social fact, whereas writing is an existential attitude. One main character of the story, Galkin, holds that great writers are only successful graphomaniacs. There is some truth in this paradox: from a strictly "earthly" point of view, talent, which distinguishes the writer from the graphomaniac, is perhaps less important than the vital need for self-expression that both have in common.

The theme of writing is seen in a similar light in *Ljubimov,* in which the narrator plays an even more important role than in *Sud idët*. Here he appears not only in asides, but actually in the fabric of the story itself. For *Ljubimov* is a *skaz,* in which the vocabulary, intonation, sentence structure (not to mention parentheses and digressions) belong to a fictional character, with sharply defined social and cultural traits: the city librarian Savelij Kuz'mič Proferansov, a country intellectual whose language is a savory mixture of literary clichés, stereotyped Soviet diction and remnants of popular beliefs. Closely tied to the events he relates (the secession of Ljubimov, a small provincial town that symbolizes eternal Russia, under the direction of the self-taught mechanic Leonid Tixomirov), Savelij Kuz'mič himself plays on one hand the traditional role of narrator-witness, authenticating the events he describes. But the fantastic nature of these events reduces this function to pure convention. Accordingly, the role of the author, responsible for the very existence of the story, becomes predominant. Although apparently confining himself to the modest role of a chronicler, Savelij Kuz'mič, like the narrator of *Sud idët,* feels responsible for what he writes, and trembles at the thought of being called to account for it. Thus, even more than in *Sud idët,* the story he relates becomes "derealized" — reduced to the level of guilty fantasy, the product of a subversive imagination. When the story ends, and the dissidence of Ljubimov has been suppressed, the city of Ljubimov no longer exists, has never existed. All that is left is *Ljubimov* the book, for which Savelij Kuz'mič carries full responsibility. The book has become his own subject matter. There is no reality of reference but the text itself.

Thus, the theme of writing as an existential need is connected with a poetics of the text as material object, independent of any external reference, an autonomous living organism, governed by its own laws:

> . . . a book which goes backwards and forwards, advances and retreats, sometimes moves close to the reader and at other times runs away from him and flows like a river through new countries, so that as we sail along, the head starts to whirl from the sheer abundance of impressions, even though everything passes slowly enough before our eyes, allowing us to view it at leisure and then watch it till it drops out of sight; a book which has a number of themes but only one trunk, and grows like a tree, embracing space with the totality of its leaves and air, and — in the manner of the lungs which have the shape of an inverted tree — breathes by expanding almost infinitely, only to contract again down to a small point; a book whose meaning is as inscrutable as the soul in its innermost kernel.[2]

Golos iz xora (*A Voice from the Chorus,* 1966–1972), for which this image serves as introduction, is of all the books of Abram Terc the one that comes nearest to this ideal of the text as an object. Its very form is as if it were the trace left by a wholly material process of construction, akin to collage. The fragments of which it is made up, whether the words, sayings or sentences of the prisoners forming the "chorus," or the thoughts that are the "voice" of the author, all appear as ready-made "things," having only to be assembled like the pieces of a mosaic or the bricks of a building. If *Golos iz xora* opens with this image (continued in the body of the work through a number of other images of the text as material object), it is no doubt because what is involved is an inaccessible ideal. A text is made up of words, which are never purely material, and by men, who can never completely remove the mark left by their hands. Perhaps the text-object is a contradiction in terms. But then, is not the need to write a form of yearning for the impossible?

* * *

The notion of the text as an object is not unfamiliar to the poetician, since poetry in general has been defined as an organization of the text by means of the significant, that is by the material side of language. But if so, this notion is contrary to the very essence of prose. This brings up the whole problem of prose as an art, and of a specific poetics of prose. Here is how Abram Terc treats the question, with reference to Gogol':

> Gogol' overcame the language barrier, resorting not to the speech that we use but rather to the inability to speak normally, which is also what prose is in its fullest sense. Not noticing that, he discovered that prose, like all art, pre-supposes a transition to an unknown language, which in this exotic capacity is the equal of poetry . . .[3]

And more specifically:

> The prose writer does not master language from the beginning, as does the poet with his divine babble, sent down from above, from birth on, taking, if necessary, the bull by the horns. The prose writer must look around, clear his throat, get into the conversation, that is, create a language before he starts living. For that purpose, among other things, he frequently helps himself by bringing in a second narrator . . .[4]

Thus, the form of the *skaz,* to which Gogol' resorted in his beginnings as a prose-writer, appears to be connected with the very essence of the art of prose. For, like poetry, *skaz* does not take the word "literally," as a pure and neutral signal for a meaning, but rather as a material object endowed with independent properties. But while poetry is mainly concerned with the "natural" properties of this object (its physical, articulatory or acoustic form), *skaz* is sensitive to its "cultural" properties, that is, to what it retains of the geographical, historical, social and psychological contexts in which it has been used. The word, from the point of view of the *skaz,* is not a SOUND, but a VOICE. In this sense, *skaz* is only one particularly characteristic form of "novelistic speech" (*romannoe slovo*), as defined by Baxtin.[5]

Skaz in a narrow sense, attributed to a narrator of a different, and usually lower, cultural level, appears in only a few of Abram Terc's stories: *Kvarti-ranty* (*Tenants,* 1959), in which the narrator is an aged "house spirit" (*domo-voj*), *Pxenc,* in which he is the inhabitant of another planet, and especially *Ljubimov.* But even in *Gololedica,* in *Ty i ja* (*You and I,* 1959), in *Grafomany,* the story is always told by a specific, individualized character, with HIS voice and from HIS point of view. One might say that for Andrej Sinjavskij, "making prose" always means taking on a role, putting on a mask (this is one of the explanations of the need for a pseudonym). This always involves adopting someone's tone, assuming someone's voice: language for him is always "lived in." This is the meaning of the figure of the mythical ancestor Samson Samsonovič Proferansov (in *Ljubimov*), who, from time to time, takes possession of the pen of his descendant, the chronicler Savelij Kuz'mič, slipping in his footnotes, or even intervening in his narrative. He is, in some way, the genius of the Russian language, a vehicle of cultural tradition and a cluster of historical "voices."

From this we can better understand the meaning of another paradox, this one uttered by the graphomaniac Galkin, which reveals an essential aspect of the theme of writing in Abram Terc's works:

> People talk about "making one's mark," "expressing one's personality." But in my opinion every writer is occupied by one thing alone: self-elimination. That's why we labour in the sweat of our brow and cover wagon-loads of paper with writing — in the hope of stepping aside, overcoming ourselves and granting access to thoughts from the air. They arise spontaneously, independently of ourselves. All we do is to work and work, and to go further along the road, suppressing ourselves from time to time and giving way to them. Then suddenly — you know, it always happens suddenly, at once — you realize: this piece you composed yourself, and it's no good, while that one isn't yours and you don't dare, you haven't the right, to do anything to it, you may neither change it nor improve it. It's not your property! And you draw back in bewilderment. You're staggered. Not by the beauty of the achievement. Simply by terror at your own non-participation in what has taken place. . .[6]

To imitate the speech of someone else, to "play" it as one would a role, is the easiest way of "self-elimination" (*samoustranenija*). But the same goal can be reached in other ways, as witness *Mysli vrasplox* (*Thoughts Unaware*, 1965), with their fragmentary, lapidary form, both improvised and set, suggesting sudden revelations, coming from outside, which must be gathered as is, without changing a single word. The art of the fragment, of the aphorism whose value entirely depends on its spontaneity, is above all the ability of being open to a speech that is so rich and perfect that you are stunned, and hesitate to call it your own. In this sense, the "author's voice" in *Golos iz xora* is also "another's voice," just as that of the camp inmates who form the "choir." We can thus say that, paradoxically, the work represents a sort of ideal model or abstract schema of Baxtin's definition of the novel as an orchestration of another's words.

It can also be noted that what distinguishes the graphomaniac Straustin, protagonist of the story *Grafomany*, from a "real writer" is that he takes Galkin's paradox for a plagiarist's confession:

> I listened carefully to Galkin's frank confessions. I even found them very interesting. So that's the way it was! He doesn't even consider it his property? That must be taken into account. . . . But who then is that author . . . ? Who does he borrow it all from?[7]

The graphomaniac is unaware of the feeling of dispossession that the true writer feels when faced with a work that transcends him and in which he no longer recognizes himself. It is just this feeling that is the stamp of art and the reward of the artist.

From this conception of writing as "self-elimination" we can better understand the paradoxical and, it should be added, somewhat provocative formula that shocked some sensitive but superficial critics: "Emptiness, that is the content of Puškin."[8] This emptiness is precisely the ability of the real writer to silence his earthbound self and be open to inspiration. It is this complete receptivity, this absolute freedom from one's self that makes Puškin, in Sinjavskij-Terc's eyes, the unsurpassable model of the artist: no other poet, he contends, is less encumbered by himself, more immediately and fully open to that "voice from the outside" that metamorphoses writing, always individual, relative, arbitrary and variable, into something absolute, necessary, imprescribable, "not made by human hands" (*nerukotvornoe*).

*   *   *

Taken to the extremes, the notion of "the text as an object" leads to what the futurists baptised as *zaum*: the production of texts based on the material side of language, purified of all external reference and preexisting meaning. It is therefore not surprising that there exists such a thing as a "Tercian" *zaum.* Thus, the very title of the story *Pxenc* and the words (*gogry tužeroskip*) used at its conclusion by the hero to evoke his distant, half-forgotten, planet of origin. Or, in *Sud idët,* the cynical lawyer Karlinskij's edifying lecture to the young conspiratrice Katja:

> Counter . . . xism . . . ism, ism, ism . . .
> Principle . . . incible . . .
> Jective . . .
> Manity . . . lution . . . Pferd . . .[9]

Here, a "transmental" (*zaumnyj*) text is constructed not from phonemes, but from abstract suffixes caricaturing the pseudo-ideological logomachy of stalinism.

But if one admits, as we have suggested, that prose, in Terc's understanding, deals with VOICES rather than SOUNDS (as does poetry), then it will be understood that the specific shape of "Tercian" *zaum* is abracadabra and non sequitur ("*coq-à-l'âne*"), in which the effect of "transmental language," devoid of external reference, comes from combining into a single paragraph, sometimes a single sentence, words and bits and pieces of sentences pulled out of different discourses. Thus in *Ty i ja*:

> It was snowing. A fat woman was picking her teeth. Another fat woman was gutting a fish. A third was eating meat. Two engineers were playing a Chopin duet. Four hundred women were simultaneously giving birth in the maternity homes.
> An old woman was dying.[10]

Here, the comic effect of this juxtaposition of disparate scenes comes from the purely formal, verbal link that associates them ('picking' and 'gutting' are translations of the same Russian verb *čistila*; the Russian text has "one (woman) . . . a second . . . a third . . . four hands . . . four hundred . . .").

We find a page constructed on similar principles in *Gololedica*:

> The woodcock plummeted from the birch-tree, as though pulled on a string. I pressed the trigger and, taking aim, saw that it was sitting on a branch, a great black cock, and looking at Diana. We climbed from our horses and galloped off. Katya in her pink bonnet waves good-bye from the veranda: "Come back safe!" Jumping into the saddle, I run down the steps and pull on my boots. "It's time to get up, master, it'll soon be daybreak," Nikiphor shouts into my ear. I clasp his fat calves in my hands: "Don't leave us, for God's sake, I implore you for the sake of your son . . ." He looks away, white with anger: "Someone might see us, ma'am." I took the scalp between my teeth and started swimming. In the middle of the river I felt sick. With my teeth still clenched, I begin to sink . . .[11]

Here, in addition to the juxtaposition of phrases taken from different stories, the effect of non sequitur is achieved by inverting chronological order.

Finally, in *Grafomany*:

> Above us a sky with a woman's smile and violet as the plum of the lieutenant called Greben was resting on the green grass. General Ptitsyn, not wiping away the rare soldierly tears which were rolling like hailstones down his cheeks, uttered the command: I love you, darling Tonya, and their lips fused in a fiery kiss. And he sensed in his soul the kind of curd-tart and mushroom pies, with half a dozen strong gherkins, cold as icicles and smelling of fresh dill, salted away in the early spring, when you want to join nature in weeping with joy and cry: O Russia! Whither art thou rushing? while blessing the first downy, tender, pink snow to fall on the black, muddy, slippery cart road.[12]

Here, pieces of literary clichés used by half a dozen graphomaniacs reading their works at the same time are mixed together in a nonsensical hodge-podge.

All the above passages are motivated by the narrative context. In *Sud idët* and *Gololedica,* they are the fruit of a fantastic hypothesis: the hero is endowed either with an X-ray vision enabling him to see several scenes simultaneously, or with a gift of second sight which places him simultaneously in several previous incarnations. But in *Golos iz xora,* in which the esthetic Abram Terc is most clearly revealed, we find a similar passage, without any motivation:

> . . . A new mode of discourse might be born from loss of memory. As you struggled to regain it, floundering in the quicksands of oblivion, dragons and the Baba-Yaga might come to mind again.
>
> A bird which a half-wit first saw in a dream later turned up in the zoo. "I know you, Nastasya!"
>
> I loved that pheasant so much I would gladly have turned into it myself.[13]

Here we have something akin to the surrealistic automatic writing. Consciousness no longer provides for the continuity of the utterance, which has to structure itself spontaneously out of a plurality of emerging voices. It is up to language itself, left to its own dynamics, to impress us with some original combinations. In fact, motivated or not, these "absurd" texts, in which language asserts its autonomy towards every possible referent, are pieces of bravura, verbal feats of prowess, sample representations of the impossible, the yearning for which underlies all writing.

Actually, of all the images which, in *Golos iz xora,* assimilate the written text to a physical, palpable, material reality, to a concrete space both created and occupied by the writer, one of the most frequent is that of the text as an acrobatic performance, a sleight-of-hand trick, a feat similar to that of a tightrope walker or prestidigitator:

> One must know how to twine rope out of a phrase. And then walk on it as on a tight-rope. In the air. Without holding on to anything.[14]

And again:

> Cannot a sentence, with all its subordinate phrases, be likened to a box which contains a duck, a hare, an egg, the death of Koshchey the Deathless (or the love of Helen of Troy)? Can it, in short, be turned into a labyrinth, or, better, into a *matrioshka,* rolling itself into a ball and running into the depths of itself by means of various "that's" and "which's" filling its intricately composite body with a soft light coming from inside, from its very core, like the soul — whence, which, where, because, which once more, and unless, then this that or the other? . . .[15]

The structure of the sentence-object is here compared to that of the fairy tale (*skazka*), for which there is an obvious fascination in the fourth part of *Golos iz xora,* and in which Abram Terc sees something intermediate between magic and sleight-of-hand:

> The difference between a fairy-tale and a *bylina* is that magic is converted into physical force. They are like two different circus acts . . .
> In general, almost all that is left of the fairy-tale is now to be found in the circus. Magician — conjurer — thief: the evolution of an image. I started with the circus. And with the circus I must end.[16]

Actually, it is the image of the circus and the figure of the prestidigitator that link the character of the writer to that of the thief, and most effectively accounts for the pseudonym of Abram Terc (who, as is known, is a legendary thief of Odessa, hero of an underworld song). Kostja, the hero of his first story, *V cirke* (*At the Circus,* 1955) to which the above quotation refers, is surely not just a thief in the "western" sense of the word. He is rather a dreamer, whose insatiable soul cannot find any occupation worthy of itself, and is fascinated by the image of the circus and its magicians. At the restaurant where he is feasting, after he has drunk his "275 grams," Kostja feels

> As if he were walking a tight-rope four hundred metres up in the air and, though the walls were tottering and threatening to collapse, he walked with a light, springing, measured gait and in a perfectly straight line. The audience stares and holds its breath and puts its hopes in you as if in God: "Keep it up, Konstantin. Don't let us down, Konstantin Petrovich. Show them what's what."

> And you must, you simply must show them some feat — some *salto mortale* or other stupendous trick, or perhaps just hit upon and utter some word, unique in life, after which the world will turn upside down and in the twinkling of an eye assume a supernatural state.[17]

At the restaurant, this need for a total, absolute and definitive feat of prowess that will reveal to the whole world something unique inside you and that you feel but cannot express — this need can only be met through an enormous scandal. The real accomplishment of his dream will be the final *salto-mortale* he performs, mortally wounded by a guard's bullet, while trying to escape. His death clearly suggests that the thirst deep within him is that of the impossible.

* * *

Such is the metaphor of the writer which has given birth to the figure of Abram Terc. It helps us to understand and to resolve the apparent contradiction between the two motivations of writing illustrated by the stories: the need to express oneself, as figured by the image of the bottle in the sea or the graffiti in public toilets, and the contrasting need to "self-eliminate," to get rid of one's self with its earthly weight. Abram Terc himself explains this contradiction when he speaks, in *Golos iz xora,* of the works that sent him to prison:

> Everything he ever wrote he did so about and by means of himself, pulling it all out of his own — very insignificant — person, as a conjurer pulls a duck or a gun out of an empty top hat, all the time marvelling at his own resourcefulness.[18]

Self-expression, for a writer, is not realizing capital, but receiving a fortune. It means expecting from writing a metamorphosis, in other words a miracle and a grace. Writing, Abram Terc says modestly, is just sleight of hand. But deep within himself he knows it is a prayer.

NOTES

1. Abram Tertz, *The Trial Begins,* translated by Max Hayward (Glasgow: Fontana Books, 1977), p. 45.

2. Abram Tertz, *A Voice from the Chorus,* translated by Kyril Fitzlyon and Max Hayward (Glasgow: Fontana Books, 1977), p. 4.

3. Abram Terc, *V teni Gogolja* (London: Overseas Publications Interchange, in association with Collins, 1975), p. 323.

4. Ibid., p. 324.

5. Cf. M. Baxtin, *Voprosy literatury i estetiki* (Moscow: Xudožestvennaja literatura, 1975).

6. Abram Terc, *The Icicle,* translated by Max Hayward and Ronald Hingley (London: Collins and Harvill Press), pp. 175–76.

7. Ibid., p. 176.

8. Abram Terc, *Progulki s Puškinym* (London: Overseas Publications Interchange, in association with Collins, 1975).

9. Abram Terc, *The Trial Begins,* p. 66.

10. Abram Terc, *The Icicle,* p. 112.

11. Ibid., p. 32.

12. Ibid., p. 179.

13. Abram Terc, *A Voice from the Chorus,* pp. 216–17.

14. Ibid., p. 132.

15. Ibid., pp. 211–12.

16. Ibid., pp. 196–97.

17. Abram Terc, *The Icicle,* p. 92.

18. Abram Terc, *A Voice from the Chorus,* pp. 130–31.

(Translated by Alexandre Guérard)

Ehrhard Bahr

THE LITERATURE OF HOPE:
ERNST BLOCH'S PHILOSOPHY AND ITS IMPACT ON THE
LITERATURE OF THE GERMAN DEMOCRATIC REPUBLIC

Ernst Bloch in memoriam:
8 July 1885–4 August 1977

Opinions are divided about Ernst Bloch's contribution to philosophy. The question has been raised: Was he a philosopher in the strict sense of the word who conducted philosophy as methodological scholarship in the tradition of Kant and Hegel, or was he a prophet and a mystical thinker who provided wisdom in the tradition of Jacob Boehme and Johann Georg Hamann?[1] The debate about this question is far from being settled, but there is unanimity as far as his achievements as a writer are concerned. Nobody denies that he was a great writer. In an allusion to the title of Goethe's first version of his Wilhelm Meister novel — *Wilhelm Meister's Theatrical Mission* (*Wilhelm Meisters Theatralische Sendung*) — critics have spoken of "Ernst Bloch's Poetic Mission."[2] But whereas Goethe's protagonist proved to be unable to found a German national theater, Ernst Bloch may have been one of the most important contributors to the rise of a new or second German national literature, though this had not been the ultimate goal of his mission. The emergence of the literature of the German Democratic Republic and its advance to international prominence and reputation during the last twenty years can be traced back to Ernst Bloch and the impact of his philosophy. The literature of the German Democratic Republic can be subsumed under Bloch's principle of hope, or, in other words, the literature of the GDR is the Literature of Hope.[3]

Ernst Bloch, who died on 4 August 1977 in Tübingen at the age of ninety-two, wrote his magnum opus, "The Principle of Hope" (*Das Prinzip Hoffnung*, 3 vols., 1955–1959), in exile in the United States. Oxford University Press was interested in publishing the manuscript under the title, "Dreams of a Better Life," but this project never materialized. Otherwise, his book would have first appeared in English in the United States. The first two volumes were published in the GDR in 1955, the complete work of three volumes finally in Frankfurt, West Germany, in 1959.[4]

When Ernst Bloch returned to Germany in 1949, he took up residence in that part of Germany which seemed to offer him the best chances for a realization of his philosophy of hope. At that time, in the West, under the leadership of Konrad Adenauer a restoration of the old power structures and old ideologies seemed to be taking place, while in the East the exiles from Nazi Germany appeared to be in charge of a democratic reconstruction of Germany. An anti-Fascist socialist unity party that appealed to the collective spirit and the tradition of the popular front of the thirties had been founded. A socialist land reform had been carried out, and the ownership of heavy industry and the production of raw materials and energy had been transferred, at least in name, to the people. Later developments towards bureaucratic dictatorship and the party state system could not be clearly foreseen at that time.[5]

In 1949, the Federal Republic of Germany appeared to Bloch, in comparison to the GDR, as "democratized Fascism."[6] He, therefore, accepted a chair of philosophy at the University of Leipzig, and was an instant success with many East German students and young intellectuals who had just returned to the lecture halls of the universities from the P.O.W. camps. Bloch's residence in Leipzig was of great importance due to the fact that the majority of GDR writers either studied at the University of Leipzig or were members of the Johannes R. Becher Institute, founded in Leipzig in 1955 to assist in the development of young socialist writers.[7] Even if they were not philosophy majors, the students could not escape the influence of Bloch in the Leipzig of the fifties, had they wanted to do so. Another important influence was Hans Mayer, an admirer and supporter of Ernst Bloch and professor of German literature at the University of Leipzig, who also taught creative writing at the J. R. Becher Institute.

Gerhard Zwerenz, a contemporary German writer and former student of Bloch, has described the fascination which Bloch held for the young generation of writers in the GDR, when he wrote about his first meeting with the philosopher. His report reads like an account of a revivalist:

> . . . and then I saw the man. He was short with a stocky body. His hair fell in his face. Wearing thick glasses, he ran down the hall and almost knocked me over. Only in the last moment could I avoid a collision. . . . At that instant, I realized that I had to study philosophy.[8]

Bloch became a father figure for the young generation in the GDR. As Zwerenz, who has a working class background, said himself: Bloch became his second father. "This event happened," according to Zwerenz, "without any of the embarrassing intimacies of family life. This father was not a gigantic, strange and threatening figure. This new and other father was exciting, stimulating, in short: a constant intellectual provocation."[9] Zwerenz considered it the most important event of his life when he selected this new father figure in Leipzig. His experience is cited here in detail because it is typical for his generation, and recurs in similar fashion in some of the writings under discussion.

Meanwhile, the intellectual life in the GDR had fallen under the same type of party direction that was typical for all the other changes between 1949 and 1956, when the GDR entered into the phase of becoming a Communist party state and the Socialist Unity Party (SED), for all practical purposes, became the established state party.[10] The short-lived "thaw" of 1956, under the impact of the Twentieth Congress of the Soviet Communist Party, was welcomed especially by Bloch, among many others. He made his thoughts clear about Stalinism and the party state in public lectures in Berlin and in his contributions to the Leipzig philosophy journal, *Deutsche Zeitschrift für Philosophie*.[11]

However, the establishment of the party state was able to consolidate its force within a short time. Under the impact of the Hungarian uprising in the fall of 1956, the Socialist Unity Party initiated a rigid campaign against all forms of deviationism or revisionism, with Ernst Bloch becoming one of their prime targets. He was forced into retirement, his philosophy was condemned as mysticism, and some of his students were sentenced to prison terms, unless they were able to escape to West Germany. Wolfgang Harich, the editor of the *Deutsche Zeitschrift für Philosophie,* was sentenced to ten years' hard labor. In the following years, some of the leading intellectuals in the GDR left for West Germany, among them critics such as Hans Mayer and Alfred Kantorowicz, and writers such as Uwe Johnson and Gerhard Zwerenz. When the Berlin Wall was built in August 1961, Ernst Bloch, who happened to be visiting the Federal Republic, decided not to return to Leipzig. He accepted a guest professorship at the University of Tübingen where he lived until the end of his life in 1977.

The most characteristic feature of Bloch's philosophy is its preoccupation with hope, or, negatively speaking, its concentration on the human ability of never becoming completely disappointed in spite of all experience to the contrary. Man is for Bloch not to be defined as "thinker" or "toolmaker" or even as "worker" and "producer" in the Marxist sense, but as "forever hopeful." Man in his definition is the creature who hopes, who fantasizes and dreams about a better life in the future, and who strives to make his dreams become reality. Hope is for Bloch the constitutive element of human existence.[12] Or, expressed in the terminology of logic: S is not yet P, subject is not yet predicate, in other words, man is the creature who strives to become something which he is not yet, the stress being on the two words "Not Yet" with their potential for the future. To be human means being on the way to something.[13]

For Bloch, the most important subject of philosophy is the future. Ever since 1883, when Friedrich Engels published his treatise *Socialism: Utopian and Scientific* (*Entwicklung des Sozialismus von der Utopie zur Wissenschaft*), utopian thinking had become a proscribed topic and had been declared unfit for use by socialist theoreticians. The term "utopia" was replaced by "perspective," especially in aesthetic theory.[14] Bloch opposes this Marxist condemnation of utopian thinking and tries to rehabilitate the term within Marxist philosophy by introducing the dialectic concept of "concrete utopia," i.e., a utopia which contains a concrete chance of realization with the past and the present as bases. Tracing utopian elements of the past, Bloch establishes the dialectic concept of a "memory of the future." Past and present obtain new functions with regard to the future. This process mandates a new time structure for philosophy and art. Translated into the framework of the historical process the concept of "concrete utopia" is used to support the thesis that the only realistic or concrete chance for man to attain his goals lies in Marxism, in short: in the socialist transformation of the world. Marxism, in Bloch's definition, "is the practice of concrete utopia."[15]

Regardless of the doubts about the validity of Bloch's principle of hope as a philosophical subject, it must be acknowledged that it had a far-reaching influence on GDR literature as a thematic motif and a structural principle. This influence, however, was not due to the circumstance that the principle of hope could perhaps offer the GDR writer an easy formula for escaping the prescribed confines of Socialist Realism, or a facile pseudo-Marxist cover-up for basically reactionary tendencies, or even a naively consoling doctrine to survive all adversities as a kind of Marxist Candide. It is important to notice that the principle of hope is neither a simplistic type of optimism which could easily be exploited by an authoritarian regime to cover up present failures, mismanagement and denial of freedom and justice by directing attention to a future that will never come. Nor is it a naive type of stoicism that could be used by an individual as a convenient justification for his passivity in the presence of intolerable conditions. The principle of hope is directed against the simplistic optimism and "socialist perspective" that was demanded from all artists in the GDR. It is a dialectical concept that tries to take into account the differentiations and contradictions of social reality as well as the frustrations of human progress without being excessively optimistic or persistently stoic. As such it was understood by most of the GDR writers. It offered them a more sophisticated interpretation of their situation and the meaning of literature than the doctrines of Socialist Realism, as prescribed by the party state. The other reason for Bloch's great influence is undoubtedly his gift as a writer. The GDR authors recognized the great literary artist in Bloch. No one had spoken with such a prophetic voice in German literature in a long time.

Examining GDR literature within this context, one will perhaps find no other work exemplifying the influence of Bloch's philosophy as distinctly as Christa Wolf's novel, *The Quest for Christa T.* (*Nachdenken über Christa T.,* 1968), "one of the few great [literary works] in the German language since the war," as the *London Times* called it.[16] It is important to notice that the author, born in 1929, studied German literature at the University of Leipzig under Hans Mayer. Her novel presents the principle of hope not only as theme, but also as structure. It is a story about the past, yet it has utopian direction; it is about an unexemplary life, yet it expresses hope. The narrator reconstructs the life and personality of her former schoolmate, Christa T., and quotes from her letters, diaries and literary sketches. There is nothing extraordinary in the life of Christa T.: she goes to school in the late forties, finishes her university studies at Leipzig, as her author and narrator did, with an excellent thesis in the early fifties; she becomes a teacher, gets married, has three children and dies of leukemia at the age of thirty-five at the beginnings of the sixties. She sacrifices her writing for her marriage and children, and dies before she can fulfill the vision of herself. But her short life and early death are not a waste. They are a gain insofar as the narrator and the reader can learn from her experience. Through the process of remembering and narrating bits and pieces of her life, the past of Christa T. is summoned into the narrator's present in order to build her and her readers' future. Thus, the Proustian "Remembrances of Things Past" are dialectically redirected, according to Bloch's principle of hope, toward the construction of a better future. The plot of the novel, as meager as it is, is only of secondary importance. Of prime relevance is the process of reevaluating the past for the purpose of creating a better future.

As the narrator states at the beginning of the novel: "[Christa T.] must be protected . . . against being forgotten. . . . [It is] useless to pretend it's for her sake. Once and for all, she doesn't need us. So we should be certain of one thing: that it's for our sake. Because it seems that we need her" (7, 9).[17] Christa T. represents the concept of the "Not Yet" in Bloch's philosophy, but also the potential utopia that is delineated in the struggles of her life. Her death, as the narrator hopes, is not going to be an end, but a new beginning. She speculates that one day people will want to know who Christa T. was and what it is she represented. Throughout the novel, there appears as a leitmotif Christa T.'s impatient question: "When, if not now?" (89, 90, 127). At the conclusion of the novel, the narrator takes up her question, demanding the realization of Christa T.'s "concrete utopia." The novel ends with the imploring words that seem to echo Bloch's language and philosophy: "When, if not now?" (235).

The question that is raised by Christa T.'s life and death leads to the problem of hope as a theme of the novel. The key sentence of the work is Christa T.'s laconic statement when she tried her hand at creative writing: "The Big Hope, or the Difficulty of Saying 'I'" (214). This almost Brechtian sentence points to the difficulty of self-realization within a socialist society. The second sentence at the beginning of the novel raises the problem: "The quest for [Christa T.]: in the thought of her. And of *the attempt to be oneself*" (7). The last four words are in italics, and are repeated with reinforced conviction towards the end of the novel: "*To become oneself, with all one's strength*" (188). What Christa T. wished for was the coming of a Socialism that would give the individual its due. The narrator calls it "the coming of our world," adding the observation: "And she had precisely the kind of imagination one needs for a real understanding of it" (66). There are discussions about the "paradise" on whose threshold they believe to be standing. The difficulty of saying "I" under present conditions leads the protagonist not to despair, but to the realization of what ought to be changed. As the narrator comments: "Christa T. began, very early on, when one thinks about it today, to ask herself what change means. The new words? The new house? Machines, bigger fields? The new man, she heard people say, and she began to look inside herself" (71 f.). Negative insights do not result in nihilism, but in hope. The narrator describes Christa T. as a visionary, yet as being all for reality: "That's why she loved the time when real changes were being made. She loved to open up new senses for the sense of a new thing" (221).

However, there are also disappointments. Fascist behavior in the form of conformism and brutality resurfaces in the new society. The narrator and Christa T. arrive at the conclusion: "Paradise can make itself scarce. That's the way of it." (67) But the future is never left out of sight and conceived of as potential for change. The question is raised as to what the world needs to become perfect, and the narrator sums up the utopian message of the novel by answering, it is the presumptuous hope of people like Christa T. that they might be necessary for the perfection of this world.

It is obvious that Christa Wolf chose Bloch's philosophy of hope because it offered her an artistic principle and an opportunity of criticizing the present stage of socialism in the GDR without relinquishing her faith in its future. For the party state and its officials, however, the novel proved to be too progressive, and only with reluctance and a delay of four years did they agree to a second printing, though the copies of the first edition had been sold within one year.

In her last novel, "Patterns of Childhood" (*Kindheitsmuster,* 1976), an account of a short trip to Poland which turns into a long journey into the narrator's past, Christa Wolf employs the same time structure as in her previous work, but her time consciousness has changed. The patterns of the narrator's childhood during the Nazi years still determine her socialist present, and therefore, she has become uncertain about the future. Without an understanding of the different layers of time and experience, which threaten to split the personality of the narrator into three different persons, it appears futile to build a new society. The novel ends on a note of uncertainty by posing a number of questions.[18]

The other novelist to be mentioned in this context is Irmtraud Morgner, born in 1933. She is perhaps the most militant feminist writer in the GDR, though her work is not informed by feminist ideology as such, but rather by Bloch's principle of hope. Being an author in the tradition of Jean Paul and E.T.A. Hoffmann, she places her trust in imagination and fantasy. For her, narrative fantasy is not an end in itself, but fulfills an emancipatory function.

Studying German literature in Leipzig during the fifties, Irmtraud Morgner must have attended some lectures by Ernst Bloch. In her second novel, "The Marvelous Journeys of Gustav, the World Traveller" (*Die wundersamen Reisen Gustavs des Weltfahrers,* 1972), there are some unmistakable references to a professor of philosophy at Leipzig which could fit only Ernst Bloch. The narrator's report about a professor who spoke for hours in extraordinary and perfect sentences, like a poet, reminds the reader of Zwerenz's account of his first meting with Bloch:

> A lot of white hair fell from his low forehead. He leisurely chose his words, was never in a hurry. . . . Actually, he couldn't teach his students philosophy, but only himself. He didn't spread the gospel of knowledge, but of simplicity, work, power, and passion. Sometimes he . . . described concepts which one should have. He spoke in images. . . . A legendary figure (14–15).[19]

What the narrator learns from the professor is the understanding of imagination as productive power of the oppressed.

Irmtraud Morgner's first novel, "Wedding in Constantinople" (*Hochzeit in Konstantinopel,* 1968) is an example of this principle. Bele, the protagonist, a young woman, travels with Paul, her fiancé, a promising nuclear physicist, to a small seaside resort in Yugoslavia which she calls in her playful fancy Constantinople. It is a honeymoon before the wedding which is to take place after their return to Berlin. What appears first as a rather uncomplicated and unpromising adventure, becomes a very important experiment for Bele. While Paul, who feels rather sure of Bele's love and understanding, is only interested in his scientific work and aspirations, Bele wants to get to know him better and build with him a better future. But Paul is under the mistaken illusion that she loves him because he is a brilliant scientist, while in reality Bele loves him because she considers him to be a brilliant lover. As far as intelligence is concerned, she is not intimidated by him, but feels being on an equal level with him, though she cannot fail to notice that in this male oriented society he feels superior to her.

In order to make him understand her love and attraction, Bele tells him a number of fairy tales and absurd stories, fantastic dreams and reminiscences, but to no avail. She employs the model of Sheherazade in order to liberate not only herself, but also her future husband. Powerless as she is, she puts her imagination to work in order to facilitate her freedom and equality. But her experiment fails. Paul persists in behaving like a sultan. Their "concrete utopia" which appears to be so close at hand escapes them. Bele leaves Paul on the day of their return to Berlin. Paul never understands what he has lost: the anticipation of utopia in a love relationship. Bele's imaginative stories are a liberation from the oppression of women in society and an anticipation of a better future, but Paul is only interested in the supposedly male world of scientific and political projections.

It is important to notice in this context that the fairy tale forms "a constituent part of Bloch's philosophy," and is also "an indispensable component of Bloch's Marxism."[20] At the very end of his "Principle of Hope" Bloch declares that only "Marxism . . . takes the fairy tale seriously."[21]

Irmtraud Morgner's next novel, "The Marvelous Journeys of Gustav, the World Traveller" (1972), is a narrative in the tradition of Sindbad's, Gulliver's or Münchhausen's exaggerated stories about their travels and exploits. It clearly follows the tradition of the "voyages imaginaires," but the reader is not presented with utopias, but rather with anti-utopias. Gustav, the narrator's grandfather, a retired railroad engineer, takes his old trusty locomotive, named Hulda, on seven fantastic trips to a number of societies and realms which offer alternatives to Gustav's life in the GDR. He finally decides for his homeland as the best possible society in the present world. This conclusion appears to be a rather safe ploy to justify a fantastic and utopian narration within the confines of Socialist Realism. But even this justification allows for subtle opposition to the world as it exists. In the preface Grandfather Gustav is described as a liar, but not by nature: "[Lying] as the productive power of the oppressed was working in him" (15).[22] The reader cannot avoid the impression of dissatisfaction on the part of the female narrator with a society that still breeds liars. Her identification with her grandfather leads to the conclusion that women are still oppressed in the GDR as were men like her grandfather who date back to times before the GDR was founded and who cannot change their old behavior. Therefore, the novel can conclude with a strong feminist statement, declaring that women have a poorly developed historical consciousness because they have been excluded from history: "In order to live as human beings, i.e., to enter history, women first have to withdraw from history" (172).

Morgner's last novel, "The Life and Adventures of the Woman Troubadour Beatriz According to the Eyewitness Reports of Her Minstrel Laura" (*Leben und Abenteuer der Trobadora Beatriz nach Zeugnissen ihrer Spielfrau Laura,* 1974), is a response to this observation. The author attempts to change this situation by choosing as protagonist a historically verifiable character who withdraws from history (because of the neglect of women as historical persons) in order to reenter history some eight hundred years later. The protagonist, Beatriz, is a 12th-century woman troubadour who finds life so unbearable in the male-dominated medieval society that she withdraws from it in order to return to life in the twentieth century at the height of the French student revolution of May 1968. Beatriz quickly learns German in order to read the most important passages on emancipation in Marx's early writings. After the student revolution has failed in France, Beatriz accepts an invitation to the GDR which she welcomes as the "promised land" and "paradise" where the exploitation of women by men has been abolished. However, to her great disappointment she discovers that though women in the GDR have equal rights in all areas of work and social responsibility, men still dominate and exploit women in literature and in domestic life. Her GDR guide and informant is Laura, a construction worker and tram conductor, who functions as Beatriz's minstrel (*Spielfrau*).

The novel has been called a feminist's *Doktor Faustus,* "not only because of its bold use of montage technique, but also because of the striking parallels between the relationship of Beatriz and Laura in this work . . . and that of Adrian Leverkühn and Serenus Zeitblom" in Thomas Mann's novel. Similar to the composer who tries to achieve a "breakthrough" in modern music in order to create a composition that will liberate human beings, the woman troubadour attempts a "breakthrough" in the art of narration in order to produce a literary work of art that will bring about the emancipation of women. Beatriz's final story "The Joyful Tidings of Valeska," a story about a miraculous sex change which leads to the abolition of stereotyped sex roles,

"has the same key significance at the end of the novel as does Leverkühn's final composition."[23]

Morgner's novel established precisely that dialectical relationship between concrete reality and utopia which is so central to Bloch's philosophy. The disappointing reality of the contemporary woman's life in the GDR is set in contrast to Beatriz's fantastic stories which point to the utopian potential in the present and its realization in the near future. The central dialectic of the novel begins with Beatriz's utopian vision and its conflict with the complex conditions of the GDR reality. While her utopianism is modified through Laura's realism, her minstrel's pragmatism is charged with Beatriz's utopian energy. Through the mutual modifications of their outlooks the social process which effects change becomes visible, and the utopian vision that Beatriz has introduced to the GDR reality results in a refusal to accept conditions as they are. Reality is interpreted in terms of Bloch's philosophy as a process out of a past that must be reconstructed in relationship to a future that will bring new possibilities for human relationships and productivity. Employing this concept of reality as development towards a "concrete utopia," Irmtraud Morgner initiates, through means of her fantastic narrative, the control of women over their own history and productivity. The GDR functions in this context as a country where such miracles can take place. The first and last sentences of the novel point to this proposition (which is undermined in subtle fashion by the circumstance that it is announced in a fantastic tale which subverts the established relationship between fact and fiction).[24]

In the field of drama, Bloch's influence on literature cannot be established as clearly as in the novel. Nevertheless, Peter Hacks and Heiner Müller, the two leading GDR dramatists, exhibit tendencies in their works which may be traced back to Bloch's philosophy of hope. Peter Hacks, born in 1928, is one of the few GDR writers who were educated in West Germany. He did not study at Leipzig, as did Christa Wolf and Irmtraud Morgner, but at Munich, and he emigrated to the German Democratic Republic in 1955, after completing his graduate studies with a dissertation on *Biedermeier* drama. Though he began his career as a dramatist in the tradition of Brecht, he followed the precepts of GDR dramaturgy and its demands for positive socialist heroes with such vengeance and diligent cunning that it finally brought him into conflict with the official critics of the GDR Writers' Union.

His early plays demonstrate the force of history through the characters of so-called great men, such as Duke Ernst of Swabia in "The Chapbook of Duke Ernst" (*Das Volksbuch von Herzog Ernst*, 1953), Columbus in "The Onset of the Indian Age" (*Eröffnung des Indischen Zeitalters*, 1954), and Frederick II of Prussia in "The Miller of Sanssouci" (*Der Müller von Sanssouci*, 1957). But then a change took place in Hacks' dramatic production which is based on some theoretical considerations that reveal his closeness to Bloch's philosophy. In 1966 he declared that the image of history, as conceived by the

aesthetic consciousness, is the "humane utopia" which does not exist in historical reality. It is understood as a counter-design (*Gegenentwurf*) of the world, existing, as also Bloch had described it, "in the past and in the future, perhaps only in remembrance and in hope."[25] Hacks believes that the subject of modern art is the relationship between utopia and reality: "Utopia cannot exist in any other way but in a reality developing towards this utopia. The only mode of perfection open to reality is the development towards perfection."[26] Art is the anticipation of utopia. The individual is never sufficiently emancipated and sociable that he could not be improved.[27] It cannot be denied that these reflections on art read like a paraphrase of Bloch's philosophy. The mere mentioning of the word "utopia" in the GDR of the sixties must be understood as a clear reference to Bloch.

After two transitional plays, "The Battle of Lobositz" (*Die Schlacht bei Lobositz,* 1955) and "Of Problems and of Power" (*Die Sorge und die Macht,* 1960), Hacks entered a new phase of dramatic production with three comedies that reflect his concept of art as anticipation of utopia. His first work of this period, *Moritz Tassow* (1965), a blank verse comedy, deals with the problems of land reform and the collectivization of farms. After the defeat of Nazi Germany, Moritz Tassow, a former swineherd, takes over the estate of the local Junker and establishes a farming commune. However, current party policies prescribe the division of the old estates into small individual farms, although large integrated communes may be more productive. While the members of the party insist on compliance with the party directives, Moritz Tassow holds on to his utopia. In the end, the representatives of the party prevail, and the land is subsequently divided among the farmhands. But Tassow has the satisfaction that he is ahead of his time. The land reform of 1945 was finally replaced in the GDR by the drive for collectivization of 1960. But in 1945, Tassow has to withdraw, like his Goethean model, from this clash with party functionaries, the men of action, and he retires to writing, yet he continues the fight for his utopia against the Antonios of his age.[28]

In the next two comedies, *Amphitryon* (1967) and *Omphale* (1970), Peter Hacks resorts to mythology in order to dramatize his concern for a "humane utopia." The Amphitryon plot, well-known to theater audiences through the treatment of Plautus, Molière, Heinrich von Kleist and Giraudoux, is changed insofar as Alkmene prefers the god to the human being, because Jupiter represents the utopian dimension of man. He is what men are, "and something beyond them" (213), incorporating the "humane utopia," whose essence consists of love and the striving towards perfection.[29] The comedy lacks the tragic element of the Kleistian version, affirming the potential of human growth and development towards perfection. Since Amphitryon fails to develop this potential, Alkmene knowingly chooses the god over her husband, because Jupiter achieves what her husband was meant to be. When Amphitryon argues that there are limits to human achievements and only "a god is

able to be a human being," Jupiter answers with the metaphor of border crossing (*Grenzüberschreitung*) which is so vital to Bloch's "Principle of Hope": "You are limited. But recognizing one's limits, / Means transcending them. . . . / Don't accept your deficiencies as self-evident. / . . . That's what your love for Alkmene / . . . should have taught you" (277). But Amphitryon is not totally uneducable; he and Alkmene experience through divine intervention their growth toward their "humane utopia" in spite of all their human shortcomings.

In Peter Hacks' other blank verse comedy *Omphale* (1970), the exchange of male and female dresses and attributes between Hercules and Omphale is presented as a positive event symbolizing their emancipation from the traditional sexual stereotypes of "man" and "woman." Hercules becomes Omphale, and Omphale becomes Hercules, both forming a new union on a higher level of human growth. But this new synthesis is only a private utopia which is short-lived, unless the two partners establish contact with society. Individual love and growth become meaningless without social interaction. Hercules and Omphale have to return to their former roles, he as dragon slayer, and she as mother of heroes, in order to restore their social standing. Their return is not a defeat, but constitutes an enrichment of their former personalities who now dare to become what they are not yet. The last two words echo one of the basic ideas from Bloch's philosophy. For the present historical reality, Hacks appears to be saying, this Herculean feat of becoming a new human being is impossible to achieve, but society is set into motion by this model development in a direction which will make the "humane utopia" possible in the not too distant future.

Heiner Müller, born in 1928, is perhaps the most important dramatist in contemporary German literature. His plays, dealing with industrial conditions and problems of the production process in the GDR, appear unaffected by Bloch's philosophy of hope. But in his most recent play, "Germania Death in Berlin" (*Germania Tod in Berlin*, 1977), Müller introduces the concept of hope into his dramatic collage of German history from the first century to 1953. According to Müller, Germany manifests itself through the fraternal strife of two inimical brothers from the time of Arminius and Flavius to the divided Germany of the twentieth century. While one of the brothers loves freedom and fatherland and wants to liberate his people from servitude, the other brother is concerned only with his individual wealth, glory and honor, and thinks only about his personal freedom. This constellation repeats itself throughout German history with the defeat and death of the altruistic brother at the hands of the egocentric brother. However, the unselfish brother never gives up hope in spite of defeat and death. The author appears to be clinging to the last vestiges of hope in German history. In the last scene, the bricklayer Hilse, a counter-figure to Gerhart Hauptmann's quietist weaver Hilse in his drama, *The Weavers* (*Die Weber*, 1892), is stoned almost to death by members of a juvenile gang, who ridicule his socialist work ethic. When he finally dies of cancer, Hilse sees in his hallucinations Rosa Luxemburg return from her grave and red flags fly over a united Germany. He asks the girl at his bedside, whom he mistakes for Rosa Luxemburg, about the children playing bricklayer and capitalist. With triumphant laughter he affirms that no child wants to play the part of the capitalist anymore. In contrast to his namesake's meaningless death in Hauptmann's *Weavers* — the old weaver is killed by a stray bullet after refusing to take part in the revolt against the ruling class — bricklayer Hilse knows what he fought and died for, even though his final goal remains visionary. Thus, Müller's last drama serves as a "laboratory of social [and historical] imagination," as he called it, which is not too far removed from Bloch's philosophy of hope.[30]

The discussion of the above novels and dramas has clearly established the influence of Bloch's philosophy of hope on some of the most prominent representatives of GDR literature. One could add other works to this list, such as Jurek Becker's novel, *Jakob the Liar* (*Jakob der Lügner,* 1969), in which the protagonist spreads hope among the inmates of a Nazi controlled ghetto during World War II by claiming to have a radio which broadcasts the approach of the advancing Red Army. Though this claim is an evident lie (one of the hardest tests of hope), it nevertheless produces resistance to the occupation forces and an ethical improvement of life among the ghetto dwellers until their final departure for a concentration camp.[31] But this additional work only proves again the same point that can be summarized under the broad generalization of the literature of the GDR being the "Literature of Hope."

Another important point which in the above discussion is mentioned only by implication, is the inherent danger of utopia as restoration and affirmation of the established power structures. What remains to be discussed is the question of the degree to which GDR writers have resisted this temptation. Bloch's "principle of hope" includes disappointment as an essential element of hope. It is not only a fact that hope can be frustrated, but it is also an ethical imperative that one must admit disappointment when preconditions of hope no longer exist. Emerging from such disappointments in a dialectic process, hope may regain itself through the contradictions of reality.[32]

The recent events in the intellectual life of the GDR, concerning the exile of Marxist poet-singer Wolf Biermann, offer an illustration of the keen awareness on the part of the GDR writers of Bloch's "principle of hope" and its dialectic nature. In 1976, Biermann was refused permission to return to the GDR after giving a number of concerts in the Federal Republic of Germany. The case became a rallying point of the progressive intellectuals in the GDR. After signing protest statements against the expulsion of Biermann, many were forced to leave the country or were expelled from their professional organizations. Since 1976, more than twenty authors, musicians, composers and actors have been forced or encouraged by their government into leaving their homeland, among them Sarah Kirsch, Reiner Kunze, Jürgen Fuchs, and many others. Some critics have spoken of a new German exile literature.[33]

One of the key words in the discussions and commentaries was the word, "hope." Reiner Kunze, one of the best known writers now in West German exile, who refused the designation "emigrant" for himself, has talked in an interview about the trust and hope which readers in the GDR place on literature, and about the resurgence of hope he felt, when crossing the border. Kunze, who had received the Büchner Prize from the German Academy of Language and Literature in Darmstadt in 1977, felt reminded of the fate of the 19th-century author and quoted from the letters of Büchner after he had fled from the dangers of political reprisals and imprisonment in Germany to Strasbourg.[34] Günter Kunert, another writer who still resides in Berlin-East, in a public letter has declared that there can be no kind of hope as long as his government continues its practice of treating artists and writers according to the American slogan "Love it or leave it." As he explained in terms of Bloch's philosophy, for him the utopia of a socialist society has been realized in principle: "Life can only become better, more beautiful, more plentiful, more varied." But there is still a gap between reality and ideal which is central to the creative process. The tension between reality and ideal constitutes for him the basic element of art. The artist's integrity demands that he truthfully reflect this tension in the individual work of art. This truth is his desire and determines his inspiration as well as the success of his work. "With the exodus of artists of integrity the moral legitimacy [of the state] disappears."[35] Similar statements were made by Peter Hacks and Heiner Müller, though Hacks did not join in the protest against the expulsion of Biermann.[36] Heiner Müller was called a representative of "petrified hope."[37] According to a report by Reinhard Baumgart in the West German weekly *Die Zeit* Christa Wolf has not given up hope yet. Arguing, however, in negative fashion, she said that the writer will relinquish his integrity if he does not believe in anything anymore. Then he will write anything to order. She declared that she had not yet been able to go so far as to believe in nothing, although in this attitude she felt like a fossil.[38]

Finally, in Wolf Biermann's recent commentary to the GDR dissidents' manifesto, which was published in the West German news magazine *Der Spiegel* in January 1978,[39] the term "hope" stands out most prominently against "false hope," created by Stalinism. It is "socialist hope" which cannot be destroyed by Stalinism, and it is "communist hope" which is not only trampled down again and again, but also reproduced again and again as counter-reaction to Stalinism. According to Biermann, the lesson of the Prague Spring of 1968 was not the suppression by tanks, but the obvious and proven fact that a socialist state can be revolutionized much more easily than an established capitalist state. Therefore, Biermann placed his hope on the tensions and contradictions in the GDR, because, as he said with an unmistakable reference to Ernst Bloch, "contradictions are hope" ("die Widersprüche sind die Hoffnung").[40]

NOTES

1. J[oachim]. G[ünther]., "Ernst Bloch," *Neue deutsche Hefte,* 24 (1977), 667-670.

2. Hans Mayer, "Ernst Blochs poetische Sendung," *Ernst Bloch zu ehren,* ed. Siegfried Unseld (Frankfurt / M.: Suhrkamp, 1965), pp. 21-30.

3. For a history and survey of GDR literature, see Konrad Franke, *Die Literatur der Deutschen Demokratischen Republik* (München: Kindler, 1971); Fritz J. Raddatz, *Traditionen und Tendenzen: Materialien zur Literatur der DDR* (Frankfurt / M.: Suhrkamp, 1972); Hans Jürgen Geerdts (ed.), *Literatur der DDR in Einzeldarstellungen* (Stuttgart: Kröner, 1972); Hans-Dietrich Sander, *Geschichte der Schönen Literatur in der DDR* (Freiburg / Br.: Rombach, 1972);Werner Brettschneider, *Zwischen literarischer Autonomie und Staatsdienst: Die Literatur in der DDR,* 2nd ed. (Berlin: Schmidt, 1974); Hans-Jürgen Schmitt (ed.), *Einführung in Theorie, Geschichte und Funktion der DDR-Literatur* (Stuttgart: Metzler, 1975). Regarding lyric poetry the author's thesis is supported by John Flores' monograph, which identified Bloch's philosophy as "the most important impetus" in the literary discussions since 1955 and which demonstrated in detail how Bloch influenced some GDR poets, such as Franz Fühmann, Peter Huchel and Günter Kunert (see *Poetry in East Germany: Adjustments, Visions, and Provocations, 1945-1970,* Yale Germanic Studies, 5 [New Haven: Yale University Press, 1971], pp. 9; 111-114, 173-177). Günter Kunert just published a poetry collection under the title *Unterwegs nach Utopia* (München: Hanser, 1977). The author's thesis regarding drama and novel is supported by recent articles and monographs by Christine Cosentino, Andreas Huyssen and Christa Thomassen on individual authors such as Peter Hacks and Christa Wolf (see Christine Cosentino, "Geschichte und 'Humane Utopie': Zur Heldengestaltung bei Peter Hacks," *German Quarterly,* 50 [1977], 248-263; Andreas Huyssen, "Auf den Spuren Ernst Blochs: Nachdenken über Christa Wolf," *Basis,* 5 [1975], 100-116; Christa Thomassen, *Der lange Weg zu uns selbst: Christa Wolfs Roman Nachdenken über Christa T. als Erfahrungs- und Handlungsmuster* [Kronberg/Ts.: Scriptor, 1977]). The author is indebted to the above studies.

4. For an introduction to Bloch's philosophy see Ehrhard Bahr, *Ernst Bloch* (Berlin: Colloquium, 1974); Silvia Markun, *Ernst Bloch* (Reinbek: Rowohlt, 1977); and the introductions by Harvey Cox and Jürgen Moltmann to the selection from Ernst Bloch's works *Man on His Own: Essays in the Philosophy of Religion,* transl. E. B. Ashton (New York: Herder & Herder, 1971), pp. 7-29. The author is indebted to these two introductions.

5. For a history of the GDR see Stefan Doernberg, *Kurze Geschichte der DDR,* 3rd ed. (Berlin: Dietz, 1968); Arthur M. Hanhardt, Jr., *The German Democratic Republic* (Baltimore: Johns Hopkins Press, 1968).

6. Hellmuth G. Bütow, *Philosophie und Gesellschaft im Denken Ernst Blochs* (Berlin: Osteuropa-Institut, 1963), p. 45.

7. John Flores, *Poetry in East Germany,* p. 13.

8. Gerhard Zwerenz, *Kopf und Bauch: Die Geschichte eines Arbeiters, der unter die Intellektuellen gefallen ist* (Frankfurt / M.: Fischer, 1971), p. 101.

9. Ibid., p. 129.

10. Hanhardt, *The German Democratic Republic*, pp. 43–66.

11. Bloch held a lecture series "Differentiation in the Concept of Progress" in 1955 and the famous Hegel lecture on 14 November 1956 at the Humboldt University in Berlin-East.

12. See Harvey Cox's foreword in Ernst Bloch, *Man on His Own*, pp. 7–18.

13. Adolph Lowe, "S ist noch nicht P," *Ernst Bloch zu ehren*, pp. 135–143.

14. See Hans Koch (ed.), *Zur Theorie des sozialistischen Realismus* (Berlin: Dietz, 1974), pp. 616–621. Cf. Georg Lukács, "Das Problem der Perspektive," *Schriften zur Literatursoziologie*, ed. Peter Ludz (Neuwied: Luchterhand, 1961), pp. 254–160.

15. *Das Prinzip Hoffnung*, vol. 1 (Frankfurt / M.: Suhrkamp, 1959), p. 16.

16. Quoted from the book jacket of the English translation by Christopher Middleton, *The Quest for Christa T.* by Christa Wolf (New York: Delta, 1972). The pagination refers to the German text *Nachdenken über Christa T.* (Neuwied: Luchterhand, 1971). For further studies on Christa Wolf see Andreas Huyssen, "Auf den Spuren Ernst Blochs," *Basis*, 5 (1975), 100–116; Christa Thomassen, *Der lange Weg zu uns selbst* (1977) and Alexander Stephan, *Christa Wolf* (München: Beck, 1976), esp. pp. 59, 92. The author is especially indebted to Huyssen's article.

17. All further pagination in the text refers to the German original, published by Luchterhand, Neuwied, 1971.

18. Hans Mayer's verdict that Christa Wolf writes about a writer's courage in suppressing the truth is not only vicious, but tragic (see *Der Spiegel*, 11 April 1977), because Christa Wolf is the last great hope of GDR literature (Efim Etkind).

19. Irmtraud Morgner, *Die wundersamen Reisen Gustavs des Weltfahrers* (Berlin / Weimar: Aufbau-Verlag, 1972), pp. 14–15. All further pagination in the text refers to this edition.

20. Hermann Bausinger, "Möglichkeiten des Märchens in der Gegenwart," *Märchen, Mythos, Dichtung: Festschrift Friedrich von der Leyen*, ed. Hugo Kuhn & Kurt Schier (München: Beck, 1963), p. 21.

21. *Das Prinzip Hoffnung*, vol. 3 (Frankfurt / M.: Suhrkamp, 1959), p. 1621. See also John Flores, *Poetry in East Germany*, pp. 111f.

22. Pagination refers to the text of the German original.

23. Patricia Herminghouse, "Women and the Fantastic in Recent GDR Literature: The Case of Irmtraud Morgner," "Women in German," unpublished newsletter, 1977, p. 6.

24. Biddy Martin, ibid., p. 7.

25. Peter Hacks, *Das Poetische: Ansätze zu einer postrevolutionären Dramaturgie* (Frankfurt / M.: Suhrkamp, 1972), p. 131. For further study of Peter Hacks' dramas, see Horst Laube, *Peter Hacks* (Hannover: Velber, 1972); Wolfgang Schivelbusch, *Sozialistisches Drama nach Brecht: Drei Modelle: Peter Hacks, Heiner Müller, Hartmut Lange* (Neuwied: Luchterhand, 1974); Peter Schütze, *Peter Hacks: Ein Beitrag zur Ästhetik des Dramas: Antike und Mythenaneignung* (Kronberg / Ts.: Scriptor, 1976); Winfried Schleyer, *Die Stücke von Peter Hacks: Tendenzen, Themen, Theorien* (Stuttgart: Klett, 1976) and Christine Cosentino's article, cited in footnote 3. The author is especially indebted to this article.

26. Peter Hacks, *Das Poetische*, p. 10.

27. Ibid., pp. 10–11.

28. See Peter Demetz, *Postwar German Literature: A Critical Introduction* (New York: Schocken, 1972); pp. 135–137.

29. Peter Hacks, *Vier Komödien* (Frankfurt / M.: Suhrkamp, 1971), p. 213. All further pagination in the text refers to this edition.

30. Heiner Müller, *Germania Tod in Berlin,* Texte 5 (Berlin: Rotbuch Verlag, 1977). See also the review by Klaus Völker in *Frankfurter Allgemeine Zeitung,* 16 December 1977, and the following reviews of the Munich production of the play: Anonymous, "'Gnade, mein Führer.' Aus Heiner Müllers Stück *Germania Tod in Berlin,*" *Der Spiegel,* 17 April 1978; Peter von Becker, "Schlachthauspostille und Tanz der deutschen Vampire," *Süddeutsche Zeitung,* 23 April 1978; Georg Hensel, "Schlacht-Szenen aus der DDR," *Frankfurter Allgemeine Zeitung,* 22 April 1978; Ernst Wendt, "Heiner Müllers Texte 1–6: Ewiger deutscher Bürgerkrieg," *Der Spiegel,* 17 April 1978.

31. Jurek Becker, *Jakob der Lügner* (Neuwied: Luchterhand, 1970), pp. 31, 48, 103, 125, 133, 142, 183. See also Jurek Becker, "Wäre ich hinterher klüger? Mein Judentum," *Frankfurter Allgemeine Zeitung,* 13 May 1978.

32. See Ernst Bloch, "Kann Hoffnung enttäuscht werden?," *Gesamtausgabe,* vol. 9 (Frankfurt / M.: Suhrkamp, 1959), pp. 385–392.

33. Peter Roos (ed.) et al., *Exil: Die Ausbürgerung Wolf Biermanns aus der DDR: Eine Dokumentation,* with a preface by Günther Wallraff (Köln: Kiepenheuer & Witsch, 1977); Fritz J. Raddatz, "Drüben wird der Geist ausgetreten: Die zweite deutsche Exil-Literatur," *Die Zeit,* 19 August 1977. Cf. Marcel Reich-Ranicki, "Der alte Ärger und die neue Taktik," *Frankfurter Allgemeine Zeitung,* 24 August 1977.

34. Reiner Kunze, "Ich bin kein Emigrant: Seit ich über die Grenze bin, habe ich frischen Lebensmut. Ein Gespräch mit dem Lyriker," *Die Zeit,* 28 October 1977 (US-edition).

35. Günter Kunert, "Offener Brief aus Ost-Berlin: Ein Schriftsteller ohne Inspiration erzeugt Flugsand: Ein Dokument wachsender Ratlosigkeit der Autoren in der DDR. Die Entwürdigung von Menschen: Auf keine Art irgendwelche Hoffnung," *Die Zeit,* 12 August 1977 (US-edition). In 1979 Günter Kunert moved to West Germany for an indefinite period of time.

36. Reinhard Baumgart, "Das Lahand ist still — noch! Ein fast unendlicher Brief aus Berlin, Hauptstadt der DDR," *Die Zeit,* 25 November 1977 (US-edition). See also "Die grauen Tinten des Peter Hacks," *Der Spiegel,* 24 January 1977.

37. Reinhard Baumgart, op. cit.

38. Ibid.

39. *Der Spiegel,* 2 January 1978, 9 January 1978. The manifesto charged that the GDR is a one-party dictatorship. It urged the withdrawal of all foreign troops from both Germanys and the installation of a multi-party democracy.

40. Wolf Biermann, "Westzucker und Ostpeitsche: Der ausgesperrte DDR-Sänger Wolf Biermann an die Autoren des 'Manifests'," *Die Zeit,* 3 February 1978 (US-edition). This interpretation is reinforced by Wolf Biermann's recent poem on the first anniversary of Ernst Bloch's death, entitled "Ernst Bloch ist ja tot" and published in *Die Zeit,* 8 September 1978 (US-edition), as well as by his recent articles on his exile in the Federal Republic of Germany, published in *Die Zeit,* 15 and 22 September 1978 (US-edition). See also Gerhard Zwerenz, "Ernst Bloch ist tot — es lebe die Hoffnung," *Frankfurter Rundschau,* 5 August 1978.

Henrik Birnbaum

ON THE POETRY OF PROSE:
LAND- AND CITYSCAPE 'DEFAMILIARIZED' IN
DOCTOR ZHIVAGO

Proza — trudneyshaya forma poezii.
Andrei Bely[1]

Chto zhe sdelal ya za pakost',
Ya ubiytsa i zlodey?
Ya ves' mir zastavil plakat'
Nad krasoy zemli moyey.
Boris Pasternak[2]

1. *Doctor Zhivago*: Controversial Assessment and Place in Overall Œuvre

Much — both complimentary and derogatory — has been said and written
about Boris Pasternak's novel *Doctor Zhivago*. Its genesis can, with certainty,
be traced back to the late thirties though it is known that the poet contem-
plated writing a major piece in prose and had been conceiving of certain
related themes and drafting some sections even much earlier.[3] The bulk of
Doctor Zhivago was presumably written between the end of the Second
World War and the year of Stalin's death, thus between 1945 and 1953. A
preliminary version was completed by the summer of 1954[4] and the definite
form two years later, appearing in print first in 1957 (in a pirate printing and
shortly thereafter in a legitimate edition released by Giangiacomo Feltrinelli
of Milan) and then, again, in 1958 (the so-called Michigan edition), with
several subsequent printings and a host of translations to follow. Some have
praised the book that brought its author the Nobel Prize (which he however
had to decline) as the culmination of a remarkable career of poetry and lyrical
prose (in addition to an impressive output of empathic translations of foreign
poetry and drama). Others have criticized Pasternak's principal work, and the
one he himself was most proud of,[5] both on ideological and aesthetic grounds.
The critics have pointed out, among other things, that the book is lacking in
dramatic power and, in some respects, in realism (beginning with the apparent
unlikelihood of the many, typically Pasternakian coincidences of life, some of
them symbolically charged, and down to the presumably false ring in the
speech of some minor figures in the novel). They have further remarked that it
can be considered a novel in a narrow, traditional or formal sense only with
considerable qualifications, particularly if compared to the great Russian
novelists of the nineteenth century, a tradition which Pasternak obviously in

some, admittedly, modified way indeed meant to continue with his book. Others have countered by pointing out that this novel more fairly and appropriately ought to be compared with the "modernist" prose of writers like Andrei Bely or James Joyce. Now, with the perspective of time and a continuous flow of published Pasternak scholarship — some, not all, meeting high standards — to enlighten us, it is becoming ever more clear that *Doctor Zhivago*, with its eminently poetic qualities (whatever its ideological shortcomings[6] and structural flaws[7]), should perhaps be assessed not so much as a specimen of that great art of the Russian novel which, as we know, has also produced genuine masterpieces in the twentieth century and, especially with Solzhenitsyn, even after Pasternak. Nor does it do full justice to Pasternak's book if we compare it primarily with prose works which transcend the limits of the traditional novel such as those by Bely or Joyce, to mention the two typical examples just referred to.[8] Instead, *Doctor Zhivago* ought to be viewed, above all, against the broad background of the total poetic œuvre of the writer himself — including (but not confined to) his earlier, highly lyrical prose. Or, more specifically, the novel can indeed be compared to and measured by the level of artistic accomplishment attained in the more limited previous output of Pasternak's prose whose inherent poetic devices and means have been so incisively and perceptively analyzed, in strictly semiotic-poetic terms, by Roman Jakobson in his famous, trailblazing essay of 1935 on the Russian poet's early prose.[9]

The artistic qualities and the whole poetic conception — as well as indeed perception — of *Doctor Zhivago* are highlighted, of course, by the twenty-five "Poems of Yuri Zhivago" which formally constitute the last, seventeenth chapter of the book but in fact form an integral part of it, its symbolic condensation and heightened poetic expression, or, as some would read it, the very core and substance justifying, as it were, the preceding prose chapters of the novel as merely a commentary and elaboration.[10]

Doctor Zhivago marked both the climax and, by its immediate political (and, for its author, personal) consequences, the end of the brief Thaw following Stalin's death which, after some fainthearted beginnings, had been ushered in the year after (1954) by Ilya Ehrenburg's novella from which this mere episode in the unpredictable course of Soviet literature derives its name. Obviously, the highly artistic prose of Pasternak's novel is, essentially, a literary phenomenon of the postwar period and as such a proper topic for our conference. At the same time, it is the continuation and extension of one writer's work begun as early as just before the First World War. That poetic writing had already reached a first, generally acclaimed peak in 1922 (the same year that also saw the appearance of *The Childhood of Luvers*) with the publication of *My Sister Life*, actually written in the wake of the 1917 February Revolution and reflecting the mood which these turbulent events had created among some of the young artists and intellectuals; in a way, therefore, that poetry was an inspired and enthusiastic response to the liberating experience of early 1917. A straight line runs from the theme and the general atmosphere of *My Sister Life* to *Doctor Zhivago,* the Brother of Life, and there are many points of close affinity between the two books, the slim volume of poetry and the lyrical but lengthy panorama and biography in prose, published thirty-five years apart.[11] In this sense, then, the present paper falls under the rubric of "evolution," rather than "experiment," the two facets of the overall theme for this volume.

2. Semiotic (Structural-Poetic) Background

To most of us, verbal art in its purest, most unadulterated form still means poetry — potent poetry in the formal, narrow sense of verse (including free verse). But by the same token, artistically shaped prose, being the secondary, derived, and therefore marked category of verbal art in relation to poetry proper, is the more demanding, the more difficult-to-master form of poetic language, as verse is its primary and 'natural' (or unmarked) category, both historically and, what is of greater significance for the purpose of the present discussion, typologically. Hegel, the renewer and refiner of logical dialectic (in the framework of German idealist philosophy), had already stated in his Berlin lectures of the 1820s: "Die *Poesie* ist älter als das kunstreich ausgebildete prosaische Sprechen."[12] It is in this sense, also, that Andrei Bely's dictum about "prose being the most difficult poetry," cited as a motto at the head of this paper, is to be understood (see above, with n. 1). And, taking this point of view a bit further, Yuri Lotman, in his book on the structure of the artistic text, summed up his reasoning along, essentially, the same lines by concluding: "*Thus artistic prose arose against the background of a poetic system as the negation of that system.*"[13] And in his subsequent book discussing the analysis of the poetic text he had more to say on this topic, suggesting, among other things, that "poetic speech . . . was originally the only possible language of verbal art. The 'dissimilation' of the language of belletristic literature, i.e., its separation from ordinary speech, was attained by this means. Only later did 'assimilation' begin. From this already sharply 'dissimilar' material a [new] picture of reality was created. A model-sign was constructed by the devices of human language. If language functioned in relation to reality as a reproducing structure, then literature constituted a structure of structures." And, resuming and paraphrasing his earlier conclusion, Lotman goes on to declare: "Thus, *the esthetic perception of prose is possible only against the background of poetic culture.* Prose is a later phenomenon than poetry, arising in a period of chronologically more mature esthetic consciousness."[14]

Recently, in his contribution to the 8th International Congress of Slavists (Zagreb, September 1978) discussing "the Poetics of Prose," in a section labeled "Lotman and the minus-device" where he takes as his point of departure the Tartu scholar's earlier, 1964 variant of his discussion of poetry and prose (contained in his *Lektsii*), Edward Brown mentions the innovative aspect of Lotman's approach and solution. However, he notes that in support of the claim that verse language "was initially the only possible language for verbal art" one could, of course, adduce the fact that for Aristotle the subject of "Poetics" was exclusively verse and that, as Brown puts it, "for very long periods in literary history prose was confined to lesser, semi-literary kinds of writing, and was rarely admitted to the precincts of art."[15] In this context, particularly, medieval textual material comes to mind where, as regards prose, it may on occasion be extremely difficult to draw a sharp line between writing in general ('practical' or 'ordinary language') and literature proper (in the narrow and precise meaning of verbal art in nonmetrical form).[16] Yet, and with all due respect to the originality of Lotman's approach and his elaboration (and illustration) of this particular point of view, the claimed innovative aspect of his findings must perhaps be at least somewhat qualified in the light of the previously cited quotations from Hegel and Bely (assuming at least that Lotman has not been unaware of Hegel's pointed statement of an, after all, well-known historical fact and of Bely's aphoristic dictum — the latter, incidentally, merely being one of the capsule formulations found in Bely's extensive writings on literature and literary theory). In view of such sophisticated pieces of Old Russian literature as the controversial *Igor' Tale,* the *Supplication of Daniel the Exile,* and the short *Tale of the Destruction of the Russian Land* (also known as *Discourse on the Ruin of the Land of Rus'*), all written, I would argue, in highly artistic, rhythmic and embellished prose (discussed in my paper cited in n. 16 and, of course, more than merely well known to the expert on Old Russian literature Yuri Lotman), one may possibly have some reservations about the claim that "prose in the modern meaning of the word arises in Russian literature with Pushkin." Yet, this statement, if viewed in its overall European historical context and considering the half millennium or so preceding Pushkin, is of course essentially true, as is, in particular, Lotman's subsequent suggestion that "it [viz., prose] simultaneously unites the idea of high art and of non-poetry. Behind this stands the esthetic of 'real life' with its conviction that the source of poetry is reality."[17] In his 1970 book, Lotman then went on to state, now talking about the age of realism in nineteenth-century Russian literature, "when the Puškinian tradition was transformed, as it appeared in those years, into a historical tradition no longer felt as a living literary fact, *when prose triumphed over poetry to such an extent that it was no longer perceived in relation to poetry* [author's emphasis, H. B.], a turnabout occurred and poetry once again emerged. The beginning of the twentieth century, like the beginning of the nineteenth, saw Russian literature under the sign of poetry. And poetry in turn was the background against which the growth of artistic prose in the 1920s was perceived." This, and the subsequent observation that "in succeeding periods the broad movement toward the prosification of artistic culture, on the one hand, confirmed the authority of 'non-art' (reality, everyday life, the document), and on the other hand made a norm of *the reproduction of life* [italics supplied by author, H. B.] by means of art,"[18] — an observation which is both accurate and keen — lead us straight to Pasternak and his *Doctor Zhivago*. The novel must thus be seen as a reaction to the Symbolist poetry of the "silver age" and the subsequent, poetry-internal counterreaction (most notably in the poetry of the Futurists, but to a considerable extent also in that of the Acmeists) — both of which had profoundly influenced the young Pasternak. It signals, moreover, a turning to the poetry of life itself, life as a positive, rich, and fulfilling experience, and at the same time a turning away from some facets of the writer's own earlier experiments in prose, during the 1920s. By the same token, *Doctor Zhivago* can be conceived of both as an attempt, unsuccessful perhaps (and certainly less convincing than the masterful pieces of the early Solzhenitsyn), to continue the great realist tradition of Russian nineteenth-century literature (in particular, Tolstoy, but, on a different plane, Chekhov also) and to combine and synthesize into a higher form of verbal art Pasternak's own previous creativity, as a poet and as a prose writer. Further, as pointed out by me elsewhere, it would seem that it most probably was precisely *Doctor Zhivago* (more than anything else written by the later Pasternak) that the group of perceptive Soviet scholars (Yuri Lotman and Vyacheslav Vs. Ivanov among them) concerned with analyzing the structure and evolution of culture at large had in mind when, discussing works by Pasternak (other than the novel banned in the Soviet Union), they noted that "his later works are dominated by a dialogue orientation toward the interlocutor-as-hearer (toward the potential reader, who must understand everything being communicated to him)." Again, as always in the complex and contradictory patterns of cultural evolution, the development from an orientation toward the speaker (characteristic of Pasternak's earlier, cryptic and esoteric poetry and prose) to an orientation toward the hearer (best exemplified by *Doctor Zhivago*) is not the only possible one in a certain epoch. The reverse trend can be observed, among Pasternak's contemporaries, in Osip Mandelstam and, because of her longer life-span and literary career, even better in Anna Akhmatova's œuvre; compare her not easily decoded *Poem Without a Hero* with some of her earlier poetry.[19]

It will be remembered that Yuri Tynyanov and Roman Jakobson in their 1928 manifesto had suggested that Victor Shklovsky head a renewed (and now somewhat differently conceived) Formalist movement, a new *Opoyaz*. It was the same Shklovsky who, publicly recanting shortly thereafter, in January of 1930, by raising his "Monument over a Scholarly Error" (which, it should be added, along with some pretty denigrating self-criticism, also contained a brilliant, if one-sided analysis of earlier Formalism),[20] had opened his famous essay on "Art as Device," originally published in 1917, by the laconic dictum

"Art is thinking in images." And, while subsequently substantially qualifying, if not rejecting, this claim, he hastened to add that one could hear this phrase from a highschool student while it also may serve as the point of departure for a learned philologist about to construct a literary theory.[21] As is well known, it was in this essay that Shklovsky, developing and, in some instances, taking issue with ideas on literary theory set forth by Alexander Potebnya, formulated his key notion of the literary device of 'defamiliarization' (or 'estrangement,' in Russian *ostraneniye,* in German *Verfremdung*) and illustrated it first and foremost with examples taken from Tolstoy but then also with instances culled from various other writers, genres, and times (including some folkloric kinds of writing reflecting oral tradition).[22]

According to Shklovsky, "thinking in images" applies only to 'prose images'. In both these and in what he termed 'poetic images,' deformation of reality is achieved by 'defamiliarization,' the artistic device par préférence. As regards imagery as it pertains to verbal art, Roman Jakobson as early as in an article of 1921 "On Realism in Art" had, in discussing one particular ("progressive") current of nineteenth-century realism, identified as one of its characteristic devices "the condensation of the narrative *by means of images drawing on contiguity, i.e., the path from the proper term toward metonymy.*"[23] Though not yet suggesting in this short essay that metonymy is the predominant trope of prose as such but only identifying it as a device cultivated by a specific grouping of writers within the broader literary style of realism — in Russia, the so-called Gogolian school — this article, along with some other early statements on metonymy as an artistic device,[24] was the germ of Jakobson's continued concern with the problem of metaphor and, in particular, metonymy and their mutual — polarized — relationship, couched in aesthetic-semiotic terms.[25] In his next, more elaborate discussion of the metaphor/metonymy distinction, illustrated with examples primarily from the early prose of Pasternak (notably, *The Childhood of Luvers* and *Safe Conduct*), Jakobson goes on to suggest, more generally, that "there is an undeniably closer relationship on the one hand between verse and metaphor, on the other between prose and metonymy." Pointing out that verse relies on association by similarity, to wit, rhythmic (and other phonic) similarity or parallelism enhanced by a similarity (or contrast) of images, he then states that "an intentionally striking division into similar sections is foreign to prose." Instead, he suggests that "the basic impulse of narrative moves from one object to an adjacent one on the paths of space and time or of causality; to move from the whole to the part and vice versa is only a particular instance of this process . . . For metaphor the line of least resistance is verse, and for metonymy it is prose whose subject matter is either subdued or eliminated."[26]

In discussing this position of Jakobson's, based, in this instance, on highly idiosyncratic prose — that of the young Pasternak — Edward Brown, while in general agreement with it and suggesting that a careful examination of narrative prose as a whole (that of Tolstoy, Turgenev, Bely, among the Russians; Flaubert, Dickens, James, among the Western Europeans, as well as many others) would bear out the overall validity of Jakobson's distinction, nonetheless qualifies his agreement in one regard. "Rather than prose itself, is it not *narrative* for which metonymy has a marked affinity?" he asks. And he goes on to suggest that "the dominant figure in *Eugene Onegin,* for instance, is surely metonymy. A poetic narrative, then, would offer both rhythmical parallelism and movement 'on the paths of space or time or of causality'." In other words, the poetic narrative, Brown submits, offers language material for its own sake while at the same time moving along 'the axis of contiguity.' The aesthetic function of poetic language as well as the ordinary vs. poetic language dichotomy itself are therefore crucially pertinent to a narrative in poetic (or, to be more precise, in metric, versified) form such as Pushkin's chef d'œuvre. What is less clear, it would seem, is whether this dichotomy is demonstrably relevant also to plain narrative prose, that is, to prose other than that of writers whose language is an 'autonomous value'; of those, Brown mentions, among the Russians, Gogol, Remizov, Rozanov, Bely, and Zamyatin.[27] The references to "language material offered for its own sake" and to "writers whose language itself is an 'autonomous value'" bring to mind the notion that while for purposes served by everyday language the speaker/ writer selects and concatenates the sound segments and meaningful entities of the message from the totality of the particular code (Saussure's *langue*) used, in verbal art the code as a whole with all its potential associations and interrelations in absentia, constitutes the message.

To the Russian writers with an 'autonomous value' of their language, enumerated by Brown, I would add, of course, Pasternak. And I can hardly think of a piece in 'poetic prose,' epic and, at the same time, highly lyrical, which would fit the two facets of prose (ordinary or discursive and, contrasting with it, artistic) better than *Doctor Zhivago.* Here metonymy (carrying on the narrative) and metaphor (evoking feelings and moods) alternate and transform — sliding and shading, as it were — into each other. And though the rhythmic and otherwise phonic similarity and recurrent patterns are most immediately perceivable in the "Poems of Yuri Zhivago" (where, among other things, they also include the device of in part highly sophisticated rhyme), the sheer power of the language as sound is there also in Pasternak's prose, in the first sixteen chapters of *Doctor Zhivago.* It is enhanced here, as in the poems, by the powerful, sweeping imagery, carrying the reader along and away. Here metonymic images of semantic contiguity of the poetic syntagmatics in praesentia, in space and time (if only as traces and memories or by sensing the future) or by causality (grasping the inner meaning and inherent connections between events or situations) alternate with metaphoric images of semantic similarity — or its opposite: contrast — of the associative (or disjunctive) paradigmatics in absentia, enriching and expanding the aesthetic experience of the reader. For although obvious and long-recognized, it bears stressing here, once again, that the literary text as read, understood, and perceived by the reader is not a closed system, a ready-made piece handed over by the author to the consumer of his product. Rather it is an open system: a challenge, an inspiration, an invitation and encouragement to enter, with the writer, into the process of creating art or, better yet, to become a co-creator of art. For, as Benjamin Hrushovski has aptly put it, "a work of literature . . . is not to be identified with a text as a fixed object. . . . there are many things readers have to add to the actual language presented on the pages of a book. A work of literature is a text to be read by a reader. The reader 'realizes' the text, links up things which are not explicitly connected, makes guesses, fills in gaps, constructs points of view, creates tensions, etc." And, as we are told, "in the 'realization' of a text by a reader there are two major aspects: *understanding* of the meanings presented in the text and *experience* of the non-semantic, rhetorical, or poetic effects of the text."[28]

With the later Pasternak's deliberate orientation toward (and concern for) the hearer/reader alluded to above (cf. also n. 19), *Doctor Zhivago* provides, I would suggest, a particularly telling example of both aspects, the semantic 'understanding' and the poetic 'experience.' In the first sense, the novel is an account of an epoch, or rather of the transition from one epoch, the pre-Revolutionary, into another, that of the Revolution and the Civil War and their immediate consequences in Yuri Zhivago's lifetime. Also, in its "Epilogue," the book tells of people and events during and after the Second World War, when Tanya, the laundry girl and Yuri's daughter with Lara, and his brother Yevgraf, now Major-General Zhivago, are the living memories after him, but, in a higher meaning, his preserved poems, in the hands of his two old friends Dudorov and Gordon, are the real — metonymic — trace of Yuri Zhivago's onetime existence on earth. Viewed in this way, therefore, *Doctor Zhivago* is an account of a slice of history in one country — Russia — the people, their fates, and events in that particular time and space. In a second sense, however, *Doctor Zhivago* is an attempt to convey, and to share, an experience, an aesthetic-symbolic perception which, it should be added, also includes religion. In the former sense, Pasternak may not have fully succeeded with his book; in the latter, I would submit, he has (which is not tantamount to sharing his religious feelings and convictions). Landscape and cityscape, the serenity of nature and the pulsating rhythm of urban life, their lights and their shadows, provide the setting for much, if not most, of the unusually rich imagery of *Doctor Zhivago*.

3. Landscape 'Defamiliarized' in *Doctor Zhivago*

In his famous essay on "Art as Device," referred to above, Victor Shklovsky had set out by quoting the definition of art as "thinking in images" and, soon qualifying this all-too-general statement somewhat, had gone on to characterize and illustrate what he considered one of the chief techniques, if not *the* primary device, of art altogether — 'defamiliarization' (*ostraneniye*). The only other device, according to him, of comparable significance is the 'impeded form' (in Russian, *zatrudnyonnaya forma,* also *zatrudnyonnyi yazyk* 'impeded language,' *zaderzhaniye* 'retardation'), designed to increase the difficulty and duration of perception and thus to heighten its aesthetic function.[29] And, as we have seen, Roman Jakobson early made the distinction between two basic kinds of images (or tropes, figures) in verbal art, metaphor and metonymy.[30] Do these two concepts and their definitions, that of 'defamiliarization' and that of the metaphoric and/or metonymic image, coincide or substantially overlap? Jakobson's precise definitions in linguistic, or rather semiotic, terms cited above (in nn. 22 and 25) suggest that, indeed, they do overlap to a large extent. Pasternak's imagery, his metaphors and metonymies encountered in *Doctor Zhivago* 'defamiliarize' everyday or otherwise normally familiar objects by connecting them metonymically with and/or likening them to — that is, for an instant or two substituting them metaphorically with — something else, less familiar or unexpected by the reader who has just been about to settle down to his usual — automatized — way of looking at things. Individual elements and larger fragments of a landscape, as well as landscapes seen as wholes, so frequently described in *Doctor Zhivago,* can serve to exemplify this poetic device and the near-overlap of (Shklovsky's) 'defamiliarization' and (Jakobson's) imagery ranging between 'the metaphoric and metonymic poles.' What follows is a sampling of such imagery in *Doctor Zhivago,* with some further instances, for lack of space, being indicated by page reference only.[31]

Cold and snow, these eternal ingredients of the Russian winter landscape complete with the characteristic blizzard, scary and forbidding, particularly when seen through the eyes of a just-orphaned child, meet the reader on one of the very first pages of the book. The ten-year-old Yura Zhivago, who, during his mother's funeral, standing on her grave with his contorted face and stretched-out neck had given the impression of a "wolf cub . . . about to howl" (7–8), stares into the white blank of the winter night from the window of the monastery cell where his uncle had taken him immediately after the funeral. Already the evening is foreboding:

> There was nothing in the kitchen garden except acacia bushes around the walls and a few beds of cabbages, wrinkled and blue with cold. With each blast of wind the leafless acacias danced as if possessed and then lay flat on the path. (8)

But in the middle of the night, when Yura is wakened by the knocking of the storm against the window, the landscape outside seems even more eerie:

> Outside there was no trace of the road, the graveyard, of the kitchen garden, nothing but the blizzard, the air smoking with snow. It was almost as if the snowstorm had caught sight of Yura and, conscious of its power to terrify,

roared and howled, doing everything possible to impress him. Turning over and over in the sky, length after length of whiteness unwound over the earth and shrouded it. The blizzard was alone in the world; it had no rival. (8)

The image of "the air smoking with snow," powerful by its metaphoric / metonymic contrast snow: smoke (/ fire), is not merely a stylistic turn introduced by the English translator, but has its exact equivalent in the language of the original (*vozdukh dymilsya snegom*). It should further be noted that the all-enveloping whiteness of snow can of course, and should probably, be interpreted as a metonymic or possibly metaphoric symbol of death and its universality, so closely and recently experienced by the child Yura (and, with and through him, by the reader). A similar image of the snow that is "general all over Ireland" can, incidentally, be found in Joyce's *Finnegans Wake*.[32] Death, the opposite of life — the book's leitmotiv — is otherwise only rarely touched upon in *Doctor Zhivago*. Toward the end of the book, though, after Yuri Zhivago's death, it is metonymically associated with the vegetable kingdom, "the nearest neighbor of the kingdom of death." As such, death is both opposed to and organically connected with "the mysteries of evolution and the riddles of life that so puzzle us" and "are contained in the green of the earth, among the trees and the flowers of graveyards." And the life-related mystery of resurrection is once more alluded to when the writer mentions Mary Magdalene who "did not recognize Jesus risen from the grave, 'supposing Him to be the gardener . . .'" (410). Cf. also Yuri Zhivago's two poems — the next to last — with the rubric *Magdalene* (Magdalina). Compared to the blinding Russian snowstorm terrifying Yura the child, the description of the cold winter night in the streets of Moscow before the First World War, as perceived, years later, by Lara and Yura on their way to the Sventitskys' Christmas party (and metonymically related to the poem *Winter Night*), strikes one as almost idyllic and friendly and, at any rate, anything but suggestive of fearful feelings (cf. below).

We find another, no less contrasting and 'defamiliarized' imagery in the brief description of a garden as seen (by Nikolai Nikolayevich Vedenyapin) from the windows and balcony door of the Sventitskys' house in Moscow:

> Purple shadows reached into the room from the garden. The trees, laden with hoarfrost, their branches like smoky streaks of candle wax, looked in as if they wished to rest their burden on the floor of the study. (36)

Here, to be sure, the original has the adjective meaning 'lilac(-colored)' (*sirenevye*) where the translator uses 'smoky', but the contrast between the branches in "heavy hoarfrost" (*v tyazhelom ineye*) and the streaks of "solidified stearin" (*zastyvshego stearina*) again suggest a similar metonymic / metaphoric contrast (hot/liquid stearin : cold/hoarfrost; liquid : solidified) as the previous between snow and smoke.

Nature and landscape, or a segment thereof, do not always provide the primary term of comparison or association in Pasternak's imagery. Instances of a reverse procedure are also frequent in *Doctor Zhivago*. Thus, love, another variation on the novel's basic theme of life (along with resurrection, previously mentioned, and other, less overt ones) and its object, here the young Lara, can be likened to a Russian summer landscape. About Pasha Antipov we read:

> He was so childishly simple that he did not conceal his joy at seeing her, as if she were some summer landscape of birch trees, grass, and clouds . . . (45)

Of course, the comparison of a young loved woman with the beauty of nature is not uncommon in literature; perhaps, the concept of 'defamiliarization' is therefore not really applicable here. But a piece of nature, submerged in water and for that reason alone a bit mysterious, can also serve for more everyday descriptions such as that of the ground floor of the Gromekos' house:

> Its pistachio-colored curtains, gleaming piano top, aquarium, olive-green upholstery, and potted plants resembling seaweed made it look like a green, sleepily swaying sea bed. (49)

Here, the very mention of the aquarium, that transparent miniature model of the depths of the sea, and of the "plants resembling seaweed" anticipate and, metonymically (in the first instance) and metaphorically (in the second), lead up to the emerging overall image of a "green, sleepily swaying sea bed."

Naturally, images of the Russian landscape emerge in *Doctor Zhivago* in particular when the reader is taken to the countryside, to the estate at Duplyanka of young Lara's parental friends, the Kologrivovs; in the small, and gloomy but almost idyllic town of Meluzeyevo, built behind the front by the troops in the fertile, black-soil country where Doctor Zhivago and Nurse Antipova work together and where their love affair begins; and, more than anywhere else, in the Urals, at Varykino where their love bursts into full bloom but which also witnesses their parting, and in the nearby provincial town of Yuryatin. At first, Varykino, the place of their happy love, appears not directly, as seen and experienced by Yuri and Lara, but metonymically, merely as a memory, a place of longing, remembered by the ailing Anna Ivanovna, Tonya's mother, from her own childhood, as told to the youngsters Yura and Tonya:

> Yura could easily imagine those ten thousand acres of impenetrable virgin forest as black as night, and, thrusting into it like a curved knife, the bends of the swift stream with its rocky bed and steep cliffs . . . (61)

For the huge forest, whose blackness is imagined by Yura to be that of the night, a metonymic — and fairly common, if not trite — image is used by the

author (for the forest is indeed black, or can at least seem so, just as is the
night); but for the "swift stream" and its curved shape he resorts to a metaphor
which involves 'defamiliarizing' such an everyday object as a knife (which in
fact shares little, if anything, with a river). In this passage, therefore, metonymy and metaphor slide typically into each other.

Forest landscapes occur a few more times in *Doctor Zhivago,* described or
interpreted by the novel's hero. Thus, for example, when Zhivago is telling his
friend Gordon how he had once seen the Tsar at the front:

> Zhivago described the landscape, the mountains overgrown with mighty firs
> and pines, with tufts of clouds catching in their tops, and sheer cliffs of gray
> slate and graphite showing through the forest like worn patches in a thick fur.
> (102)

The simile or, rather, the 'defamiliarized' similarity metaphor serves here, as
so many times elsewhere in the book, primarily the purpose of making the
description more real, of adding realism by using a "displaced" graphic image
taken from everyday life. A similar effect is also achieved just a few lines
further on when the total impression of nature combining with the results of
human activity is conveyed as melting into one whole, enhanced by a general
— real or imaginary — slow rising movement and the double repetition of the
same color designations (matching, as it were, the two occurrences of 'everything'):

> Mist hung over the valley, and everything in it steamed, everything rose
> slowly — engine smoke from the railway station, gray vapors from the
> fields, the gray mountains, the dark woods, the dark clouds. (102–3)[33]

And, toward the end of the book, in the concluding, fifteenth chapter, the
forest symbolizes health and freedom, life and God, in contrast to the fields
which stand for illness, the devil, and, ultimately, death. This contrast sadly
mirrors the difference between the young, healthy Yuri and the aged (though
not yet old) and decrepit Zhivago, on his last journey back to Moscow and
after his arrival there, and, in a way, that between the young Vasya Brykin, his
companion on part of that journey and for a while in Moscow, and himself —
the former adjusting well to life in the NEP period, the latter ever more
resigned and inept for life altogether:

> The woods and the fields offered a complete contrast in those days. Deserted
> by man, the fields looked orphaned as if his absence had put them under a
> curse. The forest, however, well rid of him, flourished proudly in freedom as
> though released from captivity. — The fields appeared to him as something
> seen in the fever of a dangerous illness, and the woods, by contrast, in the
> lucidity of health regained. God, so it seemed to him, dwelled in the woods,
> while the fields echoed with the sardonic laughter of the devil. (389)

The life-giving power of nature as perceived through the many shifting forms of the Russian scenery is a recurrent theme in *Doctor Zhivago,* of course. For example, we read about Lara arriving at Duplyanka and walking from the railroad station to the estate:

> Here she stopped and, closing her eyes, took a deep breath of the flower-scented air of the broad expanse around her. It was dearer to her than her kin, better than a lover, wiser than a book. For a moment she rediscovered the purpose of her life. She was here on earth to grasp the meaning of its wild enchantment and to call each thing by its right name, or, if this was not within her power, to give birth out of love for life to successors who would do it in her place. (66)

Or, reaching beyond nature on earth, the visible universe can be felt to influence life decisions, as in the description of Pasha Antipov's doubts while looking up to the stars in the nocturnal sky over the small town of Yuryatin in the Urals pondering what went wrong in his marriage with Lara:

> It was a clear, frosty autumn night. Thin sheets of ice crumbled under his steps. The sky, shining with stars, threw a pale blue flicker like the flame of burning alcohol over the black earth with its clumps of frozen mud. (92)

In the first reference to the stars in this episode, their "pale blue flicker," by being likened to the 'defamiliarized' "flame of burning alcohol," is somehow brought closer to the reader's imaginative perception. And, moments later, sitting on an overturned boat,

> He looked up at the stars as if asking them for advice. They flickered on, small or large, quick or slow, some blue and some in all the hues of the rainbow. Suddenly they were blotted out, and the house, the yard, and Antipov sitting on his boat were thrown into relief by a harsh darting light, as though someone were running from the field toward the gate waving a torch. An army train, puffing clouds of yellow, flame-shot smoke into the sky, rolled over the grade crossing . . . (93)

As in so many other instances in the book, the interference of man and *his* creations changes the serene scenery of nature or the universe and an image — here, the metaphor of the running torch-bearer — is used to sharpen the reader's perception of that sudden change.

The descriptions of the grandiose, eternal while ever-changing Russian landscape — the woods, waterfalls, the expanses of snow, the coming of spring, and others — especially in the Urals, at Varykino and en route there, and in West Siberia (in the "Forest Brotherhood" of the partisans to which Yuri involuntarily came to belong), are many in *Doctor Zhivago,* of course. These descriptions lend the novel its eminently poetic qualities, matched only by the lyrical feelings of its main protagonists, Yuri and Lara, feelings frequently evoked and sustained by their own visualizing and experiencing the beauty of nature of which they feel a part. And, time and again, the descriptions of the landscape are enhanced and a direct line of perception with the reader is established, as it were, by the author's resorting to his favorite poetic device of introducing 'defamiliarized' images, usually visual but occasionally also acoustic, metaphoric or metonymic, or in some combination of the two. Thus, for example, while temporarily off the train which is to bring Yuri, his wife Tonya, her father, and others to their Uralian refuge, the party, busy sawing wood, experiences the arrival of spring in the forest in a very immediate, physical sense:

> The wood smelled of damp and was heaped with last year's leaves like an unswept room where people have been tearing up letters, bills, and receipts for years. — The wood echoed to the hoarse ringing of other saws; somewhere, very far away, a nightingale was trying out its voice, and at longer intervals a blackbird whistled as if blowing dust out of a flute. Even the engine steam rose into the sky warbling like milk boiling up on a nursery alcohol stove. (201)

Unfortunately, within the limits of a short paper it is not possible to quote in full all or even many of such descriptions. In refraining from doing so, we therefore can here only refer to some — not all — of these passages by indicating the pages in the English version of the novel where they can be found and merely hinting at their content.[34]

However, in closing this brief account of landscape 'defamiliarized' in *Doctor Zhivago,* it would seem appropriate to dwell for a moment upon at least one more description of nature encountered in the book. Here, though, it is not nature or a particular landscape that is in the foreground, made clear, sharp, and pristine by the use of a 'defamiliarized' imagery from everyday life and experience. Instead, a phenomenon of nature, "the current of a mighty river," serves as the metaphor to describe and characterize, along with music, language, and artistic language in particular, as well as the very process, the inspired moment of creating verbal art:

> Language, the home and receptacle of beauty and meaning, itself begins to think and speak for man and turns wholly into music, not in terms of sonority but in terms of the impetuousness and power of its inward flow. Then, like the current of a mighty river polishing stones and turning wheels by its very movement, the flow of speech creates in passing, by virtue of its own laws, meter and rhythm and countless other forms and formations, which are even more important, but which are as yet unexplored, insufficiently recognized, and unnamed. (363-4)

4. Cityscape 'Defamiliarized' in *Doctor Zhivago*

As we have already seen, the Russian small town, Meluzeyevo or Yuryatin for example, can be conceived as forming part, to some extent at least, of the Russian landscape, of nature itself, in *Doctor Zhivago.* Additional passages to illustrate this point could easily be quoted. But more often perhaps landscape and the small town panorama, nature and town life, blend and shade into each other as so often they do also in real life. Thus, we read about Yuryatin and Lara's feelings for it (while living there in her marriage with Pavel Antipov):

> She liked Yuriatin. It was her native town. It stood on the big river Rynva, navigable except in its upper reaches . . . — The approach of winter in Yuriatin was always heralded by the owners of boats, when they took them from the river and transported them on carts to the town, to be stored in back yards. There they lay in the open air waiting for the spring. The boats with their light upturned bottoms in the yards meant in Yuriatin what the migration of storks or the first snow meant in other places . . . — Larisa Feodorovna liked Yuriatin's provincial ways, the long vowels of its northern accent, and the naïve trustfulness of its intelligentsia, who wore felt boots and gray flannel sleeveless coats. She was drawn to the land and to the common people. (91)

But also later, just before Yuri Zhivago joins Lara in Yuryatin, nature and the landscape outside town are felt to be part of life in the picturesque town:

> Merchant Street rambled crookedly downhill, overlooked by the houses and churches of the upper part of Yuriatin. — At the corner there was the dark gray house with sculptures. The huge square stones of the lower part of its façade were covered with freshly posted sheets of government newspapers and proclamations . . . — After the recent thaw it was dry and frosty. Now it was light at a time of day when only a few weeks before it had been dark. The winter had just gone, and the emptiness it had left was filled by the light that lingered on into the evenings. The light made one restless, it was like a call from afar that was disturbing, it put one on one's guard. (313)

Similarly, Meluzeyevo, the gloomy but for Yuri and Lara almost idyllic little town behind the front, presents a picture of half town, half countryside:

> The small town was called Meliuzeievo and lay in the fertile, black-soil country. Black dust hung over its roofs like a cloud of locusts. (111)

And:

> It was a two-story house on one of the best sites of the town, at the corner of the main street and the square . . . Its position gave it a good view of the neighborhood; in addition to the square and the street it overlooked the adjoining farm (owned by a poor, provincial family who lived almost like peasants) as well as the Countess's old garden at the back. (114)

Or:

> It was getting dark. Outside, the houses and fences huddled closer together in the dusk. The trees advanced out of the depth of the garden into the light of the lamps shining from the windows. The night was hot and sticky. (118)

All the flowers smelled at once; it was as if the earth, unconscious all day long, were now waking to their fragrance. And from the Countess's centuries-old garden, so littered with fallen branches that it was impenetrable, the dusty aroma of old linden trees coming into bloom drifted in a huge wave as tall as a house . . . — An enormous crimson moon rose behind the crows' nest in the Countess's garden. At first it was the color of the new brick mill in Zybushino, then it turned yellow like the water tower at Biriuchi. — And just under the window, the smell of new-mown hay, as perfumed as jasmine tea, mixed with that of belladonna. — . . . and beyond the black barns of Meliuzeievo the stars twinkled, and invisible threads of sympathy stretched between them . . . — Everything was fermenting, growing, rising with the magic yeast of life. The joy of living, like a gentle wind, swept in a broad surge indiscriminately through fields and towns, through walls and fences, through wood and flesh. (119)

By now the moon stood high. Its light covered everything as with a thick layer of white paint. The broad shadows thrown by the pillared government buildings that surrounded the square in a semicircle spread on the ground like black rugs. — Narrow dead-end streets ran off the square, as deep in mud as country lanes and lined with crooked little houses. Fences of plaited willows stuck out of the mud like bow nets in a pond, or lobster pots . . . In the small front gardens, sweaty red heads of corn with oily whiskers reached out toward the rooms, and single pale thin hollyhocks looked out over the fences, like women in night clothes whom the heat had driven out of their stuffy houses for a breath of air. — The moonlit night was extraordinary, like merciful love or the gift of clairvoyance. Suddenly, into this radiant, legend-ary stillness, there dropped the measured, rhythmic sound of a familiar, recently heard voice. (120)

But, of course, if the eloquent praise of the Russian landscape is one of the great assets of *Doctor Zhivago,* it is not the description, empathic and loving as it may be, of the Russian small town that is the book's other chief positive characteristic. In addition to being a hymn to the beauty and power of nature as encountered, over and over again, in the Russian countryside, *Doctor Zhivago* is first and foremost a tribute to Pasternak's own native city, to Moscow, its pulsating and hectic life, its pre-Revolutionary bourgeois idyllic-ness and proletarian shady side as well as its modern post-Revolutionary urbanism, its peculiar beauty, composite of many various elements, as it mirrors and echoes contemporary life itself. Also, in the imagery used for describing the Moscow cityscape and the segments of which it is made up, the poetic device of 'defamiliarization' finds a more frequent and genuine applica-tion than is the case with the at best slightly 'defamiliarized' metaphors and metonymies used in depicting the situation in and the impression conveyed by small towns such as Meluzeyevo or Yuryatin. In this respect, too, therefore only the description of Moscow can match, in artistic terms, that of nature of the Russian landscape.

Almost at the outset of the novel, in chapter two (22–3), the author provides the reader with a few glimpses of the atmosphere in and around the Montenegro Hotel in "the most disreputable part of Moscow" where Komarovsky has arranged for the déclassée widow Madame Gishar (Guichard) and her children, Rodya and Lara, to stay. And, again, soon thereafter when we are told of the "unrest among the railway workers on the Moscow network," an air of big city hustle and proletarian living is conveyed:

> It was a cold overcast morning at the beginning of October, and on that day the wages were due . . . — In an endless line, conductors, switchmen, mechanics and their assistants, scrubwomen from the depot, moved across the ground between the wooden buildings of the management and the station with its workshops, warehouses, engine sheds, and tracks. — The air smelled of early winter in town — of trampled maple leaves, melted snow, engine soot, and warm rye bread just out of the oven (it was baked in the basement of the station buffet). Trains came and went. (26)

A little later in the book, just after Lara has been seduced by Komarovsky and is on her way home and then, after she is already home, the weather, this signal from nature as perceived in the city, as though the first signs of spring, provides a contrasting (and comforting) backdrop to her desperate thoughts and mood:

> The weather was on the mend. Plop-plop-plop went the water drops on the metal of the drainpipes and the cornices, roof tapping messages to roof as if it were spring. It was thawing. — Outside the window the water drops plopped on and on, the thaw muttered its spells. (41)

The Russian winter night — that classic landscape out there in free nature depicted by Pasternak and a host of other Russian poets and writers so many times — can be brought in to the big city, to Moscow, and described in that "domesticated" setting as well. Pasternak has done precisely that in *Doctor Zhivago,* painting the streets of Moscow at Christmas time not only once, but twice — as seen by Lara, and, a few moments later, as perceived through the eyes of Yura:

> Only now . . . did she take a look around her. It was winter. It was the city. It was night. — It was bitter cold. The streets were covered with a thick, black, glassy layer of ice, like the bottom of beer bottles. It hurt her to breathe. The air was dense with gray sleet and it tickled and prickled her face like the gray frozen bristles of her fur cape. Her heart thumping, she walked through the deserted streets past the steaming doors of cheap teashops and restaurants. Faces as red as sausages and horses' and dogs' heads with beards of icicles emerged from the mist. A thick crust of ice and snow covered the windows, and the colored reflections of lighted Christmas trees and the shadows of merrymakers moved across their chalk-white opaque surfaces as on magic lantern screens; it was as though shows were being given for the benefit of pedestrians. (68)

A language more saturated, within the confines of a few sentences, with rich imagery, both metaphoric (". . . like the bottom of beer bottles," ". . . as red as sausages . . . ," ". . . as on magic lantern screens") and metonymic (". . . like the gray frozen bristles . . . ," ". . . as though shows were being given . . .") can hardly be conceived of. And shortly thereafter, the very same scenery, now seen by Yuri Zhivago:

> Yura looked around him and saw what Lara had seen shortly before. The moving sleigh was making an unusually loud noise, which was answered by an unusually long echo coming from the ice-bound trees in the gardens and streets. The windows, frosted and lighted from inside, reminded him of precious caskets made of smoky topaz. Behind them glowed the Christmas life of Moscow, candles burned on trees, and guests in fancy dress milled about playing hide-and-seek and hunt-the-ring. (70)

And interrupted only by a few reflections on Blok as the poet of the Christmas spirit in all domains of Russian life, Yura goes on observing:

> As they drove through Kamerger Street Yura noticed that a candle had melted a patch in the icy crust on one of the windows. The light seemed to look into the street almost consciously, as if it were watching the passing carriages and waiting for someone. — "A candle burned on the table, a candle . . ." he whispered to himself — the beginning of something confused, formless; he hoped that it would take shape of itself. But nothing more came to him. (70-1)

Here, in Yuri's perception of the nocturnal Moscow cityscape at Christmas time, there is less density of metaphoric images than in the writer's account of Lara's world of 'defamiliarized' associations. Note, however, the metaphor of the windows as "precious caskets of smoky topaz" (an image, incidentally, for a change operating with the very opposite of 'defamiliarization') and the only half-articulated metaphor of the candle light as "look[ing] into the street almost consciously, as if it were watching . . . " By the same token, there are other artistic devices at work here. Thus, for example, notice the fact that after the opening remark about looking around and seeing what Lara had seen before, the first perception is not a visual but an acoustic one: the sleigh's noise echoed by the trees. And in musing about Blok, there is, one may surmise, implicitly both a metonymic connection and comparison between Blok and Pasternak himself and, more specifically, the reference to Blok as reflecting the Christmas spirit "in this northern city" (in the Russian original, *Doktor Zhivago,* 81: *v severnom gorodskom bytu*) may perhaps be seen as contrasting Blok's (and Bely's) Petersburg with Pasternak's Moscow. And, toward the end of the quoted passage, the metonymic connection with the poem said to have been written subsequently by Yuri Zhivago in Varykino — *Winter Night (Zimnyaya noch')* — is of course quite explicit (cf. 363 and

445-6; and above, in the discussion of the snowstorm witnessed by young Yura in the winter night right after his mother's funeral).

A few pages later, Lara, in an early flashback, visualizes pre-Revolutionary Moscow once more, the Moscow of her arrival, when she and her family were sinking into the gloom of an impoverished life but when she also already had a premonition of her subsequent discovery of the city, and her temptation by it:

> She often thought of the night of her arrival in Moscow from the Urals . . . She was riding in a cab from the station through gloomy alleys to the hotel at the other end of town. One by one the street lamps threw the humpbacked shadow of the coachman on the walls. The shadow grew and grew till it became gigantic and stretched across the roofs and was cut off. Then it all began again from the beginning. The bells of Moscow's countless churches clanged in the darkness overhead, and the trolleys rang as they scurried through the streets, but Lara was also deafened by the gaudy window displays and glaring lights, as if they too emitted sounds of their own, like the bells and wheels. (80)

Something similar happens to Yuri Zhivago. When returning from Meluzeyevo to the "Moscow Encampment" and to his family in those days of the October Revolution or shortly after, it seemed to him, when in later years recalling this day —

> he did not know whether this was the original impression or whether it had been altered by subsequent experiences — that even then the crowd hung about the market only by habit, that there was no reason for it to be there, for the empty stalls were shut and not even padlocked and there was nothing to buy or sell in the littered square, which was no longer swept. (140)

And though the scenery of Moscow at the time of and immediately after the Revolution is not an aesthetically appealing one, the writer, in his realistic description, is able to convey at least a measure of picturesqueness even of the ugliness of the street:

> Behind them, the setting sun warmed their backs. In front of them a draft horse clattered along, pulling an empty, bouncing cart. It raised pillars of dust, glowing like bronze in the rays of the low sun . . . The doctor was struck by the piles of old newspapers and posters, torn down from the walls and fences, littering the sidewalks and streets. The wind pulled them one way and hoofs, wheels, and feet shoved them the other. (140-1)

And, as in the forlorn remoteness of the provincial town of Chekhov's *Three Sisters,* Moscow takes on a new, overpowering dimension for Yuri Zhivago, living, as he does, with Lara in her faraway Uralian hometown of Yuryatin, particularly after he learns that his wife Tonya and their son (whom Yuri has never seen) are back in the capital. Two bad dreams, one after the other, torture him — both set in Moscow, which in so many ways symbolizes the opposite of Lara and the unspoiled nature she represents:

> He was in Moscow in a room with a glass door. The door was locked. For greater safety he was keeping hold of it by the handle and pulling it toward himself. From the other side, his little boy, Sashenka, dressed in a sailor suit and cap, was knocking, crying and begging to be let in. (326)

But Yuri,

> with tears pouring down his face . . . kept hold of the handle of the locked door, shutting out the child, sacrificing him to a false notion of honor, in the name of his alleged duty to another woman . . . (327)

Moments later, Zhivago is asleep again, once more dreaming a fear-ridden, longing dream about Moscow where this time Lara appears as the hostess, their intimacy reduced to a cold, impersonal relationship:

> He dreamed of a dark winter morning in a bustling Moscow street. Judging by the early morning traffic, the trolleys ringing their bells, and the yellow pools of lamplight on the gray snow-covered street, it was before the revolution. — He dreamed of a big apartment with many windows, all on the same side of the house, probably no higher than the third story, with drawn curtains reaching to the floor. (327)

But if here Moscow, temporarily out of reach, both attracts and represents a menace to Yuri Zhivago, he intones, toward the end of the book, in the closing chapter, a veritable love song to it, a love song in prose, to be sure, but powerful and expressive nonetheless. It is preceded by a few general thoughts about art — the art of language in particular — and the big city in our modern age. Recognizing that after revolution and war Moscow has remained (into the mid-1920s) a city in disrepair, he states:

> But even in this condition it is still a big modern city, and cities are the only source of inspiration for a new, truly modern art. — The seemingly incongruous and arbitrary jumble of things and ideas in the work of the Symbolists . . . is not a stylistic caprice. This is a new order of impressions, taken directly from life. — Just as they hurry their succession of images through the lines of their poems, so the street in a busy town hurries past us, with its crowds and its broughams and carriages at the end of the last century, or its streetcars and subways at the beginning of ours.[35] — Pastoral simplicity doesn't exist in these conditions. When it is attempted, its pseudo-artlessness is a literary fraud, not inspired by the countryside but taken from the shelves of academic archives. The living language of our time, born spontaneously and naturally in accord with its spirit, is the language of urbanism. (406)

And after this artistic credo he goes on to sing the praise of his — Pasternak's own — Moscow:

Moscow, blinded by the sun and the white heat of its asphalt-paved yards, scattering reflections of the sun from its upper windows, breathing in the flowering of clouds and streets, is whirling around me, turning my head and telling me to turn the heads of others by writing poems in its praise. For this purpose, Moscow has brought me up and made me an artist. — The incessant rumbling by day and night in the street outside our walls is as inseparable from the modern soul as the opening bars of an overture are inseparable from the curtain, as yet secret and dark, but already beginning to crimson in the glow of the footlights. The city, incessantly moving and roaring outside our doors and windows, is an immense introduction to the life of each of us. It is in these terms that I should like to write about the city. (406–7)

The imagery of this and the preceding passage is not exceedingly rich — but it is striking and potent: there is the simile of the succession of images in Symbolist poetry and the succession of vehicles, old and new, in a busy city street; the image of Moscow, blinded and "breathing in the flowering of clouds"; and the parallel between, on the one hand, the incessant rumbling of the city life and traffic in its relation to the modern soul and, on the other, the metonymic connection between the first tones of an overture and the as yet mysterious and dark but already glowing curtain of the opera.

Here, more than elsewhere in the book (in which the author, in a departure from his earlier attitude, sought to identify with the reader; cf. above), the writer seems nonetheless to be speaking primarily for himself, the poet and his role, rather than for man in general (identifiable with the reader), his claim made on behalf of everyone (". . . an immense introduction to the life of each of us") notwithstanding. It is no accident therefore, I would suggest, that it is in this context that the poem *Hamlet,* unique and apart, which opens the Zhivago cycle, is mentioned as possibly belonging "to this category."

If the view, spiritual and real, of Moscow in these last notes of Yuri Zhivago is both exciting and explosive, it is with a different, more peaceful image of the city that the book draws to a close and, finally, fades out. Sitting, after the Second World War, at an open window "above Moscow, which extended into the dusk as far as the eye could reach," Dudorov and Gordon, Yuri's two old friends, with his writings in their hands, ponder over the past and venture a glance into the future:

And Moscow, right below them and stretching into the distance, the author's native city, in which he had spent half his life — Moscow now struck them not as the stage of the events connected with him but as the main protagonist of a long story, the end of which they had reached that evening, book in hand. (431)

Here, then, Moscow, the metonymic framework or "stage" of all the events, thoughts, and moods of the novel (regardless of whether they actually took place there or were merely related and associated with the city by the paths of time and space, or by causation), suddenly, and as a final poetic effect, is itself transformed into an all-overshadowing metaphor, the metaphoric protagonist of the whole story. By the same token, Yuri Zhivago's extant poems, this quintessence of his—and, one may add, Pasternak's own—life experience (cf. n. 5), now in the hands of a remembering posterity, represented by Dudorov and Gordon, turn into the ultimate metonymic symbol of the book as a whole (cf. also n. 10).

Sensing the freedom of the soul already present and the future which "had tangibly moved into the streets below them . . . thinking of this holy city and of the entire earth" and of the surviving characters of this story and their offspring, the two old men "were filled with tenderness and peace" and an unheard music of happiness flowed "all about them and into the distance." (432)

Here, in a last synthesis, Pasternak's Orthodox Christianity (to which the reference to Moscow as "this holy city" alludes and which, it should be remembered, he sincerely embraced as amply testified to in *Doctor Zhivago*) merges with his pantheism beyond and above any particular confession and strongly anchored in his ties — real, symbolic, and religious — with his ambience.

5. Man and His Ambience in *Doctor Zhivago*

It was suggested before that *Doctor Zhivago* represents the best example of the later Pasternak's orientation toward the hearer/reader (and away from his earlier more one-sided preoccupation with the speaker/writer). Perhaps, though, it would be somewhat more accurate to characterize *Doctor Zhivago*, as well as some other of Pasternak's later works noted by the group of Soviet cultural semioticians (cf. also n. 19), as "dominated by a dialogue orientation toward the interlocutor-as-hearer," to quote their apt formulation. For, while the Russian writer's concern in his novel is clearly with man as such, and not only with the poet (or, more generally, the artist), the particular relationship obtaining between man in general and the poet — with the role of the poet (here represented by Yuri Zhivago) viewed as that of setting an example and acting as mediator (with unmistakable overtones of destined sacrifice and suffering for mankind) — is also very much in the foreground of the novel. Some remaining primary concern with the poet and his specific mission, as expressed also in the poem *Hamlet,* was already noted above.[36]

By and large, however, it is the predicament of man — and not only of the poet — and man's life on earth that is the central theme of *Doctor Zhivago*. In this sense, therefore, Pasternak's novel is thematically akin both to Hamlet, the symbol of the precarious existence, and to the Faust motif. In this context, I would venture the contention that, although the Hamlet theme is explicitly mentioned in the book itself (in the poem with that title) and *Doctor Zhivago* has even been interpreted as a Russian Hamlet[37] and there exist doubtless allusions to the Hamlet-Christ affinity of self-denying sacrifice in the book,[38] the Faustian theme is there as well; and that in spite of Pasternak's own criticism (in the words of Nikolai Vedenyapin, occasionally acting as the author's mouthpiece) of the intrinsic falseness in dealing with the mysteries of the universe "even in *Faust*," Goethe's *Faust* no doubt.[39]

Elsewhere, I have attempted a comparison, revealing similarities as well as differences, between *Doctor Zhivago* and a modern *Faustus,* Thomas Mann's novel.[40] Among the striking differences is one particularly relevant to the present discussion: Pasternak's understanding of and deep-felt empathy with man's surrounding, his ambience, in the nature of the Russian landscape and in the modern setting of the Russian capital alike; by contrast Thomas Mann displays only minimal awareness of and sensitivity for the physical world in which his characters are set, and nature in particular.[41] Another important and not unrelated difference is of course the two authors' concept of the poet, the writer, and the artist in general. As is well known, Mann took a rather dim (and, for that reason, self-critical) view of the artist who for him was scarcely more than a dubious magician, an illusionist.[42]

There are nonetheless significant similarities between Pasternak's and Mann's last great prose works, their *Zeitromane aus Exilsicht* as I have tentatively called them. But these shared facets do not lie in the way they understand the function of art in life or, for that matter, in the religious domain (since Pasternak was a believing and practicing Christian while Thomas Mann was not). By the same token, there is, it would seem to me, another sphere, another world view which *Doctor Zhivago* indeed shares — not with Thomas Mann's *Faustus*-Leverkühn, but with Goethe's *Faust* and its author. I am referring here both to the pantheistic religious feeling (rather than faith in the narrow sense) which Goethe and Pasternak shared, and, what goes with it, their capacity of integrating, physically and spiritually, with the world around them and with nature specifically, a capacity endowing them with a sense of safety and security (cf. Goethe's *Naturverbundenheit* and his *Naturgeborgenheit*). For the German of the late 18th and early 19th centuries, the additional, modern dimension of space — the cityscape so crucial for Pasternak's artistic interpretation of contemporary life, its rhythm and its demands — did not yet exist to the same extent, of course. Possibly, the idyllic small town (say, Strassburg or Weimar) and what then must have seemed as big cities (such as Frankfurt, Leipzig, or Rome, even if by today's standards they would hardly qualify as more than medium-sized towns at the time) may for Goethe, as modern Moscow for Pasternak, have supplemented and, in part, substituted for his organic contact with unspoiled nature. For both, Goethe and Pasternak, there existed a metonymic relation between the poet, and man as such, and his ambience. And, the metonymically charged poetic prose text as a whole can and does, in the last analysis, assume the qualities of and turn into one all-encompassing metaphor.[43] So life itself, if interpreted artistically, may be viewed as a great symbolic metaphor for something else, only darkly sensed and perceived for the time being. The final lines of Goethe's *Faust,* metaphoric and cryptic at once and transcending all temporal bounds, are just as apposite a closing accord, in every word, for *Doctor Zhivago* — that hymn to life, with its richly strewn images, the sequentially built metonymies interlaced with nova-like flashing metaphors of which the unique visions of 'defamiliarized' land- and cityscape of Pasternak's beloved Russia constitute but a particularly striking instantiation — as they are for that other symbol of man and life whose transfiguration they tell:

> Alles Vergängliche
> Ist nur ein Gleichnis;
> Das Unzulängliche,
> Hier wirds Ereignis;
> Das Unbeschreibliche,
> Hier ist es getan;
> Das Ewig-Weibliche
> Zieht uns hinan.

NOTES

1. A. Bely, in: *Gorn* 2–3 (Moscow, 1919), 55 (in the essay "O khudozhestvennoy proze," 49–55). In English translation, the quotation reads: "Prose is the most difficult form of poetry."

2. B. Pasternak, *Stikhi 1936–1959. Stikhi dlya detey. Stikhi 1912–1957, ne sobrannye v knigi avtora. Stat'i i vystupleniya* (= *Sochineniya* III), Ann Arbor, 1961. In English prose translation, the stanza reads: "So what abomination have I committed, / Am I a murderer and scoundrel? / I have made the whole world cry / over the beauty of my country."

3. See G. Struve, *Geschichte der Sowjetliteratur,* 2nd ed., Munich, 1958, 217, fn.40; *id.,* in: *Studies in Russian and Polish Literature: In Honor of Wacław Lednicki,* The Hague, 1962, 240–1 and 246–7, fn.10 (in a paper entitled "Sense and Nonsense about *Doctor Zhivago*"); *id.* (jointly with B. Filippov), in: B. Pasternak, *Proza 1915–1958. Povesti, rasskazy, avtobiograficheskiye proizvedeniya* (= *Sochineniya* II), Ann Arbor, 1961, 350 (for exact references identifying the first publication of the early prose pieces in *Ogonyok, Tridtsat' Dney, Volya Truda,* and *Literaturnaya Gazeta*) and 358–60 (for discussion). Cf. now further esp. H. Gifford, *Pasternak: A Critical Study,* Cambridge, 1977, 176–8.

4. Cf. Pasternak's own statement in the prefatory note to the prepublication of some of the Zhivago poems in *Znamya* 1954: 4, 92: "Roman predpolozhitel'no budet napisan letom."

5. Cf. Pasternak's own words at the end of one of the variants of *An Essay in Autobiography* (*Vstupitel'nyi ocherk,* also known as *Avtobiograficheskiy ocherk*) adduced in *Sochineniya* II, 352–3: ". . . sovsem nedavno ya zakonchil [*var.* ya

zakanchivayu i gotovlyu k pechati] samyi vazhnyi svoy trud, edinstvennyi, kotorogo ya ne styzhus', i za kotoryi smelo otvechayu, roman v proze so stikhotvornymi dobavleniyami 'Doktor Zhivago.' Razbrosannye po svem godam moyey zhizni i sobrannye v etoy knige stikhotvoreniya yavlyayutsya podgotovitel'nymi stupenyami k romanu . . ." See, moreover, also for example the writer's statements in the letters quoted in Gifford, *op. cit.,* 179.

6. As is well known, *Doctor Zhivago* has not only been denounced as anti-Soviet and hence unpatriotic in the Soviet Union, but its notion of religion (and Christianity in particular) and concept of history (notably, that of Russia) as well as Pasternak's position on questions of politics, patriotism, and nationalism have been criticized by serious, a priori not necessarily hostile scholars and critics unrestrained by any political conditions or considerations. In particular, the Russian writer's attitude to the "Jewish question," with its ramifications, has both come under severe attack and, partly as a reaction thereto, also been defended. For further details, see, e.g., my discussion in *Doktor Faustus und Doktor Schiwago. Versuch über zwei Zeitromane aus Exilsicht,* Lisse, 1976, 31–56 ("Religion und Geschichte," "Patriotismus, Politik and die nationale Frage"), esp. 43–4 and 54–6 (on Pasternak's attitude to the Jews and his view of their role in history and in Russian society in particular — by some decried as assimilationist in the extreme and hence anti-Zionist). On this controversial problem (as well as the related question of his father's, Leonid Pasternak's, interest in and understanding of Judaism and Jewishness), see also several articles in *Slavica Hierosolymitana* I (1977) by L. S. Fleishman and D. Segal. Instructive in this respect is in particular Segal's essay "Pro Domo Sua: The Case of Boris Pasternak" (199–250) even if one does not have to agree with all of the author's contentions.

7. For an instance of a harshly critical assessment of *Doctor Zhivago* as a novel by a writer generally very positively disposed toward Pasternak and highly appreciative of him as a poet (and as a human being), see A. Gladkov, *Meetings with Pasternak: A Memoir* (M. Hayward, transl. & ed.), New York & London, 1977, 145–71, esp. 151 and 159–65; cf. further in M. Hayward's Introduction, 24–30, commenting also on N. Mandelstam's qualified critique of *Doctor Zhivago* (esp. 25). The Russian edition of Gladkov's recollections appeared under the title *Vstrechi s Pasternakom,* Paris, 1973. For some early, sketchy but brilliant theories of the genre of the novel, concerned primarily with its formal structure and in large part using Russian illustrative material, see G. Lukács, *Die Theorie des Romans,* 1st ed. in book form, Berlin, 1920 (originally published in 1916, in: *Zeitschrift für Ästhetik und Allgemeine Kunstwissenschaft;* 2nd ed., with a newly written, highly self-critical preface by the author, Berlin, 1963); V. Shklovsky, *O teorii prozy,* 2nd ed., Moscow, 1929, 68–90 ("Stroyeniye rasskaza i romana") and 177–204 ("Parodiynyi roman: 'Tristram Shendi' Sterna," originally published as *Tristram Shendi Sterna i teoriya romana,* Petrograd, 1921). Contemporary outlines of a theory of the novel can be found, for example, in R. Alter, *Partial Magic: The Novel as a Self-Conscious Genre,* Berkeley-Los Angeles-London, 1975, viewing the novel in terms of descriptive poetics, or in J. Culler, *Structuralist Poetics: Structuralism, Linguistics and the Study of Literature,* Ithaca, N.Y., 1977 (paperback, 2nd printing; 1st ed., 1975), 189–238 ("Chapter 9: Poetics of the Novel"), another incisive though controversial treatment. A new, semiotic theory of the novel underlies also the book by M. Bakhtin, *Problemy poetiki Dostoyevskogo,* Moscow, 1963, where the novel is conceived of as a complex, polyphonic structure made up of interrelated sets of signs. As is well known, the problem of defining the novel as the most

characteristic and significant literary genre of modern times was discussed by Bakhtin in many of his writings, some of which — both such previously published and unpublished — are now available in the posthumous volume *Voprosy literatury i estetiki. Issledovaniya raznykh let,* Moscow, 1975. For a brief discussion of the place and legitimacy of evaluation and value judgments, aesthetic and extra-aesthetic, in the study and science of literature, see, e.g., B. Hrushovski, *PTL* 1 (1976), xxi–xxii (in his introductory editorial essay "Poetics, Criticism, Science: Remarks on the Fields and Responsibilities of the Study of Literature").

8. Of Bely's works, both *Petersburg* and, to some extent, *Kotik Letayev* come to mind (the latter published only in 1922, the same year as Pasternak's *The Childhood of Luvers* with which Bely's short "autobiographical" novel has much in common). By Joyce, both *Ulysses* and, especially, *Finnegans Wake* suggest a comparison. While Pasternak, obviously, was quite familiar with Bely's writings, it is less certain that he had any close knowledge of Joyce. Thus, in an interview granted Ralph Matlaw ("A Visit with Pasternak," *Nation,* September 12, 1959, 134–5), Pasternak is said to have told the American literary scholar that *Doctor Zhivago* had "nothing to do with Joyce" and that he knew only vaguely of *Finnegans Wake.*

9. See "Randbemerkungen zur Prosa des Dichters Pasternak," *Slavische Rundschau* 7 (1935), 357–74. An English version of this seminal paper appeared in the volume *Pasternak: Modern Judgements,* D. Davie & A. Livingstone, eds., Glasgow, 1969, 135–51, as "Marginal Notes on the Prose of the Poet Pasternak" (corrected 2nd ed., London, 1971).

10. However, such an interpretation would hardly square with Pasternak's own view of his work as apparent from many private — but recorded — statements of his on the subject, and as borne out, for example, also by the passage from *An Essay in Autobiography* adduced above (n. 5) as well as by the two quotations from his letters cited by Gifford, *op. cit.,* 179. Possibly, though, one may venture a metonymic interpretation (more on metonymy, cf. below) of the function of the "Poems of Yuri Zhivago" and their relationship to the bulk of the novel, constituting, as they do, "traces," in time, in space, and as cause, of the events and moods reported and described in the prose portion of the book.

11. Cf., for example, the poem *Vesenniy dozhd'* and the Meluzeyevo episode in *Doctor Zhivago* (chapter five). See further on this O. R. Hughes, *The Poetic World of Boris Pasternak,* Princeton & London, 1974, 167, with the reference (in fn. 105) to the anonymous article "Zhivago's Defence" in the March 11, 1965, issue of *TLS;* Gifford, *op. cit.,* 50–2 and 197. It is also Gifford who (*ibid.,* 48) likens Zhivago to 'the brother of life.' On the difficult, sophisticated poetic syntax of the poem *My Sister Life,* with conclusions relevant to the entire cycle, see, for example, F. Björling, "Aspects of Poetic Syntax: Analysis of the Poem 'Sestra moja—žizn' i segodnja v razlive' by Boris Pasternak," in: *Boris Pasternak: Essays,* (N. Å. Nilsson, ed.), Stockholm, 1976, 162–79. A good deal sensible and not-so-sensible (in part even outright nonsensical) has, incidentally, been made of the assumed symbolism implied in the name of the hero and the theme and assertion of life that breathes from almost every page of the novel. Cf., e.g., E. Wilson, "Doctor Life and His Guardian Angel," *The Bit Between My Teeth,* New York, 1965 (1966), 420–46, esp. 425–6; see further also *ibid.,* 448 (in another essay, "Legend and Symbol in *Doctor Zhivago*"; both pieces had previously been printed separately, in *The New Yorker* and in the *Nation,* the second also repeated in *Encounter*). For both some appreciative and critical comments on Wilson's two essays, see Struve, "Sense and Nonsense . . . ," 244–50, including a reference

to Pasternak's own response (when made aware of Wilson's suggestion of symbolism) denying any symbolic intentions and special significance of the name Zhivago, as reported by Ralph Matlaw (cf. above, n. 8). But note also Wilson's, to my mind, rather compelling remarks on some of the possible reasons, overt and covert, behind Pasternak's public stance such as the one obviously taken in the Matlaw interview; *The Bit Between My Teeth,* 470-2. See further in my aforementioned essay (cf. n.6), 20-1, where two particularly telling passages from *Doctor Zhivago* in praise of life itself are quoted, suggesting, it would seem, that a mere coincidence as to the choice of that particular name, claimed by Pasternak, may indeed not be easy to accept. Possibly, the poet's insistence to that effect could somehow reflect his well-known aversion to what he considered, throughout most of his productive life, an improper intrusion and futile dissection of the creative act and the literature flowing from it by the "professionals." An unequivocal link between the name Zhivago and the theme of resurrection also present in the novel (and, obviously, only a Christian-inspired variation on the theme of life) is perhaps less readily demonstrable, and that in spite of Robert Payne's pertinent suggestion (in his basically quite poor book *The Three Worlds of Boris Pasternak,* New York, 1961, 169-70) and Edmund Wilson's to be sure keen observation about a play on words at the very beginning of the novel, echoing both the Russian version of the Bible and the Russian Orthodox Liturgy (*The Bit Between My Teeth,* 443). For some very far-reaching conclusions regarding the name symbolism of Yuri (: St. George) Andreevich (: son of St. Andrew the Apostle) Zhivago ("Life," "Alive") as reflecting the pattern of the hero's own life, see M. F. and P. Rowland, *Pasternak's Doctor Zhivago,* London & Amsterdam, 1967, 10-11.

   12. See G.W.F. Hegel, *Werke,* Bd. 15: *Vorlesungen über Ästhetik* III, Frankfurt / M, 1970, 240 (1st, posthumous ed., Berlin, 1838, 239).

   13. Ju. Lotman, *The Structure of the Artistic Text* (R. Vroon, transl.), Ann Arbor, 1977 (= *Michigan Slavic Contributions,* No. 7), 94-104, esp. 101. For the original Russian version, see Yu. M. Lotman, *Struktura khudozhestvennogo teksta,* Moscow, 1970, 120-32, esp. 128; available also as *The Brown University Slavic Reprint* IX, with an Introduction by T. G. Winner, Providence, R.I., 1971. Virtually the same formulation was used by Lotman in his earlier book *Lektsii po struktural'noy poetike: Vvedeniye, teoriya stikha,* Tartu, 1964 (= *Brown University Slavic Reprint* V, with an Introduction by T. G. Winner, Providence, R.I., 1968), 47-58, esp. 55.

   14. Yu. Lotman, *Analysis of the Poetic Text* (D.B. Johnson, ed. & transl.), Ann Arbor, 1976, 22 and 24; for the original Russian version, see Yu. M. Lotman, *Analiz poeticheskogo teksta: Struktura stikha,* Leningrad, 1972, 23-33, esp. 23-4 and 26. It may be noted, incidentally, that what Lotman has to say about (ordinary) language as a structure reproducing reality and about literature, i.e., verbal art, as a "structure of structures" finds a parallel of sorts in linguistic 'creativity' in the Chomskyan or, rather, post-Chomskyan (that is to say, semantic-syntactic rather than exclusively syntactic) sense as opposed to — and as a necessary prerequisite for — verbal creativity in the poetic (artistic, aesthetic) sense. Similar, though certainly not quite the same, considerations apply to what is at the heart of composing — i.e., creating — music, dealt with by Leonard Bernstein in his six Charles Eliot Norton Lectures delivered at Harvard in 1973 and drawing heavily — too heavily, I would submit — on Chomskyan linguistics (of the 'standard theory' kind); cf. L. Bernstein, *The Unanswered Question: Six Talks at Harvard,* Cambridge, Mass. & London, 1976. For further discussion, see my paper "On Linguistic Creativity," to appear in the testimonial volume for Edward Stankiewicz (Columbus, Ohio, 1980).

15. See E. J. Brown, "The Poetics of Prose," in: *American Contributions to the Eighth International Congress of Slavists, Zagreb and Ljubljana, September 3-9, 1978*, Volume I: *Linguistics and Poetics* (H. Birnbaum, ed.), Columbus, Ohio, 1978, 205–21.

16. Cf. the formulation of this very problem at the outset of my paper "The 'Supplication of Daniel the Exile' and the Problem of Poetic Form in Old Russian Literature," *Russian Poetics* (T. Eekman & D. S. Worth, eds.) (to appear).

17. Yu. Lotman, *Analysis* . . . , 24; cf. also the same wording in *Lektsii* . . . , 51. Incidentally, it should also be noted that in the first part of his assertion quoted here, Lotman qualifies his statement by specifically speaking of "prose in the modern meaning of the word." In a sense, therefore, artistic prose of the medieval, Old Russian period should be excluded by definition.

18. Ju. Lotman, *The Structure* . . . , 96 and 97 (in the Russian version, 123 and 125).

19. See Ju. M. Lotman, B. A. Uspenskij, V. V. Ivanov, V. N. Toporov, A. M. Pjatigorskij, *Theses on the Semiotic Study of Culture (as Applied to Slavic Texts)*, Lisse, 1975, 11–12; see also H. Birnbaum, *Doktor Faustus und Doktor Schiwago* . . . , 27.

20. See Yu. Tynyanov & R. Jakobson, "Problema izucheniya literatury i yazyka," *Novyi Lef,* 1928, No. 12, 35–7, esp. 37 (sub 9). The Russian text is also reprinted in: Yu. N. Tynyanov, *Poetika. Istoriya literatury. Kino,* Moscow, 1977, 282–3, with detailed, revealing background comments, 530–6 (written in close collaboration with V. V. Ivanov). It is somewhat surprising to note that both in the earlier reprint of the original Russian version published in the U.S. (*Michigan Slavic Materials,* No. 2, Ann Arbor, 1962, 99–102) and in the English edition of these programmatic theses, the last, ninth one — suggesting that a renewed *Opoyaz* be headed by Shklovsky — has been omitted; see *Readings in Russian Poetics: Formalist and Structuralist Views* (L. Matejka & K. Pomorska, eds.), Cambridge, 1971, 79–81. Cf. further V. Shklovskiy, "Pamyatnik nauchnoy oshibke," *Literaturnaya Gazeta,* No. 4 (27 January 1930), 1. A German translation ("Denkmal zur Erinnerung an einen wissenschaftlichen Irrtum") appeared in the volume *Formalismus, Strukturalismus und Geschichte: Zur Literaturtheorie und Methodologie in der Sowjetunion, ČSSR, Polen und Jugoslavien* (A. Flaker & V. Žmegac, eds.), Kronberg/Taunus, 1974, 74–80. As pointed out by the editors in the introduction to this collection (13), there exist, despite Shklovsky's overt break with his Formalist past, some ideological-theoretical links between his 1930 article and the Tynyanov-Jakobson manifesto. It is also known that Shklovsky had expressed a departure from his earlier positions previously, especially in a public debate in 1927; cf. *Novyi Lef,* 1927, No. 4, 46, and, in the immediately preceding issue of the same journal, his article "V zashchitu sotsiologicheskogo metoda," subsequently included in his collection of essays, *Gamburgskiy schot,* Moscow, 1928. For a general assessment of the early Shklovsky's impact on the theory of prose, see the excellent essay by R. Sherwood, "Viktor Shklovsky and the Development of Early Formalist Theory on Prose Literature," in: *Russian Formalism: A Collection of Articles and Texts in Translation* (S. Bann & J. E. Bowlt, eds.), New York, 1973, 26–40. For further information on the "nonmonolithic" character of Russian Formalism and on Shklovsky's early — and more recent — doubts as to his own erstwhile definition that "a work of literature is pure form," see also in the preface to the collection of Tynyanov's writings, *Poetika* . . . (1977), 10–11. On Jakobson's early nonmechanistic concern with human communication in structural terms (esp. the distinction between addresser and addressee) as reflected in his article on realism in art (first published in Czech in 1921;

cf. n. 23, below), see L. Matejka's preface (without pagination) to the selection *Readings in Russian Poetics* (= *Michigan Slavic Materials,* No. 2), Ann Arbor, 1962.

21. V. Shklovskiy, *O teorii prozy* (2nd ed.), Moscow, 1929, 7–23: "Iskusstvo, kak priyom," esp. 7–10 (the 1st ed. of this book appeared in Moscow in 1925; for the first time, this particular essay was published in a collection, *Sborniki po teorii poeticheskogo yazyka* II, St. Petersburg, 1917).

22. *Ibid.,* 13–20. For a critical discussion of *ostraneniye* (as conceived by Shklovsky and his critique of Potebnya's image concept), see, e.g., V. Erlich, *Russian Formalism: History — Doctrine,* The Hague, 1955 (2nd ed., 1965), 150–1; K. Pomorska, *Russian Formalist Theory and Its Poetic Ambience,* The Hague, 1968, 36, pointing also to a subsequent, more precise formulation, in linguistic terms, by Jakobson ("The function of poetry is to indicate the lack of identity between the sign and the object," 1933/34, in the essay "Co je poesie?") and making reference to the connection between this facet of Formalism and the psychological approach of Potebnya (which had served as a point of departure for Shklovsky but subsequently also was noted, for example, by L. Vygotsky); R. Lachmann, "Die 'Verfremdung' und das 'neue Sehen' bei Viktor Šklovskij," *Poetica* 3 (1970), 226–49; F. Jameson, *The Prison-House of Language: A Critical Account of Structuralism and Russian Formalism,* Princeton, N.J., 1972 (1974, paperback ed.), 43–98; and, most recently, E. J. Brown, *op. cit.* 207–212 (cf. n. 15, above) as well as M. Chlumský, "V. Chklovski — Saussurien avant Saussure?" *Die Welt der Slaven* XXII, 2 (N. F. I, 2), 245–56 (suggesting an elaboration by Shklovsky of the concepts of the word and the linguistic sign prior to becoming acquainted with the corresponding notions as formulated by Saussure). As is well known, the contrast 'defamiliarization' vs. 'habitualization' of the Russian Formalists found its counterpart in the opposition 'foregrounding' vs. 'automatization' of the Prague School poetics.

23. See *Michigan Slavic Materials,* No. 2, Ann Arbor, 1962, 34 (in Jakobson's article "O khudozhestvennom realizme," published here for the first time in its original Russian version; it first appeared in a Czech translation, "O realismu v umění," *Červen* 4 (1921), 300–4, and, a few years later, in an Ukrainian version in 1927, in *Vaplite* 2 (1927), 163–70). The English rendition of the Russian wording is mine and, incidentally, differs slightly from that adduced by Edward Brown, *loc. cit.*; the emphasis, marked here, is the author's.

24. In painting — mentioned in an article on Futurism in the August 2, 1919, issue of the magazine *Iskusstvo*; in film — in a discussion of the predicament and potential of that art form in the first issue of the journal *Listy pro umění a kritiku* for 1933.

25. At considerable length Jakobson elaborated on the opposite (though interrelated) notions of metaphor and metonymy in his brilliant essay on the prose of the early Pasternak (quoted in n. 9, above); here, incidentally, can also be found some particularly perspicacious remarks on Khlebnikov and Mayakovsky. Subsequently, Jakobson has returned on several occasions to the topic of metaphor and metonymy, especially in *Fundamentals of Language,* The Hague, 1956, 76–82 ("The Metaphoric and Metonymic Poles") where, among other things, the possibility of a variety of transitional and combined usages of the two tropes, of similarity and contiguity, positional and semantic, is emphasized, thus allowing for the creation of "an impressive range of possible configurations" in verbal art (77). Even if the trend is toward metaphor in poetry proper and in romanticism, and toward metonymy in prose and in realism, these dichotomic notions cannot usually be isolated other than artificially in their pure form in any piece of literature of some length; hence Jakobson's 'bipolarity' (with 'pole' in the approximate sense of point of gravitation) rather than a clear-cut

either/ or, mutually exclusive unipolar choice. In later work, Jakobson has touched on the metaphor/ metonymy distinction in verbal art several times; so, for example, in his "Closing Statement: Linguistics and Poetics," *Style in Language* (T. A. Sebeok, ed.), Cambridge, Mass. – New York – London, 1960, 350–77, esp. 368–70; and in his pioneering sketch "Quest for the Essence of Language," *Diogenes* 51 (1965), 21–37, esp. 33 (reprinted in his *Selected Writings* II, The Hague, 1971, 345–59, esp. 355), where we read this terse semiotic definition: "The metaphor (or metonymy) is an assignment of a signans to a secondary signatum associated by similarity (or contiguity) with the primary signatum." Cf. this definition with Jakobson's prior semiotic reformulation of the poetic technique of 'defamiliarization' or, more generally, his formulation of the function of poetry (in the broad sense) quoted above (in n. 22). On the integration of Jakobson's recurrent preoccupation with the metaphor/ metonymy distinction into the wider range of dichotomies and dialectics reformulated or established by him in the course of a life-long inquiry into the nature of language, and, particularly, on its place in the 'in absentia' vs. 'in praesentia' contrast and its relationship to the aphasic disorders of similarity and contiguity, see L. Matejka's discussion in *IJSLP* XX (1975/3), 116–17. For a concise (re)formulation of the metaphor/ metonymy distinction in linguistic terms (with implications for poetics), see also J. Kuryłowicz, "Metaphor and Metonymy in Linguistics," in: *Sign — Language — Culture* (A. J. Greimas, R. Jakobson *et al.*, eds.), The Hague & Paris, 1970, 135–6, identifying, on linguistic grounds, metonymy as "the fundamental and overall phenomenon" in relation to the metaphor. Generally on metaphor and metonymy, taking Jakobson's theory as a starting point, see now also in particular D. Lodge, *The Modes of Modern Writing: Metaphor, Metonymy, and the Typology of Modern Literature*, Ithaca, N.Y., 1977, 73–124 ("Part Two: Metaphor and Metonymy"). For a critique of Jakobson's poetics, see recently esp. J. Culler, *op. cit.*, 55–74 ("Chapter 3: Jakobson's Poetic Analyses") where it should be noted, however, that the criticism is directed primarily against Jakobson's poetics of poetry proper (verse) and that the author's own theoretical position, (closest to, it would seem, though also not uncritical of, the *nouvelle critique* and, in particular, that of Roland Barthes and Jacques Derrida) is highly controversial. For thought-provoking recent discussions of metaphor in semantic — linguistic and philosophical — terms, see W. Abraham, *A Linguistic Approach to Metaphor*, Lisse / Netherlands, 1975, and S. R. Levin, *The Semantics of Metaphor*, Baltimore & London, 1977, the latter in particular including a comparison with and a critique of earlier treatments. For a semiotic approach to metaphor, see further Yu. I. Levin, "Struktura russkoy metafory," *Trudy po znakovym sistemam* 2 (Tartu, 1965), 293–9; English translation: "The Structure of the Metaphor," in: *Soviet Semiotics: An Anthology* (D. P. Lucid, ed. & transl.), Baltimore & London, 1977, 203–9; and for a broadly sociological and cognitive view of the metaphor, R. H. Brown, *A Poetic for Sociology: Towards a Logic of Discovery for the Human Sciences*, Cambridge, 1977, 77–171. Recently, some of Jakobson's basic assumptions about metaphor and metonymy have been scrutinized and in part further developed and modified by Michael Shapiro; see his essay (written jointly with Marianne Shapiro) *Hierarchy and the Structure of Tropes*, Bloomington & Lisse, 1976; esp. 5–14 ("The Ontological Structure of Tropes"); *id.*, "Deux paralogismes de la poétique," *Poétique* 28 (1976), 423–39, esp. 426–32; and in his forthcoming study *Journey to the Metonymic Pole: The Structure of Pushkin's 'Little Tragedies,'* esp. part one ("Theoretical Prolegomena: 1. The Dominant and Tropes, 2. Metonymy"). Of particular importance for our discussion here is Shapiro's statement appearing toward the end of part one: "Metonymy cannot, of course, be artificially sealed off from the other major trope, metaphor. Indeed, a metonymy, even at the point of its original creation in literary texts, is already on the way to becoming a metaphor. Metaphor is defined as that trope in which the (simultaneously) established hierarchy of signata is either reversed or neutralized. Thus the very definiens of metonymy itself can become the precondition for metaphor, since the figural meaning must predominate over the literal in order for the figural situation to obtain. Moreover, both tropes can coexist in the same linguistic vehicle, thereby facilitating a quicker slide of an original metonymy into the category of metaphor . . . two coexistent figural components . . . are themselves, naturally, not unranked: the metaphoric component markedly dominates the metonymic. This rank order, notably, is consistent with the principle that metonymy tends strongly to be superseded by metaphor. This means that metonymy is the more basic, less complex of the two tropes." The latter conception does not have to imply a contradiction to the previously made claim (ranging from Hegel through Lotman) that artistic prose is secondary, derived, and marked in relation to poetry proper (i.e., verse) within the overall range of poetic language. For truly poetic prose abounds in both, of course, metaphor as well as metonymy. *Doctor Zhivago,* this "poem in disguise," as David Lean, the perceptive director of the film version of Pasternak's book, has called it, provides an excellent illustration of precisely this combination of, and sliding between, the two chief tropes of poetic language. Moreover, in the final analysis, the metonymic text as a whole can, in fact, be viewed as metaphor; cf. D. Lodge, *op. cit.,* 109–11. That, too, applies eminently to *Doctor Zhivago*; see also below, in section 5.

No attempt has been made here, following Jakobson, to distinguish between metaphor and the broader concept of simile as, in my view, every poetically charged simile by definition is (or becomes) a metaphor. It should be noted, however, that this view is by no means unanimously accepted. Thus, for example, Northrop Frye has taken great pains to define the distinction between metaphor and simile as one between models of mythical vs. realistic literature, a distinction somewhat reminiscent of that made by Jakobson between metaphor (the preferred trope of poetry and romantic literature) and metonymy (the trope characteristic in particular of prose and realistic literature). Yet another conceivable — though here not adopted — formal distinction between metaphor and simile is that the former term be reserved for one-word or, at any rate, one-term expressions, thus rendering the metaphor in effect an artistically used substitute or synonym replacing a common, ordinary notion, while the latter term, simile, would be limited to denote an explicit, usually two-word or two-term comparison, frequently marked by a linking comparative conjunction (e.g., *as, as if, as though, like* in English; *kak, kak budto, slovno, budto, tochno* in Russian).

26. Quoted from the English translation ("Marginal Notes . . . ," 1969, 143; for full reference, see n.9, above). Cf. also the in part very similar phrasing in *Fundamentals of Language,* 82. On metonymic structure in the prose narrative of the early Pasternak, see also, e.g., M. Aucouturier, "The Metonymous Hero or The Beginnings of Pasternak the Novelist," *Books Abroad,* 44: 2 (Spring 1970), 222–7.

27. See E. J. Brown, *op. cit.,* 213.

28. Cf. B. Hrushovski, "Segmentation and Motivation in the Text Continuum of Literary Prose: The First Episode of *War and Peace* (English Version)," *Papers on Poetics and Semiotics* (B. Hrushovski & I. Even-Zohar, eds.) 5, Tel-Aviv, 1976, 1–39; the quotation is from page 2. See further also *id., PTL* 1 (1976), iv ("The response of a reader or a listener to a specific work of literature," in his editorial, introductory essay "Poetics, Criticism, Science: Remarks on the Fields and Responsibilities of the Study of Literature").

29. Cf. V. Shklovskiy, "Iskusstvo, kak priyom" (cf. n. 21), 13–22, esp. 13 and 21–22.

See further also *id.,* "Svyaz' priyomov syuzhetoslozheniya s obshchimi priyomami stilya," in: *O teorii prozy,* 24–67, esp. 32–60 ("Stupenchatoye stroyeniye i zaderzhaniye," "Motirovka zaderzhaniya," "Obramleniye, kak priyom zaderzhaniya").

30. Note, incidentally, that when characterizing metaphors as one kind of (poetic) images, the terms 'metaphor' and 'image' are not taken here in their technical sense used in the semiotic of Charles S. Peirce where the class of 'icons' (or 'hypoicons,' along with 'indices' and 'symbols' making up the range of signs) is further subdivided into three distinct subclasses: 'images,' 'diagrams,' and 'metaphors.' Cf. *Collected Papers of Charles Sanders Peirce* I/II (C. Hartshorne & P. Weiss, eds.), Cambridge, Mass., 1965, 134–73 (=2. 227–2. 308), esp. 157 (=2. 275). This terminological discrepancy needs in particular being pointed out here as Jakobson, after settling in the U.S., has been strongly influenced by this great American thinker (whose importance for linguistic semiotics he can be said to have rediscovered), an influence only comparable with that of Edmund Husserl on the earlier Jakobson.

31. The page references, given by page number in parenthesis immediately after each quotation, are all to the paperback edition *Doctor Zhivago* (Signet 451–E6531, New York), the authorized reprint of the hardcover English language edition published by Pantheon Books, Inc., New York, 1958. Considerations of space also rendered impracticable to quote the adduced passages in their original Russian wording, along with their English translation, something that in view of the forcefulness of Pasternak's diction and the compelling choice of words, sounds, and rhythm of his figurative language would of course have been preferable.

32. See D. Lodge, *op. cit.,* 133, fn.

33. Actually, in the Russian original, the effect of associations and identifications, tensions and contrasts is even greater, achieved, as it is, by repeating the same sound sequence (*par*) representing essentially — yet in each instance not quite — the same notion ('steam,' 'vapor'), two phonetically different elements close in meaning (*kuri: dym* 'smoke,' in addition to the just mentioned *par* with a related meaning) as well as the means rendered also in the English translation (B. Pasternak, *Doktor Zhivago. S poslednimi popravkami avtora,* Ann Arbor, 1958, 122): *Parilo. Par* stoyal nad kotlovinoy, i *vsyo kuri*los', vsyo struyami *dyma* tyanulos' vverkh *parovoznyi dym* so stantsii, *ser*aya is*par*ina lugov, *ser*ye gory, *tyomn*ye, *tyomn*ye oblaka.

34. Compare, for example, the landscape descriptions of nature breaking into spring as watched from the train to the Urals (195 and 198–9); the description of the hills, "huge and dark in the distance, like proud shadows, silently scrutinizing the travellers" from the Torfyanaya station to the estate of Varykino (223); the description of the nocturnal scenery at Varykino in Yuri Zhivago's own notes (236–7); and his account for the "first signs of spring" intermingled with his musings about *Eugene Onegin* and the reasons for the use of the expression *solovey-razboynik* in the well-known Russian epic folk-song (suggesting "a metaphor based on similarity of sound" or, as the Russian original more tersely has it, a "sound image," *zvukovoy obraz*; see 238–9, and, further, B. Pasternak, *Doktor Zhivago,* 295); the scene of sunset, complete with a nightingale calling "Wake up!" with an allusion to the "Awake!" and the theme of resurrection of Easter Sunday (253–4); the description of the warm night in the small Siberian town of Khodatskoye with the nearby Vozdvizhensky Monastery, combining visual and acoustic imagery, especially when describing how "a dark low sweet humming drifted from the deepest of the monastery bells" which "mixed with the dark drizzle in the air" and "drifted from the bell, sinking and dissolving in the air, as a clump of earth, torn from the river-bank, sinks and dissolves in the water of the spring

floods" (156–7); the coming of autumn (and the premonition of winter) in the partisans' Fox's Thicket, using historical imagery of medieval towns in addition to visual
impressions and the sensations of scent and taste (284–5); the lingering of the summer
in the forest where the rays of the setting sun in the forest were piercing it and "the
leaves, letting them through, glowed green like transparent bottle glass" (286); and the
description of the coming of winter, with snow and gusty winds, including several
metaphoric/metonymic images: "Then the clouds would part like windows . . ." "The
vapors skidded like smoke over the pine woods; their resinous needles were as
waterproof as oilcloth. Raindrops were strung on the telegraph wires like beads . . ."
(300).

35. What in the English translation, speaking of "subways," may seem as an
anachronistic oversight on the part of Pasternak — the Moscow Subway System, the
Metro, was, as is well known, not even begun to be constructed until the later 1930s
(and completed only after the Second World War), while Yuri Zhivago writes his
pertinent notes in the 1920s, after his return to Moscow in 1922 and before his death in
1929 — in the Russian original, mentioning *vagony svoikh gorodskikh, elektriches-
kikh i podzemnykh zheleznykh dorog* (B. Pasternak, *Doktor Zhivago,* 500), is a bit
more ambiguous and would, in any case, allow for an acceptable interpretation. For,
after all, some of the urban and suburban streetcar and railway network of Moscow
may indeed have been subterranean (*podzemnyi*) in the 1920s. In a recent article, "The
Urban Theme in Recent Soviet Prose: Notes Toward a Typology," *Slavic Review* 37: 1
(March 1978), 40–50, G. Gibian quotes, by way of a point of departure, this very
passage from *Doctor Zhivago* as an example of the continued preoccupation of Soviet
Russian prose with urban thematics, along with its current infatuation with rural
topics (in the writings of the *derevenshchiki*). While one can only subscribe, of course,
to Gibian's contention that "Soviet literature today can be understood best through
an awareness of the dialectical relationship between rural and urban thematics" (41),
Pasternak's prose, and his great novel in particular (now already somewhat removed in
time), obviously provide ample illustration of both, land- and cityscape, rural as well
as urban setting and symbolism.

36. On Pasternak's conception of the poet, see, especially, O. R. Hughes, *op. cit.,*
21–33 ("The Poet and the World") and 78–167 ("Time and Eternity," "Responsibility
of a Poet"); K. Pomorska, *Themes and Variations in Pasternak's Poetics,* Lisse, 1975,
51–63 ("The Fate of the Artist") and 81–8 ("Doctor Živago: Concept of Human
Fate"); V. Erlich, *The Double Image: Concepts of the Poet in Slavic Literatures,*
Baltimore, Md., 1974, 133–54 ("'Life by Verses': Boris Pasternak"; an earlier, shorter
version of this chapter was published under the title "The Concept of the Poet in
Pasternak," *SEER* XXXVII: 89, June 1959, 325–35); H. Birnbaum, *Doktor Faustus
und Doktor Schiwago,* 12–14; and C. Milosz, *Emperor of the Earth: Modes of
Eccentric Vision,* Berkeley–Los Angeles–London, 1977, 62–78 ("On Pasternak Soberly," esp. 64–71 and 74–8, "The Image of the Poet" and "The Poet as a Hero"; this
essay first appeared in *Books Abroad* 44: 2 [Spring 1970], 200–9).

37. Cf. V. Frank, "A Russian Hamlet: Boris Pasternak's Novel," *The Dublin
Review,* September 1958, 212–20.

38. See O. R. Hughes, *op. cit.,* 146–9, with some references to earlier prefigurations
in Pasternak of the Hamlet-Christ theme in *Doctor Zhivago.* On a Christ = Poet, rather
than Christ = Zhivago identification in the book, see also P. A. Brodin, *Nine Poems
from Doktor Živago: A Study of Christian Motifs in Boris Pasternak's Poetry,*
Stockholm, 1976, *passim.*

39. See B. Pasternak, *Doctor Zhivago,* 39; cf. further H. Birnbaum, *op. cit.,* 59. On the Hamlet (and Faust) theme in Pasternak's own life and writings, *Doctor Zhivago* in particular, see further V. Markov, "An Unnoticed Aspect of Pasternak's Translations," *Slavic Review* XX (1961), 503–8, esp. 505–6.

40. See H. Birnbaum, *op. cit.*

41. Cf. also H. Birnbaum, *op. cit.,* 35 and 50. In other novels by Mann, his lack of interest in nature is, if possible, even more obvious. Thus, one could cite, for example, *The Magic Mountain* where virtually nothing of the ever-present Swiss Alpine landscape is described.

42. Cf. H. Birnbaum, *op. cit.,* 47; see further also, for instance, H. Wysling, *Thomas Mann heute: Sieben Vorträge,* Berne & Munich, 1976, 94–111 ("Schwierigkeiten mit Thomas Mann"), esp. 97–104 ("Kunst und Leben als Illusion," "Künstlerpsychologie — Künstlerverdächtigung," "Intellektualismus und elitärer Kunstbegriff").

43. Cf. D. Lodge, *op. cit.,* 109–11 ("The Metonymic Text as Metaphor"). Note, in particular, this statement: "In the metalanguage of criticism, metonymy ultimately yields to metaphor — or is converted into it" (111). Cf. further also the previously quoted formulations concerning the relationship of metonymy and metaphor used by Shapiro (n. 25, above).

Addendum to note 20: It should be noted, however, that the full text of the Jakobson-Tynyanov manifesto, that is, including its ninth point, was reprinted by Jakobson in his paper "Yuriy Tynyanov v Prage," published in Jakobson's *Selected Writings,* V: *On Verse, Its Masters and Explorers,* The Hague, 1979, 560–8, esp. 564–6. From this memoir it also becomes clear that this much celebrated document of literary theory actually was drafted rather hastily during Tynyanov's visit to Prague, and that it was not preceded by any lengthy, close cooperation between the two scholars.

Marianna D. Birnbaum

AN ARMCHAIR PICARESQUE:
THE TEXTURE AND STRUCTURE OF
GEORGE KONRÁD'S *THE CASE WORKER*[1]

In its simplified surface content Konrád's novel is *A Day in the Life of a Social Worker*. The reader follows comrade T., a middle-aged, middle-class social worker during a routine day of his professional life with all the worries, horrors and inhumanities, smaller and greater tragedies such a day normally encompasses. At one apartment where the tenants, old clients of T., have committed suicide, he decides to stay for a while to try and find someone who would take over the temporary care of the couple's imbecile child. Waiting in a decrepit armchair, T. muses about how his life would change if he chose to remain with the child forever in the shabby room of the Bandulas. As the afternoon draws to an end, a neighbor appears and agrees to care for the child. T., tired, but wiser for his contemplations, returns home to his family.

* * *

1. Texture: Metaphor, Metonymy, Subtext

Many authors of modern fiction, especially those of the *nouveau roman,* reveal the world as nothing but a series of systems of articulation. Konrád's novel, however, is based on intimate contact between text and everyday experience, and in this sense it is no deviation from the traditional novel. His 'special effects' are embedded in the texture of his highly poetic prose, in the unexpected metaphors and metonymies, which create the "sudden rapture of dislocation" (Culler, 192[2]); they are reinforced by the conflict between the confessional first person singular of narration and the superimposed, false esthetic distance. Among the jungle of intricately woven tropes only a few can be discussed within the scope of this paper.

Of the many views regarding their role and function, metaphor and metonymy will be conceived hereafter as follows: *Metaphor* is an unexpected, total comparison, an imposed identity on an object or on an action. In its fundamental alienness it interrupts contiguity between sequential items in a discourse, and the greater the gulf between the object and its newly asserted identity, the stronger the disruptive effect of the metaphor (Lodge, 111–12[3]). In its particular position the metaphor functions as a synonym "in the singularity of the moment." Bound by its ontic status, the object lacks the freedom of metaphor which first makes the object void of its form and content, then replaces its previous semantic influence with its own, independent or dissociated meaning. The effectiveness of a metaphor is enhanced if the *absence* of the replaced object is clearly felt in the *presence* of the one replacing it. In addition, the new amalgam (i.e., minus-word + absorbing synonym) creates a radiation in both directions in the text, comprehensively rearranging and redirecting the links in the chain of objects or actions, both in its semantics and form. Thus, metaphor is sharpened by the lack of spatio-temporal proximity. *Metonymy,* however, depends on contiguity and combination. In the following it will be demonstrated that Konrád's text leans toward metonymy in order to create metaphor. Further, it will be shown that his local metaphors are generally subordinated to synecdochic descriptions within metonymic chains which, in turn, ultimately create total metaphors. Metaphorical metonymies (symbols) interlace the entire novel, with *space* and *time* the principal metaphors in it, until, in the end, the metonymic text "submits to a metaphoric interpretation" (Lodge, 111).

In modern fiction space and time often assume a disproportionately important function, frequently becoming the most significant carrier of the author's message, competing with, and at times surpassing characterization. This perhaps reflects the increasing need of today's artist to return to a greater degree of subjectivization than is possible within the framework of the realist novel without the necessity of romanticizing his protagonists.

Space and time can create distance — experience can subjectivize both. Distance can be reduced or expanded, time can be speeded up or slowed down in the mind and feelings of the individual. Reality and its truth become relative in the process of subjectivization, outer chronology is amended or substituted by an inner one, space loses its size and can transform itself into *soul-space* only. This means that the everyday and the imagined, the pedestrian and the enchanted are allowed to flow together and appear as equals, creating some of the essential features of modern fiction. This liberates narration of the confinements of chronological order and permits the artist to use the concept of time and space as real or as metaphoric. It is just a seeming transgression of nature, since imagination itself is within nature. As Derrida (186[4]) pointed out, "imagination, which excites other virtual faculties, is nonetheless a virtual faculty: the most active of them all." Imagination allows the writer to use reality as real, as a supplement, or as contrast to his ideas of it. He is free to establish an arbitrary scale of importance for his information or, if he so chooses, can present all elements of his information as equally important. His model of the universe, distorted or fragmented, will have, if the work is well written, an inner validity which is for its reader a perfect replacement for verity (Culler, 193).

Konrád uses the outside world simultaneously as reality and as "reality effect" (Barthes, 84–9[5]), and space and time as the most important metaphors in it. Space is therefore used on a real and on a metaphoric level. Real space in the novel is the city and its public buildings, T.'s office, the house in which Bandula lives, the square that he looks down to from the window, all of which, in their role of occasional memory fragments, constitute the backdrop for the hero's imaginary adventures. Space is used as metaphor to describe the hero's diminishing desire for mundane values: ". . . Here between these four walls I find everything needed for life; nothing superfluous remains" (114[6]). Or,

> There is more of everything in my room than there should be, even space. At first I thought it was cramping, even moving carefully, I collided with the sharp edges of the furniture. . . Now I have more and more space at my disposal; the room expanded, its limits have receded . . . When I stand with my back to the window, the opposite wall vanishes from sight, and it seems to me that I should have to walk a long way to reach it. This room is big enough for my lifetime. There are nooks and crannies that I will never explore, unusual space — it's frightening (122–3).

It is obvious that space becomes unreal not in terms of *size* but in terms of *place*. It is no longer the room T. is investigating; it is his own soul. It is the hidden corners of his thoughts that he fears, it is his own mind which he will never have enough time to fully explore. Space also becomes a metaphor for punishment, its reduction turns into the image of a jail, self-imposed, and not truly spatial. He is serving a sentence by examining his values, and this is confirmed as T. looks at his 'visiting' family, ". . . their faces still resemble mine, their skulls resemble my shaven, convict's skull . . ." (125). The hero reaches the smallest space from the largest, he moves into it through the broad unit of the city, down his office, the house, the apartment, to the "decrepit rocking chair at the head of the bed" (60[7]).

The game with space starts first as real, ". . . if I were trapped in this room . . ." (62). With his steps toward self-recognition the hero begins to realize that "it is not duty" that keeps him there (103), but he is staying because he is running away from the failure of his whole life. Thus he uses the imaginary space as refuge.

> On the whole I have no desire to absent myself from here for any length of time (130).*

At the end of his experience in his *soul-space,* he confesses that it was a "long day full of temptation" (143). Since he resisted temptation to fulfil his desires and turn his longings into new behavior, what has he learned?

> . . . stretched out on this bed still moist with the sweat of a couple buried at public expense, watching over the slumbers of a little idiot boy, I see my limitations one shade clearer (144).*

Thus, to emphasize it again, space is primarily used by Konrád for soul-searching and as a symbol of man's bondage by empiric limitations.

Space is also used by Konrád as microstructure. The starting point of imaginary excursions during the afternoon is the chair. From this reduced space, which the hero uses as a position of observation, the plot will progress, and to it the hero will return. Thus the chair, like the formulaic beginning of folktales, functions as a signal to the reader, marking the starting of a new episode. The microstructure of the episodes could be represented by the following diagram:

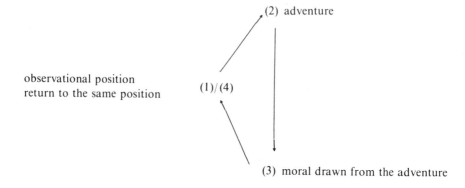

A third manner in which Konrád utilizes space is within a given metonymic chain. Describing how T. decides to stay with the child, the following sequence grows out of a simile:

> Here I crouch . . . in this room . . . that is no more real than a house abandoned the previous night by drunken soldiers moving up to the front, leaving nothing behind but a muddy tailor's dummy with its eyes shot out, a lampshade full of shit, several torn leather armchairs, vases smelling of rum, Grandma's wedding photography touched up with a goatee, a shattered mirror (propped up by two chubby bone-white, rococo, decapitated angels), and finally, dangling from the chandelier with crystal pendants tinkling lightly in the draft, a hanged tomcat, the emaciated demon of the house . . . it would be no more absurd on the first day of peace to open the windows of such a house where soldiers had whiled away time stuffing toothpaste in their navels, and tearing up children's sheets to make bandages for their frost-bitten feet, to shovel away rubbish and scrub the floor with lye, than to do so here in this unemployed room, petrified even in its chaos . . . (101–28).

A new dimension of space appears in this segment, a *space in time* is developed through such metonymic chains. After each metonymic excursion the narrator returns to the starting point (here the room) and reaffirms his contact with the reader. He forms a renewed alliance; information is again shared. By his returning to the very same word (with which the simile + chain was created) the reader is reassured, a new space, a momentary resting place is granted to him by the narrator. Waiting until the reader, having absorbed and assimilated the new information contained in the previous chain, is again conversant with the text, the narrator will rush ahead with the next referential object only to repeat the pendulum-like process. The metonymic chains are therefore turning into a kind of space between narrator and reader and add to the peculiar rhythm of the text which is studded with such separations and reunions. Thus penetration and withdrawal on the structural level are repeated on the linguistic level of texture.

Penetration into the imaginary, and withdrawal from it, is achieved by yet another method — the alternate use of the present tense and the conditional. In a sequence of episodes describing the imaginary delivering of the child to an asylum, Konrád's narrative technique seems particularly interesting when his use of the means of predication is investigated. The reader is prepared by the 'conditional' posing of the problem: ". . . If there were room for him, I should call a taxi . . ." The transitory state following it is created by staccato phrases, predication is expressed by elliptic, participial constructions.

> The kicking child in my arms, legs sawing, hands clutching at the air, over my head the torn parasol of shrieks.*

The next segment has finite verbs but they are assigned to objects or abstractions, not to people:

> Higher still hovers the dusty griffin of the office in indifferent serenity, on its wings the symbol of authority, a summon in his beak. Not a soul walks the corridors, but from the public toilet to the battered door at the stairwell suspicion rakes the corridors.*

Finally the sentence, "I knock at one of the doors" completes the transfer to the new place which exists in the hero's head only (66-7). Following the course a day-dreaming mind would run, the slow build-up is abruptly broken by a signal from the outside world; the hero catapults back to the conditional mood without any in-between stage.

The imaginary trip is undertaken several times, on each occasion different associations and, in turn, different metonymic chains are released. In one variant the cityscape seems to be in the center of the traveler's attention (73-4), the hero paying homage to the pulsating city, while in another a conversation with the taxi driver will form the kernel of the episode (70). Added to the constant change of present and conditional, the hero contributes to the permanent shifting with his own alternating roles, turning from observer into participant and back. Motion and change are often emphasized by vocabulary. A 'prose poem' about dusk in the city begins with a transferred predicate — "The evening surrenders to night" — not far removed from cliché. But after the machines "discharge" the people, rhythm is created by the use of monosyllabic verbs chosen from a single system of associations (a semantic paradigm) to describe their motion through town.

> . . . . They trip along . . . flap along . . . bound along . . . stamp along . . . fall
> back . . . surge forward . . . swing . . . rush on . . . (156).

At the end of the 'poem,' a metaphor for *home* is built on the heavily synecdochic sequence of metonymies. The feeling of permanent change is enhanced by the constantly changing angle of observation, varying from a view from *above* to a view in the *midst*.

As if a camera would first move, then suddenly stop to take stills, so does the narrator present a scene at the home for retarded children. First only the eye of the camera moves, the objects are 'frozen':

> . . . midget heads . . . frilled hairlips . . . lipless mouths open to the jaw . . . a
> rigid lidless eye . . . crippled limbs, atrophied to the bones . . . six-fingered
> hands . . . objects more loathsome than the swill waiting to be removed from
> the back door of a soup kitchen (76).

A floodlight is thrown on each deformed creature; in twenty lines they are looked at as if they were dummies in a horrible wax museum.[9] The camera has made its first round, and suddenly the picture fills with motion: one gnaws on a strap, the other masturbates, the third systematically bashes his head against the wall; crawling, rushing, fist-shaking, screaming and wriggling with their bodies, they are all moving about in a frenzy, a horror show made up of freaks. Having first been introduced to the motionless figures, by now the reader immerses himself in the scene in terrified fascination. Unexpectedly, while a staff member explains the physiological deficiencies of a brain sample swimming in formaldehyde, the reader is suddenly jerked back from the spell by the narrator's side remark, ". . . even on this imaginary visit his presentation is too technical" (77). Due to the ingenious approach, many of these episodes gain a large degree of autonomy, become independent units in the text emitting their own energies.

Alternation between real and imaginary is also the most important feature in Konrád's handling of *time*. When narrated time and time of narration coincide, their convergence is marked by nodes of realism in the text, discrete segments in the story-line, when the officious voice of the social worker and the descriptive efforts of the narrator are meant to be closest together.[10] In most instances, however, not just two but several time aspects are simultaneously active.

Real time, one day, and especially the one afternoon at the Bandulas, appears as a frame for the entire story. In a sense it is eternal time, signifying any day, anywhere in the world, and, at the same time, it is *today*, since the narration is in the present tense. Narrated time is projected back to the past, its depths going to the earliest memories of the oldest characters in the novel.

Simultaneously, it is cast ahead in the future, bifurcating into plans and imaginary experiences already completed. The passing of imaginary time is marked by the hero's changing habits rather than by overt references to it. Between turning off the radio to segregate himself from the news and until T. is turning away from the window in order to withdraw from the visual intervention of the world, weeks, or even months, could have gone by. From learning the language of the deaf-mutes in order to detach himself from ordinary human communication and to digging himself into a corner of his bed, any number of days could have passed. Even this timeless time, undemanding as it is, is interrupted by thoughts about the hero's prior life, comments about people and events that once have held importance for him. These interpolations add to the ambiguity of the length of time imagined which is only once described, in a curiously bucolic style, perhaps reflecting the hero's general contentment with his situation:

> Tender lettuce has arrived, followed by perverse sour cherries, and shortly thereafter by peaches with cool outer garments that only ask to be removed. Already squadrons of wasps are maneuvering over the grape crates. Full moons have passed before my window, the aggressive Ram with his lowered horns has long since fled, and in his place Aquarius sits, ready to pass judgment. I am not making much progress with the child (125).*

This metonymic sequence stands as a metaphor for the passing of an entire year during which the make-believe visits of his family contribute to the reader's conceiving of it as real. New episodes, genuine and illusory, running in relay, aid in obscuring the time reference within this second frame of the novel. Stretching and shrinking time create a horizontal movement, advancing to the future or retreating to the past, a vertical one. The interaction of the two, often contemporaneous effects form yet another distinct pattern of rhythm in the text.[11]

Investigating Konrád's use of time in terms of Lotman's 'game-model' (250[12]) reveals that the author takes advantage of the possibility of conceiving of time as a conditional entity which can be turned about, and, especially, 'replayed,' achieving a synthesis between actual and conditional behavior.

Apart from *space* and *time,* the novel also contains overt tropes, as well as local metaphors, and similes which grow into metonymic chains: T. says,

> Though I am well acquainted with it, neither my hair nor my skin, nor my clothes are impregnated with the smell of poverty, that yellow star (103).

The sentence is, strictly speaking, deviant, yet semantically enhanced by the metaphor. Causal relationships are condensed, synecdochic details create a metaphorical metonymy, the symbol of discrimination:

(1) Poverty does not smell	≠	old clothes, unwashed hair do
(2) People feel that poverty marks them for discrimination	=	people were marked by the yellow star for discrimination
(3) The yellow star is visible on the exterior of the person	=	poverty is visible on the exterior of the person
(4) The yellow star in Hungary was worn on the chest where also flowers are worn. The yellow star does not smell.	(=)	flowers are missing from the sentence; flowers smell

The elements of which the image of poverty is built are in the text. The metonymic function of the metaphor is derived from extra-textual structures of which the yellow star is just one component. It would have a largely different informational value in any other relationship. The smell of flowers, a further extra-textual element, is present in the form of a 'minus-device' (Lotman, 55[13]). The attitudinal content is further extra-textual information, marking the phrase and its new identity.

The holocaust is often used by Konrád as a basis against which metonymic chains are pitted. In the following it is used to illustrate man's lack of understanding of his own mortality:

> . . . they build themselves gallows, dig themselves a pit, take off their clothes without batting an eyelash, and covering their genitals with their hands, await the last command; five minutes before they are to die the whistle blows for them to gallop around the icy yard . . . (59)

The image comes from recent history; the problem is the psychology of the victim who in his complacency becomes an accomplice to his own murder. This discussion is however left out of the text, the narrator simply returns to his earlier topic and picks it up where he has left off before the metonymic chain was introduced.

In another scene, the narrator looks at livestock carriers with their caged cattle and horses and identifies them with police cars and "aluminum tombs" and "on a central corridor six dark cells with imposing locks, and in each one stands a man" (73). A cliché association — man and cattle, cattlecar and people in it — rob this sequence of its novel power. Due to frequent combination, just as there are dead metaphors this has become a 'moribund' metonymy.

In cases of comparison, the new is always compared to the familiar. The airplane used to be compared to the bird, and not vice versa. Konrád is drawing on the same method. At the slaughterhouse where the hero works he is visited by a journalist. "Auschwitz, Auschwitz," whispers the visitor in despair. Here a metaphor (with a metonymic charge) forces itself upon the reader to be taken as the *familiar* to which *new* notions are compared.

Several metonymies are built on cultural models of which war and war-related images are especially forceful. In one segment, Bandula's apartment — as was earlier shown — is changed into a place one day after the siege. Referring to their suicide, "their right to life" is affirmed by the narrator as "they had their place in the world, even if it was no bigger than the bullet holes in the roughcast of our houses" (43). His own seeking refuge in Bandula's apartment is a simile which grows into a metonymic sequence about a general left alone on the battlefield:

> My pretexts are caved in, my subterfuges relocated, I wait like a desperate commander. His tanks have burned out, his planes have crashed, his infantry has fled, and now he is sitting by the dead telephone in his paralyzed fort; knowing there is nothing to be done . . . (111)*

The hero's alleged autobiography also contains memories of military service; however, it is soon clear to the reader that the narrator renders a collective biography of all who fight in wars, and the moral is that on the lowest level of destruction it matters little which side was right (17).

War toys in a shop window are T.'s first exposure to society as he leaves Bandula's apartment to return home. Their new significance for the hero is communicated in a description similar to what is referred to as *ostranenie* in Russian Formalist criticism (157).

The episodes in the novel present a panorama of human misery. In their totality, the horrors of life seem to be as exaggerated as the sufferings of the child hero in Kosinski's *Painted Bird*.[14] It is also meant to achieve the same effect: the events get separated from their victims and grow into one mortifying symbol of pain people inflict upon one another. Each episode is a capsule tragedy, intensified by the guarded neutrality of the narrator. The awfulness of the events does not increase in the course of sequentialization, but without the reader's noticing it the control of neutrality gradually loosens. By the time T. decides to stay with the child many of the cynical comments disappear and are replaced by statements of timid compassion. It is noteworthy that metaphors disappear at times when the most terrible tragedies happen, showing that the extreme does not need or can stand any further intensification. The last moments of a blind old man are recorded as follows:

Yes, he said, "life is expensive." One morning B* polished off a bottle of lye, and for good measure a glassful of nicotine solution. Not wanting to soil the bed, he sat down on the stone floor of the kitchen to die and tied a handkerchief around his mouth to prevent his death rattle from being heard from the outside. . . . On a page torn out from a school copybook he wrote: "Sell my best suit to pay for the funeral." (29)*

Like a short newspaper report, the text is bare, reduced to the most concise communication. The studied objectivity of narration with its coolness and terseness triggers exactly the desired response in the reader who, of course, also realizes that the man cannot even be buried in his best suit, the minimum of dignity. Had the hero of this episode wailed and cried, all emotional work would have been done by him alone. But 'restrained' by the narrator in a situation which calls for tears, the reader responds for him. It is an old "trick of the trade" but only the very good writers can use it successfully.

Essentially there is nothing 'objective' in this work. The act of selecting and ordering the material alone is a subjectivization, carefully camouflaged by the author. The aura of 'equal importance' is maintained even at the point when the narrator reaches the core of his story, his visit to Bandula's apartment. It is introduced as one of the many episodes with the child described as "their five-year-old crouched naked and hairy in his bed, slimy with excrement" (30).*

In some instances, special information is a *sine qua non* for enabling the reader to make the "proper" metaphoric interpretation. Strewn about the text, and identifiable only for the initiated, are the author's metonymic private jokes, not unlike those of the late Nabokov. A couple of examples should illustrate this. The self-description of the hero ". . . a fair to middle technician of the machinery dealing with social tensions" (90) is a parody of an earlier oft-quoted slogan by Stalin, "The writer is the engineer of the soul." To discredit the metaphor, Konrád chooses his own from the same set of technical vocabulary, thus establishing a metonymic relation between the two, the second his own, charged by the first.

In one of the episodes, the life of Anna, the cotenant of the Bandulas, is given in brief. Only the student of Hungarian literature will know that her character contains traits of her namesake, the great love of Gyula Juhász, an important lyrical poet of this century. Anna allegedly singled out Juhász by making him the only man with whom she did not share her bed, and, while she was receiving her overnight visitors, the poet stood outside pressing kisses on the doorhandle. Anna of *The Case Worker* similarly rejects Bandula's advances. T. is chiding her, ". . . You would let him whimper outside your door that you opened to everyone else . . ." (151). It is her character which calls attention to the fact that Bandula's portrait also contains some features of Juhász.[15]

Even if couched in 'magic prose,' Konrád writes corrective fiction, his main topic being man and his existential concerns. At the bottom of each episode lies the author's indignation over poverty, injustice and alienation. His comments on people and their often crippling relationships are reflected in the concise image, ". . . They wear leather gloves to hide their prosthetic hands but take them off when they want to caress someone" (64). Both interpolated monologues and separate episodes persistently express the same concern. At times contrasting, at times enhancing one another, text and topic form a special relationship in the segments where the author talks about cruelty.

In an exposé on children, the author chooses to present his views in a deliberately distorted, cynical manner, using the irritating first person plural of elementary school teachers and hospital staff:

It is not proper to throw the newborn baby into the garbage pail. It is not correct to let your infant starve. If a baby is ill, one should call a doctor. It is not advisable to tie a baby to its crib, sit him down on a hot stove, shut him in the icebox, put his fingers into an electric socket . . . Let's refrain from raping teen-aged girls, particularly our own. While making love let's not crush our sleeping child against the wall . . . let's not call his mother a whore, his father a bastard . . . let's not threaten him with our service pistol . . . let's not leave him behind on the train . . . (90-1).*

The absurdity of the narrator's style underscores the absurdity of behavior which he relates. Thus by the device of contrastive presentation a subtext is created which is actually more powerful than a compassionate plea would have been since it is charged by the tension between 'code' and 'message,' between the 'proper' lexical items and 'improper' semantic connotations in the same text. Instead of "surface realism in internal absurdity," the same multiple effect is achieved by the opposite: surface absurdity in internal realism.[16]

A similar result is achieved by the method of a 'quasi-neutral' rendition of the hero's activities after he has decided not to abandon the child even for a brief period. He imagines that he will do piecework at home, making garter-belts or fur monkeys by the thousand. The mechanical description of his work is interrupted by the "outside" information of the reader: namely, his knowledge that millions actually spend their entire working lives in precisely such a machine-like manner.

The anthropomorphization of objects and reification of people in the novel express the author's frustration over distorted values, over tendencies in modern society to equalize people and things. One of the first episodes tells about an old woman who came to T.'s office building to apply for supplementary benefits. She could not enter the building because she was unable to force the heavy iron door's new spring. Disheartened she went home, wrote a letter to this effect, and hanged herself.

The director was furious and scolded the superintendent, who instructed the fitters to put in another spring. A month later this was done (5).

Eight and a half lines follow in which the hero explains how the other employees managed to use the door until it was fixed, and mentions that he himself was able to tame "this noisy, churlish contraption." A horrible and at the same time trivial story is told in a manner that is reminiscent of Kafka's *In the Penal Colony* in which pedantic concentration on the object creates a chilling distance between the tool of murder and the victim. The display of indifference on the part of the narrator is to emphasize the author's message. Yet, as is often the case with Konrád, the story was not placed at random at the beginning of the novel. It has an additional function to the one described: the door literally leads the reader into the building, and to the next episode which starts in the lobby.

Naturally, anthropomorphization of objects can have many different artistic functions. In another segment of the text it contributes to the impressionistic description of the city, full of motion, patches of color:

> Under the canopy of vapor light, late shopping baskets, battered dinner pails, torn leather-bags passed by (52).

Yet here, too, lines follow in which people are sucked in by their doorways, the street commands the pedestrian, the table, the chair the homecomer. Objects, things determine the lives of people. In his dream in Bandula's room T. conceives of ultimate freedom as,

> Here between these four walls complex movements fall away from me, things push me away, and indivisible time reveals itself (114).*

People and things are equalized in their deterioration and decay. They live in houses where,

> what once was smooth and sturdy is crumbling away, what was ingeniously functional sticks out naked and ashen ... Discolored name-plates, walled-up windows, shattered blinds, . . . urine-stained rosettes, sagging gutters and cables . . . (47)

The houses are inhabited by people who,

> have given up lying comfortable in bed, or stretching out, or making love in peace ... the plaster flakes off them, the drain leaks on their necks, rats gnaw on the baby's toes, the sick urinate on the healthy (47).

Interaction eliminates the difference between animate and inanimate, and they become interchangeable and inseparable at the same time (Lodge, 98–103[17]).

In another episode,

> An iron folding door daubed with gray, hideously gnarled wooden steps, the formerly glassed inner door has been mended with rags and newspaper. Inside a one-legged man is sitting in the dark, weeping. I take his grandchild away with me (49).

Description of an object is admixed with the capsule story of the fate of two people in one paragraph. A catalogue of items, no metaphors (except for gnarled wooden steps, virtually a cliché), the paragraph describes total despair.

The reader is told of the hero's personal commitment in the segment in which he compares himself to a "toothless janitor," who is woken up one night by the doorbell, only to find an abandoned infant at his feet. Cursing, and furious that he, and not some other janitor was picked, "come right down to it, he secretly approves of the unknown person's choice" (22).

Konrád transforms the realities of daily life into multileveled symbols through which he descends into the depth of the self. He uses the individual plots, as well as his comments, recomposed into plots as a road on which the hero progresses toward finding himself. He explores the religious and ethical concepts of our lives, investigates the social, national and personal values of the 'episodists,' and seeks an answer to the meaning of life and human responsibility in it.[18] In this sense the novel is about the possibility of choice, which Konrád sees as "minute air bubbles immured in limestone: such are the neglected opportunities of free will" (90).

In the novel, life's occurrences are shown in their occasional, dislocated or distorted significance. Thus, the simplest daily actions are presented wrapped in their philosophical functions, while in other instances the most vexing ontological questions are reduced to pedestrian, daily chores. Such constant redirection of expectation, such upside-down arrangement of traditional priorities forces the reader to follow very consciously the narrator's path toward self-exploration and recognition. T. uses make-believe experiences to hold off reality, yet precisely these show him up as a failure. He is sucked up by the experiments which slowly penetrate to the sphere in which his deepest beliefs of his self were cherished, and render the convictions first powerless, then destroy them. The sham values of social respectability and professional achievements, his crutches all through his life, fall away from him when he finally faces himself in the shabby room of Bandula. His few moments of victory are still spent during the charades — these are the only moments when he has control over his own life. At the end, he will not have the courage to transform his new insight into behavior. He will accept his own insufficiency and surrender to society. He has a cause but he realizes that he is a coward. He lacks the freedom of choice, granted only to idiots who are not burdened by the past.

> We have much to learn from idiots, the siblings of all things . . . How elegantly they discard their memories — like used busline tickets — so that the freshness of individual encounter will not be contaminated by pitiful attempts at recognition (78).*

One unit serves as the capsule reconstruction of the entire novel, as such modeling the model. T. thinks of a rabbi who has found that he can no longer talk about God to his congregation in true conviction. He therefore decides to leave them, and take to the road in disguise. Unable to answer a dying woman about the meaning of life, he chooses to become mute. Unable to listen to the sorrows of a young mother who lost her infant, the rabbi decides to turn deaf.

Living alone in the forest he comes upon a wounded ferret whom he nurses back to health. One day a condor plummets from the sky and carries off the ferret in front of the rabbi's eyes. "At that the rabbi thought to himself that it would be better if he closed his eyes too." Yet deaf-mute and blind he could only sit and wait for death. Instead, he got up and returned to his congregation. "Once again he preached to them on the subject of good and evil, according to Yahweh's law. He did what he had done before, and waxed strong in shame" (131).

The parable is a reduction of Konrád's novel to its moral message, inserted without any relationship to the hero's imaginary activities, thus it is 'real' in every sense of the author's intentions, making the entire book become its frame.

It is, naturally, very tempting to also draw a metaphorical relationship between the two main characters of the novel, that of T. whom the reader follows all the time, and that of Bandula of whom he only knows through the hero's attitude toward him. Like everybody and everything in the story, Bandula is totally shaped by the perspective of the narrator (Guillén, 259 [19]), while the hero himself is the sum total of what he says about himself, and how he is viewed, according to him, by others. New aspects and meanings to his character are created by and during the process of his recording these views.

The two *personae* can be also viewed as two aspects of the one hero, or even as opposing paradigms of human behavior leading us again to the problem of choice. When the thin support of 'normalcy' disappears from Bandula's life, he gives up totally. As his middle-class existence with its protective rituals, so similar to T.'s, collapses around him, Bandula lacks the desire to reconstruct a mere semblance of it for himself. From a respected citizen he turns into a grotesque outcast, with a wife and imbecile child, a thorn in the neighborhood, a pathetic, yet irritating misanthrope also in the eyes of the case worker. T., who has gone through the war, and some humiliation in his job similar to those of Bandula (at a certain point they both have to deal with corpses, showing a similarity in their work), clings doggedly to traditional values. At the beginning of the novel, family, status and comfort mean a lot to him. In the course of his self-examination, he gradually becomes aware that the occasions when he could be effective, when he and authority "are one" (110), are very rare. Most of the time he can do nothing for those who need help, and then, he confesses, ". . . I am as pathetic as the client who has just left me — and a hypocrite to boot" (110). It is first Bandula who points it out to him, "you rarely think of yourself — only, let's say, when you have a toothache" (41). It is Bandula all the way who has the greatest influence on the hero's sudden change of behavior, and this should warrant another thought about the 'message' of the novel.

One can look at the two characters as two potential modes of coping with social and ontological experiences, each leading to its logical conclusion.

Bandula necessarily commits suicide because his view of life cannot sustain him any further. The case worker will go on living and reconciling, and for that matter always compromising, because he can only become a maximalist in his daydreams. As he returns to his family, the reader understands that of the two, Bandula is the stronger but also the less human, precisely because he was unable to compromise. If the two are metaphors of human behavior, then the child of which each had temporary custody has also to be viewed in his own metaphorical meaning.

Then the child, the imbecile boy, who is almost a reversed Casper Hauser in the eyes of his father, is the symbol of humanity, of life, surviving by its own imperfection, its hopelessly blind powers and ponderables. He is the symbol of humanity and society for whom those who have chosen to go on living have to accept a permanent responsibility and do the best they can.

2. Structure: *The Case Worker* and the Picaresque

The Case Worker can be, naturally, analyzed in isolation, or in its relation to Konrád's other works, as well as in its affiliations with Kafka, Joyce, or the writers of the *nouveau roman*. Here, however, I would like to demonstrate the novel's structural affinity to the *picaresque,* which on the surface would seem to differ greatly from *The Case Worker.*

Literary structure is essentially, as Barthes puts it, "a composition by the controlled manifestation of certain units and a certain association of these units."[20] The special subcode in which these units are organized can be called genre within which a variety of further subcodes appear and are utilized simultaneously. Since we accept that each work of art is a particular and unique model of the universe (Lotman, 50), we have to approach it with its own tools deriving from its own system, and prove that it indeed belongs to one particular, historically determined artistic code. Thus, in the following, I shall show that *The Case Worker* can, and should, be analyzed in its relationship to the particular subcode *picaresque.* For that purpose I am not using the archetype of the genre, but the cluster of picaresque conventions which, when the work is removed from its national and historical setting, should be applicable to Konrád's novel, primarily in structural, but secondarily also in their thematic and stylistic features. Pitted against this model, *The Case Worker* offers the reader an additional angle of observation, and a rearrangement of several concepts already identified in the novel.[21]

As is known, the literary genre *picaresque* deals with the lives of rogues and adventurers. It is of Spanish origin, and as most scholars claim, its archetype is *Guzmán de Alfarache,* by Matteo Alemán. Along with Guzmán, and also by association with it, the earlier, *Lazarillo de Tormes* is frequently mentioned, the two together constituting the prototype of the "género" to which Cervantes had already referred (Sieber, 6–11[22]). Thus, this enduring genre is assumed to have emerged in the late sixteenth century from the confessions of a criminal and the life story of the anonymous Lazarillo, their shared features being *sequences of seemingly unstructured plots.* The picaresque is also about the hero's moving up in society which is, at the same time, exposed for its hypocrisy and false values.

What can therefore Konrád's *case worker* and the *picaro* have in common? The *picaro* sets out to fight his way up to respectability and richness. Not unlike the folk-hero, by his very first steps of separation from his place of origin, the *picaro* moves to change his fortune. Contrary to this, Konrád's hero is locked in the day-by-day constrictions of a smallish job, in one city, and the most important events of the novel take place in one dingy room, while 'real' time is reduced to one afternoon.

To avoid any misunderstanding, it is important to keep in mind that not the *picaro,* the hero, but the *picaresque,* the model, will be investigated. While the structure of *The Case Worker* will be shown to directly follow the picaresque conventions, its hero will, as I hope to prove, move on a reverse course.

Let us first look at the use of *time* and *space.* Admittedly, in terms of 'real' space the *picaro* participates in multiple adventures in many places while the *case worker* sits in an armchair. Yet the events take the reader out from the armchair, out from the room, into the homes and lives of scores of people, into public squares, pubs and streets of his own city, as well as into foreign countries. Thus, imagined or real, space is equally important in the *picaresque* and in *The Case Worker.* The *picaresque* encompasses decades, often the entire life of the hero. *The Case Worker* concentrates on one day. Yet the events taking place in the time span allotted to them are structured in the same manner. Real and recalled by memory, or imagined and involving the future, rather than the past, both have the same *two-temporal perspective, one serving as a frame for the other.* Thus, not the direction but the relationship between 'narrated time' and 'time of narration,' the dual time perspective, is the important common feature.

Just like *The Case Worker,* the *picaresque contains a chain of episodes, related in the first person, often interrupted by the narrator's comments.* Stuart Miller's description of the genre applies unqualifiedly also to *The Case Worker*: "Characters appear and disappear to no effect, forever forgotten. Usually the protagonist does not seek any stable relationship between himself and another. . . If he does, he is usually frustrated. No mysterious order emerges to bind events together and to bring them to some end. In the picaresque plot viewed as a whole nothing strictly speaking *happens.* The picaresque plot merely records fragmented happening, after fragmented happening" (Miller, 12 [23]).

A cavalcade of social types, many of them from the outer fringes of society, appear in the episodes while the digressions are devoted to the narrator's views on the relativity of justice, of honor, and the meaning of life. Konrád's book, as we have seen, contains the same types, and similar comments, yet it is not the individual plot but the total *model,* the *episode/comment alternation,* which constitutes the important, shared feature. The peculiar rhythm based on these alternating segments and the increasing tempo of events, so typical of the genre, are equally present in the scheme of *The Case Worker.* Here, too, structure is seemingly loose, like in the picaresque, which Guillén compares to a "freighttrain" connected only by the hero.[24] Superficially viewed, the individual episodes of the *picaresque* are linked together capriciously, yet upon closer scrutiny, a careful ordering of them is discovered. Each unit enhances the one it precedes, and guides the hero ahead to the end, to the ultimate message of the work. The chain of episodes in Konrád's novel is just as meticulously controlled, *including* the deliberately created aura of arbitrariness about them.

There is still an ongoing discussion whether the episodes or the narrator's comments should be considered the main part of the *picaresque.* Is it the totality of the subplots or the digressions of the narrator that actually constitute the essence of the work? This is a question which can also be asked about *The Case Worker.* Only the reader's point of view will determine whether the core of the novel is expressed in the episodes or in the comments and moral judgments of the narrator, to which the subplots then only serve as an illustration. Naturally, this question seeks an answer regarding the 'message' alone. When investigating the 'code,' it becomes obvious that only the combination of the two components, the episodes *and* the comments, will result in the unique structure of the *picaresque,* making the 'code' truly also the 'message.' The same is valid for *The Case Worker,* in each instance the elimination of either component would destroy the entire work.

As the Spanish *picaresque* emerged in translations, it immediately began to induce the creation of imitations which have moulded themselves to the historical and social realities of the countries in which they were written.[25] The narrow, autobiographical aspect of the genre soon disappeared and the role of the *picaro* doubled, having become a satirist and, at the same time, the object of satire (a role that also characterizes the Bandula/T. relationship, as discussed earlier).

Such fiction as Grimmelshausen's *Simplicissimus* (1668), LeSage's *Histoire de Gil Blas de Santillane* (1715-35), Defoe's *The Fortunes and Misfortunes of the Famous Moll Flanders* (1722), all utilized the by then established conventions, broadening the earlier popular *liber vagatorum* with philosophy and social comment, pertinent to their own milieu. These works of which the above three are only examples to make the point, remained faithful to the common ambiance of the *picaro.* Even when written with humor and irony, they depict a sad world, full of injustice and despair. The heroes or heroines, integral parts of this world, turn every trick that enable them to reach success, primarily expressed in money and status. Yet with all the events the *picaro* participates in he remains a very evasive hero. He has many character traits, but they do not appear before the reader in any order; they come out at random, as if emphasizing his internal instability. This, as was shown, is also true for the hero of *The Case Worker*. The *picaro* is "neither a round nor a flat character," claims Miller (45), and Chandler, in his by now classic on the *picaresque,* calls the *picaro* an anti-hero, who "is everything and nothing; everything in what he does, nothing in character" (46).

In the course of a number of casual relationships T. shows the two, the active and the passive, aspects of his personality. His active component is putting people and efforts into motion — at least at an initial stage. The passive one sits back and observes what happens inside the lives and systems brought into motion, and refrains, as much as possible, from getting involved with them. This quality is also characteristic of the personality of the *picaro*.

"Identifying the narrator is one of the primary ways of naturalizing fiction," says Culler (200). Compared to much of the *nouveau roman* where it becomes the reader's task to reconstruct the narrator and bring coherence to the text, Konrád's narrator is readily distinguishable. Most of the thoughts presented can easily be attributed to him. Yet, in the traditional sense of fiction we know very little of the hero. In the conventional novel, the protagonist is the most developed character, and the others occurring in the work are described through their touching the hero's life. Their qualities and characteristics transpire primarily through their interaction with the protagonist. In *The Case Worker* the exact opposite takes place. Detailed, often clinically analytical observations of the 'others' are rendered, while the persona of the hero/narrator remains in relative anonymity. He wears the cloak of the bureaucrat, not in the pejorative but in the original sense of the word, and for the better part of the text he also uses the language of a state official. In a few places, however, there is a distinction between story and presentation, between referential object and views of the narrator. Such alternation of two emotive systems, while enhancing the ambiguity of the figure of T. (or for that matter the figure of the *picaro*), intensifies the relationship between episodes and comments. The arcane hero adds the *lack of information* to his personality, and with his consistent resistance to reader anticipation (Lotman, 51) creates the desired tension. The hero of *The Case Worker* is as opaque as the *picaro*; in terms of vital information we know very little about him indeed.

> . . . I live with my family in a pleasant part of town, in an apartment commensurate with my professional status, with neighbors of like social standing . . . (103).

T.'s full name is never revealed, he remains comrade T. for most of his clients, his family never addresses him, and he does not seem to have any friends. He is once referred to as Doctor T. by an old woman who might have just used the title to flatter him (9). Little is said about his education, and his previous professional experiences seem to have been rather "caused" than chosen.

Earlier a public prosecutor (86), demoted, he became an inspector supervising exhumations (87), a job he exchanged for the slaughterhouse (88), before he landed the job as a social worker, "a representative of public order, half jurist, half functionary" (90). At the beginning of the novel, the *case worker* occupies a position of comfort and respectability which the *picaro* strives to achieve. The end station of the *picaresque* hero is the beginning of the journey for comrade T., which will be a reversed trip all the way. His life is stable but empty, his days are without joy, happiness is just the absence of tragedy.

> ... My family life is orderly ... my loved ones do not sleep with axes under their pillows ... my wife is not in jail ... nobody pours lye in my wine ... I am generally well liked (103–4).

Even in this fragmentary description a similarity to the *picaresque* is observable. Due to the corrective aspect of the genre, the *picaro* renders an inverted picture of the world (Chandler, 43). The cynical overtones are, however, sharper in the traditional *picaresque*.

The fundamental loneliness of the hero, who at the end will remain within society (alone, but not alienated) is another shared feature of T. and the *picaro*. Guillén calls the *picaro* a halfway-outsider (393), a person who can neither assimilate to, nor reject his fellow men, who, therefore, often takes the role of an observer. The elemental need of participation draws him into variegated adventures, each making an impact on him.

In *The Case Worker,* the relationship of structure and immediate social framework shows the influence of the *picaresque* conventions. Its hero, sitting in the armchair, watching over an imbecile boy, fabricating his private charades, is different from the *picaro,* a rogue permanently promoting his 'upward mobility.' T. is seemingly passive. Events come to him, parade in front of him, pull him along for a while, and let him off after each involvement.

Whether glued to an armchair or being in the middle of the action, Konrád's hero shares the experiences of the *picaro*: life's chaos meets him in each event. There is mobility in his stagnation, an inner mobility. He makes his moves in the afternoon, in the chair of the Bandulas. He starts on the journey of the *picaro* by deciding on a new path in life. The journey is imaginary, therefore true to his deepest aspirations. T. chooses to revolt against the dreariness of his existence by deciding to abandon his comfortable environment and stay with the orphaned child. Playing with his own faeces, drivelling in his filthy bed, the imbecile boy is more human, more reassuring for T. than his well-bred, mechanical doll-like children, the pride of his middle-class home.

The *picaro*'s effectiveness is determined by how capable he is to adjust to his ever-changing ambiance. Each case is an experiment, and his efforts are recorded in the episodes. Comrade T. executes the same experiment in his chair. From there he pays his imaginary visits in town and participates in new events, in his new, projected role. His adjustment to his chosen milieu is also a successive experience. Its end result is his total adaptation, demonstrated at the make-believe visit of his family when the hero realizes that he has lost the desire to and the traditional means of communicating with them (123).

As Konrád's hero travels in the reverse, it is only logical that he should start his journey by staying. In a static position he nevertheless can turn into Bandula, can project a life with Anna, etc. Role playing is frequent in the picaresque convention, but there the hero extends his influence through his various roles, while T. is progressing toward a reduced, simplified life style. Thus another feature is shared, though in the reverse.

If we accept Herrero's definition of the picaresque to be in its essence "an extended sermon," it is obvious that the *picaro* and Konrád's hero reach the same insight at the end of their respective stories.[26] By the conclusion of the *picaresque* the *picaro* has completed his journey upward in society, a moment which often coincides with his finally *accepting himself. The Case Worker* moves in the opposite direction. Rejecting social respectability, he strives to becoming a member of the society of the poor and the outcast, and through this, he finally *understands and accepts himself.* After many trials and tribulations, the *picaro* realizes that he is no better and no worse than his fellow men. On his self-searching inner journey, T. arrives at the same conclusion, only at the opposite end of the social spectrum. On his way home from his afternoon vigil he sees a world in which the difference between his "clients" and himself is minimal, and, above all, accidental. With this realization his integration, too, is completed: he sees life as an ultimately isometric experience. Čiževsky speaks about the "spiritual rebirth" of the *picaro,*[27] which should, I suggest, rather be reduced to a mere 'reconciliation' with the world.

In *The Case Worker* the reader assimilates information from each episode on the basis of its independent validity until the sum total of the individual phenomena leads him to discover the governing principles of the novel. He does this 'simultaneously' with the hero who 'finds himself' through the relating or creating of the episodes. The incidents and episodes are therefore *functions,* whose artistic ordering will shake the hero's *a priori* notions, and enable him to recognize life's meaning. The hero who by his namelessness and activities transforms his individuality also into a *function,* remains in this aspect especially close to the *picaro.* The reader's identification is not with him but with the socio-psychological generalizations he represents. It is not a recognition of the *persona* but of the *features,* common to the existential experiences of man to which the reader responds. The same applies to the *picaro,* as was recognized by Jung who wrote

> ... Eine kollektive Personifikation wie der Schelm geht aus der Summierung von individuellen Einzelfällen hervor und wird vom Einzelnen wiederum als bekannt begrüßt, was nicht der Fall wäre, wenn es sich um eine individuelle Ausgeburt handelte.[28]

To conform to Renaissance ideals, the *picaro* attempted to change society, to remake man even if to his own distorted values. *The Case Worker,* whose professional function would be the same, moves again in the opposite direction. Rather than attempt to change others, he himself decides to conform, his action symbolizing more than his temporary disillusionment with immediate social conditions.

The popularity of the *picaresque* very soon created the *anti-picaresque*[29] in which all social achievements were proven sham. Later still, the *anti-picaresque* turned back to an authentic autobiography; a typical example of this is Orwell's *Down and Out in London and Paris,* playing in a milieu similar to Konrád's book. In Orwell, society is presented with detailed naturalism but the personal, moral comments of the author are reduced. Konrád's *The Case Worker* is different, because the author changes his daily experiences (he has worked as a superintendent in a child welfare organization) are remodeled, reordered, and transmitted to the reader in 'magic' prose. In this sense, Konrád is further away from the *anti-picaresque,* the modern variant, than from the original, Spanish tradition.[30]

Structure and, to some extent, character have their roots in the picaresque convention but Konrád's language breaks away from the language of the genre, being richer and often, as earlier discussed in this paper, on the borderline of prose and poetry. The poetic charge of his prose is what disguises the picaresque structure. Poeticity was less far removed from the early *picaresque* than it is from, say, *The Thief's Journal* by Genet. As Ricapito very properly observed, "in the *picaresque,* reality is never copied but is either imitated poetically, or deliberately deformed."[31]

Lotman claims that an entire work can be viewed as one sentence or even as a single word non-reducible in terms of meaning. This is markedly true for the *picaresque,* Spanish type or modern. Any link taken out of the "magic chain" breaks the whole into fragments and robs it of its intrinsic energy.

* * *

At the end of his "journey," in a poetic and moving monologue, T. calls upon all underprivileged, "whose wildest dream is to be next to last" and the

> eternal underdogs, those who don't write the letter because they can't make up their minds how to address the recipient . . . those who never get picked for either team on the school playground . . . who get the leftover pudding or wife . . . who bathe, dust and copulate once a week . . . who often cry into mirrors . . .

to come to him. Back in his 'real life,' the identification he has made with Bandula is transposed to a deep identification with all in need. T. now claims to be one of them, and offers his help on a different level than before:

... Let all those come who want to; one of us will talk, the other will listen; at least we shall be together (173 [32]).

The novel is about a social worker, written by an artist who has worked as a social worker. Therefore it is only natural that it contains its author's comments on the profession and its inherent shortcomings, and on the possibilities of bettering the quality of life.

Does the novel also contain the comments of the artist on the artist? It does indeed: in fact in one of the first metonymic excursions of the hero. Musing on his back in Bandula's bed, T. watches the ceiling, on which he discovers broken lines, suggesting all kinds of images. They soon turn 'real,'

> ... The horses are drawing a hearse ... in the middle an old man in black raincoat ... a strolling graphologist ... a forgotten musical clown, possibly a dealer in stolen goods, in any event an old man in a black raincoat, lifts high his silver saxophone, tosses back his head and blows. Out of the instrument pour shaggy figurines in black raincoats, no doubt peddlers or strolling graphologists or possibly even forgotten musical clowns or dealers in stolen goods, lifting minute saxophones (61).

The chain of thoughts recalling wandering musicians (in a Fellini-like image), turns into a metaphorical metonymy, a symbol of the artist who, above all, will write about himself.

NOTES

1. *The Case Worker* is George Konrád's first novel. It was published in Hungary in 1969 (*A látogató*), and has since been translated into several European languages.

2. J. Culler, *Structuralist Poetics: Structuralism, Linguistics and the Study of Literature.* Ithaca, 1976; henceforth, Culler.

3. I use *metaphor* in a similar but not identical sense as D. Lodge does in *The Modes of Modern Writing: Metaphor, Metonymy and the Typology of Modern Literature.* Ithaca, 1977; henceforth, Lodge. The phrase "in the singularity of the moment" is a free adaptation of Hegel's term. He used it in dealing with action losing its meaning when isolated from its context; see M. Makkai, "Against Reductionism and Purism: Tertium Datur," *Essays on Explanation and Understanding,* ed. by J. Manninen and R. Tuomela. Dordrecht, 1976, 29.

4. J. Derrida, *Of Grammatology,* Baltimore, 1976.

5. R. Barthes, "L'effet de réel," *Communications,* 11 (1968), 84–9.

6. In the following, quotations will refer to *The Case Worker,* tr. by Paul Aston, New York, 1969. Whenever I found the translation to be inaccurate, I have emended it. These emendations are marked by an asterisk following the quotation.

7. Before total immersion in his role, the hero still watches the activities outside Bandula's window with interest. The reduction of needs starts with "If instead of

Bandula I was lying among scratchy breadcrumbs on that wire spring . . . " (85), thus contemporaneously with his identification with Bandula. This is logically followed by the admission of staying by choice (103), until the room becomes large enough to have "life reveal itself in it" (114). At this point his taking notes stops (117), and although he still listens to the radio, he turns away from the window (117–18). When the occasional lover enters the room, life with her and the idiot child is reduced to touching (119). The room being too large, the next step is his withdrawal to the bed (121–2). The narrowing of space is so graphic that no diagram could present it more persuasively.

8. *Simile* is here conceived of as a combination of two or more notions enhancing contiguity, thus affiliated with metonymy. An unexpected simile may provide, however, an abrupt semantic shift, and consequently a break in contiguity. On such occasions simile functions as metaphor.

9. Cf. Lodge (79) referring to R. Jakobson's brilliant observation regarding 'metonymic' filming and 'synecdochic' close-ups.

10. The 'official' tone is also an artistic *imitation* of bureaucratic language or of the jargon of the sociologist. An actual professional communication would sound more as follows: "In the total number of cities [of Hungary] more than fifty percent of the population with earning power has not completed the eighth grade of public school, or its previous equivalent, four years of either general middle school or *gymnasium*. This layer constitutes the lower stratum of our vertically stratified society. The majority of skilled laborers, unskilled workers and agricultural laborers belong to it. This is the level of the lower income groups, of families living in inferior housing." The quotation is from one of the more easily digestible segments of a sociological work co-authored by George Konrád (István Szelényi and György Konrád, *Az új lakótelepek szociológiai problémái* [*Sociological Problems of New Housing Developments*], Budapest, 1969, 31.

11. Real time in which man functions in his daily existence is the subject of one long, contemplative passage,

> . . . petty, dispersed, fraudulent time of the alarm clock, the time that lurks in wait from morning to night . . . that is lost no matter how hard we try to save it . . . the time we cherish even when we waste it . . . the daily time . . . that jumps into buses . . . punches time cards . . . A man can make peace with his everyday time . . . ignore it now and then. Or else, stricken with its horror, he can croak of it day after day, from morning to night (54) *

12. J. Lotman, *Szöveg-model-típus* (*Text-Model-Type*), Budapest, 1973. On "feature transfer" and its role in the semantics of metaphor, cf. S. R. Levin, *The Semantics of Metaphor,* Baltimore, 1977, 62.

13. J. Lotman, *The Structure of the Artistic Text,* tr. by R. Vroon, Ann Arbor, 1977 (*Michigan Slavic Contributions,* 7); henceforth, Lotman.

14. J. Kosinski, *The Painted Bird,* Boston, 1965.

15. This is what Lotman calls the "secret, conspirative" meaning of the text (*Szöveg* . . . , 253).

16. Lotman's statement on the multiple effect achieved by "surface realism in internal absurdity" as condensed by E. M. Thompson, "Jurij Lotman's Literary Theory and Its Context," *Slavic and East European Journal,* 21, no. 2 (1977), 225–38, esp. 232. The concept was developed by Lotman in the course of analyzing A. K. Tolstoy's poem "There sits beneath a canopy . . . " (cf. Y. Lotman, *Analysis of the Poetic Text,* ed. and tr. by D. B. Johnson, Ann Arbor, 1976, 219–28) but the phrase, as used by Thompson, is not in the translation.

17. Lodge provides similar examples from the prose of Dickens. In *Bleak House* and *Oliver Twist* the more 'realistic' townscape is in opposition to the romantic plot, especially in the latter case. In *The Case Worker* it is poetic language that is used to describe poverty. It is full of alliterations and anaphoras which the English translation can only partially render. The author stresses the typically poetic elements in his prose, thus "the border not only fails to disappear but on the contrary takes on greater significance" (Lotman, 102).

18. As we shall see, these are the essential questions the 'original' *picaro* asks himself. He, too, is seeking answers to how to act, in what to believe, and these are his most important motivating forces.

19. C. Guillén, "Toward a Definition of the Picaresque," *Actes du IIIᵉ Congrès de l'Association Internationale de Littérature Comparée, Utrecht, 1961*, The Hague, 1962; henceforth, Guillén.

20. R. Barthes, "The Structuralist Activity," *European Literary Theory and Practice: From Existential Phenomenology to Structuralism*, ed. by V. W. Gras, New York, 1973, 159.

21. "The fact that the text is associated with a given genre, style, age, author, and so on, changes the entropy value of its isolated elements; this fact not only forces us to view extra-textual connections as something wholly real, but also indicates certain ways for measuring this reality" (Lotman, 51).

22. H. Sieber, *The Picaresque*, London, 1977; henceforth, Sieber.

23. S. Miller, *The Picaresque Novel*, Cleveland, 1967; henceforth, Miller.

24. Guillén, 386-7.

25. For a detailed discussion of this point, cf. W. F. Chandler, *Romances of Roguery*, New York, 1961 (1899); henceforth, Chandler. Also, Sieber, 36-62. See further J. Striedter, "Der Schelmenroman in Russland," *Veröff. d. Abt. f. sl. Spr. u. Lit. d. Osteuropa-Instituts d. FU Berlin*, Bd. 21 (1961); F. Monteser, *The Picaresque Element in Western Literature*, 1975; and *Pikarische Welt*, ed. by H. Heidenreich, Darmstadt, 1969.

26. M. Herrero Garcia, "Nueva interpretación de la novela picaresca," *Revista de filologia española*, XXIV (1937), 349.

27. D. Čiževsky, "The Unknown Gogol," *Slavic Review*, XX (1952), 482.

28. *Pikarische Welt*, 247.

29. Already Chandler recognized that the *picaro* is "the anti-hero of society" (14). His semi-alienated status (many researchers believe that Lazarillo's author, as well as Alemán, were Marranos) made the character later perfectly fit to fill the frame with modern, equally critical functions.

30. The use of personal experience brings the author of the first popular picaresque to mind. Not unlike Konrád, Alemán possibly met the subjects of *Guzmán* in his official role as professional investigator. In 1593 Alemán was appointed by the Crown to find out about the condition of galley slaves who worked in the quicksilver mines of Almadén. Most probably part of his report to the court was based on personal interviews (Sieber 18). Many of Konrád's cases could have been based on personal encounters as well. Although several centuries separate them, their concern for the poor unites the two writers. Alemán's interest in the plight of the exploited is testified to by his correspondence with Cristóbal Pérez de Herrera, one of the important social reformers of his time. Konrád's continued interest in social reform is proven by the sociological study he co-authored (cf. n. 10), and his recent book, *The City Builder* (tr. by I. Sanders), New York, 1977.

31. J. V. Ricapito, *Toward a Definition of the Picaresque.* Ph.D. thesis, Los Angeles, 1966, 633.

32. The last imaginary excursion is the most personally tainted part of Konrád's novel. Before returning home, T. questions the validity of his decision to stay with his family, his job, and in the country. This is done on two levels, each involving the railroad station which he passes on his way home. The first level is presented through an unsympathetic description of an expatriate who has visited Hungary and is leaving again.

> . . . Red stockings, red dress, black cloak, black hat, white-painted mouth,
> green eyeshadow, dog, porter, relative, "I send you those dresses . . ." (163)*

It reflects the negative feelings of many who stayed in the country against those who left. The second level investigated the difference between life at home and life of a *genuine* Westerner. T. follows a face in the window of a Transeuropean Express, on an imaginary vacation at seaside hotels, fishermen "and Swedish girls who think of nothing but bathing" (165), only to conclude,

> . . . when he gets back into the habit of standing in line in the dark vaulted corridors of public buildings, not daring to tell the pipe-smoking, ear-scratching clerk that he has been waiting a long long time to get the document stamped, then I should say, there will no longer be much difference between us . . . (166)

Thus the imaginary last trip ends with the satisfaction of disenchantment. It enables the hero to make his compromise easier. Although it simplifies the issues, it allows him to stop questioning himself about the validity of his decision, and lets him view East and West together, equalized under the umbrella of omnipotent bureaucracy.

Vera Calin

POSTWAR DEVELOPMENTS OF THE
PREWAR TRADITION IN ROMANIAN PROSE

The emergence of Romanian literature in secular literary culture was a phenomenon delayed by historical and spiritual circumstances. It is usually located sometime before or during the romantic period. The climax of this prolonged process, marked by ups and downs, coincides with the interwar years when Romania produced a number of writers — mostly poets — of European renown who experimented with the most advanced poetic formulae, became representatives or even promoters of the poetic avant-garde and were recognized as such. They achieved recognition beyond the borders of their native land, which they chose to leave and represent abroad. The reasons for which the simultaneous explosion of creativity in the field of prose-writing was for a very long time ignored beyond the boundaries of Romania pertain to a series of circumstances. The main reason explaining this discrepancy, this status of a strictly local phenomenon to which the Romanian narrative prose was reduced in spite of its openness to the impact of modernism, was due to its much less spectacular evolution in comparison with that of the poetic avant-garde. Between the two World Wars the Romanian narrative followed a course of development parallel to that of the most innovative trends of Western Literature. However, it never attained the radicalism of the avant-garde with its aggressive polemicism and "widespread use of subversive or openly disruptive artistic techniques,"[1] and therefore never meant to overthrow the whole system of current social and poetical values. Nonetheless, both Romanian poetry and prose testify to that interwar up-to-dateness manifest in more than one East European literature, which, while pressing on the rhythm of any normal evolution, succeeded in keeping abreast with the most recent Western literary tendencies. "Synchronism" is what the Romanian prewar critic Eugen Lovinescu called this integration of Romanian literature into West European culture and adherence to the "spirit of the age" in his *History of Romanian Modern Civilization*. This "saeculum" is regarded by the same critic as a homogeneous reality governed by the standards of urban civilization.[2]

Since this study is confined to the domain of literary prose, I want to emphasize from the very beginning that, within the frames of what Lovinescu characterized as synchronization, prose-writing in prewar Romania amounted not only to works of striking variety and complexity, but that these works were perfectly mature and up-to-date in relation to Western cultural standards. Still, a few distinctions seem necessary to me.

Possessed as they were with the idea of "urban homogenization," Lovinescu and the writers gravitating around his literary circle rejected the traditional Romanian story or novel which depicted rural life, sometimes in a spirit of conventional idealization. Bringing that archaic world into 20th-century literature accordingly amounted to a cultural conservatism and was an artificial way to affirm national specificity.

Despite the modernist trend inaugurated and encouraged by the "ideologist of modernity,"[3] the rural novel survived, illustrated — sometimes from antagonistic viewpoints — by numerous writers, but most brilliantly by two of the superlatively representative Romanian interwar prose-writers: Mihail Sadoveanu and Liviu Rebreanu. The former, the author of more than one hundred novels, began his creative activity at the turn of the century and went on uninterrupted until the late 1950s. He treated country-life as well as historical matter in the manner of an ancient oral bard and remained to the very last the prototype of the story-teller. Both his historical fictions and his rural stories or novels represent implicit and unconscious means of rejecting the new urban and technological civilization he instinctively resented as traumatic. Actually, he completely lacked the prerequisites demanded by modernist criticism. In his epics he accomplished, in the manner of the old bards to whose family he definitely belonged, a unique fusion between historical tradition and rural contemporary reality, between man and nature, a synthesis of striking originality, although indebted to the folklore ballad.

Peasant life was in the center of Rebreanu's creation as well. But the latter's objective, impassive, shockingly brutal prose, completely deprived of that note of lyricism which imbued Sadoveanu's narratives, turned him into a favorite of Lovinescu's circle, which viewed him as one of the creators of the Romanian modern novel. All the aspects of a dramatic period (the peasant upheavals at the turn of the century) are conveyed in the same ostentatiously noncommittal tone, in that dry and matter-of-fact style which both crudely and unemotionally describes horror without avoiding the repulsive simile, but definitely bans any emotional epithet, thus justifying the characterization of naturalism or verism often applied to Rebreanu's social novels. In these frescoes of rural life, the narrative technique remains linear and metonymic, in perfect consonance with what Jakobson considered stylistically characteristic of realism.

But neither Rebreanu's unemotional outlook on peasant life nor his programmatically chosen exterior narrative angle would have justified his being ranged among the modernists. His metaphysical novel *Adam and Eve* (1925) had already disclosed another dimension of Rebreanu's artistic personality, the one manifest in his attraction for occult and esoteric knowledge. The novel uses the myth of reincarnation by means of metempsychosis. A proof of the author's awareness of the romantic heritage, this parable paved the way for Rebreanu's further investigations of the subterranean levels of morbid human conscience, which he undertook in the novel entitled *Ciuleandra* (the name of a Romanian frantically-Dionysian folk dance). The novel deals with a case of neurosis — the result of a sinful heredity (naturalism, of course). The scenery of the main character's dissolution and final breakdown is a psychiatric ward, in which the victim of heredity fragmentarily relives, by means of flashback technique, the events of his life. Naturally, in this atmosphere of insatiable curiosity for cultural novelty, the city novel and the complexity it involved was bound to prevail. The novelist's keen interest in twisted and sophisticated, even morbid, characters, in profound psychological dramas and intellectual dilemmas accounts for the rapid development and precocious maturity of the "analytical prose" which a Romanian critic — G. Ibrăileanu — opposed to "creative prose" (creative of new "objective" universes).[4] The psychological novel of that period accepted the most varied techniques experimented with by Dostoevsky, Proust, Joyce, and Huxley (inner monologue, stream of consciousness, disruption of time sequence, montage, etc.).

The most passionate defendant of modernism was Camil Petrescu, an ebullient and scintillating spirit of varied aesthetic and philosophical concerns, a playwright, a challenging essayist, a novelist, and in all these hypostases, an aggressively adept theorist of new themes and techniques, above all "the new structure" of fiction. In one of his essays he categorically stated that ". . . epic literature such as was written until Proust no longer belonged to the structure of modern culture," moreover that "compared to the evolution of science and philosophy during the last forty years literature had remained anachronistic." Types and plots had, he further asserted, become geometrically stereotyped, for the writers' supreme ambition was to create characters. This was, according to C. Petrescu, the result both of Cartesianism and Leibniz's doctrine of monads. The "new structure," the perfection of which was attained by Proust, "is supposed to take into account the fundamental indetermination of the human being, the erosion operated both by time and effervescent sensitiveness upon the geometrical outline, upon the petrification of the human being into geometrical forms."[5]

Of his two prewar novels, *The First Night of War, the Last Night of Love* (1930) and *Procrustes' Bed* (1933), the latter is most relevant for Petrescu's understanding about the inconsistency, mobility, and relativity both of the human being and of the criteria according to which it is classified. It is an example illustrative of what the author terms modern architectonics and also of what a contemporary Romanian critic calls "the shifting focus," i.e. the continual change of the narrative point of view.[6] Ladima, the main character, a poet and journalist, a misfit in the trivial and materialistic world he lives in, crushed by its platitude and spirit of compromise, never appears as a physical or moral individuality, but is recreated, reconstructed in varied ways by those who knew him: an intelligent and sophisticated woman, a semi-prostitute, a magistrate, thus becoming an evanescent creature in a world dominated by relativism. The whole novel grows around a void, an absence, like an atoll surrounding the crater of a sunken volcano; this recalls the structure of some of Faulkner's novels which develop around an essential ellipsis, such as *Sanctuary* or *Absalom, Absalom!* To multiply the points of view Petrescu uses the footnote only for creating "the documentary illusion," in reality allowing the author to arbitrate between different viewpoints and parodying the veristic seriousness.[7]

In his essays C. Petrescu insistently expressed his belief in the social mission of the intelligentsia and in the advent of noocracy. Hence his conviction that the qualities, the inner life, and the quests of the intellectual enabled the latter and only him to become the possible hero of a literary work lucidly dealing with the dynamics of passion, the impact of ideas and the existential problems of modernity.

George Călinescu was a *homo universalis* of the Renaissance type, a brilliant critic and essayist, a literary historian who knew how to turn that scholarly yet ineffably charming book *History of Romanian Literature* (1941) — owing to his permanent and unpredictable demon of analogy — into a History of World Literature. He belonged to the unequalled masters of the literary portrait, the portrait in progress. In his *History of Literature* as well as in his essays he used the portrait as he did the paradox as methods of criticism. His imagery — in his studies, essays, or novels — was fostered by his inexhaustible and organically assimilated scholarship which his imagination used as a poet would his store of sensations. In his writings aphoristic expression abounds, deprived of any attempt at moralizing: "Really genial creations are always parricidal," he states, alluding to Don Quixote having killed Cervantes. Such rhetorical preferences as well as several defenses of Classicism (among them the essay "The Significance of Classicism," 1946) account for his being ranged among the "classicists" and in opposition to the modernist tendency represented by Lovinescu. This label oversimplifies. A certain stylistic superabundance, a kind of piling or cumulative technique, the avalanche of references and quotations in the works of the essayist and literary historian ("criticism," he used to say, "is the art of using quotations") sound extravagantly baroque and are apt to remind us of Montaigne's or Burton's cascades of bookish enumerations. An exuberant relish for shockingly paradoxical connections may also be termed as baroque or perhaps as mannerist: "Nero may very well have been a lunatic, yet he had the Pyrrhic instinct enclosed in a profoundly lyrical soul."[8]

Of his two prewar novels, *The Wedding Book* (1933) and *Otilia's Enigma* (1938), the latter was considered a triumph of classicism and the archetype of the Balzacian novel in Romanian literature owing to the multitude and power of the portraits it contained, portraits, according to many critical opinions, aiming at a classic universality — the miser, the hypocrite, the upstart.

In fact, the first lines of the novel might have introduced any of Balzac's novels into the complex and labyrinthine world of the *Comédie Humaine*:

One night in early July, 1904, not long before one o'clock, a young man of about eighteen years, wearing the uniform of a high-school student, turned into Antim Street coming from Apostles' Street carrying a kind of not very big suitcase which must have been very heavy, since, tired as he was, he kept moving it from one hand to the other.

Like Balzac, Călinescu most certainly knew how to use "the language of furniture, buildings, streets, and neighborhoods."[9] Although he did not share Camil Petrescu's dislike for the omniscient novelist, Călinescu may still baffle the adepts of his classicism. There are in the novel *Otilia's Enigma* as many girls named Otilia as there are characters in the book, just as the number of Albertines in Proust's *Recherche* equals that of the men and women having known the young woman named Albertine.

The wonderful outcome of what Lovinescu chose to call "Synchronism," which foretold the further evolution of Romanian literature in the direction of modernity, seemed suddenly to be brought to a stop not so much by the outbreak of World War II as by the subsequent political and ideological realities of the East European countries. What eventually happened in Romanian literature is intensely symptomatic of some possible options of the East European writers who had reached artistic maturity in the prewar period. Some of them chose to adapt unorthodox trends and manners to the demands of a controlled literature whose stylistic label in the years of Stalinism was Marxist Socialist Realism, a formula which soon was to become equal to official academism.

Answering the question about the continuity of Romanian prewar tradition into the postwar years and about the writers' ways of rallying to or refusing "the principle of order, control, and repression"[10] first and foremost requires a discussion about their degree of acceptance of the political concept of art, or, more bluntly, of their submitting to the policy of controlled art.

Some of the writers mentioned above died shortly after, before, or during the war. Some others emerged after a long eclipse — an eloquent eclipse — at some moment of some post-Stalinist thaw; others chose silence, impenetrable and meaningful silence. Some left the country, self-exiling themselves and writing in a foreign language, as did Mircea Eliade and Eugène Ionesco. But most of the outstanding Romanian prewar prose writers continued their creative activity, using pathetic strategies and subtle devices in order to preserve their original vision, their multi-leveled and -angled narrative techniques, their epic architectonics, now regarded and rejected as formalist, decadent, or even heretical manifestations. The above phrases represent a very rough statement. Actually, the gamut of possible attitudes was very rich and the strategies and compromises necessary in the new political context were incalculably numerous and of very different degrees.

Geo Bogza, the ex-surrealist poet who had in the early 1930s demanded on behalf of "creative exasperation" the advent of the Reporter as a creator of anti-literature, became the author of a series of poetic reportages, which he continued to write after World War II.[11] The ex-avant-garde poet, who had begun his career as a literary reporter in the years prior to the Second World War (*Lands of Stone, Fire, and Clay,* 1939), maintained the same pattern of reportage in *The Book of the River Olt* (1945) and continued with a series in which the lyrical, visionary note had stylistic recourse to a "technique of intensification,"[12] a special type of hyperbole meant to transfigure, from a cosmic or geological perspective, everyday, even trite reality into a fantastic existential experience.[13] Concomitantly, he pursued a journalistic activity materialized in a serial of feuilletons published weekly in the periodical *Contemporanul.* Every Friday, for seven consecutive years, his articles of an unclassifiable variety (prose alternating with verse or even drawings, short comments, or substantial essays elaborating on the event of the week, on an apparently banal episode, on literary issues, meditations fostered by psychological, social, existential, cosmic experiences) were published in the *Contemporanul* with the rhythmicity of a heart beating — like the very pulse of life.[14] There is a passionate unmistakable sincerity and a poetical quality about this journalistic prose. It bears the mark of its author's vision stylistically exteriorized in a very specific type of overstatement which seems the result of the will to repeat genesis, to reconstruct the world according to new classifications and criteria:

> A roe, a living being, is perhaps, in a both righter and more poetical order of the world, closer to an airplane than to a hippopotamus, in whose proximity zoology pinpoints it.[15]

The alternation of the category of the gigantic on the one hand and that of the minuscule and fragile on the other ranges among the invariants of Bogza's poetical prose. A pathetic fighter for human dignity:

> (I do not know whether sometimes, at the anniversary of one or five thousand years of the cosmic era, an exhibition will be organized where the matter constituting varied cosmic worlds will be exhibited, but if that is going to happen, the inhabitants of other universes will have the opportunity to realize how imbued with blood our earth is.)[16]

Bogza is the author of numerous meditations on human conditions:

> (If I were to live in another universe in a world with less painful and blamable aspects, the great reproach I would address to God would not regard his hiding himself from us, nor the certitude of our death, but the fact that we turn to corpses, that he did not for our sake discover an end defying the laws of organic chemistry.)[17]

But in all his hypostases and moods the ex-poet and present reporter is permanently aware of the miracle of "this fantastic adventure which is life on earth, once begun by an amoeba and finally attaining human conscience."[18]

The multivalence of those literary reportages, the connotations of those articles — some of them genuine parables — most of them politically interpretable and interpreted, amounted to Bogza's journalistic activity coming to an end. He eventually collected all the feuilletons published during those seven years (1966–1973) in a volume entitled *Lighthouse Guardian* (1974).

At first glance, Zaharia Stancu went through the same evolution from poetry to poetical prose. Between the two World Wars he published several volumes of lyrics in a rather traditional vein if compared to the aggressively outrageous expression of the poetry punctuated by sexual imagery written by the vanguard to which Bogza belonged. Aggressive tones were audible in many of Stancu's lampoons, for he was involved in political debates and for a time gravitated around the anti-fascist and proletariat reviews. Of his prewar novels, *Men in Tophat* (1941) was identified as a "roman à clef" and as such was applauded by a scandal-greedy public. Eventually, when, in the years of the people's republic, Stancu became a member of the Academy and the president of the Writers' Union, *Men in Tophat* was praised for its realistic description of a both snobbish and immoral milieu of the prewar upper bourgeoisie.

In the postwar years Stancu stuck to a narrative formula which he brilliantly illustrated in the first novel (*Barefoot,* 1948) of an autobiographical cycle. This is a lyrical evocation, undertaken from the viewpoint of a child, of rural life at the turn of the century and concomitantly of the same events Rebreanu realistically evoked in his *Uprising,* namely the peasants' mutinies of 1907. The hallucinatory note, the evocation of the brutal and tragic events in the shape of memories long buried in the confused mind of a child account for those events being removed from historical reality to the realm of dreams and fever. All these (and we must add the poetry of recollection) are ingredients of a lyricism which raises certain chapters of the book to the level of prose poems, as does the chapter entitled "The Grass." Most definitely the metaphorical nature of poetry has with Stancu superseded the usually associative manner of the narrative. Moreover, the prevailingly paratactic dispositions of the phrases insure a rhythm enhanced by certain recurrences pertaining to the rhetoric of the anaphora. The impact of causal relation being thus diminished, Stancu's *Barefoot* can hardly be located within the sphere of historical fiction and sometimes even within that of narrative proper. A sample may be enlightening:

> The wind is blowing from the Danube — a warm wind. And the wind has brought with it clouds. And the clouds have brought warm rain, spring rain. The good rain has put new life into the earth. The boundless fields have come back to life. There is everywhere a smell of new fresh grass, a smell of young leaves and of wheat, which has grown over two spans high above the earth. New, fresh grass has sprung up on the graves of the men that were shot and buried, deep underground.[19]

The following novels, thematically sequels to the first, although sometimes located in urban political or journalistic milieus, recurrently return to the roots: the Danube and its century-old traditions. For there is a subterranean level in Romanian literature out of which most rural narratives — and not only rural — draw their implicit mythic substance. That is what Thomas A. Perry means when he writes in a survey of Romanian literature entitled *A Study in Literary Migration*:

> Interwoven into the straight linear account in Rebreanu's *Uprising* is the old Romanian motif of conflict and death rooted in Dacian mythology. In an overlay of the historical present, a subliminal world in which age-long emotions have lain buried emerges from time to time in a whirlwind of violence and then recedes as the hubbub of the world takes over again. In Stancu's *Barefoot*, beneath Darie's wanderings before the German invasion lie the fabric of all Romanian experiences with invaders, and visions of the Persians, Romans, etc., which surface periodically.[20]

Rather than a historical fresco, Stancu's cycle represents one single lyrical novel, written over and over again by a poet haunted by his recollections, continually moving his inner and objective experiences from the area of prose to that of poetry — be it lyrical prose — thus succeeding in keeping his hands clean as a writer, if not as a representative of the cultural establishment.

The multivalent personality of George Călinescu continued that amazingly extensive and hectic activity which had characterized his creativity in the prewar years. He did not renounce any of the explorations he had been engaged in. He wrote essays, but instead of dealing with the *Anatomy of Angels, The Seraphic Soul,* or *The Magic of Alchemy,* he focused on monographs of Romanian classical writers (a genre he had superlatively illustrated before the war with his massive *Life and Work of Mihai Eminescu,* a reconstruction brilliant both in point of scholarship and literary originality of the life and work of the greatest Romanian poet), on studies such as *The Aesthetics of the Fairy Tale* or on essays on world literature. In all of these postwar works, his baroque analogies and paradoxical connections, his similes meant to produce "meraviglia," and his portraits in progress, drawn with that bias for the burlesque, are at the level of his prewar manner. As a publicist he continued his activity in the same vein of witty magniloquence which had distinguished the prewar output of the columnist. He entitled his chronicles (previously known as *The Misanthrope's Chronicle*) *The Optimist's Chronicle,* whose optimist occasionally became as virulent, acid, extravagant, and fond of paradoxes as his predecessor — the Misanthrope — and whose optimism was often of an unambiguously spoof character. Since Călinescu was ostentatiously an adept of augmentative expression, his inimitable but, lately, often imitated style remained to the very end marked by that propensity toward abundance, expressive exaggeration, and hyperbole. However, his extensive scholarship, his stylistic audacity, and his power of grasping the deep implications of a trite incident enabled him to convey, by means of his hyperbolic utterances, unexpected connotations, as happens in his brief comment on the both tragic and grotesque destiny of Chekhov's unassuming employee who sneezed onto his supervisor's bald head: "The man who bespattered his supervisor with saliva and eventually died of terror is a Shakespearean hero, moreover I should say to make my idea clear, a Homeric one."[21]

In his two massive postwar novels, *Poor Ioanide* (1954) and *The Black Chest* (1960), ample in proportions, luxurious in savory details, Călinescu went on practising that symbiosis of unrefrained frenzy and lucid observation. He did not abandon any of his biases or idiosyncracies: his attraction for the bizarre and the grotesque, his understanding of style as a magnificent spectacle. He only carefully avoided that social environment which would have obliged him to focus on the "positive hero," gravely emphasizing the latter's superior ethics and behavior. He therefore applied his comically oriented observation to the world of the ex-upper-class, of those sighing after the lost paradise or servilely coming to terms with the new regime. He voluptuously portrayed ridiculously ferocious fascists or else turned to the jungle of the "old" university where he could study some of the social phenomena which had always roused his irony, among them the dynamics of social climbing. Călinescu's burlesque bias proved an efficient antidote to the stereotypes of progress, and even the most "progressive" of his characters, the architect Ioanide, is treated from shifting angles: admiringly for his constructive passion and his artistic achievements, slightly ironically every time the "progressive" intellectual attempts to accept the artistic suggestions of the cultural bureaucrats who politely control his creation. Both in *Poor Ioanide* and *The Black Chest* the sincere or hypocritical adhesion to the new order of the ex-exploiters as well as of the representatives of the new establishment is marked by very subtle variations in the political clichés they use. The author's irony at those verbal stereotypes and the mentality they rhetorically express is implicit.

The "new way of life" of the ex-rulers fascinates Călinescu's sense of the absurd and the scenes describing the expedients of the former diplomats, landowners, and rich art dealers in order to cope with the unpredictable conditions of the new society bear the unmistakable mark of Călinescu's humor. The ex-count turned into a porter, the prince requalified as a mechanic, and ladies of aristocratic, even princely origin meet at the flea market where they sell their belongings while discussing worldly matters and pedigrees.

The label "Balzacian structure" usually applied to Călinescu's novels proves its total inadequacy when used to describe the structure of *The Black Chest*. The novel implies at least two temporal perspectives. The romantic convention, already stale, of the letters discovered in a drawer — the drawer of the chest Ioanide buys at the flea market — is but a technique enabling the author to proceed to numerous temporal shifts and to ignore the traditional chronology and unilinear time of the realistic narrative. To parenthetically conclude these brief remarks on the works of one of Romania's most outrageously original spirits: Călinescu's last artistic manifestation (he died in 1965) was the performance under his direction of his absurdist play about the non-existent French King Louis XIX by the researchers of the institute of which he was chairman.

Camil Petrescu, the adept of modernism and noocracy, had in the prewar years written plays and novels about complex and tormented characters who, whether historical or not, were almost demonically possessed with their ideas and more often than not failures as regards the possibility of social adaptation to mediocre middle class philistine criteria and to verbal platitude. Clearly Petrescu's noocratic utopia or, for that matter, his literary themes and techniques could not be tolerated during the Stalinist period, when intellectuals were at best downgraded to the role of temporary fellow travellers and a priori suspected because of their elitism, their horror of the commonplace, and rejection of current behavioral or linguistic standards.

Petrescu's kinship with his heroes obliged him to seek escape in the past. In 1948 he wrote a play whose hero was a Romanian historian, a scholar of crystal purity, a spirit that admitted no kind of moral or intellectual transactionism, moreover a martyr of the cause he had dedicated himself to. Bălcescu was, like most of Petrescu's characters, and in his own messianic way, obsessed with "ideas" and involved in the 1848 Wallachian Revolution. Eventually the young historian became the hero of a vast prose trilogy, *A Man Amongst Men* (1955–1957). Thus one of the most articulate and outspoken defenders of modernity sought refuge in the "revolutionary" past. I do not wish to regard Petrescu's epic about the 1848 revolution from a prejudiced angle, dictated by the necessities of my thesis. Nor do I want to indulge in a somewhat biased view of Petrescu's trilogy and regard it as merely the result of the author's shifting the implications of his belief in the mission of the intellectual back into a period of social turmoil and revolution out of fear of censorship. Petrescu was intensely preoccupied with creating historical and local color. He enjoyed the psychological picturesqueness of the epoch, knew how to set crowds into motion and to create the documentary illusion by means of footnotes and by inserting the texts of numerous authentic proclamations, treaties, etc., into the fabric of his narrative. No one can deny the author's wish to be "true" to historical reality which in the writer's mind had value in and by itself. But from the vantage point I have chosen, it seems obvious that everything in this novel — historical events, collective movements, encounters, and clashes — converges to the center of radiation represented by the man whose messianic spirit and intellectual pathos proved decisive for the lines of development that were to lead to the social explosion. Petrescu's noocratic utopia, a very controversial concept, is implicit in his epic about Bălcescu's participation in the events of 1848.

At this point it may be worth stressing the intimate relationship, the organic affinity between commitment to modernity and the "resurrection" of the past, during periods of cliché-ridden ideological control, and of reductionist interpretation of Marxist determinism. Such a type of escapism into the nearer or remoter past, be it individual (childhood) or collective (history) enabled more than one Romanian writer to maintain his thematic preferences and stylistic structures and to avoid compulsory adherence to thematic schematism and slogans. Paradoxically, retrospect (withdrawal toward the safer regions of childhood, i.e. recourse to a naive perspective) and retreat to the historical past have proved efficient alibis contrived by Romanian postwar prose writers, subtle strategies allowing them to adhere to non-traditional, sometimes strikingly heretical experiments.

In terms of modern psychology or psychoanalysis, as Read remarked, the function of the past became that of an outlet for otherwise repressed tendencies or feelings of artistic frustration, in other words, a means of avoiding political taboos and an efficient and even aesthetically fruitful compensatory solution. Most East European literatures have, under Stalinist oppression, discovered the advantages and the artistically stimulating character of this disguised outlet, the past, for very contemporary anxieties and existential interrogations.

But the retreat from the present must be emotionally and intellectually apt to suggest the author's inner world and artistic universe, in other words have connotative power as regards the invariants of his creation and the components of his sensitivity. Otherwise, such a retreat remains but a para-artistic strategy meant to maintain the writer in the field of publishable literature, thus necessarily leading to a lowering of standards.

Ion Marin Sadoveanu, the homonym of the great Sadoveanu, distinguished himself as the author of a novel pervaded by the perfume of the approaching "fin de siècle" which, in the Bucharest of the turn of the century — the Little Paris of the Balkans — was characterized by a very specific blend of Western refinement and up-to-dateness, on the one hand, and Balkanic picturesque morals and inertia, on the other. Sadoveanu's *End of the Century in Bucharest* (1944) succeeds in portraying, with guilty admiration for his "joie de vivre" which implied leisure, dissipation, and decadent hedonism, a representative of the old Romanian aristocracy, the boyar Banu Barbu and, concomitantly, with the same undertone of humorous criticism, in drawing the portrait of a shrewd parvenu, the upstart who cynically ruins his protector, while admiring his charming personality, his elegant, nonchalant ways, and even showing an inner feeling of gratitude for the man who had taught him how to move in that "slippery world" of the aristocracy. The ambiguous attitude of the writer toward his protagonists and their social behavior was naturally "unsatisfactorily" neutralized by the retreat into a past so deprived of exemplary value and revolutionary impulses as was the "belle époque." To attain what was called "Marxist timeliness," I. M. Sadoveanu undertook to revive an "episode" of ancient history, namely a slave insurrection in a city (Histria) built by the Romans of the present territory of Romania (*The Sea-Bull*, 1963). It was an artistic failure.

Most unexpectedly and paradoxically, any kind of alignment strategy proved inadequate for that towering personality, Mihail Sadoveanu, the creator of a mythical universe within which Romanian history and ahistoric peasant life were linked to each other within a permanent ritualistic continuity. The mythical vision of history, nature, rural life, the lyricism implicit in Sadoveanu's attraction for archaic forms of life still surviving in prewar Romania, such as pastoral life based on transhumance (*The Hatchet, 1930*), and the writer's sympathetic description of the lonely life of the shepherd or the fisherman, had to be left behind as obsolete features in any evocation of postwar village life. Sadoveanu's two novels dealing with the violent changes in rural social relations brought about by the march toward communism (*Păuna Mică*, 1948 and *Mitrea Cocor*, 1949) were, except for a few episodes in which the lyricism of the old bard was still identifiable, conventional apologies of the metamorphoses of rural life under the new leadership.

To avoid silence and not to let himself be forced into conformity, Sadoveanu switched to his prewar themes: nature, that mythified geography of his country mysteriously evoked in narratives such as *The Land Beyond the Mists* (1926) and, quite predictably, to history mythically transfigured. In his 1951 novel *The Flower Island,* he amplified an old lyrical narrative, *The Empire of Waters,* thus returning to his solitary fishermen of the Delta of the Danube, primitive beings living in perfect identity with nature. The invasion of this geologically petrified world by "contemporary" characters becomes immaterial to the atmosphere of the story, being the obvious result of an exterior and circumstantial impact. A historical novel published in 1952, *Nicoara Horseshoe,* an episode of the Moldavians' struggle against the Turks, was but a renewed version of a prewar narrative, *The Falcons,* a version in which the alliance between the 17th-century Moldavians and the Cossacks against their common enemy was somewhat emphasized, as was the solidarity between the military leaders and the mass of the people. Still, time and again, we identify the fabulous atmosphere of Sadoveanu's prewar historical narratives.

The trajectory of the Jewish writers after the Second World War, of those writers dealing with the specific condition of the ghetto, deserves being mentioned in this context. Their creative activity represented a rich chapter in Romanian prewar literature, a chapter my colleague, the outstanding contemporary Romanian critic Ov. S. Crohmălniceanu, elaborated on at length in his *Romanian Interwar Literature* (vol. II, 1972). Crohmălniceanu is the first postwar Romanian critic focusing on the novelists who created, in their very specific manner, a mixture of humor, bitter irony and tragic gravity, features amounting to that grotesque vision Shalom Aleichem accustomed his readers to: the tense, sad and sometimes hilarious everyday life of the prewar ghetto. Ion Călugaru wrote in that Chagallian vein[22] a trilogy about a Moldavian semi-rural borough. The life of the ghetto, the relations between the Jews and the Gentiles are in Călugaru's novels interpreted by a child soon grown into a teenager. The Jewish ghetto of Bucharest was stridently and grotesquely evoked in the novels of I. Peltz, while in his *Ghetto 20th Century* (1934) Ury Benador undertook a lucid analysis of all the phenomena pertaining to the Jewish segregation, an analysis amounting to an enlightening literary document on the religious and cultural invariants of Romanian Jewry.

After World War II, the ghetto as a spatial reality and as a version of the age-old topos of the enclosed space disappeared, owing partly to the Jewish emigration and partly to the assumption that communism had satisfactorily solved the problem of ethnic minorities. Jewish anxieties and emotional issues, specific problems and even psychological, if not geographic, segregation survived. Yet the literature of the Jewish condition was doomed to extinction. Regretfully, the numerous prose writers who had described the Jewish world stopped writing or else switched "to their worst luck" as Crohmălniceanu thinks,[23] to neutral or unequivocally committed themes. Călugaru wrote a socialist-realist novel entitled *Steel and Bread* (1951); Benador abandoned the 20th-century ghetto for a life of Beethoven. The problems of Romanian Jewry belong to a closed chapter in contemporary Romanian literature.

Since the question at issue in these remarks is the survival of prewar tradition under the postwar circumstances created by communist culture, I felt I had to devote a large part of my survey to the main trends in Romanian prewar prose.

Most of the writers belonging to the prewar generations I was concerned with and whose impact on postwar prose justifies elaborating on the topic of "new developments" died in the late 1950s or in the 1960s. Stancu lived through the early 1970s. Bogza is alive. His was the anguished question about the destiny of Romanian culture after those "mountains" had disappeared:

> Thinking about all that happened in our culture during the last quarter of a century, about so many mistakes which might not have weighed so heavily had they not been followed, owing to the implacable passage of years, by the disappearance of a whole generation — profoundly humanistic in its structure and spirit — it seems to me there is nothing we need more, at the present moment, than to again tie the broken thread.

There was actually no inbridgeable gap between most of the prewar writers who remained artistically active until the 1960s and those postwar writers who did their utmost to avoid the all-pervading censorship during the Stalinist period or to avail themselves of any moment of post-Stalinist tolerance and even of that see-saw movement, that alternation of freeze and thaw characteristic of the cultural policy of so many East European countries after the

Second World War. In fact, the terms of the problem are much more complex and sometimes even intricate, owing to the sinuous evolution of more than one Romanian postwar writer, but an example may explain a few puzzling phenomena referring to the dynamics of certain impacts discussed here. I am thinking of the great number of young critics and prose writers who, feeling free to choose their model, consider themselves as belonging to Călinescu's "school." Fascinated as they are by that synthesis of profound scholarship and explosive imagination displayed in the prose of the "maestro" whom they try to imitate, they justify the use of the verb "to Călinescianize" in the reviews written by Romanian contemporary critics, themselves encouraged toward lexical invention by Călinescu's defining the stylistic mannerisms of Petrarch's followers as "Petrarchizing."

Bogza's example stimulated a large output of poetical reportage, while Stancu's autobiographic cycle was the inspiration for numerous novels which do not allow the reader to draw a separating line between prose and poetry, on the one hand, and hazy recollection and objective reality, on the other.

But the point I should try to make at the end of these remarks is that most of the prose writers I selected to illustrate my thesis with, while ensuring the evolution of the prewar tradition in contemporary Romanian prose, became *ipso facto* responsible for a number of literary experiments. Although prompted by the circumstances of the political context, those experiments remained valid *qua* artistic facts and were as such taken over by the postwar generations. What began by being merely a flexible strategy meant to preserve the writer's artistic identity often acquired an autonomous aesthetic status and amounted to noteworthy results. The possibility of maintaining topicality and avoiding obsolescence by means of escapism into the past is only one example among many others.

Generally speaking, it may be asserted that the Romanian prewar tradition in prose, as well as in drama and poetry, was an antidote both against the *pompier* academism with which socialist realism may be equated, and the corruption of taste by that specifically communist version of *kitsch* which — in the period of Stalinist dogmatism — many Romanians improvised, or to which even gifted writers paid their tribute.[24]

Undoubtedly the aesthetic problems of the younger generations of Romanian prose writers, those who began their creative activity in the atmosphere of Stalinist intellectual terror, have their own degree of specificity and cannot be reduced to the adoption and continuance of prewar tradition. But that is another story.

NOTES

1. Matei Călinescu, *Faces of Modernity,* Bloomington: Indiana University Press, 1977, p. 96.

2. Ov. S. Crohmălniceanu, *Literatura română între cele două războaie mondiale,* vol. I, Bucharest: Minerva, 1972, p. 26.

3. I. Negoitescu, *E. Lovinescu,* Bucharest: Albatros, 1970, p. 6.

4. G. Ibrăileanu, *Creaţie si Analiză,* Viata Româneasca, n. 2–3, 1926.

5. Camil Petrescu, "Teze si antiteze," apud I. Vitner, *Semnele romanului,* Bucharest: C. R. 1971, p. 65.

6. Silvian Iosifescu, *Mobilitatea privirii, Naraţiunea in secolul al XX–lea,* Bucharest: Eminescu, 1976, p. 262.

7. *Ibid.,* p. 263.

8. George Călinescu, "The Universe of Poetry," in *Studies in Poetics* (translated by Andrei Bantaş and Anda Teodorescu), Bucharest: Univers, 1972, p. 94.

9. Ov. S. Crohmălniceanu, *op. cit.,* p. 543.

10. Herbert Read, "Introduction" to *Surrealism,* edited by Herbert Read, New York – Washington: Praeger Publishers, 1971, p. 25.

11. Matei Călinescu analyzes this evolution in the chapter about the avant-garde in his book *Eseuri despre literatura modernă,* Bucharest: Eminescu, 1970, p. 178.

12. Ov. S. Crohmălniceanu, *op. cit.,* p. 308.

13. *Ibid.*

14. Geo Bogza, *Paznic de far,* Bucharest: Minerva, 1974, p. 5.

15. *Ibid.,* p. 12.

16. *Ibid.,* p. 47.

17. *Ibid.,* p. 49.

18. *Ibid.,* p. 58.

19. Zaharia Stancu, *Barefoot,* edited by Frank Kirk, New York: Twayne Publishers, Inc., 1971, p. 228.

10. Thomas A. Perry, *A Study in Literary Migration,* Shantih, New York, vol. 3, no. 4, 1971, p. 2–3.

21. George Călinescu, *Studii si Conferinţe,* apud Vera Calin, *Pornind de la clasici,* Bucharest: E.S.P.L.A., 1957, p. 225.

22. Ov. S. Crohmălniceanu, *op. cit.,* p. 348.

23. *Ibid.,* p. 350.

24. The analogy between *kitsch* and socialist realism is discussed in the chapter "Kitsch" in Matei Călinescu's book *Faces of Modernity.*

Guy de Mallac

THE VOICE OF THE STREET IN
PASTERNAK'S *DOCTOR ZHIVAGO*

> [History] . . . is the centuries of systematic
> explorations of the riddle of death, with a
> view to overcoming death.
> *Doctor Zhivago*[1]

> [History is] another universe, made by
> man with the help of time and memory in
> answer to the challenge of death.
> *Doctor Zhivago*[2]

> *Doctor Zhivago* is a political novel in the
> same sense that *A Tale of Two Cities, Le
> Rouge et le Noir,* or, for that matter, *War
> and Peace* are political novels. It diag-
> noses the effect political situations have
> on men and women. But, contrary to Dick-
> ens, Stendahl, and Tolstoy who handle
> the intrusion of politics as an extraneous
> assault, as a physical penetration which,
> however ruthless, cannot change the tex-
> ture of human lives, Pasternak sees this
> intervention as a chemical, nay, a nuclear
> process affecting and destroying the liv-
> ing tissue of reality.
> Victor Frank[3]

In Pasternak's work the street can sometimes be a variation on a *topos* of the
urban landscape, as in the fresh and original statement "I come from the
street, where the poplar is amazed . . . "[4] — where the street's feelings are
conveyed through the poplar's amazement. The street, metonymically speaking, can also stand for the numerous simple people who are active in it; in this
sense, the voice of the street makes itself heard through the viewpoint of such
personages.

In *Doctor Zhivago,* we have a broad and complex spectrum of ideological/
political views, with interesting cases of shifts in the views of individual
characters (e.g., Antipov/ Strelnikov, Kologrivov, Komarovskii, Tiverzin). A
majority of the characters evince strong concern for what happens in Russia
— and in the case of the more "popular" characters, this is clear evidence of the
concern of the street for events in the street. The voice of elemental, rural

Russia, which was heard so strongly in Pilniak's novel *The Naked Year* (1921), is similarly present in Pasternak's novel.

Over the decades the poet's famous exclamation in *My Sister, Life* "What millennium is it . . . out there (*na dvore*)?"[5] has oftentimes been inaccurately interpreted as reflecting the persona's remoteness or standoffishness in relation to current historical events. The claim is made here that personages in *Doctor Zhivago* manifest considerable involvement in the events *na dvore*, "out there" on the street. And in particular, some of the voices from the street deserve to be heard carefully — those that serve to set forth Pasternak's conception of history.

The novelist's views on history are presented by various spokesmen in a few key passages of *Doctor Zhivago*. These are Nikolai Nikolaevich Vedeniapin, Zhivago's uncle, a priest returned to lay status who has become an apostle of a Tolstoyan type of socialism; Zhivago himself; Lara; and the remarkably well-read girl of Iuriatin, Sima Tuntseva. These characters express opinions that variously reflect the fundamental attitude of the author — to that extent *Doctor Zhivago* is even an overly *monologal* novel, in the terminology of the Soviet scholar Mikhail Bakhtin.[6]

Zhivago's conception of man's spiritual destiny is closely linked to the gradual disruption of the pact he originally concluded with socialism. As disillusion followed disillusion, he opened his eyes to the trickery underlying Bolshevik dogmatism, and evolved his own more authentic vision of man.

As we consider the stages of the hero's fascination for the social ideas of his time, it is therefore important to trace the chain of upheavals which the author and his generation experienced, in order to see how his views gradually evolved — to be later reflected in the novel.

The world in which Pasternak grew up and which first left its imprint on him was that of the Russian intelligentsia before 1914. Because both his parents were distinguished artists, Pasternak grew up in an extremely cultivated and cosmopolitan milieu of artists and intellectuals. The dazzling inspiration of Scriabin vied with the philosophical conversation of the sage of Iasnaia Poliana and the magic of Vrubel's coloring, to leave indelible marks in the mind and heart of the poet. Some of his subsequent reactions and views are clearly indicative of an early contact with that milieu.

However, it would be wrong to see in Pasternak purely and simply an anachronistic survival of a past epoch and its bourgeois culture, a judgment which has become a commonplace of Soviet Pasternak criticism and which also constitutes the basis of Isaac Deutscher's critique of *Doctor Zhivago* as a work archaic in both idea and style.[7] The vigor with which the writer denounces the defects of the old regime, especially the social privileges and omnipotence of money, is sufficient proof to the contrary. One could not seriously contend that Pasternak has given far too idealized an image of czarist Russia, much less that *Doctor Zhivago* is, as Deutscher argues, conditioned by a nostalgic desire for return to a bourgeois accommodation to that past.[8] Some would much rather accuse him of making concessions to socialist realism when, in the first part of *Doctor Zhivago,* he depicts a world in which men of doubtful reliability lead prodigal millionaires to their ruin, or wealthy bachelors play the evil genii of young orphans. Also, in *Doctor Zhivago* he gives the floor to the businessman Samdeviatov, who in discussing the old regime finally explodes:

> . . . Gluttons and parasites sat on the backs of the starving workers and drove them to death, and you imagine things could stay like that? Not to mention all the other forms of outrage and tyranny. Don't you understand the rightness of the people's anger, of their desire for justice, for truth?[9]

These words from a man prospering under the new conditions created by Bolshevism echo the judgment of Zhivago, the young doctor returning from the German front in 1917:

> . . . there was really something unhealthy in the way rich people used to live. Masses of superfluous things. Too much furniture, too much room, too much emotional refinement, too many circumlocutions. I'm very glad we're using fewer rooms. We should give up still more.[10]

The voice of the street in the novel thus denounces the bankruptcy of various values of the old regime.

Even though he does not follow the official Marxist point of view about the timeliness of the revolution in all its aspects, Pasternak does nonetheless agree it was a pressing necessity on the social plane. The heroes of *Doctor Zhivago,* like an important segment of Russian student youth at the beginning of the century, turn to socialism in their search both for an absolute and for a method of curing the country's political situation. Socialism is for them

> . . . the sea of life, the sea of spontaneity . . . life as you see it in a great picture, transformed by genius, creatively enriched. Only now [since the revolution] people have decided to experience it not in books and pictures but in themselves, not as an abstraction but in practice.[11]

In the beginning this enthusiasm is manifested by a wild admiration for the revolution that has suddenly "exploded right into the very thick of daily life." Zhivago, for his part, manifests an attachment to the revolution in the first months following the establishment of the new regime by sustaining a humble fidelity to his work at the hospital, while the "fashionable" doctors drop "those people." (They ask Zhivago: "So you're working for *them*?")[12] As Raymond Aron has pointed out, the political and artistic *avant-gardes* have often been able to play a common game since they dream of an adventure carried out in common with an eye to the same liberation: "The artist denounces the Philistine, the Marxist, the bourgeoisie. They can think of themselves as solidary in the same combat against the same enemy."[13] But this alliance is based on a misapprehension, as we shall have occasion to see in the case of Pasternak and the Russian intelligentsia.

The search for an absolute — that is what socialism was for so many of Pasternak's generation. It is significant that the French critic Jean Duvignaud devoted to Pasternak an article entitled "Le Don Quichotte de notre temps," in which he states that ". . . this distance between Zhivago and the world, this distance between Pasternak and Soviet society, is the very distance which separates Cervantes and his dreams." Duvignaud furthermore states that:

> Like all writers attracted to socialism and revolution, . . . [Pasternak] dreamt
> of a complete, absolute communication between men . . . a world was going to
> appear in which each consciousness, transparent to other consciousnesses,
> would be fully recognized for what it is. A world was going to be born in
> which man, communicating freely with man delivered from his "alienation,"
> would find the spontaneity and innocence characteristic of a humanistic
> society.[14]

Alas! this lovely dream was soon to collide with a materialization quite different from what was expected. In Zhivago's opinion (and in this respect he is symbolic of Pasternak), socialism, the "sea of life," would but generate a fermenting of elementary forces *directed toward a greater flowering of life.* Reality proved him wrong.

The exalting episode of the abortive revolution of 1905 could sustain such hopes. To that event Pasternak dedicated his long poem *The Year 1905.* In it, the poet perceives as "through a dream" the past and present of the eternal Russian revolution. This vision is not focused around the revolutionary intelligentsia. Besides Sofiia Perovskaia and the heroic students, muzhiks, factory workers, and the sailors of the *Potemkin* stand in the foreground. Benjamin Goriély quite rightly notes that these events of 1905, contemporary with Pasternak's youth, are described in the exalted tone of youth, well suited to the psychology of the Russia of that time, and he comments: "Youth of the bourgeoisie, youth of the intellectuals, youth of the working class, youth of the political parties, youth of ideas. What an intoxicated snowfall!"[15] The poet sees in the riot the unleashing and explosion of a profound, uncontrollable force, symbolized by fire, "the inferno . . . flooding and swelling" in the last pages of the poem. This work constitutes both a rupture with his previous poetry and an attempt at conciliation with the regime.

The next important episode was the war of 1914, a cataclysm to which Pasternak apparently traces all the evils that befell his generation. One of the indirect sequels of this war was the launching of the revolution of 1917.

While Pasternak (as he has been reproached) fails to treat in sufficient detail some of the most exciting, controversial issues which agitated Moscow in 1917,[16] he does excel in conveying the atmosphere in Moscow during the years immediately following the revolution, and the long series of mishaps of the "forest brotherhood" in Siberia. Also, for many topical and anecdotic details of Chapter Seven of *Doctor Zhivago* ("Train to the Urals"), Pasternak very skillfully utilized historical sources — such as a relation entitled "A Journey from Petersburg to Siberia in January 1920," published at the time in an émigré publication of documents.[17] These are particularly successful instances of transmutation of experience into art, of documentary into fiction.

It would be unfair to reproach Pasternak, as did the editorial board of *Novyi mir,* with having given a completely distorted image of the events of 1917. The editors of this journal, in the open letter they addressed to Pasternak in November 1958, consider it a grievous fault that he mixed up the two revolutions of February and October 1917 by lumping them together instead of depicting them separately, and showing all the differences in social significance that created an enormous distance between the bourgeois revolution and proletarian revolution. It is interesting to note that a Communist free from allegiance to Bolshevism from Moscow, such as Isaac Deutscher, also reproaches Pasternak for confusing the two revolutions. The truth is that Pasternak "strode through history," as Yves Berger put it;[18] his aim was to write a *sui generis* epic, not a pedestrian chronicle or annals. Was it therefore necessary for him to define the hero's attitude to "the overthrow of autocracy, the coming to power of Kerensky, the July events, Kornilov's revolt, the October uprising, the seizure of power by the Soviets and the disbanding of the Constituent Assembly," as the *Novyi mir* editors would have him do?

One should point out in this connection that Pasternak *does* have specific merits as a chronicler. These merits were singled out by a competent observer who praised the writer's description of "Russian geo-strategy." Few students of literature may have thought to look up in the January 1960 issue of the *Revue de défense nationale* the article of a French strategy expert, Colonel Jacques Dinfreville, entitled "The Partisan War in *Doctor Zhivago.*"[19] Dinfreville congratulates the novelist on the detailed report he has provided of the combat methods of the partisan army. The military leaders seem intensely alive, he emphasizes, having no appearance of "made-up characters"; surrounded by their *spetses* (military specialists), "bodyguards, spies, agents provocateurs," they conduct their campaign vigorously. Disadvantaged by the unhomogeneous composition of their army, to which the central powers grant but few resources, they use "a scientific technique of coercion" on their men and absolutely classical guerilla tactics on the enemy. The author of the novel rightfully emphasizes the determining moral factor, nor does he forget to recall the topographic peculiarities of the unusual operational setting of the *taiga*. This perceptive analysis rightfully "rehabilitates" Pasternak as a chronicler-novelist.

Nevertheless, it is not on the plane of chronicle-writing that Pasternak most intensely revives the events of 1917. It is in a poetry of a paradoxically intimate and delicate turn whose musing seeks out the profound afflatus at work in the overthrow of every order, including the political. Bowra reminds us that for Pasternak, as well as for other futurists (Maiakovskii and Khlebnikov in particular), "the Revolution was a prodigious manifestation of natural forces which had hitherto lain dormant in Russia," a manifestation completely in accord with Pasternak's dynamic conception of life. Pasternak's poetry contains some of the characteristics of the revolutionary period which inspired it, but they are reworked after his own fashion, which is quite different from that of Maiakovskii.

Pasternak lived his political experience so intensely that he expressed external events as he felt them, eager to gather their meaning through the framework of his own dialectic, whence the transposition of these events onto the palette, so limited at first glance, of his lyric emotion. From this perspective, the importance of historic events seems to be reduced to that of natural events. As one commentator observed:

> ... This is precisely the importance that [Pasternak] ... finds in them. They are indeed natural events and therefore full of majesty and mystery. They are a special manifestation of the strange powers that can be observed in physical nature.[20]

Commenting on the poem "Summer" (composed in 1917), Sir Maurice Bowra emphasizes that the political events, forming a part of the harmonious rustic scene, "are also its climax and its culmination." What must be augured from the dawn and the rising breeze, symbols of a new order, in the poem "May it be" of 1919? Pasternak is convinced, as Bowra says:

> that such an eruption of natural forces must in the end be right and prevail, he finds in them a source of vitality and energy. What matters for him is this release of nature's powers which bring man closer to itself.[21]

To the very extent that he considers political events *from afar,* as though they were a far-away realm, Pasternak can say that in *My Syster Life* (the collection containing the above poems) he has succeeded in creating "expressions not in the least contemporary as regards poetry." This type of poetry exemplifies the ideal he opposes to that of Maiakovskii. It is not at all surprising, then, that the poet who had sung only a certain exotic quality of the Revolution, that the philosopher who had meditated only on its logical presuppositions and historical preparation, should be brought brutally back to earth when confronting his dreams with the actual realization of that revolution and its sordid, shabby aspects. Nadezhda Mandelstam has discussed the uncanny idealistic fascination exerted on Mandelstam, Pasternak, and "the most worthy" of their generation by the very notion of Revolution; according to her, they "feared the Revolution might pass ... [them] by if, in ... [their] short-sightedness, . . . [they] failed to notice all the great things happening before our eyes."[22]

Disillusionments kept accumulating for the intelligentsia overtaken by the events of the revolution — that intelligentsia of which Pasternak was an integral part and of which Iurii Zhivago is the symbol. Of the whole process of establishing Marxism in Russia, the part that weighs heaviest on Zhivago is the dragging out of the transition period, with its sequel of disorders and confusion — a situation which exemplifies what the political scientist G. Ferrero labeled "destructive revolution."[23] For decades the Soviet rulers loudly proclaimed the necessity for transforming the country, preparing the way for Marxism, building the city of the future, and during all those years the Russians were obliged to live a life of sacrifice in what were often inhuman conditions, hoping their grandchildren would see paradise realized here on earth. In the name of this people too long deluded, Zhivago explodes: "Man is born to live, not to prepare for life." For the Communists, "transitional periods, worlds in the making, are an end in themselves." These passages awaken an echo of Camus' voice accusing the revolutionaries of sacrificing living men to an allegedly absolute good, to a historical end.

This transitional situation is indefinitely prolonged because "those who inspired the revolution aren't at home in anything except change and turmoil." It is an epoch when true values go unutilized, when only "the resourceful" succeed; Russia is governed "by civilians . . . [and] lawyers." The cruel struggle between Reds and Whites, an ethic of reprisals, the reigning terror, and famine soon drive out all civilization. "That period confirmed the ancient proverb, 'Man is a wolf to man' . . . . The laws of human civilization were suspended. The jungle law was in force."[24]

Once a regime has been set up under these conditions, or rather in spite of them, what are its far-reaching repercussions on human life? Two fundamental criticisms emerge from Pasternak's work: the Soviets force the hand of life, of reality; they choke off all flowering of the personality, the normal condition of life in society.

By their intransigence, the Soviets overturn the universally accepted norms of life and the most natural features of interpersonal relations. "It isn't natural, it's like the ancient Roman virtue. . . . They are made of stone, these people, they aren't human, with all their rules and principles."[25]

Having left a starving Moscow, Zhivago, en route to the Urals with his family, no longer recognizes the habitual face of things nor the accustomed behavior of men. "Where is reality in Russia today? . . . It has been so terrorized that it is hiding. . . . what's going on isn't life — it's madness, an absurd nightmare." Nothing functions any more according to human laws. The Soviet ideologists portrayed in *Doctor Zhivago* (non-party men though they are) act as fanatics, concentrating wholly on their program, thinking only of realizing their theories. Carried away by their fixed ideas and their will to alter everything to accord with them, they are blinded to the real facts:

> . . . What kind of people are they, to go on raving with this never-cooling, feverish ardor, year in year out, on nonexistent, long-vanished subjects, and to know nothing, to see nothing around them?[26]

On closer examination, however, was not the disillusionment of the intelligentsia inevitable? The editors of the French magazine *Arguments,* after having emphasized that "Pasternak belongs . . . among those who, at a certain moment in their lives, thought that communism represented a 'chance' for humanity," are satisfied with adding, "we would be inclined to say that in order to understand Pasternak and his novel, one must have gone through the communist experience, or have come quite close to it."[27] It seems to me that whether we are Marxists, non-Marxists, or ex-Marxists, the essential question is: Why does Zhivago abandon socialism? Why did he *necessarily* have to be disappointed by its practical application?

Renato Poggioli has quite correctly pointed out that "Ivan Karamazov accepted God while rejecting the world He had created: Doctor Zhivago similarly accepts the postulate of the revolution while rejecting many of its corollaries."[28] Stalinism is certainly a corollary which Zhivago finds most offensive. If another commentator could say that *Doctor Zhivago* is not so much an *anti-* and a *pre-*Soviet novel, it is because its heroes, in their political views, certainly go as far as the whole pre-revolutionary Russian intelligentsia did, but never much farther. The socialism that Pasternak portrays in his poem "Waves" is clearly presented as a remote and, ultimately, unrealizable ideal, which the poet is inclined to contrast with all the pettiness around him. It is an ideal that essentially belongs to the "far-away realm of socialism," but which, paradoxically and unexpectedly, turns out to be close at hand. Its essentially hazy nature results from the fact that it is seen through a smoky screen of theoretical discussions.

In brief, the intelligentsia's disappointment with the actual liberation process was the inevitable consequence of its dream of a far too ideal liberation. The type of revolution they had in mind never materialized because its very conception was mythical. Through a congenital necessity, unforeseeable by the idealistic intelligentsia, the revolution that actually occurred was to give birth to tyrannical power — as Raymond Aron has pointed out: "Revolutionary power is by definition tyrannical power. . . . The tyrannical phase lasts for a shorter or longer time depending on the circumstances, but it can never be spared. . . ."[29]

In a fictional context Pasternak has denounced the basic misapprehension of the believers in the abortive revolution of 1905:

> By virtue of a self-deception permissible in our day too, they [these intellectuals] imagined that the Revolution would be staged again, like a once temporarily suspended and later revived drama with fixed roles, that is, with all of them playing their old parts. This illusion was all the more natural that, believing deeply in the universally popular nature of their ideals, they all held the opinion that it was necessary to test their own conviction on living people. Becoming convinced of the complete and, to a certain extent, environmental oddity of the Revolution from the standpoint of the average Russian outlook, they could justly be puzzled as to where fresh amateurs and devotees for such a specialized and subtle undertaking could emerge.[30]

Confident that socialism would resemble a play given by a handful of conscientious amateur actors reciting the formulas memorized in advance in pre-war salons and cafés, the intelligentsia was bound to find the interludes following the October Revolution extravagant or grotesque. The intelligentsia represented by Zhivago adhered to a liberalism which, although generous, was in the last resort inadequate in the face of the irruption of disturbing social and political phenomena in the wake of 1917.

Within the plot development of *Doctor Zhivago,* Pasternak gives an interesting insight into the social psychology of the generation depicted in the novel. The social movement depicted is from the aristocratic mansions of the Zhivago and the Gromeko families to the outdoor life of Zhivago's daughter, the laundry-girl Tania, a waif roaming the streets, from the "upstairs" level of the Gromeko townhouse to the "downstairs" level of the lodge of the porter Markel. In the first part of the book, Markel was already the mediator between the Gromeko-Zhivago family and the events in the street. In the latter part of the novel, it is Markel's daughter Marina — and no longer the aristocratic Tonia or the *déclassée* Lara — who is the feminine presence in Zhivago's life, acting as mediator between him and the everyday realities of existence. The pervasive presence of the new social reality, as represented by Tania and Marina, is depicted as necessary, though part of the disruptive pattern of events.

Although the Revolution is presented in the novel as much needed "surgery," the ensuing upheavals are envisaged by the protagonists as a vast, fundamental uprooting necessarily bringing about a waste of vital substance and constituting a rupture in a sort of original pact between man and the world. The catastrophic outlook evidenced by Pasternak in *Doctor Zhivago* is closely linked to his conception of fate. The theme of fate is not developed in this novel explicitly, it is more an "atmosphere" in which events unfold, a structuring principle of the plot. In this connection, one commentator distinguishes two possible conceptions of fate: the first (the Greek *anagkē*), that of a blind, capricious force; the second, that of a reasonable law of being, an objective order of life. This latter conception, based on a mysterious bond between necessity and liberty, between the objective order of the world and man's creative will, is undoubtedly the one prevailing in *Doctor Zhivago.* It seems to me, however, that the two conceptions are in fact closely linked in the novel; events in it are envisaged by the protagonists as having "the strangeness of the transcendental, as if they were snatches torn from lives on other planets that had somehow drifted to earth."[31] The cataclysms of the First World War and the Revolution are envisaged as a real apocalypse; here, fate is made implacable (although rational in a certain sense), and the frightened creatures can only go to ground in some corner spared from divine wrath. It thus becomes clear, from the portrayal of these cataclysmic events in the novel, that Pasternak relates very strongly to them as a participant (whereas Tolstoy, as was noted by Victor Frank, merely conveys God's eye-view of history).[32] This refutes the main thesis of Deutscher's argument about the non-participation in revolutionary events of the novel's characters. True, these participants are everyday characters, not extraordinary actors, like Kutuzov, Napoleon, and Alexander — nor do they participate in the action of major battle scenes, as is found in *War and Peace.* Pasternak's approach — the description of the Revolution from the viewpoint of the common man, a rather insignificant historical figure — is nonetheless a fully valid approach to epic depiction. To be sure, such an approach has cheated the esthetic preferences of a reader like Akhmatova, who was unhappy that Pasternak's protagonist was such an ordinary, run-of-the-mill, un-striking personage; she could not agree with Pasternak's concept of Zhivago as an "average" man, feeling that literature should raise its heroes above the crowd.[33] In Pasternak's view, Zhivago was truly the man in the street.

In the foregoing discussion of Pasternak's attitude vis-à-vis historical developments in his country, some of the observations that have been made concerning his vision could have been formulated from a Marxist or near-Marxist viewpoint; furthermore, they have in fact been put forward (in a more damaging form) by critics protesting in *Pravda* and *Literaturnaia gazeta.* However, do Marxists offer anything in the way of a more coherent, reasonable attitude toward history? It is fitting that we examine this matter here, since it is in its confrontation with Marxism that Pasternak's humanism takes on all its meaning and implications. Not because it exists and is valid only as a counter-truth or antidote, but because any form of humanism wishing to assert itself as such in the twentieth century must do so in terms of Marxism in one way or another, and define its position in relation to it. Raymond Aron asserts:

> Every action in the middle of the twentieth century implies and involves taking a position with regard to the Soviet venture. To elude this taking of a position is to elude the tyranny of historical existence.[34]

What is true of action is at least as true of intellectual reflection. Thus Sartre, in his *Critique de la raison dialectique,* points out how imperative it is to take into account "the reality of Marxism."[35]

In *Doctor Zhivago,* Pasternak depicts all the stages of enthusiasm experienced by his heroes for Marxist doctrine. (As Deutscher pointed out, Pasternak portrays no Communist Party member in good standing[36] — thus Strelnikov is the strongest ideological antithesis to Zhivago.) Iurii Zhivago has no difficulty in subscribing to the assessment of Marxism made to him by Strelnikov (shortly before the latter's suicide). In the face of the debauchery, depravity, and social injustice of which the disreputable and poor districts of every capital were a flagrant display, barricades and socialist publicists were in the last resort powerless. ". . . Marxism arose, it uncovered the root of the evil and it offered the remedy, it became the great force of the century."[37]

Zhivago's experiences from 1917 on did not permit him to go further, however, than these concessions to Marxism. As he witnesses the practical application of Marxism, his opposition increases. It is a radical opposition, because beyond the Soviets' concrete realizations, it is directed against the philosophy underlying them. For Zhivago, ". . . Marxism is too uncertain of its ground to be a science. Sciences are more balanced, more objective. I don't know a movement more self-centered and further removed from the facts than Marxism."[38] The problem raised by Pasternak in this passage is that of "scientific socialism," of the claims of Marxism to be a scientifically proven system, and we know how fundamental this claim is for the champions of Marxism-Leninism.[39]

It is not appropriate here to attempt yet another "final" evaluation (after so many others) of the claim put forward for Marxism. I will restrict myself to underlining certain limitations of the Marxist conception of history, insofar as the latter is brought up for discussion in Pasternak's novel. It is worthwhile attempting to elucidate the seemingly paradoxical reproach that Pasternak's characters address to the Bolsheviks: he accuses them of disregarding history by remaining at the level of nature — such, in effect, is the meaning of the reminder that "man does not live in nature but in history."[40]

This reproach seems astonishing at first sight if one considers the cardinal importance of history for the forefathers of Bolshevism. For Marx, Reason must emerge from history. Because he situates the historical process objectively, outside of the Mind, Marx makes the Mind subject to various phenomena of History. Because of the completely materialistic character of the content of History for Marx, production relations and social reality strictly determine human consciousness, and consequently every event of history. And when in the *Economic and Philosophic Manuscripts* Marx makes it clear that communism will be the end of the conflict between man and nature, does he not thereby grant that at the end of the historical process, man will be in nature?[41] History therefore has a physical teleology, just as its content is made up of the sum of physical determinisms. The historical outcome of the Dialectic will be an adequation of consciousness to its content, and vice versa, and therefore a return to the undifferentiated condition of animal life.

When, on the other hand, Pasternak says that man is in History, he does not mean a historicity excluding transcendence, in the Marxist manner. For the Marxists, indeed, man is so essentially historical that social practice "is identified with human reality," and all transcendence is rigorously excluded.

In the last analysis, the schematic and verbalistic aspects of the Hegelian-Marxist conception of history made it scientifically inexact: as Sartre points out in the *Critique of Dialectical Reason,* history as it is actually lived offers resistance to *a priori* schemata.[42] It is indeed possible to discard such schemata and envisage history in the broader perspective of human evolution. This is Pasternak's position, considering history as a kind of organic phenomenon.

Pasternak does not envisage history according to any pre-established schema; he grasps it in its total ordination. As a growing organism, humanity advances — with much bumping and groping, it is true. Pasternak does not consider history as the materiality of the various empirical facts composing it; History manifests itself in its orientation, according to its spiritualized, transfigured sense. There is no doubt that he thus comes quite close to Berdiaev, with whose works, however, he was not well acquainted.[43]

Is it not this attitude that he has in mind when he talks about the historical method of the Marburg school, which consists in considering the logical significance of this or that period of history? History is of interest to the historian only to the extent that it can be "laid bare to [his] logical commentary,"[44] and not through its specificity or historicity in themselves. Besides, man's historicity has too often been reduced to the simple consciousness of historicity. In seeking the meaning of history in history alone, a certain type of humanism failed grossly. Thus the spectacle of history induces the Marxist to adopt a relativizing conception of man: he is only the product of the material content of the world, which is historically manifested according to the dialectical process. This minimizing conception runs the risk of giving rise to skepticism about man within man himself. Pasternak has rather an absolutizing conception of history, in the sense that for him history, the meeting-place of the temporal and the eternal, is what reveals man in his true dimensions. For him, man's historical dimension is not so radical and obvious that it is rigorously proven by action unfolding itself. It it were, it would be condemned to total "exteriority." Indeed, such a radical historicism would be characterized by temporal dispersion and would lead in the end to the suppression of history.

It is in *Doctor Zhivago* that Pasternak formulated his conception of history. When collated, "Father" Vedeniapin's reflections and Iurii Zhivago's tirades, as well as Sima Tuntseva's digressions, form a surprisingly coherent vision of history. There are thus grounds, here again, to consider these three characters as spokesmen of the single opinion of the author. We do not find in Pasternak as well-developed or systematic a statement as that which Tolstoy gives in the epilogue of *War and Peace,* a veritable treatise on the meaning of History. Pasternak proceeds in the manner of an impressionist painter: numerous strokes create the total impression if one just stands back far enough. The numerous lyrical and symbolic allusions represent an esthetic system effective enough to make us overlook the absence of a strongly developed dimension of psychological portrayal.

Pasternak talks about a primitive state in which nature asserted itself in its absolute virulence:

> Nature hit you in the eye so plainly and grabbed you so fiercely and so tangibly by the scruff of the neck that perhaps it really was still full of gods. Those were the first pages of the chronicle of mankind, it was only just beginning.[45]

It is truly the epoch of the alienation of man, who felt so out of place on a hostile earth; of the alienation in the cosmogonies then flourishing, by which man related himself, as well as the earth, to the "spirits of fire and water."

The first great civilizations led to a religious syncretism; the plurality of gods in Rome abolished the reign of fear: "This ancient world [the world of cosmogonies] ended with Rome, because of overpopulation. Rome was a flea market of borrowed gods and conquered people. . . ."

However, the ransom for that liberation was severely felt, because it occurred only as a result of the human promiscuity of a decayed civilization, the vestige of a "high-class culture" in the process of disappearing — to use Oswald Spengler's terminology. Rome was only

> . . . a bargain basement on two floors, earth and heaven, a mass of filth convoluted in a triple knot as in an intestinal obstruction. Dacians, Herulians, Scythians, Sarmatians, Hyperboreans, heavy wheels without spokes, eyes sunk in fat, sodomy, double chins, illiterate emperors, fish fed on the flesh of learned slaves. There were more people in the world than there have been ever since, all crammed into the passages of the Coliseum, and all wretched.[46]

All that the ancients knew was

> . . . blood and beastliness and cruelty and pockmarked Caligulas who do not suspect how untalented every enslaver is. They had the boastful dead eternity of bronze monuments and marble columns.[47]

Such contrasts may seem exaggerated; however, they must be put into context. The two passages quoted are inserted in an argument whose essential aim is to describe a more humane conception of history and civilization, which took shape after the Roman era. What Pasternak is stigmatizing, in relegating them to the past from which they arose, are the tribal alienation, "the reign of numbers," the "patriarchal alienation" of a degrading submission to rulers and tyrants, the pompous inanity of a national glory which enslaves what is most noble in man. Declamations about leaders and peoples belong "to the Biblical times of shepherd tribes and patriarchs."[48] The "Caligulas" (the rulers and tyrants who elicit such degrading submission) referred to in *Doctor Zhivago* stand for one particular infamous leader toward whom Pasternak personally felt "horror" — Stalin. This is made clear by statements Pasternak made to Gladkov during World War II, in which it is obvious that "Stalin" is meant when he said "Caligula."[49]

The fact that *Doctor Zhivago* is in a very specific sense a condemnation of the *Stalinist* era of Communism has not escaped such an acute ideological observer as Deutscher, who reproached Pasternak with projecting the "horrors of the Stalin era" back into the era of early Bolshevik rule.[50] Incidentally, this acknowledgement by Deutscher that Pasternak in his portrayal of post-revolutionary events in effect described the Stalinist era and dwelled on it comes as a contradiction to his own statement that Pasternak's mind "had stopped" in the early 1920s and that the writer had thus misinterpreted "the calendar of the revolution."[51] Deutscher completely missed the plain fact that one of Pasternak's conscious aims in writing *Doctor Zhivago* was to denounce the horrors of Stalinism. It is really Deutscher who in his naïveté betrays ignorance of the *Soviet* calendar — in the early 1950s (and even at the time of the Thaw) it was inconceivable yet to have an explicit description of the Stalin era in a literary work. Whence Pasternak's subterfuge, purportedly giving a description of the 1920s and in effect portraying Stalinism. This approach also reflects a feeling which Pasternak must have had that the horrors of Stalin's days had their roots in the first few years of the Bolshevik rule.

Doctor Zhivago is the orchestration of a deep-seated ideological conflict which affected the whole of Russia. To the extent that it reflects that conflict, the novel is the voice of Russia — while it is also the culmination of what has been termed the "remarkable, silent duel" which opposed Pasternak and Stalin.[52] From the memoirs of both Aleksandr Gladkov and Ivinskaia, it is clear that the writing of *Zhivago* was conceived by Pasternak as an act of political courage. In his book Pasternak denounced the philistinism (*meshchanstvo*) that had prevailed in Soviet literature and culture under Stalin. In the mid-1950s he felt strongly not only about the excesses of the cult of personality (*lichnost*) period, but about the continued facelessness (*bezlichie*) and uniformity of the philistinism that, by sheer force of inertia, endured under Khrushchev — this is made clear in a poem he penned in 1956:

> The cult of personality's been unthroned
> But the cult of hollow words holds sway
> And the cult of faceless philistines, perhaps,
> Has magnified a hundredfold. . . .[53]

According to Zhivago, Stalinism was culturally bankrupt because it made an organized effort to revive an era which was relegated to obsoleteness as a result of the spiritual progress of mankind:

> . . . Rome was at an end. The reign of numbers was at an end. The duty, imposed by armed force, to live unanimously as a people, as a whole nation, was abolished. Leaders and nations were relegated to the past.[54]

The fundamental divergence between Stalin's and Zhivago's philosophies has to do with the respective significance they grant to the rights of *homo publicus* as opposed to *homo privatus*. Such a conflict is in essence similar to the one set forth by Arthur Koestler in *Darkness at Noon* (1941) — which for decades was the only full-length treatment, albeit in fictional form — of the plight of Pasternak's protector Bukharin.

In Pasternak's view, the key element in the history of mankind, which generated a new attitude, was Christianity — the successor of such decisive moments in man's history as Egypt, Greece, and the theology of the Old Testament.[55] Against the background of this new ideology, Stalinism appears as regressive. Christianity is presented in *Doctor Zhivago* as a deed "still being accomplished by all who are inspired" and "not yet superseded by anything else"; it is depicted as an endeavor indissolubly linked to a new humanism, to the promotion of "individual human life." It is Christ who established history as it is understood today, "Christ's gospel is its foundation . . . There was no history in this sense among the ancients." In striking phrases, Pasternak defines what history is for him: "history . . . is the centuries of systematic explorations of the riddle of death, with a view to overcoming death." History is "another universe, made by man with the help of time and memory in answer to the challenge of death."[56] This is the goal which polarizes higher human activities, the ultimate triumph of life, as considered in its most immediate as well as its more advanced forms.

The "impetus" moving in this direction requires a "spiritual equipment": it is again to the Gospel that Pasternak traces its fundamental ideas. These ideas are:

> . . . To begin with, love of one's neighbor, which is the supreme form of vital energy. Once it fills the heart of man it has to overflow and spend itself. And then the two basic ideals of modern man — without them he is unthinkable — the idea of free personality and the idea of life as sacrifice.[57]

These three notions — the idea of the free individual, love of one's neighbor, and life as sacrifice — are the pivotal points in Pasternak's ideology.[58]

NOTES

1. Pasternak, *Doctor Zhivago* (New York: Pantheon, 1958), 10.
2. *Doctor Zhivago,* 66.
3. Victor Frank, "Boris Pasternak," paper read at Pasternak Symposium, St. Antony's College, Oxford University, December 1962.
4. Pasternak, *Stikhotvoreniia i poemy* (Moscow and Leningrad: Sovetskii Pisatel, 1965), 187.
5. *Stikhotvoreniia i poemy,* 111.
6. Bakhtin coined the concepts of *monologal* and *dialogal* in his fundamental work *Problems of Dostoevsky's Poetics* (1929).
7. Isaac Deutscher, "Pasternak and the Calendar of the Revolution," *Partisan Review,* Spring 1959. Quoted here from Davie and Livingstone, eds., *Pasternak: Modern Judgements* (London: Macmillan, 1969), 240-58.
8. Deutscher, "Pasternak and the Calendar . . . ," 243, 248.
9. *Doctor Zhivago,* 261.
10. *Doctor Zhivago,* 170.
11. *Doctor Zhivago,* 147.
12. *Doctor Zhivago,* 197.

13. Raymond Aron, *L'Opium des intellectuels* (Paris: Calmann-Lévy, 1955), 54–55.

14. Jean Duvignaud, "Le Don Quichotte de notre temps," *Arguments,* December 1958, 7.

15. Benjamin Goriély, study of *The Year 1905* in Pasternak, *L'An 1905* (Paris: Debresse, 1958), 23.

16. Deutscher, "Pasternak and the Calendar . . . ," 246.

17. "Poezdka iz Peterburga v Sibir v ianvare 1920 g.," *Archiv russkoi revoliutsii,* third ed., III (Berlin: I. V. Gessen, 1922), 190–209.

18. Yves Berger, *Boris Pasternak* (Paris: Seghers, 1958), 75.

19. Jacques Dinfreville, "La Guerre des partisans dans le *Docteur Jivago,*" *Revue de défense nationale,* Paris, Jan., 1960, 4–50.

20. C. M. Bowra, "Boris Pasternak, 1917–23," *The Creative Experiment* (London: Macmillan, 1949), 150.

21. Bowra, "Boris Pasternak, 1917–1923," 153.

22. Nadezhda Mandelstam, *Hope Against Hope: A Memoir,* trans. by Max Hayward (New York: Atheneum, 1976), 126.

23. According to Ferrero, "destructive revolution" (as opposed to "constructive revolution") is caused "by the collapse of one principle of legitimacy and the absence of a legitimacy of replacement." It is to the destructive revolution that he attributes "the responsibility for terror, wars, and tyranny." (Raymond Aron, *L'Opium des intellectuels,* 19).

24. *Doctor Zhivago,* 296–97, 310, 378.

25. *Doctor Zhivago,* 299, 301.

26. *Doctor Zhivago,* 381–82.

27. *Arguments,* Paris, Dec. 1958, editorial, 2.

28. Renato Poggioli, "Boris Pasternak," *Partisan Review,* Fall 1958, XXV: 4, 549.

29. Aron, *L'Opium des intellectuels,* 50.

30. Pasternak, *The Last Summer,* 31–32.

31. L. A. Zander, "Filosofskie temy v romane B. L. Pasternaka 'Doktor Zhivago'," *Vestnik russkogo studencheskogo khristianskogo dvizheniia,* Paris, New York, No. 52, I, 1959.

32. Victor Frank, "Boris Pasternak."

33. Olga Ivinskaya, *A Captive of Time,* trans. by Max Hayward (New York: Doubleday, 1978), 190.

34. Aron, *L'Opium des intellectuels,* 66.

35. Sartre, *Critique de la raison dialectique* (Paris: Gallimard, 1960), 15, 23, 107, 139.

36. Deutscher, "Pasternak and the Calendar . . . ," 253.

37. *Doctor Zhivago,* 460.

38. *Doctor Zhivago,* 259.

39. V. I. Lenin, *Chto takoe "Druzia naroda" i kak oni voiuiut protiv sotsialdemokratov?, Polnoe sobranie sochinenii,* izd. 5-oe (Moscow: Gos. izd. polit. lit. 1958), 139–40.

40. *Doctor Zhivago,* 10.

41. Marx, *Ökonomisch-philosophische Manuskripte aus dem Jahre 1844,* in Marx and Engels, *Historisch-kritische Gesamtausgabe,* ed. V. Adoratskii (Berlin: Marx-Engels-Verlag, 1932), Erste Abt., Bd. 3, 111–23, 150–72.

42. Sartre, *Critique de la raison dialectique,* 81.

43. Pasternak, *A Safe Conduct: Collected Prose* (New York: Praeger, 1978), 45.

44. From his study, *The Meaning of History* (1923), it is clear that for Berdiaev history is the highest spiritual reality, and as such, is not given empirically in the form of simple material facts, because it does not exist in that way. Historical memory, in spiritualizing and transfiguring it, reveals what constitutes its inner nature, and shows itself truly endowed with a soul.

45. *Doctor Zhivago*, 43.

46. *Doctor Zhivago*, 43.

47. *Doctor Zhivago*, 10.

48. *Doctor Zhivago*, 10, 43, 412–13.

49. Aleksandr Gladkov, *Vstrechi s Pasternakom* (Paris: YMCA, 1973), 54.

50. Deutscher, "Pasternak and the Calendar . . . ," 254–55.

51. Deutscher, "Pasternak and the Calendar . . . ," 240.

52. *A Captive of Time*, 135.

53. *A Captive of Time*, 142.

54. *Doctor Zhivago*, 413.

55. *Doctor Zhivago*, 411.

56. *Doctor Zhivago*, 411, 43, 413, 10, 66.

57. *Doctor Zhivago*, 10.

58. Cf. Guy de Mallac, *Boris Pasternak: His Life and Art* (Norman: University of Oklahoma Press, 1980), Chapters 15, 16, and 17.

Postscript

At the time when this paper was delivered, I did not yet have access to the excellent study by Christopher J. Barnes, "Boris Pasternak i revoliutsiia 1917 goda" (*Boris Pasternak 1890–1960: Colloque de Cerisy-la-Salle, 11–14 septembre 1975,* Paris: Institut d'études slaves, 1979, pp. 315–37). Here I would like to at least refer interested readers to it.

Thomas Eekman

MODERNIST TRENDS IN
CONTEMPORARY SERBO-CROATIAN AND
SLOVENE PROSE

In the years around 1900, modernism (the "moderna") entered the South
Slavic literatures and sweeping changes took place in the poetic expression of
each of these nations.[1] New formal devices and techniques, new themes and
images, a new poetical sensibility that had recently developed in West European and Russian poetry made themselves felt on the Balkan Peninsula too,
and answered a need for renewing the worn out forms and contents in South
Slavic poetry. Thus Serbian and Croatian, as well as Slovene, Bosnian, and
Bulgarian verse became a more prominent aspect in the culture of these
nations. Vladimir Nazor, Oton Župančič, Jovan Dučić and Pejo Javorov, to
mention just a few names, can compare very well with some of the foremost
lyricists in other European poetic traditions.

In prose the impact of new international trends seems to have been less
strong in those years. Apparently, the effect of the predominant nineteenth
century schools was very tenacious and the South Slavic prose writers did not
feel the urge to abandon the traditional strongholds of realism and (in some
cases) naturalism. Even romanticism, though vehemently rejected by previous
generations, was still very much alive and continued its role as a literary
heritage. This does not mean that no attempts were made to write prose in an
original way, but there was no comprehensive movement comparable to that
in poetry, no strongly felt need to experiment.

In Europe and America the art of novel writing, and of prose in general,
went through several new stages and was the subject of experimentation and
intensive discussions in the years before the First World War and during the
interwar period; this interest in the theory and the form of the novel continued
to be very lively in the decades after World War II.

To sum up in a few lines the (generally known) main points in this development: the interior monologue, used in 1887 in a short novel by Édouard
Dujardin, but already present, though in a less elaborate form, in some earlier
works (in Turgenev's *Smoke,* 1867, for example), was borrowed and further
developed into the "stream of consciousness" novel by James Joyce, who, in
his turn, was followed by many others. This was not a movement away from
realism; on the contrary, it was argued that this technique rendered reality
more richly, subtly and convincingly as it encompassed not merely the realia
of the external world, but followed as closely as possible the workings of the
mind of one or more characters, including the mind's illogical, irrational,

enigmatic aspects. The purpose of all these innovations was to bring the reader closer and make him privy to the very essence of the hero.

The same purpose was served by the use of first person narration, which is, of course, a method well-nigh as old as prose itself, but which became much more common in our century than ever before. Instead of presenting the omniscient author's or narrator's point of view, it became more customary, since the late nineteenth century, to render the "post of observation," as Henry James called it, of the hero or of several heroes. "A good deal of recent fiction," writes Jonathan Raban (1968), "is obviously written with a view to experimenting with the conventions of narrative, exposing the kind of mechanics of story-telling which we would normally take for granted."[2]

Characteristic of the European-American twentieth century novel are, among other things, an increasing tendency to turn away from the external events and to concentrate on the hero's inner, psychological drives and a rejection of the rectilinear time sequence in favor of a construction in which the chronology is more complex. The novel is no longer composed in the form of a simple succession of occurrences, but can simultaneously take place on two or more parallel planes or can be chopped up into separate fragments. The techniques of montage and collage are applied. Joyce's *Ulysses,* Proust's *A la recherche du temps perdu,* Belyj's *Peterburg* and other works are landmarks in this evolution; these writings "evolved a complex form evocative of the complexity of life."[3] Particularly in French literature of the last forty years the experiments went further. The "anti-novel" arose, with its anti-hero as a manifestation of the writers' feelings of defeat, frustration, disillusionment in society. "The anti-hero and the anti-novel sum up modern man's literary and social sense of powerlessness," writes Paul West.[4] As a reaction to the psychological probings of the modernists, the anti-novel would simply note and register the material world surrounding the heroes, limiting its scope to a mere "reism." Next to these "chosistes" there were authors who would tackle the question of the hero's identity or the loss of it, sometimes portraying characters without identity, without a name. The *nouveau roman,* anti-metaphysical and anti-psychological, evolved from Camus', Beckett's and Ionesco's absurdist writings and went, in part, back to Breton and other surrealists.

It seems that now, by the end of the seventies, all these trends and fashions have lost a great deal of their glamor and attractiveness, yet they have been extremely influential in many European countries. And this is the reason why I mention here the above well-known phenomena. During the first decades of our century these new novelistic tendencies did not have any tangible impact in South-Eastern Europe, even though there may have been some (pre-) expressionist symptoms in Serbo-Croatian prose and drama writing around World War I. The interwar period produced some more experimental and innovative creations. The foremost Croatian writer Miroslav Krleža introduced elements gleaned from German expressionism in his early dramas. In his novel *Povratak Filipa Latinovicza* (Filip Latinovicz's Return, 1932) he made intensive use of the *monologue intérieure*. His hero is a hypersensitive artist engrossed in cheerless musings about the "infernalization of reality."

Miloš Crnjanski, who was to develop into one of the foremost Serbian prose writers, started his career with the *Dnevnik o Čarnojeviću* (Diary about Čarnojević, 1920), a partly expressionistic novella in which the horrors of the first World War and the hero's vicissitudes in it are depicted in brief, rapidly alternating, sensuous images of a clearly modernistic stamp. These authors, following the footsteps of Proust and other European writers, turned away from the still prevailing realist and naturalist traditions — the types of prose in which the surrounding reality is presented as having its intrinsic objective quality. They rejected the mere depiction of objects and phenomena, but endeavored to show to what degree the mind of their hero is occupied with these objects and phenomena. The modern novel has therefore been called "anti-epic,"[5] because the numerous digressions, giving the workings of the hero's mind a dominant position in the novel, diminish its epic, purely narrative character. In practically all instances, the actual content has lost its primacy, the author presents to us the internal world of his heroes or concentrates on technical, structural, formal problems, mindful of André Gide's maxim that "la forme est le secret de l'œuvre."[6]

Another interesting, though much less known work in this vein is the novel *Dan šesti* (The Sixth Day) by the Serbian poet and prose writer Rastko Petrović. The work was not printed until 1955–1956, when it was serialized in the Belgrade literary monthly *Delo*; then it came out in book form in 1961. But it was written in the thirties: the first part in 1932–1935, the second in 1938, when Petrović worked in the Yugoslav diplomatic service in Washington (where he died in 1949).

In the first part the arduous retreat of the Serbian army and large numbers of civilians in 1915 through the Montenegrin and Albanian mountains is the central theme. Petrović developed in this text a rather ambitious and complex type of prose, with frequent shifts of scene and changes in viewpoint, with a kaleidoscopic succession of characters, flashbacks, interpolated memories and associations, philosophical reflection and psychological analysis of some of the heroes, and with inner monologues printed in italics — in other words, exactly the type of novelistic technique and novelistic method that was applied by modernist prose writers in various parts of Europe.

The Sixth Day is not a broad historical, epic novel about this Serbian tragedy: the author is exclusively preoccupied with the incredible hardships suffered by the participants in this trek of over two months, and especially with the fate of his protagonist, Stevan. During the journey Stevan is mostly alone or with an accidental companion, and thus Petrović anticipates by ten to thirty years the numerous accounts of similar roads to Calvary during the partisan war as described in postwar Yugoslav literature — for example, by

Mihailo Lalić in *Svadba* (The Wedding), *Lelejska Gora* (The Wailing Mountain), and *Hajka* (The Chase), or by Vjekoslav Kaleb in *Divota prašine* (The Wonder of Dust).

The second part of the novel was found after Petrović's death; it was written in Washington and deals with contemporary American life. In this polished, refined prose, in which the hero's subtle, often melancholic meditations find expression, the modernistic qualities we discovered in the first part have receded and given way to a more conventional narration.

The second World War was a trying period for Yugoslav letters, in which artistic expression was stifled altogether in most parts of the country and made increasingly difficult in some others, and in which a great number of poets and writers perished. Then, in the years after 1945, a very much streamlined literature arose, adapted to the exigencies of the new communist regime and the doctrine of socialist realism. Writers were required to paint a heroic, but one-sided picture of the tragic and confused circumstances of World War II on Yugoslav soil.

Even though the conflict with the Kominform of 1948 put an end to this period of ideological bondage, it took the Yugoslav men of letters four to five years to recover the basic rights and liberties that are the prerequisites of a variegated and worthwhile artistic creativity. For years the writers would adhere to straightforward, strictly realistic depiction and narration without indulging in experimentation or endeavors to renew their style or methods.

Around 1953–1954 the first attempts at innovation in the field of prose writing appeared in print. A good example is *Daj nam danas* (Give Us This Day) by the versatile Serbian literary critic, essayist and novelist Radomir Konstantinović (born 1928). Issued in 1954 with a revised edition in 1963, it marked a rupture with the realistic tradition and presaged the advent of an avant-garde movement. It is a lengthy text in which only allusions are made to what actually is going on and the reader has to make a constant effort to follow the associations in the hero's mind (it is, of course, in first person narration).

Konstantinović's next novel, *Mišolovka* (The Mouse Trap) of 1956, is a similar bulky work in which the hero lives on the edge of two worlds, the real world and that of his imagination; the borderlines between the real and unreal, the rational and irrational are blurred and made unrecognizable. Unrest and fear become almost material, palpable entities to him. Both these books are attempts at analyzing and fathoming the hero's psychology; one could call these attempts, for the persevering reader, at least partly successful. However, in his subsequent works, like *Ahasver ili traktat o pivskoj flaši* (Ahasverus or a Treatise on a Beer Bottle, 1964), which indeed is a treatise, rather than a work of fiction, the endless monologues, the long sentences (some of them over two pages long) with no division into paragraphs, the constant stream of words with virtually no action (though manifesting Konstantinović's intellectual marksmanship and verbal skill) become tiresome.

An equally prolific and successful novelist who was increasingly involved in applying new devices in his prose was Vojin Jelić, born in the small town of Knin in Northern Dalmatia, which figures in many of his works under the disguise of "Kamovo." In 1953 his novel *Andjeli lijepo pjevaju* (The Angels Sing Beautifully) came out. It is divided into three separate parts, in the main connected by the time and place of action rather than by the action itself or the heroes. The time is just before World War II and during its early days, the place Kamovo. Both the first and the second part are presented in the form of autobiographies. The third and most extensive part is written in the third person. Jelić uses a rather intricate and circumstantial narrative style; his sentences are longer and more complex than was usual in Serbo-Croatian prose works of the fifties.

In creating a new, peculiar manner of expression in his prose he went a step further in his next novel with the euphonic title *Nebo nema obala* (The Sky Has No Shores, 1956), in which simple realistic narration is superseded by a lyrical, metaphorical, figurative style with a sometimes far-fetched imagery and an odd sentence structure. Jelić was one of the first to introduce various features of avant-garde prose writing into Yugoslav literature. It is a partisan novel, but its *recherché,* even labored language with a highly stylized dialogue and the unreal, sometimes surrealistic passages interlarding the story distract the reader's attention from the plot.

These features are more subdued in *Pobožni djavo* (The Pious Devil) of 1975, representing the notes of a fictitious young man, again an inhabitant of Jelić's home town "Kamovo." The style is again intricate, allusive, and characterized by constant unexpected transitions and exclamations and the interpolation of songs and other texts. In part it is the protagonist's soliloquy, much in the tradition of Dostoevsky's "Man from the Underground" and Duhamel's Salavin. Jelić's language is ornate, picturesque and quite his own, though remotely reminiscent of the everflowing pace and dynamism of Miroslav Krleža's language. A minimum of plot and action is offset by a stream of opulent disquisitions.

Živko Jeličić from Split (born in 1920) is another author who was among the first to apply modern techniques and methods in his writings. He started out as a poet, but from 1958 onwards, when his first two novellas appeared, he devoted himself exclusively to prose. The novellas, *Kap stida* (A Drop of Shame) and *Staklenko* (approximately: Mr. Glassy) — the latter was published separately as a short novel in 1964 — immediately placed Jeličić in the ranks of the modern experimentalists in Yugoslav prose. Both works virtually do without a real *fabula* and chiefly consist of portrayals and analyses of the main characters. The setting is a Dalmatian urban ambience; dialectisms and neologisms are profusely used.

Mr. Glassy is a highly imaginative and sensitive young man who sees through the persons with whom he comes into contact; he also realizes his own translucence. The images of glass, window, mirror, reflection or vitreosity recur throughout the text. There are flashbacks, intermezzos of various kinds, an alternation of first and third person narration and other modernist devices. The style is more traditionally realistic in the lengthy passages in which the inhabitants of the fishing village where Staklenko and his girlfriend spend a summer play the main role, speaking the čakavian dialect interspersed with Italian.

Mlaka koža (Tepid Skin, 1960) continued these tendencies, but it is much more elaborate and ambitious, consisting of eight hundred pages of detailed descriptions and observations (sometimes quite striking), an endless series of studies in minute depiction, in part rather obscure. "Here and there this novel by Jeličić is abundantly soaked in irony and cynicism," writes Djuro Šnajder, "and all the characters act grotesquely . . . It is a pity that Jeličić — at the moment when, according to his basic conception, the "liberated" persons ought to evolve before our eyes into well defined entities — builds up his scenes and situations on innumerable, quite freely selected details; through all this "wood-carving," this chiseling, and this playing with "psychological flexibility," the unity is hard to visualize, one detail swallows the other, inventions (and they do exist in this novel) become ineffectual. Thus persons do not develop into characters, they only evoke a slightly shaded atmosphere, and the design of a sentence dissolves into a mass of bubbles which vanish at the first touch."[7]

Among Jeličić's subsequent writings are a number of "scenarios," each preceded by a list of characters, like a play, with short, laconic, sometimes elliptic descriptive sentences and a dialogue printed in italics. Of more momentum are the novels *Ljetnih večeri* (In Summer Nights, 1966) and *Šašava luna* (The Stupid Moon, 1973). They largely consist of circumstantial descriptions and the rendering of every spoken word: all of this is wrapped in modernistic external, graphic forms. The events of the first day of *The Stupid Moon,* which could be mentioned on less than a page, are drawn out over about a hundred pages. There is again an abundance of dialect and colloquial language and of curses, with some dialogue in Italian. It is regrettable that the disproportionate length of some of Jeličić's works and their condensed descriptive style make them rather difficult to digest.

In Slovenia Ciril Kosmač (born in 1910), a realistic prose writer who had several books published before the war and in the early fifties, changed and renewed his methods in the novel *Balada o trobenti in oblaku* (1956). Its main character, the writer Peter Majcen, leads two lives: a normal everyday life, in which he is forced to engage in meaningless conversations with stupid, vulgar people, and a life of his imagination, in which he enjoys spinning the thread of the novella he is planning to write (this second life, the text of the imagined novella, is printed in italics). Gradually these two worlds seem to merge. The trumpet and the cloud perform symbolic roles. In an almost mysterious way the two stories amalgamate towards the end. The story in italics is a horrifying war episode. The characters are somewhat schematic, anemic, which may be the result of a deliberate compositional effort; the work has a certain thrilling, mysterious quality and touches upon questions of inspiration and creativity, the dividing line between dream (imagination) and reality. The attention is not so much focused on the events of the war, but on moral questions and personal dilemmas.

It would be easy to continue this list of post-war Yugoslav writers who contributed to a change in the character of the novel. The short stories of Ivan Kušan (born 1933), for example, one of the most prominent and versatile younger Croatian prose writers, written between 1956 and 1969 (collected in the volume *Veliki dan*: The Great Day, 1970), attest to his role as one of the earliest renovators of Croatian prose in the late fifties and sixties. Some of the stories, told in the first person, contain little plot or action and impart to the reader the fine-spun innermost thoughts of a man who is "not quite absolutely normal," as is said of one of the heroes. By far the most extensive text in this volume, "Moj potop" (My Deluge), written in 1956–1958, is actually a novel. It presents to us a lower middle-class man, a typical petit bourgeois, the violinist Tomislav Parić, who is shown alternately from the outside (in third person narration) and the inside (first person), with a multitude of details about his behavior, his thoughts and his environment. There *is* a plot of sorts in "My Deluge," as the hero one day takes a train and runs away from his everyday surroundings, his problems and quandaries. The use of italics, the rendering of diverse, alternating streams of thought, each interrupting the previous one and starting without a capital letter — all these devices, familiar to us from French and Anglo-American literature, were still relatively new in Yugoslav letters when Kušan wrote this work. Kušan's imagination, remarks Djuro Šnajder, "has shown itself in anti-rationalistic, inexact objectivations, in psychological clairvoyance. The cognition of his hero is inundated by misgivings, by a notion of fatality, and by presentiments of extraordinary intensity. To this writer the human being is the greatest miracle and secret, susceptible to miraculous discoveries . . . In man, spaces are extending from insight to insight, from premonition to discovery, and this movement is supernaturally, mystically, fantastically imbued in pain as in faith: suffering is the price for entering into the world of the Real, there is no other way and there cannot be one."[8]

Kušan did not make extensive use of these technical and structural innovations in all his works; they are absent from his novels *Toranj* (The Tower, 1974) and *Naivci* (The Naive Ones, 1975), in which a humorous (and, in the latter, a satirical) tone prevails. His playing with the time sequence can be seen in the fact that *Naivci* starts with the ninth and tenth chapters, only thereafter the other chapters follow in a regular order.

The above examples are no literary masterpieces; writers like Jelić and Jeličić could be termed second-rate authors, and Ranko Marinković, for example, with his short story collection *Ruke* (Hands) and the novel *Kiklop* (The Cyclops), is a greater artist and has more significance for the development of post-war Croatian and Yugoslav prose. However, the examples are typical of the new trends manifesting themselves in the mid-fifties. They show that Yugoslav avant-gardist prose dovetailed into the modernist tendencies of the West. The nature of these trends can be summarized as (1) the predominance of a personal, narrator's account of both his inner life and the external world with which he is confronted; (2) a tendency toward the small detail at the cost of the plot or story line (these trends can be labeled as neo-realist); (3) a preference for the fantastic or supernatural, also the irrational; and (4) a continuation of surrealistic prose as it was practiced by some, mostly Serbian, writers of the interwar period. As part of the "neo-realist" trend I would include the works which A. Flaker has described as "jeans prose" — those in which the author portrays or puts himself into the shoes (the jeans) of a youngster, or more generally of uneducated, very simple people, often using their speech, their dialect or jargon.

In the sixties virtually all novelists who respected themselves seem to have been engaged in some form of modernistic writing. The vehement debates carried on in the fifties pro and con avant-gardistic prose writing gradually subsided. Some authors adopted only certain features of the new novel (Oskar Davičo, Aleksandar Tišma, Petar Šegedin, Ranko Marinković, to mention just a few names), others dedicated themselves more completely to contemporary ways of expression (Slobodan Novak, Jožo Laušić, Mirko Kovač, Danilo Kiš, etc.). The trend to replace an objective authorial attitude, as was the norm in the traditional 19th-century realistic novel, by a purely subjective narration is clearly present in part of postwar Yugoslav prose, whereas some other writers tended to exclude all subjectivity and attempted to let the objective world, the world of objects, reign supreme.

That older writers, imbued in the realist tradition, participated in these innovative endeavors can be exemplified by Petar Šegedin and Ivan Dončević, both born in 1909. In Šegedin's *Crni smiješak* (The Black Smile, 1969) the perplexity and loneliness of the human being faced with the riddle of existence and death and the theme of the passing of time are central. The best part of the book is perhaps the fragment "Žamor mora" (The Rustling of the Sea), which had already been published a few years earlier. In it, a Chekhovian mood (notably that of a story like "The Lady with the Dog"), a tormented Dostoevskian probing into the deep layers of an individual's conscience and thinking, and a Pirandello-like interest in the hopelessly inscrutable human soul and in the relation of the author (the "I") with his characters are blended together, moulded into modern narrative forms (with more than one plane of narration) and told in Šegedin's characteristic, leisurely, somewhat garrulous and repetitive, yet effective narrative manner.

Ivan Dončević had in the thirties gained the reputation of being one of the socially-oriented realistic writers and confirmed this reputation by the volume of short stories about the war, *Bezimeni* (The Nameless) of 1955 and other publications. A more ambitious, interesting, and significant work is his novel *Mirotvorci* (The Peace Makers, 1966). It was followed by *Krvoproliće kod Krapine* (Bloodshed near Krapina, 1968), a humorous work without deep implications, but not without some structural and technical novelties. Dončević showed with this book that he wanted to keep up with contemporary trends and endeavors to modernize the technique of the novel. The main development is narrated by the central hero in the first person, but each of the characters is provided with a short biography (in third person narration) in the form of footnotes printed in italics. The novel contains a dream in dialogue form with a great many characters, including Boccaccio and Sigmund Freud, but also a lamp. The plot is very slim — it is the story of one day in the life of a mediocre Zagreb employee (a legal adviser in a furniture plant). There is a great deal of reflection and use of the "stream of consciousness" procédé; and references are made to the life stories of the main protagonist, his wife, his would-be-lover, and his director. The work is not a masterpiece, but manifests a considerable widening of the diapason of Dončević's abilities as a prose writer.

The Slovene poet and prose writer Matej Bor (pseudonym of Vladimir Pavšič, born in 1913), author of the first illegal book of partisan lyrics in Yugoslavia and of numerous plays dealing with topical socio-political problems, wrote his only novel, *Daljave* (Far Distances), in 1961. The action evolves around two male characters, the meek partisan, Blaž Oblak, and the strong-willed renegade, Mirko. The dichotomy of these contrasting characters provides the basis for the rather complex plot. The realistic action is intertwined with imaginary scenes and visions. Like in so many prose works about the war that were produced at some temporal distance from the events, the personal, psychological interplay of the heroes is more important in it than the war situation during which the action takes place (partly in retrospect). Love and eroticism are no minor ingredients of the work; the attitudes and feelings of both heroes towards the girl Amalija are rendered in detail. Events from the partisan war are shown in a somewhat unreal, ghostly way. The point of view in the novel constantly changes, shifting between Blaž's perspective, that of Mirko, that of Amalija and those of two or three other characters (for the two men, first person narration is used). Blaž is lying on his death bed in the beginning of the novel, too sick to speak, only able to write in the air with his hand. He is writing his reminiscenses which are then described through flashbacks. Thus Bor created a new variety of story telling: after the story in letters, in diary form, in *skaz,* in dialogue or in inner monologue, here is the story written with a finger in the air.

Far Distances is a rather ambitious work, with frequent jumps in time, flashbacks, shifts of viewpoint and narrator, sophisticated dialogues and inner monologues. There is too much retardation, the text is too lengthy (with no division into chapters) and contains too many digressions, descriptions and reflections, and all characters speak and think in the same way, so that it is hard to tell them apart. Nevertheless we have to recognize this work as one of the most serious and elaborate attempts at modernizing postwar Slovene prose.

Another coryphaeus of realistic prose who altered his method and approach in the course of the sixties and came close to the modernists was Dobrica Ćosić (born 1921), who had become famous with his romantic-realistic novel about the partisan war *Daleko je sunce* (Far Away is the Sun, 1951). He considerably enlarged his stylistic devices and way of expressing himself in his next novel, *Koreni* (Roots, 1954) and even more so in the extensive work, *Deobe* (Partitions, 1961), that followed. In the latter he renounced the use of quotation marks and partly also of periods, which in this case intensifies the impression of chaos and confusion that reigned in the ranks of the četniks he described. Monologues go on for pages without any stops, capitals or new paragraphs; this works rather laboriously. But the work shows Ćosić's astounding richness of vocabulary (the obscenities and swearwords stand out), his mastery of language and his skill in the art of novel construction.

Equally interesting, but totally different is his novel *Bajka* (The Fairy Tale) of 1966. The fantastic element takes possession of the hero-narrator; he is confronted with Satan who, under the name of Andjamo, dominates the whole book. In this work Ćosić "attempts, in a tense intellectual concentration of moral evaluation and poetic allegory, to create a visionary work with a considerable admixture of the fantastic, which was supposed to communicate ever-valid truths and fears for the future of the human race, led to the brink of annihilation."[9] In his major work, *Vreme smrti* (The Time of Death, 3 vols., 1972-1975), Ćosić abstains from any further experimentation of this kind.

Krsto Špoljar, from Croatia (1930-1977), manifested no literary pretensions until his novel *Gvožđje i lovor* (Iron and Laurel) appeared in 1963. The plot has receded to the background here, and one's attention is focused upon the thoughts and experiences of the main hero and his relations with the world around him. This main hero is the "First Person" who tells the story; he is a fifteen-year-old boy in a small town during the last stages of the second World War. The pervading theme of the novel is the frustration the narrator experiences vis-à-vis his pals, and other people in general — his feelings of guilt, jealousy, shame, suppressed admiration for some of his friends, loneliness — his realization of his own inferiority, cowardice, superfluousness, and ugliness. This is communicated in great detail, in long and involved sentences, with numerous metaphors, similes, and digressions.

His next novel, *Vrijeme i paučine* (Time and Cobwebs), came out in 1970; it placed Špoljar even more firmly among the avant-garde in contemporary Croatian prose. The scene shifts constantly from April, 1941 — the first days of the war in Yugoslavia — to May, 1945, the first days after the liberation. The narrator (sometimes also presented in the third person) is a high school student at the end of the war; the second main character is his "red-haired uncle," a reserve captain at the outbreak of World War II and a Croatian patriot. Notwithstanding its setting in these eventful times, there is very little action; instead, there are long-winded soliloquies and meditations, presented in a compact style with endless sentences; chapter II, for example, starts with a sentence eleven pages long. In its polyphone, multi-plane structure, *Time and Cobwebs* is typical of the direction prose innovation was taking in the sixties and early seventies. The following fragment may give an idea of the character of Špoljar's style; it is the cemetery scene with which the book opens:

I could leave the cemetery most quietly, what are these crazy tales about dead people good for anyway? — *the present time*

. . . deep, deaf silence, stable as something palpable, a creature or, really, a person, invisible but definitely present, the silence fills in a suffocating way and without any exception this crepuscular space about which I cannot even say that it is the real home of those countless ones who disappeared and got lost in the dust of oblivion who were part of that time (a dead, really a dead time) in which we nonetheless somehow lasted together, foreigners but reciprocal owners of life, I am convinced that the silence here is eternal, petrified in its constant future, and most accurately in the slightest detail I felt (a firm sharpness of perception notwithstanding my pain) that the silence did not give way before the cracked tolling of the tin bell with its piercing sound hanging in the empty, bare and peeled tower of the little mortuary church almost putrefied by the evil of old age, neither would it give way before the singing of some creature whose black pontificals embroidered with gold and silver curls and the letters IHS marked him as a priest, and not even before the strokes of the spade, the scrape produced by its penetration into the humid, but yet sandy soil, the grating of the stone plate with moss scattered over it when it was moved, it did not recede before the people either and their hoarse voices squeezed by their murmur . . .[10]

Gordo posrtanje (Stumbling Proudly), a novel by the Bosnian writer Vojislav Lubarda (also born in 1930), is equally typical of the new trend in novel writing under discussion. One of the two time levels (printed in italics) is the war period in Bosnia, characterized by a most atrocious internecine struggle; one gets an insight into the extremely complex and chaotic situation, when Serbians ("Vlasi") and Moslems ("Turci"), communists and četniks (both Serbians), Serbians and the Croatian ustaše fought and massacred each other, but sometimes also turned into allies. The other temporal plane is twenty years after the war; a latent family conflict is interwoven in the action related to the war situation.

In Slovenia similar tendencies developed. In some novels by Vladimir Kavčič (born in 1932) a Kafkaesque element is clearly present; they develop the theme of loneliness-within-the-crowd. The inner movements of the heroes are sounded and described with much subtle detail; increasingly he deals with moral problems that preoccupy the minds of his characters, determining the tenor of their lives, torturing or even destroying them. *Ognji so potemneli* (The Fires Have Darkened) of 1960 is the story of two brothers returning to their desolate native home; their parents and their two sisters have been killed in the second World War. One has fought against the Germans in the French *maquis*; the other has lived through the war in their native village. The confrontation with his elder brother evokes feelings of guilt in the latter, and towards the end of the novel he kills a local traitor from the war years, sets their own house on fire and then commits suicide. This highly dramatic work is constructed on three levels: in the first place, the outer reality, the alternation of events, motions and emotions in a regular, rectilinear time sequence; secondly, the thoughts of the two heroes, all that goes on in their minds and hearts (printed in italics); and finally the memories of both of the war periods (put in parentheses). Although the actual time is several years after the war, the plot is inspired by it, as in many of Kavčič's creations.

After *Tja in nazaj* (There and Back) of 1962, which is devoid of any experimental or even non-conventional elements, he wrote *Od tu dalje* (From There Onwards, 1964), evoking the ghostly ambience of a Kafkaesque city which tends to dehumanize and depersonalize the individual. Kavčič's hero, whose name here and in several other works is Dimitrije, finds employment in an obscure, but powerful Institution; however, he has no idea what sort of work he is supposed to do. The text contains long conversations, but little progression. At the end Dimitrije succeeds in escaping from the lifeless overregulation of this city by swimming across the river. However, in the sequel, *Onkraj in še dlje* (Beyond and Still Further), printed in a magazine in 1965–1966 and issued in book form in 1971, he finds that the city on the other bank is likewise governed by a mysterious Institution from whose tentacles he cannot escape. This work, too, is highly allegorical and novel, modern in its plot, setting, and underlying ideas, although not so much in its structure or technical aspects. The general theme of the two books is the total alienation of the individual in an insensible, ineluctable socio-political system full of absurdities.

Another Slovene writer, Rudi Šeligo (born 1935), went into a quite different direction from Kavčič in his search for new novelistic forms. He wrote a number of short stories before he launched his first novel, *Stolp* (The Tower) of 1966. In his stories one sees a gradual evolution from a realistic prose, minutely rendering all details, both of an external, objective reality surrounding his heroes and of their inner life — to what has been termed "structural prose," a form of "reism," where not only objects but even persons are viewed as inanimate matter. The heroes are portrayed from the outside, as soulless mechanisms. What all his prose works have in common is the attention he is paying to the smallest details, like a very slowly moving, scanning movie camera. His first successful story was called "Kamen," meaning "rock," but here it is, characteristically, the name of the hero. In "Žil" (Jules) of 1967, the method, used by other writers before him, of describing in detail an ordinary day in the life of an ordinary man is employed — from daybreak and his awakening up to late in the evening. Typical for this reistic or mechanical approach is "Velika Simona veliki šahist" (Big Simona Great Chessplayer, 1967), in which the heroine is a cashier, who is only seen as sitting all the time behind a glass window at a cashier's desk in a restaurant.

Concomitant with such a static method is, inevitably, a lack of action, not to speak of plot or denouement: like in so many experimental prose works, the movement in Šeligo's fiction is almost reduced to zero. In the novel *The Tower* the day of a group of workers, filling trucks with sand, is the camera's objective. It is first person narration, therefore the reism is modified and mitigated by a personal, more emotionally involved point of view. Here and there passages in italics render the main hero's thoughts and feelings. Yet a high degree of objectivity is maintained. The dialogue of the spade workers is rendered in the way a play is printed, without connecting text. In this novel Šeligo joined the group of young Yugoslav prose writers who direct their spotlight on the simplest, uneducated members of society and try to identify with them (first person narration is a device which enhances this identification). However, Šeligo does not attempt — as Majdak and some others do — to exactly render the speech, the jargon of his simple heroes. In 1975 he produced his first big novel, *Rahel stik* (Feeble Contact), which is characterized by a highly complex, ingenious composition and a more lyrical style than in his previous works.

Among the Serbian writers belonging to the same generation a similar movement to renew the forms of the novel and short story can be seen. Next to Danilo Kiš, Branimir Šćepanović and Borislav Pekić one could mention here Mirko Kovač (born 1938) with his collection of stories *Gubilište* (The Scaffold, 1962), the novel *Moja sestra Elida* (My Sister Elida, 1965), described as "not a novel in the classical sense of the word, but a tragic poetical vision of human darkness and despair,"[11] and the four novellas *Rane Luke Meštrevića ili povest rasula* (The Wounds of Luka Meštrević or a Story of Decay, 1971). The fourth of these novellas, "Životopis Malvine Trifković" (The Life Story of Malvina Trifković), is also separately published and can be considered a short novel. In these novellas one finds a strong tendency to neglect the narrative connection and to replace it by a mosaic of fragmentrary information. They are presented as authentic accounts evoking the life of bygone centuries in an old Hercegovinian town; but at the same time they abound in fantastic scenes, unreal details and surrealistic, delirious passages. Many sentences are not directly related to the plot; all the time new persons are introduced, without any character drawing. In "Životopis Malvine Trifković" (which has a clearer narrative line) the texts of fifteen manuscripts, actually letters, are rendered from which the figure of the heroine and her life story gradually emerge.

To avoid even more repetition than the above vignettes of contemporary writers contain already, I shall refrain from quoting more examples of modernist writing within the same generation, and point only in passing to one of its most talented representatives, Radomir Smiljanić in Serbia (born 1934), who made a reputation with a whole series of novels. Especially a trilogy with the strange titles *Neko je oklevetao Hegela* (Somebody Has Calumniated Hegel, 1973), *U Andima Hegelovo telo* (In the Andes Hegel's Body, 1975), and *Bekstvo u Helgoland* (Escape to Helgoland, 1977) drew attention. The hero, Hegel Miliradović, is a strange, half unreal figure, admired and venerated by a group of adherents like a *guru,* but at the same time shown by the narrator to be an insignificant, ridiculous man, a braggart and even a thief. The whole action of these novels is fantastic, unreal, unserious.

Some writers introduce fewer irrational elements into their works and seemingly adhere to the rules of realism; however, this is not the classical realism that endeavors to present an objective, true picture of "life-as-it-is," but a method which only shows reality as the narrator perceives it, his subjective vision of the surrounding world, presented through the procédé of "strange-making" or defamiliarization. As an example one might point to Dragi Bugarčić (born 1948), who in his two novels, both printed in 1975: *Zaharije u Beču* (Zachary in Vienna) and *Pustolovine Želimira Besnickog* (Želimir Besnicki's Adventures), follows the vicissitudes of a young man of lower middle class milieu and paints his predicament in an insecure, chaotic world.[12] He was the first in Yugoslav literature (with, to some degree, Miodrag Bulatović) to tackle the problem of the "guest worker" in foreign countries.

The material mentioned or briefly discussed here could be supplemented or replaced by other texts; but it seems to me that it is sufficiently typical and representative, evincing an unmistakable trend in Yugoslav prose writing, of the sixties in particular, to move away from the traditional patterns and to modernize itself. Even though this trend is characterized by a great variety of styles, themes, personal idiosyncrasies and approaches, there are certain tendencies most of the prominent Yugoslav writers of the period 1956–1975 have in common — some of them purely formal or even graphic, some structural (the most striking feature being the strong predominance of either the descriptive or the psychological, analytic element over the elements of plot, narrative development, fiction), and finally some thematic. Death and transitoriness, alienation and loneliness are dealt with in hundreds of varieties, and this trait the Yugoslav literatures obviously have in common with the Western literatures. The nightmarish experience of the second World War on Yugoslav soil, an inexhaustible source of traumatic inspiration in the literature of this country, has lent a specific coloring to the way these themes are pursued. These efforts to modernize are not always successful, not always of the highest quality and sometimes no more than mere experiments, but they nevertheless show an abundance of true literary talent and point to the integration of contemporary Yugoslav prose into the prevalent international literary trends of our days.

NOTES

1. Cf. T. Eekman, "Parallel Developments in the Poetry of the South Slavs (late 19th–early 20th centuries)," in *Aspects of the Balkans, Continuity and Change,* Contributions to the International Balkan Conference, UCLA, ed. Henrik Birnbaum & Speros Vryonis, The Hague: Mouton, 1972, pp. 370–396.

2. Jonathan Raban, *The Technique of Modern Fiction, Essays in Practical Criticism,* London: Edw. Arnold, 1968, p. 26.

3. Paul West, *The Modern Novel,* London: Hutchinson, 1963, p. 34.

4. *Ibid.,* p. 429.

5. Stanko Korać, *Hrvatski roman izmedju dva rata,* Zagreb: August Cesarec, 1974, p. 157.

6. André Gide, *Œuvres complètes,* Paris: NRF, 1932–1939, vol. VII, p. 500.

7. Djuro Šnajder, *Uvod u najnoviju hrvatsku prozu,* Zagreb: Matica hrvatska, p. 238.

8. Djuro Šnajder, *op. cit.,* p. 173.

9. Predrag Palavestra, *Posleratna srpska književnost, 1945–1970,* Beograd: Prosveta, 1972, p. 228.

10. Krsto Špoljar, *Vrijeme i paučina, Sentimentalni odgoj na hrvatski način,* Zagreb: Matica hrvatska, 1971, p. 7.

11. Predrag Palavestra, *op. cit.,* p. 308.

12. Cf. Nikolaj Timčenko's review of *Zaharije u Beču* in *Književne novine,* Beograd, December 16, 1976.

Efim Etkind

MIXAIL BULGAKOV, OUR CONTEMPORARY

A literary work can be evaluated from two opposing points of view: (1) One can examine the conditions of its coming into existence and the role which it plays in the creative evolution of the author or (2) one can examine the readers' reception and the role which the work plays in the literary movement of the period.

Most frequently both points of view are interconnected: The creative history of a work turns out to be one of the aspects of the societal life of an epoch, and reader reception is one of the facets of the history of the work, of the formation not only of its reputation but even of its text. However sometimes these two points of view are not connected: This is the case when, on the one hand, the creation of the work and, on the other, its publication, that is its influence on readers, are separated in time.

The problem of works whose publication has been delayed and occurs long after their creation is particularly intriguing for the literary historian. Theoretically, two contrasting fates are possible: (1) The work appears in another epoch, in which its ideas or its artistic form are perceived as archaic. In this case, the work is like a museum piece, a *pamjatnik,* no longer capable of participating in the current literary life and struggle. (2) The work appears in an epoch in which its qualities astonish its new contemporaries with its topicality, at times even artistic daring; and it is immediately included in the ongoing process, determining the paths of literary development.

An example of the first variant is V. Kjuxel'beker's tragedy *Prokofij Ljapunov,* which the author conceived in the beginning of the thirties of the 19th century and completed in 1834; it appeared one hundred years later, in 1938, in the Leningrad journal *Literaturnyj Sovremennik.* The intent of this play about imposture and Russian "Faustiana," as Kjuxel'beker himself wrote in one of his letters, could, a century later, interest only a historian; the play itself, despite its Schillerian tone, was capable of attracting only a professional erudite: the Russian reader of 1938 had other concerns, far from Kjuxel'beker's "Faustiana."

An example of the second variant is the poetic heritage of André Chenier. The Jacobin dictatorship executed the poet in 1793, and at that time he was known to the French reading public only through a small portion of his works. A quarter of a century later, in 1818, Chenier's verses were published and immediately became the topic of conversation not only in France, but also everywhere else in Europe. One would be hard put to exaggerate its significance for the French Romantics and for Pushkin. Balzac, in his novel *Lost Illusions,* has given a memorable description of the public's unexpected discovery of this great lyric poet, resurrected at the very moment when he was most needed by society and literature. It is possible that if Chenier's elegies had appeared in the 18th century, they would have remained unappreciated and not understood; there is no doubt that in the history of French letters they belong to the Romantic epoch, and that André Chenier is not a younger contemporary of Voltaire but the older brother of Victor Hugo, Musset, Lamartine, Vigny, Barbier.

"Delayed" writers is a term one can use to refer to the historico-literary problem which concerns us here. In the first instance, an author who was already an archaist in his own time and who, after a hundred years, has turned out to be infinitely distant from the reading public is "delayed." In the second case, the author is considerably ahead of his time, but then, after twenty-five years he is still in the avant-garde.

Mixail Bulgakov belongs among such "delayed" writers. His novel *Master i Margarita* was begun in 1928, completed in 1939, and published in 1966–67. This novel was as significant for Bulgakov's creative life as *Faust* was for Goethe and *Demon* for Lermontov. In each of these cases, the work is one into which the writer has placed his whole being and on which he has labored until his death. All this is relevant to the author's subjective circumstances; but, despite the significance of the work for the writer, it could still be incomprehensible to the reading public a quarter of a century later.

In 1934, the talented poet Pavel Vasil'ev wrote a poem "Xristoljubovskie sitcy," which had programmatic significance for him but which remained in manuscript form for twenty-two years; it came out only in 1956 in the journal *Oktjabr'.* The brilliance of the verse, the energy of the language are typical of Vasil'ev, unique and unexpected:

> . . . kružok
> Ix byl ukrašen junoj devoj —
> V šelku ee kipela plot',
> Ona deržala kružku v levoj,
> A v pravoj vetčiny lomot'.
> A rjadom,
> Ot zakata krasen,
> Igral gornist v syrjuju t'mu,
> On byl ogromen i prekrasen,
> No ne xvatalo
> Glaz emu . . .[1]

However, Vasil'ev's poem did not appear when it should have, in the mid-thirties, and when it did appear in the year of Krushchev's "thaw" it proved to be irrelevant. Nothing could save it — neither the tragic fate of the author, who was executed by a firing squad in 1937 at the same age as Lermontov had been when he was killed, nor his reputation as one of the most brilliant talents of his generation, nor the panegyric by one who was chary of his praise, B. Pasternak, who then, in 1956, compared Vasil'ev with Majakovskij and Esenin ("He was comparable with them, especially with respect to Esenin's creative expressiveness and the power of his gift, and he promised so much..."). And still "Xristoljubovskie sitcy" remained buried in *Oktjabr'* as a sad memorial to the deceitful poetry of the thirties when, after the First Congress of Writers and Ždanov's speech, "artistic" constructions following the recipes of Socialist Realism were born.

A decade later, already after the end of the "thaw," in another rather right-wing journal, *Moskva,* the first part of M. Bulgakov's novel, *Master i Margarita,* appeared (1966, no. 11); the last part came out two months later (1967, no. 1). The editorial board took this bold step at a time when the journal was on the verge of failure, when the number of its subscribers and readers had catastrophically dwindled. Apparently, the managers of *Moskva* knew very well what would result from the appearance of the first part; indeed, the number of subscriptions improbably increased, almost doubled, in 1967. That was the spontaneous reaction of the people who sought to read Bulgakov's novel "from cover to cover" without delay. In the course of several years, book binders were burdened with a single common task: People brought them both published parts to be bound into one volume, the book which not a single publisher was allowed to produce. The whole world already knew about *Master i Margarita:* the YMCA in Paris had already brought out a reprint of the text from the journal while the publishing house Posev in Frankfurt had produced two complete editions in Russian (1969–1970). Foreign translations had already appeared: English (Mirra Ginsburg, N.Y., 1967; M. Glenny, N.Y., 1967, & London, 1967), Bulgarian (Liliana Minkova, 1968), Danish (Jørgen Harrit, 1968), Dutch (Marko Fondse, 1968), Finnish (Uuli-Liisa Heino, 1969), French (Claude Ligny, 1968), German (Thomas Reschke, 1968 and 1970), Greek (Andrea Rikake, 1971), Hebrew (1969), Hungarian (Klára Szöllősy, 1969), Japanese (Yasuo Yûko, 1969), Italian (Vera Dridso, 1967), Macedonian (Tanja Uroševič, 1970), Norwegian (Martin Nag, 1967), Polish (Irena Lewandowska, Witold Dąbrowski, 1969), Portuguese (Ruy Bello, 1969), Romanian (Natalia Radovici, 1970), Serbo-Croatian (Milan Čolić, 1968), Slovak (Magda Tákočová, 1968), Spanish (Amaja Lacasca Sancha, 1968), Swedish (Lars Eric Blomqvist, 1971), Turkish (Aydin Emeç, 1968) — in a total of twenty-two languages. We should also add a language of the Soviet Union — Estonian (M. Varik and J. Ojamaa, 1968). The novel became known to the whole world. In many countries, articles about it appeared — in English alone, for the two-year period 1967 and 1968, more than sixty reviews were noted (see Ellendea Proffer's bibliography, Ardis, 1976, pp. 91–92, nos. 882–952). Students write term papers about it, graduate students — dissertations, professors — monographs, editors — prefaces; other writers compare Bulgakov to Goethe, Dostoevskij, and Swift. The servile publishing house of the GDR, Kultur und Fortschritt, issued *Master i Margarita* in 1968 with Ralph Schroeder's postscript, titled "Bulgakov's novel *Master i Margarita* in the mirror of Faustian models of the 19th and 20th centuries," where the name Bulgakov is placed side by side with Dostoevskij, Thomas Mann, and Gor'kij, and the novel itself is treated as an unquestionable classic. The Yugoslav director Aleksandar Petrović made a film based on Bulgakov's novel in 1972 (a joint Italian-Yugoslav production). Soviet critics have written lengthy articles about the novel; entire critical monographs have appeared in journals and newspapers (A. Al'tšuler — *LG* 7, II, 1969; M. Čudakova — *VL,* 1973, no. 7; V. Lakšin — *NM,* 1968, nos. 6 and 12, *Pamir,* 1972, no. 4; G. Makarovskaja and A. Žuk — *Volga* 1968, no. 6; P. Palievskij — *NS,* 1969, no. 92; L. Skorino — *VL,* 1968, no. 6; I. Vinogradov — *VL,* 1968, no. 6). Such writings have also appeared in the Russian press outside the Soviet Union.

But the novel *Master i Margarita* did not appear as a separate volume in the Soviet Union. And, as more time passed, as more foreign editions, studies, dissertations, films, and operas appeared, the politics of the Soviet publishing houses seemed even more astounding.

Until November 1966, everything was clear: *Master i Margarita* was a forbidden manuscript. For some reason, someone considered it anti-Soviet (why? who?) and it was forbidden to mention it. In the first volume of *Kratkaja literaturnaja ènciklopedija* (1962) there is a note about M. Bulgakov, not even forty lines — that is, ten times less than about the emigré Bunin, fourteen times less than about Brjusov, as many lines as about another Bulgakov — Valentin, who was only the personal secretary of Lev Tolstoj and, it might be mentioned, also an emigré of many years. Of course, the author of the note, Ju. Osnos, knew about *Master i Margarita,* but he did not mention it — the only thing that he imparted to the reader in the form of an evaluation is that in the stories of the early Bulgakov "the non-acceptance of reality was reflected by the writer, who was incapable of discerning the true face of the times behind the 'grimaces of NEP'" (*KLÈ,* vol. 1, 1962, column 769). This characterization is fully relevant to *Master i Margarita*: "non-acceptance," "he was incapable of discerning" . . . — such is the reason for the censorial prohibition.

What could be done? A prohibition is a prohibition. But, in 1966, this pretense of ignorance about Bulgakov's major work was thwarted. The book — to everyone's amazement — appeared in the journal *Moskva.* It appeared with censorial abridgements, with K. Simonov's diplomatically polite preface, with A. Bulis's "covering" postscript — in short, with every possible precaution. The saying was: "Don't think the worst; we are publishing an old Soviet novel which we haven't had time to publish until now — we had more pressing matters to take care of. Moreover, there isn't anything special in this book — it's just a novel (like all novels), satire plus fantasy." The publishers of the novel could respond to the amazed readers in the same manner as Bulgakov's cat Begemont loves to answer. In reply to the question, "Who sent the telegram?" the cat replies, "Why, I did. So what else is new?" just as though it were the most normal thing in the world to have a cat send out telegrams. The editor of the journal *Moskva,* E. Popovkin, arranged the publication of the novel in such a way as to say: "Well, we are publishing Bulgakov's book. So what else is new?"

It was, after all, precisely this irrational, even fantastic, aspect of Soviet reality that Bulgakov had in mind and it is surprisingly reflected in the fate of his manuscript. The famous writer wrote his book in secret over a period of twelve years — twelve of the total of fifteen years during which he was occupied with writing — and if his secret had been uncovered, Bulgakov's fate would have been similar to that of his hero, the Master: arrest, destruction of the manuscript, a camp, and then death or, at best, a mental asylum. But the manuscript of this important book remained a secret carried by the author through 1935, 1937, and 1938, the years of the great terror.

Further, the manuscript lay for a quarter of a century, almost untouched, in the care of Bulgakov's widow, his Margarita. It survived not only the years of the great terror but also other years, such frightening years as — the war, the *Ždanovščina,* anti-cosmopolitanism, the terror of 1949–1953 . . . It survived, although it passed at times into different hands. For example, in the Tashkent evacuation of 1943, several writers read a part of the manuscript, the Moscow satirical part. Apparently, E. S. Bulgakov hid the biblical part especially well. It was read by A. A. Axmatova, whose poetic necrologue to Bulgakov was published at the same time as his novel, in 1966, twenty-six years after these verses were written:

> Vot èto ja tebe, vzamen mogil'nyx roz,
> Vzamen kadil'nogo kuren'ja;
> Ty tak surovo žil i do konca dones
> Velikolepnoe prezren'e . . .[2]
>   (1940)

In what other work of Bulgakov's, created in the last years of his life ("do konca dones"), is his contempt revealed with such force?

Many knew about *Master i Margarita* (a contributor to *Moskva,* E. Laskina, did not hide her long-standing intentions concerning publication from her friends), but the secret was kept. It was kept for a quarter of a century. And this in itself is remarkable. It was not without reason that Voland taught Margarita that "manuscripts do not burn."

Further, the manuscript became a journal publication. The censors (or editors, in this case they are synonymous) reworked it in order to, so to speak, "defang it." All of the parts (paragraphs, phrases, portions of phrases) in which there were direct or indirect references to the following were expurgated: NKVD, the police and their agents, especially ugly features of the Soviet way of life (Torgsin), female nudity. Aside from that, the editors removed all those passages which allowed the transference of the notion of devilry to Soviet reality. The editorial corrections themselves are fantastic in their absurdity and even plain stupidity — thus, Korov'ev, mocking the Muscovites, would be able to censor the text of the novel. For example: "Here through the open door the *naked* Natasha came running, *clapped her hands and called to Margarita* ..."(367); "'I hate it, that novel, answered the Master, '*I have gone through too much because of it*'" (370); "The lady was half-barefoot, in some sort of transparent, obviously foreign, slippers which were torn into pieces. *Yuck! you! in slippers! . . . For, you know, the lady was naked! Well, the cloak was thrown directly over her nude body!* What a place!" (374).[3] There is a familiar logic in the editing (abridgements); however, this logic itself is schizophrenic, phantasmagoric and hence close to Bulgakov's devilry. The Soviet publishers' treatment of Bulgakov's text does not contradict the "satanic episodes"in the novel; to the contrary, they foretell it.

In the same year, 1967, that the mutilated "Master"appeared in the journal *Moskva,* the publisher, Scherz Verlag (together with Giulio Einaudi), issued a booklet containing the items red-pencilled by the censor — to be sure, without any indication as to the relevant pages. At the same time, these red-pencilled items were widely disseminated in "Samizdat"; tens of thousands of those who possessed bound copies of the journal text carefully pasted in little strips with the deleted phrases. I have not seen a single copy which has not undergone such a repair process — such strange looking books, swollen with numerous strips of paper. With this pasting-in process, even readers far removed from literature scrutinized the text and asked themselves or others: "Why did *they* do that? They were afraid of the words 'naked' or 'nude body'? They don't allow the word 'police'?" One of my colleagues, a physics instructor, with amazement showed me the beginning of the chapter "Flight": "Invisible *and free*! Invisible *and free*!" (298). The word *free* was expunged twice. "Why," asked my colleague, "can't a witch, flying on a broomstick, rejoice in her freedom?" Probably Soviet censorship has never ever exposed itself in this way. My ingenuous physicist suddenly unwittingly observed that this means that Margarita was formerly "not free," and that the censors (or editors) are afraid of the word "free" in particular. Considering further the following: "*Naked* and invisible, flying around . . . " (301), my colleague laughed. "Is it possible," he wondered, "that the word 'naked' frightens them, even in the presence of the word 'invisible'? After all, the latter renders the former harmless!" Or, a little further on, he was even more amused by the following red-pencilling in the remark by Nikolaj Ivanovič, who had been transformed into a hog and straddled for flight on the Sabbath by the servant Natal'ja: "'I demand to be turned back into my usual shape!' the pig suddenly grunted, half-angry, half begging. 'I refuse to take part in an illegal asse mbly! Margarita Nikolayevna, kindly take your maid off my back!'" (309). Is it possible that pronouncing the word "illegal" would give the reader a dangerous thought? I can assert with confidence that all the "pasters in" laughed at the censor-editor and saw in his activity a parody similar to the parodied speech of the cat Begemont. This parody of censorship was an unprecedented genre of satiric literature; though at one time Heinrich Heine did think of it as well. The twelfth chapter of his book "Le Grand" looks like this:

> German censors.............................
> ....
> ....asses...............
> ....

Who, then, exposed to laughter the mysterious censorial-editorial practices, with their wild belief in the magical strength of a seditious word, with their bigoted fear of obscenity, with their panicky horror at "uncontrolled associations" and "subtexts"? First, the anonymous authors of the parodied constructions themselves; second, having appeared from who knows where, from thin air, the victims — the expunged words and phrases which themselves, having been put in their rightful place, called for vengeance. Who disfigured Bulgakov's text? Who preserved the expunged items and put them into circulation? All this somehow happened by itself — or through the interference of an evil spirit. This then is the peculiarity of Soviet reality, that it is irreal, puzzling. Everything that was happening in the literary and scientific life of the USSR invariably carried such a puzzling, otherworld quality, especially after Bulgakov's demise, during the postwar years. Why did Zoščenko's harmless tale about the adventure of an ape evoke apocalyptic consequences — the Ždanov pogrom, the Central Committee's resolution concerning the journals *Zvezda* and *Leningrad*? It is impossible to logically comprehend these facts. Why were Zoščenko's humor and Axmatova's tragic lyric poetry put together in one resolution? Why did Šostakovič's opera *Katerina Izmajlova* suddenly turn out to be an object of political persecution, while several years later the music of that very composer was proclaimed as the zenith of classical music? Why did the long recognized theorist of literature, mythology, and folklore, Academician Aleksandr Veselovskij, who died in 1906, suddenly become an enemy of the Soviet regime? How did it happen that the party leadership, having set out on a campaign against the cosmopolitans that they themselves had dreamed up, developed a sudden blindness and confused the two Veselovskij brothers, attributing to Aleksandr the comparativist methodology of the younger brother Aleksej, author of the book *Zapadnoe vlijanie v russkoj literature* (1883)? Who suddenly found it necessary to reinterpret the novel of the Soviet poet Boris Pasternak in a counterrevolutionary spirit and set against its author the collective farmers, metal workers, auto mechanics, village teachers, and writers, who had not even laid eyes on this novel and yet were furious at the "traitor Pasternak"? Why was Academician Marr at first proclaimed the single coryphaeus of Marxist linguistics, and then, later, its own violent subverter? Why did the secret police at first put the opponents of Marr into camps, and then, later, his supporters? Why? . . . Why? . . . *One hundred thousand why's,* the title of a children's book, could be applied to the Soviet irreal reality in its entirety. Henceforth, for brevity, we will call it "Soviet irreality."

This is the secret of the topicality of *Master i Margarita*; this is why this book became the literary hit of the last decade. We will now discuss this point in greater detail.

Bulgakov's book — in the form of a tragicomic fantasy — shows the reader "the Soviet irreality" of the thirties. Satan and several of his assistants appear in Moscow, sowing panic among the populace through unexpected miracles: they destroy the laws of space and time, physiology and psychology; they are capable of foreseeing the future and even changing it. All these deeds overturn the primitive, materialistic logic, the vulgar rationalism of the Soviet intellectuals. When Mixail Aleksandrovič Berlioz, sitting on a bench in Patriarch's Park, first sees a figure materializing from thin air, the author says about him:

> Berlioz' life was so arranged that he was not accustomed to seeing unusual phenomena. Paling even more, he stared and thought in consternation, 'It can't be!'
> But, alas it was, and the tall, transparent gentleman was swaying from left to right in front of him without touching the ground.
> Berlioz was so overcome with horror that he shut his eyes . . . (12–13)

Berlioz, the first victim of Satan's interference, is the most consistent rationalist among the novel's characters. He is a dialectician, an atheist, an erudite, and, importantly, free of the least doubt in the correctness of his knowledge. But everything is not as simple as he thought. Berlioz, having self-assuredly negated that which "cannot be," would perish under the wheels of a tram; he would slip in a puddle of sunflower seed oil, spilled by Annuška. This was preordained for him, although this "could not be." In an argument with a pseudo-foreigner, that is, with the devil, Berlioz proves to be bereft of individuality. This is perhaps the most important feature of this well-educated literary *činovnik*; he speaks not in his own name, but in the name of some sort of "us": ". . . neither of us believes in God," "we're atheists," "in our country there's nothing surprising about atheism . . . ," ". . . with all respect to you as a scholar, we take a different attitude on that point" (19, 25). Thus, by condemning Berlioz's rationalistic narrowmindedness, Bulgakov condemns the collective world view of Soviet society, of those who do not know how to think independently and, instead, accept something shared by all of "us." But one should not draw conclusions about Bulgakov's religiosity: he does not maintain any belief whatsoever; he only disaffirms the self-assurance of vulgar all-knowingness. The position that "something cannot be" is fatuous because everything, even Satan, is possible. Rationalists of the Soviet school have learned to explain everything in terms of the simplest cause-effect relationships. Thus, the investigator puts forth sensible explanations for obviously irrational occurrences: ". . . and the detective was convinced that Berlioz had thrown himself (or had fallen) beneath the car while under hypnosis" (425). It is easy to explain any incredibility in this way; but miracles still do occur: in Moscow the devils are the masters.

But even such irrational circumstances are, it would seem, real — that is to say "real devilry." It was also subjected to censorial terror for it is linked with the NKVD. This Soviet-police reality first appears, strangely enough, in the ancient Judean episode, when the procurator, having questioned Yeshua, speaks to the centurion in Latin: "This criminal calls me 'good man.' Take him away for a minute and show him the proper way to address me. But do not mutilate him" (29).

Anyone who imagines the speech pattern of an NKVD investigator will recognize these phrases. And further along in the interrogation of Pontius Pilate everything is *familiar*: for example, the background questions he asks, and even the attempts to save the accused: "Listen, Ha-Notsri, the Procurator said, looking at Yeshua somehow strangely: the face of the Procurator was terrifying, but his eyes betrayed anxiety. 'Have you ever said anything about great Caesar? Answer! Did you ever say anything of the sort? Or did you not? . . .'"

Such cases, although rare, have occurred from time to time, where the investigator has tried, even partially, to aid the alleged criminal and remove from him at least the charge of slander against the leader, against "the great Caesar." The entire interrogation and even Pilate's inner monologue, thinking about himself as follows, is in this familiar vein: "the hegemon had examined the case of the vagrant philosopher Yeshua, surnamed Ha-Notsri, and could not substantiate the criminal charge made against him. In particular he could not find the slightest connection between Yeshua's actions and the recent disorders in Jerusalem. The vagrant philosopher was mentally ill, as a result of which the sentence of death pronounced on Ha-Notsri by the Lesser Senhedrin would not be confirmed" (38–39).

If, in this text, we replace *Yeshua Ha-Notsri* and the *wandering philosopher* with Russian names, *Jerusalem* with Moscow or Kiev, *procurator* with investigator, *Lesser Senhedrin* with Special Deliberation, the text will be directly relevant to the Soviet reality of the thirties — its stylistic characteristic is apparent. Sometimes Bulgakov stylizes somewhat in imitation of the Bible. The procurator concludes a fully Soviet interrogation, which has turned into a philosophical dialogue, with a stylized remark, also Soviet in spirit but switched to another tonality: "Do you imagine, you miserable creature, that a

Roman Procurator could release a man who has said what you have said to me? Oh gods, oh gods! Or do you think I'm prepared to take your place? I don't believe in your ideas! And listen to me: if from this moment onward you say so much as a word or try to talk to anybody, beware! I repeat — beware! " (43).

The circumspection of the speech, the pathos of the repetitions, exclamations of the type "O gods! gods!," the reference "miserable" — all this is a stylized put-on, under which is visible the shrewd, two-faced Soviet investigator. The duality of the style reflects the duality of the subject. However, the style-base, which is subject, on the one hand, to recognition by the reader, and, on the other, to concealment from the leadership, is indubitable. In some sections of the narrative, it comes to the surface, as, for example, in Pilate's conversation with the High Priest, where Pilate tries to change the decision of the spiritual authority and have Var-Ravvan instead of Ha-Notsri executed: "In view of all these facts, the Procurator requested the High Priest to reconsider his decision and to discharge the least dangerous of the two convicts and that one was undoubtedly Ha-Notsri . . . " (46). In other places, the biblical stylization overwhelms the text. But the duality is always present. And it is also indicated in the names which have been changed but are still recognizable; for example, Yeshua Ha-Notsri instead of Jesus of Nazareth, Eršalaim instead of Jerusalem, Va-Ravvan instead of Varrava (=Barabas), Iuda iz Kiriafa instead of Judas Iscariot. Bulgakov's names are phonetically closer to the Hebrew names than those in the Graecized Gospels; but their function is to sound "displaced" and seem like words not from religious usage but from a historical treatise. *Jerusalem* is discernible behind *Eršalaim,* and *Moscow* behind *Jerusalem.*

Soviet phraseology is otherwise presented through the direct speech of the devils, who represent different variants of it. The most interesting among them is the cat Begemont, who personifies the boorish bureaucrat, the militant citizen, and the supervisor who inspires trepidation — all this in one individual. The cat is "the size of a pig, black as soot and with luxuriant cavalry officer's whiskers" (65). This is how the cat speaks: Having responded (this was already mentioned above) to Poplavskij, Berlioz' uncle from Kiev, that it was he who had given the telegram, and having added: "'. . . what else?'" the cat drily continues, 'I, it would seem, am asking in good Russian, what else?' But Poplavskij didn't give any answer. 'Passport!' bellowed the cat and stretched out a bloated paw . . . 'Which department issued the document?' the cat asked, staring at the page. There was no answer. 'Department 412,' the cat answered his own question, pointing his paw across the passport which he held up with his feet. 'Well, of course, I know that department. There they issue passports to anybody. While I, for example, wouldn't have issued one to someone like you! . . .' The cat got so mad that he threw the passport to the floor. 'Your presence at the funeral is cancelled,' continued the cat in an official voice. 'Try to go to your place of residence'."

Each intonational nuance is authentic: from the boorish-bureaucratic tone of "I, it would seem, am asking in good Russian" to the word "document," to the impersonal "is cancelled," the seemingly courteous paraphrase "try to go" and the bureaucratically lifeless "place of residence." The cat's line of speech is continued when he, playing chess with Voland, using live figures, is forced to surrender to a devil who is stronger than he: "I give up," he says, "but I give up only because I cannot play in an atmosphere of persecution on the part of envious people" (327). This episode with living chess figures is symbolic, and the cat Begemont or, rather, the cat Bureaucrat is especially funny and terrifying here. Finally, the cat fulfills his bureaucratic function when Nikolaj Ivanovič asks him for a document certifying where he spent the night: "'What for?' asked the cat sternly. 'To show my wife and *to the police,*' said Nikolai Ivanovich firmly [the italicized items were deleted by the censors, E. E.]. 'We don't usually give certificates,' replied the cat frowning, 'but since it's for you we'll make an exception.' Before Nikolai Ivanovich knew what was happening, the naked Hella was sitting beside a typewriter and the cat was dictating to her: '"This is to certify that the bearer, Nikolai Ivanovich, spent the night in question at Satan's Ball, having been enticed there in a vehicular capacity." Hella, put in brackets after that "[pig]." "Signed — Begemont."' 'What about the date?' squeaked Nikolai Ivanovich. 'We don't mention the date, the document becomes invalid if it's dated,' replied the cat, waving the piece of paper. Then the animal produced a rubber stamp, breathed on it in the approved fashion, stamped 'Paid' on the paper and handed the document to Nikolai Ivanovich. He vanished without a trace . . . " (368–69).

Here, phantasmagoria is combined with the most "everyday" reality of the Soviet establishment. Bulgakov's conjuring lies in this: It would seem that the devilry should contrast with more than the usual, trivial bureaucratic life; however, the narrative is so constructed that the absurdity of this life naturally gives rise to devilry, for the absurd in and of itself is phantasmagoric. If Gogol's Nose could run a department, for Bulgakov an empty, headless suit fills the absurd functions of a bureaucrat. Stepan Lixodeev sees the sealing-wax seal on Berlioz's door and immediately surmises that "Berlioz has done something," but what? He recalls some article, some "slightly equivocal conversation which had taken place, as far as he could remember, on April 24 here in the dining room when Stepa and Berlioz had been having supper together. Of course their talk had not really been shady (Stepa would not have joined in any such conversation), but it had been on a rather unnecessary subject. They could easily have avoided having had it altogether. Before the appearance of this seal the conversation would undoubtedly have been dismissed as utterly trivial, but since the seal . . . " (104). Thus, from day-to-day activities devilry grows: a sealing-wax seal, a suspicious conversation on an irrelevant subject, an unexpressed thought about treason, and the arrest of an interlocutor. Given the conditions of devilry, the path from any conversation to a sealing-wax seal appears quite natural. And if they can arrest you for any conversation, then even "a most robust black cat" can appear in a mirror and also just as suddenly disappear, and then reappear "a glass of vodka in one paw and a fork, on which he had just speared a pickled mushroom, in the other."

Chapter 9 of part I, "Koroviev's tricks," is characteristic in this sense. Its hero is Nikanor Ivanovič Bosoj, "chairman of the tenants' association of No. 302A Sadovaya Street, Moscow, where the late Berlioz had lived" (120), for whose dwelling space there appeared a multitude of claimants — in two hours thirty-two applications were made. Up to this point, everything is within the limits of reality; however, the excitement surrounding the vacated dwelling space acquires the character of a nightmare. Devilry begins to arise in the stack of applications: "Among them was a description, shattering in its literary power, of the theft of some meatballs from someone's jacket pocket in apartment No. 31, two threats of suicide and one confession of secret pregnancy" (121). N. I. Bosoj takes a standard folding ruler, climbs up to apartment No. 50 to measure it and there he meets Korov'ev, who, upon being asked whether he is an official of some sort, lapses into disgusting verbosity, foretelling some sort of chicanery: "'Ah, Nikanor Ivanovich! . . . Who is official and who is unofficial these days? It all depends on your point of view. It's all so vague and changeable, Nikanor Ivanovich. Today I'm unofficial, tomorrow — presto! I'm official! Or maybe vice versa — who knows?'"(122). Korov'ev wants to rent the vacated apartment for Voland who is on tour in Moscow, but Bosoj cannot make up his mind — "foreigners were normally supposed to stay at the Metropole . . . "(124), and he "insisted on clearing the matter with the Tourist Bureau" (125). To this, Korov'ev replies: "Of course! . . . It must be done properly. There's the telephone, Nikanor Ivanovich, ring them up right away!" And suddenly everything is favorably resolved — the Intourist bureau immediately agrees. Nikanor Ivanovič receives the money for the rent and also a bribe, about which Bosoj subsequently claimed something amazing: "the package jumped into his briefcase of its own accord" (127). Subsequently, the following events occurred: information against Bosoj ($400 in the lavatory!) was phoned in, a search, the mysterious disappearance of the contract from the briefcase, arrest, the gloating of the residents.

Devilry? Of course. But the phantasmagoric squabbles surrounding dwelling space, the omnipotence of bribes, the grovelling before foreigners — all are real facts from which devilry grows. Four decades after Bulgakov, Vladimir Vojnovič wrote *Ivan'kiada,* a documentary story in which there are no devils or witches, and in which reality is no less irreal than in Bulgakov's novel. The readers of *Ivan'kiada* perceive the satirical chapters of *Master i Margarita* as fully contemporary.

Moreover, over the years the irreality of Soviet reality has even grown. In the book *Zapiski nezagovorščika* I related a story, similar to Kafka's novel, concerning the fate of a single phrase. Bulgakov apparently had not read Kafka, but his perception of Soviet everyday life exposes the absurdity which is its major characteristic. The absurdity is growing, devilry also. Mixail Bulgakov, a writer of the thirties, was born as the author of *Master i Margarita* at the end of the sixties and became one of the most popular Soviet authors in the world during the seventies. The amazing characteristic of his prophetic novel has turned out to be not the lessening but the growth of its timeliness.

NOTES

1. 'Their circle was adorned by a young maiden — / Her body was seething in silk, / She held a cup in her left hand, / In her right hand a piece of ham, / And next to her, / Red because of the sunset, / A hornplayer was playing in the moist dark, / He was big and beautiful, / But his eyes / Were missing . . .'

2. 'I give this to you, instead of roses for your grave; / Instead of incense smoking; / You lived so sternly and were carrying to the end / A magnificent contempt . . .'

3. Pages references are from the Posev edition, Frankfurt/M, 1974. The italicized words were removed from the journal text. In some passages, the English translation by Michael Glenny (New York: Harper and Row, 1967) has been consulted.

Aleksandar Flaker

SALINGER'S MODEL IN EAST EUROPEAN PROSE

Since my book on jeans-prose[1] discusses in greater detail Salinger's novel *The Catcher in the Rye* as a paradigm of certain phenomena in Central and East European prose that can be related to the paradigmatic structure of the American novel, in this paper I will deal in particular only with some features of Salinger's work that are also found in the works of Central and East European authors. I would like to stress at the very beginning that the division into "West," "Central" or "East European" prose is today rather arbitrary, and indeed these terms are adopted more for pragmatic reasons than for any methodological beliefs they might imply. Moreover, the author of both the book and the paper must apologize that the borders of the phenomena observed by his linguistic knowledge are necesssarily limited to Slavic literatures and the German literature in the GDR. The author of a Hungarian review of my book on jeans-prose has already remarked:

> In any event: the author draws an unbroken mountain-range onto the map of today's history of world literature — especially East and Central European — a map which so far has been sketched just in rough outline. What we particularly miss in this book is exactly the Hungarian literature . . .
> Nevertheless, this book helps us to better understand some features and currents in our younger literature. After we have read this book the works of such authors as István Csörsz, István Császár, György Asperján, Miklós Munkácsi, Péter Dobai — and I could certainly continue this listing — take on for us a world-wide perspective and fall within a new sequence of phenomena.[2]

Miklós Szabolcsi, a prominent Hungarian comparativist, wonders whether this prose type was created in Hungary under the influence of Salinger or Oleša, or "as an answer to the challenge of identical or similar socio-historical circumstances."[3] The first part of the question is, of course, classical in the comparative study of literature, whereas the second part of it, towards which this Hungarian scholar is obviously more inclined, reflects sociological determinism. Nevertheless, we do not intend to answer these questions here. They cut too deeply into basic methodological questions of literary scholarship in general to be subjected to precipitous consideration. However, at the very beginning it should be pointed out that, according to our research, in the geographic area which we have conditionally set up, jeans-prose is directly influenced by Salinger's novel only in some of its features. In most of the cases the direct "influence" of Salinger could not be ascertained, and in some cases even the authors themselves cite other writers as their models: to mention but the names of Alan Sillitoe, Jack Kerouac, or from the francophone area those of Françoise Sagan (*Bonjour, tristesse*) and Raymond Queneau (*Zazie dans le metro*). Let us also mention that Croatian authors also claim Gertrude Stein's experiences to be their model. As for direct contact with Salinger, two names can be unquestionably cited: those of the Russian Aksënov and the German Plenzdorf. Aksënov on several occasions mentions Salinger among the writers who influenced him (Salinger's novel was translated into Russian in 1960). Plenzdorf built the structure of his text (first conceived as a screenplay, later transformed into a theater-play, and ending up as a novel *Die neuen Leiden des jungen W.* [*New Sorrows of Young W.*], 1972) on the relationship of the existent literary works: Goethe's *Werther* and Salinger's *The Catcher in the Rye*. Plenzdorf's mention of Defoe's *Robinson Crusoe* in this text is not accidental either.

The degree to which the presence of Salinger's novel was felt as it circulated some time ago in Central and Eastern Europe is testified to by a voice in the discussion going on in Czechoslovakia in the sixties, which are marked (at least for that country) by a process of significant opening in the literary domain:

> In the field of human relationships, in ethics, in psychology we people have a surprising amount of things in common. This is also reflected in books. As an example I would like to cite one such praise-worthy book, J. D. Salinger's *The Catcher in the Rye*. In it Salinger was successful in a rare, kingly creation of a character. His Holden Caulfield has brothers all over the world, and certainly has them even in Czechoslovakia. The author lives in America, is philosophically inclined towards Buddhism, and, in addition, has devised a character that expresses a part of us all — if we are not yet tired and sclerotic. Yet Holden Caulfield primarily represents our sixteen-year olds, that is to say, the youth that live thousands of kilometers east of him in an entirely different social setting.
>
> Here too there exist Holden Caulfield clubs which neither a school inspector nor an organ of public security could detect, simply because their members haven't even heard of the book. There are Holdens without being conscious of their own existence. To conclude, Holden is a state of mind, Holden is a type of sensibility, Holden is the negation of an adult world.[4]

I think we should give credit to Jaroslava Blažková for perceiving certain conditions needed to create the model of jeans-prose. We should also realize that her statement contains the answer to the question why in our consciousness this model centers around Salinger's novel as its paradigm. For we are dealing here primarily with that type of a young narrator, also spread in the literature of the fifties and sixties within European literatures, which has essentially determined the model we have named jeans-prose. In such prose it is this young narrator (regardless of whether he appears in the first or third person) who builds a style of his own, based on the spoken language of urban youth (frequently infused with elements of slang), and who denies traditional and existent social and cultural structures.

This prose model is defined by a basic opposition non-adult: adult which for its part is further divided into the following components: individual (Salinger's case) or more frequently a loosely connected, i.e. unstructured, group of young people who are opposed to the institutions (family, educational apparatus, cultural institutions, firmly established vocations, and, more rarely, even the police); then, a very typical opposition whose poles are represented on one side by the culture of the young, mainly based on mass media and the style of clothing (here jeans, of course, symbolize the culture), and on the other by the "museum" culture of adults with its canonized art and literature. Yet, the most obvious basic opposition for this type of prose is the one between the two types of languages, as is, for example, clearly expressed and made blatant in the structure of both Plenzdorf's text and the Croatian novel by Slamnig *Bolja polovica hrabrosti (The Better Half of Courage)*, 1972. It is important to stress that the opposition between the two kinds of *languages* used is the very criterion which renders this prose type distinct from that of the 19th-century model of "fathers and sons." Thus, in jeans-prose only the world of the young is present, whereas the second member of the opposition, in other words the adult world is either implied, together with its representative characters (for example we do not get acquainted with Holden's parents), or appears just marginally. This is the reason why conflict within the plot is rarely encountered. Consequently, we should not ascribe to such a prose type generation conflicts as its constituent elements nor should we seek in it anything that indicates social differences. The conflict between adolescents and adults arises mainly on the level of culture (of course, in the broadest sense of the word) as a conflict of outsiders or representatives of the margin of society (particularly the characteristic hooligans in the Polish variant of jeans-prose) with a firmly structured society which however does not imply any more prominent social antagonisms. This lack of plot conflict is related to the significant motives of escapism from the structured world: Holden quits school, but hesitates to return to his parents. As a result the plots in this prose type are very often based on journeys (from Salinger's and Holden's wandering through New York all the way to Rolf Schneider's *Reise nach Jaroslaw* [*Journey to Jaroslaw*], 1974), with pronounced spatial escapism — fleeing from parents — and on the contrast between two types of cultures (Polish and German, thus bringing the opposition onto the national plane).

Since the opposition non-adult : adult is in this prose type transferred into the sphere of culture, taken in its broadest sense, the basic type of narrator appears in front of the reader as an immature intellectual, a pupil (from Salinger's Holden and Aksënov's novel *Zvëzdnyj bilet* [*Ticket to the Stars*], 1961, to the girl narrator from *Beleške jedne Ane* [*Notes of a Girl Called Anna*], 1973, by the Serbian writer Momo Kapor, and to Gittie from Schneider's novel), or a student (Aksënov, *Kollegi* [*Colleagues*], 1960, Slamnig, *Bolja polovica hrabrosti*). Such a young person, standing at life's crossroads, has to finish school or university studies and choose his own way in life accordingly. The narrator or protagonist in jeans-prose neither has a broad education nor encyclopaedic knowledge, yet can, as a rule, develop his ironic attitude towards the traditional kind of Erziehungsroman or Bildungsroman, towards "all that David Copperfield kind of crap" (J. D. Salinger, *The Catcher in the Rye*, Boston [36] 1972, p. 1), towards Goethe's *Werther* (Plenzdorf), towards canonized national tradition in general (cf. also the attitude of Croatian prose-writers toward "folklore" epics or the attitude of Slamnig's Flaks towards the language used in 19th-century Croatian literature, or else the mocking tone of Aksënov's narrators towards Russian realistic painting, and so forth). At the same time such a narrator is ready to display his loyalty for a certain type of literature, ranging from Fitzgerald's *Great Gatsby*, which appears in Salinger's novel, to Salinger's *The Catcher in the Rye* featuring in Plenzdorf's text or to Hemingway's *For Whom the Bell Tolls* which is incessantly mentioned by Schneider's Gittie. What is even more stressed in this prose type is the adherence to the cultural community of youth created by present-day mass media which, at least in the area of subculture, have abolished state and national borders. Thus, in jeans-prose we can find the whole range of singers, performers and composers of pop, from Louis Armstrong and Ella Fitzgerald to Jimmy Hendrix and Frank Zappa, or else film stars and directors, from Gary Cooper and Fellini to Marlon Brando and, of course, the personality unavoidable for this type of prose: James Dean.

A very typical stylistic technique in jeans-prose concerns the narrator's language, which tends towards the infantile. This feature is also found already in Salinger's paradigmatic novel. The major part of Slamnig's prose works, especially those fragments dealing with the narrator's childhood, is characterized by this feature. Childish naiveté is brought into contrast with the "inanities" of adults, i.e. with the world which Salinger's Holden would call "phony." At least two very popular books of contemporary Serbian prose are based on this infantile style and view of the world. One of them is the "novel" by Bora Ćosić *Uloga moje porodice u svjetskoj revoluciji* (*The Role of My Family in World Revolution*), 1969, in which by imitating the style of childish diary entrances he brings about a rather special dehierarchization of events, objects and characters that pertain to the historically decisive time of the Second World War and the liberation of Belgrade. The second book is Kapor's *Beleške jedne Ane* which, via the mind of a "girl in jeans" and by means of a style that comes close to that of school compositions (one of Anna's "school compositions" appears in the book, just as Holden's "Essay on Egyptians" does in Salinger's work), dehierarchizes and shifts the social reality of contemporary Belgrade, ridicules the mythologization of phenomena, and laughs at the contemporary "socialist-type establishment" and its consumerism which is felt as much in the tendency to accumulate material goods as in the cultural sphere. Both of these Serbian books show a tendency, present in this prose and already noticeable in Salinger's novel, to use narration reminiscent of *causerie,* i.e. to emulate the adolescent type of oral narration which somehow breaks the logical succession of phenomena in time, and limits the space to a narrow urban environment.

The tendency towards oral type narration in some works of jeans-prose can be attributed to a fundamental situation in the narrator-author relationship. Therefore, it is not by chance that besides Holden as a narrator the writer also figures on the pages of Salinger's novel in order to listen to the story told (of course, orally) by the young narrator:

> I'll just tell you about this madman stuff that happened to me around last Christmas just before I got pretty run-down and had to come out here and take it easy. I mean that's all I told D. B. about and he's my brother and all. . . He used to be a regular writer, when he was home (p.1).

This narrator-author relationship motivates the style of Kapor's feuilletonistic prose from the very beginning (*Beleške jedne Ane* first appeared as feuilleton in a Belgrade magazine):

> You're really cute! In fact, I like you because you know how to listen to people. I mean, you look straight into a man's eyes and you sort of really listen to him. The others are mainly preoccupied by themselves. Am I bugging you? You know, tonight is my night for babbling. It's just that I feel that something like a flood of words is flowing out of me . . . (M. Kapor, *Beleške jedne Ane,* Beograd 1973, pp. 5–6).

The imitation of oral-type narration is in jeans-prose most frequently attained by the well-known device of syntactic parceling which should evoke the spontaneity of such narration.[5] Such chopping up of the sentence syntax is already found in Salinger's novel, and also in the early prose of the Croatian author Šoljan (as early as the nineteen-fifties), as well as with Aksënov, and, it goes without saying, with Plenzdorf. Therefore, if the prose of those authors were translated into one language, their uniform style would be made obvious, even if they belong to different national literatures and periods of time.

The spontaneous oral narration, as a starting point in the stylistic of jeans-prose, presupposes a listener whom the narrator addresses in order to maintain necessary contact. This allows for the use of frequent spoken-language clichés which are particularly typical of the English (and especially American) spoken language and to which Salinger resorts in shaping the narration of his Holden. Thus, already on the first pages of his novel we meet colloquial clichés like:

> If you really want to hear about it. . . If you want to know the truth. . . I'm not saying that. . . I'm not going to tell you. . . I'll just tell you. . . You probably heard of it. . . (pp. 1–2).

Another, even more characteristic feature of jeans-prose is the presence of implicatives, i.e. the expressions of broad but unspecified semantic scope, which originate in the spoken language. The person addressed knows to what these expressions refer and what contact is implied. To the mannerisms of Holden's narration belong such implicatives as:

and all, and all that kind, anything like that, this stuff. . . (pp. 1-2)

Expressions of the "all that" type are present also in non-English jeans-prose literature. Thus, the equivalents to Salinger's colloquial implicatives can be found in Šoljan's early prose, which abounds in expressions such as *sve to* 'all that,' *takve stvari* 'such things,' and also in the prose of the Serbian author Grozdana Olujić (in her novel *Glasam za ljubav* [*I Vote for Love*], 1963) who often speaks about *te stvari* 'those things,' or else uses implicatives of the type *nešto mi se nije išlo* 'somehow I didn't feel like going,' or *nešto kao pitanje* 'sort of a question,' which belong to the type of Salinger's "sort of." There is no doubt that Salinger has directly influenced the colloquial utterances of Plenzdorf's Wibeau whose style incorporates a multitude of German equivalents of Salinger's English colloquial implicatives, such as *oder so* 'or so,' *oder wer* 'or somebody,' *oder was* 'or something,' *und all das* 'and all that,' and others. A comparative stylistic study would certainly show to what extent this prose has adopted English syntactic and phrasal elements which are in any case typical of the jargon of the young in the whole of Europe. These common syntactic and phrasal elements have developed as a solidarity symbol to the subculture whose main manifestation are blue jeans — again, of American origin. Such a study could, for example, establish the degree to which the Slovenian author Rudi Šeligo in his short story *Šarada* (*Charade*) (from the collection *Poganstvo* [*Heathenism*], 1973) imitates, if anything, just the English colloquial language when he ascribes to his narrator Gretta the frequent use of the adjective *ušiv* 'lousy' (*ušivo življenje* 'lousy living,' *ušivo sonce* 'lousy sun' and others), which might be influenced by the English expression "lousy" (also frequent in Salinger), and how much his language has been directly influenced by Salinger when Gretta labels all "inanities" that surround her by the same adjective *trapast,* which would echo Salinger's "phoney."

However, the orientation towards the use of the spoken language of urban youth and towards the stylization of its slang is by no means caused by a wish on the part of the jeans-prose authors to stress their "pro-Western" or even "pro-American" orientation. This inclination stems from its own, so to say, inherent demands. Thus, in discussing contemporary Polish prose and referring to Salinger's paradigm, a Polish critic wrote in 1973:

> What matters most in Salinger is language. It is satiated with slang, which by its syntax, lexicon and phonetics makes manifest its distance from standard language, that of school and of official culture. The utmost colloquial style of the language should guarantee its "authenticity," shield it from the "hypocrisy" of such literature which hovers in its bookish skies entirely detached from anything that exists in its "full reality". . . The use of slang is a gesture of scorn towards the established hierarchy of values, an act of

disparage directed against society, and, at the same time, the proof of one's own rebellion, and the affirmation of the individual, the independent and the different. It represents the rejection of any mask in the name of truth. The social function of the writer as someone who contributes to strengthening harmony and order, such as are grafted into human brains by school and educational systems, is thus totally brought into doubt.[6]

It goes without saying that authors' use of urban youth speech has, in different social settings and literatures of different traditions, resulted in a range of varieties. Thus, the Croatian authors Slamnig and Šoljan use, in a moderate degree, the elements of the substandard syntex of oral speech accompanied by certain lexical signals and English syntactic constructions. Aksënov, for his part, stylizes to a higher degree the jargon of the Russian student community, making use of characteristic idioms and phrases, whereas Plenzdorf directly imitates Salinger's paradigm. As for the variety of Momo Kapor's language, it consists in the condensation of jargon-type stylemes. Another variety is based on mannerisms of direct narration moulded into the urban hooligan slang which comes, for example, from Warsaw cobblestone streets with the Pole Marek Nowakowski, or from the Zagreb street-life with the Croatian authors Majetić (*Čangi off Gotoff,* 1970; the first edition of the novel, entitled *Čangi,* was confiscated in 1963) and Majdak (*Kužiš, stari moj* [*You Dig, Buddy*], 1973, with the pronounced stylizing of the Zagreb kajkavian urban dialect).

In different social settings also different degrees of opposition have been provoked against this prose type because it disturbed the "established hierarchy of values." The opposition was raised in the name of the defense of literary language "purity," as, for example, in Soviet literature where the critics rejected Aksënov's "mannerism" in his stylizing of student slang. As another motive appears the claim that the "hero" of jeans-prose is not representative enough since he is regularly shaped outside the "working process." (Thus, for example, a Ukranian critic has counted that twelve out of sixteen heroes figuring in the short stories published in the magazine *Vitčyzna* [*Fatherland*] "don't do anything for a living"[7]).

At the time when this opposition started to fade away and when the linguistic purism was overcome, there regularly arose sexual puritanism, which so far has not been eliminated, we can say, from most of the area of Central and Eastern Europe (in this respect literature in the GDR and Poland is more "libertine" than in the USSR). However, in the literature of, for example, Yugoslavia, a successful campaign was led against sexual puritanism, and in that regard a major service was also rendered by the translations of Henry Miller's novels. It is in connection with the translation of Miller's *Tropic of Cancer* that the Croatian author of jeans-prose Antun Šoljan advocated the rendering of English four-letter words into Croatian by their numerous Croatian equivalents:

And those who consider this question to be trivial, should remember that behind the hypocritical mask of the guardians of purity many other taboos, less naive, less obvious, and consequently more dangerous are hidden. Let them remember that there where things cannot be called by their names, the clear light of truth cannot shine.[8]

Šoljan published his feuilleton entitled *Petoslovnica. U traženju izgubljenih riječi* (*Five-Letter Word. In Search of Words Lost*) in 1966. Only three years before, it was still possible for the Public Prosecutor (in Yugoslavia there exists no preventive censorship) to bring legal action against Majetić's novel on account of "pornography." Only four years after Šoljan's feuilleton, Majetić's novel was published, not only in its full resonance but also supplemented by a section in which its hooligan protagonist has a discussion with a prison guard, and where even the report from the court trial of its author is interpolated.

Much less opposition was incited by the insistence on the jeans-prose narrator or protagonist's conforming to contemporary civilization — in fact by the emphasis upon "youth" cosmopolitanism. Here also lexical anglicisms, abounding in the spoken language of the young, very often signal such conformity. As an example, we can cite Slamnig's novel *Bolja polovica hrabrosti* where the narrator's language is characterized mainly by anglicisms in order to contrast with the language used by the older Croatian generation in which germanisms appear too often. Present-day anglicisms also appear in profusion with Plenzdorf, now mainly pertaining to mass culture notions (*Kinofan,* "movie fan," *Show, Happening* and so on). As signals of participation in the cosmopolitan community of the young items of clothing also have their place in jeans-prose. Thus Aksënov characterizes his Georgian youth from the Black Sea coast in this way:

> Without wiping himself — there wasn't even a trace of a towel — he would put on worn-out jeans produced in Tbilisi, tie around his neck a scarf given as a gift from some German girl, get his feet into the sandals and leave for the kitchen.

or

> He had on, that evening, an Italian nylon shirt, Polish trousers and a pair of shoes from West Germany which were sent from Moscow by his cousin — to put it briefly, he was in full regalia (*Mestnyj Xuligan Abramašvili* [*Local Hooligan Abramašvili*], 1964, a short story appearing in the collection *Žal', čto vas ne bylo s nami* [*It's a Pity You Were Not With Us*] Moscow 1969, pp. 218, 227).

Nevertheless, jeans-prose has never developed structures suited to take on socio-analytic functions. Its protagonists are regularly shaped as outsiders, "traitors" (that happens to be the title of Šoljan's novel from 1961), fugitives from school or family, bohemians or hooligans, eternal travellers unwilling to change either world or society but, instead, search for themselves or for their temporary "gangs," through evasion, a new Arcadia lying outside social structures: in holiday landscapes (Šoljan, Aksënov), in communion with nature (the Pole Stachura) or in secluded sheds somewhere within big cities where they can sing their jeans-solidarity songs (Plenzdorf). Such characters of "transit passengers" (Šoljan) are not, naturally, capable of bearing, centered around them, the structure of a complete socio-analytic novel. As a result, this kind of prose has predominantly catered to the short story type of literary forms which tend towards cyclization (Šoljan's *Izdajice* [*Traitors*]), sometimes approaching the style of the newspaper feuilleton (Kapor), whereas the inclination towards the spoken language brings this prose closer to dramatic forms (Plenzdorf's text was first conceived as a screenplay and met with success in its theater production; Majdak's novel *Kužiš, stari moj* was put on stage in Zagreb, and a film was also made based on it). Therefore, we can hardly speak about the jeans-novel, existing as a distinct literary form, not even in the sense of Salinger's paradigm, except when it is built upon the traditional type of novel dealing with "reeducation" and socialization of youth (Aksënov's novel *Kollegi*; *Zvëzdnyj bilet*; the first version of Majetić's novel *Čangi*). The title of Šoljan's longer story *Kratki izlet* (*Short Excursion*), 1965, in which the author already moves away from the model of jeans-prose, perhaps best characterizes the forms of this prose type. In its clearest cases, it is mainly a short-winded prose, based more upon linguistic artifice than upon the contrast of its characters, more upon the negation of social structures coming from the margin of society than upon their analysis, more upon ironic attitude towards social and cultural values than upon the offering of new values. Yet, in spite of all, jeans-prose carried within itself certain messages for the world. One should be deft to detect them in it. On the level of utterances they read:

> We look clear into the matter. We'll clean these words. Now, this is the most important: to fight for the purity of one's own words, one's own eyes and soul. And out to track down the old junk (V. Aksënov, *Kollegi, Žal', čto vas ne bylo s nami,* p. 17).

> Neither time, nor events, nor cannons, nor words, nothing could change the last survivors of our tribe — our tribe multiplies, proudly, invincibly, freely. We are still around. We could still gather once, knowing of each other, though we live scattered on distant points of this globe. Nothing is yet lost forever (A. Šoljan, *Izdajice,* Zagreb 1961, p. 153).

> By that I mean to say that jeans are a frame of mind and not a pair of trousers (U. Plenzdorf, *Die neuen Leiden des jungen W.,* Frankfurt a/M, 1973, p. 27).

NOTES

1. *Modelle der Jeans Prosa,* Scriptor, Kronberg/Ts. 1975; *Proza u trapericama,* Liber, Zagreb 1976.
2. M. Szabolcsi, "Próza — farmerban," *Nagyvilág,* 1977, 10, p. 1563.
3. *Ibid.,* p. 1564.
4. Jaroslava Blažková, "Literatura a Holdenové světa," *Souvislosti a perspektivy prózy,* Československý spisovatel, Praha 1963, pp. 78–79.
5. On syntactic parceling in the "young" Russian prose, cf. K. Koževnikova, *Spontannaja ustnaja reč' v epičeskoj proze (na materiale sovremennoj russkoj xudožestvennoj literatury),* Praha 1970.
6. J. Prokop, "Miłość do desygnatów," *Teksty* 6, 1973, pp. 36–39.
7. V. Faščenko, "Novela z napivfabrykativ," *Vitčyzna* 1971, 10, p. 141.
8. A. Šoljan, *Zanovijetanje iz zamke,* Zagreb 1972, p. 220.

George Gibian

FORWARD MOVEMENT THROUGH BACKWARD GLANCES:
SOVIET RUSSIAN AND CZECH FICTION
(HRABAL, SYOMIN, GRANIN)

Nothing is supposed to be new under the sun; and "Plus ça change, plus c'est la même chose." If these two old sayings are true, how is an artist ever to create something original? Is it really impossible to be an innovator, or just very difficult?

The question of literary influence was considered banished — as vulgar and fallacious in its presuppositions — for a couple of decades, in the dominant, sophisticated academic circles in the United States. It has now, after this extreme and obviously untenable ostracism, returned to us again. In the many books of Harold Bloom, for instance, sometimes so obscure as to be unintelligible, always complex and provocative, the problems of literary influence and heritage, and of the relationship between literary fathers and sons, and grandparents and grandchildren, are among the chief concerns.

These reflections are relevant to the Soviet and East European literary scene today. Certain basic features remain the same, in the last decade, as they have been for twenty years before that; others have changed considerably. The intense hopes for radical liberalization which arose after Stalin's death (from about 1954 to 1956) have now given way to resigned acceptance of either a stable, or at best a very slowly and unevenly improving cultural situation. This may be the chief general fact of all, the *krupny fakt,* which seeps like a gas into all the nooks and crannies of cultural endeavor, and colors the intangible milieu and hence affects what is being written.

Many writers have emigrated or been made to emigrate: this is the second big fact. A few others have been allowed to travel repeatedly to the West and to return, not only the most reliable ones, but also some interesting writers, free souls, such as Aksyonov. Among the results of this greater amount of foreign contact has been far easier access to Western and formerly repressed Russian literary works. Rehabilitated authors — such as Babel, Olesha — are now far more normally accepted dwellers in Russian literary culture.

The third major factor is the ubiquitousness, or at least the broad spread, of dissent, in the sense of radical, strong disaffection with the status quo — any far-reaching criticism of things as they are — expressed or implicit.

Among the various aspects of recent East European literature which deserve being studied, I submit, are the various ways in which writers have been saying something new, or have moved forward in new ways, by returning in some sense to the past. On the level of literary form and convention, they have returned to the past by working within, or alluding to, and noticeably following, or reworking, literary conventions of past periods. Such regressions can under certain circumstances constitute an innovation, a forward movement away from currently dominant literary manner.

On the level of subject matter, the past can be returned to, to suggest three different ways as examples, by the author's going back to recreate historical material or events from his or the characters' childhood or youth (in a way which emphasizes the pastness of the past); or the past itself can become an object of inquiry, with its significance for the present being probed in the literary work; or survivals of the remote past (for example, archaic, premodern ways of behaving, thinking, and talking) can become the focus of literary representation.

The various ways of looking backward, and thereby paradoxically trying to say something new and innovative are, I suggest, one of the distinctive features of Soviet Russian writing in our time. There are new feelings about what in the past is worthy of being dwelled on, and about what the nature of time is.

There is much less of this to be found in Czech literature since 1969; very different circumstances have prevailed there. For purposes of comparison, let us begin, however, by examining the work of one Czech prose writer who stands out by his fascination with certain survivals of the past and in whom we find latent or tacit innovations through going to the past.

Bohumil Hrabal was forty-three years old when his first publication appeared — two sketches issued as a supplement of a bibliophile edition, in 1957. Six more years passed before his next publication took place, in 1963, when he was almost fifty and had been writing for twenty-four years. The numerous works which followed became extremely popular in Czechoslovakia. Then, after 1970, came silence — until September 1976, when *The Haircutting* was published.[1] It had been known through unofficial circulation, along with *I Waited on the King of England,* which, at the time of writing this essay, has not yet been printed anywhere.

Hrabal's works are digressive and exuberant. They praise life, yet show fascination with horrors and absurdities, too. He has literary analogues in the Czech past, but hardly in the present. He reminds one of Jaroslav Hašek and of what the Czechs call *hospodský kec,* a tavern tall tale or joke. He comes out of the tradition of the oral story. He reminds us also of some works by Jakub Deml, and has repeatedly expressed his admiration for him; he included selections from Deml in his anthology of Czech prose, *Hrabal uvádí* (*Hrabal Presents*). He frequently praises five writers — Kafka, Klíma, Weiner, Deml, and Hašek.

His works rely heavily on a flood of language encrusted with metaphors and conceits. His moods vary from the gentle to the exuberant. The general tone is set by a mixture of rhetorical, mostly oral devices: lyrical apostrophes, far-fetched similes, almost baroque conceits. His favorite topics are sensuality of a macabre sort, which includes both instances of shocking grossness and of the goodness of life.

When one reads short passages of Hrabal which embody some of his linguistic flights, one feels one has hold of something essential in Hrabal, whereas a few lines of Kundera, Vaculík, Páral, or Havel do not convey so much of their distinctive quality. Their special voice resides rather in theme or plot, an attitude towards experience, an ordering of parts, one in relation to another, and these qualities emerge only as the reader goes along, out of the long run process of reading. They are macrofeatures; Hrabal's essence is in the subparts, in microfeatures.

Hrabal's favorite subjects include gargantuan feasts, the topsy turvy absurdity of life, and pastoral idylls. As his novel, *I Waited on the King of England,* has it, "the absurd becomes the marvellous." He also values expertise, *élan,* fantasy, imaginativeness, the grotesque, the horrible, and the wildly poetic.

His texts are unlike either English-American or standard Czech literary style. He resembles more Irish story telling — some of Joyce or Donleavy — and the Latin American verbal cataract of a Marquez. In Russia, Leskov in the nineteenth, Zoshchenko in the early twentieth century, and Syomin in the 1960s resemble Hrabal.

Hrabal's folk language, as a Czech critic, Frynta, has pointed out, has a strong dose of absurd confrontations, black humor, destruction of conventional myths, and ignoring of taboos.[2] It is a surrealism of the preliterary stage, composed of urban Czech folklore. Other Czech writers who have stood out since the sixties have looked elsewhere for their innovations; Škvorecký is the least remote from Hrabal, but even he does not venture into Hrabal's domain of fantasy and hyperbole. Hrabal has looked for innovations in folk humor. He constructs his epics out of the verbal skills of ancient folk bards' excess; together with the tavern, oral imagination, and in his plots, he has moved back to episodic, picaresque strings of anecdotes. Such unity as there is comes from the persistent basic features: his admiration for certain qualities of vitality and repeated use of the same stylistic devices.

In an essay in *Domácí úkoly* (*Home Work*), he speaks of non-literary elements in contemporary Czech prose, and praises those characters who speak not only as it is customary to speak in their milieu, but as it gives them pleasure or joy (*radostí, nejen zvykem*). He admires the stalwart people —like Syomin's heroes — who when knocked down, may be counted out, but get up and fight again another time. He says in one essay, "Believe as I do in the parade and craziness of life." Elsewhere he wrote, "Humor is an oscillation between the irrational and the real. . . . I see in our popular humor a model of how to resist the gloom which springs from intellectualism. . . . For me life is a big feast which was given to me as a present" (*Domácí úkoly,* p. 65) and "I should like to transfer into literature that which a happening does: disruptions through accident, dropping out of a part, provocation. I must enjoy myself when I work, and that is the meaning of a happening." (p. 69). Hrabal seeks liberation, or if one may be pardoned for using modish terminology, the carnivalization of life.

The Haircutting is a hymn of praise to a woman of the pre-1918 era, in real life Hrabal's own great aunt. Like most of Hrabal's previous works, *The Haircutting* is full of colorful, wild stories, and it is told in the first person, by the chief character, in rich popular idiom. Hrabal's hyperbolic leanings are also strongly in evidence. The mood of the story, however, is unusually gentle. It has some of the pastel, tender qualities of Božena Němcová's nineteenth-century Czech classic, *Babička* (*Grandmother*), although the differences between the two heroines make such a comparison a paradox.

As the barber cuts her hair, he calls it "This relic of old Austria," and the cutting of it, designated by the quaint, old fashioned term *postřižiny*, is a turning point in the story. The new short hairdo, which the heroine calls the "Josephine Baker one," is "her soul, her portrait" now. A new age has come; she submits. Hrabal probes pre-1914 Bohemia, with its now extinct mores and social distinctions.

The haircutting marks the end of one kind of Anna and the birth of a new one, whose story we are not told. It signals the coming of a new regime, a new style. As Czechoslovakia replaces Austria-Hungary, Hrabal shows, comically, that everything is being shortened. The heroine notices shorter working hours are being discussed, fashions in the tails of dogs are shorter (and she proceeds, with her typical exuberance, to shorten her dog's tail with overly ample bribes of cream rolls from the sugar bakery); and her hair, too, will be shortened. Like so many of the decisions of Hrabal's characters and particularly this heroine, her decision is both absurd yet correct, irrationally arrived at, but brilliantly appropriate. The pattern of which she has become aware is located in disparate categories, yet her leap to the conclusion that it is also time for her hair to be cut is warranted. The extravagance or "length" of the ways of the old Austrian Empire is out; a new moderation is in. She is being moved by a structuralist perceptiveness worthy of a Levi-Strauss, a Barthes, or a Lotman.

It is not to the future life symbolized by short hair, but to the rendering of that period to which her long flowing hair was appropriate, that the story is devoted. It is in the historical and epic past that Hrabal finds his heroine, the embodiment of *élan,* but married to a husband who is the incarnation of caution and moderation. She responds vehemently to everything in her surroundings which can be a stimulus to fun. She is gargantuan in her readiness to leap at anything vital. "Blood and saliva," she repeats, as if those two fluids were her dominant humors. She is at home in the world of the senses and of nature. In turn, horses look at her, she says, "as if they were communicating with me." She trusts her instincts — "I always asked myself first, no matter what I did, and I always said yes to myself, and this inner yes-saying of mine . . . crossed into my blood."

Pre-rational, atavistic, spontaneous human reactions enthrall Hrabal. They are both of the past and of the people. He describes the heroine as if she were a goddess of *joie de vivre,* and she herself displays mythopoeic leanings. She sees a man roasting malt in the brewery as "some kind of a god out of a primeval myth of the globe." Religious motifs crop up frequently as analogues to simple everyday acts. What might have been told as a small town anecdote becomes a mini-myth: Dr. Gruntorád in his youth caught his wife in their bedroom with an officer. The officer escaped through the window. As he jumped on his horse, he stuck a willow twig which he had been carrying in his boot into the ground. The twig grows into a huge willow tree, which covers the whole house and acquires mythic venerability. Hrabal's oral style (direct addresses to the reader, non-literary forms of words, repeated conjunctions, formulas) also produces an effect of ritualization.

The Haircutting is Hrabal's journey back to a woman's harmonious existence bathed in a warm, colorful past, with long hair symbolizing the essence of that age — always submissive to it and accepting of it. There is horror and brutality in this story, also, but far less than in some other works of Hrabal's. The grotesque and absurd elements which coexist side by side with, or even within, Hrabal's idyllic scenes, give the work its special flavor, and keep him from being maudlin. The power of fantasy unifies it all — typified in the conclusion to *The Haircutting,* a lyrical passage about local architectural monuments which no longer exist, and are being appreciated in imagination.

The Haircutting is most unpretentious; it can be read as a simple, pleasant story of the old days of Bohemia and as a portrait of a delightful, vivacious woman in a small Czech town. It is also a series of anecdotes. Yet behind its historical recreation of all the robust humor and zest of days now long gone, there is unity to the episodic structure. Standing squarely in the oral Czech story telling tradition of Hašek and Deml, it is nevertheless a hagiographical eulogy. The heroine with her marvellous hair, amidst all the anecdotes, the men, and the incidents of a brewery steward's wife, is a model of the feminine, robust, secular, earthly saint. The text is a hymn to physical desire, play, enjoyment.

*
*   *

Vitali Syomin is a Soviet writer some of whose work is also an apotheosis of the survival, into our days, of unintellectual, traditional — and, in his case, the Russian people's — vitality and fightingness, and is therefore somewhat comparable to Hrabal. He is an exception among Soviet Russian authors in not being an inhabitant of either Moscow or Leningrad, but rather very much at home in Rostov on the Don. He is known particularly for stories published over the years in *Novy Mir*: *Asya Alexandrovna* (No. 11, 1965); *Our Old Women* (*Nashi starukhi*), (No. 9, 1966); *Zhenya i Valentina* (No. 11–12, 1972), and others. *Seven People in One House* (*Semero v odnom dome*), with which we shall concern ourselves, was published in *Novy Mir* (No. 6, 1965).

The narrator of this eighty-page *povest'*, Vitya, is an educated person, a former teacher, now a journalist, who married into the family; everybody else belongs to the working class and is of peasant origin. The heroes of the book are first, so to speak, the setting itself — the house in which the family live, and secondly, Mulya, the widowed mother-in-law. (Vitya is married to her daughter Irka.) The story consists of incidents in the lives of members of the family and their friends. Drinking, swearing, and slang dominate the action.

Mulya's family, as the story reveals them, and above all Mulya herself, have a clear-cut code of behavior: one is loyal to the family and respected according to one's know-how, primarily as applied to building and maintaining a house (mixing mortar, repairing fences and shutters). The predominant virtue is vitality: self-assertiveness, energy. The characters are far from being saints. They are not only a collection of hard-working laborers, but also, on occasion, crooks, drunks, and even murderers. One of the conflicts between the narrator and Mulya's family occurs when he feels the truth should be told the police about a killing he had witnessed, whereas the family take it for granted one will cover up for an insider. Their amorality, from an intellectual outsider's point of view, is striking:

> Ninka always amazed me, because she was through and through at home in the world against which I, according to my profession, was obliged to fight. If I should say "People steal in all the stores," this would be a tragic acknowledgement of the fact that all the exertions of teachers, newspapersmen like myself, writers, the highest state authorities, all those who teach what is good and what is bad, had been in vain. When Ninka asserted, "People steal in all the stores," she did not feel either bitterness or disillusionment. She lived in that world. No better and no worse than the others. That is all. (p. 83)

The characters like everything to remain set and traditional. A gypsy is expected to act like a gypsy, a worker like a worker, along lines set down by folk stereotype and tradition. They do not gloss over things, but look straight at them and accept them, whether it is the promiscuity of one character, or a stabbing by another.

A struggle for power is clearly going on between the women and the men. Mulya just as evidently is the most powerful person in the house. The narrator has only admiration for female superiority in strength (in another story, Syomin created a similar situation in which a stepson acquires awe for the fighting strength and loyalty of his stepmother). Mulya is like the strong mortar which the men mix — she holds the walls of the family together. She is above all a worker and a fighter. Syomin's Amazon reminds us of the heroine of Leskov's *Voitel'nitsa* (the "Fighter Woman"), just as Syomin's narrative forms recall Leskov's in that and in other stories. Vulgar and amoral that she is, Mulya deserves to stand alongside Solzhenitsyn's hagiographic portrait of a spiritual and selfless woman, Matryona in *Matryonin Dvor*.

Intellection is scanty in this work (in contrast to Granin's continual turning to analysis and comment in the text which we shall discuss next). Syomin presents dialogues, anecdotes, stories, with only a minimum of conclusion-drawing by the narrator Vitya. What guides the conduct of his characters is not consciousness and reason, but tradition and instinct. Syomin shows them motivated by ingrained patterns of behavior based on ancient Russian peasant ways, transported by the fundamentally unchanged rural population to the fringe areas of urban life. Proverbs are resorted to for guidance; behavior of others is mostly noted, but not dissected. Colorful, metaphoric advice is given — if these are not too grandiose terms to apply to such peppery exclamations as "Don't shit steam, you'll burn your legs," said to someone who was being too angry.

Syomin places us in a world of graphic thinking, and folk formulas. The tale begins and ends with the same scene of drinking; the entire body of the work is a flashback, a series of recollections. But we are not dealing with a sophisticated work of self-reflexive literary experimentation. This is no twentieth-century modernism, no playing with technique, no *Finnegan's Wake*. While the men are drinking vodka in the opening and concluding scene, they argue over such appropriate topics as whether one gets drunk more quickly from cut alcohol (*spirt*) or from vodka, and such superstitions as the belief that a cigarette smoked after vodka makes one twice as drunk as two mugs of beer.

A more general topic comes from the newspapers. *Izvestiya* had an article by a Polish professor comparing statistics of male and female mortality which claims that in all ages, women live longer than men. An extended discussion of possible causes ensues: war, smoking, alcoholism. One of the men says, "Why go far afield? Raise your hand if you have a father." Only one of the four men has, and they tell him it does not count, because his father is not living with him. And then the stories begin — of fathers killed, run away, of Mulya's exploits and sufferings. Six women and one man are living in the house, but since Vitya is an intellectual and not a jack of all manual trades such as a man ought to be, in Mulya's eyes he does not even count as a man. She blithely refers in his presence to there being no man in the house. Yet, the narrator realizes, she would not really want to share any of her power — not even if there were what she would consider a real man in her house.

The stories illustrate life in the terrible years of Russia's history, with starvation, war, Stalinist repression, crime, German atrocities. Syomin concludes his work back at the table, after much smoking and drinking, with Mulya asking Vitya to tell the others to go home, since he, Vitya, will have to go to work next morning only at nine, but Mulya at six. This is Vitya's concluding thought: "I kept thinking of how Tolka asked those who had fathers who were still alive to raise their hands, and about what Mulya said about herself — tomorrow people have to work." Death and the necessity to work — these are the two final, enduring facts which this pathetic, comic, folksy story brings home.

The modern age, technology, politics, and intellection are ignored by Syomin. Perennial concerns — animal, instinctual — remain. Surviving and feeling at home in one's house are the chief things. A very old woman, Manya, remembers the Tsars Nikolay and Alexander III, but "the point was not in Alexander and Nikolay. What was important was that Manya survived them. That was understandable to all. Uncle Petya felt it, and I felt it, I looked at the yard, the house, I recalled it as it used to be in those days, and more and more felt that I belonged here. I liked that feeling, to be at home, in this shack, in this street." (p. 136)

Nest-making is the overriding necessity for these characters. When Vitya's wife is pregnant, she forgets about everything else and only tries to size him up to see if he will have the know-how to get enough room for them to live in.

If the female heroine is the powerful and hard-working Mulya, the male hero is a neighbor, Uncle Vasya: "He has talented hands, and how strong and calm he is." (p. 97) He picks up a quarrelsome fellow and calmly tosses him over the fence. It does not matter if he can only read at the grade school level, out loud, pronouncing "with expression." Vitya overhears him trying to read one of his newspaper articles this way, and he gives up reading after five minutes and goes out. This is a putdown not for Uncle Vasya, but for the article.

Medicine in this story is also old-fashioned and folksy. Aloe with honey and vodka cures a woman who had been ready for the grave when regular doctors and health spas were treating her. Superstitions are many, such as the belief that if a woman plans to do the wash and is about to dry it outside, and the sun is shining, it means her man loves her. (p. 77)

Siniavsky said that Russian writers are trying not to write novels, but to rewrite the gospels. This is not Syomin's chosen task. He is not writing prophetic and hortatory works, but showing the survival of ancient Russian *byt*, the details of how simple people live in this world, in almost animal, instinctual traditional ways. There is nothing modern about his narrative form either. His manner of story-telling could be from the middle of the nineteenth century; the folkways of his characters are still older. It is through going back to those particular aspects of the past, told in Leskovian fashion, that Syomin stands out among the other writers of the last couple of decades. He is interested in that past which is embodied in national, folksy characters surviving like an anthropological calque right into his own days.

* * *

In many ways antithetical to Syomin, in subjects, attitudes, and forms, yet similar in his fascination with time and the past is Daniil Granin, our next Soviet Russian example. He has written so much, so well, and the themes and forms of his works are so varied and rich as to make him an author of exceptionally high importance in trying to understand what has been happening in Soviet Russian prose today.

Granin has been a prominent Soviet-published author for over twenty years. His "Opinions of One's Own" ("Sobstvennoe mnenie," *Novy Mir,* August 1956) was one of the key works of the period of the Thaw. It embodied its central moral, psychological, and artistic concerns better — more concentratedly and poignantly — than *The Thaw* by Ilya Ehrenburg, which has given that period its commonly accepted name.

Granin's tales and novels dealt with scientists and technocrats (*Iskateli*), on the one hand, and private experiences (*Posle svad'by*), on the other. His documentary writings are also voluminous and important.[3]

Now, in the 1970s, after two decades of literary eminence in the Soviet Union, and service as secretary of the Leningrad Union of Writers, his works reveal thematic and artistic concerns the significance of which extends beyond Granin himself, to the Russian intellectual and literary climate of our time in general. They mark a shift in the *Zeitgeist*; a change in Russian sensibility since the start of what I propose to term the Stabilization Period; he is one of its best morally and artistically questing published writers. I am suggesting dividing post-World War II Soviet literature into four periods: 1. Zhdanovism and last years of Stalin; 2. The Thaw; 3. The Pendulum or See-Saw period, from about 1958 to 1970 (with swings of alternating liberalizations and freezes); and 4. The present Stabilization or Post-Solzhenitsyn Period, a plateau, without sudden changes, but with protrusions of fascinating concerns and investigations. One of these is the turn towards the interrogation of the past, such as Granin's in "Obratny bilet" ("The Return Ticket," *Novy Mir,* August 1976, pp. 3–48).

"The Return Ticket" is part story, part essay. Granin presents the past as surviving in living connections with, and influences over, the present. The work discusses, for example, the Dostoevsky historical preserve, the "memorial," in the town of Staraya Russa, but it is itself another, verbal memorial to Dostoevsky, whom Granin cites as the exemplary creator of novels about memory and the preservation of the past among the living.

The work is rich in ideas and materials of many kinds. Granin does not merely affirm, as he does, that "parents survive (or continue: *prodolzhayutsya*) in their children," but he also presents us with "the palpability (his term is *oshchutimost'*) of this parental dwelling within us." (p. 45) There is the suggestiveness of sensory descriptions and of specific experiences, rendered in narrative form. But in addition there is much interrogation; we are in a world of mature, complex reflection. Some of the current *derevenskaya proza* seems jejune and thin in comparison.

Since it would not be realistic to expect all readers to be familiar with this work, a brief summary should come first.

The narrator — someone like Granin himself — is visiting a friend, Andrian, a philosophical inhabitant of Staraya Russa. He travels still further, to the village of Kislitsy, where he had lived as a child with his father. He reflects about his own grandson, about his trip to Kislitsy, and about memory and forgetting.

Andrian and the narrator had visited an old teacher of Andrian's in still another small village, Lazenky. The narrator recalls his visit to Dostoevsky's house in Staraya Russa, his talks with the Dostoevsky scholar and museum director Georgi Ivanovich, and events in Staraya Russa history, and he visits places where the action of *The Brothers Karamazov* is supposed to have taken place. He reflects on many subjects, such as the reasons why writers locate their works in real places. He cites passages from Alyosha Karamazov's speech about memory, dreams of his father, thinks of his father's life (second marriage, work as a forester), recalls other former friends, Staraya Russa as it had been in the days of NEP, converses about the length of time it takes forests to become established, about holding on to the past and things as they used to be versus the desire for change and improvement. Among other topics of his meditations are: relations between fathers and their children, Dostoevsky's to his father, Dostoevsky's to his characters, Andrian's tyrannical father's opposition to his wish to become a philosopher, and the narrator's own father's relations to him as a child. The last page of "The Return Ticket" links an illustration in a volume of *The Brothers Karamazov,* of Alyosha speaking to children surrounding him, with the desire of the post-World War I generation to remove prewar photographs and other objects from their lives; he concludes by emphasizing the influence of childhood memories on the formation of those people who persevere in remaining human and good despite all blows which life has dealt them.

The very brief and incomplete summary of the topics which Granin takes up, in the order in which he does so, inevitably will seem disjointed; the text does jump from one topic to another. Yet there is order and unity under the surface heterogeneity.

This work, confusing as it may seem when examined in its twists and turns, is quite lucid in its general direction when we look at its point of departure and conclusion. The first page states, "The country of my childhood had been destroyed, my childhood had perished." (p. 3) The last page ends with the affirmation of the lasting positive influence of good childhood memories (one's parents in real life. Alyosha Karamazov's sermon to the children in the novel) on the entire subsequent life of an individual. This conclusion perhaps sounds excessively moralistic and uplifting, when thus taken out of context. The story is not at all jarringly didactic. Between the two points, the melancholy beginning and the encouraging ending, Granin meanders among many different forms of narration. What starts as a short story (first person narration, dialogues) soon shifts to travelogue (descriptions of a village, small town, large town, Leningrad), to reminiscences, essays of reflection and speculation, social comment, character sketches, conversations. There is constant movement, from one narrative mode to another.[4] There is no stasis, no rest; all is in flux and eternal movement. For Granin, all things flow.

The beginning of the story contains a comment on the current plethora of *derevenskaya proza*. The names of tiny villages which the narrator lovingly lists (Khakhily, Visyuchy Bor, and so on) stir his recollections of childhood, and they remind us also of the ancient Russian place names which attract the narrator of Solzhenitsyn's *Matryonin Dvor* and of Turgenev's localities in *The Hunter's Sketches.*

Granin's journey into the past at the outset seems like a conventional piece of fashionable *derevenskaya proza* — a return to the past, to childhood, to the countryside. Andrian refers explicitly to the narrator's trip as a *poezdka v rodnye mesta* and asks, "Don't you have a fresher theme? Let literary lions (*molodtsy*) who don't have anything left to say write about that." (p. 5) He continues derisively: "They cherish nostalgia for the country because they have gotten themselves snazzy (*shikarnuyu*) apartments and now have to ride in elevators and take baths in bathtubs." But after this polemic aside, Granin takes his story far beyond the confines of most *derevenskaya proza,* into areas of complex thought and feeling.

The range of reference is extremely broad. Granin weaves into his work allusions to Gorky, to Zoshchenko's quasi-psychoanalytical quests into his youth, to the scholar Mikhail Bakhtin. He gives historical statistics about Staraya Russa, deplores the dearth of Soviet studies of religious literature, cites *Eugene Onegin* and *Crime and Punishment.* Many places, events, and literary details are included. Granin's loose, all-embracing form opens the door to all experience and many possible stances towards it. It is kept from flying apart centrifugally by the centripetal questioning by the author. Throughout, there is an unusually high proportion of interrogations, addressed by the narrator to his material. He persistently tries for an *osmyslenie* of the material — the finding or giving of significance to it.

The time scheme shifts repeatedly. We find ourselves in the present, then veer to the world of *The Brothers Karamazov,* to Leningrad after 1918, after 1945, to Staraya Russa today, to the narrator's childhood, to his father's childhood, to various other points of his father's life, to Andrian's life in the days of NEP, and the early days of Staraya Russa five hundred years ago.

Andrian at one point refers to a time machine (p. 44); the entire story is a time machine in which the narrator wafts us along with his reflections and experiences through numerous periods.

Nothing in the story is unilinear and direct. It is richer in questions than in affirmations and answers. What are the reasons for Granin's abundant range of heterogeneous references? He seems obsessed with the instability of our world, aware as he is of change all around him: the destruction of an old town or region (due to wear and tear or to war), and the aging and passing of individuals, and of whole historical epochs. He is not fascinated with the spectacle of this phantasmagoria for its own sake but because he is searching, in this dance of life, for a stable point.

Granin finds this only in connections. Everything taken alone, by itself, shifts, changes, and perishes in this story, but it also stands in a relationship to something else, and in this system of links, there is enduring comfort. It has to do with the moral formation of human individuals — Granin's focus and conclusion.

These seemingly separate elements (things or people) are not really isolated, but exist meaningfully in their connections with, and effects on, other factors. They are scattered in space and time, and span, in addition to real life, the world of literary fiction (one's own father, Dostoevsky as author of *The Brothers Karamazov,* and Alyosha as his character, are equally enduring and forceful grains — facts — in our memory and hence in our life). The connections between the various places, things, and characters to whom Granin refers are those of moral effects, interwoven in memory.

Granin's way is to look at various successive aspects of each relationship. "How you turn everything around," Andrian once throws in his face. (p. 47) He does not view human beings as completed or stationary, but sees them in process, being made. The soil under Staraya Russa constitutes the present town and vice versa. "All the earth of this very old Russian town is composed of the dust of roads, houses, stoves, cellars, it preserves birchbark writings, fragments of swords and pots, glass and stones, pieces of skins and banners, remnants of people's houses, cathedrals, blacksmith's shops, watchtowers, highway turnstiles, saltworks, forts, Arakcheev's barracks." (p. 42)

In Granin's scheme, there is no teleology, no progress-oriented, unilinear or dialectical time, Hegelian or Marxist. We are in a world of co-existence, where past and present, in eternal change, nevertheless are linked, through memories. Fathers and sons, history and the present, die, yet live and continue to affect life.

In 1956, in "Opinions of One's Own," Granin had presented as the climax of his story the hero's moment of *anagnorisis,* his perception of his life-long self-deception and cowardice. In other works, he probed a variety of intellectual, moral, and even practical, bureaucratic problems of the lives and careers of engineers and industrial managers. Documentary prose also began to captivate him, and continues to absorb him.

Parallel to these several preoccupations came stories centered on perennial emotions, in the setting of contemporary Soviet life. "Rain in a Strange Town," for example, transmutes Chekhov's *Lady with a Dog.* It places love between people — married but not to each other — into Soviet reality. Granin is fascinated by the survival of primeval emotions, in changed form, in contemporary Soviet Russia.

The backward look, which in "Rain in a Strange Town" is addressed to Chekhov's love theme, is directed in "The Return Ticket" at a multiplicity of past relationships. Now Granin seems almost obsessed with the past. We have seen how many spiritual and physical ancestors populate his stage. The matrix in which these numerous elements are embedded and related to each other is the Montaigne-like, essayistic speculation by the narrator.

The past supplies food for ruminations about links. Here we have no inventors and managers cut off from their antecedents. There are searches for temporal connections. Granin in this work perceives life as a thick network of relationships cutting through time, a tapestry which seems to have its center of gravity, or its focal point, inside a mind. This is a most subjective work. Ideas, recollections have the most intense reality. Perhaps like old Rembrandt in his last period, and many other artists in various media, Granin is now moving both into the past and into introspection.

"The Return Ticket" belongs to the history of Russian spirituality as much as it does to the history of belles-lettres.

*

*   *

There are other explorations of the past in recent Soviet literature which are as complex as those of Granin. Yuri Trifonov in *House on the Embankment* (*Dom na naberezhnoy, Druzhba narodov,* No. 1, 1976) strips away historical layers and interweaves the personal and professional lives of several characters — primarily two, an upward mobile, weak young man, and the descending son of privileged governmental officials.[5] Trifonov's journey into the past is focused, as in most of his tales of the last decade, on analysis of moral turpitude — mostly sins of omission, betrayals — slowly emerging before us, made to seem understandable, natural, rather than melodramatically villainous, yet not any less repulsive.

His short novel demonstrates that innovation and quality are not necessarily directly related. *House on the Embankment* is a conventional Soviet prose work when we tick off its various features one by one — construction, theme. The pressure to denounce, to conform from elementary school to advanced literary institute, the *Bildungsroman* breadth spanning two generations, the repeated meetings of the two old schoolmates, the seeping of Stalinist denunciations from the highest to the lowest levels of society, professional and personal intermingling of concerns — all these topics have been used over and over in Soviet literature since 1954, but the complexity, subtlety, and power of Trifonov's ways of dealing with them in this novel surpass Soviet parallels, and make us wonder if one could not think of him as the Henry James of today's Russia.

Quite different, yet also complex, and most self-conscious, is the return to the past of Andrey Bitov. Only portions of his novel *Pushkinsky Dom* have been published in various journals in the USSR.[6] Some are novelistic, others include more literary theory than narration. One of these, appropriately enough, was published in *Voprosy literatury* (no. 7, 1976). Bitov presents, in various narrative ways, through a number of reflecting prisms of commentary and varying temporal and personal points of views, the amatory and literary pursuits of his hero, who is a literary scholar. His protagonist writes a paper, while doing his *aspirantura,* on three poems, by Pushkin, Lermontov, and

Tyutchev, all written when each poet was twenty-seven years old; Bitov's hero is also twenty-seven; he sees in these poems, about prophets, discussions of similar questions of philosophy of life. Bitov's work (story or essay) presents speculations about poetry, literary scholarship, life in general. It is a mixture of novel, theory of literature, and wide-ranging reflection, such as has few equals. The intricacy and self-consciousness of Bitov's purposes can best be illustrated by a lengthy quotation from his own two-page statement about his novelistic scheme:

> All narration is carefully divided into two interrelated lines, the hero's and the author's . . . the novel and "comments." The three parts of the novel are wedge-shaped in construction. The first and second narrate, in parallel form, the hero's life from the beginning to the present time, to the moment where the third, concluding part starts. The second part in that sense is a "version and variation" of the first. Only the first is told retrospectively, as of today, when historical appraisals of the process in which the hero participated have become known to us. The second is an attempt to tell the same history within the hero, when he has no idea about the history in which he is immersed. . . .
> The first part, "Fathers and Sons," becomes a history of a family, and our country's history makes it possible for us to double the Turgenevan themes, on account of a whole generation's having been excluded from participation in the historical process, and of the sudden meeting of three generations at the same time in the middle of the 1950s. . . . All parts, as is proper in a museum, are given big titles and are accompanied by epigraphs from corresponding novels. The title of the third part is a hybrid of the late Pushkin with the young Dostoevsky, the epigraphs here are a turning away from Pushkin to Sollogub, like the action itself. The third part, after the hero reaches his own real time, is a struggle between two lines, the hero's and the author's. They intersect more and more often, the control is shorter and shorter, until the author's time and the hero's time finally coincide. At that point naturally everything ends, since it cannot continue any longer.
> The effort to reach contemporaneity of action, undertaken in the first two parts, which as it were take place at the same time, is undertaken once more within the second part: a sequential representation of the hero's three women, who exist simultaneously in all his times. . . . In this manner, the composition itself suggests that the basis of the plot is time itself, that it is time which is being investigated, that time gives birth to the form.[7]

Fascination with time and returns to the past have not been rare in Russian literature in its history.[8] Tynianov in his famous collection of essays showed how the archaizers of the early 19th century were really innovators. Reprises of the picaresque tradition, for example, are strewn over the history of Russian as well as Western literature (Thomas Mann's *Felix Krull,* Saul Bellow's *Augie March,* and many others). Soviet prose writers today have their particular ways of being original by returning to some aspects — thematic or formal — of the past. The variety as well as the frequency of works in which they attempt this is striking.[9] It has been one of the ways in which they have recently found it most natural to move out along new lines: by taking backward glances. In the Soviet context, this represents a marked shift away from stereotypes of progress, forward movement, unilinear time, which mark official thought — away from all teleology and towards a sense of time as simultaneity.

NOTES

1. Bohumil Hrabal, *Postřižiny* (Prague: Československý spisovatel, 1976), with numerous minor changes from the unofficially circulated typescript.

2. Emanuel Frynta, "Náčrt základů Hrabalovy prozy," ("A Sketch of the Bases of Hrabal's Prose"), postcript in Bohumil Hrabal, *Automat svět* (*Cafeteria "The World"*) (Prague, 1966) pp. 319–330. I am also indebted to Václav Černý's excellent essay, "Za hádankami Bohumila Hrabala," *Svědectví* (Paris, No. 51, 1976), pp. 537–567 ("The Riddles of Bohumil Hrabal.")

3. Lev Plotkin, *Daniil Granin: Ocherk tvorchestva* (Leningrad, Sovetsky pisatel, 1975), is a useful monograph about Granin's work up to the story "Rain in a Strange Town." In *Interval of Freedom: Soviet Literature during the Thaw, 1954–57,* (Minneapolis: University of Minnesota Press, 1960), I discussed Granin's technological works, pp. 44–45, 65–66, 135–136.

4. The literary effects achieved by a multiplicity of narrative methods and voices in Solzhenitsyn's *Gulag* were the subject of my article, "How Solzhenitsyn Returned his Ticket," in Kathryn Feuer, ed., *Solzhenitsyn: A Collection of Critical Essays* (Twentieth Century Views, Englewood Cliffs, N.J., 1976), pp. 112–119.

5. Klaus Mehnert, "Moskau 1976 (1). Beobachtungen und Gespräche," *Osteuropa* (No. 10, October 1976), pp. 884–889, gives a fine account of the novel and its importance.

6. At the time of writing, the publication of *Pushkinsky dom* in Russian has been announced as forthcoming by Ardis (Ann Arbor, Michigan) late in 1978.

7. Unpublished typescript in my possession.

8. The unjustly neglected novel by Veniamin Kaverin, *Pered zerkalom* (*In Front of the Mirror*) (Moscow, 1972), which is one of the most interesting works of the post-Stalin period, also is saturated with backward glances. Valentin Kataev has written two important memoiristic novels, *Svyatoy kolodets* (*Holy Well*) (Moscow, 1966) and *Trava zabven'ya* (*Grass of Oblivion*) (Moscow, 1967). Deming Brown's recent and excellent *Soviet Russian Literature since Stalin* (Cambridge: Cambridge University Press, 1978) devotes its entire ninth chapter to literature which "reexamines the past."

9. In the course of the discussion at the conference, Professor Efim Etkind suggested there were still other fruitful fields of investigation into Soviet literary concerns with the past, among others the biographies in the series *Lives of Remarkable Men* (*Zhizn' zamechatel'nykh lyudey*), particularly the lives of Chaadaev by Aleksandr Lebedev and of Saltykov-Shchedrin by Andrey Turkov.

Michał Głowiński

THE GROTESQUE IN
CONTEMPORARY POLISH LITERATURE

I

It is possible to examine the grotesque from many perspectives. Here, with regard to contemporary Polish literature, I shall consider it to be a specific relation to social consciousness and I shall also attempt to show its functions.

If such a point of view is adopted, then the first and most fundamental characteristic of the grotesque is the fact that it comes into conflict with the accepted ideas preserved in social consciousness (or with ideas imposed upon that consciousness), that it negates long-standing convictions as to the structure of the world, of human behavior, of history, of social life, of psychology, and that, subsequently, it questions official axiological systems. For the grotesque the most fundamental is the destructive facet. The grotesque incorporates elements belonging to an accepted or imposed social consciousness, yet it separates them from the context in which they occur: while retaining the constituent parts it destroys the whole. The incorporated element loses its traditional meaning, becomes problematic and is presented in a new light. The grotesque, however, is not content to merely analyze the world, or rather its socially established views into its primary factors. This is only the first stage of the process. The second stage is also inevitable: out of these isolated parts must emerge a new whole, governed by its own laws. These laws have a polemic character, for the rules of the grotesque become clear not only in the use of individual elements, but, above all, in the general principles in which they are linked.

As a negation of the accepted form of social consciousness the grotesque relates in one way or another to the texts in which that consciousness is verbalized. From this point of view it is a certain type of relationship of one text to another. In other words, in the grotesque the element of parody is always fundamental for it negates not only the accepted view of the world but also its linguistic expression (which after all is an essential component of this view); they are in fact inseparable phenomena. The parody of texts which transmit the established, official view of the world is particularly significant in Polish literature of the grotesque.

Viewed as an element of literary communication the grotesque is a kind of agreement with the reader. It is an agreement which requires him to deviate from the ordinary world view and to accept a certain type of game based on handling, in a particular way, that which is, or which is supposed to be, recognized as rational, natural, or evident. All grotesque, then, assumes a certain attitude on the part of the reader; if that attitude does not crystallize, then it is difficult to discuss a conception of the grotesque. This agreement is marked by an essential feature: it is always formed in opposition to the official forms of culture and to official ideology. Many theoreticians of the grotesque have already drawn attention to this fact; credit for emphasizing it is due above all to Bakhtin.[1] It seems, however, that one cannot limit "nonofficial-dom," according to that scholar, only to the realm of carnivalization and popular laughter. This "nonofficialdom" is a component element of any pact that a grotesque work concludes with the reader. History has shown that there has been no official ideology — political, social, or religious — which would adopt the grotesque. The grotesque, once it becomes official, ceases to be grotesque and can be at the very most only one of the components of makeshift satire. (Bakhtin aptly opposes the grotesque to satire, linking the latter to rhetorical laughter.) The grotesque by its very nature is antitotalitarian.

II

Tendencies toward the grotesque are among the most important phenomena in Polish literature of the twentieth century and are without precedent. They appeared, admittedly, to replace literary creativity of the lower strata of society at the turn of the sixteenth century to which renewed attention was drawn only in the interwar period. They also found expression in the work of the great Romantics, above all in drama, but this was limited merely to a few instances. It is only the twentieth century which marks the invasion of the grotesque. The phenomenon is even more striking since in Poland surrealism did not exist as a separate movement and the poetic avant-garde of the twenties and thirties had on the whole the character of constructivism. How, then, do we explain the unusual role of the grotesque?

It appears that a major factor was the radical change in the role of literature after 1918. At a time when Poland lacked independence, literature was always more than merely just literature, it was a national institution. In a society which could not decide its own fate literature fulfilled the role of a basic moral authority, it was a transmitter of tradition, and it established programs for action and gave direction. (I disregard the well-known and obvious fact that contemporaneous poetics, particularly that of realism, also did not favor the grotesque.)

With independence regained in 1918 literature was freed from its previous obligations. Not only did writers immediately recognize this fact but they welcomed it with particular joy. Literature could now become simply literature as everywhere else, as in any normal society. It could become impartial. And it was precisely in this literature that the grotesque came to occupy a prominent place.

It should be mentioned, however, that grotesque tendencies already appeared in the last phase of Young Poland, that is to say, in the closing phase of symbolism. They attest to the change in the conception of literature; new emphasis was now placed in particular on the element of play and irony. The literary tone was distinctly lowered and literature was denied by the aesthetic ideals of the waning epoch which had led it above all toward expressivity. Tendencies of the grotesque can be found already in the early poetry of the greatest Polish symbolist, Bolesław Leśmian, as well as in the creative work of a little-known writer, Roman Jaworski, undoubtedly a precursor of the great writers of the grotesque. He published only two books. A volume of stories, *Historie maniaków* (Maniacs' Tales, 1909) was a programmatic manifesto of the literature of the ugly, a literature based on the play of contrasts and improbabilities. This volume contains thoughts on the grotesque as the salvation of art. The novel, *Wesele hrabiego Orgaza* (The Wedding of Count Orgaz, 1925), was the first work to appear in Poland telling of the annihilation of European civilization, a work grotesque in the full meaning of the word. The savior of culture was to be a butcher from Chicago, who had organized in Toledo a great mystery play in the vein of the Dionysian rituals of ancient Greece. The mystery play did not yield any results however, as civilization, doomed to annihilation, could not be saved. Grotesqueness is manifest not only on the level of the plot and ideology. Grotesque is the entire construction of the novel as well as its strangely beautiful language, composed of the most different stylistic elements. The grotesque questions not only the novel as a genre: in effect it questions literature as such.

And here we are already approaching that current which during the interwar period was the most fundamental: the grotesque of the catastrophic and its most outstanding representative, Stanisław Ignacy Witkiewicz.[2] His grotesque, both in drama and in the novel, is not only a game, a joke or even only the previously calculated shock effect on the reader accustomed to literature of a different sort, a "serious" literature, which does not destroy the established view of the world (such as the grotesque works by the Skamander poets, e.g., Tuwim). For Witkiewicz the grotesque represents a certain ideology. The example of Witkiewicz clearly shows how wrong are those theories of the grotesque which place language beyond its limits and which confine the grotesque to the representation of the world in the literary work,[3] or which contrast "thematic grotesque" with "the grotesque of language."[4] The point of departure for the grotesque in Witkiewicz is its relation to language. He mixes the most varied styles in such a way as to have motivation neither in the literary tradition, nor in the societal conceptions as to what constitutes proper speech, speech which corresponds to the speaker's social position, setting, situation, and topic. It is also impossible to reduce it to the burlesque, which is characterized by the fact that matters usually treated in a dignified style are treated in a vulgar style. The grotesque language of Witkiewicz relies upon a consistent mixing of styles ranging from the style of a philosophical treatise to the vulgar language of a street brawl. At times such mixing occurs within one sentence in which, for example, a poetic expression will appear next to a vulgar one.

The grotesque of Witkiewicz in the sphere of language alone can give the impression of disorder; disorder, however, it is not. It follows certain rules, although they are negative rules, relying on the reversal of that which is recognized as appropriate. The fundamental characteristics of Witkiewicz's grotesque are apparent even in the formation of his language. We stated at the outset that the grotesque is based not only on the analysis of a socially accepted world view (language included) but that it is also a construction. However, in different types of the grotesque the proportions vary. In the case of Witkiewicz, the *pars destruens* is more essential than in any other of the writers discussed here; this incidentally applies to a greater degree to the novels than to plays. One of the most basic factors of construction is the collage, the arrangement of various elements, each with different characteristics and properties. An example of this is Witkiewicz's play *Nowe wyzwolenie* (New Liberation, 1920), composed, as it were, from ready-made parts taken from Shakespeare's Richard III and Wyspiański's *Wyzwolenie* (Liberation).

The grotesque in Witkiewicz is closely linked to his theory of art. In the case of the drama it comes above all from his conception of "pure form." According to him, pure form is primarily that which deviates from mimetic aesthetics; it is not based on "imitation." The grotesque, with which Witkiewicz incidentally did not deal in his treatises on the theory of art, would be that kind of "deformation" which makes impossible the continuation of a naturalistic poetics. Here, we note parenthetically, also appears one of the basic characteristics of the grotesque in twentieth-century Polish literature: it was treated as a negation of realistic aesthetics, as a sphere of modern and original forms. Witkiewicz did not connect the novel with the idea of pure form, rather, he called it a "bag" and asserted that it can hold everything which the writer puts into it. And that bag became precisely the grotesque mixture of things.

In the novels mainly, but also in some of the plays, can be seen the connection of Witkiewicz's grotesque with that set of ideas which were of great significance for Polish interwar literature and are usually termed catastrophism. The grotesque is associated with the conviction that European culture finds itself in a period of decay, that it is subject to decomposition, and that its basic values have become worthless. It is in a state of constant threat from, among others, the forces of totalitarianism. The play *Gyubal Wahazar* (1921) is the grotesque vision of a dictatorship, and Witkiewicz's last play, *Szewcy* (The Cobblers), is the grotesque vision of a totalitarian reality. Catastrophism is characteristic of a substantial part of Polish poetry of the thirties, but it is not always seen as related to the grotesque.

The focal point of Polish grotesque literature is the work of Witold Gombrowicz. There are several reasons for that. In his work converge all lines —

those which come from his predecessors as well as those which are directed toward the future — for Gombrowicz's work has countless successors and epigones. Moreover, it is the greatest achievement in Polish literature of our century, its most original contribution. When discussing Gombrowicz we are speaking already of entirely contemporary literature. A large portion of his work was published only in the fifties and sixties.

The grotesque derives from the very essence of that conception of literature which Gombrowicz elaborated. It is the fundamental component of his aesthetics, or for that matter not only of his aesthetics, but also of his understanding of man and of the human condition. The world of human relationships (and in Gombrowicz all that is human implies human relationships, is a play between "I" and "others") is devoid of the element of naturalness. In it there is nothing that could be considered neutral and self-evident; there is, therefore, no level that could be defined as degree zero. Everything in the life of the individual and of society belongs to the realm of artificiality and non-naturalness. The task of literature is not to assimilate or conceal that artificiality, but to reveal and intensify it. And it is precisely here that the grotesque is born, from its "non-natural" and "artificial" essence. In Gombrowicz's conception it is not the violation of that which could be considered "normal" since in reality nothing of the kind exists and it thus does not imply a "deformation." The specifically conceived "form" governs everything, defining the relation between people, their behavior and reactions. The grotesque is also a form in a sense, for everything is form. However, as a result it overcomes existing and accepted forms, it allows one, as it were, to rise above them, including those forms which are considered characteristic for Polish culture. Gombrowicz is deeply rooted in it, but at the same time he tries to embrace it from a certain distance, which found its expression in his most consistently grotesque work, namely, the novel *Trans-Atlantyk* (Transatlantic).

With Gombrowicz the grotesque is a matter of language, of the relationship of one text to another, thus, of parody. This is characteristic of all his writing from his first short stories to his last works. His whole œuvre is one great criticism of language as the domain of artificiality, as a factor which defines man, for it introduces into his statements that which is traditional, existing and accepted. It is not possible, however, to free oneself from language; at most one can reveal its nature, mark one's own distance and nonconfidence vis-à-vis it. But Gombrowicz does this in a differeent manner than Witkiewicz, not as a matter of stylistic mixture. When the students in one of the fragments in *Ferdydurke* speak in sentences patterned after heavy Latin sentences, it is something more than just a student joke. It shows Gombrowicz's attitude toward language: speech does not closely correspond to the situation in which the utterance takes place. The programmed artificiality is merely an intensified artificiality, characteristic of all speech, an artificiality of which we are unaware. That affected speech is not only a linguistic game, it defines the whole world presented in the work. It is a critique of the socially accepted models, just as that world which is presented (the plot, the heroes, etc.) is a vote of nonconfidence in existing patterns and conceptions. Gombrowicz's grotesque questions plot as the traditional meaningful system in which events lead to a univocal solution, while this system itself constitutes the logical and ordered whole.

The most important element in Gombrowicz's grotesque is the great role played by parody.[5] Parody is a form of criticism of language, or rather, of certain of its configurations as established in culture. His whole œuvre from beginning to end is built on parody. Its range is unusually wide: Gombrowicz parodies the great works of world and Polish literature, Shakespeare and Proust, Mickiewicz and romantic drama. More than that, he also parodies the forms of "lower" literature, the forms of the popular story or of Old Polish literature of the nobility such as the *gawęda* (tale) or the "village story." In *Trans-Atlantyk* and in *Pornografia* (Pornography) parodies of *Pan Tadeusz* play a great role.[6] The parodied models are juxtaposed in a striking fashion. One of the early stories is at the same time a parody of both *A la recherche du temps perdu* and the sentimental novellas of Maria Konopnicka. Most important, however, is something else: the grotesque effect arises not from parody itself, but from the fact that because of parody there emerges a literary world which questions our conventional ideas and which attacks the everyday sense of rationality. This in particular is due to the fact that the parodied "form" does not adhere closely to the story plot; somehow the topic cannot be told in that "form." Gombrowicz delights in resorting to archaic literary genres. It is difficult — as in *Pornografia* — to describe occupied Poland using the means which was supplied by the "olden village story"; it is difficult — as in *Operetka* (Operetta) — to present social upheaval using means employed by the operetta form marked, as Gombrowicz put it, by "divine idiocy." Neither of these works, however, is what it seems, namely, a simple village story, or, precisely, an operetta. The writer confides: "To capture in the operetta a certain passion, a certain tragedy, a certain pathos, without imping-ing on its sacred stupidity — that is no small task! " Here we find ourselves at the very core of Gombrowicz's grotesque.

As has been already stated, the work most truly grotesque (and hence most consistently parodistic) is *Trans-Atlantyk*. This is a peculiar story about a young man who by accident in 1939 finds himself in Argentina, told in a caricatured Polish of the seventeenth century and related to the picaresque novel. The story is a reconstruction of the Polish gentry world, as it were — at the antipodes. There occur duels and hunts, the mentality of the Polish gentry remains in unchanged form (being to some extent the Polish mentality per se), the characters speak as figures from the *Pamiętniki* (Memoirs) of Jan Chry-zostom Pasek and they behave in the same manner.[7] Artificiality reaches its apogee; parody, never transformed into unequivocal satire nor being only a caricature, gives rise to the grotesque. Gombrowicz questions a set of traditional values acknowledged by a certain social group; he reduces to the absurd a world which that group has created and recognized as having value. Destruction goes hand in hand with construction. *Trans-Atlantyk,* although fashioned from such varied material, is composed with a precision more characteristic of a poem than of a novel.

III

Let us repeat: Gombrowicz's œuvre is of fundamental importance for the development of contemporary Polish literature and, above all, for the tendencies of the grotesque characteristic for that literature. That significance became manifest early, with the publication of *Ferdydurke* (1937). It is precisely that novel — the one still best known — which had the broadest impact; its expressions and phrases have entered common parlance. It turned out that the categories of the grotesque created in it apply to different social situations, that they can be extended in a variety of ways for various purposes and in different styles. That first great work of Gombrowicz was therefore the turning point not only in the development of his art, but also in that of the contemporary Polish grotesque.

It would seem that in a society treated severely by history, in which literature was assigned various ad hoc functions and utilitarian tasks, the grotesque would have no chance for development. At most it could be due to the individual initiative of a lonely artist, the more so since in the official literary programs there was of course no place for it. As we now know it happened otherwise. And the fact that the grotesque appeared and played such an important role in spite of all expectations, and at times even in spite of all circumstances, attests not only to its genesis but to its role in society as well. It became in the Polish context an expression of a non-conformist attitude, both vis-à-vis traditional ideas and intellectual and artistic habits, and vis-à-vis official literary programs. (This latter applies in particular to the mid-fifties, after the bankruptcy of socialist realism, which was the only poetics permitted in 1949–54.) Incidentally, we are talking here not about literary programs in the narrow sense. What is important is that the literature of the grotesque does not have the prerequisites to become an official literature, to be transformed into an instrument of propaganda; all attempts to subordinate it are doomed to failure to begin with. And it is precisely that fact which determines the social role of the grotesque, at times even independent of what constitutes its immediate subject matter.

For the grotesque in contemporary Polish literature there are in principle no inaccessible areas: the field of its penetration is unusually wide. It ranges from history to the present and its tones are the most varied — from catastrophic horror to playful indifference, from polemics to entertainment. In grotesque works there are constructed extraordinary worlds, worlds far removed from ordinary experience, but in addition everyday life is shown in the categories of grotesque smallness.

The grotesque of everyday life is the discovery of Miron Białoszewski. He took as the subject of his works that which in literature had hitherto been considered to be virtually undeserving of description, provocatively insignificant events, seemingly unimportant and meaningless. He tells of them in a language crippled in its very root, a language which so far had not been admitted to literature. This is the smallness of the grotesque: its grotesqueness emerges precisely from telling about that which, it would seem, is not worth telling. Białoszewski questioned not only the hierarchy of thematic values — such a hierarchy in one form or another always accompanies literature. He also questioned literature itself, reducing it to language which parades its antiaestheticism. Writing about shallow banality in a consciously crippled language, Białoszewski in a grotesque manner denied the very idea of literariness. This therefore is how one of the limits of the area would appear where the grotesque came to prevail.

A second limit: a great and tragic experience, say in particular the years of Nazi occupation. Białoszewski wrote his remarkable *Pamiętnik z powstania warszawskiego* (A Memoir of the Warsaw Uprising, 1970) — to be sure not a truly grotesque work. This does not mean, however, that the years of the occupation — a major and repeatedly treated topic in Polish literature — lie beyond the scope of the grotesque. Something else took place. This refers not only to writings such as Stanisław Dygat's novel *Jezioro Bodeńskie* (Lake Constance, 1946) written in Gombrowicz's vein, or Kazimierz Truchanowski's novel *Zmowa demiurgów* (The Conspiracy of the Demiurges, 1947), a grotesque allegory which points out in its fantastic plot the mechanisms of totalitarianism. The grotesque was a literary style which came into being during the occupation or told of it while created later. It is true that one could not speak in a grotesque manner about everything that happened. No grotesque work was written about the extermination of the Jews, or about the concentration camps. It is even difficult to conceive of such a work. Nevertheless, the grotesque captured at least fragments of that area. That is a peculiar kind of the grotesque; its peculiarity was somehow to be the equivalent of an unusual reality, marked by inconceivable and unpredictable contrasts. Two examples: In the spring of 1943 when the Warsaw Ghetto was burning, close to its walls there was a happy little town with carousels and lively music. (In literature this fact achieved the status of symbol: Czesław Miłosz dedicated to it his famous poem "Campo di Fiori," not grotesque, incidentally, but moralistic.) The other example: On an advertisement pillar in Warsaw, next to a list of executed people was hung a bill advertising the premiere of the operetta *Das Land des Lächelns* (a fact noted in memoir literature). If such juxtapositions had appeared in a literary piece from before 1939 they would have been regarded as grotesque hyperbole, while the work itself would have been accorded prophetic qualities, as is occasionally done with Kafka's "Penal Colony."

Literature could not remain indifferent to the macabre "grotesque" as life itself wrote it. Among the countless works which in one way or another dealt with the years 1939–45, there were attempts to capture that "grotesque," to create a vision of a world in reverse. Perhaps the most outstanding achievement in this field are three grotesque stories by Jerzy Andrzejewski, written during the war but published only in 1955 in the volume, *Złoty lis* (The Golden Fox). They tell of everyday life in occupied Warsaw, of unusual situations that resulted from the fact that everything had to be a matter of conspiracy. What was significant here, however, was not its heroic aspect, but the level of absurdity to which the exigencies of the occupation could lead. Andrzejewski found a very adequate solution to the problem he had set about to solve. He resorted to the form of the archaic novella, the story about unusual events and adventures, concerned with neither motivation nor probability. That form (known, say, from Cervantes' "Novelas ejemplares") allowed for the combination of unusual events, but also kept them at a certain distance. And here the mechanism which is characteristic of the Polish grotesque becomes manifest. It is a mechanism which was first tried out by Gombrowicz and later continued and developed by Mrożek. It avails itself of an archaic literary genre which is "inadequate" and which, by the same token, becomes a factor which forms part of the grotesque, one of the most significant components of the style of the grotesque.

When discussing the areas dominated by the grotesque we cannot avoid history, or rather, historical myths, those, in particular, which were firmly anchored in social consciousness. History plays a large role in contemporary Polish literature, though not because it is past-oriented. Given the specific conditions of that literature, the topics taken from history allow one to speak of essential things — history became a source of parables. This, however, is not the case with the grotesque. What is at work here is above all the model of *Trans-Atlantyk,* in which Gombrowicz transferred historical Polish attitudes to the present and placed them in an exotic ambience. The grotesque has a deheroizing character; the romantic hero ceases to be a hero or can even perform in a circus. I am thinking here in particular of two pieces representative of this group: Mrożek's play *Śmierć porucznika* (Death of the Lieutenant) and the novel by Kazimierz Brandys *Wariacje pocztowe* (Postal Variations, 1972). These works gave an accurate account of the weak points of social consciousness and soon became the target of sharp attacks especially on the part of conservative opinion. They were reproached for "desecrating what is held sacred." I may add parenthetically that the historical grotesque, taking place in *la belle époque,* usually in Austria, provides an occasion for literary jest. Examples are the novels *Droga do Koryntu* (The Road to Corinth, 1964) by Andrzej Kuśniewicz and *Czaszka w czaszce* (The Skull in the Skull, 1970) by Piotr Wojciechowski. They are written in a very precise style and are also influenced by Gombrowicz in a sense. However, this is limited primarily to borrowing from him elements characteristic of the spectacle.

This, therefore, is how one could present the areas to which the grotesque can be applied. However, the basic object of the grotesque is the Polish "here and now"; it became an important phenomenon of the literary life. Its significance became apparent during the period of the so-called Thaw in the mid-fifties when socialist realism was rejected and ridiculed, and when it not only ceased to be the only officially sanctioned style, but simply vanished. Yet it left strong traces and gave rise to various reactions. One of the most important reactions and one which had the greatest consequences was precisely the grotesque. During this time Gombrowicz's *Ferdydurke* and his short stories were revived in Warsaw; also, his postwar works *Trans-Atlantyk* and *Ślub* (The Marriage Ceremony) were now published. This was an important event which determined the direction of Polish literature. The renewed appearance of Gombrowicz's works hastened the growth of grotesque tendencies and they became one of the great patterns. Polish grotesque literature of that time was a reaction against socialist realism in more than one sense. For one, socialist realism did not recognize the grotesque — it had no place for it. The only attempt to integrate the grotesque into socialist realism — Jerzy Andrzejewski's *Wojna skuteczna* (The Effective War, 1953) — was not a success. The grotesque could only become didactic satire, which is tantamount to turning into its opposite.

The grotesque became an important literary — and not only a literary — phenomenon in the second half of the fifties. At that time it seemed to be an excellent antidote against boredom and the propagandistic character of socialist realism. It was even more attractive by the fact that it was linked to an idea which at that time had a magic effect, the idea of "modernity." Modern was everything which was not contained in the aesthetics of socialist realism and which added the traits of modern art, in particular, in its avant-garde trends. For the grotesque, then, there appeared an especially opportune situation; the literary public had been waiting for it and now approved of it.

It was precisely during this period that the work of Sławomir Mrożek received general attention. Mrożek perhaps most consistently analyzed and exposed the schematic nature of socialist realism. He parodied in a most consistent fashion its language and reduced to absurdity patterns of behavior, particularly in his first volumes of short stories, *Słoń* (The Elephant, 1957) and *Wesele w Atomicach* (The Wedding at Atomice, 1959). In the comic hyperbole of his earlier stories and plays the reader would recognize those immediate experiences. In the story "Żyrafa" (The Giraffe), the learned ideologist asked by a little boy what a giraffe is does not give an immediate answer but must first ascertain what the classics of Marxism had to say about it. When he finds nothing about it in their writings he reached the following conclusion:

"There is no such thing as a giraffe . . . Neither Marx nor Engels, nor any of their great followers have written anything about giraffes. That means that a giraffe does not exist." For the Polish reader such grotesque definitely was not then and is not now merely a game of scholarly wit.

The grotesque in Mrożek's case, as incidentally in the majority of grotesque writers, is, again, directly connected with parody. In *Słoń* and *Wesele w Atomicach* one finds above all parody of official language, of the language of propaganda, a language radically schematized, full of hackneyed expressions, and in its essence ritualistic.[8] Mrożek carries that language to the absurd laying bare that feature which Orwell called "newspeak." Coupled with parody the grotesque becomes a criticism of the official language and, consequently, a defense of language against corruption. And in Poland this is perhaps one of the most fundamental functions of the grotesque, and not only of the grotesque but of all literature. This tendency manifests itself in numerous ambitious undertakings of contemporary Polish literature, not all of them necessarily grotesque. The above-mentioned ordinary language of Białoszewski is in a sense a criticism and defense of language; a critique of language can also be found in the work of the younger generation of poets such as Ryszard Krynicki, Stanisław Barańczak, and Adam Zagajewski.

Criticism of the language of propaganda is part of the permanent stock of grotesque works, for it is a permanently live issue. Parody of the established patterns of socialist realism could not possess that permanence mainly because it was not deeply rooted in social consciousness. It cannot, therefore, be a negative point of reference a dozen or so years after the decline of that trend. Mrożek understood this very well and did not continue what he had already elaborated in the first collections of his short stories and in his early plays. He significantly extended the scope of his grotesque writing, reached for historical patterns, and in particular added to it certain universal dimensions. In his plays and stories he creates an unusual situation which is the point of departure for the plot. In this he undoubtedly follows Gombrowicz's example. In his play *Emigranci* (The Emigrants) the interplay between the intellectual and the simpleton has a grotesque dimension. The starting point here is the situation of confinement and alienation. In *Rzeźnia* (The Slaughterhouse) it is the fate of an artist that is grotesque in a world in which Paganini turns out to be the butcher and Philharmonic Hall is transformed into the slaughterhouse. In *Tango* and in *Niezwykłe wydarzenie* (An Unusual Event) the grotesque world is built on the same idea, characteristic of Mrożek: a specific system is disturbed by the unexpected intrusion of a foreign element which proves to be destructive. In his latest stories (from the volume *Dwa listy* [Two Letters, 1974]) the grotesque turns into a macabre game in which the basic questions of human existence are highlighted.[9]

One can note a similar phenomenon in Różewicz's plays.[10] The grotesque is already evident in his early poetry which presents a wrecked and senseless world. It is a record of experiences during the occupation. In viewing them, the poet avoided all heroization; what absorbed him was the vision of a mutilated world. Różewicz's plays are perhaps closest to existentialism. The grotesque is born in the destruction of individuality, in its fragmentation into various separate social roles (*Kartoteka* [The Personal File, 1959]). Probably Różewicz's best play, *Stara kobieta wysiaduje* (The Old Woman Alights, 1968) takes place in a café which is transformed into a rubbish heap. It is, however, not an existential rubbish heap modeled after Beckett; it is a totalitarian rubbish heap. In it the Guardian of Order turns out to be the most important figure.

In the grotesque universality is united with the particular; it is characterized by a nonconformism vis-à-vis established values and officially approved manners of speaking. The question arises as to how literature of the grotesque can develop in situations which are not always favorable. It seems that it holds a rather peculiar position. It commands a greater margin of freedom than works representative of other poetics. It can do so because it has been acknowledged that this literature does not directly relate to social realities, that it by nature is "odd," "unreal," "fantastic." One way or another, its social role is immense. To a certain extent one can compare it to the role of the jester at the royal court. The jester was allowed to say more than not only any courtier but also than any other member of society. Carrying the jester's insignia he had his own privileges. He was entitled to state so-called bitter truths. But he did not cease to be the jester even when criticizing the king. In this role of jester is expressed the greatness of the grotesque which retained its independence from official ideologies and visions of the world while subjecting them to doubt. Its weakness, however, is also evident, because in order to accomplish that it cannot relinquish that very role of the jester. That jester-like quality, however, does not fully exhaust the whole phenomenon.

Wolfgang Kayser in his classic interpreted the grotesque as the expression of an alienated world. This is undoubtedly true. But in depicting that alienated world the grotesque somehow overcomes it. It does so by the fact alone that in a more or less direct manner it speaks about that world. This function of the grotesque seems to be particularly evident in contemporary Polish literature. Perhaps it would not be an exaggeration to say that in a certain way the grotesque fulfills a function similar to that which in antiquity was performed by tragedy: it is catharsis.

NOTES ·

1. M. Bachtin (Bakhtin), *Twórczość Franciszka Rabelais'go a kultura ludowa średniowiecza i renesansu* (The Creative Work of François Rabelais and the Folk Culture of the Middle Ages and the Renaissance), Cracow, 1975 (English translation

by H. Iswolsky: *Rabelais and His World,* Cambridge, Mass. & London, 1968). See further A. Clayborough, *The Grotesque in English Literature,* Oxford, 1965.

2. L. Sokół, *Groteska w teatrze Stanisława Ignacego Witkiewicza* (The Grotesque in the Theatre of Stanisław Ignacy Witkiewicz), Wrocław, 1973.

3. Such a position is taken by L. B. Jennings, *The Ludicrous Demon, Aspects of the Grotesque in German Post-Romantic Prose,* Berkeley & Los Angeles, 1963. As to the formation of the notion of the grotesque, see F. K. Barasch, *The Grotesque: A Study of Meanings,* The Hague – Paris, 1971; cf. further Ph. Thomson, *The Grotesque,* London, 1972.

4. L. A. Forster, "The Grotesque: A Method of Analysis," *Zagadnienia Rodzajów Literackich* 1966, vol. IX, 1 (16).

5. I deal with this in more detail in the essay "Parodia konstruktywna" ("Constructive Parody") in the volume *Gry powieściowe* (Fictional Games), Warsaw, 1973.

6. See the article by S. Chwin, "'Trans-Atlantyk' wobec 'Pana Tadeusza'" ("Transatlantic" in Relation to "Pan Tadeusz"), *Pamiętnik Literacki,* 1975, Vol. LXVI, 4.

7. On Gombrowicz's attitude toward the cultural traditions of the Polish gentry, see J. Błoński's essay "Sarmatyzm u Gombrowicza" (Sarmatism in Gombrowicz), in the collective volume *Tradycje szlacheckie w kulturze polskiej* (Gentry Traditions in Polish Culture), edited by Z. Stefanowska, Warsaw, 1976.

8. Two articles by A. Bereza deal with this question: "W kręgu 'walki' (O problemach stylizacji)" (In the Realm of 'Dispute'—On Problems of Stylization), in the collection *Z teorii i historii literatury* (On the Theory and History of Literature), edited by K. Budzyk, Wrocław, 1963; "Parodia wobec struktury groteski" (Parody in Relation to the Structure of the Grotesque), in the volume *Styl i kompozycja* (Style and Composition), edited by J. Trzynadlowski, Wrocław, 1965.

9. See the essay by J. Błoński, "Mrożek filozof. Próba interpretacji fantastyki współczesnej" (Mrożek the Philosopher: An Attempt at Interpreting Contemporary Fantastic Literature), *Pamiętnik Literacki,* 1977, vol. LXVIII, 3.

10. On the grotesque in contemporary Polish drama cf. Z. Jastrzębski, "O pojęciu groteski i niektórych jej aspektach w dramacie polskim doby obecnej" (On the Concept of the Grotesque and Some of Its Facets in Present-day Polish Drama), *Dialog,* 1966, 11.

George Gömöri

THE MYTH OF THE NOBLE HOOLIGAN:
MAREK HŁASKO

Marek Hłasko's collection of short stories *First Step Among the Clouds* (*Pierwszy krok w chmurach*), published in 1956, belongs without doubt to the most interesting debuts of the fifties. His stories made an impact with their outspokenness, occasionally verging on brutality; the frankness with which he spoke about social conditions and problems of young people in Poland was strikingly new to readers force-fed on Socialist Realist idylls or "production novels." In 1958 he won the Polish Publishers' Award but already before that his name had come to be associated with the wave of "black literature" — the pessimistic portrayal of reality which won its legitimacy during the first Thaw. At the time of the publication of his first collection Hłasko was only twenty-two years old; two years later, because of his defiance of Polish censorship, he was more or less forced to become a political refugee in the West. The rest of his life he spent in different countries — France, Germany, Israel, and finally, the United States — in a desperate search for a new identity. At one point he was ready to return to Poland but the authorities refused to let him back. He died in Wiesbaden in 1969. The circumstances of his death suggest suicide or at least near-suicidal carelessness. He was thirty-five years old when he died.

Hłasko's work (which includes several short novels, an autobiographical sketch and about thirty short stories) can be approached from various angles, some more fruitful than others. For example, one could see in him a representative of the Polish "angry young men," the battered generation — the "lost" epitaph had been already reserved in Poland for the previous generation, that of the "Columbus Boys"[1] — which had experienced the war as a child and grew up uneasily balancing between the conflicting demands of State and Family, Ideology and Reality. Although there were certain elements in Hłasko's prose which he shared with other writers of his generation these were by no means decisive. By 1956 he had constructed his own myth, he had an outlook, an approach to reality expressed in a style unmistakably his own. At this point one could dislike his naive and crude "philosophy" but still like his prose — a basic sincerity and strength of purpose shone through his most provocative passages.

Basically, Hłasko was not a political writer. His awareness of this is clearly discernible from the pages of *Twenty-years Old, Beautiful Young Men* (*Piękni, dwudziestoletni,* Paris, 1966), his "precocious autobiography." Nonetheless, the better half of the book is taken up by the discussion of the political feelings, jokes and complexes of Poles in the fifties. But then this is the context in which he grew up, these are the facts he remembers. In his recollections he would disclaim responsibility: "I am only a witness of the prosecution; the case itself is indifferent to me as long as the trial is interesting."[2] An exaggeration perhaps; but I do not think Hłasko was an admirer of democracy or of the free enterprise system either (in spite of his pro-American sympathies). To understand his revulsion to the monolithic political system in Poland which later on found expression in *The Graveyard,* we need not go too far. Although he came from a middle-class family, Hłasko earned his living for some time as a lorry-driver and his experiences from these years left a strong imprint on his way of thinking. Working at Bystrzyca Kłodzka or at the Central Railway Station in Warsaw he learned a thing or two about Polish reality: to begin with, the popular maxim that honest hard work will get you nowhere and that the Socialist system of distribution works only thanks to the existence of an 'alternative market' and a 'black' system of exchanging goods. He also learned to disrespect the State which in those years was exploiting the worker more unscrupulously than the capitalists had ever done before. Hłasko claims to have understood the system and to have started thinking "in dramatic categories"[3] while working for a Warsaw construction firm. His connection with the secret police also helped — if not exactly ideologically, at least in finding his own style. This strange claim was made by Hłasko in his memoirs where he told how he had been recruited as an informer by an officer of the Polish Security Police and how he became, in his own words, an "informer *à rebours*"[4] writing nasty reports on staunch Communists while praising sky-high the ideological reliability of people totally hostile to the regime. Moreover, he can recommend this "genre" to others; in his opinion there is nothing that can teach you so much clarity and terseness of style as the regular composition of reports for the police.

On the basis of such experiences Hłasko saw Polish reality now in depressingly dark, now in grotesque terms. The only thing that kept him going under such conditions was youth and his harsh vitality which even bouts of drinking and fits of depression could not destroy. Much of the gloom went into his first authentic stories (I discount "Baza Sokołowska" on account of which he later felt ashamed) such as "We are Flying into the Sky," "First Step Among the Clouds" and "The Most Sacred Words of Our Life." These stories described episodes in the life of young people whom society — that is outsiders, people not participating in their private mystery — shocked and humiliated by destroying the psychological foundations of their love. "Society debases love" has been, of course, a well-known theme in modern European literature; what made it particularly relevant in this case was the fact that "society" here was not simply the malice or envy of others but also the objective circumstances, the terribly cramped living conditions of Warsaw, the tiredness, inertia or dour cynicism of people who had been through so much during the German occupation and the following years. At this stage Hłasko's heroes were mainly workers or young people, not particularly articulate or sophisticated, but ordinary folks with simple enough desires and expectations that were pathetically low. In a short story written in 1956 ("A Port of Desires") the seaman hero formulates the philosophy behind these expectations:

> Life is a dirty hell and people foul everything. You have the worst scare in such moments when you feel that something good is beginning to happen in your life.[5]

The plight of luckless young people is the theme of Hłasko's most popular long story, *The Eighth Day of the Week* (*Ósmy dzień tygodnia*). The main problem of the young in Warsaw is that they find no place where they can be truly alone, where they can make love undisturbed. Peter has no proper place of his own but lives in a den in the ruins of a house which he shares with three friends; Agnieszka, his girlfriend, lives with her parents, brother and a subtenant in a small, crowded flat. The mother is bedridden, the father is worn out and intimidated, the brother is a drunk. There is but little hope for improvement, which is striking, considering the date: it is 1956, well after the Twentieth Congress. At one point Peter says: "We are all tired. The two things that bind people together in Poland are vodka and weariness."[6] The abuses of political power and the everyday struggle for the bare necessities have undermined people's values — cynicism is widespread and infectious. That is why the young idealists attach so much importance to love. The main characters have lost their faith in politics: Peter was jailed in 1952 (we never learn why), and Agnieszka's brother, Grzegorz, is an ex-functionary of the Communist Youth organization which by now is completely compromised and discredited. Yet in a sense Agnieszka is the worst victim of the regime. She cannot sleep with Peter, whom she loves, for the sheer lack of a roof, so after much frustration she gives herself to the first comer, a man whom she met by chance in a bar. *The Eighth Day of the Week* reflects the ways in which human life is deformed and debased in a society where, allegedly, "man is the highest value."

The only antidote to the bitterness and frustration created by such conditions is humor. Marek Hłasko is one of the funniest writers in post-war Polish literature. His is a ribald and often black humor, related not so much to Wiech (the author of popular feuilletons about characters living in the less fashionable districts of Warsaw) as to Zoshchenko, and to the Hungarian writer P. Howard, neither of whom were known to Hłasko. The common source of this humor is the world of cheap novels, Westerns or adventure stories about legionnaires or gangsters. Young working-class Poles, part-time hooligans from Wola and Marymont, would often pose as these heroes, so it is not impossible that some of Hłasko's characters really spoke in the way he described them. In his memoirs Hłasko mentions Damon Runyon, claiming an affinity with this colorful chronicler of guys and dolls on Broadway, but the Polish writer's humor is more coarse and cruel and it draws heavily on political themes as well.

This is apparent in *The Graveyard* (*Cmentarze,* 1958, American edition, New York, 1959) where after a night spent in a police cell for drunkenness, the whole world of Kowalski (an ex-partisan and a Party member) turns into a nightmare. He is dismissed from his job, he is kicked out of the Party, and finally his daughter commits suicide; he cannot find consolation among his wartime Communist friends either. Yet strangely enough, the nightmare is more grotesque than just tragic — it is a tragic farce. There is the scene of a Party meeting in Kowalski's factory where a man is taken to account for keeping a dog called "Samba" (a clear indication of his pro-American sympathies!). Another worker incites the wrath of the meeting for publicly questioning a crude version of the Darwinian theory of evolution. A painter whom Kowalski visits during his quest for truth has now turned sculptor: he produces hundreds of Stalin's busts for a shooting-booth in the suburbs where people queue up to vent their frustrations. Hłasko's explanation why he wrote a grotesque rather than a tragic book is interesting — surely one cannot write a truly tragic story about this kind of totalitarianism.[7] The reason for this lies in the incalculability, the sheer arbitrariness of the Stalinist system. While in Hitler's Germany you knew exactly where you stood, whether you were accepted or persecuted by the regime, this was not true in Stalin's Russia where yesterday's heroes were today's "enemies of the people," where tormentors could be speedily transformed into victims and former victims could emerge in commanding positions. When the logic of changes is infathomable, one comes very close to a world of absurdity.

The Graveyard was — according to Hłasko — based on authentic facts; everything described in the book did take place sometime during the fifties. The plot however describes these nightmarish happenings in succession and they ruin Kowalski in a matter of days. Because of this, *The Graveyard* should be regarded perhaps as a parable about Stalinism, its central figure, Kowalski, cast in the role of Everyman, or that of the biblical Job whose patience is tried and found wanting by the powers that be. For if we apply the yardstick of strict realism to the novel, we are bound to see it as a caricature of the real Poland of the fifties; but good caricatures only stress and magnify typical features. Hypocrisy, police intimidation, careerism, drunkenness — all these were components of the reality which Hłasko tried to capture in this grotesque tale.

Next Stop — Paradise (*Następny do raju,* Paris, 1958; American edition, New York, 1960) was written about the same time but it reveals more about Hłasko's central myth and the nature of his preoccupations. If Kowalski was a very ordinary man, the characters in this novel are all unusual: they exist on the margins of society. Their work involves the delivery of logs from the forest to the nearest town. The roads are hazardous and the lorries very old, ready to break down or fall to pieces any minute. Human life is cheap on this job — by the end of the story three drivers are dead, a fourth one is arrested by the police for stealing timber, and only Zabawa, an embittered and stubborn Communist, and Warszawiak, a tough young man from the capital, survive the ordeal. The atmosphere of the book is not unlike Clouzot's and Yves Montand's film *La salaire de la peur* in which the heroes drive lorries full of ecrasite and can be blown up in a matter of seconds. While Zabawa's main aim is to fulfill the plan, all the other drivers just want to survive and get out of the mountains as soon as possible. It is in this story that we first come across Hłasko's strong, tough and reckless heroes whose downfalls are usually brought about by a woman. They are coarse and foul-mouthed "cowboys" with simple, almost childish desires. Most of them feel attached to their lorries; Warszawiak is not only a fast driver, but something of a speed-maniac who would say, with a touch of Hemingway in his voice: "At least in a car I can feel like a man."[8] The appearance of an attractive woman in this all-male territory spells danger. Zabawa's wife desperately wants to leave the mountains and go back to town — to achieve this she will do anything. Warszawiak has an ambiguous relationship with her: he is almost the only man on the base with whom she does not make love, whom she hates; yet he tries to help and protect her in various ways. It is the "sheriff's wife" syndrome from a somewhat faded Western. Hłasko readily admits that he has been influenced by Westerns which he admires but he considers this a good influence since "the genesis of the Western is an obsession with justice: a lonely man has to destroy evil, and brute force."[9] On the other hand, Hłasko does not quite adhere to the convention of Westerns: while in most films the hero is either a good man, or at least a reformed outlaw, Hłasko's protagonists are neither particularly good, nor repentant about their past. They often perform acts of gratuitous cruelty (e.g. Warszawiak's treatment of the prostitute in *Next Stop — Paradise*) and present a callous exterior to the world. Their saving grace lies in their courage and determination to carry out whatever task they had set for themselves. This task can be defined in either negative or in positive terms. Dov Ben Dov, the hero of *All Were Turned Away*, [10] simply wants to keep out of trouble and find an honest job in Eilat, for he is out of jail on parole and knows that a mistaken move might cost him years of freedom. As for Abakarov, the Russian airman in *Dirty Deeds* (*Brudne czyny*, Paris, 1964), he is obsessed with the idea of revenge which he must carry out in order to honor the memory of a dead friend.

Men have their work, their harmless or mad obsessions, but women want something different, they are always after something else. In Hłasko's fiction it is always a woman who messes up the life of the hero, or (in *Next Stop — Paradise*) that of several characters. Hłasko resents this, although he realizes that most women are in fact only paying back in kind, for their life had been ruined earlier by some man. Perhaps the most appropriate thing to be said about Hłasko's relationship to women is that it is a curious love/hate relationship with a strong tendency to emphasize hatred or the hopelessness of any long-term relationship — Hłasko seems to imply that the latter is impossible both on psychological and on biological grounds. In *Dirty Deeds* he meditates on a trait in women which he calls "their desperate whorishness." This is the corollary to women's desire to have "a whole man," for "A lonely man always represents a totality which a lonely woman can never represent; a woman can never find support in herself — in her body, her habits and her stupidity — something which millions of lonely men, content with a dog, money or alcohol, are capable of finding. And this is why there is such a lot of fortuitousness in the life of women which is regarded by men only as whorishness, only that and nothing else; but that is an effort made again and again, always ending in failure, a trial to accept another voice and another body, even if that voice or body wants to kill or destroy [you] ..."[11] Since a man is regarded as a self-sufficient entity whose need of women is mainly biological and not permanent, one can understand Abakarov's derisive evaluation of women (addressed to his German girlfriend, Catherine) in the same novel: "I have never really liked any of you, even a little or even for a moment. This may be so, because you really have the illusion that you can do something for a man. It was good with you because you gave me sleep. And this terrible exhaustion."[12] Behind Abakarov's swagger and misogynistic talk hides his fear that he might be deflected from his planned course of revenge (Catherine wants to leave Israel with him) and also "the collective wisdom" of men unhappy, demoralized or *morally castrated* by their love or concern for women.[13] This, in a sense, is thought to be worse than physical death which is the fate of some of Warszawiak's mates in *Next Stop — Paradise*. There Wanda, the temptress, is only an additional stimulus in the daily struggle against nature which involves the drivers in risking their lives, but people like Dov Ben Dov in *All Were Turned Away* are damned from the very beginning because his wife deserted him and is now expecting the baby of another man. The worst that can happen to you, implies Hłasko, is the loss of your pride and self-esteem. This can happen, of course, as a result of political terror, or of immoderate consumption of alcohol, but it is much more likely to happen as a result of the "love trap."

And conversely — if men treat women "generically," as samples of a coveted but dangerous biological species, women will also look at men in the same way. Most women in Hłasko's fiction are easy to possess and the hero lays them by using simple, manly stratagems. Women, according to this myth, are not attracted to men by the latter's superior intellect or firmness of character; they appreciate other things such as strength, rugged good looks and constant devotion, or else (depending on circumstances) just money. Cruelty, even brutality they can forgive; cowardice — never. This is still the well-worn pattern of the Western but there is more to it: Hłasko's women actually resent anything that dedicates their man to a higher purpose. Perhaps they sense (rightly?) that such dedication may undermine and destroy their private happiness. The snag is that most men worth their salt do not want that sort of "happiness" — they have other, more idiosyncratic ways of self-realization or self-destruction.

The portrait of the Lonesome Avenger or the Noble Hooligan would not be complete without certain other features. Technological fetishism is one of them. The motor-car and/or the aeroplane have a near-magic significance for Hłasko's heroes. They are powerful symbols of authority and wish-fulfillment. Just as the cowboy is attached to his horse, so are Hłasko's men attached to their machines, they know them intimately and enjoy handling them whether they drive lorries (*Next Stop — Paradise*), a jeep (*All Were Turned Away*) or fly an aeroplane (*Dirty Deeds*). Hłasko himself seems to be mesmerised by the possibilities that modern technology offers; in the afterword to *Next Stop — Paradise* he enthuses as follows: "The automobile is the most beautiful thing invented by 20th-century man — the only thing thanks to which it is possible to run away from life, from oneself and from others."[14] One has to come from a technologically underdeveloped society to wax that enthusiastic about the blessings of the car which is still an important status symbol in Eastern Europe and which was owned by exceedingly few people in the Poland of 1958.

Apart from automobiles there is another thing that means much for the Noble Hooligan and that is friendship. Again, the atmosphere of the Western is discernible: one might dedicate a life to avenging a friend who was murdered by outlaws or by the law itself, and one perseveres on this mission to the bitter end. Friendship, in the long run, is more important (because it is more sincere and lasting), than love. This view is particularly stressed in novels written outside Poland — in *All Were Turned Away* the friendship of Dov Ben Dov and Israel Berg is the only serious human bond in the whole novel, whereas in *Dirty Deeds* the memory of his friendship with Izaak provides constant ammunition to Abakarov's obsession; at one point he tells Catherine that he came to Israel in the first place because his friend, a Jew (Abakarov is not Jewish) wanted to be in the land of his people. Friendships endure even the otherwise fatal appearance of women and this happens even in Eilat, the Wild West of Israel, where there is a desperate shortage of the fair sex. In Hłasko's insistence on friendship as an important value there may be sentimental personal reasons (in his memoirs he refers to Edward Bernstein, a friend of his youth, as his "best friend," just as his first love remained his "only real love") but loyalty to a friend is also part of the myth of the Noble Bandit, a myth subconsciously, and after a while consciously, fostered by Marek Hłasko. And it is in *Dirty Deeds* where concepts such as male pride, loyalty and endurance are dominant that Hłasko reminds us most of another distinguished Polish expatriate, Joseph Conrad. Even his style, until then reminiscent of Hemingway with short, clipped dialogues and axiomatic formulations of quasi-philosophical views, turns more opaque, while the moods and emotional states of the main protagonists are described with careful eloquence.

Also here for the first time an element of genuine tragedy appears in Hłasko's fiction which partly makes us forget the fragility and the naive self-centeredness of his myth.

For ultimately Marek Hłasko's central myth strikes the reader as anachronistic. It is possible to write an entertaining book or a couple of good stories about the tough guys fighting it out in the Sudeten Mountains or at the "Coney Island" of Eilat; one can play-act the Noble Hooligan in Targówek or even in Los Angeles but what this pose hides is an inadequacy, a fear of others and a hatred of the whole world of the "not-I." Hłasko had shown considerable talent and most of his early writing was successful in capturing the specific mood of post-war Warsaw, a new town full of embittered, worn-out, tragic people with their special brand of humor, people who nevertheless participated in the daily comedy of life. *Dirty Deeds* shows a further stage in the development of his artistic sensibilities — it might have become the starting point of a new departure which never happened. *Sowa córka piekarza,*[15] Hłasko's last novel, was a disappointment: instead of following up his probe into individual psychology, into the nature of interhuman relationships, Hłasko fell back on the clichés of his early work. Perhaps the complexity of the sixties and the loss of his old artistic hunting-grounds was too much for him. In spirit he remained a Romantic, a slowly aging and superfluous rebel against East and West, a displaced alcoholic with the looks of a Slavonic Marlon Brando. The possibility of a comeback was there but it failed to materialize. Hłasko died young like James Dean, like Cybulski, and left behind a personal legend and a small *œuvre,* incomplete and uneven but nonetheless impressive and very readable. No picture of Poland in the nineteen-fifties can ever be complete and authentic without the bleak humor, the youthful pathos and the scornful challenge of the Noble Hooligan, Marek Hłasko.

NOTES

1. The name comes from Roman Bratny's book *Kolumbowie, rocznik 20* and it denotes the generation born in the nineteen-twenties.
2. Marek Hłasko, *Piękni, dwudziestoletni,* Paris, Instytut Literacki, 1966, p. 13.
3. Ibid., p. 14.
4. Ibid., p. 45.
5. Marek Hłasko, *Opowiadania,* Paris, Instytut Literacki, 1963, p. 100.
6. Ibid., p. 47.
7. *Piękni, dwudziestoletni,* p. 144.
8. Marek Hlasko, *Next Stop — Paradise,* London, Heinemann, 1961, p. 8.
9. *Piękni, dwudziestoletni,* p. 12.
10. Original title: *Wszyscy byli odwróceni.* It was published by the Instytut Literacki in Paris, 1964. This is the first of Hłasko's novels written in Israel where he lived for about two years between 1959 and 1961.

11. Marek Hłasko, *Brudne czyny,* Paris, Instytut Literacki, 1964, p. 256.
12. Ibid., p. 295.
13. Ibid., p. 297.
14. *Next Stop — Paradise,* p. 193.
15. It was published by Księgarnia Polska in Paris, with no date.

Michael Heim

HRABAL'S AESTHETIC OF THE
POWERFUL EXPERIENCE

Since Jaroslav Hašek's *Good Soldier Schweik* is the work of Czech literature best known outside Czechoslovakia, Western critics faced with new Czech works tend to place them in the Schweik tradition. The parallels they draw are often tenuous at best; Hašek is simply not all things to all Czechs. There is one Czech writer, however, who has very definitely picked up where Hašek left off. His name is Bohumil Hrabal.

Hrabal does not imitate Hašek. The valiant but finally unsatisfying attempt made by Karel Vaněk to complete *The Good Soldier Schweik* after Hašek's death illustrates the perils involved in imitation. True, Hrabal uses the same point of departure (the barroom story or *hospodská historka*) for the same purpose ("to transfer the material of life from the existential world to the level of comedy")[1] — in other words, for catharsis), but his basic approach is different. Hašek was an unconscious dadaist. Apparently unaware of the existence of the dada movement, he practiced its preachings as fervently as its most enthusiastic adepts, directing his very deliberate irrationality against the forces of an over-organized society. Hrabal, born a generation later (during the First World War, when Hašek — and dada — were in their heyday), is a conscious surrealist, a follower of the strong Czech surrealist movement that survived the Second World War and has remained active to this day. His surrealist stance is most evident in a story like "Want To See Golden Prague? " ("Chcete vidět Zlatou Prahu? "), where the guiding intelligence is a surrealist poet, but it pervades everything he has written. Like most surrealists he turns his irrationality inward and focuses on the individual. The individual transforms it into an effective means of coping with life's vagaries.

Among the stories that made Hrabal one of the most widely read Czech authors of the mid-sixties, "Palaverers" (Pábitelé) occupies a special place. The title — a nonce word which, though not coined by Hrabal, was adapted by him to suit his purposes[2] — entered the parlance of his readers overnight. They accepted it as the essence of all his garrulous, preposterous, innocent, passionate, bumbling, wise, zany, human characters. In "Handbook for the Apprentice Palaverer" ("Rukověť pábitelského učně"), a piece he wrote in 1970 as a preface to the first American edition of a selection of his stories,[3] Hrabal provides perhaps the definitive word on what it means to practice his brand of palavering. Rather than list schools attended, jobs held, and honors accrued, he runs together a series of impressionistic and seemingly incongruous self-definitions: ". . . I am the solid bell of imbecility cracked by the lightning of knowledge, my objectivity acquires extreme subjectivity, which I consider an accretion of nature and the social sciences, I am a negative genius, a poacher in the meadows of language, I am a game warden of comic inspiration, a tried and true ranger in the fields of the anonymous anecdote . . . I am a corresponding member of the Academy of Palavery . . ." Clearly Hrabal's concept of what palavering involves is central to his concept of art.

Oddly enough, however, neither the word *pábitel* 'palaverer' nor any of its family (*pábit* 'to palaver,' *pábení* 'palavering,' *zpáben* 'palavered') appears in "Palaverers" or in any of the stories in the collection that bears its name.[4] Why did Hrabal single out the characters in "Palaverers" as the first official representatives of the genus and the title characters in the title story of his second volume?

"Palaverers" differs substantially from Hrabal's other early stories in two respects: It is one of the few with a first-person narrator and the only one touching directly on the subject of art. Not only the title, therefore, but also the narrator and the basic theme contribute to make the story a programmatic work, a statement of the author's aesthetic.

As the narrator unfolds his story, he makes it clear he is an outsider, a Prague friend whom the budding painter Jirka Burgán has invited home to his village for advice. Not only is the narrator from the city, he is an intellectual, and the Burgáns' blind faith in his judgment identifies him further as a representative of the art establishment. To some extent the narrator is playing the role of raisonneur: he acts as the author's mouthpiece, expressing amazement, admiration — any of the emotions Hrabal wishes to call forth in his reader. In so doing he stands apart from Hrabal's usual third-person narrators, who serve little more than to set the scene and fill in the gaps between speeches. His first-person status also enables him to enter actively into the action, but here he parts company with the raisonneur. Instead of persuading the protagonists to appreciate his values, he is persuaded by them to respect and even practice theirs. At first the narrator tries to warn Mrs. Burgán that the scythe planted in old Mr. Burgán's skull may cause infection; he tries to make ordinary, rational sense of the antics Jirka goes through to set the mood for his paintings; he marvels at the idea that flabby Mrs. Burgán with one eye hanging lower than the other and a sagging lower lip once posed as a naked bronze statue in the fifth act of *Troilus and Cressida*. But as his day with the Burgáns proceeds and he shares their world, he comes to accept the special way in which they experience life. In the process the reader accepts it as well. For Hrabal has made his narrator an intellectual not only to set him off from the Burgáns, but to ease his audience — much of which can identify with the intellectual's position — with the least possible culture shock into the habitat of *homo palaverus*.

If this sort of narrator is out of the ordinary for Hrabal, so is the direct concern with art. Though art as such plays a part in other Hrabal stories (in the guise of the "absolute graphics" enthusiast in "The World Cafeteria"

("Automat svět") or the surrealist poet in "Want To See Golden Prague?" for example), nowhere else does it form the fundamental theme. "Palaverers" is fundamentally a study in aesthetics. The narrator is an art critic. From the start he recognizes the superiority of Jirka's technique: "The way you juxtapose blue and red. Why the Impressionists would be proud of your colors" (31). And before the day is out he accepts Mr. Burgán's explanation of his son's success: ". . . our boy doesn't have any formal training, so he makes up for it with experiences he feels deeply" (30–31). The aesthetic underlying all Hrabal's early stories and the idea of palavering as such is the deeply felt experience, the powerful experience.

Hrabal's aesthetic of the powerful experience bears a certain resemblance to the Russian formalist idea of *ostranenie,* defamiliarization, seeing with innocent eyes. Both aim at undermining conventional perception; both delve beneath the surface for new insights into the world. Jirka's natural ability to see brilliant color under the all-pervasive layer of cement dust is a metaphor of the deeper vision Hrabal is after.[5] It recalls Natasha's ability in *War and Peace* to cut through the "dust" of conventionality and see the opera quite differently from the rest of the audience. But while Tolstoy uses the device to evoke scorn and derision (the reader learns how convention dupes him), Hrabal turns it into a vehicle of high spirits, exhilaration (the reader discovers art where he least suspected). The aesthetic of the powerful experience is in fact imbued with an irrational optimism. The true palaverer finds things better than they seem to others, and since the true palaverer is also an artist — literally in the case of the prototype Jirka, figuratively in the case of most of Hrabal's other characters — art serves as a safety valve against the rigors of the human condition. The goal of the aesthetic of the powerful experience lies not in reproducing reality, but in bypassing reality. Its main concern is not life, but something larger than life. When Jirka decides to do a statue of Bivoj, a legendary Czech hero, he asks his puny father to model for him. The result — a musclebound giant.

Closely related to irrational optimism and every bit as essential to the aesthetic of the powerful experience is excess, hyperbole. Again Jirka's Bivoj statue provides a good illustration, and it is the puny muscleman himself who states Hrabal's primary aesthetic axiom in a nutshell: "Our son is always exaggerating . . . It's the artist in him" (27). To be a creative artist, in other words, is to exaggerate.

Although in "Palaverers" the objects Hrabal builds his aesthetic around are visual — painting and sculpture — it lends itself without major modification to verbal art as well. In fact, the story may be read as an extended metaphor for Hrabal's literary credo.

Part of Mrs. Burgán's palavering routine consists of muttering a gentle "Rascals" each time the recruits stationed nearby set off one of their hand grenades. When the narrator tries to prime it for her, she lays her hand on his sleeve and says, "Not you . . . It's a game we play" (31). What she means is that the fun the family makes of one another and the outside world, its palavering, is a game, is art, and that like all games (including the war games on the hill), like all art, it has its own rules. The rules governing Jirka's graphic art apply to the entire family's verbal art. In both cases a negatively marked slice of reality — dust pollution in the former, sound pollution in the latter — is bypassed by the good graces of hyperbole: the riot of color he uses to coat his canvases on the one hand, the helicon he plays to combat the thunderous silence the family must endure on Sundays — the only day the recruits are off duty — on the other.

All Hrabal's early stories follow this pattern. Mr. Burgán — flying through feces, straddling his motorcycle for two hours in a thistle patch, escaping from a swarm of wasps with a scythe sticking out of his skull — is not alone. He forms part of a fellowship that includes the hero of "Angel Eyes" ("Andělský voči"), who writes a letter to his insurance company with the salutation "Dear Dirty Bastards and Murderers" (38); and the little boy at the end of "The Notary" ("Pan notář") who stuffs into his mouth a used prophylactic he has just fished out of the river; and the coal heaver in "A Prague Nativity" ("Pražské jesličky") who says, ". . . in the past thirty years I've loaded so much coal in my scuttle that if I put all those cellar stairs end to end I could climb clear up to the moon" (135). The Hrabalian powerful experience naturally lends itself to hyperbole.

Within the context of Hrabal's early stories the "Palaverers" narrator plays an unusually large role. His function, however, is to demonstrate that the constant intervention of a conventional literary narrator is superfluous, that the powerful experience suffices in and of itself. The narrator represents the "academy" with its official, sometimes even bureaucratic requirements and restraints; Jirka and his family represent an art free of dogma. That the narrator himself senses the dichotomy becomes clear when, asked by Mrs. Burgán whether Jirka ought to go to Prague to study, he lowers his eyes in embarrassment and replies, "Prague is like a pair of obstetric forceps . . . and these pictures, they're no child's play. They are the finished product" (32). Jirka has no need of directives from Prague, the academy, or anywhere else. His art is not rule-free — no art is free of rules — but it is free of all inhibitions imposed from without (and especially from above) and the schematics they encourage.[6]

By the end of the story the Burgáns have won the narrator over to their side. Hrabal charts his progress by registering his changing attitude toward the cement dust. Even before introducing himself, the narrator introduces the dust: "It was drizzling cement dust, and all the houses and gardens were coated with finely ground limestone" (23). After talking a while with Mr. Burgán, he describes a cart moving along the road, completely engulfed in dust: "The driver just kept singing his cheerful song inside the cloud of dust. Suddenly the gelding on the right gave a jerk on the reins . . . and shook down a good hundred pounds of cement dust" (24). His brief exposure to palavering has begun to have an effect on him; he takes optimistic note of the singing emerging from the midst of the dust and comments hyperbolically on the amount of dust falling from the tree. Full conversion, however, comes only with the final image, the final words in the story. Just as Mr. Burgán is about to vacuum an aster bush so that his wife can make up a bouquet for the narrator to take back to Prague, another hand grenade goes off on the hill and ". . . a small white cloud formed just above the clearing. It was like a white hawthorn bush in bloom" (34).

With this image the narrator demonstrates that he has accepted the dust on the same terms as the Burgáns; he sees it through their eyes. He has caught from his hosts the eminently infectious aesthetic of the powerful experience, the creative exuberance that empowers the palaverer to turn the petty into the sublime. Surely it is Hrabal speaking in the person of Mr. Burgán when the latter characterizes his son's art with the words "minimum cause, maximum effect" (32), for these words contain the kernel of Hrabal's art as well.

NOTES

1. See Emanuel Frynta's rich analysis of the urban oral folklore element in Hrabal's works in his afterword to the Hrabal anthology *Automat svět* (Prague: Mladá fronta, 1966), pp. 319-331.

2. Writing in the literary weekly *Literární noviny* (March 14, 1964, p. 2), the poet František Hrubín recounts how one day while he and his friend, artist Kamil Lhoták, were leafing through a weekly from the days of Franz Josef they came upon a feuilleton that particularly caught their fancy. It pictured the Czech Parnassian poet Vrchlický, by this time ailing and well on in years, tossing away his fiftieth or sixtieth cigarette of the day and sighing, "This palavering is having a bad effect on me." Hrubín and Lhoták took a liking to the word and began peppering their conversations with it. At first they used it to refer to anything off-beat or eccentric an elderly person happened to do, then to anything eccentric anyone did. Before long, when someone they knew fell in love, they said he was palavered; when someone had a bit too much to drink, they called him palavered too. Finally, anything anyone threw himself into with gusto they qualified as palavering. Since Hrabal belonged to their circle, he must have heard the word quite often. In his hands, however, it took on a very specific meaning.

3. Bohumil Hrabal, *The Death of Mr. Baltisberger* (New York: Doubleday, 1975), pp. xiii-xvii. The preface has not appeared in Czech. Page numbers following translations in the present article refer to this edition, which contains, along with "Palaverers": "Romance" ("Romance"), "Angel Eyes" ("Andělský voči"), "A Dull Afternoon" ("Fádní odpoledne"), "Evening Course" ("Večerní kurs"), "The Funeral" ("Pohřeb"), "The Notary" ("Pan notář"), "At the Sign of the Greentree" ("U zeleného stromu"), "Diamond Eye" ("Diamantové očko"), "A Prague Nativity" ("Pražské jesličky"), "Little Eman" ("Emánek"), "The Death of Mr. Baltisberger"

("Smrt pana Baltisbergra"), "The World Cafeteria" ("Automat svět"), and "Want to See Golden Prague?" ("Chcete vidět Zlatou Prahu?").

4. Bohumil Hrabal, *Pábitelé* (Prague: Mladá fronta, 1964). "Pábitelé" was reprinted in the *Automat svět* anthology cited in note 1 above. *Automat svět* also includes stories from Hrabal's first collection, *Perlička na dně* (*Pearls at the Bottom*) (Prague: Československý spisovatel, 1963).

5. Another Hrabal story, "Diamond Eye" (also originally from *Pábitelé* and anthologized in *Automat svět*), deals with perception in an even more literal sense. Sixteen-year-old Vendulka, the main character, is on her way to Prague for an operation that may enable her to see for the first time in her life. Her picture of what goes on around her is constrained only by the limits of her imagination, and her imagination is virtually limitless. What will happen to her flights of fancy if the big-city doctors restore her sight is as much up in the air at the end of "Diamond Eye" as what will happen to Jirka's art if the big-city academicians tamper with the aesthetic of the powerful experience.

6. John Fowles treats much the same problems in the title story of his collection *The Ebony Tower* (Boston: Little Brown, 1974), pp. 1–114. His manner and style are entirely different, his framework and conclusion remarkably similar. In both "The Ebony Tower" and "Palaverers" a sophisticated artist (Fowles's London-based Williams is a painter, teacher, and critic) makes an excursion to the countryside to visit an "instinctive" artist (Williams goes to the Breton woods to interview a crochety renegade English painter), and in both works the magic of the setting — or rather, the direct, fundamentalist approach to artistic creation it fosters — leads the initially self-assured sophisticate to a profound revaluation of his art: Fowles's character realizes how cold and schematic his own abstract work has been; Hrabal's recognizes the value of untrammeled expression. It is almost as if Western Europe in Fowles and Eastern Europe in Hrabal were owning up to their post-war aesthetic excesses. Fowles takes the revaluation process much farther than Hrabal; his work is a novella, ten times the length of Hrabal's short story, and his main character goes on to think through his whole life in the light of what he has learned about his art. But both authors have used a similar point of departure to make a similar point, namely, that art cannot be straitjacketed.

D. Barton Johnson

A STRUCTURAL ANALYSIS OF SAŠA SOKOLOV'S
SCHOOL FOR FOOLS:
A PARADIGMATIC NOVEL

I. Theme and Basic Oppositions

School for Fools is the first novel of Saša Sokolov, a Russian writer born in 1943 who has recently followed his novel into exile and now lives in the United States.[1] The book has been widely reviewed and surprisingly well received, especially considering its restricted distribution and its demands on the reader. The late Vladimir Nabokov, a man not known for the generosity of his critical judgments, described the short novel as an "enchanting, tragic, and touching book."

The novel is a first person account, retrospectively narrated, of the mental landscape of a nameless, schizophrenic adolescent who, now in his twenties, tells his story with the assistance of an author-persona. Through the kaleidoscopically chaotic prism of the young man's schizoid mind we see a number of incidents reflecting both his disordered perceptions and his attempts to come to terms with his psychic abnormality vis-à-vis the surrounding world. These experiences are manifested primarily in his relationships with his parents, with certain members of the dacha community where the family summers, with his doctor, and with members of the staff of the "School for Fools" that he attends. The father dislikes and resents his abnormal son while the boy's kind but unimaginative mother acts as a buffer between them. The protagonist has apparently spent a number of periods in a mental institution where he is attended by a Dr. Zauze. Allied with Dr. Zauze in the narrator's mind are Nikolaj Gorimirovič Perillo, the petty tyrant in charge of the School for Fools, and his deputy, Šejna Solomonovna Traxtenberg, who stalks the school corridors dragging her club foot. Opposed to these two figures are two other of the school's staff who occupy cardinal positions in the boy's mental life. One of these is Veta Akatova, the biology and botany teacher, whom he loves and whom he fantasizes as his bride-to-be. She and her father, a rehabilitated entomologist and Academician, live in a nearby dacha as does the boy's other idol, the iconoclastic misfit Pavel (who is also called Savl) Norvegov, the geography teacher. Norvegov has died at some point during the boy's school years and most of the lad's recalled conversations with him postdate his death and are entirely imaginary as are his relations with Veta and her father. The biology teacher, Veta, and the geographer, Norvegov, serve as the respective focal points of the disturbed adolescent's efforts to reach a psychological accommodation with the elemental human experiences of love, sex, and death.

The theme of the book resides in its fundamental opposition Irrationality/ Rationality with the former being the positively defined or marked member. This most basic dichotomy is manifested through three parallel, superimposed, but scarcely less central polarities: Madness/ Sanity, Freedom/ Bondage, and Nature/ Institutions.

The narrator-protagonist's madness is such that the two halves of his personality are in constant dialogue with each other. In general, the major voice "A" is the narrator and the second, minor voice "B" is a hectoring presence that constantly demands further details, offers corrections and accuses the major voice of both fundamental and trivial fabrication while decrying "A"'s efforts to push "B" into the background. In some senses voice "B" is that of rationality, pointing out the primary narrator's confusion of reality and fantasy. Voice "B" asserts that their psychiatrist, Dr. Zauze, has charged him with following "A" at all times and attempting "to merge with him into a single whole, a single being with inseparable thoughts and aspirations, habits and tastes" (R71/ E98). In certain other scenes, however, the voices whose respective identities are not in any way formally signaled in the text seem to switch roles. At times it seems that the two identities go their own ways in complete mental and physical dissociation, while at others both halves are fully aware of the activities, thoughts, and memories of the other. Although it would be attractive to distinctively ally each of the voices with one of the basic polarities, Irrationality/ Rationality, there do not appear to be sufficient grounds for doing so.[2]

Dr. Zauze has advised the narrator that it is only through the full integration of the two parts of his personality that he will be cured, or as the doctor puts it, find *pokoj i volju* ("peace and freedom") (R71/ E98). This bit of counsel curiously echoes that of the boy's idol, the geography teacher and aging hippie Pavel who in one of his many impassioned orations tells the collective narrator *Znajte, drugi, na svete sčast'ja net . . . no zato . . . est'že v konce koncov pokoj i volja . . .* ("Know this, my friends, there is no happiness on earth . . . but then . . . there is, finally, peace and freedom.") Since we live but once "live in the wind, young folk" (R19/ E27).[3] Although both men draw upon Puškin's phrase, their messages are quite different and even diametrically opposed, for Dr. Zauze is the spokesman of rationality, of the dread psychiatric hospital, while Pavel Norvegov, who bears the epithet *vetrogon* ("wind-driver") is the prophet of the wind, of the forces of the irrational.

It is a further fragment of Puškinian subtext that prompts the reader toward a more explicit awareness of the triune manifesting aspects of the novel's fundamental thematic opposition. In the midst of one of the narrator's numerous stream-of-consciousness deliria we find the phrase "God grant that we do not go mad" (R75/ E104) evoking Puškin's "God grant that I not go mad" — a poem that has many points of resonance with theme and incident in Sokolov's novel. In the poem, Puškin speaks of the powerful appeal of madness, identifying it with the creative gift ("I would sing in a fiery frenzy, / I would abandon myself in the fumes / of incoherent wondrous dreams") and likening the nature-enraptured poet, free in his madness to "A whirlwind, ploughing the fields, / Smashing the forests." Puškin regretfully concludes, however, that madness would ultimately mean not happiness and freedom, not the voice of the nightingale and the delights of nature, but the derision of the sane, incarceration and the clank of fetters. The poem thus prefigures all of the major thematic dichotomies of Sokolov's *School for Fools*.

The Madness/Sanity polarity of Sokolov's novel has already been touched upon in our preceding comments on the boy's insanity, as has the opposition of the forces representing the irrational and the rational. The second thematic opposition, Freedom/Bondage, flows directly from the first, for, as in the Puškin poem, the narrator sees freedom as a correlate of madness, and bondage as an aspect of sanity. The former identification is made explicit in two passages in the novel. One of the symptoms of the narrator's insanity is what he terms his "selective memory." Although his selective memory makes it impossible for him to experience time in a normal fashion, it has one great virtue. As he tells his mother, "this kind of memory allows us to live as we wish, for we remember only what is necessary to us . . ." (R85/E117). On another occasion the boy comes home and announces to his bewildered mother that he is a graduate engineer with his own car. When his mother asks if he is not the same schoolboy who that very morning had threatened to sew his mouth shut rather than eat his school lunch sandwiches, the boy replies with dignity "I don't know if one can be an engineer and a schoolboy together, perhaps some people can't, some are unable, some haven't been given the gift, but I, having chosen freedom, one of its forms, I am free to act as I wish and to be whoever I want either simultaneously or separately . . ." (R77–78/E107). For the narrator, his madness is a form of freedom, freedom from the slavery of reality and its monolinear chronology.

The third manifesting aspect of the Irrationality/Rationality thematic dichotomy is the Nature/Institutions opposition. The boy's family owns a summer dacha and much of the more lyrical writing in the book concerns the beauty of this rural setting with its river and abundance of flora and fauna. So profound is the boy's love of natural beauty that he undergoes a quasi-mystical, quasi-psychotic experience of merging with it and becoming a water lily, *Nymphea alba*, whose name he assumes. Flowers, plants and birds are an omnipresent motif and one of the protagonist's dreams is to become a naturalist, specifically an entomologist in emulation of Arkadij Akatov, the father of Veta, his beloved.

It is not by chance that all of the major positive characters live in the area of the summerhouse settlement and that all of them have names derived from those of natural phenomena. Most are associated with the wind, a figure used by Puškin as a metaphor for the wild, free forces of creativity. This agency of nature assumes the status of a (and perhaps even the) major character in Sokolov's work even appearing in a semi-personified, semi-deified guise as the *Nasvlajuščij Veter* 'the Ill-Boding Wind'). Norvegov, the globe-spinning geographer, is its major spokesman and the other affirmative characters are, in a surprisingly literal sense, its children. Counterpoised to the foregoing are institutional forces. Most prominent among these is the "School for Fools" with its endless (and much decried) homework assignments and a staff that cruelly holds out to mentally defective students the hopeless ideal of becoming engineers. Typifying the school is the idiotic and elaborately intricate *tapočka* system, introduced by the "tired and gloomy" director, Perillo, who insists each student change into special slippers while at school. Also typifying the "unnatural" institutional forces is the omnipresent threat of Dr. Zauze and the psychiatric hospital which Perillo holds over the boy's head. Perhaps the most odious representative of these rationalist, enslaving, institutional forces is the father who both by personality, as a cavilling misanthrope, and by profession, as a senior state prosecutor, is the quintessential institutional man.

II. Structure and Style

A. External Structure

The structure and style of the novel require commentary if for no other reason than that its form and content are tightly interwoven. *School for Fools* contains five chapter divisions, each of which has a very loosely defined but perceptible focal point, albeit with digressions which dominate long sections and overflow into other chapters.[4] With the exceptions of Chapter II, which is a series of realistically written vignettes of people living in the dacha settlement and those connected with them, the chapters are written in semi-episodic sections generally ranging from one to five pages in length. Each section is a single paragraph. Continuity even within the sections is haphazard and shifts of subject matter are frequent, being triggered by aleatory associations made with immediately preceding words or phonetic patterns. The greater part of the narration is in more or less well formed sentences although at times the narrator lapses into agrammatical stream-of-consciousness monologues. Portions of the narrative are addressed directly to various of the other characters, although not infrequently the reader is left to ascertain the identity of the addressee since they are not overtly identified. Much of the narration is set within two long dialogues, one set within the other and both containing long digressive episodes. The innermost, between the deceased Norvegov and the boy, has as its subject matter the boy's attempts to learn about sex. Inset within this inner dialogue is the story of Norvegov's demise and his posthumous attempts to recall this fact and the events leading up to it. The larger frame dialogue is between the boy and Akatov in which he asks the father for Veta's hand in marriage. Both of these conversations are imaginary and although here, as throughout the novel, different voices are represented it is clear from stylistic evidence (particularly certain distorted word forms and syntactic turns) that the boy is the single voice underlying the other characters — not excluding that of the author-persona. Stylistically, the writing runs the gamut from slang and subliterary colloquialisms to very high style indeed with a heavy admixture of Russian Church Slavonic.

Folklore elements are abundant. Especially prominent is the tale of the menacing bear with the wooden leg whose dragging gait is echoed in the ominous onomatopoeic element *skirlý* which symbolizes the mysterious sex act for the protagonist. Another folkloric element is to be observed in the use of fixed epithets for many of the characters. The mother is invariably described as "our kindly, patient mother"; a doomed classmate of the narrator, Roza Vetrova, bears the epithet "sepulchral flower"; Perillo, the principal, is invariably "tired and morose"; the resemblance of Akatov, the naturalist, to a "round-shouldered tree" is ritualistically mentioned.

In spite of its subject matter the novel has many moments of humor. Occasionally these are in scenic incident but more often in passages involving parody and word play. In one scene, the boy who is visiting Norvegov's dacha tells his teacher he is reading "several volumes of a contemporary classic" (R41/E59) given him by his father. On hearing the name, Norvegov rushes over to the river and dunks his head — apparently to avoid mind pollution. It is left to the reader to recall that the river is the Lethe, the river of oblivion. Mention has already been made of the Puškinian element in the book. Sokolov's literary antecedents are, however, more to be sought in the stylistic peculiarities of that other progenitor of modern Russian literature, Nikolaj Gogol'. In one case the debt is explicitly acknowledged. In a long inventory of people awakened by the passage of night trains the concluding entry is:

> . . . the dockmen, who think they hear the sound of an unfastened boat chain, a splash of oars, a rustle of sails, and then, throwing over their shoulders buttonless Gogolian overcoats, emerge from their dockhouses and stride across porcelain shoreline sands, and dunes, and grassy embankments; the still, faint shadows of the dockmen are cast on the reeds and the heather, and their home-made pipes gleam like bits of rotted maple wood, attracting astonished moths (R12/E17).

This seizing upon a passing character arising incidentally in the course of a description, who then suddenly and briefly comes to life before receding into oblivion is a typically Gogolian device.[5]

The most pervasive source of humor in the book is word play. The list of awakened sleepers mentioned above also includes such pairings as *umnyx professorov i bezumnyx poètov, dačnyx izgoev i neudačnikov — udil'ščikov rannej i pozdnej ryby* ... R11).[6] The boy recounts how his father has him copy extracts from newspaper editorials so that he will become better versed *v voprosax vnešnej i vnutrennej kalitiki* R97)[7]; elsewhere reference is made to the *otdel narodnogo oborzovanija* (R125)[8]; the bookstore slogan [*kniga*] *ukrašaet inter'er* mushrooms into ... *inter'er, èkster'er, fokster'er* (R118),[9] and so on.

B. Internal Structure

In the traditional realistic novel the narrative is carried forward by the plot, a series of motivated, causally connected incidents, which move unidirectionally along a linear time line.[10] In essence, this is necessarily so, for the very concepts of motivation or causality are dependent upon a linear time sequence. The motivation of an event must obviously precede the event itself and without motivation there can be no plot. It is precisely these facts that result in the assignment of the traditional "realistic" novel to the syntagmatic axis of language.

Škola dlja durakov stands apart from these fundaments of the traditional syntagmatic novel by the device of having a madman as its narrator. This does not in itself, however, enable the writer to escape the above-mentioned confines of the traditional novel. This has been made possible by assigning the narrator a very special sort of madness in which the central aberration involves time and memory, the precise elements underlying plot and chronology. A frequent motif in the protagonist's narrative is his comment "in general in our mind something is wrong with time, we don't understand time properly" (R15/E22–23). This is connected with his other major psychic peculiarity — his "selective memory." The narrator's specific sort of psychosis motivates the a-rational shape and flow of the narrative. As an example: voice "B" asks "A" if he remembers meeting the teacher Norvegov on a train platform some years before. "A" does, but the reader is thrown into confusion several lines later when it develops that Norvegov had already been dead for over two years at the time of the encounter (R18/E26). The narrator feels time to be the source of his madness and even formulates his own theory of time. He notes the artificiality of calendars with their sequential and counterfeit numbering of days. In (his) reality, each person has his own unique calendar that consists of a sheet of paper with a multitude of randomly scattered dots, each representing one day, but not any particular day: "... the days come whenever one of them feels like it, and sometimes several come all at once. And sometimes a day doesn't come for a long time. Then you live in emptiness, not understanding anything, quite sick" (R23/E33–34). This theory of time underlies the a-chronology of the narrative and is manifested at every level — thematically, in the non-sequentiality of related scenes, and even grammatically. So central is this aberration that in many passages, as in the following, the narrator refuses to commit himself to any single temporal marker: ...

nedavno (siju minutu, v skorom vremeni) ja plyl (plyvu, budu plyt') na vesel'noj lodke po bol'šoj reke. Do ètogo (posle ètogo) ja mnogo raz byval (budu byvat') tam . . . (R24).[11] In another example: *Ja ženjus', očen' skoro, vozmožno včera ili v prošlom godu* (R121).[12]

The protagonist's obsession with time is reflected in still other ways. The boy rejects the idea fostered by the school that he, like all Soviet youth, should become an engineer, for what is the point of concerning oneself with such trivia as *čertit' čerteži černymi černilami kogda so vremenem ne očen' xorošo* (R73).[13] As a matter of urgent priority he calls for the establishment of a "supercommission" which will "straighten out the matter of time." At another point the boy strides into the school toilet carrying his "plans for the transformation of time" in his briefcase (R80/E111).

We have remarked that the particular areas of delusion manifested by the narrator shape the structure of the narrative in that it is freed from the strictures of linear chronology, hence of causality and plot. This, by implication, raises the question of the mechanism by which the narrative proceeds within each episode.[14] To provide grounds for addressing this question, we shall attempt to summarize one of the episodes in the narrative. This is a hazardous undertaking, for in the very process of summary an impression of unity and coherence is produced which underplays the seemingly chaotic and discursive nature of the narrative.

The boy's family shares an apartment entry hall with Šejna Traxtenberg. In this entry hall the boy finds two large railroad furniture-shipping crates. Fascinated by anything even remotely connected with trains the protagonist idly wonders about the train and branch-line by which the crates arrived in the city. At this point, the author-persona interrupts, saying "Dear student so-and-so, I, the author of this book, have a pretty clear picture of that train — a long freight" (R30/E43). This introduction is followed by a three-page passage in which the author creates an entire new world. The train stands on a siding. Various commissions inspect it, chalking their findings on the sides of the RR cars. Bored, one man starts to use the side of a RR car as a blackboard to calculate his retirement and pension. As he reaches into his pocket for a piece of chalk, the author interrupts in mid sentence inserting ("here I should note in parentheses that the station where this action takes place could never, even during the two world wars, complain about a lack of chalk . . .") (R31/E44). This introduces a list of thirty-eight real and unreal items that the station lacks but, he continues, there is no shortage of chalk. In fact, the station, the river, and the town are all named *Mel* ('chalk') and chalk mining is the sole industry of the settlement. The entire life history of the village is revealed. The residents not only live by chalk, they die from an industrial disease caused by it. The page-long digression ends, the parentheses close, and the pension calculations resume. This vignette is followed by a discussion of other examples of chalk graffiti on the cars accompanied by imaginary biographies of the authors. Finally the train leaves the siding and speeds through the countryside displaying its chalk inscribed texts to the gaze of all Russia. The train finally arrives at its destination and the scene switches to the RR shipping office. Here in midsentence the boy interrupts the author and launches a several-page account of his nocturnal visit, under the name Te Kto Prišli ('Those Who Came'), to the home of the head of the RR shipping room to inquire about the crates. The visit is rendered as a stream-of-consciousness saga of how the official's wife bought the pyjamas he wears and only at the end of the section do we return to the furniture crates when the man invites Te Kto Prišli to visit the shipping office where the workers are listening while one of their number recites Japanese poetry. The next section describes the poetry reading and we are treated to actual quotations of Russian translations from such works as Nobel Prize winner Yasunari Kawabata's *Snow Country*. In their ensuing discussion the workers are transformed into characters with Japanese names and personalities. At length they revert to themselves when their boss, on behalf of Te Kto Prišli, asks about Šejna Traxtenberg's crates and orders a notification letter sent to her. In the final section the boy is standing in the entryway (which is empty since the crates have not yet arrived) reading the letter reporting their arrival. The episode, which has consumed nearly a quarter of the first chapter (itself of about forty-five pages) drifts off into oblivion with the "B" part of the boy's personality upbraiding the "A" component for reading other people's mail.

Among the things that might be noted about the episode is that it has no relevance to anything that precedes or follows it. The very introduction of the shipping crates is incidental and the internal progression of the episode is also a matter of chance association. The boy is launched on his fantasy by the sight of the RR shipping containers. When the author-persona takes over the narration he visualizes the chalk scrawls on the cars leading to his reconstruction of their origin and the creation of a whole town. In the scene at the RR shipping office after the arrival of the crates various railyard sounds drift in through the window. The metallic sounds suggest to the boy the ringing of a bicycle bell which signals the arrival of the dacha mailman and hence by association the arrival of any caller. This in turn leads to the night visit to the home of the pyjama-clad official. This stream-of-consciousness subepisode is presumably a deranged refraction of the purchase of a pair of pyjamas by the narrator's mother for his father since the latter appears in a similar pair near the end of the novel (R87/ E144). The boy's identity as Te Kto Prišli apparently evolves from his response, *Te Kto Prišli,* to the official's *Kto?* when he answers the knock at his door. The following "Japanese" section is presumably suggested by the vaguely oriental sound of the name, Te Kto Prišli, and so on.

Our examination of the internal flow of the episode and of the transformations of the characters suggests that the narrative progresses through what might be called a sort of associative dream logic that falls beyond the boundaries of chronology and causality. More generally, the writing and narrative technique display many of the features commonly associated with the surrealist movement. The resemblance is even more striking when some of the didactic writings of André Breton, the founding father of Surrealism, are examined. One of Breton's explications is as follows: "Surrealism is based on the belief in the superior reality of certain forms of association heretofore neglected, in the omnipotence of the dream, and in the disinterested play of thought."[15] More concretely, these ideals are manifested in such innovative modes of artistic organization as "free associations, violated syntax, non-logical and nonchronological order, dreamlike and nightmarish sequences, and the juxtaposition of bizarre, shocking, or seemingly unrelated images."

These statements seem a not inaccurate description of Sokolov's work. It is, however, in the surrealist approach to certain basic questions of existence that the most striking parallels may be found. In Breton's "*Second Surrealist Manifesto*" we read "Everthing leads us to believe there exists a spot in the mind from which life and death, the real and the imaginary, the past and the future, the high and the low, the communicable and the incommunicable will cease to appear contradictory."[16] *School for Fools* could well stand as a fictive avatar of this philosophical pronouncement. The positive role of the irrational is very prominent in Sokolov's novel in attitude, subject matter, and technique. It is "a tale told by an idiot" and written by a man who has explicitly rejected rationalism as a primary mode-of-being — a stance that is amply reflected in his novel with its principled disregard for the traditional narrative devices of chronology, motivation, and plot. In connection with the surrealist tenet of psychic automatism in the creative process it is certainly of interest that Sokolov reports that he does not revise his output apart from deletions.[17] All things considered, it does not seem amiss to regard Sokolov's *Škola dlja durakov* as a late Russian flowering of the surrealist novel.

III. Paradigmatic Analysis

A. Recurrent Elements

Roman Jakobson has advanced the theory that narrative prose tends to fall along the syntagmatic horizontal axis of language and, consequently, manifests an essentially metonymic function. This is particularly true of the realistic novel with its dependence on linear time and plot. Conversely, certain non-realistic modes of writing are assigned by Jakobson to the paradigmatic vertical axis of language and manifest a basically metaphoric function. Such literary movements as Romanticism, Symbolism and Surrealism fall along this latter axis.[18]

Our discussion of Sokolov's novel with particular attention to the absence of a time/plot line and its assignment to the surrealist tradition suggests that the most fruitful critical approach to the novel might be in terms of concepts associated with the paradigmatic axis of language. Before proceeding, however, it would be well to make some final observations about plot and time in the context of the theory of the syntagmatic and paradigmatic axes. Plot, which is the major constitutive element of the realistic novel, is clearly a prime syntagmatic phenomenon in narrative just as is the sentence in lower level linguistic theory.[19] Perhaps most obviously of all narrative elements it rests on the process of combination and manifests the relationship of contiguity. Plot, like sentence, is sequential and time-dependent. The very concepts of causality and motivation upon which plot and plot movement hinge are meaningful and indeed conceivable only given at least tacit linear chronological sequence. There are also more general implications for the dimension of time in fiction that arise from the syntagmatic or paradigmatic orientation of the work. These polarities have as their respective correlates diachrony and synchrony. The narrative of the traditional syntagmatic novel proceeds diachronically; that of paradigmatically oriented novels synchronically. This distinction is of particular interest in the light of our subsequent comments on the fundamental structuring of the two types of narratives. The assignment of a novel to the paradigmatic axis has certain implications parallel but opposed to those mentioned above in connection with the 'syntagmatic novel'. If plot is primarily a syntagmatic function, what is its paradigmatic equivalent?

Paradigmatics is based on the phenomenon of similarity but similarity itself has an epistemological prerequisite. Antecedent to the idea of similarity is that of comparison which in turn depends upon repetition or recurrence.[20] It would seem reasonable to propose that just as chronologically linear, motivated sequences of scenes are the basic structural principle of traditional, realistic, syntagmatically oriented novels, so the achronological, unmotivated superimposition of recurrent scenes is the fundamental structural principle of paradigmatically oriented narratives. In the former, the narrative action is diachronic; in the latter — synchronic or, perhaps more accurately, a-chronic. An examination of *Škola dlja durakov* shows that while there is no plot there are many scenes which are wholly or partially recurrent and which by virtue of their similarity may be said to constitute paradigmatic sets. This element of repetition which exists not only on the level of scenes but of images and motifs is the fundamental structural principle of Sokolov's *School for Fools*.

The most striking recurrent scene in the book involves the narrator's attempts to inform himself about the mechanics of sex by querying his mentor Savl (or Pavel) Norvegov. During this after-school interview, Savl Petrovič is sitting in profile on the windowsill of the men's toilet of the school. Smoking, he sits with his knees drawn up so that his chin rests on them and so that he can warm his feet on the steam radiator which is below the window. This scene occurs, recurs, or is invoked nine times in the course of the short novel.[21] It is first alluded to in an interior dialogue in which "B" is mocking "A"'s love of Veta for both "A" and "B" are ignorant of the sex act. "A" remarks that "we once asked Pavel Petrovič if he had had women" (R72/E100). The imagined conversation with Norvegov then drifts off to other topics. The following recurrences touch on various sex-related themes such as Norvegov's outrage at the obscene graffiti on the toilet stalls and the reason he lurks in the toilet after school hours. In an intermediate series of recurrences the subject matter changes. Pavel experiences a loss of memory and asks the boy to help him fill in the gaps. In doing so it develops that Savl at some point in the past had been under threat of dismissal and during this interval had died. In the final occurrence of the scene Pavel finally responds to the boy's questions about sex by giving him "an excellent translated brochure by a German professor on marriage and the family" (R155/E209-210). In fact, the booklet tells the boy nothing apart from the vaguest generalities.

The image of Savl's profile in his characteristic pose resonates with a number of similar recurrent images in the book. Among these is the image of the boy himself, similarly posed, sitting in the grass reading (R40-41/E57-58). This somehow merges into the logo of a Soviet publisher of children's books which depicts a similar image, a dark youth against the background of a white dawn. This in turn is associated with the publisher's slogan *Kniga za knigoj* 'Book after book.' This slogan combined with the visual image merges in the boy's mind into one of his recurrent fantasies in which he sits for ten years in the appropriate posture reading "book after book" until he has become a handsome, very well-read young engineer who finally arises from his reading to visit his fiancée, Veta, in his new car. Thus the image of Savl on the toilet windowsill reverberates throughout the novel.

A second such scene is the account of a commuter train trip by the boy and his mother to a music lesson. This scene occurs only four times but each one is in increasing detail although the same key elements appear in all. The earlier occurrences are buried in stream-of-consciousness monologues hypnogogically induced by the sound of train wheels. The third occurrence focuses on another portion of the hypnogogic fantasy (a date with Veta) and it is only with the fourth occurrence that the context and incidents of earlier fragmentary scenes become fully intelligible. As this example suggests, Sokolov's writing, like that of many other avant-garde writers, is more oriented toward the careful re-reader than to the casual reader. Most of the major scenes, many with tangential subscenes which are also recurrent, are to be found more than once. Sometimes portions of the wording are identical, sometimes slightly or substantially modified.

This same pattern is to be observed in the case of recurrent images and motifs. Some of the recurrent images involve complex sets of attributes, some or all of which are mentioned at each appearance of a character. Traxtenberg-Tinbergen is often accompanied by such a constellation, particularly in her appearances in her alternate identity as Tinbergen, the witch. In this latter guise her attributes include: (1) the children's rhyme *Tra ta ta, tra ta ta, Vyšla koška za kota,*[22] (2) dancing in the apartment entryway an. ~chool corridors, (3) her association with the *Skirlý* folk tale (by virtue of her club foot). One or more of these (and several other) attributes are automatically introduced whenever reference is made to her although they have no conceivable relevance to the incident at hand.

As we remarked above in connection with the mutation of the recurrent scene of Savl Petrovič's pose, repeated images and motifs sometimes show signs of syncretism symptomatic of the narrator's derangement. One example of such is the image of the *devočka s prostoj sobakoj* 'girl with a plain dog'. This figure first occurs as one of the sights seen by the boy as he bicycles about the dacha settlement (R48-49/E68-69). The image reappears in the same form in a city cemetery where the boy and his mother are visiting his grandmother's grave. The boy mentally greets the girl, remarking to himself that he sees her here every visit (R91/E125). The image occurs again in a modified form in a description of the kitsch statuary in front of the boy's school. One of the figures is a *devočka s nebol'šoj lan'ju* 'girl with a small doe,' a recollection that is challenged by "B" who insists the sculpture depicts the girl petting her "plain dog." Subsequently, in the course of an interior monologue, the figure appears in transformed variants as a *devočka s malen'koj rodinkoj* 'a girl with a tiny birthmark' and as a *dačnicu s glazami vetrenoj lani* 'a dacha girl with the eyes of a light-hearted doe, (R88/E121). These sets finally blend with yet another, perhaps the most crucial and the one underlying the entire figure in its variant forms. Veta, the narrator's beloved, lives in a nearby dacha. He dreams of visiting her but is afraid of her father's dog which is termed *prostaja sobaka.* The example is instructive for it suggests that the members of paradigmatic sets which are based on similarity (i.e. a recurrent scene or image) are further linked to each other by transformation.

A final example at the phrase level shows a somewhat different sort of set in which the recurrent element is a verb phrase serving to define the communality of disparate subjects. In the cemetery scene the boy, an ardent butterfly collector, wanders off in pursuit of a specimen but as he overtakes it the "*Babočka . . . sovsem propadaet . . .*" (R91).[23] The word has caught the boy's fancy, however, for a few lines later as he watches a RR locomotive cross a bridge, the verb evolves into the ritualistic phrase *propadet-rastaet* ('vanish-melt away') which subsequently recurs in a number of different contexts. Here the phrase becomes a leitmotif which follows the imagined progress of the train through the countryside. All "disappears — melts away" (R91-92/E126-127). The phrase is picked up later to describe cars passing over a bridge (R123/E168). In its final appearance it depicts drops of water falling from the oars of a rowboat and merging back into the river — *propadet-rastaet.* As well as unifying the disparate events described into a paradigmatic set, it evokes an elegiac mood enveloping the different events.

The above recurrent scenes and images (and a great many more could be adduced) can be viewed as manifesting units of paradigmatic sets. Consisting of superimposed recurrent elements, they produce their aesthetic impact through their cumulative effect rather than through syntagmatically moving the narrative forward toward a denouement. Such paradigmatic sets are the basic structural units of the novel.

B. Characters

Paradigmatics also proves to be an insightful approach to the narrative's characters. We shall examine two such areas in particular. One is the phenomenon of doubling or pairing which is widespread in the novel. The other deals with the origin and phonetic organization of the names of the characters and, perhaps, of the very characters themselves.

All of the narrative's major characters are internally paired, that is, they have alternate names and/or identities: Narrator/Nimfeja Al'ba, Pavel/Savl, Arkadij Arkad'evič Akatov/Leonardo da Vinci, Traxtenberg/Tinbergen, Mixeev/Medvedev.

The case of the narrator involves multiple pairing. As we have noted the two halves of his nameless schizoid personality are in antagonistic dialogue. Apart from this he has two pseudonyms. One, Nimfeja Al'ba, he acquires as a result of his transformation into the water lily of that nomenclature. This identity is part of his delusional system and appears frequently. His appearances as Te Kto Prišli are, with a single exception, restricted to the episode described above.

Norvegov who bears the given name Pavel in the early pages of the book soon becomes Savl although he remains Pavel to persons other than the narrator and to Roza Vetrova, the geographer's schoolgirl mistress. The point of transition from Pavel to Savl is quite specific. Admonishing himself for cowardice, the boy feels that he must strive to be honorable like " *Pavel, on že i Savl* " (R28/E40). This is an inversion of the passage in *Acts,* 13, 9–10. ("Then Saul, who is also called Paul . . .") These verses serve as the first of the book's three epigraphs and describe Paul's tirade against a false prophet, Elymas the sorcerer, who attempts to thwart Paul's conversion of a Roman proconsul. As a result of Paul's imprecation the false prophet is blinded. The biblical episode as such does not seem to have any particular relevance to the events of the novel but rather draws a parallel between the vituperative apostle and his iconoclastic and equally eloquent Russian dual-namesake. There is, however, a sense in which they are united in being spokesmen for higher, albeit very different powers. This matter will be touched upon later.

The most complex case of pairing, that of Arkadij Arkad'evič Akatov and Leonardo da Vinci, is the least explicit but all the more intriguing for that reason. The grounds for the identification of the two characters as one are: (1) the two names (in their full forms) are close, albeit imperfect anagrams; (2) both men are identified as entomologists and the narrator aspires to be a colleague of Akatov (after he marries his daughter Veta) and reports that he worked as an apprentice in Leonardo's workshop; (3) both Akatov and Leonardo (and only these two characters) address the boy as *junoša* 'youth'; (4) in his workshop Akatov has a large photograph of Veta which figures in his conversation with the boy; when Leonardo seeks the narrator's advice about what features he should give the face of the Mona Lisa which he is working on, the narrator suggests Veta's features as a model. Thus Akatov and Leonardo both create Veta for the protagonist; (5) both men are the addressees of long sections of the boy's narrative. The reason for this elaborate bit of mystification is unclear. All of the other character pairings are, at least from the reader's point of view, explicit and the common identity of the bearers of the names is clear. Akatov and Leonardo are completely separate for the reader and are apparently unaware of each other's existence (or non-existence.)

The Traxtenberg/Tinbergen relationship which roughly parallels her respective roles as deputy principal and witch has been mentioned elsewhere, as has her association with the *Skirlý* folktale. By reason of her deformed foot she is also linked with the image of the witch Baba-Jaga whose traditional fixed epithet is her *kostjanaja noga* 'bone leg.'[24] The same sort of folkloric features that characterize Tinbergen are also prominent in the final pairing, that of the postman Mixeev/Medvedev. Mixeev, in addition to his alternate name, Medvedev, may have still another identity for it is posited that he is, or is closely associated with, the force called the *Nasylajuščij Veter,* the Ill-Boding Wind. Mixeev/Medvedev is depicted as an elderly man whose beard flies in the wind as he bicycles about the dacha settlement distributing mail. To some of the more imaginative residents it seems that his face radiates the wind and that he may indeed be the *Nasylajuščij Veter* who also rides a bicycle and sends a devastating wind into over-populated dacha areas (R11/E16). There is also a latent reflection of Mixeev/Medvedev as a surrogate of Hermes, the messenger of the gods. In a stream-of-consciousness monologue the two figures are mentioned within a few lines of each other although they are not linked (R13/E19).

Although all of the above characters are internally paired, there are, as we have noted, substantial differences in the nature of the internal relationship. In some cases such as that of Traxtenberg/Tinbergen each aspect has fairly distinct, but not mutually inconsistent attributes. In others, such as that of Pavel/Savl there seems to be no distinction. The twinned aspects of each character are largely (but not entirely or consistently) similar just as their names are semi-anagrams. The relationships are paradigmatic.

That the concept of "the double" is important to the author is evinced in yet another way. The third of the book's three epigraphs also draws attention to this idea. It is a quotation from E. A. Poe's story "William Wilson": *To že imja. Tot že oblik.*[25] Poe's tale contains some interesting parallels to Sokolov's novel. Like *Škola dlja durakov,* it is in the form of a memoir whose author tells of a relationship at a private boarding school with a look-alike schoolmate who shares the writer's name, birthday and apparel and differs from him only by his hoarse whispered voice and his sense of decency which leads him to admonish the narrator and foil many of his malicious undertakings. Among the points of congruence between the tales are a sour-visaged headmaster who administers the institution's Draconian laws and a monstrous school clock. The story ends with the memoirist slaying his imaginary double, i.e., his own conscience, in a fit of rage at being once again thwarted by him. It would seem that Sokolov's choice of the epigraph serves merely to call attention to the double theme and that in the final analysis the most plausible explanation of the splitting of so many of the characters into two entities is simply that it is a projection of the narrator's own schizophrenia.

The non-paired characters, like their paired counterparts, fall into positive and negative groupings. Among the former (who are all female) is the boy's "kindly, patient" but nameless mother. The two remaining positive characters are Veta Akatova who is the beloved of the narrator and Roza Vetrova who is a classmate of the narrator at the *School for Fools* and the mistress of Savl Norvegov. Both of the women are the love objects of doubled characters.

The forces of evil are represented by three unpaired male characters: the boy's nameless father, the prosecutor; the psychiatrist, Dr. Zauze; and Nikolaj Gorimirovič Perillo, the school headmaster. To these we must add Šejna Traxtenberg, Perillo's deputy. It is of interest that of the names given all are non-Russian, foreign, and of phonetic types that do not permit declension in Russian.

An examination of the means by which certain of the characters are first introduced into the narration reveals a curious phenomenon. Several of the characters are first adduced in a stream-of-consciousness monologue the contents of which, totally obscure at the time of reading, are subsequently seen to foreshadow a number of the narrative's most prominent characters, scenes and motifs. The characters, or at least their names are generated in the onrush of the word flow, first being cited as chance objects, or sounds, and then evolving into the personal names of the character subsequently associated with them. The most striking example of this process is that of Veta Akatova, the boy's biology teacher and beloved.

The context for the seminal interior monologue is a commuter train trip from the dacha RR station to town in which the repetitive sounds of the wheels induce a hypnogogic state in the narrator-passenger. Fragments of the monologue are as follows: *Èto pjataja zona, stoimost' bileta tridcat' pjat' kopeek, poezd idet čas dvadcat', severnaja vetka, vetka akacii ili, skažem, sireni, cvetet belymi cvetami . . . , večerom na cypočkax vozvraščaetsja v sad . . . , potom cvety zakryvajutsja i spjat, . . . ; vetka spit . . .* (R11).[26] This is followed by a digression on the branch's night trains and whom they disturb. The *vetka* 'branch' is then addressed directly:

utrom prosnis' i cveti, potom otcvetaj syp' lepestkami v glaza semiforam i pritancovyvaja v takt svoemu derevjannomu serdcu smejsja na stancijax prodavajsja proezžim i ot'ezžajuščim plač' i kriči obnaživajas' v zerkal'nyx kupe kak tvoe imja menja nazyvajut Vetkoj ja Vetka akacii ja Vetka železnoj dorogi ja Veta beremennaja ot laskovoj pticy po imeni Najtingejl . . . vot berite menja . . . èto sovsem nedorogo . . . ja sama rasstegnu vidite ja vsja belosnežna . . . osyp'te že pocelujami . . . ja Veta čistaja belaja vetka cvetu . . . ne kričite ja ne kriču èto kričit vstrečnyj . . . tra ta ta čto tra kto tam ta gde tam tam tam Veta vetla vetly vetka tam za oknom v dome tom tra ta kom o kom o čem o Vetke vetly o vetre tararam tramvai *tramvai* ai večer dobryj bilety bi lety čego net Lety reki Lety ee netu vam ai cveta c Veta c Al'fa Veta Gamma i tak dalee . . . (R 12).[27]

The train of association begins with the railroad term *severnaja vetka* 'northern branch' which immediately gives rise to the botanical motif *vetka akacii* 'branch of acacia' with its *belymi cvetami* 'white flowers'. The *vetka/cvetok* 'branch/flower' interplay continues throughout the scene and the book as does the homonymic play on *vetka*. The first *vetka spit* 'the branch sleeps' reverts to the railway motif but the second clearly refers to the flowering shrub which is transformed into a woman, a flowergirl, who is selling her wares and her person at the station. Here she recapitulates her transformations: *Vetka železnoj dorogoj* 'Vetka of the railroad,' *Vetka akacii* 'Vetka of the acacia' and Veta, the flowergirl-prostitute. This in turn trails off into what appears to be gibberish but is actually a rhythmic sequence paralleling the sound of the train's revolving wheels and invoking several of the key motifs in the narrative — *vetka* 'branch,' *vetly* 'willows,' *veter* 'wind' and *ta* 'that' (for *ta ženščina* 'that woman' — Veta). At this point the conductor (*konstriktor*) comes through the car, saying *Dobryj večer* 'Good Evening' to the passengers and requesting their tickets. The word *bilety* 'tickets' immediately falls prey to the rhythmic pattern of the clacking wheels and is fragmented into *bi* and *lety,* the latter becoming a new motif whose ramifications eventually constitute a second cluster of meanings similar to the *vet* cluster but with its own set of referents. The new phonetic motif is quickly displaced by a return to the *vet* complex which is enriched by the fragmentation of *cveta* 'flower' into *c Veta* and the recasting of Veta as a character in the Greek alphabet — *Al'fa, Veta, Gamma.* The passage concludes with yet another contextual shift with the train moving along the track of the stellar constellation Veta.

There are a number of things to be considered about this hallucinatory introduction to one of the novel's main characters. The first is that the reader has no prior knowledge of the character or of her relationship to the narrator. Her identity is not established until nearly forty pages later (R52/E73). Similarly, the significance of the Greek letters *Al'fa, Veta, Gamma* is necessarily lost on the reader for in addition to not knowing who or what Veta is, he does not know that *Al'fa* is a surrogate for Al'ba, the surname of *Nimfeja Al'ba,* the narrator's alter-ego. More generally it might be noted that the character, Veta, is introduced by a process of dream-encoding and that even if the reader were in a position to decode the dream transformations (i.e. RR *vetka* 'branch' → *vetka akacii* 'branch of acacia' → *Veta Akatova*) he would still be in the dark for the end product of the decipherment proves to be a token in an as yet unknown language. A final matter of import is that the passage describes (in an extremely elliptic way) a scene which recurs in variant forms four times in the novel.[28]

The introduction of the character Leonardo da Vinci occurs subsequently in the same monologue. The train clatters on and the sound of the wheels evokes the rhythmic patter *ne to ne ta ne to ne ta ne to ne ta netto brutto Italija ital'janskij čelovek Dante čelovek Bruno čelovek Leonardo xudožnik arxitektor entomolog . . .* (R 13).[29] The patter suggests the terms *netto* and *brutto* (net weight and gross weight), which are used in rail shipments and are of Italian origin. These evoke Italy and Italians ending in Leonardo — artist, architect and entomologist. Here again the reader cannot know he is being introduced to a major character in the narrative. Even less so than in the case of Veta, for the accompanying text makes it clear that Leonardo is the historical figure: *. . . esli xočes' uvidet' letanie četyr'mja kryl'jami stupaj vo rvy Milanskoj kreposti i uvidiš' černyx strekoz . . .* (R13).[30] Just as the introduction of Veta, the biology teacher, is accompanied by her own motifs, i.e., *vetka (akacii)* 'branch of acacia', *vetla* 'willow', *veter* 'wind', and the constellation *Veta,* Leonardo, who, as we have shown above, is identical with Arkadij Akatov, the entomologist, is assigned his own motifs and phonetic emblems, *letanie* 'flying' and dragonflies.[31] The *"le(t)"* element which figures in the name of his alter ego, Leonardo, and profession (the study of *letajuščie nasekomye* 'flying insects') and in peripheral motifs such as *leto* 'summer', the period when insects fly, and the river name *Leta,* the Lethe, on whose banks his residence stands, is prefigured in the final lines quoted above in which (in masked form) the train conductor asks for the passengers' tickets — *bilety* (R12/ E18).

The technique whereby Akatov/ Leonardo is introduced into the narrative also parallels that used for his daughter Veta in that it pre-echoes a major scene in which the narrator formally asks Akatov for Veta's hand in marriage (R108/ E148). Following the above and interspersed among other more or less irrelevant thoughts we read *. . . xoču strekoz letanie v vetlax . . . v guščax vereska gde Tinbergen sam rodom iz Gollandii ženilsja na kollege i vskore im stalo jasno čto ammofila naxodit put' domoj vovse ne tak kak filantus . . . na Vetočke železnoj dorogi tra ta ta tra ta ta vyšla koška za kota . . .* (R13).[32] This passage, again in transmuted dream form, expresses the narrator's fantasy that he will marry Veta, the entomologist's daughter, after he himself has become an entomologist and their professional colleague. The rhythmic patter of the train wheels again penetrates the boy's doze and this time generates the Russian children's rhyme *Vyšla koška za kota* 'The kitty wed the tomcat' which becomes the couple's epithalamium. It is of interest that in the proposal scene which is prefigured here the nature motifs which accompany all three characters are combined. The narrator prefaces his imaginary betrothal request to Akatov by stressing that the three of them are united by their common interest in nature, in *vse rastuščee i le tajuščee, c vetuščee i pla vajuščee* (R108).[33] As we have indicated by our underscoring, the phonetic and semantic motifs that are associated with the father and daughter are again adduced here while the narrator, whose alternate identity is that of the white water lily *Nimfeja al'ba,* is symbolized by the word pla*vajuščee* 'that which floats.'

The preceding two examples of the technique of character introduction involved their generation in the course of a hypnogogic interior monologue. The final case that we shall examine differs in that the character evolves from an item in one of the book's many lists. In a surreal scene the narrator opens the door into the entryhall of his apartment and finds Leonardo standing in the moat of the Milan fortress observing the flight of dragonflies. The narrator tries to slip back unnoticed into his flat but Leonardo (whose apprentice he is) catches him and gives him a long homework assignment list. Among the items in the list are a series of commands such as "to transform a cicada into a butterfly, . . . day into night . . . a vowel into a sibilant," and so on. Leonardo concludes his assignment by saying: *a krome togo, posadi u sebja v sadu beluju rozu vetrov, . . . podari učitelju Pavlu beluju rozu, . . . poraduj svoego starogo pedagoga — vesel'čaka, balagura i vetrogona* (R21).[34] Leonardo then records a long lyric oration by Pavel which begins *O Roza, . . . belaja Roza Vetrova, milaja devuška, mogil'nyj cvet, kak xoču ja netronutogo tela tvoego.*[35] Once again we see the introduction of a character by transformation of an object, a rose, into a name. The identity of Roza Vetrova becomes known to us only much later in the narrative and the case is fully parallel to that of Veta who likewise undergoes transformation from flower (*vetka beloj akacii* 'branch of white acacia') into the character, Veta Akatova.

All three of the characters whose genesis we traced have associations with the wind; Veta and Roza Vetrova by virtue of their names and Arkadij Arkad'evič Akatov through his incarnation as Leonardo and their shared preoccupation with wind-borne creatures. It is further significant that Leonardo remarks at the end of his list of assignments *pri pomošči mel'nic proizvedu ja veter v ljuboe vremja* (R22: Sokolov's italics).[36] Postman Mixeev/ Medvedev's association with the wind has been previously remarked and it might reasonably be assumed that it is not by chance that his latter name contains the 'wind digraph' "*ve.*"[37] The narrator also has intimate ties with the wind. Prominent among them are his associations with his idol, Norvegov, the *vetrogon* 'wind driver' and prophet of the *Nasylajuščij Veter* 'The Ill-Boding

Wind' and with Veta whose very name bespeaks the wind. Further, the narrator's alternate name, Nimfeja, faintly echoes *veja* "blowing" which, of course, is a paronym of *veter* 'wind.' Most obviously the narrator-*durak* is related to the wind through self-proclamation. In a diatribe (addressed to Savl on the toilet windowsill) against the stupidities of his other teachers, the boy concludes: *my spešim zajavit' vam lično, dobryj Savl Petrovič, . . . čto ne somnevaemsja v suščestvovanii Nasylajuščego . . . my kričim segodnja na ves' belyj svet: da zdravstvuet Nasylajuščij Veter!* (R81–82).[38]

Norvegov, of all of the major characters, is most closely identified with the wind and may justly be termed its prophet. Not only is his fixed epithet *vetrogon* but his name, Norvegov, is an anagram of the epithet.[39] *Vetrogon* has two meanings. One, that of a flighty unstable person easily driven before the wind, is frequently alluded to in the novel. The other, a technical meaning, is that of an apparatus that creates a strong current of air — a wind generator. Norvegov is associated in the text with windmills. Joking about his frailty, he says that his doctors have forbidden him to go near windmills but he is unable to resist them as they stand alongside his house (R18/E26).

All of the positive characters might well be called the children of the wind, of the *Nasylajuščij Veter*. As we have shown, they are related to the wind (and to each other) by common phonetic elements in their names and in their associated motifs. As literary characters they lack both depth and individuation and like folktale characters almost seem to represent Proppian functions rather than multidimensional personalities. Sokolov's treatment of his characters seems to strike a certain resonance with the view of character expressed by Russian Formalist theoreticians who held that literary characters are merely by-products of the narrative structure, that they are compositional rather than psychological entities.[40] In a sense, Sokolov's characters (and we are speaking here only of the "wind" characters) are but aspects of the central primal force of the narrative, the *Nasylajuščij Veter*. For this reason we shall now turn to a more detailed examination of this seminal character in the novel.

Like many of its offspring, the *Nasylajuščij Veter* has dual character: benevolent to its friends, awesome to its enemies. This is demonstrated early in the novel when Norvegov counsels his young charge(s) "to live by the wind" for, he says, it is by no means a bad thing to be a *vetrogon*. He continues: *Ibo čego ubojus' pered licom večnosti, esli segodnja veter ševelit moi volosy, osveščaet lico . . . , a zavtra — lomaet nenužnye vetxie, postrojki, vyryvaet s kornem duby . . .* (R19).[41] As he speaks, his rage mounts: *Bojtes' Nasylajuščego Vetera, gospoda gorodov i dač, strašites' brizov i skvoznjakov, oni roždajut uragani i smerči* (R19).[42] In one of his final appearances Savl again invokes the wind: *Nyne kriču vseju krov'ju svoej, kak kričat o grjaduščem otmščenii: na svete net ničego, na svete net ničego, na svete net ničego, krome Vetra!* (R 149).[43]

These and other references show the *Nasylajuščij Veter* to be a purifying, cathartic power that will scourge its enemies and those of its creatures from the face of the earth. The wind is a force of nature and, as we have noted, all of its fictional children are somehow connected with *vse rastuščee, letajuščee, cvetuščee i plavajuščee* 'all that grows, flies, flowers and floats.' For these characters and presumably for Sokolov, their creator, nature stands in opposition to human institutions and the restrictions on freedom they entail. Returning to the basic thematic oppositions that we posited at the beginning of our analysis we see the *Nasylajuščij Veter* as being genetically allied with one of them, Nature, and metaphorically with a second, Freedom, and acting against all manifestations of their contrasting polarities, Institutions and Bondage. The identification of the *Nasylajuščij Veter* with the thematic dichotomies may be carried still further, however, for the literary and psychiatric precedents for linking madness and winds are numerous.[44] Even without such external evidence, however, the materials of our narrative suffice to support such a conclusion. The insane protagonist and his circle of "wind friends" are warmly and sympathetically portrayed in contrast to the dour depiction of those representing the voices of sanity, that is, the father (the court), Perillo and Traxtenberg (the school) and Zauze (the hospital). They are the voices of institutionalized (and institutionalizing) humanity and, hence, of servitude.

All three of these thematic antinomies can be subsumed under the still more fundamental opposition of Irrationality/Rationality. Irrationality, particularly in its manifestation as madness, has a long literary history of being linked with the poetic gift, with creativity; rationality, with repression. It does not seem unwarranted to identify the *Nasylajuščij Veter,* the main character of the narrative, with Irrationality and even, from the narrator's and author's point of view, with creativity. As we pointed out at the beginning of our analysis the novel makes a specific allusion to Puškin's "God grant that I not go mad" in which madness is linked with the poetic gift.

The *Nasylajuščij Veter* has yet one more association which might be tentatively put forward. We have previously noted that Pavel and Savl, the alternate Christian names for Norvegov, the spokesman of the wind, are derived from those of the New Testament figure and that it is this figure who is the subject of the first of the novel's three epigraphs. The major part of the epigraph is Paul's imprecation against the Jewish sorcerer. The curse is, however, prefaced by the words "*No Savl, on že i Pavel, ispolnivšis' Duxa Svjatogo i ustremiv na nego vzor, skazal.*"[45] It is this "being filled with the Holy Spirit" that gives Paul his power to smite the sorcerer blind by his words. Just as the biblical Saul, who is also Paul, is filled with the enabling Holy Spirit, so the novel's Pavel, who is also Savl, is filled with the spirit of the *Nasylajuščij Veter,* which empowers him to deliver his eloquent diatribes against the Philistines of his world.[46] It is also noteworthy in this context that the language of Savl Petrovič's philippics is rich in Church Slavonicisms.

There is also linguistic support for equating the *Nasylajuščij Veter* with the *Svjatoj Dux*. *Dux* is derived from the verbal root meaning 'to blow' and variants of the phrase *veter duet* are frequent in the text. Taken together the above observations provide considerable support for the identification of Pavel Norvegov and the biblical Paul and, more importantly, of the *Nasylajuščij Veter* and the Holy Spirit. It should be emphasized, however, that the associations are metaphorical and in the absence of information to the contrary, one should be extremely cautious about setting Sokolov's novel in a theological context.

Before turning to a quite different aspect of the novel it might be well to review briefly some of the paradigmatic aspects of the characters. Preliminarily, it might be remarked that the various thematic dichotomies that are united in the hyperopposition Irrationality/Rationality form antonymic paradigmatic sets. All of the positive characters by virtue of their manifold association with the *Nasylajuščij Veter* stand on the Irrationality side of the dichotomy. Their enemies stand with equal firmness on the side of Rationality. The opposing camps form two paradigmatic sets internally united by many factors. This is most obviously so in regard to 'the children of the wind' with their thematic and anagrammatic kinship with nature. It is equally, although less elaborately, true for the creatures of Rationality with the common thread of their non-Russian names and their consequent morphological defectiveness.

C. Metalinguistic Phenomena and Lists

The paradigmatic axis of language is based on the concept of selection. "Selection," Jakobson has written, "implies the possibility of substituting one for the other, equivalent to the former in one respect and different from it in another."[47] Selection and substitution are but two aspects of a single operation. Expanding on this thought, Jakobson's commentator continues: "Selection is an internal relationship based on the SIMILARITY of the SUBSTITUTION SETS (including paradigms) while similarity ranges from the near identity of synonyms to the close relationship of antonyms, from resemblance . . . to analogy, from metalanguage to metaphoric use of terms . . . from synonyms to heteronyms (and the whole problem of translation in general), from paraphrase to circumlocution."

In the strict sense, the terms 'metalanguage' and 'metalinguistic' are used when we are speaking of the relationship between message and code as in utterances of the type "*Pup* means a young dog" or "*Pup* is a three-letter noun." More loosely speaking, however, the terms are used to describe "language about language" or even "writing about writing." It is mostly in this latter sense that we shall use the words here although some of the phenomena to be discussed do warrant the more rigorous definition. In either case, the topics under examination fall along the paradigmatic axis of linquistic and literary structuration.

Writing about the process of writing plays a prominent role in *Škola dlja durakov*. The opening words of the novel establish the motif of the autonymic, self-referential character of the writing — a motif which persists throughout the novel and which comes to a crescendo at the narrative's conclusion. The novel's first sentence is: *Tak, no s čego že načat', kakimi slovami?*[48] The "B" component of the narrator prompts voice "A": *Vse ravno, načni slovami: tam na pristancionnom prudu.*[49] "A" counters with *Na PRISTANCIONNOM?*,[50] and observes — *No èto neverno, stilističeskaja ošibka, Vodokačka nepremenno by popravila, pristancionnym nazyvajut bufet . . . , no ne prud, prud možet byt' OKOLOSTANCIONNYM.*[51] After further quibbling "A" launches the story: *Xorošo, togda ja tak i načnu: tam, na okolostanncionom prudu* (R7).[52] This is not the only metalinguistic discussion of a stylistic point to be found in the book and Vodokačka, the teacher of Russian language and literature at the "school for fools" is elsewhere cited as an authority in the narrator's debates with himself on matters of composition.[53] As in the above example, one half of the narrator's identity often abruptly demands clarification and amplification of various textual points by the other half. This metalinguistic aspect of the text is what we might call intra-narratorial. The text also contains metalingual dialogue between the narrator and the author-persona. We have previously remarked on one of the two major authorial intrusions in the narrative.[54] The second major intrusion occurs near the end of the novel as the boy imagines that happy day when the mail will bring a letter from the Academy of Sciences notifying him that he has won their entomological prize for his winter butter-fly collection. He has just begun his fantasy with *Odno iz utr . . .* 'one morning,' when the author breaks in: *Učenik takoj-to, razrešite mne, avtoru, perebit' vas i rasskazat', kak ja predstavljaju sebe moment . . . u menja, kak i u vas neploxaja fantazija . . .*" (R156–157).[55] At the conclusion of this lengthy intrusion the narrator warmly congratulates the author on his talents and thanks him for having "taken on himself the labor of writing such an interest-ing tale about me, about all of us" (R161–2/E218). The author expresses his gratitude and his all-consuming desire to please his readers and his characters but expresses his apprehension of the boy's father and the latter's crony Perillo. He fears that they may have *him* sent *tuda* 'there', to Dr. Zauze, and contemplates the use of a pseudonym (a *minodvesp*) but rejects the idea as unworthy of Savl, that *rycar' bez straxa i upreka* 'knight *sans peur et sans reproche*' (R162–163/E219). This descent of the authorial persona into the world of his characters is perhaps the strongest evidence that the figure of the authorial persona is not to be confused with the author of the book. It is still another dimension of the irreality of the events of the narrative and, more importantly, a demonstration of the ostentatiously artificial nature of *School for Fools* as a work of art.

From this point on, the author-persona and the narrator-*durak* become active and overt collaborators in entitling the novel and mapping out the few remaining pages. It is decided that if the title *Škola dlja durakov* is to be adopted more material about the school must be included and that a description of one of Veta's biology classes would be appropriate. This is to be composed by the boy and his words . . . *s čego načat', kakimi slovami* 'how to begin, with what words' (R164/ E221) echo the first words of the narrative. The author comes to his aid and suggests *I vot* 'And then,' and these words, repeated, introduce us to the final episode. At its end, the author again requests the boy's permission to interrupt, for *pora zakančivat' knigu* 'it's time to end the book' (R169/ E228) because he, the author, is running out of paper. He mentions, however, that if the narrator wishes to add further incidents, they can go out to buy more paper. This they do: "slapping each other on the back and whistling foolish songs, we walk out into the milliped street and in some miraculous manner are transformed into passersby" (R 169/ E228).

This device of writing a book about writing a book, while by no means novel, is an ultimate example of a metalingual and, hence, paradigmatic phenomenon.

Allusion and subtext are also metalinguistic phenomena in that they comment on the text from the viewpoint of other codes. Indeed it has been suggested by Jurij Lotman that it is through the contrastive interplay of different codes that works of art attain their effect.[56] Sokolov's novel is extremely rich in allusion. Of particular interest in this context are the epigraphs which afford the author the opportunity to offer external comment on his work without having to cope with the problem of incorporating such materials into the narrative flow. Sokolov uses this device in a way particularly appropriate to the kind of book he has written. Ordinarily, epigraphs are chosen in order to underscore the theme of the book. Sokolov, as a writer more concerned with technique than content, has picked at least two of his three epigraphs with a view toward alerting the reader to certain central devices. Although the first, more traditional epigraph establishes the image of a central character and, perhaps, points out the parallel we have suggested between the *Svjatoj Dux* 'Holy Ghost' and the *Nasylajuščij Veter,* the remaining epigraphs signal two of the most characteristic technical devices of the narrative. The Poe quotation underscores the profoundly pervasive double motif. The other epigraph, which we have not yet examined, is as follows:

> Gnat', deržat', bežat',obidet',
> slyšat', videt' i vertet', i dyšat'
> i nenavidet' i zaviset' i terpet'.
> > Gruppa glagolov russkogo jazyka,
> > sostavljajuščix izvestnoe isklučenie
> > iz pravil; ritmičeski organizovana
> > dlja udobstba zapominanija.[57]

This group of verbs is virtually meaningless from the point of view of the thematic aspect of the novel, for its significance lies purely in the form. The two relevant aspects are to be found in the list format and in that the list contents are rhythmically organized. The epigraph points to one of the most striking devices of Sokolov's narrative — its use of rhythmically organized lists.

Škola dlja durakov contains some sixty rhythmically organized lists. The use of lists (or catalogues or inventories as they are sometimes called) as devices in literary works has a history ranging from Homer through James Joyce. That Sokolov is aware of this tradition is evinced by two references to the famous Homeric catalogue of ships in the *Iliad*. In one of the interior monologues the sequence Al'fa, Veta, Gamma occurs as one of the contexts for the name of the narrator's beloved, Veta. This leads him to lament that no one had taught him Greek and, as a result, "we cannot sensibly enumerate a single ship" (R13/E19). Later in the novel, reflecting on his sudden amnesia while boating on the river of oblivion, the narrator punningly counsels himself: *Beri grébi i grebí domoj, v Sirakuzy perečisljat' tavričeskie korabli* (R142).[58] Sokolov's lists display an enormous variety in terms of subject matter, internal conceptual organization, and grammatical format. In length, they range from three items to over a hundred. The following which may serve as an example of one of the more straightforward sorts of list, describes a group of dacha commuters as they get off the evening train: *Ustalo, otduva-jas', vytiraja lica platkami, tašča portfeli, avos'ki, ekaja selezenkoj*(R7).[59] One of the items in this list leads to the question of the contents of the string shopping bags: *Čaj, saxar, maslo, kolbasa; svežaja, b'juščaja xvostom ryba; makarony, krupa, luk, polufabrikaty; reže sol'*(R7–8).[60] Even lists as simple as these display points of interest. The stark list of nouns in the second example is suddenly enlivened by the "fresh fish with the flapping tails." The internal organization of the items is also worthy of scrutiny. One would assume that *sol'*'salt' would most appropriately go with *čaj* 'tea' and *saxar* 'sugar'. *Maslo* 'butter' which one might expect to be separated from the former items by a semicolon is in a single series with them as is *kolbasa* 'sausage', while the latter, a meat, is isolated from the closely related *ryba* 'fish.' A reexamination of the ordering suggests that it has a phonetic and rhythmic, rather than a logical or semantic basis. Grossly speaking, the items *čaj* 'tea' through *ryba* 'fish' are unified by an "*a*" assonance while the remainder of the series rests on a phonetic pattern involving "*k*" and the non-high vowels, particularly the labialized '*u*' and '*o*.' Such organizational principles are to be found in many of the lists. The grammatical diversity of these short lists, the one with its sequence of adverbial gerunds and their complements, and the other with its list of nouns is striking.

Grammatical parallelism, both syntactic and morphological, is also promi-nent. Lists are to be found in almost every case: *reka medlenno struilas' mimo . . . vmeste so vsemi svoimi rybami, . . . s otražennymi oblakami, nevidimymi i grjaduščimi utoplennikami, . . . s pustymi konservnymi bankami i tjaželymi*

šapkami monomaxov, . . . s jablokami razdora i grušami pečali . . . (R44).[61] At
times this leads to somewhat bizarre effects as in the following case where
Norvegov advises the boy (who is bringing him a letter) to keep hailing him
from the far side of the river "*poka . . . učitel' Pavel ne uslyšit, . . . ne vyjdet iz
doma, . . . ne peregrebet Letu, . . . ne obnimet, . . . ne skažet dobryx
zagadočnyx slov, ne polučit, net, ne pročitaet . . . pis'ma, ibo ego, vašego
učitelja, netu v živyx . . .* (R42).[62] The sequence is a ludicrously extended *poka
. . . ne* + perfective verb construction with the continuing meaning "until" but
the introductory *poka* becomes so remote in the course of the twelve item list
that the discontinuous constituent *ne* gradually shades into the ultimate
negation of the ending, i.e., that Norvegov, the teacher, is "no longer among
the living."

Semantically the lists and their contents are highly variegated: passing
sights, sounds, smells, articles, activities, graffiti, metaphors, comparisons,
and so on. One list, nearly a page long, is an imaginary projected biography of
the recurrent "girl with the plain dog" (R48–49 / E68–69) in the form of a series
of verb phrases. Occasionally a list item serves as the source of a Gogolian
digression which rises, swells, and then fades back into the list (p. 211
above). At other times, however, important motifs or characters are introduced. We noted above how the character Roza Vetrova evolved from Leonardo's list (a catalogue unequalled for the complexity of its internal structure) of homework assignments for the boy.

The fundamental function of the inventories is poetic in the most general
sense although it must be noted that at times the lists rise to the level of genuine
poetry as in this final example. Norvegov is in essence telling his protégé that
life is not wholly absurd, that it does contain a modicum of meaning, a secret
which neither of them knows but which they must seek whether it be:

v gor'kix li kladezjax narodnoj mudrosti,
v sladkix li rečenijax i rečax,
v praxe otveržennyx i v straxe približennyx,
v skital'českix sumax i iudinyx summax,

v dviženii *ot*	i v sostojanii *nad,*
vo lži obmanutyx	i v pravde obolgannyx,
v vojne	i mire,
v mareve	i murave,
v stadijax	i studijax,
v styde	i stradanijax,
vo t'me	i svete,
v nenavisti	i žalosti,
v žizni	i vne ee —
vo vsem ètom	i v pročem sleduet xorošen'ko razobrat'sja,

v ètom čto-to est', možet byt' nemnogo, no est' (R42)[63]

Such lists constitute paradigmatic sets from two points of view. One is that their constituents show a high degree of parallelism in their morphosyntactic structure. The second is that they evince further internal parallelism in that they are phonetically and rhythmically organized.[64] These latter levels of organization interact with the semantic organization of the lists, for semantically disparate items are thrown into formally parallel patterns that serve to accentuate startling semantic juxtapositions.

There is yet another sense in which Sokolov's lists can be viewed within the context of the paradigmatic axis. In ordinary prose language, particularly in narrative, which is primarily a syntagmatic function, only one member of a paradigmatic set is ordinarily selected for each contextual slot. The other members of the set exist only tacitly, *in absentia*. *Škola dlja durakov* escapes from this straitjacket, for through the use of the device of poetic lists Sokolov has found a way to realize not just one of the possible realizations of the paradigmatic set, but a number, often a large number of the potentialities.[65]

IV. Concluding Comments

Our analysis has attempted to demonstrate that Saša Sokolov's *Škola dlja durakov* is a fundamentally paradigmatic work that can best be approached and understood in that conceptual framework. In concluding our discussion we shall draw upon Sokolov's book to illustrate a general, theoretical point. If we take Sokolov's surrealist narrative as an example of the paradigmatic novel and, using a hypothetical traditional, syntagmatic novel for comparative purposes, examine them against the two linguistic axes, we will observe that the two kinds of works make very different kinds of demands on the reader. These demands derive from the differing implications of the dominant axis in each type of book.

In the traditional realistic prose narrative the syntagmatic plane is dominant and the paradigmatic plane is severely restricted. Normally on the latter plane only one member of any paradigmatic set is realized at a given point in the text. The reader, by his knowledge of the code that he shares with the writer, must supply at least some of the missing members of the set if he is to experience the work at any depth, i.e., as literature. This tacit 'filling in' of the absent members of a paradigmatic set is traditionally referred to under the heading of 'connotation.' The ability of the reader to activate such sets is one index of how well a person reads — assuming that aesthetic appreciation is his intent. This 'filling in' is an activity that the reader must bring to the text.[66]

In *Škola dlja durakov,* the syntagmatic plane is sharply attenuated. This is manifested in the absence of linear chronology (and, with it, motivation) and in the consequent replacement of causally connected scenes (plot) by static, recurrent episodes; in its pervasive doubling of characters in phonetically based sets; in its rhythmic lists; in its paronomasia; in its simultaneous presentation of verb forms in all three tenses, and so on. Here the reader is supplied with several members of a paradigmatic set but, to a considerable extent, is left to his own devices to supply a syntagmatic framework for what he reads.

The reader of the traditional, syntagmatically oriented novel has a simpler task for two reasons. For one, merely by sharing a code with the author, he will have at least some of the absent set members in his linguistic repertory; for another, the traditional realistic novel can be read, after a fashion, with minimal recourse to absent paradigmatic set members. The matter is more complex for the reader of the paradigmatically oriented work for the syntagmatic data that he must supply are stored in a much more open-ended and abstract way than are the paradigmatic data. Projection is far more problematic. This is one reason many readers find paradigmatic writing unintelligible. Although it is doubtless in part through its failure to conform to traditional expectation, the paradigmatic novel makes far more heavy demands on the reader, for if he is to have narrative (in the traditional sense) he must project it for himself. Just as in the traditional novel the reader must project missing members of a paradigmatic set, so must the reader of much experimental writing project a syntagmatic framework onto the text. This can be schematized as follows:

	A *Realistic Novel*	B *Sokolov's Novel*
Syntagmatic (S):	+	-
Paradigmatic (P):	-	+

Axis

In A, the reader has the S-axis and must project the P-axis.
In B, the reader has the P-axis and must project the S-axis.

This schema would seem to provide a theoretically based framework for distinguishing certain kinds of modernist fiction from that of the traditional realistic novel and its descendants.[67] It also affords a conceptual framework for the appreciation, study and analysis of such writing.

Roman Jakobson has defined the poetic function as a projection of the principle of equivalence from the axis of selection into the axis of combination, i.e., equivalence is promoted to the constitutive device of the sequence.[68] Sokolov's poetic novel with its intense focalization on the paradigmatic axis clearly illustrates the observation that equivalence is promoted to the constitutive device of the sequence. One might wish to add a corollary to Jakobson's dictum that in the case of highly paradigmatic novels such as Sokolov's, it is for the reader to project, within the existing code, his own axis of combination, that is, a syntagmatic axis from the paradigmatic constituents of the work. In closing we would like to note that in his emphasis on the paradigmatic axis Sokolov stands with some of the great modernist writers of the twentieth century. The later Joyce and, among the Russians, Andrej Belyj come to mind. Whatever the defects of Sokolov's *Škola dlja durakov*, it must be accounted a remarkable achievement for any young writer and all the more so for one who grew up in a society where the winds of artistic change have been stilled for nearly half a century.

NOTES

1. Saša Sokolov, *Školja dlja durakov* (Ann Arbor, 1976). English quotations are from Sasha Sokolov, *A School for Fools*, tr. Carl R. Proffer (Ann Arbor, 1977). Cited English passages have sometimes been altered to bring them into closer conformity to the Russian original. Page citations follow the convention (Rxx / Exx), referring to the Russian and the English texts respectively.

2. This question has been examined in detail by Fred Moody in his "Madness and the Pattern of Freedom in Sasha Sokolov's *A School for Fools,*" *Russian Literature TriQuarterly,* XVI, pp. 7–32.

3. The schizoid narrator refers to himself as "we." Norvegov, who is part of the boy's delusional world, always addresses him in the plural.

4. The chapters are: I. *Nimfeja* ('Nymphea'); II. *Teper': rasskazy, napisannye na verande* ('Now: Stories Written on the Veranda'); III. *Savl*; IV. *Skirlý*; and V. *Zaveščanie* ('Testament').

5. This aspect of Gogol's style has been described by Vladimir Nabokov, *Nikolai Gogol* (New York, 1961) pp. 75–85.

6. 'sage professors and insane poets, dacha irregulars and failures — anglers for early and late fish' (E17).

7. 'in questions of external and internal polshittysticks' (E133).

8. 'the department of national education' (E170).

9. '[a book] adorns the interior'; '. . . the interior, the exterior [and] the fox terrier' (E161).

10. This is not to say that the chronological progression is necessarily arithmetic. Flashbacks, flash-forwards and parallel-time sequences are all common in the traditional novel but in the final analysis it is generally possible to reconstitute an orderly temporal sequence.

11. '. . . not long ago (just now, in a short time) I was floating (am floating, will float) down a big river in a rowboat. Before this (after this) I was often (will be) there . . .' (E34).

12. 'I'm getting married, very soon, maybe yesterday or last year' (E165).

13. 'belaboring blueprints with blue ballpoints when time is all messed up' (E101).

14. The parallel but larger question of progression at higher narrative levels is treated below under the heading "Recurrent Elements."

15. Patrick Waldberg, *Surrealism* (New York, 1975) p. 72. The immediately following characterization is from M. H. Abrams, *A Glossary of Literary Terms,* 3rd ed. (New York, 1971) p. 168.

16. Waldberg, p. 43.

17. Personal communication to the author.

18. Roman Jakobson & Morris Halle, *Fundamentals of Language* ('s-Gravenhage, 1956) pp. 76–82. Jakobson's remarks on surrealism may be found on p. 78 of the foregoing and also in his "Closing Statement: Linguistics and Poetics" in *Style and*

Language ed. Thomas Sebeok (Cambridge, 1960) p. 351. Although the comments in both cases refer to visual art their relevance to verbal art is obvious, especially in that surrealist painting derives from surrealist writing. On this last point, see Waldberg, pp. 14–15.

19. This analogy has been developed in detail particularly by the French structuralist theoreticians A. J. Greimas and Tzvetan Todorov. See Terence Hawkes, *Structuralism and Semiotics* (Berkeley, 1977) pp. 87–99 for a convenient survey.

20. For a discussion of these matters, see Jurij Lotman, *Analiz poètičeskogo teksta* (Moskva, 1972) pp. 39–40. Also in English as Yury Lotman, *Analysis of the Poetic Text* tr. D. Barton Johnson (Ann Arbor, 1976) p. 37.

21. See the following pages: R73–74/E101–102, R80/E111, R82/E113, R99/E135, R112/E152, R123/E168, R146/E198, R149/E202 and R154/E208.

22. 'Tra ta ta, Tra ta ta, The kitty wed the tomcat.'

23. 'The butterfly . . . vanishes utterly . . .' (E126).

24. N. M. Vedernikova, *Russkaja narodnaja skazka* (Moskva, 1975) p. 51.

25. 'The same name! the same contour of person!'

26. 'This is zone five, ticket price thirty-five kopecks, the train takes an hour twenty, northern branch, a branch of acacia or, say, lilac, it blooms with white flowers, . . . in the evening it returns to the garden on tiptoe . . . then the flowers close and sleep, . . . the branch sleeps . . . ' (E17).

27. 'wake up in the morning and flower then wither scatter your petals into the eyes of the semaphores and while dancing in time to your wooden heart laugh in the stations sell yourself to passersby and to those departing weep and keen naked in the mirrored RR car compartments what is your name I am called Vetka I am Vetka of acacia I am Vetka of the railroad I am Vetka pregnant by the tender bird named the Nachtigall . . . here take me . . . it costs very little . . . I myself will unbutton see I am all snowwhite . . . shower me with kisses . . . I am Veta chaste white branch I flower . . . don't shout I am not shouting it's the train coming . . . tra ta ta what tra who there ta where there there there Veta willow willows branch there beyond the window in the house that tra ta whom about whom about what about Vetka willows about the wind tararam tramway *tramway* ai evening good tickets billets bil let why not Lethe river Lethe it isn't for you ai colors ts Veta ts Al'fa Veta Gamma and so on . . . (E18/19).

28. The scene is briefly described on p. 217 above.

29. 'ne to ne ta ne to ne ta ne to ne ta netto brutto Italia Italian person Dante person Bruno person Leonardo artist architect entomologist . . .' (E19).

30. *'if you want to see flying with four wings step into the moats of the Milan fortress and you will see black dragonflies'* (E19).

31. Leonardo/Arkadij is also the inventor of a flying machine resembling a gigantic black dragonfly (R22/E31).

32. 'I want dragonflies flying in willows . . . in thickets of heather where Tinbergen himself born in Holland married a colleague and soon it became clear to them that *ammofila* does not find the way home the same way *filantus* does . . . to Vetočka of the railroad tra ta ta tra ta ta the kitty wed the tomcat . . .' (E19). The phrase starting from *vskore im stalo jasno* . . . 'soon it became clear to them . . .' is a paraphrase of a passage in Niko Tinbergen's book *Curious Naturalists* (New York, 1956) pp. 104–105. The eminent Dutch naturalist who subsequently serves as the source of the name of Traxtenberg's alter ego is here a third, transient cognomen of Akatov/Leonardo.

33. 'everything that grows and flies, flowers and floats' (E147).

34. 'and moreover, plant the white rose of the winds in your garden; . . . present

teacher Pavel the white rose, . . . delight your old pedagogue — the jovial man, the jester, the wind driver' (E30).

35. 'O Rose . . . white Rose of the Wind, dear girl, sepulchral flower, how I want your untouched body!'

36. 'with the help of windmills I can produce wind at any time' (E31).

37. The connection is strengthened by the fact that the *ved* of Medvedev occurs as one of the book's variant forms of Veta (R71).

38. '. . . we hasten to declare to you personally, dear Savl Petrovič . . . that we do not doubt the existence of the Ill-Boding one . . . this day we shout to the whole wide world: long live the Ill-Boding Wind!' (E112–113).

39. Allowing for the pronounciation of the final *v* of Norvegov as an *f,* his profession, *geograf* 'geographer,' is also a partial anagram of his proper name and his epithet. Even his alternate sobriquet *fljuger* 'wind vane' displays a tinge of anagrammatization.

40. Victor Erlich, *Russian Formalism,* 2nd rev. ed. (The Hague, 1965) p. 241. Erlich's discussion is directed specifically to heroes but applies with still greater force to secondary characters.

41. 'For what do I fear in the face of eternity if today the wind ruffles my hair, freshens my face . . . but tomorrow — destroys unneeded dilapidated buildings, rips up oaks by the roots . . .' (E27).

42. 'Fear the Ill-Boding Wind, you sovereigns of cities and dachas, cower before breezes and drafts for they breed hurricanes and whirlwinds' (E28).

43. 'Now I cry out with all my blood as one cries of vengeance to come: in the world there is nothing, in the world there is nothing, in the world there is nothing — except the Wind!' (E202).

44. Shakespeare's *King Lear* and Cervantes' *Don Quixote* come to mind. The latter work has other points of resonance with *Škola dlja durakov.* Savl Petrovič, like Quixote, has a penchant for both real and metaphoric windmills.

45. 'Then Saul, who is also called Paul, filled with the Holy Spirit, set eyes on him, and said.'

46. One further parallel is that Savl, like Saul of Tarsus, leaves a testament for his followers. The novel's fifth and final chapter is entitled *Zaveščanie* 'Testament' referring to Savl's bequest of his skeleton for display in Veta Akatov's classroom.

47. The preceding theoretical comments are drawn from Linda Waugh, *Roman Jakobson's Science of Language* (Lisse, 1976), p. 33. The immediately following observations on metalinguistic phenomena are from Elmar Holenstein's *Roman Jakobson's Approach to Language: Phenomenological Structuralism* (Bloomington, 1974) pp. 162–163.

48. 'All right, but how do you begin, what words do you use?'

49. 'It makes no difference, use the words: there at the station pond.'

50. 'At the *station* pond?'

51. 'But that's incorrect, a stylistic mistake. Vodokačka would certainly correct it, one can say "station" snack bar . . . , but not pond, a pond can only be *near* the station.'

52. 'Good, then I'll begin that way: there, at the pond near the station' (E 11).

53. See pages R95 and 97/E131 and 133 for examples. The character Vodokačka, although several times mentioned, never actually appears in the narrative. She is, however, one of the "wind and water" figures. Like them she has two names: Valentina Dmitrievna Kaln and the acronymic derivative *Vodokačka* (R95–96).

54. See p. 213 above.

55. 'Student so-and-so, allow me, the author, to interrupt you and tell how I imagine to myself the moment . . . like you, I have a pretty good imagination . . .' (E212).

56. Lotman, pp. 106–113.

57. 'To drive, to hold, to run, to offend,/ to hear, to see and to turn, and to breathe,/ and to hate and depend and endure. // A group of Russian verbs / constituting a certain exception / from the rules: rhythmically organized / for ease of memorization.'

58. 'Take the oars and row home to Syracuse to enumerate the Taurian ships' (E192). Sokolov's lists may also have more recent antecedents in Gogol whose presence informs his writing in other ways. See Carl R. Proffer's comments on Gogol's use of Homeric lists in *Taras Bulba* in his *The Simile and Gogol's Dead Souls* (The Hague, 1967) pp. 177–178.

59. 'Weary, breathing heavily, wiping their faces with handkerchiefs, carrying briefcases, string bags and throbbing with spleen' (E12).

60. 'Tea, sugar, butter, sausage; fresh fish with flapping tails; macaroni, buckwheat, onions, prepared foods; more rarely — salt' (E12).

61. '. . . the river slowly streamed past along with all its fish, . . . with its reflected clouds, its invisible and emergent drowned bodies, . . . with its empty tin cans and heavy caps of Monomakhs, . . . with its apples of discord and pears of sorrow . . .' (E62–63).

62. 'until . . . the teacher Pavel hears, . . . comes out of his house, . . . rows across the Lethe, . . . embraces you, . . . says kind and mysterious words, receives, no, doesn't read . . . the letter for he, your teacher, is no longer among the living' (E60).

63. 'in the bitter fonts of folk wisdom, / in sweet adages or dicta, / in the dust of the damned or the dismay of the beloved, / in the bags of bums or in Judas' sums, / in movement *from* or position *over,* / in the lie of the defrauded or in the truth of the defamed, / in war or peace, / in mirage or sward / in stages or in studios, / in shame or sufferings, / in darkness or in light, / in hatred or pity, / in life or outside it — / into all of this and much else one must thoroughly delve, / in all this there is something, perhaps not much, but something' (E59–60).

64. Rhythm which rests on the repetition of similar prosodic elements is a paradigmatic phenomenon. For a discussion of rhythm and rhythmic organization as an aspect of the paradigmatic axis, see Lotman, pp. 37–43.

65. This idea was first suggested to me by the comments on lists in James Joyce's *Ulysses* made by Robert Scholes in his *Structuralism in Literature* (New Haven, 1974) pp. 188–189.

66. Also critical is the extent to which the paradigmatic sets of the reader and the writer share the same constituency.

67. This concept is explored in D. Lodge, *The Modes of Modern Writing: Metaphor, Metonymy, and the Typology of Modern Literature* (Ithaca, N.Y., 1977).

68. Jakobson, "Closing Statement. . . ," p. 358.

Vida Taranovski Johnson

IVO ANDRIĆ'S *KUĆA NA OSAMI*
('THE HOUSE IN A SECLUDED PLACE'):
MEMORIES AND GHOSTS OF THE WRITER'S PAST

When he died in 1975 at the age of 82, Ivo Andrić had been Yugoslavia's foremost writer for three decades. He was a national institution. Recognized as a talented storyteller in the twenties and thirties, he achieved national prominence in 1945 with the publication of his three novels, *Travnička hronika* (*The Bosnian Story*), *Na Drini ćuprija* (*The Bridge on the Drina*), and *Gospodjica* (*Miss*). Worldwide recognition came in the form of the Nobel Prize for Literature in 1961. Although he published approximately one hundred stories and fragments in the three decades after World War II, only one longer work, *Prokleta avlija* (*The Devil's Yard*) and a handful of short stories received the undivided critical acclaim accorded his earlier fiction. The evolution to delicate psychological portraiture and a more refined form was hailed by critics. Yet the fact that recent criticism has tended to reevaluate Andrić's early "classics" and has ignored much of his later literary endeavors is evidence of a lingering doubt that Andrić's early Bosnian stories and novels would ever be surpassed. After *Lica* (*Faces*), a collection of primarily old stories and only one or two new ones, appeared to mixed reviews in 1960, Andrić actually published very little. Thus the writer himself may have been responsible for this imbalance in critical attention. In the sixties it might have seemed that Andrić's prodigious talent had finally exhausted itself.

The posthumous publication in 1976 of a large body of previously unpublished fiction invites comparison and demands a reevaluation of Andrić's creative life. One work in particular, a collection of eleven stories titled *Kuća na osami* (*The House in a Secluded Place*) attests to Andrić's continuing productivity and evolution in fiction. At the same time a highly retrospective and a fundamentally innovative work, this is Andrić's last and most ambitious attempt in short fiction. On the one hand, *Kuća na osami* offers a panoramic view of his most enduring themes, motifs, and character types. On the other, it is basically different in composition from all of his other prose. The vast majority of Andrić's stories were first published individually and only later combined into loose, "open" collections. Although perhaps unfinished, *Kuća na osami* is a coherent whole, clearly conceived and executed as an indivisible "closed" cycle of stories. Most importantly, in this work Andrić is delving for the first time into the writer's memory and exploring his own art of storytelling in a self-conscious and highly personal, autobiographical manner. Memory and storytelling in fact become the main thematic link among the stories, which Andrić uses to make his final pronouncements on both his life and his art. *Kuća na osami* thus functions in three frames of reference: fictional, metaliterary, and autobiographical.

In terms of composition only *Lica* (*Faces*), the last collection published in Andrić's lifetime, can be regarded as a forerunner of *Kuća na osami*. Both collections are a series of brief sketches, anecdotes or character portraits with basically static narrative structure. Moreover, in both an introduction precedes the stories. Here the author states his purpose and defines the overall composition of the collection. The story "Lica," from which the earlier collection derives its title, depicts the diversity of human faces which haunt the writer's imagination. In the "Introduction" ("Uvod") to *Kuća na osami* a similar narrative persona appears as the writer who is literally attacked by visions of widely different yet equally mesmerizing faces (*lica*) and personalities. Here the similarity ends.

In *Lica* the narrative viewpoint does not remain constant and the elusive figure of the narrator-writer disappears completely in many of the stories. In fact, there are no formal connecting links between the stories. Uneven in aesthetic value and quite disparate in substance, these stories virtually proclaim their independence of each other. Especially since almost all of the stories were first published separately, the idea of putting them together strikes the reader as an afterthought. Yet the fact that Andrić attempted to motivate this grouping of stories and took some steps toward achieving a compositional whole makes *Lica* an important predecessor of *Kuća na osami*. Moreover, in *Lica* Andrić is moving closer to using his own voice, that of the writer, to tell his tales. But he seems to hesitate in fully implementing this narrative technique. In *Kuća na osami,* on the other hand, he is completely at ease with a narrator who is clearly the writer's second self. It is precisely this figure of the narrator-writer, whose presence weaves through all the stories, which creates this successful collection.[1]

In *Kuća na osami* Andrić for the first time uses both a single primary setting as a "frame" for all of the stories and a single primary narrator as his storyteller. As is traditional for "frame" stories, he uses the introduction to authenticate his storyteller, his characters and the setting, as well as to define the compositional framework of the collection. Immediately upon describing a strange and colorful house in Bosnia and identifying these writings as recollections (*sećanja*) from a summer spent there, the narrator establishes himself as a writer through the comprehensive description of the mechanics of his craft, the ruses and maneuvers he uses to recapture the threads of the previous day's story. The details of this ritual — absent-minded glances around the room, feigned indifference while stalking his story like a hunter stalks his prey — are vividly and humorously portrayed. Yet, at times, images of faces or snatches of conversations assail him so vividly and with such force that he has to exorcise these visions by capturing them on paper. The "Introduction" thus ends with the presentation of the compositional framework for the whole collection.

Kuća na osami offers a procession of unforgettable characters, tormented "souls" who intrude upon the writer in order to tell their true stories. The visitors are ghosts who come back from the dead to settle accounts, to expose the true nature of their suffering — the tragedy of a complex inner life hidden behind banal external appearances. Thus, each story is a revelation and a reevaluation of a life. The narrator-writer plays the seemingly passive role of a captive listener, imprisoned by memories in the strange and secluded Bosnian house. Most of the stories are framed by the expected or actual arrival and departure of the visitor.[2] The narrator also connects the stories by frequent reference to the communality of his characters, often pointing out their similarities and differences. Thus, the overall compositional unity is further supported both by the narrator's explicit insistence on the connecting links between the stories and by the structural parallelism of the individual stories themselves.

The setting which frames the stories functions as the second major unifying element in the cycle. What unites the visitors, at least superficially, is the house. The narrator mentions that "what they have in common is only that they gathered around my house in Sarajevo from time to time and left an invisible but real trace there."[3] Each visitor, then, represents a recollection associated with the house. Each is in some way memorable. Each is one of many. The repeated references to the house are a formal unifying device which allows the writer a free hand in portraying a wide variety of characters. Thus the diversity in personal histories, social origin, character traits and personalities, which is emphasized throughout, does not detract from the compositional integrity of the work as a cycle. These differences turn out to be superficial because all of Andrić's characters share a similar fate.

Although the use of setting as a formal device to connect the stories is quite transparent, its thematic significance is not. The narrator's insistent return to the house in every story combined with its very long and detailed description at the very beginning of the "Introduction" demand closer analysis. The very first sentence tells the reader familiar with Andrić's fiction that this is his steep and rocky Bosnia: "It is a two-story house on the steep Alifakovac, near the very top, set somewhat apart from the others." (XV, 9). Since *na osami* means "by itself, in a secluded place," the title then seems to refer to this particular house, a fact which underscores its thematic importance. The very detailed physical description that follows reveals an odd mixture of old Bosnian and new Austrian architecture:

All this was built in the nineties — in 1887 exactly — when even the local people started to build houses 'according to plan,' with an Austrian look and layout and were partly successful in this. If it had been only ten years earlier, this house would have been built totally in the old Turkish manner like the majority of the houses on the Alifakovac, and not in the German manner like the houses in the plain around the Miljacka [river]. Then the wide hallway at the entrance to the first floor would be called an 'ahar' and the balcony on the second floor a 'divanhana,' and all this would not have the hybrid look of a structure where in the process of building, man's desires and plans took one course, aimed towards something new and unknown, and his hands, eyes, and whole inner being drew him in another direction, to the old and the familiar. (XV, 9–10)

The house physically embodies Bosnia's cultural dualism. It is a palpable and enduring monument to the clash of Eastern and Western cultures found in all of Andrić's Bosnian fiction. In endless twists and permutations Andrić draws out the tragic consequences of Bosnia's unique and ephemeral existence on the border of two civilizations. Here, in his last work, this conflict is presented in a more positive vein as the house itself is in fact charming, a workable testament to the forced accommodation of diverse influences.

Through the image of the house, Andrić evokes the hybrid nature of Bosnia, which is reflected not only in its culture and society as a whole, but in its individual inhabitants as well. Thus the description of the house acquires a psychological dimension. It foreshadows the conflict of the characters, which from the beginning must be viewed in terms of the specific setting. This internal relationship between character and setting is particularly prominent in Andrić's early prose in which grotesque, monumental characters reflect the mysterious and exotic atmosphere of Bosnia. In this collection a succession of enigmatic, larger-than-life characters is directly tied to an equally strange house. Precisely because the house is so unusual, the reader is not shocked by the apparitions that come to inhabit it temporarily.

In Andrić's early fiction Bosnia not only functions as a setting for the majority of his stories but also emerges as a major theme, even the main protagonist. In other words, it operates on both a formal and a thematic level. While the historical-ethnographic entity provides the formal setting, a highly subjective, mythical Bosnia becomes a major theme and such a powerful presence that it attains the status of an autonomous being on a par with the characters themselves. The human characters, monumental and grotesque, indeed often appear only to be expressions or extensions of its complex, mysterious nature, in Andrić's own words, of its "dark beauty." In the post-war stories Andrić for all practical purposes abandoned this Bosnia in favor of more contemporary themes and a variety of settings, only one of which was Bosnia. The Bosnia of these stories loses its exotic and fascinating atmosphere and is generally free of the overruling legendary design of the earlier fiction.

In *Kuća na osami* Andrić seemingly reverts back to the Bosnian theme. But here the Bosnian setting loses the geographical and historical concreteness of the post-war Bosnian stories and the unifying mythical dimension of the early Bosnian fiction. Although it is the primary setting, the main action in several of the stories actually takes place outside of Bosnia.[4] Yet *Kuća na osami* still seems to be a retrospective on Andrić's early Bosnia because it remains as a kind of symbolic landscape, a frame of mind or angle of vision from which the writer chooses the material for his stories.

Thus, it is not surprising to meet again those alienated and tormented beings who inhabit Andrić's Bosnian world. The stories themselves are a series of finely nuanced portraits of a motley crew of dreamers, inveterate liars and drunkards, recluses, libertines, ruthless rulers and social outcasts, tormentors and victims. Characteristically for Andrić, two of these — the nineteenth century historical figure Alipaša Rizvanbegović Stočević ("Alipaša") and the Bosnian storyteller, Ibrahim-efendija Škaro ("Priča" ("A Story")) — had already appeared in previous works: Alipaša in one of the fragments of the unfinished novel *Omerpaša Latas,* and Škaro in a fragment, "Razgovor predveče" ("An Early Evening Conversation"). While Zuja, the main protagonist of the last story "Zuja," does not appear in any of Andrić's earlier fiction under that name, her story bears a remarkable resemblance to one of the subplots of "Mara milosnica" ("The Pasha's Concubine"), an early Andrić masterpiece.[5] Not only does Andrić reintroduce individual characters and plot elements, but he intertwines familiar types of characters and motifs to create new variations on old themes. An examination of the individual stories themselves will demonstrate to what extent they represent a review and synthesis of Andrić's short fiction from both the pre-war and post-war periods.

The first story, "Bonvalpaša ("Bonvalpasha") is a character sketch of a fascinating adventurer, the French nobleman Claude Alexandre de Bonneval, a soldier of fortune who adopts the Moslem faith as an act of expediency. He is immediately recognized by Andrić readers as a type of character, the convert to Islam ("poturčenjak"), a man without family or country, who became particularly prominent in Andrić's last, unfinished novel *Omerpaša Latas* (*Omerpasha Latas*). Although he is established as a nineteenth-century historical personage, the facts of his convoluted existence and his political machinations are only briefly told. There is no action to distract the reader's attention from his magnificent, simultaneously repulsive and attractive countenance. His every feature is described in minute detail, broken down into its constituent parts in an attempt to capture the magnitude of the character. He emerges from this scrutiny as one of Andrić's most vivid and vital creations, a massive and grotesque figure frozen in time, a worthy rival of the mesmerizing, monumental Djerzelez Alija and other early Bosnian heroes. Not even the narrator-writer can resist his persistent, exuberant as well as obnoxious attempts to enter his house and his story. He is in fact the first person whose story is told.

Already in the first story a pattern is beginning to form. In style and technique, in the meticulous attention to detail and static rather than dynamic narrative structure, this story is reminiscent of Andrić's more recent writings. But the expansive, larger-than-life protagonist evokes the exotic, legendary atmosphere which permeated so totally Andrić's early Bosnian fiction.

Another historical figure from the nineteenth century, the ruthless vizier of Hercegovina, Alipaša Rizvanbegović Stočević, appears in the second story,

"Alipaša." The inscrutable and dignified Alipaša shares the monumental proportions though not the emotional temperament of Bonvalpaša. As in "Bonvalpaša" the historical facts are presented in a cursory manner, and are offered only as background material for the spiritual odyssey of Alipaša. While Bonvalpaša had spent his whole life in unrestrained pursuit of pleasure, in a state of hedonistic euphoria, the haughty Alipaša's last days as a disgraced prisoner are marked by an epiphany which reveals to him the eternal and universal truths of human existence. Paradoxically, in his physical degradation and spiritual torment Alipaša attains that true grandeur and dignity which he never possessed as the undisputed ruler of Hercegovina. The thematic focus of all the stories in the collection is an inner, previously hidden existence, characterized by fear, pain, and anguish, yet punctuated by moments of ecstasy and transcendence. The confrontation between the internal and external, subjective and objective reality is Andrić's most enduring theme, and its concomitant, *zanos* (ecstasy), his earliest motif.

In "Baron Dorn," the third story, the baron shares the aristocratic birthright with his predecessors, a fact duly noted by the narrator. However, he does not possess either their power or grandeur. In fact, baron Dorn would have been just another inefficient and insignificant Austrian bureaucrat were it not for his single, all-consuming passion — lying. In his attempts to transform his ludicrous and naive lies into "that masterpiece of mendacity — truth," (XV, 40) he is elevated from his pedestrian existence. He experiences moments of elation, which are inevitably followed by despair. While his own countrymen ridicule him, baron Dorn finds a receptive audience among the Bosnians for whom the telling of tales is a way of life. They introduce him to Bosnian brandy (*rakija*) to which he quickly succumbs. In other words, his life takes a predictable course in the Bosnian setting. Foreigners in particular, but native Bosnians as well, are destroyed by this illness, alcoholism, with remarkable regularity. Beginning with Andrić's first story, "Put Alije Djerzeleza" ("The Way of Alija Djerzelez"), *zanos* is often an alcohol-induced euphoria. Drinking becomes only the external manifestation of unexplained and inexplicable spiritual torments which either surface or are exacerbated in the morbid atmosphere of Andrić's Bosnia.

The major passion which ruled the universe of Andrić's early fiction was sensual. The fourth and fifth stories in *Kuća na osami,* "Geometar i Julka" ("The Surveyor and Julka"), and "Cirkus" ("Circus"), are stories of infidelity and unrequited love. Beginning with "Put Alije Djerzeleza," relationships between the sexes seemed doomed. Love, if it exists at all, is pathetic or tragic but never happy. The surveyor in "Geometar i Julka" is an uninteresting and unpleasant little man in appearance. Yet he tells a tale of adultery that is both pathetic and moving. Tormented by his wife's infidelities, but more importantly by her complete disregard for him as a human being, and afraid that he might one day kill her, he takes his own life instead. "Cirkus," the sordid story of a circus director's degradation by his cruel and faithless wife, leads to his unsuccessful murder attempt and eventual disgrace and death. This is the inner reality of the glamorous circus world which has haunted Andrić from childhood. Beginning with "Ćorkan i Švabica," (Ćorkan and the German Girl") the circus motif is associated with transcendence of reality, with *zanos.* As usual the glittering fantasy world of the child turns out to be tarnished.

Continuing with the motifs of childhood recollections, alcoholism and suicide, the sixth story, "Jakov, drug iz detinjstva" ("Jakov, the Childhood Friend"), is a tale of a man driven to suicide by a hereditary addiction to alcohol. Typically for most of Andrić's early Bosnian stories, alcoholism here is treated as a form of hereditary degeneracy, the thinning of the blood of Bosnian families who perpetuate and pass on vices, obsessions and psychic derangements. But in its repetitive, militant condemnation of this Bosnian "poison," this story proves to be the weakest in the collection. Andrić again returns to the openly didactic, socially conscious narrative voice that he had adopted without much success in his post-war topical stories.

Both Jakov and Ibrahim-efendija Škaro, the protagonist of the next story, "Priča" ("A Story"), are physically and spiritually transformed by alcohol. Jakov's paranoia, his guilt and fear of life alternate with feelings of elation, power, and insight, on that borderline between sanity and insanity, normality and abnormality, induced by alcohol. In this euphoric state he is able to look into that "other side [of life] with all its wonders" (XV, 76). Ibrahim-efendija is a hermetic personality who has great difficulty committing himself verbally. Drinking frees him from his constricted existence, literally loosening his tongue so that he becomes a wondrous storyteller who weaves spells over his listeners. Ibrahim-efendija does accomplish what baron Dorn had unsuccessfully strived to do all his life: to create truth out of lies. He creates a whole new reality out of his spellbinding tales, because his listeners are convinced that "only in these tales [life] finds its true form and total meaning" (XV, 90). Ibrahim-efendija uses his talent to transform reality, both for himself and for his audience. In this way he manages to escape life's hardships and to deceive fate. More importantly, he assures himself of immortality for he continues to live in his stories: "he lives sometime and somewhere still, like a tale" (XV, 90). In this story Andrić explores most fully and explicitly a major unifying theme in the cycle, the theme of art and the metamorphic and cathartic power of storytelling.

As the stories in the collection continue to unfold, the reverberation of motifs and variations on familiar themes becomes increasingly obvious. Escape from imaginary or real torments, from a harsh and cruel existence, the second thematic thread which weaves through all the stories, is most successfully presented in "Robinja" ("The Slave Girl"), perhaps the most memorable story and certainly the most self-contained in the collection. "Robinja" is the haunting tale of a slave girl who takes her own life. The girl, a prisoner captured in a Turkish raid on a village in Hercegovina, is caged and waiting to be sold. Characteristically for Andrić's early Bosnian stories, the thin, wasted libertine who is bargaining for her is contrasted to his healthy, well-endowed victim. In her physical stature the slave girl is reminiscent of Anika in "Anikina vremena" ("Anika's Times"), the girl from Trebinje in "Za logorovanja" ("During the Encampment"), and the woman from Mostar in "Olujaci"("Olujaci"). While Anika only orchestrates her own murder, the slave girl takes her own life in a supreme gesture of self-will. She seeks to obliterate her spiritual agony in sharp physical pain as she slowly and methodically presses her head between the wooden bars of her cage. The oblivion which she finds is awesome in its immediacy and finality, both for the character and for the reader. The story itself, a graphic presentation of this process of self-destruction, is one of Andrić's most powerful and terrifying creations.

"Robinja" represents a kind of structural italics in the collection. It is the only story not completely framed as a visit or a recollection. In all the other stories the narrator reappears at the end to present the character's departure or comment on it. The effect of his reappearance is to physically and emotionally distance the reader from those disturbing visions from the past. The endings of the stories dispel the negative stamp which marked the lives of the characters. In "Robinja" the return from the past to the narrator's present does not occur. Thus the emotional tension built up by the slow exposition of the physical process of the suicide is never released. Although on the level of plot there is relaxation of tension through her death and the end of her suffering, the reader is not released from the emotional grip of its impact.

The reader is still under the influence of this story when he is faced with "Životi" ("Lives"), the ninth tale in the collection. Because the narrator did not provide an adequate transition, one expects some thematic similarities between the stories "Robinja" and "Životi." Yet the characters and subject matter are totally different. In fact the two stories which are most closely linked on the thematic level, "Priča" and "Životi," are separated by "Robinja," a seemingly unrelated story. Like Ibrahim-efendija in "Priča," the protagonist of "Životi" was successful in his attempt to "escape his real life"(XV, 106). As a young man he had reached a crisis realizing that only two courses of action were open to him — madness ending with suicide or withdrawal from life. So he moved to a secluded house, and became a passionate collector of rare objects and antiques. He lived in superficial contact with people, hiding behind the mask of an eccentric. While the protagonists in "Priča" and "Životi" both lead a hermetic life emotionally, the slave girl in "Robinja" is physically contrained. They escape by creating invisible barriers around themselves, mental prisons which they carry with them to the grave, while the girl ironically is freed from her prison by taking her own life. The story "Robinja" thus plays a contrapuntal role to the preceding and following stories. These three stories present most clearly the theme of escape from man's heaviest burden: living.

"Ljuvabi" ("Loves"), the penultimate story in the cycle, once again returns to the theme of tragic and tormented love, in which the characters are polarized into victims and tormentors. Although here the sexual roles are reversed — woman is the victim and man the aggressor — the same basic elements are present as in the earlier stories "Cirkus" and "Geometar i Julka": passion, violence, death. The prostitute who tells of her love for a man who beats her brutally herself sees no solution to her life except more violence and death. The agony of her life is complex. Pain merges with pleasure for the beatings which she receives transport her onto a higher level of existence. Labelling the woman a masochist would only simplify what is a complex and poignant tale. The point of the story is that *zanos,* feelings of elation and transcendence, appear in the most unpredictable situations. This, of course, has been true of all of Andrić's fiction.

While in "Ljubavi" the violence was part of a strange and tormented love relationship, in the last story, "Zuja," it is totally stripped of feeling and becomes an impersonal and inhuman sexual assault. A servant girl indulging in her favorite pastime — leaning over a bridge mesmerized (*zanesena*) by the cascading water below — is attacked silently and brutally by a passerby, a faceless monster of a man. It is ironic that this last story in the collection recalls so vividly the terrifying sexual violence and the ominous atmosphere of such early Bosnian stories as "Za logorovanja" and "Mara milosnica." Yet the manner in which Andrić presents this story material is reminiscent not of his early period, but of his more recent writing. The description of the rape in "Zuja" and of the suicide in "Robinja" is more graphic yet more restrained than similar descriptions in the early stories. For example, in "Za logorovanja" the portrayal of a rape is much less precise and more impressionistic. The reader suspects that Andrić is accenting the elements of atrocity and perversion for their shock value in this story, as well as many of his early Bosnian stories. In these last stories, particularly in "Robinja" and "Zuja," there are no grotesque or exotic gestures to heighten the effect of this violence. Instead, the experience is presented in detail from the viewpoint of the victim. Its impact upon the reader is more immediate and deeply moving.

Although not all stories in *Kuća na osami* are of equal esthetic merit — "Robinja," "Alipaša," and "Bonvalpaša" are masterpieces of portraiture clearly superior to "Jakov, drug iz detinjstva" — they do function successfully within the context of the collection. The interweaving of motifs and character types unites the stories on the thematic plane just as the setting and the narrative persona connect them on a formal level. The recurrence of familiar characters and themes calls attention to the retrospective nature of the cycle, particularly in the reappearance of motifs associated with the early Bosnian stories: the combination of violence and sex, the traditional Bosnian obsessions with alcohol and tall tales, hereditary and social degeneracy. Love is tormented, relationships between the sexes are doomed. Both love and sex are often perverse, abnormal in some way, and their consequences are always disastrous. Death by murder or suicide, if not realized in the story, nevertheless remains as a potential or predictable resolution of the human dilemmas presented. The repetition of these elements resurrects that ominous and mysterious atmosphere of the early Bosnian stories whose monumental protagonists were victims of similar passions and psychic disorders. But it is noteworthy that Andrić combines larger-than-life figures typical of the early stories (in "Alipaša," "Bonvalpaša," and "Robinja") with the more modest figure of the "little" man (in "Cirkus," "Geometar i Julka"), more characteristic of the immediate post-war stories. Although *Kuća na osami* primarily seems to be a retrospective of Andrić's earlier fiction, in fact it represents a synthesis of both his pre-war and post-war writing in thematic terms.

It is evident, however, that Andrić treats his material differently, in the manner characteristic of his post-war fiction. The changes in style, narrative technique and structure, noted by critics, are here developed and refined further. Only in one story, in "Jakov, drug iz detinjstva," the awkward didacticism of Andrić's post-war topical stories can again be recognized. The evolution to more analytical prose, to static rather than dynamic narrative structure, exposed rather than hidden motivation are all formal characteristics of his more recent fiction.

The happy endings and forced optimism of the immediate post-war stories, influenced by the political and cultural climate of the times, have completely disappeared in this, Andrić's last work. They had sounded a false note because they were inconsistent with the complex world view that permeated all of Andrić's previous fiction. In *Kuća na osami,* once again, human existence consists of a timeless and universal cycle of agony and ecstasy. Whatever its cause — a single traumatic experience, hereditary degeneracy, social decay or inexplicable fears and phobias — the result is an inevitable split between an internal and external reality. Paradoxically, in the midst of a seemingly hopeless existence, even in physical pain and spiritual degradation, there are moments of elation and transcendence, a heightened awareness if not an increased understanding of life. Each story represents either a revelation of such moments or a reevaluation of tormented, anguished lives.

These reassessments of human traumas are a type of ritualized exorcism both for the narrator-writer and for the characters themselves. It is through the cathartic process of storytelling that the ghosts who visit the writer find peace as in the case of baron Dorn, the surveyor and the circus director. The baron comes to tell his tale because he sees in the writer a man who understands his predicament and does not consider it hopeless. The surveyor in "Geometar i Julka" and the circus director in "Cirkus" come to fill in their stories in the writer's memory, because "everything in life must be illuminated from all sides" (XV, 70). It is of course not only the characters, but Andrić himself who is exorcising visions from the past, visions that are both personal and literary.

Although Andrić finds a clever device for parading familiar characters and synthesizing themes in this retrospective work, by identifying the narrator as a writer and the characters as his creations, he begins to explore the metaliterary questions of his own storytelling art, and the nature of fiction. In the very end of the "Introduction" the narrator-writer openly states that the tormented souls who visit him are "characters from stories" (XV, 12). He thus exposes the literary device and questions the nature of his characters' existence. Yet these imaginary beings who appear in a clearly fantastic situation — they come as ghosts — do also possess a vitality and existence outside of the writer's purview. On the fictional level, the fact that they are dead is irrelevant. In the case of Bonvalpaša and Alipaša their stories have the weight of history behind them. The surveyor, the collector of antiques, the prostitute in "Ljubavi" are all identified as real people the writer had met at some time in the past. *Kuća na osami* turns out to be not only a literary reminiscence but a personal, autobiographical one as well, because Andrić openly erases any distinction between his narrator-writer and himself.

Andrić's propensity to use his own voice in the post-war stories has already been noted. In *Kuća na osami* the clearest identification of the narrator as author occurs in the story "Životi," when Andrić places in the mouth of his narrator the exact statement he himself made in 1961 in his Nobel Prize acceptance speech.[6] The narrator-writer in this collection is not meant to be perceived as some "second self," some alter ego of the writer, but as Andrić making a final, confessional declaration of his life and art. From the physical isolation of this Bosnian house and the spiritual isolation of the artist, Andrić takes stock and settles accounts with the past:

> Whole regions or cities, streets or apartments come to me as light ethereal visions transported by memory, in their desire to find, here, on my paper, their final form and their true significance and explanation. (XV, 107)

Through the cathartic process of storytelling, in *Kuća na osami* Andrić answers questions about his literary and personal life, questions that he had not been able to deal with previously. The theme of reconciliation with life and with the past unites Andrić with his characters. That is why there is a certain mellowness of tone that permeates this work, as well as the feeling of tolerance, acceptance of life in all its forms. Andrić's message in *Kuća na osami* is not pessimistic. It is disquieting and deeply moving, yet always life-affirming.

NOTES

1. Andrić uses this type of narrative persona, the writer who relates memories of meetings from the past, as a storytelling device in the post-war period. Before World War II, he primarily utilized an omniscient third person narrator who combined traits of the historical chronicler and the Bosnian storyteller. In the early period very few stories are told in the first person, and when they are, the storyteller is a *skaz* narrator, usually identified as one of the characters from the Bosnian setting. The only major

exception is the first person narrator, an alter-ego of the author, in "Jelena, žena koje nema," a story published in three installments: 1934, 1955, 1961. The complex framing technique in which more than one character is employed to tell the story, culminating in the layering upon layering of narration in *Prokleta avlija* (*The Devil's Yard*), attest to Andrić's continuing search for an authentic voice from the historical and cultural milieu that he describes. In this work as well as in several stories written around World War II, he finds his ideal Bosnian storyteller in the monk Fra Petar. More and more in the post-war stories the absence of any stated differences between the narrator and the author, and the identification of the stories as recollections demonstrate Andrić's increasing concern for the authentication of the narrative persona as the author himself. The voice of this first person narrator becomes familiar even though it is stylistically unmarked, except for a propensity for generalizing statements in narrative asides. These asides, often set off by parentheses and a shift to the first person plural, seem to be the author's own moral and philosophical pronouncements. It is this narrative that is used in *Kuća na osami* as well as in some of the *Lica* stories.

2. In the stories "Zuja" and "Cirkus" the arrival of the visitor is delayed. But each figure is conjured up from the narrator's memory of the past, particularly of his childhood. In "Robinja," "Životi," and "Ljubavi" the visitor is not a person. It is the sea, or a city or even a street that invades the house and brings the story. However, by stating that not all his visitors are human, by creating a negative comparison, Andrić preserves a certain structural parallelism in the introductions to these stories.

3. *Sabrana dela Ive Andrića* (*Collected Works of Ivo Andrić*), XV, *Kuća na osami i druge pripovetke* (*The House in a Secluded Place and Other Stories*), (Beograd: Prosveta, 1976), p. 35. All further references to this work will be cited in the text by volume and page number. All translations from *Kuća na osami* including the titles of stories are mine.

4. In "Geometar i Julka" the setting of the main story is a train trip from Beograd to Novi Sad. Even foreign countries, Italy in "Životi" and France in "Ljubavi," function as a secondary setting. (In the post-war period a visit to a new place or travel by train is a common device which Andrić uses to set his story.) But since all the characters, all these memories, haunt the narrator in that one house in Bosnia, they are united and even invaded by its atmosphere.

5. The story of the docile and selfless servant Zuja who is the backbone of the powerful but decaying Aleksić clan seems to be only a variant of Jela's relationship to the Pamuković family in "Mara milosnica." Both women share an early traumatic experience, rape, which depersonalizes them, stripping them of any individuality and independent spirit.

6. The narrator in "Životi":

"Valja plivati. Postojati. Nositi identitet. Izdržati atmosferski pritisak oko sebe, sudare, nepredvidjene i nepredvidljive postupke svoje i tudje, koji ponajčešće nisu o našoj meri; a povrh svega izdržati još i — svoju misao o svemu tome." (XV, 107)

Andrić in his Nobel Prize acceptance speech in Stockholm in 1961: "Morati plivati. Postojati. Nositi identitet. Izdržati atmosferski pritisak svega oko sebe, sve sudare, nepredvidljive i nepredvidjene postupke svoje i tudje, koji ponajčešće nisu po meri naših snaga. A povrh svega, treba još izdržati i svoju misao o svemu tome." (XII, 68) ("One must swim. Exist. Bear one's identity. Withstand the atmospheric pressure, conflicts, unforeseeable and unforeseen actions whether one's own or others', which most often are not within our power. And above all one must withstand one's own thought about all this.")

Davor Kapetanić

THE ANTI-HERO IN CONTEMPORARY CROATIAN FICTION: THE CASE OF ANTUN ŠOLJAN

In Croatian literature the fifties marked the emergence of a young generation of writers whose creative concerns went beyond merely serving immediate political realities. They brought about a movement that would make beneficial changes in literature, leading it to its modern aesthetic and intellectual horizons. Gathered around the journal *Krugovi* (1952–1962), this generation set off on its not-too-idyllic spiritual excursion without any declarative manifesto as its common platform. But from the beginning these writers were bound by specific intentions characteristic of a homogenous group. Its representatives similarly expressed a dominant orientation toward the individual and presented a carefully planned opposition to the literary codex of that time, one that relied on social determinism and exclusively insisted on ideological purity.

During the first postwar years, the proclaimed ideal of Croatian prose was the social novel, in whose center one would find, as its dramatic agent, a hypothetical "new" man. This "new" man was almost a revolutionary saint who found true meaning, justification, and fulfillment of life in the sphere of history. The social and political implication of each gesture of the hypothetical hero was emphasized and it determined the simple, schematized polarization of the positive and negative. This polarization was the only possible means of representing reality. Preferring a question to any answer, the prosaists of *Krugovi* found no reason to accept that which was offered by the literature of social commitment. Satiated with futile searches for nonexistent heroes who, fortunately, occurred in theoretical postulations rather than in literary works, the prose writers of *Krugovi* — a group whose best-known member is Antun Šoljan — opted for the hero in dilemma. This hero is not, of course, Malraux's intellectual hero who accepted the mysticism of revolutionary action, while suspecting that the ideology of social commitment was but another species of illusion. Šoljan and the writers of his generation broke the ideological organization of the hero's image and put him in an antipathetic position, in the world of ordinary facts. Here, he finds himself in a life that is rationally ordered in spite of the occurrence of great events. As one of Šoljan's protagonists will emphatically exclaim, it is perhaps "senseless, stupid, limited life, but nevertheless life." On a line where the experience of existence opposes history, the self-conscious and responsible character of the socialist-realistic type will yield his place to his rival, the anti-hero.

In the effort to understand man in terms of the genuine scope of his life and to construct a narrative structure that would make this possible, the *Krugovi* generation could turn to their predecessors. Certainly, a stimulus could be found in the works of Petar Šegedin, an author who emerged on the Croatian literary scene in the period between the wars. In the first post-war years, though, he published works of exceptional artistic merit which were either strongly attacked or completely suppressed by the official critics. In two novels which Šegedin published during that time, *God's Children* (*Djeca božja,* 1946) and *The Lonely People* (*Osamljenici,* 1947), one finds the psychological analysis of man's existence. The *dramatis personae* of both novels are "foreigners" with broken and defeated destinies, who live isolated from the world. Their message, that man is only free to suffer, eminently qualifies them to belong to the category of the modern anti-hero.

Viewed from such a perspective, Šegedin's novels anticipated in Croatian literature the productive model of the character whose physiognomy we are interested in tracing, and who is elusive, refractory, inconsistent, at odds with himself and his society, and always surprisingly different from his socially prescribed role. Caught within one kind of predicament or another as "the fool, the clown, the hipster, the scapegoat, the scrubby opportunist, the rebel without a cause, the criminal, the poor sod, the freak, the outsider, the hero in the ashcan and hero on the leash," [1] that unheroic hero moved the imagination of almost all contemporary Croatian writers. He has a central position in the collection of short stories *Hands* (*Ruke,* 1953) by Ranko Marinković, a writer who established himself shortly before the war, as well as a quarter of a century later in the novel, *Ciao, Slobberers* (*Ciao, slinavci,* 1978) by Tito Bilopavlović, a member of the young generation of prosaists. The list of names could go on indefinitely, regardless of the writer's specific literary orientation or ideal, or the choice of either realistic or experimental forms of prose expression. It is necessary to say, however, that Šegedin's imaginative penetration into the region of the self, with all its psychological brilliance, did not initiate a total concept of the anti-hero. It was the fiction of Antun Šoljan, qualified by its specific experience of "existence," that would create a complex figure of the anti-hero who, through his development from pale pamphleteer of hope to victim, would become the most conspicuous inhabitant of Croatian prose.

One can already discover the essential type of the anti-hero at the beginning of Šoljan's literary production, with the programmatic appearance of the "extraordinary envoys." They appear in a story by the same title published in 1953:

> All of it was because of us and we knew it, but we knew that they created it unconsciously, led by instinct and local-patriotic pride, and thus we felt superior, for we are those who are familiar with the situation in its details; we are conscious of all aspects of the thing which they see only from one side; we are prepared at any moment to return to our land which they don't recognize, and to which unknowingly they must come only as strangers. Burdened with this powerful knowledge of possibility and variation, completely calm and

cold under the weight of a multi-faceted consciousness, we are impartial observers who, not for any price, will engage in a momentary drama, superior, enclosed within them, unattainable to them; we are people from a far-off island, with eyes full of warm blue climate and an exotic sea through which they never swam, whose fragrance never touched their nostrils, and so, they never thought as we do, and so, they don't know that we are different for them, and with them, and for ourselves.[2]

The romantic texture which would remain as one of the surface distinctions of Šoljan's style, and which one cannot overlook here, does not overwhelm the intense semantic meaning of this paragraph in which we find a new body of values. The constructional centers "we" and "they," on which the whole short story rests, clearly emphasize the separateness of the "extraordinary envoys"; they do not belong to the conventional social structures and their norms. But the dominant polemic relationship of these two contrastive grammatical centers offers additional information, that is, that the "people from far-off islands" are not just social outsiders, they are self-conscious voluntary exiles who abandoned society by their own choice, and not because they were discarded as rubbish. Their fundamental situation includes both estrangement and communion. Burdened with too much knowledge, they disaffiliate themselves from society, but under the set masks of "impartial observers," they hide the tragic spasm of longing for the world. One of the "extraordinary envoys" declares at the beginning of another short story by Šoljan published in 1953: "The Pavlići were a world that I wished for . . ."[3]

The image of the anti-hero, as it appears, makes him a refugee who says no to his time. He does not, however, take the position of a nihilist who, essentially pessimistic in his vision, confronts the problem of existence in the spirit of negation. Šoljan's "extraordinary envoy" senses no harmony between himself and the social world around him, but he somehow manages to affirm life:

> If you don't like your life, if it has become odious to you, if you are tired of it, if you are lonely, lost, frightened — cross over, brother. There will always be enough strength to take one more step, all the way until the last step. And even if all the steps constitute crossing over the same road, even if from this hell you can flow only into another hell, even if from the beginning of the earth it has all been the same, only into such a world is man born, only in such a world does he live.[4]

The idea expressed by the protagonist of the novel *The Traitors* (*Izdajice*, 1961), clearly presents an understanding of life which developed on the foundation of the philosophy of existentialism present in the works of Sartre and Camus.[5] Within the frame of this philosophy, he presents himself as a man who knows that although life may be useless passion, it nevertheless must be lived:

> And joining the ranks of the warriors against death, nameless and sacrificed like them, alive and healthy, against my will and against my beliefs, I entered the battle in the name of the simplest life without further questions.[6]

As if following a strictly observed contract, Šoljan's protagonists find themselves in the world and outside of it at the same time: they are tempted by all the enchanting possibilities before them, but they cannot devote themselves to a single one, completely and without reservation. Their existential instinct provokes them to test themselves, but their self-indulgent introspection leads them to their own intention and acts.

Although he is physically capable, the main character of the novel *The Traitors* loses a bet that he can climb to the very top of a pole and thus become a victor. Motivated by the desire to achieve and to prove that man does not always have to remain the victim in life, he accepts the challenge, but at the point where he sees that the goal is within reach, he changes his mind, for he becomes conscious of the fact that absolute, definitive meanings are nothing more than illusions:

> Many have climbed to the top, and many have fallen. And what has been their reward? Both the victorious and the defeated are caught in the empty chain of years — the chain in which there is neither victory nor defeat, neither climbing nor falling.[7]

This scene is indeed symbolic, for throughout the novel the protagonist-narrator as well as the other characters continually make attempts that never achieve a complete fulfillment. Their lack of fulfillment does not come from the situation in which they find themselves, but rather from their perception of the danger that lies in surrendering themselves to externally imposed standards of value. Šoljan's characters are aware that there is no armor against fate, but they must set forth on their quest to break out of the darkness of conventional illusions and go out into the light of truth. For them the old standard formulas had failed completely, and they engaged in a creative struggle to invent their own tragic formula. They seek to know the meaning of what lies in store for them, for only in this way can they come to know themselves.

Precisely at this point, Šoljan's anti-hero divorces himself from the customary image of the anti-hero in modern world literature, which defines him as a subversive who "shouts aloud his envy and hatred, mounting an attack on every belief."[8] He is also not "the self-satisfied moralistic commentator who arrives at the battlefield as the belated messenger who reports to those who have perished that a victory has been achieved."[9] He is the parabolic moralist for whom the world is only a collection of taboos, a series of myths, both ideological and personal, which he does not wish to accept. He rejects them in the name of authentic life which these myths and taboos deny. Even the way in which Šoljan modelled his protagonists and their environment suggests the possibility of such an interpretation:

> In order to analyze their behavior, comprehend the absurdity of their fears and joys, understand their struggle and hope, their weapons and enemies, I tried to offer them everything they don't have. Using the model of past writers I made them a kind of Arcadia which they themselves could never create and in it I cultivated a pure culture of rare man, which here, for lack of a better term, we can call Kavalerov.[10]

This parallel with Kavalerov, the main character of Olesha's *Envy*, is itself indicative and does not require a more detailed explanation. What should be emphasized here, however, is the environment of idleness in which Šoljan places his protagonists. In its deepest meaning, this modern Arcadia, which is merely an illusion of social escape, functions as the negative projection of the social machine, and provides the spiritual basis upon which man can discover his identity. Although man is really a part of his world, he must not allow it to transform him into a non-human object. He, therefore, escapes into a kind of temporary exile where he can feel that he is more than just a simple unit of work energy. Idleness is one of the ways in which he can achieve the maximum freedom which is necessary for the discovery of life's meaning. Even the external characteristics given to Šoljan's characters reflect this idea. For the most part, they are young people, students or artists, who, unencumbered by the obligation of a steady profession, rise above the deceptions of an unreal existence. Šoljan places them in situations of adolescent joking, flirtation, and pleasure that are free from social relations, family ties, and the responsibilities of work. One should not see them as possible descendants of the so-called Beat Generation, or interpret them as social rebels who express their negative criticism of society living their own type of utopian existence. What spurs them on is not the principle of negation or criticism, but rather the energy of the search: "Again I was on the road. . . In front of me were a thousand roads and a thousand ways to change my life."[11]

With these closing lines of *The Traitors*, Šoljan symbolically announces the theme and content of his next novel, *Brief Outing* (*Kratki izlet*, 1965), for this entire novel takes place on a journey, in other words, on a search. The narrator and his companions wander through the desolate region of Istria, hoping to discover some remarkable old frescoes. The journey, however, is a rather sad experience. One by one the travelers drop out; only two of them, the narrator and the old guide Roko, do not succumb to the temptations of doubt, fatigue, women, and wine. But at the end, when they reach their hoped-for destination, they find only a destroyed monastery, a ruin that shows them the senselessness of their journey.

Through this sisyphean message about the tragedy of human existence and the uselessness of effort, the novel represents a new characteristic of the anti-hero, which is more than just the realization that man must endure life alone. From his inception, Šoljan's anti-hero is a member of an exclusive group which is freer than the rest of society. Now left alone, abandoned by his companions, he gains that which he has always lacked, his roots:

> A whole huge voiceless army marches beside me. They are everywhere around me, in the thick darkness which teems with life. I feel a silent union with them, and even though I do not see them, I recognize them in the darkness: they who surround me are my ancestors, all of my ancestors who, sometime long ago, in the same dark corridor, passed the same uncertain road, searching for salvation from their enemies, their conquerors, their world, and from themselves . . . I know that my journey, my longings are not senseless, for I am not alone, I belong to the river that flows ceaselessly, and I carry them on, I continue their journey, not only their small private path through senseless time, but also their striving for the goal that must exist, although I have not yet seen it.[12]

In his solitude, the anti-hero finds in the feeling of national identity a protective enclave. The role of anti-hero, one which he himself has chosen, is not, as it may at first appear, in conflict with his position in a national history. On the contrary, this is the way in which he can further emphasize his obsessive pursuit of his being, for his pursuit lies beyond the confines of social conditions and the present moment. He searches for the meaning of life, all of life, and although he may not find an answer, he stubbornly persists in his metaphysical quest. The story of his ancestors allows this quest: through it he tries to create, in Hemingway's manner, a world of his own in which he can live by a self-willed code, which, as he tells us, makes possible some hope for the future:

> I often think about putting an ad in the newspaper: some sort of hope always exists for man. But I know I don't have the strength to do it. But don't be angry if, while chattering on, I say: tomorrow, tomorrow I will place an ad in the newspaper. I will do something.[13]

But the writer of an "existential adventure" will not permit his hope to grow stronger: belief in an angel of mercy is valid only there where the angel of destruction sleeps. Thus, in his last novel, *The Port* (*Luka*, 1974), contradicting the metaphor implied in his title, Šoljan closes the door: he presents a terrifying vision of hopelessness in the world of reality which is totalitarian in structure and mechanically regimented.

In this work, Šoljan inverts the model of the "industrial novel"[14] and entering into the region of concrete life, he presents a story about the building of a modern tanker port in a provincial coastal place, when oil has allegedly been found. The denouement of this novel is very simple and brings to mind that of his *Brief Outing*. When it is discovered that there is no oil, the building of the port ceases to be a profitable investment. Thematically, the novel is not an innovation in contemporary fiction, for it comes after Ivan Kušan's *Tower* (*Toranj*, 1970), which is a satire about the building of the first socialist leaning tower. Nor is it innovative in its exposition of the conflicting relationship between a new civilization and the old stable order of conventions; this had already been done in works of several prose writers. It is through its literary technique, and especially through the image of the anti-hero, whose physiognomy now reaches its final stage, that of the victim, that this novel achieves its exceptional merit and expressive artistic pathos.

Having placed the action of the novel within the frame of concrete life, Šoljan fulfills the promise of the short story "Extraordinary Envoys": he returns the anti-hero to his land. Almost in the style of a classical realistic novel, Šoljan gives his anti-hero a series of attributes: a name, a profession, family connections, the responsibility of work. Taking nothing for granted he even surrounds him with the members of the socialist establishment. At the same time he gives him all the appropriate characteristics of the anti-hero: aloofness, morality, the capability for introspection, and the sense of and desire for tradition. Moreover, he is given a place within the socio-cultural environment: he is an engineer who is building a port in his birthplace. In other words, the anti-hero is fully equipped for the final discovery of "the truth" about life and himself.

What the anti-hero finds, however, is far from the resolution presented earlier by Šoljan, though throughout the novel we can find traces of just that belief: "Something always remains in the world of possibilities, some deed will remain unrealized. It leaves a feeling of emptiness, failure, and loss. But curiosity is next. Hope. Search."[15]

Examined within the context of the whole novel, these words are nothing more than a facade of consolation, a quixotic attempt of the protagonist not to surrender without a fight. From the very first sentence of the novel: "Perhaps in the beginning it was a dream . . . ," he is caught by the vision of futility and realizes that he is a plaything for forces more powerful than his own reason or will. From the beginning he is faced with obstacles and is gradually reduced to a state of impotence, but he persists in seeking the truth and acting in life, for his only consolation is the belief that man's duty is to fulfill himself on earth. But life appears to be a farcical ordeal and the quest for identity is an impossibility.

This position of the protagonist is instrumental for the development of the novel: he begins to build a port, but instead destroys the world of his childhood; he continues with the construction even though it is impractical and senseless; he begins a love affair with a young girl whose father's death he is blamed for. And so it goes on to the symbolic conclusion of the novel where he remains hopelessly alone on the shore among the remains of the half-built port, already abandoned. He is not Joyce's Bloom who remains the "one lonely, last sardine of summer,"[16] but he is like a simulacrum, a shadow, a half-living entity. He is left with nothing but the victim's fate to accept defeat at the hands of alien and incomprehensible powers of reality. With this novel, Šoljan completes the transformation of his anti-hero from the existentialist non-heroic hero who is engaged in an obsessive search for authentic life to the man of absurdist literature who is unable to make sense of the catastrophe of his world. Šoljan's antithesis of the hypothetical man of socially-engaged prose, mentioned at the beginning of this paper, is thus taken to its final consequences.

NOTES

1. Ihab Hassan, *Radical Innocence* (Princeton, 1961), 91.
2. Antun Šoljan, *Deset kratkih priča za moju generaciju* (Novi Sad, 1969), 61.
3. Antun Šoljan, "Bijeloglavi Pavlići," ibid., 84.
4. Anton Šoljan, *Izdajice* (Zagreb, 1961), 215.
5. One, however, cannot conclude that Šoljan simply copied the ideas of Sartre and Camus. His anti-hero, unlike Mersault in *The Stranger*, will never come to the realization that nothing matters; nor will he follow the call for action as Sartre's heroes. Šoljan's anti-hero is in this respect more an expression of the real, tragic experience of the culture in which he grew up.
6. Anton Šoljan, *Izdajice* (Zagreb, 1961), 209.
7. *Ibid.*, 105.
8. Lionel Trilling, *Beyond Culture* (1961), 178.
9. Branimir Donat, *Unutarnji rukopis* (Zagreb, 1972), 255.
10. Anton Šoljan, *Izdajice* (Zagreb, 1961), 10-11.
11. Anton Šoljan, *Izdajice* (Zagreb, 1961), 215.
12. Anton Šoljan, *Kratki izlet* (Zagreb, 1965), 123.
13. *Ibid.*, 188.
14. Aleksandar Flaker, *Proza u trapericama* (Zagreb, 1976), 205.
15. Antun Šoljan, *Luka* (1974), 129.
16. James Joyce, *Ulysses* (New York, 1946), 284.

Wolfgang Kasack

VLADIMIR VOINOVICH AND HIS UNDESIRABLE SATIRES

No one likes to be laughed at. Be it political party, social rank or class, or even a single human being, nobody likes to be sacrificed to general laughter. In order to maintain a positive attitude even when being laughed at, one must at least be ready to admit his weaknesses and mistakes, take the world in stride, and also be able to laugh at oneself. The Soviet system with its Communist Party which, despite its constant zig-zag course, has always regarded itself as the best and most progressive system in the world, in its pseudo-self-confidence will not tolerate any criticism or allow any laughter about itself, its institutions, or its representatives. It cannot take satire directed at itself.

Satire is a form of literature with an immediate bearing on reality. It places, as Schiller so appropriately put it, "reality as a deficiency in contrast to ideal as ultimate reality."[1] Consequently, it portrays the negative phenomena in reality, and thus makes one aware of a perfect, or at least better, positive state. In order to understand satire, another of Schiller's ideas is essential: "It is, incidentally, not at all necessary that the latter [the positive state] be explicitly mentioned if the author only knows how to awaken the idea in the reader's mind."[2] The norm, from which the reality being attacked deviates, can be common knowledge, can be derived from what is portrayed, or can be explicitly mentioned. What is decisive is the contradiction between the ideal and the real, the distance from that which the reader (or spectator, as satire is not bound to any one genre) feels to be normal or desirable. A satirist is aggressive. He wants to fight this state of abnormality with the force of the written word, make it ridiculous, destroy it. But when he is dealing with negative phenomena, the abolition or improvement of which appear impossible, then he at least wants to diminish their weight by teaching the reader to be able to laugh at them. Vladimir Nikolaievich Voinovich (b. 1932)[3] has become one of the most important Russian satirists of the 20th century largely as a result of two of his works: *Zhizn' i neobychainye prikliucheniia soldata Ivana Chonkina* (The Life and Unusual Adventures of the Soldier Ivan Chonkin, 1963–1970; of which two of the planned five volumes have been published to date) and *Ivankiada ili rasskaz o vselenii pisatelia Voinovicha v novuiu kvartiru* (Ivankiada or a Tale about the Moving of the Writer Voinovich into a New Apartment, 1973–1975).[4] There are also satirical elements to be found in some of Voinovich's other works, for example, in "Putem vzaimnoi perepiski" (By Way of Mutual Correspondence) and "Proisshestvie v 'Metropole'" (An Event in the Metropole).[5] However, the former essentially lacks the aggressiveness characteristic of satire, and the latter, in view of the threatening situation, is only rarely penetrated by the inner distance necessary to humor. Voinovich wrote his satires out of inner necessity, no differently than M. Bulgakov, Yu. Daniel, D. Kharms, V. Maramzin, G. Shakhnovich, E. Shvarts, A. Siniavsky, the Brothers Strugatsky, and V. Tarsis. The difference in the living conditions in the Soviet Union from what is felt to be a normal state, especially from the norms whose existence is asserted by propaganda and the idealizing literature of socialist realism, is felt by such authors to be so unbearable that they simply have to put it in writing. They must free themselves of this inner tension, and according to their talents, they must portray this reality with its overwhelming deficiencies as ridiculous or fantastical or absurd.

The plot of Voinovich's *Chonkin* takes place in the summer of 1941, using the framework of a soldier senselessly standing at his post as topos. The soldier is quick to recognize that although he cannot fulfill his guard duty according to regulation without rotating shifts (after all, a person has got to eat, sleep, and tend to his business), he can nevertheless coordinate it well with life in the local community. He lives with the mailwoman Niura and meets Golubev, the almost continually drunk chairman of the kolkhoz, the peasant Gladyshev who runs experiments in house and garden, and others in the village with whom he experiences the onslaught of war. Chonkin, forgotten by his unit, is charged with being a deserter by Gladyshev, who is seeking personal revenge. When seven NKVD men show up to arrest Chonkin, he obediently fulfills his orders not to leave his post and arrests the NKVD detachment instead. Similarly, he fights against a regiment of soldiers who are after him for allegedly being a German spy until he, together with Niura, surrenders to the stronger force. Chonkin's arrest marks the end of the published parts and leaves the plot open for further development.[6]

In *Ivankiada* Voinovich describes an incident from his immediate surroundings, the struggle for apartment 66 on ulitsa Cherniakhovskogo No. 4 in the writers' co-op between himself and Sergei Sergeevich Ivanko, one of the major literary functionaries of the Soviet Union and chief literary editor for the State Press Committee. Ivanko, who shared a three-room apartment comprising 50 sq. meters with his wife and child, wanted to convert this to a four-room apartment by knocking out a wall to the two-room apartment next door which had become vacant. By doing so, Ivanko's living quarters would exceed the maximum limits of 60 sq. meters. Voinovich, who shared a one-room apartment covering 24.41 sq. meters with his pregnant wife, also had designs on this two-room apartment of 47 sq. meters. The responsible tenants' council (this refers to a Soviet form of condominiums such as the apartment in question with its own administrative body) had officially recognized Voinovich's claim to the apartment. The contents of the documentary history "Dokumental'naia Istoriia"[7] are the maneuverings of Ivanko and a few literary officials against Voinovich's legal claim and his ultimate victory.

While Voinovich has written in *Chonkin* what is known as "social satire," formerly characterized as "class satire," i.e. satirical images of the groups of people represented by institutions (the Party, NKVD, military), in *Ivankiada* he has written individual satire, commonly found in literature from the late Middle Ages until the beginning of the 18th century. Satire can have both a general enemy as its object and a specific one. However, individual satire can only have an artistic effect when the specific enemy is someone known to the reader or if he is of some far-reaching importance. The former holds true for Stalin-satire, which besides in Voinovich's *Chonkin,* is also to be found in Solzhenitsyn's *V kruge pervom* (The First Circle). The latter is found in *Ivankiada.* In his foreword, Voinovich emphasizes the typical nature of Ivanko's character: orthodox Marxists and ideological dogmatists have disappeared unnoticed — characteristic for the present is a "deiatel' novogo tipa" ('an official of the new type,' 8). Ivanko is only one example. Likewise, the ending emphasizes the generalities of this satirically-unveiled figure, where Voinovich answers with "That is he who needs it" (105) to Nekrasov's question as to who would need the bleeding of the Russian culture by means of a third emigration. Ivanko is the epitome of the inconsiderate party official who is only interested in his own material well-being, and who scorns rights and his fellow man.

Voinovich's satires are forbidden in his homeland. In February 1974 he was expelled from the Writers' Union. In the West his works have appeared in Russian and in many translations, making the author world-famous.[8] Ivanko, having been made ridiculous, left Moscow before the book was published (December 1977) and is now employed as a member of the United Nations delegation of the Soviet Union.[9]

Satirists know that the enemy, whose deficiencies they show and expose to ridicule, will react irritably. Their power lies in having the reader and thus, the masses, on their side whenever they simply advocate real truth and morals. Therefore, the consequence is often that the satirist, for his own protection, veils his plans and does not attack his target directly. He chooses rather an indirect way — by means of allegory and fantastical alienation. For his satires on the totalitarian system Yevgeny Shvarts chose the form of a fairy-tale drama, labeling it "anti-fascist." The fantasy aspects used by Andrei Siniavsky and Yulii Daniel to veil their satires on the socialist-communist system were not even considered by the writers themselves to be sufficient cover in order to even be able to show the works to a publisher in the Soviet Union. They chose pseudonyms and published in the West in order to reach the Russian reader. The degree of fantasy aspects is much stronger in the case of the Brothers Strugatsky. It was only in a few of these works that the censor, in banning them, confirmed that the grievances in the fantastical-fictional world symbolized the grievances in their own socialist society. In *The Master and Margarita* Bulgakov combines realism and witchcraft to form the grotesque, and then completes it with allegorical double-plot. The book was only published after twenty-five years in a small amount of copies due to the fact that totally banning it would have damaged the image of the Soviet Union even more, and because several of the satirical allusions had lost their relevance.[10]

Voinovich was aware of the fate of Soviet satirists. Nevertheless, he chose the path of direct satire. Although in the beginning of *Chonkin* several aspects characteristic of Russian fairy-tales are present, such as doubting the reality of the events and the hero's noble origins (22), nonetheless the work as a whole does not possess fairy-tale form. These elements diminish quickly, appearing again only at the end, when Chonkin, originally portrayed as somewhat foolish, displays his cleverness. Likewise, the transferral of the plot to the year 1941 cannot be viewed as a disguise, since he too directly refers to deficiencies of the targets which are not bound to a certain time period and are, therefore, also current. Soviet satirists only seldom employ geographical disguise (e.g. the fantastical geographical disguises of Ye. Zamiatin, A. and B. Strugatsky, and A. Zinoviev). Quite the contrary, Voinovich emphasizes the bearing on reality by means of historical fact. In *Ivankiada* Voinovich dispenses with even a hint of the protective disguise of indirect satire. The first-person storyteller is completely identical with the author. Names, addresses, and dates are real (all of them checked), and documents round out the plot. *Chonkin* is, as told in third-person narration, fictitious. The characters and their actions only exist by virtue of their being told.[11] *Ivankiada* is a true-to-life reproduction. All characters are alive and it is about their actions that the author writes.

It is precisely such an immediate bearing on reality that makes satire unbearable in the eyes of the defenders of ideology. When all traces of satirical allusion disappeared from literature after the Zoshchenko persecution in 1946, the Communist Party, represented by Malenkov, acted surprised at the 19th Party Congress (1952): "In our Soviet belletristics and dramatic works and likewise in our cinematography there is a lack of the art form known as satire. We need Soviet Gogols and Shchedrins."[12] They were not lacking, and they are not lacking. They are simply unwanted if they fail to submit themselves to instructions to falsify reality according to the principles of partiality. Satire in the Soviet Union is wanted or at least tolerated only when the target cannot be made synonymous with the System itself or with one of its substantial institutions. Characteristic of the unpublished opinion of the Russian intelligentsia as to the true attitude of the government towards satire is the following epigram:

> Potomu chto nam nuzhny
> Podobree Shchedriny
> I takie Gogoli,
> Chtoby nas ne trogali.

('Because we need more harmless Shchedrins and the kind of Gogols who wouldn't bother us.')

Let us take a look at the targets of Voinovich's venom in his satires. The widest range ever reached by Soviet satire is encompassed by Aleksandr Zinoviev in his *Ziiaiushchie vysoty* (Gaping Heights). In each of the hundreds of chapters he deals with a different area of social and political life of the Moscow intelligentsia and portrays it satirically in an indirect, yet comprehensible manner. As a satirist his intent is encyclopedic. Voinovich, too, takes up many pages in both of his satires, but with him, points of major emphasis are particularly discernible, while numerous other elements of Soviet reality are only barely mentioned in episodes and allusions.

The main target of satire in *Chonkin* is the secret police, the NKVD. Their methods of questioning, arrests on grounds of suspicion and denunciation, their power based solely on the generation of fear and, finally, their superfluousness (no one notices the disappearance of the NKVD people when Chonkin arrests them) are the primary themes and comprise substantial parts of the novel. While in "Proisshestvie v 'Metropole'" the conduct of the KGB is the main topic of the report, its powerful influence in *Ivankiada* is only suggested through hints such as that to Ivanko's being related to Semichastny, the former head of the KGB and by other details (19).[13]

The satirical attacks on the NKVD are concentrated in the second part of the book. In the first part the target is more the military with its despotic officers (15f.) and the power of the totally incompetent heads. In the second part the despotism and incapability of a general (252ff.) and the poor equipment and training of the troops at the beginning of World War II are ridiculed (274ff.). The kolkhoz system in its inability to perform is in many ways the focus of Voinovich's satire, ranging from the drunk, incompetent chairman of the kolkhoz to the dependence upon directives and falsified reporting. Actually, Voinovich is saying nothing original here, as these deficiencies have often been criticized by V. Ovechkin, Ye. Dorosh, A. Yashin, and others. Voinovich's attack on Lysenko and Michurin and their absurd attempts at hybridizing is disguised only lightly in exposing the misled village scholar Gladyshev and his tomato-potato hybrid PUKS, short for "Put' k sotsializmu" ('the road to socialism,' 58).[14]

A general attack on the Communist Party as the seat of power in the Soviet Union is not undertaken in *Chonkin*. The satire is instead directed against many characteristic phenomena of the one-party system and its control over life, against the powerlessness and dependence of the subordinate party authorities (125), against the primitive belief in party slogans. On the other hand, with the exposure of Ivanko, the party- and functionary-elite is indicted as a whole: the new ruling class, their exploitation of their offices to gain personal advantage (77), their creeping upwards and their kicking downwards (67), their hypocrisy (33), their nepotism (15, 32), their scornful attitude towards subordinates (15) and those expelled from their own class (96), and — as the overall theme — their claim and possibilities of getting around existing laws (compare especially 31, 77, 88).

The primary target of individual satire in *Ivankiada* is a certain literary functionary. In addition, however, Voinovich particularly denounces the following members of the Writers' Union: S. Yeidlin (and his wife V. Bunina), Ya. Kozlovsky, A. Kuleshov, I. Kuprianov, L. Lench, K. Simonov, V. Telpugov, B. Turganov, S. Vasiliev, as well as the KGB general in the secretariat of the Writers' Union V. N. Ilyin; the chairman of the State Committee for Book Publishing, Printing, and Sales B. I. Stukalin; and the lord mayor of Moscow Promyslov (45, 56). It is also true in most cases that the satirized object is, on the one hand, the named person and his unlawful or immoral behavior, on the other hand, the behavior of this type of the Soviet upper class — the class in general.

A special position is taken in *Chonkin* on the individual satire on Stalin. It is found in some twenty different places in the novel and is about the obligatory mention in official letters (67, 263), the mandatory toast at banquets (with a vodka made of muck, 109), the personality cult in children's education, the fear at the mere mention of Stalin's name (186), and much more.

In *Chonkin* the Party is also a target of satire because of its type of instruction. As early as 1956, in *Fabrichnaia devchonka* (A Factory Girl), A. Volodin exposed the party lies of the Stalin era with the example of false marital morals in party instruction. Solzhenitsyn struck the chapter on instruction in *V kruge pervom* from his original text, hoping that it could be published in the Soviet Union.[15] In *Chonkin* the scene about party instruction is among the first presented: the praise is given to the person who can repeat the printed text by heart as his own opinion. As in Solzhenitsyn, the essential characteristic is the absolute apathy of the participant (24–30).

Party meetings are exposed in different ways — their pseudo-spontaneous character, their schematic course, and their constant lying: "A meeting is an event where a lot of people gather and some say things they don't think and others think things they don't say" (133). Even in criticizing in this manner, Voinovich does not stand alone. In "Zatmenie" (Eclipse) Vladimir Tendriakov's character says the same thing: "Primakov, who was lecturing, spoke and didn't believe a single word, but he was of the opinion that it was necessary. We all listened to him and didn't believe either, but like him, were of the opinion that everything was in order, that it was necessary."[16] *Ivankiada* contains a satirical allusion to the pseudo-democratic meetings: "A meeting is simply a celebration; adopted, passed, supported, approved" (44). Even Erenburg in *Ottepel'* (Thaw) did not proclaim any change in this storefront democracy, but rather only admonished it: "One must not degrade everything to a recorded course of 'heard and passed'."[17] In other words, Voinovich attacks the undemocratic way of life in Soviet society. The cited phenomena as satirical objects can be multiplied. Through his own generalizations, the use of pressure against people who have signed petitions receives an even higher meaning (*Ivankiada,* 31–32).

A target similar to the satirical exposures of Stalin and his personality cult is the stereotyped party phrases spread throughout the novel *Chonkin.* A phrase like "Brought up in the spirit of boundless dedication to our party, the people, and the great genius, Comrade Stalin, I. V., personally" (67), as Gladyshev writes for Chonkin to the commander of the batallion in the form of a letter by a third party using newspaper jargon, additionally emphasizes that the content does not correspond to the thinking of its author. Expressions such as "the uncomprehending mass" (147) or "In what other country can you find such spruce, such birch . . .?" (211) or "Engineers of the human soul" (*Ivankiada,* 9) are understood immediately by the Soviet reader in their proper contexts (e.g. the foundation of party-regimentation, emphasis on Soviet patriotism, the Stalinistic formula for writers) but prove to be incomprehensible for the majority of foreign readers. Herein lie the noted boundaries of the effect of satire outside the native country or with the distance of time in between.

A few of the most important effects of the totalitarian system upon the everyday life of the Soviet citizen are explicitly exposed to ridicule by Voinovich. This is primarily the act of denunciation, the repulsiveness of which N. Pogodin portrayed on stage in 1955 in "Sonet Petrarki" (A Petrarch Sonnet). In Voinovich's novel the denunciation motif appears as the main theme in the anonymous charge against Chonkin (193) and in the undiscriminating acceptance of it by the NKVD representatives. It is also dealt with in the field of military satire (253). In this respect one also finds excessive secretiveness. Chonkin is afraid of revealing "top-secret military information" (94) when asked to tell his age and how many foot-clothes the army had. He is plagued by the nightmare of the idea of "betraying his comrades, his homeland, the people, and Comrade Stalin personally" (99). In *Ivankiada* Voinovich also concerns himself with secretiveness, but here the ruling functionaries' secret arrangements are made in their own interests and directed against the general public (19). At this point, Voinovich also attacks the evils of bribery (60), namely that the gift does not tax the giver materially — he has state funds at his disposal. Fear and cowardliness are general human weaknesses. When Voinovich repeatedly makes them the objects of satire, he is dealing with their specific characteristics within the socialist system. The chairman of the kolkhoz is afraid that the pilot who crash-landed and, later, Chonkin are really auditors in disguise (13, 69) and he believes that the NKVD detachment has come to arrest him personally (200). His guilty conscience is not only due to his negligent administration and his drinking, but also due to the objective impossibility of his fulfilling the directives and quotas ordered from above. Voinovich's criticism is here in agreement with some other authors who wrote about village life (Ovechkin, Dorosh, Tendriakov, Pomerantsev, and others). The fear of a renter in *Ivankiada* who wanted to vote like Ivanko against her convictions (39) is well-founded through customary reprisals. This is also the case with some authors who do not dare to tell a taxi driver where Solzhenitsyn's works have been published (59 f.).

It is a reasonable assumption that authors who write satirically also in some way include the field of literature. Bulgakov's *Master i Margarita* is largely a satire on literature. Solzhenitsyn dedicated Chapter 57 of *V kruge pervom* mainly to the insincerity of prescribed literature. Shakhnovich wrote a story in which two characters of a Soviet novel about factory life try in vain to get into conversation with each other.[18] They only know empty phrases. Voinovich presents the questioning of the deserving milkmaid Liusha by the village citizens about her relationship to the master of the house at the Kremlin and the description of her career as a parody on literary and non-literary Stalin portrayals (151 f.). Likewise, he reports in *Ivankiada* on the technique of promoting untalented friends of functionaries and suppressing important literary works, especially Kornei Chukovsky's handwritten almanac *Chukokkala* (70, 107–112).

In general, it is characteristic of Voinovich's objects of satire that they mostly have to do with the main social phenomena of Soviet life and scarcely with overall human weaknesses (with the exception of "Putem vzaimnoi perepiski," if one chooses at all to view this prose as satirical). Most of the objects exposed to ridicule serve as typical for the system as such.

Among the methods which a satirist can use in order to attack the perceived object of non-literary reality, there are a few basic forms. First, the satirist has at his disposal all genres — prose, drama, verse — and mixtures thereof, as well as both narrative forms, very important in their difference, especially with regard to satire, the first- and third-person structure. Voinovich is a prosewriter. In writing *Chonkin,* he chose the third-person, i.e. fiction, with occasional first-person inserts. In writing *Ivankiada* he chose first-person structure, i.e. a statement about reality in which he inserts a fictional passage. The first-person inserts in *Chonkin* have, as in Pushkin's *Eugene Onegin,* logical functions which cancel each other out: their purpose is partially to lend strength to the fictional aspects ("I made up the heroes," 21), partially to weaken the fiction, i.e. to simulate reality ("I gathered together into a pile everything I had heard which had to do with the case," 5). Such appeals to the reader, which enhance the comical aspects, appear mostly at the beginning. Later, Voinovich lets the fictional world be what it is. The fictional passage in *Ivankiada* forms a chapter of its own, the longest of all the narrative units — "Proisshestvie v solnechnyj den'" (An Event on a Sunny Day, 65). The attentive reader already becomes suspicious in the first sentence: "Sergei Sergeevich was awakened by the sun," since an event is taking place in which the narrator cannot have taken part. Near the end of the event — Ivanko is criticized by Minister Stukalin for exploiting his job to gain personal advantage — the fictionality is explicitly affirmed (74). The game is even shortened to half a page and repeated once again, this time showing a hypothetical possibility of the reaction Ivanko's boss could have had and emphasizing that this is only an imaginary possibility by hinting at the incongruence with reality. On the one hand, Voinovich needs the fictional insert in order to show in a scene how Ivanko behaved in his professional world, i.e. in a scene in which the narrator cannot have taken part. On the other hand, he needs it to show what the norms are like upon which actual behavior should be based, using the two examples of Minister Stukalin's possible behavior with regard to the accused Ivanko: he was silent instead of upholding the law.

The distinction between direct and indirect statements is especially relevant to satire. Voinovich portrays a world of deficiencies, but in *Chonkin* he enriches this direct level with indirectly portrayed inserts — through dreams. Chonkin has three of four dreams, the fourth is experienced by Gladyshev. The first, which is a nightmare about the experiences of the small soldier in the military and ends with the threat of his being shot at Stalin's orders (50–52), closes the military satire and at the same time raises it to an abstract level. The second dream (88–99), in which Chonkin finds himself at a wedding of pigs, takes political dimensions when Chonkin is forced to grunt along with the rest. By combining human and animal elements, Voinovich employs animal grotesque which reaches its peak when Chonkin's military higher-up, and even Stalin, are served on a platter as roasts with vegetables. Gladyshev's dream of the horse that turns human (157–160) supplements the Lysenko satire in an anthropological sense. Chonkin's last dream of Rousseau creeping back to nature (243) has only poetically ornamental effect in the drunken scene. The dream inserts in *Chonkin* and the fictional insert in *Ivankiada* enrich both works through their stylistic and structural changes and deepen the satirical effect.

An indirect satire, such as Voinovich offers in his dream portrayals, always contains some distortions of the object of satire. Within direct satire four sub-forms are to be found — (1) that of purely exposing the object to ridicule; (2) that of the antithesis, i.e. the confrontation of the exposed object with the norm; (3) that of degradation, i.e. the emphasis upon the object to be condemned and ridiculed by means of epithets, metaphorical language, etc.; and (4) that of hyperbole, the excessive, mostly caricatured, highlighting of its negative aspects.

In using pure exposure the satirist is openly stating what he has observed in reality. He frees it of any deceptive accessories so that the eye can clearly see the deficiencies. This form is also often called an unmasking, as the deficiency often hides behind a mask. With Soviet satire one mostly deals with unmasking, since Communist public relations center around secretiveness and propaganda.

The scene where Chonkin is drilled in the burning heat with the constant changing command "Drop! As you were! "(15 f.) is typical for this form. Every reader recognizes the accusation and the basic normal conditions without the author having to make further comment. This drilling is senseless and inhumane and does in no way tie in with the cause of the punishment, the soldier's incapability to show respect according to regulations. It also contradicts the ideals of the education of the Soviet soldier as heroic defender of the Fatherland.

Such exposures to ridicule are characteristic of the whole book. The short glance at the fate of Niura's mother, who perished helplessly as a kolkhoz peasant (43), unmasks the inhumane effects of the kolkhoz system. The high-sounding politically-doctored report written to the commander of the battalion by Chonkin who can scarcely write his name has an equally strong effect through its realism. From the telephone conversation between the village party secretary and his boss and by driving out the peasants who had come seeking advice (121–127), every reader deduces the deficiencies of the hierarchical party structure, which represses any spontaneous action. The ridiculousness of the way the System creates "deserving workers" and sends them on trips along with a group of journalists to give incentive to the masses is excellently depicted in the simple portrayal of Liusha's visit (149–155). This portrayal needed no hyperbole, no degradation, no confrontation with that which is normal.

Gladyshev's denunciation and the secret police's willingness to promptly arrest the supposed deserter Chonkin without any further checking are typical examples for the satirical unmasking of secrecy practices by their mere exposures to ridicule.

Voinovich only seldom uses this technique in *Ivankiada*. For example, he lets Ivanko's personal data, which illustrate his close relations to the KGB and the highest caste, speak for themselves (19 f.); the same holds true with regard to the direct characterization of the head of the apartment cooperative, Turganov (17–19), and the KGB-general, V. N. Ilyin (50–52). Basically, in this documental story, however, Voinovich supplements the factual rendering with a second level, thus creating satire.

Antithesis is the prevailing method in *Ivankiada*. Voinovich portrays the actions of Ivanko or his helpers more or less soberly and then contrasts them with the norm. In this way one understands such a portrayal as mere exposure to ridicule, partially makes his deductions with respect to the norm with which the action is contrasted, and then the information about the legal situation follows to strengthen the satire — as the main object of attack is the inequality of the law in the Soviet Union. One of Voinovich's simplest but typical examples of this technique concerns the preference of Ivanko regarding his vacation: "Sometimes he vacationed in Nice with his family. Have you, reader, ever had a vacation in Nice?" (24).

By looking at the macrostructure of *Ivankiada* we see that the story as a whole is based upon this principle of antithesis. Voinovich's autobiographical report on his efforts to obtain the promised apartment and the efforts of his opponents to prevent this in favor of Ivanko is confronted with the legal situation, i.e. the norm by which the reader measures its deviation and the exposed and deficient reality. This legal situation is represented by three documents which are printed in bold type in the Russian edition. Voinovich first mentions his letter to the board of the renters' collective, in which he insists upon his right to the apartment and reminds them of the unlawfulness which would be caused by the unauthorized distribution of the living space (30). After that he explains in detail, in the form of a legal opinion (with respect to the corresponding legal clauses), the existing and desired apartment situation of Ivanko and himself, unmistakably proving his moral and legal rights (38–39). And finally he brings in his letter addressed to Minister B. I. Stukalin, which summarizes the illegal and immoral behavior of Ivanko and charges him with exploiting his profession for personal gain. The accompanying letter to the Writers' Union, to which he addressed a copy, is contained in the text as well. Insofar as the actions of Minister Stukalin are concerned (70–73), there is also a fictional part which belongs to these larger counterparts with which the violations he experienced are contrasted, as it is here that Voinovich invents the ideal of the minister who acts according to the laws. By supplying a weakened ideal picture, which would have at least been bearable (74), he emphasizes the abominable qualities of the actual events. In this case they are mentioned by way of addition. The minister does not answer the letter, thus condoning Ivanko's actions.

In many places the microstructure shows the same technique. Voinovich mentions that Ivanko is called a "great writer" (33) and then informs the reader that this is the result of a single brochure encompassing forty-four pages which had been published twenty years earlier and which in no way can be considered to be aesthetic literature: *Taivan' — iskonnaia kitaiskaia zemlia,* 1955 (Taiwan — Original Chinese Territory). It is only through this information collected from the Lenin Library that the ridiculousness of the term "great writer" is made fully obvious. But even before revealing this detail the formulation "the writer Ivanko" (16) had the effect of seeming antithetical and, therefore, satirical and comical. The essence of such criticism is made clear by another example of antithesis, namely when Voinovich quotes a typical sentence of literary officials — it is not a union of the gifted, but rather a union of Soviet writers. Voinovich makes the comment that he always thought the term "gifted writer" to be a tautology (23).

Using the same technique, Voinovich emphasizes Ivanko's actions. Through dialogue we learn first that Ivanko wants to enlarge his apartment by knocking out a supporting wall, then, that this is forbidden according to Soviet building code regulations, and finally, that he obtains a permit to do so (16).

Two types of rights, one for the people and one for the upper caste, are illustrated in detail. In the same dialogue, Voinovich states how they pointed out to Ivanko what a social injustice it would be if he lived with three persons in a four-room apartment while his colleague with the same number of people in his family only had a one-room apartment, to which he answers "Well, that's their tough luck" (15). In this case the norm takes precedence over the deviation. With the help of antithetical narration Voinovich prepares his reader for the atrociousness of Ivanko's inconsiderate attitude.

The actions of other figures are also illustrated by means of the same technique of satire. Turganov explains that the renters' assembly had supposedly recommended giving Voinovich the apartment (19). At this point in time, however, the reader knows that a decision has already been made and that Turganov is lying. As antithesis to this sentence, Voinovich therefore does not present the known facts, but rather sober legal information, which only allows the board to make recommendations and the renters' assembly to make decisions. This satire is an up-to-date polemic. The author can not allow himself to miss any opportunity to call legal facts of the case to the reader's, or maybe even to the legal examiner's, mind.

The supplement to the denounced action is not always the norm; sometimes it is a commentary which heightens the meaning. In this vein, Voinovich quotes the writer V. P. Telpugov who became famous when, in reference to *Chonkin,* he demanded turning the author over to a penal institution, "even if the novel had only been planned and not even written" (52). Voinovich calls attention to the atrocity both of the demand to lock up a writer for a work which exists only in thought as well as of the abominable nods of approval from the other writers who were present.

By the use of the satirical technique of degradation, the object fought against or the designated behavior of the opponent are abased with the help of language. Through language the contrast to the ideal state is made more blatant and the reader is made conscious faster. However, if the degradation is carried on too far, then the satire loses its credibility. Basically, Voinovich portrays the representatives of the NKVD (KGB) and the military as anti-heroes. In this respect, even Chonkin himself is a portrait in satire of a Soviet soldier, a product of degradation, but in this case, in the course of action increasingly tragic elements are mixed in. The NKVD people, however, are ridiculed in every situation. The focal point of the interrogation scene is the ineffectiveness of intimidation and brute force when used against the old Jewish cobbler. The man questioned proves stronger than those questioning him. Finally, the technique of role-changing serves Voinovich's purpose in this scene: the NKVD captain Miliaga stands before his victim with knees knocking together out of fear while his victim sharply reprimands him (187). The reason for this is simply that the victim just happens to share the name Stalin, which takes away Miliaga's ability to reason.

A highlight of the degradation of the NKVD representatives is their arrest by Chonkin and Niura. The vivid picture of Niura tying the men together with a long cord serves one purpose: to make the feared and hated institution look ridiculous. There are many details which adapt themselves to the technique of degradation. The NKVD representatives arrive in the village so covered with mud that they are unrecognizable (198), one is shot in the behind (206), the captain mistakes the Soviet lieutenant who is questioning him for a German and conforms out of fear of this assumed situation crying "Heil Hitler, Stalin kaputt" (260).

In depicting the relationship of Chonkin to the NKVD representatives the technique of role-changing again appears: the person to be arrested does the arresting (208 f.), the people who normally act as overseers for those sentenced to hard labor are forced by their "captives" to harvest potatoes (234). Role-changing always makes those affected conscious of the normal situation. It is also the basic technique with which Maramzin in "Tiani-tolkai" (The Push Me — Pull You) characterizes the KGB satirically, with the difference, however, that it is not used as much by means of the technique of degradation.

Chonkin's military higher-ups and the members of the regiment that overwhelm him at the end, in particular the general, are all incompetent, corrupt figures similar to the NKVD representatives. The leaders of the regiment are helpless when they hear of an emergency landing made by a plane with engine trouble; the chief of staff even suggests having the aircraft towed off like a wrecked car (19). The soldiers who advance against Chonkin do not know how to handle Molotov cocktails (276 ff.), their general made his career through denunciation and his attributes are ignorance, rudeness, and arbitrariness. In depicting him, Voinovich supplements the technique of degradation with use of obscene expressions. Voinovich cites the Russian curse with proper clarity "tak tvoiu mat'" (268, compare 278).

Reduction is a frequent medium of satirical degradation. The practice of secretiveness has led to the fact that in the Soviet Union the secret service is only reluctantly called by name. A person is not arrested, but rather brought "Where it is Necessary." Voinovich constantly uses this metaphor. "What does that mean 'Whither it is Necessary' or 'Where it is Necessary'? For whom is it necessary and why?" (176). It is also reported that the general denounced someone "For Whom it is Necessary" (253). Metaphoric clipping, emphasized by unusual capitalization and multiple repetition, creates the humor intended and, through this, the satirical denunciation of the feared authority.

Another important example of the technique of degradation by way of reduction is the depiction of the dream in which pigs play the parts instead of people and instead of uniform statements from humans, only synchronized grunting is demanded (97). In this case, Voinovich is employing the same type of reduction which is often found in Bulgakov's works — grotesque reduction. When Voinovich refers to Ivanko as "the honorable" (99), omitting his name, this is an example of reduction through ironic degradation. When he compares the former general prosecutor of the Ukraine with a dandelion and thereafter only refers to him as "the dandelion" (9), this is an example of metaphorical clipping with a similarly degrading effect.

Voinovich is rich in details of such satire in speech, no doubt the strongest is the name PUKS for "Put' k sotsializmu" ('the road to socialism,' 61) as the term for a senseless hybrid plant, which is at the end completely devoured by a cow, which not only signifies the senselessness of this hybridization, but also the senselessness of PUKS, i.e. the road to socialism. In the Metropol-examinations the KGB representatives also had strong objections to PUKS.[19] Voinovich often uses a single word in an unusual context to achieve satirical allusions in language. For example, he says of the October Revolution that it has made it possible to "scramble up" (karabkat'sia, 60) to the glorious and stony heights of science. Not only is the term "stony" not in keeping with the usual party slogan, the verb "to scramble up" is absolutely out of place with regard to party pathos, and thus Voinovich's usage shows the emptiness of the phrase. A peasant says of Stalin that he "is standing on the mausoleum, waving with his little hand" (131). The disfiguration of the place of honor in front of the Kremlin wall by the peasant's vernacular language characterizes the simplicity of the speaker; the formulation "ruchkoi pomakhivaet" ('waving his little hand') is in such direct contrast to the image of the great leader which the Party is striving for, that Stalin himself is also drawn into the ridiculous picture. If one recalls that S. V. Smirnov had precisely at this time produced the picture venerating the super-human standing on the mausoleum,[20] then the relevance of such a satire of words becomes especially clear.

Voinovich takes pleasure in using irony for the satirical degradation of his objects. In reference to these objects, he depends on the fact that his reader will recognize the incredibility of his praise for his opponents and that the reader will not only understand that he means the opposite of what he says; he will also understand that these opposite meanings serve Voinovich's purpose of exposing the opponent to ridicule. The largest ironic passage is the false praise for the KGB as an institution which is gifted with fantasy and, therefore, accelerates literary productivity. He plays upon the endless number of criminal actions, spy activities, and acts of sabotage which investigation officials fabricate, and cites as a famous example the protocol of the trial of Bukharin (*Ivankiada* 53). The irony affects both sides: the fabricated complaints with blackmailed testimonies and falsified literature. In *Chonkin* the NKVD is the object of ironic remarks as well; for example, when he speaks of "taking care of the people," which has always been the goal of this institution (190), or when he praises the "undisputed success" of this institution reached in the "war of extermination against its own citizens" (176), or that he "must draw attention to the honor of the institution" that it does not arrest people at just any denunciation since "otherwise there would be no one left who was free" (193).

Often the irony is only to be found in epithets, such as when he speaks of "our super-state" (*Ivankiada* 8) or when he characterizes the authoritarian chairman of the apartment coop with the phrase "he promenades democratically" (46), or when he sets Konstantin Simonov apart from all other unknown writers who are tied in with the apartment controversy in that he calls him "Simonov personally" (10; compare further on Konstantin Simonov, 45 and 89).

A satirist would not be a good satirist unless he could also laugh at himself. When Voinovich discloses his good fortune that, due to the renters' council's decision, he will at last be able to get rid of his one-room apartment, he is deliberately too quick in his joy — finally he will get his own room "where I can create my immortal or otherwise disposed works in peace and quiet" (12 f.).

Of the satiric media Voinovich least uses hyperbole. He obviously worries that exaggeration via caricature could damage the serious intent. The deplorable circumstances he attacks are so obvious that they only need unmasking, not overemphasis, in order to reach the reader's consciousness. Granted, the course of action at the end of *Chonkin* possesses a somewhat caricatured hyperbolic nature when a single person arrests the whole NKVD detachment. But has it not happened often enough that a dedicated single individual accomplished the seemingly impossible, and is the satirical effect here not based much more upon the technique of degradation? In the last analysis, this is a question of the psychological evaluation of the situation, whether one chooses to view this as a distorted or unusual reality. The crippling (also in a metaphorical sense), disarming effect of a determined defender is considerable upon an attacker otherwise used to success. Voinovich depicts this with comical means.

Hyperbole as an artistic medium determines, and in a careful manner at that, the characteristics of Gladyshev, a miniversion of Lysenko. Granted, formulations such as "Gladyshev who is renowned for his docility" (10) still fall into the category of irony. Yet the whole PUKS project is totally over-caricatured. In depicting a tomato-potato hybridization, Voinovich is supposedly not exposing a sample of reality to ridicule; on the contrary, he has given his imagination free rein, just as with the fecal vodka with which Stalin is toasted. At this point hyperbole comes in touch with the technique of indirect satire, such as Voinovich uses in depicting dreams.

The analysis of Voinovich's *Chonkin* and *Ivankiada* has been limited to their satirical features. Adding these features together does not yet result in the whole work of art. They are supplemented by artistic means independent of the satirical aspects; among them, in Voinovich's case, metaphorical language plays the most important role. Voinovich strengthens a large number of compact scenes in *Chonkin* with the description of static or dynamic images. In this regard, one finds the portrayals of Chonkin gradually nearing the fence to Niura's garden (40); of his sliding towards Niura on the bench their first evening together (49); of the soldier in uniform and apron embroidering (64); of the vodka-drinking chairman of the kolkhoz with his head in the safe for secret matters (124); of the backs of the peasants getting farther and farther away while the party-speaker is watching them during his speech (138); of the throng of people (of the "Hydra"), i.e. the country people fighting for paltry barter goods (145–147); of the head milkmaid's procedure for getting out of the car — her powerful rump first (149); of the district party secretary who, out of the confusion caused by the missing NKVD representatives, pulls on his underwear over his uniform-like riding breeches (214); of the ardent potato-digging NKVD representatives with Chonkin as guard (234); and, finally, of the soldiers, in summer wearing winter-camouflage outfits and looking like piles of snow advancing to overtake Chonkin. One is always dealing with detailed images. Before describing the NKVD soldiers tied to each other with a sort of clothes-line, Voinovich goes so far as to expressly formulate: "Soon, anyone who desired could catch sight of the following picture" (208). Voinovich is concerned with vividness and he is well able to put this into words. He does not use the image to deepen the emotional circumstances, but rather to enhance the humor. It affects his Chonkin as well as the functionaries, the peasant population who are basically to be pitied due to their grave needs, and the NKVD representatives pursued by satire. Voinovich's comical images can be present to serve the satire, but they do not absolutely have to be there.

It is not difficult to derive Schiller's ideal of the norm from each individual case in Voinovich's *Chonkin* satire. The soldier sent senselessly to his post, the denunciating peasant, the drunken chairman of the kolkhoz, the party secretary, completely helpless unless someone tells him what to do, and the unlawful, crude, and inhumane secret police — all are bound by the reader to the idea of how things should be. That is the gist of this type of satire. Voinovich's episodes form an overall picture when viewed together. It is not the respective deficiencies after all which are the objects of his satire, and they do not portray any chance social blunders in the Soviet Union; rather they represent the system as a whole. Sometimes the indications which make such a generalization possible are obvious, such as in the case of PUKS, the "road to socialism." It is false in both senses. However, the reader must deduce the general meaning of each individual critique without such help. This meaning exists — and therein lies the lasting value of the book. Voinovich's satires are concrete enough to convince, and allegorical enough to have an effect even outside the country. Perhaps Voinovich was not at all mistaken with his self-ironic remark about his "immortal work."

NOTES

1. Friedrich Schiller, "Satirische Dichtung," in "Über naive und sentimentale Dichtung," *Gesammelte Werke,* edited by C. Höfer, Munich–Leipzig, 1910–26, vol. 12, p. 86.

2. *Ibid.*

3. Biographical details in W. Kasack, *Lexikon der russischen Literatur ab 1917,* Stuttgart, 1976.

4. *Zhizn' i neobychainye prikliucheniia soldata Ivana Chonkina. Roman-anekdot v piati chastiakh.* Partially printed in *Grani* 72, Frankfurt/ M, 1973, pp. 3–83; Part 1–2, Paris, 1975. *Ivankiada,* Ann Arbor, 1976.

5. "Putem vzaimnoi perepiski," *Grani* 87–88, Frankfurt/M, 1973, pp. 122–191. "Proisshestvie v 'Metropole'," *Kontinent* 5, Paris, 1975, pp. 51–97. "Ministru sviazi SSSR tov. Talyzinu N. V.," *Russkaia Mysl'* 11.4.1976, p. 3.

6. In *The Times Literary Supplement* (1.23.1976, p. 93) Geoffrey Hosking presents Chonkin very well as a literary type. Hosking also portrays the other characters very aptly and assigns the work to a literary category.

7. The page references in parentheses are those of Voinovich's works dealt with here.

8. G. Hosking, *op. cit.,* "One of the most significant and encouraging events in recent Russian literature ... KGB has impeccable literary taste and takes masterpieces seriously."

9. In the epilogue of *Ivankiada* (pp. 102ff.) Voinovich traces the further development of some of the main characters.

10. "M. Bulgakov: *Master i Margarita,*" *Moskva* 1966: 11, 1967: 1. What the censor regarded as a satire of immediate interest, i.e. as criticism which is still justified, can be guessed only to a certain degree from the deletions of this version since rumor has it that Boris Yevgenev, member of the editing staff, made room for his own contribution by shortening Bulgakov's text. The complete version appeared in Frankfurt/ M, 1969, and in M. Bulgakov, *Belaia gvardiia. Teatral'nyi roman. Master i Margarita,* Moskva, 1973.

11. Käte Hamburger, *Die Logik der Dichtung,* Stuttgart, 1968.

12. Report of G. Malenkov, *Literaturnaia gazeta* 10.7.1972, p. 2.

13. The NKVD=Narodnyi Komissariat vnutrennykh del (People's Commissariat for Internal Affairs), founded in 1934, was transformed into the KGB = Komitet gosudarstvennoi bezopasnosti pri Sovete Ministrov SSR (Committee for State Security, Council of Ministers, USSR). One of the best KGB satires is by Vladimir Maramzin, "Tiani-tolkai" (The Push Me — Pull You), *Kontinent* 8, Paris, 1976, pp. 13–47. Close to an NKVD satire are some crucial passages in Yuri Trifonov's "Dom na naberezhnoi" (The House on the Embankment): *Druzhba narodov* 1976: 1.

14. As far as the controversy about T. D. Lysenko is concerned, the two opposing views are expressed in the following basic articles and works: the one side is represented by an article in the second edition of *Bol'shaia Sovetskaia Entsiklopediia,* vol. 25 (1954), commending Lysenko and by an article in the third edition, vol. 15 (1974), which is only slightly critical of Lysenko. The other side finds its expression in Zhores A. Medvedev's *The Rise and Fall of T. D. Lysenko,* New York–London, 1969.

15. A. Solzhenitsyn, "Dialekticheskii materializm — peredovoie mirovozzrenie," in: *Kontinent* 1, Paris, 1974, pp. 125–142.

16. *Druzhba narodov,* 1977: 5, p. 130.

17. I. Erenburg, *Ottepel',* Moskva, 1954, p. 68.

18. G.. Shakhnovich, "Sluchai v biblioteke," G. Shakhnovich, *Solo na barabane,* Tel Aviv, 1977, pp. 68–74. Compare also "the typical average crime novel,""Operatsiia 'Vydra'," *ibid.,* pp. 142–148.

19. V. N. Voinovich, "Proisshestvie v 'Metropole'," *op. cit.,* p. 69.

20. S. V. Smirnov, "Svidetel'stvuiu sam," *Izbrannye stikhotvoreniia i poemy,* 2 vols., Moskva, 1974, vol. 2, pp. 150 f.

Lars Kleberg

ROMANTICISM AND ANTI-ROMANTICISM:
TRADITION IN THE FILM AND THEATER OF
ANDRZEJ WAJDA

Let us recall the final scene in Andrzej Wajda's *Ashes and Diamonds,* the unsurpassed masterpiece of Polish cinema. Maciek, the young hero, is a member of a bourgeois resistance group that has turned against the Communists after the German collapse in May 1945. Maciek has just murdered the local Party secretary and is leaving the scene of the crime when he happens to run into a group of soldiers, who open fire on him when he tries to flee. He stumbles into a courtyard filled with wash — white sheets — hanging out to dry. Suddenly we see blood soaking through a sheet behind which Maciek has hidden. The film ends with him bleeding to death on a garbage heap.

Wajda's film is black and white, but colors rendered as various shades of gray are of key importance (just as sound can be in a scene in a silent picture). The spectator is led to associate the red blood seeping through the white sheet with the colors (red and white) of the Polish flag. Maciek's painful death on the refuse heap is symbolic. Bourgeois patriotism and its romantic cult of action had gone morally and politically bankrupt and landed — literally — on the rubbish heap of history.

But there is more to the ending of *Ashes and Diamonds* than this. Parallel to Maciek's destruction runs another, equally pregnant line. The celebration of the end of the war is still going on when Maciek leaves his hotel at dawn after completing his assignment. The lingering merrymakers, representatives of both the new and the old Poland, whirl round and round on the dirty, deserted dance floor in a strange, drunken polonaise. After the scene with Maciek and the sheets the camera returns to the suggestive, retarded dance. Then back again to Maciek, who is now fleeing from his pursuers like a wounded animal. At the hotel the polonaise whirls eerily on. The doorman unfurls the Polish flag (to hang it up over the entrance). Finally we see Maciek dying in the rubbish — and hear the polonaise still playing in the background.[1]

The ending of Wajda's film is obviously saturated with symbolic meaning; it may even seem *oversaturated* to many, but more about that later. Its symbolism is also markedly literary. The red-white theme and Maciek's bloody death are connected in Jerzy Andrzejewski's 1948 novel.[2] Setting Maciek's death on (history's) rubbish heap, however, was added to the scenario, which the author and Wajda wrote ten years later. The parallel scene, in which the enchanted circle of the polonaise captivates and unites all the dancers, is entirely absent from Andrzejewski's novel. In particular the Polish spectator, however, easily recognizes it as an allusion to Wyspiański's drama *The Wedding* in which peasants and lords, seemingly hypnotized by the magic music and song of the *chochoł*, the straw man, dance together at the end of the wedding feast.

The way the two lines are interlaced and opposed in Wajda's film is fascinating. The discredited but nevertheless likable hero's linear, individual path leads inescapably to death. Opposed to it we find the collective in the hotel — a mixture of old and new, caught in the circular movement of the dance, apparently with no particular goal, perhaps incapable of action, spellbound like the people in Wyspiański's *The Wedding*. Against the poses of the collective dance, which transforms the shabby gathering into something majestic, is contrasted the reduction of the dying Maciek to a bestially grunting, thoroughly biological creature. The two scenes are at the same time united by the fact that they both express the grip of the past on the present (the dance, the flag symbolism), while if the future is represented at all, it is only by the glaring morning light.

In *Ashes and Diamonds* and many later films Andrzej Wajda makes use of symbols belonging to the language of the romantic tradition: the white horse, the eagle, the red-and-white flag, the dance, etc.[3] In short, it would be possible to go through Wajda's entire production with Sławomir Mrożek's satirical little handbook *Poland in Pictures* and check off all the clichés for "Polishness" the director had used. At the same time one would find that Wajda's romantic poetics of heroism, gestures and poses is never found alone, but is always intertwined with an opposite poetics that might be termed naturalistic, dominated by biology, blood, physical violence and filth.

The opposition and coupling of "the poetics of gesture" and "the poetics of physiology" in Wajda's film takes place not only at the surface level, in the shaping of particular images, but is also related to the themes of the films, individually and as a whole. Wajda's central topic is the historical fate of the Polish nation and the meaning of that history for the present age. The conflict he nearly always starts from is a clash between an ideal (national, political, moral) and reality (historical, material, physical). Here I shall attempt to discuss this conflict in Wajda's later works, not only in his films but also with reference to his activity in the theater, which in recent years has become increasingly important. I shall pay particular attention to the films *The Wedding* (1972) and *The Promised Land* (1975), and to the theatrical production of Wyspiański's *November Night* (1974) in Cracow.

"If there were no Poland, there wouldn't be any Poles either" runs the famous closing line of Alfred Jarry's absurd classic *Ubu Roi*.[4] Father Ubu's magnificent platitude is actually not as self-evident as it may seem, and Jarry was probably aware of the fact. For almost 125 years, 1795–1918, there really was no Poland on the map of Europe. There were, however, Poles. Their dreams of liberation and the restoration of the Polish nation generated a remarkable ideological and artistic phenomenon — Polish romaticism. The disintegration of the Kingdom of Poland was interpreted by romantic ideology as a Messiah myth. Poland was the "Christ of nations," whose suffering and death were vicarious and would be followed by a glorious resurrection. But the dream of restoration also existed in a militant, revolutionary variant: the worst oppressed of all peoples would become the standard bearer of the European revolution. The heroes of Polish romantic literature from Mickiewicz's *Forefathers' Eve* on were born and lived in the field of tension between these two myths.

The unusually strong position that romanticism enjoys even now in Poland can only be explained by the fact that it came to function as a compensation and substitute for a nation that did not exist and was not allowed to exist. There is a scene in Wyspiański's *The Wedding* which memorably expresses the real, profound meaning of "There is no Poland, but there are Poles." The Poet in the play is talking to the Bride. He tells her that "You can look for Poland all over the world and never find her." But there is *one* place where she does exist, he continues, pressing the girl's hand to her breast. "In my heart?" "Exactly. That is Poland."[5]

Poland, transformed by external historical necessity into an idea — this may be said to be the foundation of romantic mythology for generation after generation of Polish poets, writers and artists. But what happens when the idea is confronted by reality? When it becomes evident that the absolute idea (Freedom, Independence, etc.) must either be realized in the relative categories of real history or not be realized at all? This is the theme of some of the most important post-war Polish literary, cinematic and theatrical works.

The riches of Polish romanticism has been and still is a delicate inheritance in the Polish People's Republic. The idea of national liberation would seem to be acceptable in all camps, but one of its components — hate of Russia — can easily be given an anti-Soviet interpretation. The romantics' religious mysticism is of course incompatible with a materialistic philosophy. The calls to revolt and blasphemies of a figure like Mickiewicz cannot be embraced by a conservative outlook, but the romantic Titans are at the same time extreme individualists who are quite unacceptable as positive revolutionary heroes.

One is struck by the fact that romanticism is still discussed in Poland in terms of "for" and "against," rather than as a product of a particular and limited historical situation. This is also true of Marxist-oriented scholars such as Maria Janion, perhaps the leading expert on romanticism in Poland today. For Professor Janion romanticism is nothing less than the key to the twentieth century. This applies to Europe in general, of course, but to Poland in particular. She could easily have paraphrased Jan Kott and entitled *The Romantic Fever,* her latest book, *Romanticism — Our Contemporary* instead.[6]

As recently as a few years ago a heated debate broke out in Poland on the romantic tradition and its proper evaluation today, both as an historical phenomenon and a part of the living cultural heritage. One young cultural historian, Jerzy Krasuski, launched a frontal assault on romanticism, which he condemned in the spirit of George Lukács as a thoroughly reactionary and irrational movement guilty of "the destruction of reason" in the twentieth century. Behind his attack one could discern a desire to limit the space allotted to the study of romanticism in the school and university system. Maria Janion, Andrzej Walicki, and others had little difficulty in refuting his rather primitive criticism.[7]

The long review of Maria Janion's new book that appeared in the weekly *Literatura* in early 1976 provides a more interesting example of criticism of the romantic complex.[8] The reviewer, Ryszard Przybylski, does not deny for a moment that romanticism has had a central position in Polish culture, that romanticism in fact *is* Polish culture. But Przybylski regards this inescapable fact as a curse rather than a blessing. The beginning of the trouble began with the collapse of the kingdom and the partitions of the country at the end of the eighteenth century, which removed the foundations of classicism and the sound influence of the Enlightenment. Romantics of various shades and forms thereupon devoted themselves to building up a non-existent Poland out of the ruins. In other terms, the weak development of capitalism in 18th-century Poland had not yet had time to produce a positive bourgeois consciousness when the dualistic romantics arrived and destroyed everything. The birthplace of European romanticism, after all, is the gap between (bourgeois revolutionary) ideals and (capitalist) reality; the romantics' utopian and/or pessimistic visions can be regarded as attempts to "bridge" or internalize that gap. Romanticism acquired a special strength and became uniquely long-lived in Poland due to the fact that the opposition between ideal and reality found expression in terms of "national independence" versus "foreign oppression"; the abortive revolts of the nineteenth century confirmed that the ideal was unattainable — now or ever — in this world.

Romanticism, says Przybylski, has produced stubborn ideological phantoms that even today stand between the Poles and reality. With respect to contemporary culture, romanticism and its cult have produced a fixation on what the critic termed "histrionism," the genius's ecstasy over his own art. A collective weakness for exceptional individual brilliance is one element in this romantic "histrionism," which according to Przybylski still afflicts modern Polish culture. Another element is a weakness for exaggerated effects and *kitsch*. The romantic style — and above all the style of the later worshippers of romanticism — is "a prophesying at the brink of the kitsch abyss."

What, then, is Andrzej Wajda's position in the discussion of romanticism? He has not explicitly participated in the debate, but practically his entire production can be regarded as a commentary on the running discussion about the romantic heritage and its function in today's Poland.

In an interview in 1967 Wajda explained his kinship with the tradition of romanticism:

The Polish romantic artists were like the phantoms of an imaginary world; they themselves were the tribunal, the army, public opinion and ultimately the conscience of the nation. And this is why their ideas — such as the Fatherland, liberty, independence — possessed a poetical and mythological dimension rather than a concrete and political one.

This phenomenon must be understood to appreciate the behavior of the heroes of my films. They are the direct heirs to Polish romantic thought. For them, behind the words Fatherland, liberty, order, sacrifice, solidarity, there is a great poetic tradition, a great spiritual force. And this is why, when they clash with the concrete forces of history, they fail and die.[9]

The tragic collision of the ideal with reality, the romantic pose confronted by raw historical and physiological necessity — here we have Wajda's basic theme. We have already seen one example of how this theme is treated in *Ashes and Diamonds*. Now let us examine its development in three recent works. It is not only their proximity in time (premières in January of 1973, 1974 and 1975, respectively) that allows us to regard the film *The Wedding,* the theatrical production *November Night* (at Teatr Stary in Cracow) and the film *The Promised Land* as a kind of triptych. All three are based on literary works from the turn of the century (Wyspiański's plays from 1900 and 1904 and Reymont's novel from 1899). The plays and the novel are thematically connected with Cracow, Warsaw and Łódź, respectively, three cities which, to simplify matters somewhat, represent culture, politics and economy in Poland's history. Chronologically the action in *November Night* comes first, dealing with the abortive uprising of 1830. The other two are set around the turn of the century, but depict diametrically opposite events and milieus. The protagonists of *The Wedding* are a group of Cracow intellectuals, strongly influenced by romantic myths, who celebrate the symbolic wedding of one of their comrades to a peasant girl. In *The Promised Land* the action is structured around three young industrialists in Łódź who sacrifice everything and everyone around them on their way to the top, all in accordance with the expand-or-perish laws of capitalist competition.

One striking feature of Andrzej Wajda's film production lies in his need of a literary model. He has focused on themes and plots connected with romanticism from the works of very different writers. Although the mythology of romanticism is very close to him, he did not treat it directly, at its historical source until *November Night,* which is about the uprising in 1830. One is at the same time struck by the fact that Wyspiański's play is not an authentic expression of Polish romanticism either, but a *neo*-romantic work with a strong element of epigonism and stylization. In the final analysis, Wajda even approaches a tragedy as central to Polish romanticism as that of 1830 indirectly, through a work that is stylized on the model of the great romantic poets.

Wyspiański's *November Night* is a drama about the revolt of the young officers and cadets against tsardom and its representative in Poland, Grand

Duke Konstanty, the tsar's brother. The tragedy of the uprising was that even before it had been put down by the Russian troops, it had been defeated from within by the rebels' miserable planning, the older officers' skepticism toward the project, and finally a lack of popular support. When Wyspiański has the cadets gather in Łazienki Park in the first scene of the play, their only support comes from the ancient goddesses Pallas Athene and Nike in various incarnations — the marble statues in the park which have come to life at the historical moment to lead the march through Warsaw.

Wyspiański was undoubtedly a great writer, but one wonders whether he might not have wanted to be even greater. His idea of coupling together the excited rebels and the awakened gods is suggestive and effective on the stage. Rhetoric abounds, nearly — but always only nearly — attaining the heights of classical tragedy and the romantic geniuses. As the critic Andrzej Wirth has pointed out, Wyspiański's brilliance cannot be separated from his efforts to *appear* brilliant:

> Wyspiański's dramatic works are a conglomerate in which his brilliant theatrical intuition often goes hand in hand with manifestations of a rather obvious graphomania. . . . It is impossible in this case, however, to separate the "good" from the "bad"; from a theatrical point of view Wyspiański's works are an organic whole and must either be accepted or rejected as such.[10]

In Wajda's 1974 staging of the play in Cracow no attempt is made to hide the decorative goddesses and the olympic rhetoric; on the contrary, such operatic features are emphatically played up. The goddesses appear against an endless black background on cothurns, above all the mortals on the stage. And they *sing* their monologues in powerful voices (via playback) to Zygmunt Konieczny's dramatic music. Wajda has also made the rebels intensely theatrical: they pose, fence and declaim as if they kept one eye on the reactions of their future audiences.

Wajda places two persons in contrast to the cadets who have often been considered negative or even cowardly figures — Grand Duke Konstanty and the Polish general Chłopicki, who hesitates to join the mutineers. While the rebels are led by the goddesses who in Wajda's version are products of the insurgents' own imagination, dreams with no basis in reality, Konstanty is "just a man." He vacillates between loyalty to Russia and his own ambitions to become king of an independent Poland. He is afraid of the mutineers and he is bound to his (Polish-born) wife by a violent erotic passion.

Grand Duke Konstanty is of course no hero in Wajda's interpretation; he does not represent any sort of historically rational alternative to the unrealistic ideas that haunt the rebels. But he is *real*. He stands for the bodily, physiological truth as opposed to an overstrung ideology and false consciousness. We recognize from the earlier Wajda his opposition of "gesture" and "physiology," but here it is given a somewhat new ring through a change in certain lines in the final scene. In Wyspiański's original the ending is pathetic — the old imprisoned patriot Łukasiński sings the famous words of Mickiewicz's *Ode to Youth*: "Hail, dawn of freedom / with thee cometh the Sun of salvation." In Wajda's version it is instead Konstanty in the midst of falling autumn leaves who has the final word: "These trees will be putting out new shoots next spring. . . ."[11] The phantasmal events of the November night are over, but nature — biology — promises new times, new hope. The dream of freedom and the laws of nature for a brief moment coalesce.

The Polish reviewer who maintained that "*November Night* summarizes the main trend in Wajda's film production" was not exaggerating.[12] This becomes clear if the play is considered in relation to *The Wedding* and *The Promised Land*, the two films Wajda made immediately before and after the revolutionary drama. In the first case the "ideological" line and the "poetics of gesture," in the second the "naturalistic" line and the "poetics of physiology" are developed in an almost pure form.

Wyspiański's *The Wedding* is one of Wajda's recurring points of departure. We have already touched upon his incorporation into *Ashes and Diamonds* of the enchanted dance from the final scene of the play. After the success enjoyed by the film in 1958 Wajda also began to work in the theater and his work there has become increasingly important for him. In 1962 he staged his first version of the play at Teatr Stary in Cracow, followed ten years later by a film version.

Wajda made an important change in the original when he adapted it to the cinema. Wyspiański's play takes place in a farmhouse where representatives of the Cracow intelligentsia gather with the peasants of the village to celebrate the wedding of one of their number to a peasant girl. The marriage symbolizes the intelligentsia's dream of breaking out of its isolation. Wajda has added certain important scenes to the bizarre wedding company in which distance is achieved by setting the action more firmly in the Galician countryside near the Russian-Austrian border, where Russian or Austrian soldiers can at any moment appear out of the fog. In this atmosphere the band of peasants armed with scythes after the call to revolt by the ghost of Wernyhora, becomes even less realistic than in Wyspiański's original. The final dance, which unites high and low in an enchanted, hypnotic circle, was in *Ashes and Diamonds* lofty and theatrical. Here it is set outdoors in the gray light of dawn and is photographed at a distance.

Wajda's ironical distance is conspicuous in all the scenes focused on the wedding company. It is instead the scenes centered around the *dramatis personae*, as the author calls them — the fantastic figures representing projections of the dreams of the (Cracow) guests — that are intensely expressive. This merely emphasizes that all of them are the captives of their own illusions and false consciousness. The destruction of these illusions, the confrontation of "gesture" with naked reality, comes when the peasants prepare to start off and discover that their commander (the Host) has a hangover and remembers nothing of the call to revolt. Left without a leader, they are unable to do anything. At this "moment of truth" Wajda discredits the iconography of the uprising in a typical manner. As the peasants of the village fetch their scythes from the barn, the camera sweeps by an uncompleted painting in the neo-romantic style, depicting a procession of identically armed peasants (the barn is also used as a studio). Later a forest of scythe blades is shown outlined against a gray sky, a shot which can be seen as an ironic quotation from the beginning of Éjzenštejn's *October*.

If almost all the figures in *The Wedding* are possessed by their ideas, fantasies and dreams taken from national and romantic mythology, those driven by ideological motives are few and far between in *The Promised Land*. Life in Łódź is determined by capital, interest rates, rises and falls in prices. True, the young Polish nobleman Borowiecki loves his family estate and venerates his father, but this does not prevent him from selling the estate in order to build a factory. He loves his fiancée as well, but this does not hinder him from being unfaithful to her with a Jewish industrialist's wife, who supplies him with important information, and from then marrying the daughter of a German textile magnate. Borowiecki's father dies in a little apartment in Łódź in which the symbols of the old noble family — portraits, coats-of-arms, swords, etc. — lie piled together as in a warehouse or antique shop. But he dies with his honor intact. The same is true of the manufacturer Trawiński, who commits suicide rather than become an animal in the capitalist jungle. All the others, however, voluntarily allow themselves to be transformed into predators that must eat or be eaten, expand or perish. Industrialism as portrayed by Wajda is an elemental force that sweeps along with it everyone and everything, a fever that changes men into naturalistic *bêtes humaines*.

Borowiecki's and his two partners' (a Jew and a German) savage appetite for riches, however, assumes at the same time the form of an obsession or *idée fixe*, and their illusions must — in keeping with Wajda's basic theme — be as such inexorably destroyed by brutal reality. This happens in an added epilogue that completely changes the ending of Reymont's novel. In the novel, Borowiecki in his last years becomes a philanthropist on the Tolstoyan model. Wajda shows him instead as the leader of the Łódź magnates ordering the army to fire on demonstrating workers. The rough stone cast through the window of the factory's plush executive office symbolizes the destruction by the workers' revolt of the capitalists' dreams of eternal power and, historically, the shattering of that power itself.

All of Wajda's films end with the defeat of the hero. Wajda's heroes, prisoners of their ideological illusions — which are usually romantic in origin — are shattered and die when they collide with what he himself calls "the concrete forces of history," forces which, as we have seen, are often of a markedly physiological nature. These "forces of history" are therefore not expressions of an historical reason that could motivate optimism, but are rather manifestations of a brutal, incessantly destructive and regenerative Nature.

In an analysis of some of Wajda's theatrical and cinematic works Stefan Morawski has formulated the invariant central theme developed in work after work as a conflict between "good history" and "evil history"; that is, the constant defeat of "possible" good by "necessary" evil, a defeat, however, that is not total, that leaves intact a memory or dream of the realization of "the good" in the future. Morawski cites as examples Wajda's staging of Przyby-szewska's *The Case of Danton, November Night,* and the films *Pilate and Others* (based on Bulgakov's *The Master and Margarita*) and *The Promised Land.*[13]

What makes Morawski's analysis debatable is the fact that history in Wajda's films is so strikingly the same from epoch to epoch, from the French Revolution to the 1945 of *Ashes and Diamonds.* History — victorious history — is in Wajda's works neither evil nor good, it simply *is,* rolling forward like the steamroller in Jan Kott's interpretation of Shakespeare, shattering illusions and often physically crushing those who hold them. *The Promised Land* clearly shows that Wajda's viewpoint springs not from the dialectic of history but from a pessimistic relativism. In the beginning it is the older Borowiecki's feudal ideal that is destroyed by his son's capitalism; but by the end of the film young Borowiecki's wealth has itself become an illusion, a phantom that in its turn meets its (potential) destiny in the concluding workers' revolt.

If history is more or less the same since Danton was defeated by Robespierre, indeed, since Yeshua Ga-Notsri was defeated by Pilate, this implies an important logical conclusion. Wajda's most important films and theatrical productions are all based on historical subject matter, especially Polish history from the Napoleonic wars up to World War II and the resistance movement. Now, if these interpretations of different historical epochs so persistently repeat the same historical paradigm — the ideal crushed by reality — it is difficult not to extrapolate and say that the same must apply to Wajda's view of the present age. One could even maintain that Wajda — like so many other artists who deal with historical themes — uses the present as his point of departure and then projects it on convenient selected periods of the past. The truth of the matter, however, is that he does not proceed from Poland's recent history unconditionally but approaches that history as seen through the prism of what we have observed to be unusually long-lived romantic mythology. The paradigm in Wajda's (from this viewpoint) peculiarly ahistorical interpretation of history — the eternal collision of ideals with reality and the tragic defeat of the former — is of course a central element in that mythology.

If the above observation is correct, it becomes fairly meaningless to search

Wajda's films for direct topical allusions — the rebels in *November Night* as referring to the Warsaw students in 1968, the firing upon the workers at the end of *The Promised Land* as an allusion to the strikes in Szczecin in 1970, etc. The historical dramas nevertheless deal with the present, though with an important qualification, namely, with Wajda's romantically influenced *interpretation* of the present. Searching for superficial allusions to the present is far less interesting than discussing how Wajda approaches the modern age in his recent works.

Sławomir Mrożek's *The Emigrants,* which Wajda staged at Teatr Stary in Cracow in the spring of 1976, ostensibly has a very topical theme, namely, the situation of the *Gastarbeiter.* But in Mrożek's dialogue between the two emigrants AA and XX, who live together in a cellar apartment somewhere in Western Europe, there emerges — at least for the Polish audience — an opposition that ultimately derives from romanticism. This is the opposition between the intellectual and the manual laborer, between the brain and the stomach, between *pan* and *cham,* which are inseparably linked to one another in Mrożek's cellar. When the intellectual's façade of verbal brilliance finally breaks down, this is not a victory for the spirit of compromise or common sense or anything of the like, but quite simply the defeat of AA, who represents the idea of freedom, and also XX's loss of an ideal. Interestingly enough, Wajda chose Jerzy Stuhr, the young actor who played Wysocki, the leader of the uprising in *November Night,* for the part of AA.

The present age and social environment in *The Emigrants* are merely the background against which Mrożek discusses the problem of freedom. What we are dealing with here is not an interpretation of the present through the prism of romantic tradition, but simply a projection of an old Polish debate onto a plane that is more concrete than in Mrożek's earlier plays. For that reason Wajda's version says nothing new about his attitude toward the present, and little new about his attitude toward the dualism of romanticism.

It is with all the more interest, therefore, that one looks forward to the belated distribution abroad of *The Marble Man* (1976), Wajda's first film on the history of socialist Poland. There are indications that this work will mark the beginning of a new period in Wajda's creation, a period that may also include an altered attitude toward the romantic heritage. For it seems that it is only in relation to this heritage that Andrzej Wajda's art can exist.

NOTES

1. Andrzej Wajda, *The Wajda Trilogy: Ashes and Diamonds — Kanal — A Generation,* London 1973, pp. 233–239.
2. Jerzy Andrzejewski, *Popiół i diament,* Warsaw 1963, p. 382: "As through a mist he heard the flat, muffled sounds of firing. Dropping his bag he fell to the ground.

Above himself he saw a big red-and-white flag. Still higher, the blue, very distant sky. 'Where has that flag come from,' he wondered. 'What's happening?'"

3. Sławomir Mrożek, *Polska w obrazach,* Cracow 1957.

4. Alfred Jarry, *Ubu Roi.* Préface de Jean Saltas. Paris 1907, p. 181.

5. Stanisław Wyspiański, *Dzieła zebrane* 4, Cracow 1958, pp. 189–190.

6. Maria Janion, *Gorączka romantyczna,* Warsaw 1975.

7. *Kultura* 20, Warsaw 1974, pp. 1, 4–5.

8. Ryszard Przybylski, "Tyrania Króla Ducha," *Literatura,* February 19, 1976, p. 4.

9. "Entretien avec Andrzej Wajda," *Études cinématographiques,* 69–72, Paris 1968, p. 8. This special issue on Wajda contains valuable analyses of Wajda's relation to romanticism and the literary sources of his earlier works.

10. Andrzej Wirth, *Teatr, jaki mógł by być,* Warsaw 1964, p. 106.

11. Wyspiański, *op. cit.,* 8, p. 196.

12. Elżbieta Wysińska, "'Noc listopadowa' i 'Wyzwolenie,'" *Dialog* 10, 1974, p. 128.

13. Stefan Morawski, "Główny topos Andrzeja Wajdy," *Dialog* 9, 1975, pp. 135–139.

Vladimir Markov

THE PLAYS OF VLADIMIR KAZAKOV

Vladimir Vasil'evič Kazakov (born 1938), a playwright, a poet, and a prose writer, is certainly a unique case in contemporary Russian literature. Being a Muscovite and the clear product of the Russian futurist tradition, he was, at least until quite recently, all but unknown even to some experts on futurism who live in Moscow.[1] As different from his world-famous colleagues who manage to combine the reputation of a dissident with membership in the Writers' Union, Kazakov could not even dream of being accepted into that august organization (and no sane person would publish him in Russia), even though politically he is absolutely acceptable (i.e., his work has no political overtones whatsoever). As to his "world fame" (which is all but inevitable nowadays for any young Soviet man of letters who even slightly deviates from socialist realism), it is certainly one-sided: he was published in Germany (both in the original and in translation), but not a living soul knows about him in this country. Just to mention him brings the correction: "you mean Jurij Kazakov" (and even the knowledgeable will suspect one of speaking about Mixail Kozakov).

I first learned about Kazakov in 1971 when he sent me several of his plays, which he expected me both to appreciate and to publish (I did the former to a limited extent and failed him in the latter). Eventually, I received more dramas and some prose from him. In the meantime, his *Moi vstreči s Vladimirom Kazakovym* (1972)[2] and the novel, *Ošibka živyx* (1973),[3] appeared in Germany; seven of his dramas were broadcast on German radio. In all, I have typescripts of eleven short dramas by Kazakov — seven of them were written in 1970, and the rest are undated.[4] I shall concentrate on these dramas, largely ignoring his "scenes" and "historical scenes" printed in *Moi vstreči...*, which belong to an earlier period and otherwise differ considerably from the plays of 1970.[5]

Kazakov encloses a short autobiography in the writings he mails which contains an enumeration of what he calls the "events" of his life. Not only do they include books by Xlebnikov, Kručenyx[6] and Xarms, but also books by Gogol' and Dostoevskij, and — rather unexpectedly — by Stendhal. He does not list any of the contemporary European absurdist playwrights, nor does he mention Koz'ma Prutkov, whose traces can be found in Kazakov's plays.

Kazakov is an absurdist playwright *par excellence*. Instead of indulging myself in defining the genre,[7] I shall give a detailed synopsis of a typical play of his.

The play is simply called "A Drama." It begins with a character named Vladimir saying: "This is what doesn't interest me at all. What is the time now?" to which the clock answers "Coo-coo." Vladimir interprets this as two o'clock and after "Some day! Some weather! Some etc.," is ready to leave, but immediately runs into his uncle (unnamed) and stays on stage until the end of the play. The uncle begins by chiding his nephew for not greeting him politely, but the more details he gives, the more we see that he is not describing Vladimir, but rather another person. When Vladimir finally says "I think you confuse me with someone," his uncle retorts: "Not someone, but Boris Valentinovič Gorbylev," to which the nephew knowingly nods: "That's the one who is not the very same." In an aside, let us sum up briefly here that two of Kazakov's favorite themes have already been introduced: time (in a rather undeveloped manner) and, at some length, identity. In the meantime, the conversation changes after the uncle asks Vladimir where he is going and since Vladimir does not seem to know, his uncle gives him the name of the person he is going to visit. For good measure, his uncle reminds him that his name is Vladimir. Obviously encouraged, Vladimir then tells the rest: he is going to an old woman to pawn his ax, which he immediately swings as a demonstration, scaring his uncle into leaving the stage. The allusion to Dostoevskij is unmistakable, but the name of the old woman resembles that of the character in *Crime and Punishment* as little as Vladimir does Rodion (and, let us add, Raskol'nikov never planned to pawn his ax). Vladimir does not stay alone too long and announces to the audience that his fiancee, Anastasija, is coming. The girl enters with the declaration that it is an odd thing to be a fiancee all day from morning until night — and only after this does she greet Vladimir with a *zdravstvujte*. Whereas Vladimir's dialogue with his uncle, with all its illogical touches, resembled real-life conversations and had some unity, he now answers Anastasija with all kinds of irrelevant nonsense, so that she finally has to say: "You again speak about other things." When he greets her for the second time, the poor girl says: "At this time, you are always madder for a half-hour than at any other time."

A new character, the already mentioned old woman, makes a sudden appearance, but this brings little help. Even if there is some sense in the dialogue now,[8] it is often of the "anti-sense" variety. For example, Vladimir says: "Hello, Nadežda Jakovlena. Hello, is that you (*Zdravstvujte, èto vy?*)" to which she answers "*Ja èto zdravstvujte* (I am hello)" and immediately asks: "Are you alone or with your fiancee?" This is quite unnecessary because Anastasija remains on stage (and later even joins the dialogue); nevertheless, Vladimir answers that he is alone. The subject of the discussion now becomes the absent uncle and each of the characters asks in turn: "Where is uncle?" Finally, Vladimir declares that he is uncle and then quite reasonably asks: "Where is Vladimir?" Identity is in serious trouble at this moment, and even the old woman asks: "Who am I? I forgot." — with Vladimir reciting macabre nonsense poetry and Anastasija turning sentences upside-down (O Vladimir! Vladimir, o!). The briefly appearing Thief is also identity obsessed, saying

"Night. No one is around. Not even me." The at-long-last-appearing uncle sums up the situation which could serve as an epigraph to many a Kazakov play: *Zdes' kogo-to netu* ('Someone is not here'). From then on, things happen to sentences rather than to people in the play. Even when the subject of the ensuing (and rather excited) conversation is the ax, this is what the *dramatis personae* say: "I feel that I cannot any longer, but not any longer I cannot either" or, in reaction to "It is already 11:30" (which in Russian is "half of the twelfth [hour]"), someone says "It is half of the old woman; it is half of everything." Finally, Vladimir begins to passionately decline the name of Anastasija all the way from nominative to prepositional. In the meantime, the old woman disappears along with the ax. "No old woman, no ax," says uncle, to which Vladimir adds: "No me." Uncle concludes the play with the words: "Yes, Vladimir, you disappeared. You are not here. This is a grievous loss. But what can one do! As they write me in this letter: Courage!".

* * *

The setting of Kazakov's plays are seldom identified. From the words of the characters, we learn that they are in the street (because they mention wind or refer to houses) or inside a room (because, for example, mirrors are involved). The only "description" can be found at the beginning of *The Gate* (*Vrata*): "For a long time, the stage stays empty; in fact, there is no stage at all" — here there are echoes of both Gogol' and Koz'ma Prutkov.

As to the characters, they are mostly identified by name alone. Others have no names, but are identified by relationship (uncle) or profession (fireman, guard, smith). In only one play, *Heavenly bodies* (*Nebesnye tela*), do all characters belong to the same profession — that of circus performers. There is a tendency, however, to suggest nineteenth-century Russian high society with "beautiful" names like "Èvelina" or with "noble" surnames like Melik-Melkumov or Xvijuzov, reminiscent of Ostrovskij's comedies and, once again, of Prutkov.[9] There are also "numbered" characters with no names, as, for instance, the four guests in *Guests* (*Gosti*), who cannot come to the conclusion as to how many of them there are. Finally, there are collective characters (crowd, procession) as well as objects, as, for example, the stage in *The Gate,* which even conducts a dialogue with the protagonist (once again reminding us of Prutkov).[10]

In my personal opinion, action in an absurdist drama has always been a problem. Even the world-famous plays of this kind, with all their brilliance of dialogue, in the long run, may bore the audience to death. Kazakov does not seem to have theater in mind at all; his dramas are clearly closet dramas. It is often difficult to say what is going on in them. Characters speak — to themselves or to each other — but the words do not lead anywhere. They may disappear or even split into two. Occasionally there is a hint (but only a hint) of violence (the slashed throat at the end of *The Gate*), but it remains unclear whether it is real or not. There are unexpected pauses (which might be a parody of Čexov). Reaching the end of such a play, we are likely to repeat the words of one character in *The Gate*: "What was unclear, remains unclear," or to give an affirmative answer to the heroine's question in the same play: "What is going on here? Nothing?"

As mentioned above, one of the important themes in Kazakov's plays is identity. The characters not only do not quite know who they are, but also have difficulty with determining how many of them there are on stage (even if there are only four of them). We have already seen Vladimir become his uncle for a while and in *Rain* (*Dožd'*) a man exchanges places with the rain. Objects are also capable of losing their identity: in the last-named play, a character looks for his reflection not in the mirror, but on his watch (space becomes time).[11] In the world of Kazakov, even sameness is no guarantee of authenticity, and a man complains in *Rain* that in the street *vmesto doma stoit točno takoj že* ('instead of the house there stands one exactly like that'). As to the people, they keep dropping sentences like *A my vse ešče my ili ne tol'ko my?* ('And are we still we or not just we?' [*Factory Surroundings, Fabričnye okrestnosti*])[12] and *Oni suščestvujut v raznoe vremja, a ne suščestvujut odnovremenno* ('They exist at different times, and do not exist simultaneously' (*FO*)), and in the same play, a question is asked by the character who was supposed to answer it, while "the First One" keeps referring to himself as "the Second One."

One could talk at some length about differences between Kazakov, on the one hand, and Beckett and Ionesco (to choose the most famous names from the recently celebrated literature of the absurd), on the other. Of course, Beckett and Ionesco are not so easily teamed together. They are both concerned, however, with the human predicament, whereas Kazakov is not. People are the way they are in Beckett and things happen the way they do in Ionesco because the world is as it is. Beckett's absurdity is, therefore, tragic, and Ionesco's is grotesque; and both are symbolist. Kazakov's world seems to be of his own making, and there are no religious or any other "serious" overtones in his plays.

Perhaps the most important difference, and Kazakov's most unmistakable claim to originality, is that Kazakov's absurdity is sustained by (or maybe even derives from) the verbal plane. There is an astonishing variety of such verbal absurdities or their mixtures, but establishing their typology is not my intent. Some are obvious in their nature or derivation. When, for example, a character in *Guests* complains that his age does not correspond to "the rest of him" and gives, as an example, the fact of his being forty years old and yet having been born in Smolensk (which is a good example of absurdity in reverse, i.e., a normal thing is presented as an absurdity) — it may have its source in "Armenian" riddles. When, in the same play, someone says *Da, da, vy ne pravy* ('Yes, yes, you aren't right'), we recognize a familiar speech error.

When, again in *Guests,* somebody's *vysota kružilas 'ot golovy* (the height was dizzy because of the head), we are reminded of some children's poetry or folklore based on metathesis.[13] Other absurdities are based on frustrated expectation. When in *The Gate* someone begins *Segodnja zdes'* ('Today here'), we expect *a zavtra tam* ('and tomorrow there'), which never arrives; instead Kazakov gives us *a zavtra nigde* ('and tomorrow nowhere'). In *On bezumec, a my bezumcy* ('He is crazy, but we are crazy'), the expected contrast does not come about because tautology destroys it.

Kazakov's characters love questions. When one of them (in *FO*) asks: *Vy stranno govorite ili ja stranno slušaju?* ('Do you speak strangely or do I listen strangely'), the question is not necessarily absurd. Real absurdity can be found in *Vy ogloxli ili ne slyšite?* ('Have you turned deaf or don't you hear?'), but it is based on an obvious play on synonyms. More typical for Kazakov is, however, the question *Ja oslyšalas' ili oslyšalas'ja?* ('I heard wrong or was it I who heard wrong?'). Here the reverse word order does not create a question within a question; it is pure, "transemantic" absurdity. In fact, inversion ought not to be accompanied by interrogative intonation here. The two parts of the sentence are contrasted by syntax (and by the conjunction *ili*), but are identical in meaning.

We have seen in *The Gate* that Kazakov uses declension tables parodically as an absurdist device. Such things happen more than once. In the following example, we enter the area of dialogue (whereas in previous examples absurdity was "internal," based on semantic relationships within a sentence). In the same play, still parodying the textbook declension, Kazakov has his characters converse like this: — *On tušit.* — *Čem?* — *Plamja.* ('He's extinguishing. — With what? — Fire.') Here not only frustrated expectation is involved (we expect something like *Vodoj* ('With water'), but also logical incongruence.[14] Kazakov, however, does not want to say that someone *tušit plamenem* ('extinguishes with fire'). The absurdity is based on noncorrespondence of the answer to the question, and this involves grammar.

Grammar plays an important part in Kazakov's verbal absurdities. We can find absurd combinations of finite forms and infinitives (*ulybnulsja vojti,* 'he smiled to enter'; *vzdrognula ona sprosit',* 'she shuddered to ask'), theoretically possible, but hardly ever occurring forms of conjugation (*budem byt',* untranslatable, but roughly comparable to 'I am being to be'; *ja ostalsja ostavat'sja,* 'I stayed to stay'), and omission of objects (*vyšel iz,* 'he went out of'; *my govorim o,* 'We speak of'; *na časax bol'še čem bez,* 'the watch shows more than of'; *rovno bez,* 'exactly of').[15]

Omission of the expected or, its reverse, intrusion of the irrevelant, are elements of the absurd. The former could be demonstrated by Vytkovskij's dividing his life into two periods — number one and number three in *The Gate.*[16] The latter can be found in the same character's description of Anna: "the same hair, the same pig-iron (*čugun*), the same eyes and pale face." In

FO, smoke is of three colors: gray, black, and last. In Vytkovskij's three periods, however, we have something more complex than just omission. If all three periods, that is, #1, #2, #3, were mentioned, the absurdity would not be removed, because of the "idiotic obviousness"[17] of the statement, which in itself is a device of the absurd.[18]

From here we are led to what Kazakov often practices: cluster of absurdities. *FO* begins with the following dialogue: — *Ne sliškom li my idem? — A? Èto ešče ne my.* ('Don't we go overly? — What? That's not yet we'). On the surface this is simply a wrong answer to a question, something similar to the folkloric dialogues of deaf people. Actually, however, a triple absurdity is achieved here because (1) *sliškom* cannot modify *idem* 'we go' (it does here, because, presumably, *bystro* 'fast' [or *medlenno* 'slow'] is omitted); (2) the answer shifts the emphasis to *my* ('we'), which was not the subject of the question; and (3) *ešče ne my* ('not yet we') is a logical impossibility in the given situation, because there is no one else, and the only remaining possibility is "we" *in statu nascendi.* Of course, the whole thing fits Kazakov's playing with identity perfectly. The play ends with another dialogue which is also a cluster of absurdities: "— Do you hear? — I see. — To whom? — Who? — No one to no one. — Or vice versa."[19]

More examples of verbal absurdity could be added (for example, fragmentation),[20] but my aim is not to give an exhaustive description. It is, rather, simply to introduce Vladimir Kazakov, who is, with all his literary ties and ancestries, a truly original phenomenon, — himself an absurdity of sorts in the context of Soviet literature.

NOTES

1. Except Nikolaj Xardžiev.

2. Published by Carl Hanser Verlag in Munich and containing Kazakov's early works (both prose and plays).

3. Also published by Hanser as translated by Peter Urban as *Der Fehler der Lebenden.*

4. Their Russian titles are *Vrata, Drama, Fabričnye okrestnosti, Gosti, Otraženija, Tost, Dožd', Nebesnye tela, Voskresenie, Izvajanija.*

5. The influence of Daniil Xarms is obvious in them. For completeness' sake, let us add that Kazakov's prose contains parts written in dramatic form.

6. The autobiography makes special mention of Kručenyx, who not only "blessed" Kazakov for a literary career (just as Deržavin did Puškin), but also suggested that he concentrate on prose and drama, and not poetry (which Kazakov seems to have written in great quantities in still earlier stages).

7. To quote from Thomas à Kempis, "I would far rather feel contrition than be able to define it."

8. Compared to the preceding scene, when Vladimir's mind wandered.

9. This quality is much more visible in Kazakov's short plays in verse (See *Moi vstreči* . . .) which are filled with countesses and tsars.

10. And the passerby in *Vrata* may derive from the passerby in Čexov's *Cherry Orchard*.

11. Another character, in *Otraženija* (*Reflections*), more romantically, sees somebody else's reflection in the mirror.

12. From now on referred to as *FO*.

13. Cf. *Exala derevnja / Mimo mužika / Vdrug is-pod sobaki / Lajut vorotá*. ('The village was riding / Past the peasant / All of a sudden from below the dog / the gates are barking.')

14. Of course, fire is used to fight fire under some circumstances, but this hardly entered Kazakov's mind when he wrote the play.

15. A further step is providing us with that object, but in the form of the same preposition: *v neskol'kix metrax ot ot* ('in a few meters from from').

16. One could discuss the absurd use of numerals in Kazakov's plays. The hostess in *Okna* (*Windows*), for example, is "about 30, 31, 32, 33 years old"; three men sit at the table, one of them being the fourth one; "Fourteen. How much is it?" someone asks, and the answer is "Yesterday."

17. The term is Emile Cammaert's in his *Poetry of Nonsense* (London, 1925).

18. Cf. in *Okna: krov' cveta krovi* ('blood of the color of blood').

19. One can see something remotely Maeterlinckian in this finale, and this is not the only case, but, in my opinion, an influence can be excluded, although one can find a sufficient amount of symbolist imagery in Kazakov's plays (e.g., mirrors).

20. A good example could be *roj* and *vyj* in *FO,* which are not "swarm" in the nom. sing. and OCS "neck" in the gen. plur., respectively, but the second halves of *vtoroj* 'second' and *pervyj* 'first.'

Predrag Palavestra

ELEMENTS OF NEUTRAL TEMPORALITY AND CRITICAL REALISM IN THE CONTEMPORARY SERBIAN NOVEL

The aesthetic confrontations and the conflict with dogmatism, which took hold of the whole of Yugoslav culture and art a quarter of a century ago, stimulated some particularly interesting and significant changes both in literary life and in literature itself. The creative and critical experiences gained by writers in that period have proved to be valuable both for literary and historical, as well as for theoretical and aesthetic studies. A little later, similar changes also took place in other European literatures and thus on a broader theoretical context inspired the re-evaluation of the real boundaries and vital possibilities of the realistic novel. Shortly before the end of his life George Lukács, an indubitable authority in the field of Marxist criticism and one of the theoreticians of socialist realism, gave his interpretation of the new meaning of critical realism in socialist society.[1] In all the appraisals and surveys of post-war Serbian literature, in the various questionnaires and discussions, which were especially conducted in *Književne novine* and in the journal *Savremenik*,[2] writers and critics agreed almost unanimously that all the evident tendencies in the contemporary Serbian novel indicated the creation of a new tradition of critical realism. In my book *Posleratna srpska književnost, 1945–1970* (Postwar Serbian Literature, 1945–1970), on which this paper is based, as in some other studies,[3] I have attempted to point out that the resistance against the vulgar forms of both the aesthetic theory and the creative practice of socialist realism had two quite different stages and that the change in relations towards realism was reflected in the changes that occurred in the very structure of the literary text, above all in the structure of the contemporary novel.

The world to which postwar Serbian fiction turned at a time when the clash with the idealized and false romanticism of socialist realist theory had just begun, had neither the dynamism nor the completeness of real life. Instead of a forced picture of the totality of social movement, with a more or less marked perspective of the socio-historical development, a partial and metaphorically poetic picture was formed depicting the profound and tragic discord between the intrinsic and extrinsic world of contemporary man, between the individual and universal spirit, between the individual and collective consciousness. Certain experiences of writers of the so-called "new novel," which developed at approximately the same time, stimulated the inchoate process of violating the classical forms of the realistic novel, from which many former inherent qualities had been eliminated.[4] The temporal and social dislocation of motifs, the abandonment of plot and its breaking down into a multitude of episodes which ostensibly had no mutual connections whatsoever, the strict realistic verisimilitude of details in a totally diffuse and fragmented picture of the vital whole, the greater and more expressive hermetism of style and the dense symbolism of the texts, initially led the contemporary Serbian novel to a specific form of neutral temporality. This form, without any doubt, represented a type of quiet resistance to and a passive escape from ideological coercion. The internal reality of the novel was opposed to the external reality of the objective world, whose former instruments for the acceptance and evaluation of literary works were, in the main, powerless to penetrate into the new, enclosed and inaccessible world of poetic isolation and security of creative spirit. This was a world that defended itself from vulgarity, depersonalization and submerging into the common life by an imposed self-enclosure and by the mastership of aestheticizing. At one stage of the novel's development, neutral temporality deprived the postwar Serbian novel of the traditional ethical obligations that writers inherently feel towards society and the historical moment. According to the dialectical regularity of literary development, a situation recorded in French literature towards the end of the last century repeated itself when, in the name of stifled individualism, a section of writers rebelled against the vulgar artlessness of the naturalistic literary school.[5] The only ethical obligation, maintained by writers, referred to the natural humanistic postulates of art; all other ideological, class, historical, civil, as well as family-ethical obligations were skillfully avoided. As in the European avant-garde novel, the ethical consciousness of the individual, who has broken his ties with his social surroundings, was expressed indirectly and quite unobtrusively. This is completely different from the way in which the ideological position of a writer and the ideological tendency of a work were stated in committed literature or the literature of socialist realism. Changing the nature of the realistic novel, which had become more powerful and more expressive in detail rather than in its broad scope, writers of the poetic novel made a considerable effort to realize an autonomous temporal space in the work itself, raise the relationship towards ethical criteria to a more absolute level and give it a more permanent meaning, accomplishing this from within, through literary means. One section of writers, who today are among the most significant creators of the contemporary Serbian novel — writers such as Miodrag Bulatović, Aleksandar Tišma, Mirko Kovač, Branimir Šćepanović and Radomir Smiljanić — in their development underwent the experiences of neutral temporality and produced brilliant examples of new prose. With the poetic transposition of reality and with breakthroughs into the area of the unreal and fantastic, they demonstrated the power of neutral temporality to widen the possibilities of the realistic novel. Today, according to an almost universal conviction, the boundaries of the realistic novel have been widened on all sides.[6]

With the introduction of neutral temporality it was hoped that realistic prose would rid itself of the triviality and the naturalistic perpetuation of the phenomena which, strictly from the sociological and ideological viewpoint, could be used better and more naturally in other humanistic disciplines. However, this aspiration also concealed within itself certain weaknesses inherent in the poetic form of the novel. Freed from temporal rules and enclosed in an autonomous space of its own internal harmony, literature was doomed to lose its attractiveness and become uninteresting and boring. In spite of pragmatic demands from the outside, often set before literature for the sake of society, the postwar Serbian novel confirmed through its own experience that neutral temporality gave the contemporary writer the possibility to point out and express the *essence* of human situations and relationships. Furthermore, it also gave contemporary writers the opportunity to devote more attention to the essence of the phenomena of life and their effect on man than to transient social occurrences or to the momentary demands of political practice. On the other hand, however, it was also affirmed that neutral temporality could lead writers to a distinctive ethical quietism and spiritual austerity, in which literary utterances as the humanistic postulates of a literary creation lost their moral meaning.

So there was a new qualitative development in the postwar Serbian novel, a process of transformation in the tradition of critical realism, which based its relationship to the reality of existence on ethical criteria and acknowledged the aesthetics of the participation of literature in the dialectical development of human experience. The communicative function of literature, which among other things implies a moral action, demanded a change in the position of the creative process, which, at the same time, meant a change in the form of the modern novel. The restless spirit of creative skepticism, founded on a tradition of reason and scholarly consciousness, historically emboldened by man's victories and induced to resist everything that might force it to develop into a fossilized dogma, could not reconcile itself to the passive and subordinate position in which, as circumstances turned out, the literature of neutral temporality found itself. In the positions of creative freedom and autonomy of the creative work which were gained, a change in the communicative function of the literary work from poetic to critical realism represented a dialectically conditioned phenomenon in the development of modern literature. This phenomenon contains one of the most important contributions of contemporary Yugoslav and, in particular, Serbian literature to the poetics of the modern novel, in which both individual works as well as whole stylistic trends which demanded the re-evaluation and change of traditional critical criteria in the interpretation of realistic literature occur all the more frequently and clearly.

The revival and transformation of critical realism have become characteristic of the contemporary phase in the development of postwar Serbian literature. In the course of the last ten years many writers have engaged in an open critical dialogue with their epoch, leading the moral opposition against the appearance and permanence of evil in man's life as well as against social injustices in the ever-changing world. The critical tone of the realism of these writers is sometimes over-imbued with dark colors, the crudeness of street language, and with naturalistic strokes. It is a critical tone, however, that is not expressed in the classical manner by revealing and unmasking social deformities and conflicts, but by new, more intricate and more modern literary devices, in particular by the pitting of the individual sphere against the social and historic. While formerly critical realism was predominantly socially motivated, in contemporary Serbian literature it is, in the main, psychologically and ethically motivated. Critical realism turned towards the moral dilemmas and the alienation of contemporary man, who has been enervated by menacing contradictions of the dehumanizing modern civilization and by the loss of the power of hope. The tragic and dramatic experience of the universal disharmony between man and the world in which he lives, a feeling of alienation and a presentiment of worthlessness, a helplessness before the destructive forces which change rather than destroy a character, form the basis of the black realism of doubt and despair, in which, nevertheless, the spark of light both in man and on the horizons of expectation is inextinguishable. On the contrary, from the darkness where it is smothered and banked up, that flame of humanity shines with an even greater glow, by which the new realism of contemporary Serbian literature is connected with the inherent ethics of the greatest creations of the realistic tradition.

By virtue of its very nature, to which a critical tone and a moralistic tendency are inherent, satirical literature served as one of the most ideal areas for the revival and strengthening of critical realism in the contemporary Serbian novel. Unlike the journalistic level of the social chronicle, to which writers of lively intellect but of weaker creative capabilities resort, the satirical novel could perform in several ways; it could be an allegorical story, a social and psychological novel, a sociological study, or even a depiction of a fantastic negative utopia. In the novels of Erih Koš all these rich possibilities of the satirical novel are generously used; these novels are the real pioneers of critical realism in contemporary Serbian literature. Although closer to the traditional forms of realistic fiction and unelaborate in verbal decor, Koš used the spiritual, moral, and social subject matter of critical realism in almost all aspects of satirical prose, consistently maintaining the viewpoint that "every kind of realism is critical, or else it isn't realism."[7] In Meša Selimović's novels *Derviš i smrt* (The Dervish and Death) and *Tvrđava* (The Fortress), the historical framework, the oriental external decoration (elements of which sometimes helped Ivo Andrić tell even a contemporary story in a more picturesque way) and the spirit of critical realism were affirmed less explicitly than in Koš's novels *Veliki Mak* (The Big Mac), *Sneg i led* (Snow and Ice) or *Dosije Hrabak* (The Hrabak File). It was affirmed by the internal contrasting of two irreconcilable morals and two antagonistically separated and alienated worlds, the individual and the universal, whose principles clash in tragic solutions as in classical tragedies. A similar contrasting of internal and external worlds forms the basis of Dobrica Ćosić's great epic *Vreme smrti* (Time of Death), in which, as in the work of Koš, the traditional characteristics of the realistic novel are maintained in quite a strong form. These characteristics, however, are abandoned to a considerable extent in the novels of Borislav Pekić, one of the most significant contemporary Serbian writers of the critical trend. Pekić is an outstanding moralist whose style unites many positive features of the classical realistic process of novel-writing with undreamed-of possibilities of rich associative poetic prose. He achieves moralistic and critical effect equally confidently both when he uses a mythical model, as in the allegorical story *Vreme čuda* (The Time of Miracles), and when he resumes the form of the social and psychological novel in *Hodočašća Arsenija Njegovana* (The Pilgrimages of Arsenije Njegovan). The urban tone of Pekić's prose, which pulsates with rhythms of the modern city, marked further possibilities of critical realism. Such possibilities were also richly used in the themes of the novel *Vodeni cvetovi* (Water Lilies) by Sveta Lukić.

Talent for nuances and a high intellectual concentration make Pekić one of the great masters of the contemporary Serbian novel. Certain possibilities of the transformation of critical realism attracted a whole new generation of fiction writers, in which Vidosav Stevanović, Milisav Savić, Ivan Ivanović, and Miroslav Josić Višnjić have already affirmed their outstanding individuality. Refined lyrical evocations and emphasized veristic, even naturalistic accents are simultaneously interwoven in their creative processes. The method of the bare recording of living, crude and sometimes inarticulate speech of imbecile wretches and victims from the periphery of life, who are alienated from their environment and unadapted to society (which is always changing and being created) is, to a certain degree, suitable for the tragic feeling and bitter experience that this prose describes, although such a process fundamentally simplifies the technique of modern critical realism. Živojin Pavlović and Dragoslav Mihailović incurred the real hazard of equating naturalism with the method of critical realism — a process which is to a large extent characteristic of the modern novel. These two writers were among the first to openly join the revival of critical realism in the more recent Serbian novel. In Pavlović's novels *Lutke* (Dolls) and *Kain i Avelj* (Cain and Abel), as in his films, life is shown without any affectation and poeticization, in the grey mist of an unpleasant memory, sometimes even as a bare sociological description, although always with an emphasized moralistic note. A sociological foundation is also evident in the novel *Kad su cvetale tikve* (When Pumpkins Blossomed) by Dragoslav Mihailović. This story, with its external features, its plot, vocabulary, milieu and monologic form, acts as a photograph of a tragic episode from postwar life. It is, however, a novel of archetypal construction, containing many elements of classical drama, whose hero is a tragic victim of an immutable destiny. In another psychologically subtle novel by Mihailović, *Petrijin venac* (Petrija's Wreath), the directness of the narration is an immediate reflection of unambiguous relations towards life, in which neither moral nor philosophical experience is found on the surface of the banal everyday event but rather beneath its outer layer, in the harmony of tragic and dramatic conditions which in a single moment can turn any triviality into a microcosmic catastrophe and a conclusive defeat.

Even some of the onetime representatives of the poetic novel are turning towards possibilities of a new critical prose. A collection of short stories by Danilo Kiš, *Grobnica za Borisa Davidoviča* (A Tomb for Boris Davidovich), written in ethical defence of all victims of dogmatism, terror, Stalinism, Fascism or anti-Semitism, gives an example of that change of realistic approach from the neutral temporality to the critical realism. Antonije Isaković's new short stories *Tren* (A Moment), which I have recently read in manuscript, are even more permeated by the idea of open critical condemnation of ethical deformations and human tragedy in the modern world.

Utilizing the material that is relevant in its sphere, contemporary Serbian prose attempts to realize its relationship to contemporaneity and social movements by the critical and realistic evaluation of the changes both in human relationships and in human consciousness, which essentially influence man's position or fate. The confrontation with processes in the field of social, moral, and psychological relations, and the critical search for the forms, developments, and solutions of the contradictions and crises which affect society and influence man's fortune have not only widened both the thematic and stylistic scope of postwar Serbian literature, but also have brought about changes in the structure of the novel. In fact, the development of the novel has shown that revived critical realism, adapted to modern standards, can become a vital form in the rich harmony of today's creative tendencies. This is even more apparent if one bears in mind that the metamorphosis of critical realism is not only a distinctive feature of Serbian literature, but a process which has also occurred in other Yugoslav literatures, especially in the Slovenian contemporary novel.[8] A widening of the traditional boundaries of realism has occurred in many European literatures, particularly in those which have been subjected to the influence of aesthetic theory and the practice of socialist realism longer than others. These, according to the Polish aesthetician Stefan Morawski, are moving towards a delineation of mimesis and realism.[9] Likewise in Serbian literature, where the postwar novel has passed through two extremely important phases — through the closed structures of neutral temporality and the moral commitment of critical realism — this delineation of mimesis and realism has signified a broadening of the concept of realistic literature that has been supported more recently by Marxist critics and theoreticians. The relationship to realism has become a central question of Marxist literary theory. Aware of all the changes which have occurred and which are occurring in the contemporary world and in socialist society, in which literature does not accept a subordinate role of a static mirror but seeks the opportunity to express "the dynamic conception of the totality of society with individual man as the basic factor,"[10] Lukács made a positive contribution to the Marxist interpretation of the meaning of critical realism in modern literature. Lukács stated, "Since real Marxism, which is not bureaucratically and subjectively debased, is founded upon an ever-deeper study of objective reality, therefore also in the field of literature . . . it must regard critical realism as its ally."[11] Neither overrated as a primary method in the transformation and development of the sphere of contemporary realism, nor underrated as an underdeveloped and malignant offspring of outmoded literary preaching, critical realism in the present day Serbian novel only has to find its real form. The appearance and effect of critical realism are part of the revival and creative metamorphosis of the realistic tradition in which the prolific power of faith in permanent human values is maintained as the insatiable recurrent theme. The catharsis of the novel and the change of prosaic technique, the experience of neutral temporality, and the new relationship vis-à-vis realism, sharpening the critical accent of recantation and productive skepticism — these are the key points which trace the curve of development of the most recent Serbian prose.

NOTES

1. Georg Lukács, *Die Gegenwartsbedeutung des kritischen Realismus (Današnji značaj kritičkog realizma,* Belgrade 1959; *The Meaning of Contemporary Realism,* London 1962). This paper was written immediately before the Hungarian events of 1956, but was published after them. A little later, Lukács confirmed his attitudes and to a certain extent supplemented them with his essays on the novels of Alexander Solzhenitsyn.

2. The questionnaire "Nova i stara proza" (New and Old Prose), *Književne novine,* XXIX, no. 420–423, August-September 1972. The questionnaire "Opredeljenja: oblici i mogućnosti proznog izraza" (Definitions: the Forms and Possibilities of Fiction), *Savremenik,* 33/1971, 4, pp. 304-327. "Kritički realizam" (Critical Realism), *Savremenik,* 35/1972, 6, pp. 491-530.

3. Predrag Palavestra, *Posleratna srpska književnost, 1945-1970* (Postwar Serbian Literature, 1945-1970), Belgrade, 1972. P. Palavestra, "Preobražaj kritičkog realizma" (The Transformation of Critical Realism), *Savremenik,* 27/1968, 4, pp. 348-357. P. Palavestra, "Neutralna temporalnost" (Neutral Temporality), *Politika,* August 6, 1967.

4. Lucien Goldmann, *Pour une sociologie du roman,* Ed. Gallimard, Paris 1964; *Za sociologiju romana,* Belgrade 1967; and Roger Garaudy, *D'un réalisme sans rivages,* Ed. Gallimard, Paris 1963; *O realizmu bez obala,* Zagreb 1968.

5. Joris-Karl Huysmans, *Nasuprot, Predgovor napisan dvadeset godina posle romana* (A rebours, Préface écrite vingt ans après le roman), Belgrade 1966.

6. Roger Garaudy, *D'un réalisme sans rivages,* p. 161.

7. Erih Koš, "Bojne trube i mrtvačka zvona" (Battle Trumpets and Funeral Bells), *Savremenik*, 35/1972, 6, p. 492.

8. At the VIII International Conference of Writers in Piran, 1975, Dr. Dimitrij Rupel presented a paper on the novel in which the elements of critical realism in the contemporary Slovenian novel were implicitly suggested.

9. Stefan Morawski, "Zapažanja o realizmu" (Observations on Realism), a paper at the VII International Congress for Aesthetics, Bucharest, 1972. *Književna kritika*, 3/1972, 5–6, pp. 61–74.

10. Georg Lukács, "Solženjicinovi romani I" (Solzhenitsyn's Novels I), *Izraz*, 28/1970, 12, p. 623.

11. Georg Lukács, *Današnji značaj kritičkog realizma* (The Meaning of Contemporary Realism), p. 110.

Vladimir Phillipov

EXPERIMENTATION IN PRESENT-DAY
BULGARIAN DRAMA
(BLAGA DIMITROVA'S *DR. FAUSTINA*)

The new conditions created by the 9th of September 1944 Socialist Revolution in Bulgaria, and the hopes and enthusiasm generated by it, were first expressed in the works of poets, essayists and journalists. However, it did not take dramatists long to respond to the events and the mood of the day. In April of 1945 the National Theatre in Sofia staged the play *The Struggle Continues* by Krum Kyulyavkov. If not directly related to the situation and the problems of the first months after the revolution, its theme — the antifascist struggle —and the feelings accompanying it were still very much in the air at that time. This is a theme which has preserved its attraction to this very day.

The Struggle Continues was soon followed by a number of dramatic works which were close to it in subject matter and spirit. *Reconnaissance* by Lozan Strelkov is made up of almost the same ingredients as *The Struggle Continues* but is dramatically better, with characters that are psychologically more convincingly motivated. *Alarm* by Orlin Vasilev is considered by the critics to be the best in this group of plays about the antifascist struggle.

Royal Mercy by Kamen Zidarov takes us back to the years of the First World War to dramatize the conditions which divided the nation and thus prepared the way for the final crisis.

The Struggle Continues, Reconnaissance, Alarm and *Royal Mercy* represent the first stage in the development of the post-Second-World-War Bulgarian drama, which has been described by some critics as the period of "Sturm und Drang," or the period of "the clash of ideas."

Each of these plays has certain merits, but taken as a whole they display all the weaknesses in the alphabet of dramatic criticism, the most conspicuous among them being their naïveté and tendency to reduce things to black and white.

Then there followed the years of the cult of personality in our political and social life, which were years of barrenness in literature and the arts. They produced on the stage the so-called "bezkonfliktna" (conflict-free) drama, in which the forces and values opposed were those of "good" and "better," in an atmosphere of pathos, idealization and false enthusiasm.

The historic April 1956 Plenary Session of the Bulgarian Communist Party put an end to the practices of the "cult of personality" and released the creative energies of the Bulgarian people. A resurgence was felt in every sphere of life, including literature. The poets were again the first to register the new spirit.

Feeling, perhaps, that drama gave them better and wider opportunities to express their attitude to the changes in progress than poetry did, many of them invaded the Temple of Melpomene. Poets like Ivan Peichev, Georgi Dzhagarov, Valeri Petrov, Kliment Tsachev and Ivan Radoev produced a succession of dramatic works.

The new period which they ushered in is usually described as the "poetic wave," chiefly because so many of the plays were written by poets. It not only introduced new themes and values but also a better understanding of the inner life of man and of the function of dialogue. And it infused the drama with the intensity characteristic of poetry.

It was the dramatists of the "poetic wave" who were the first to start experimenting. A typical example in this respect is *A Justinian Coin* by Ivan Radoev. This, as Radoev declares in the program for the performance, is a play "with no plot" and "no logical sequence."[1] As in modern drama, Radoev freely uses the categories of time and place, the dialogue is suggestive, and the projection of characters subjective. Its source, however, is not the modern theatre. According to Radoev himself, his intention was to create a drama "derived from the structure of a poem."[2]

One finds a similar but far more restrained attempt at creating a poetic drama in *Every Autumn Evening* by the poet Ivan Peichev. Experimental by nature are also the first plays by two other poets, *The Doors Are Closing* by Georgi Dzhagarov, and *When Roses Dance* by Valeri Petrov.

In *The Doors Are Closing* Dzhagarov blends the fervor of the publicist with the intensity of the poet within the strict rules of classical drama. *When Roses Dance,* which was a great success at the time it appeared and which has recently been revived, is a musical combining lyrical beauty with the burlesque.

Of all the plays of this period the best known is Dzhagarov's *The Public Prosecutor* which has been repeatedly described as a work directed against the cult of personality. However, as was pointed out at the time it was discussed, the play is not so much about the personality cult and its abuses as about the "ethics of the communist."[3] *The Public Prosecutor* plays on two levels, the subjective and the objective, and this has determined its composition. The first scene takes place at the office of the prosecutor. It launches an intense dramatic exchange between him and an examining magistrate, which continues in every other scene from the point where it has been left off. The intervening scenes take us to the prosecutor's family to reveal additional dimensions in the character of the hero. In this way Dzhagarov creates a play of considerable psychological depth.

The "poetic wave" which covers the period of the late fifties and the first half of the sixties represents what was new and most interesting in the field of drama. There were many other plays written and produced during that period, some of them continuing existing traditions, others departing in new directions; yet it was the works of the poets which stood out and determined the character of the dramatic scene as a whole.

Around the middle of the sixties a number of plays appeared which marked a new stage in the post-war period. This was the so-called "drama of everyday life." The plays of the "Sturm und Drang" period had centered on important historical events and on political and moral principles conceived on a large scale. The pathos of heroism, of selflessness and noble ideas determined the key in which they were written. Man in them was a cog in the mechanism of movement of events, a projection of ideas, but not an individual. The "poetic wave" then shifted the interest in the direction of the human being, but its treatment of ethical problems remained somewhat abstract. Its poetic vision left out of the picture the man in the street with his everyday problems. The awareness on the part of some authors of these inadequacies in the drama from the preceding years brought into existence "the drama of everyday life," which concentrated on the small, private problems, on emotions and reactions of the average man, its most prominent quality being the impression of authenticity and sincerity which it creates. The sensitivity and understanding with which this kind of material is treated reminds one of the school of neo-realism.

According to the Bulgarian critic L. Tenev, the drama of "everyday life" is ultimately interested in society which "in the process of self-formation clashes with the destructive or affirmative roles of the individual." In the final analysis every individual is "a projection in the light of moral and social relationships."[4] Proof of this is the fact that the plays of this kind do not only deal with the small man and what he has to cope with in a life of contradictions and difficulties, but also with a number of problems which have social relevance, such as apathy, loss of ideas, tolerance of negative values, shortcomings and abuses. One of the main objects of attack in them is philistinism and self-interest. When compared with earlier dramatic works, the plays of "everyday life" show greater interest in the inner life of man and an increased professional skill. Another positive advance is the lack of both obviousness and of the tendency to moralize and "impose prescriptions from the outside."[5]

The best known examples of the drama of "everyday life" are the works of Dragomir Asenov (*Roses for Dr. Shomov, A Saturday Night Promenade, Examinations*, etc.), Nikolai Khaitov (*On This Earth, Paths*), Lozan Strelkov (*There Are Not One Hundred Truths*), Boyan Balabanov (*The Birds Fly in Pairs, Happiness Does Not Come on Its Own*), Lada Galina (*Warm Rocks*), Emil Manov (*Bridegroom*), Georgi Svezhin (*A Neapolitan Song*). Some of the plays are concerned with the problems of youth, such as *Slap in the Face* by Kamen Zidarov and *We Do Not Believe in Storks* by Nedyalko Yordanov; others with crime, such as *Call Me Up on the Telephone . . .* by Bozhidar Bozhilov.

The interest in fact and authenticity gave rise to the so-called "documentary historical drama." The best known example of this kind is *Ivan Shishman* by Kamen Zidarov. It is a drama in verse about the tragic events before the fall of Bulgaria under Ottoman domination. A number of "documentary" plays are about the period of the Resistance. Of certain interest among them, because of its experimental character, is *A Letter* by Pancho Panchev. The play, based on an actual story, opens with the reading of letters written by political prisoners before their execution. The plot centers on a highschool teacher and one of her students who have been sentenced to death for their participation in the Resistance. They are both kept in the same cell. The girl is tormented by the fact that she knows nothing about the fate of her boyfriend. The teacher manages to establish contact with other prisoners in order to procure a fictitious letter from the young man. As it turns out, he is also in the prison and the letter the girl eventually receives is real. Along with this plot there is a second, imaginary one — the young girl's memories of the different stages of her love for the young man. They are enacted against the background of the prison cell. Each flashback is centered around the balcony scene from *Romeo and Juliet,* first presented on the plane of naive awkward amateurism, then on the level of art, and finally, in real life.

Although not accurate as regards historical fact, *The Old Man and the Arrow* by Nikola Rusev is interesting from a dramaturgical point of view. This is a play about one of the early Bulgarian khans. Its scope is wide, ranging from the grotesque to the tragic. Occasionally its style reminds one of Friedrich Dürrenmatt. The most interesting aspect of the play is the quality of the dialogue — it is in a constant whirling movement which at times sweeps across problems and events of the present, particularly when sensitive and knotty questions are concerned. The critics were divided; some hailed the play while others rejected it sternly. But whatever its shortcomings, *The Old Man and the Arrow* is an original and fascinating play.

Yet another group of dramatic works which deserve attention appeared on the stages of Bulgarian theaters at the end of the sixties. The plays of Nikolai Khaitov, mentioned earlier, continue an old tradition — that of the drama about life in the countryside. The important thing in his works, however, is not the mentality of peasants, their problems, or the colorful details of their life, but some more basic qualities of that life, presented in somewhat more ideal forms. In Khaitov's play *A Boat in the Woods* the characters exist as if it were in the world of folk tales. A step further in that direction was taken by Pancho Panchev in *A Tale about the Fur Caps.* Here the material world is present as we know it, but man is not its subject. The things of substance are dissolved in a fairy-tale-like atmosphere. This makes it possible to concentrate on some abstract values and present them in a purer form. The plot of *A Tale about the Fur Caps* concerns quadruplet brothers, each standing for certain moral principles: the first — predatory instincts, the second — deception and hypocrisy, the third — laziness and careerism, and the fourth — persistence, diligence, and love. The play represents the conflict between these human qualities in the course of life. As L. Tenev observes, *A Tale about the Fur Caps* is close to the medieval moralities which are unknown in the history of our literature.[6]

Myths are an inseparable part of the folk and fairy tales; there is always an element of the unreal and the absurd in them. That is why when *Bustle* by Yordan Radichkov — a play deeply rooted in the soil of folklore — appeared on the stage, some critics immediately declared it was an imitation of the theatre of the absurd. Indeed, the play resembles in certain respects the theatre of the absurd but the source of its technique is different. Its intentions and total effect are different too. *Bustle* is a kind of narrative drama. It consists of twelve episodes. In each of them one of the characters tells the tale of the gullible old man and the sly fox. Every time, the story is given a twist in such a way that the narrator is individualized. The central theme of the play is human stupidity. It is based upon an old Bulgarian tale, the bare outlines of which are as follows: An old man went fishing. He caught so much fish that the bottom of his cart was covered with it. The sly fox saw this and decided to trick him out of it. The fox lay down on the road along which the old man was to pass and pretended to be dead. When the old man came to the fox he got off the cart, poked the fox with his foot and, deciding it was dead, tossed it into the cart. Then he went on his way dreaming happily of how surprised his old woman would be when he brought her not only a lot of fish but a fox too, which would make a wonderful collar for her coat. In the meantime the fox threw all the fish out of the cart and disappeared.

The critics were divided in this case too. Some praised the play and others found many faults in it, complaining that it was not a drama proper, that it had no "address," i.e., that it was not clear against whom and what the criticism was directed, that it was too abstract, and so on and so forth. Some of these complaints might be valid, yet they do not invalidate Radichkov's achievement. *Bustle* is a remarkable work of art displaying great talent and rare imagination.

The brief survey so far has indicated, I hope, that at a certain point in its development Bulgarian drama started ramifying in different directions. Some critics have recently complained that it shows no progress in the seventies. Without the proper perspective it is difficult to see whether they are right or not. However, one thing is clear: drama at the present moment is characterized by multiplicity and variety.

As a concrete example of what is going on in Bulgarian theatre today I propose to examine in some detail *Dr. Faustina* by Blaga Dimitrova. This play was staged in the experimental 199 Theatre in Sofia in 1972 and had a successful run for more than three seasons.

* * *

Blaga Dimitrova was born on January 2, 1922 in the small town of Byala Slatina. Her father was a lawyer and her mother a teacher. She grew up in the ancient Bulgarian capital of Veliko Tŭrnovo. In the thirties her family moved to Sofia where Blaga Dimitrova finished high school and then obtained a degree in Bulgarian literature from the Philological Faculty of the University of Sofia. At the same time she studied with the prominent pianist Professor Andrey Stoyanov. In 1951 she successfully defended her Ph.D. thesis at the Maxim Gorky Literary Institute in Moscow.

Blaga Dimitrova published her first work in 1938 in the youth magazine *Bŭlgarska Rech* (Bulgarian Speech). Her first book of poetry appeared in 1950. Blaga Dimitrova is a versatile and productive woman of letters. She is first and foremost a poet, but she has tried her hand at and made her mark in every major field of literature, including translation. Blaga Dimitrova's writing does not possess the qualities of popular literature, yet she enjoys wide popularity in her country. Her works have been examined and evaluated by all leading Bulgarian critics and she has attracted the attention of some foreign critics as well.[7]

The admiration and enthusiasm of Blaga Dimitrova for the great Bulgarian poet Elisaveta Bagryana is a well-known fact. Something of the sensitivity and searching spirit of Bagryana represents an inseparable part of Blaga Dimitrova's own poetic nature, but on the whole she overcame Bagryana's influence quite early and struck out on a path of her own. The most obvious difference between the two is in the field of poetic technique. Blaga Dimitrova opted for a kind of poetry in which the effects of sound and rhythm are subtle, elusive and quite often startling. In this respect she is closer to the "metaphysical" trend than to the dominant Bulgarian romantic tradition. She is also related to "metaphysics" in her aptitude for unusual and unexpected metaphors and turns of speech. Her poems are imagistically sharp and both emotionally and circumstantially genuine. Blaga Dimitrova has been constantly experimenting within the poetic technique chosen by her. Her departure from the poetry of E. Bagryana is also manifested in her preference for the intellectual. The modern world, and science in particular, are the main sources of her imagery.

While one finds in E. Bagryana an exquisite expression of the emotionality of a woman who is proud, independent, and complex, one discovers in Blaga Dimitrova the subtlety of feminine psychology projected against the background of ideas and positions which are militantly feminist. Blaga Dimitrova is aware of the nature and fate of women:

A WOMAN

To be a woman is a worry.
It means:
to be a beautiful smile
in the grayness of the daily round;
constancy — against a changeable wind,
and tenderness — amidst the coarsened world;
to choose among the countless earthly roads

the most courageous one —
the reckless road of the heart,
and follow it to its very end;
to find your joy in giving joy to others;
to be a lit up window waiting in the night;
to forgive the unforgivable,
and build up life from broken pieces.

To be a woman is a responsibility.
It means:
to bear the future in your womb;
continue into a baby's cry
the long and silent kiss;
to turn your arms,
stretched out for an embrace
into a cradle for a new-born life,
to hover over it at night
bright like the star-eyed night,
to pay for every happy smile with a wrinkle
and the touch of the hoar in your hair;
to infuse your beauty, tear by tear,
into the young shoot,
leaving nothing for yourself.

To be a woman is a sacrifice.

At the same time she is engaged in a constant struggle to overcome the prejudices about women in the minds of both men and women.

However, it is not feminism that determines the character of Blaga Dimitrova's art. If one has to define its basic feature in short, I would be tempted to say that it is its spirit of restlessness and vitality. She is a writer constantly "on the road" in search of the meaning of everything — the past, the present, the future, the private and the social, events at home, events in far-off countries. The Bulgarian critic Zdravko Petrov writes the following about her:

> Intellectual routine and apathy are not characteristic of her. Her spirit is filled with enthusiasm at every historical event or meeting, be it with Sartre or L. Leonov, at every tragic impulse of the epoch. She is mentally in touch with many of our century's trends of thought and is committed to the intellectual and topical problems of our day.[8]

Blaga Dimitrova was an ardent champion of the cause of the Vietnamese people. She visited Vietnam five times during the war and wrote two books and numerous poems about it. Her only child is an adopted Vietnamese girl.

One of the important developments of Blaga Dimitrova as an artist in the sixties was her concentration on herself, the quest for identity amidst the complexities of the surrounding world. This found expression in two semi-autobiographical novels. The title of the first one, *Journey to Oneself,* "is not only a thematic indication, but a complete metaphor of her poetic world, which is aware of the necessity of reconsidering trends and finding new bearings."[9] With its unusual form and approach, the second one, *Avalanche,* is also an expression of her artistic search for new techniques. Not surprisingly, it provoked arguments, objections, and rejections among the critics. The sixties also saw the appearance of exquisite love lyrics in which Blaga Dimitrova managed to preserve the individuality of her talent. The seventies brought yet new developments. Blaga Dimitrova had had some experience as a scriptwriter — she was the author of the scenario of the film *Sidetrack,* made after her novel of the same name, and now she entered the field of drama. The first play she wrote was *Dr. Faustina.*

A few years ago a serious operation brought Blaga Dimitrova to the brink of death. The poetry which appeared later introduced the sense of the tragic in her art. But this was a feeling which arose out of love for life and not from despair of it.

Blaga Dimitrova is, under a fictitious name, the main character of "The Bulgarian Poetess," a short story by John Updike. In this connection the Bulgarian critic quoted earlier writes the following:

> In this short story he [*i.e. J. Updike*] has drawn her portrait very successfully and in relief, not only her outer traits, but also the inner dimensions have been grasped. It is even strange that so many things were discovered by Updike at first sight; of course, all the risks borne by a flash of insight and revelation are present here. But unfortunately, this was done by an astute foreigner and not by a Bulgarian writer or literary critic, for very often we look and see nothing because we are involved in the petty vanities of everyday life. It was necessary for a foreigner to immerse himself in the atmosphere for a very short time in order to draw our attention to certain things. We do not always realize what kind of people live among us, what their spiritual aspirations, their joys, and literary failures are.[10]

This might be true of writers and literary critics, but certainly not of the reading public. The reading public has for many years now been aware of the personality of Blaga Dimitrova, both of her achievements and her failures as an artist.

*   *
*

Dr. Faustina has only three characters: the protagonist, a thirty-six-year-old research astronomer, her former husband and his friend from high school. The husband and the friend are about forty years old. Both are architects. Both remain nameless. The friend, who has left the country more than twenty years before the time of the action, lives in Brazil where he has taken part in the construction of the new capital of Brasilia.

The play opens in the evening of the day on which Faustina has obtained a divorce from her husband. When the curtain rises in the dusk of the drawing room of Faustina's apartment "*two cigarettes glow, conducting a Morse-like dialogue between them.*" Faustina returns home, greeting herself with the following words: "Welcome home, free bird! " She senses the smell of cigarettes, but dismisses the possibility of anyone else being in the house: "Nonsense! From today I am the only one who has a key to the door. (*Taking a deep breath*) Only I . . . (*She sinks into herself and adds with a changed voice*) Everything is over."

There follows a soliloquy in modern free verse. In a kind of reverie Faustina speaks about what it has cost her to put an end to her former way of life, and what it means to start a new life "without holding onto someone's warm and strong hand." Coming to herself, she realizes that there are people sitting in the armchairs in two of the corners of the room. Frightened she switches on the lights, but keeps her back turned to the corners where the two men are sitting. She tells herself with an assumed tone of irony: "Come on, don't be so much of a woman to people the darkness with devils." One of the men clears his throat, Faustina freezes with fear, but she quickly gets herself under control: "I've never heard ghosts cough," she says. The husband apologizes for their having smoked in the room. To her question who they are, the friend responds: "You called us and we came . . ." Faustina plucks up courage, turns round and looks at them straight in the face. The two men relax and begin laughing. She declares firmly: "Nobody has invited you! . . . ," and then, opening the windows, she waves her hands to drive the tobacco smoke out of the room: "Come on! Prove you are real devils and smoke yourselves out of here! " The husband comments: "You cannot chase us away. Your guess was correct. We are part of you! " And the friend continues: "Sometimes the part is bigger than the whole. This is one of the laws of cosmogony, isn't it? "

It is indicated a couple of times in the course of the scene that the husband and his friend are in this case figments of Faustina's imagination, but also that they have an independent existence of their own. Having thus established the nature of the "devils," the dramatist proceeds with the business of the play.

Dr. Faustina is divided into two "parts," each consisting of two scenes of approximately equal length. The first scene is about the attempts of the devils to tempt Faustina. The husband starts by declaring: "I come from the earth . . ." Then he promises her earthly joys if she signs his contract: "I'll infuse in your blood the sap of spring and you will blossom up young and fresh . . . A magic herb will make you attractive and unequaled in beauty. You will have love, warm and passionate like the black soil. You will come to know the height and depth of exultation . . ." He also offers her material acquisitions.

The friend, on the other hand, promises Faustina something different if she chooses to sign his contract: ". . . I bring the vibrations of those distant, pulsating double stars to which you have dedicated your sleepless nights in the observatory. You will be illuminated by the finest astral emanations. You will penetrate to the very heart of the secrets of the universe . . ."

The two devils vie like petty peddlers, each convinced his "goods" are better and that Faustina would prefer them to the wares of his competitor. But Faustina declares that she wants both the terrestrial and the celestial. "The old Faustus says: 'I want the impossible!'" she tells them, "And I say: 'The impossible is the only possibility for me!'" For her the one loses its meaning without the other: "What is the earth without the sky, and the vault of stars without its support on the earth?"

The two devils finally agree provided "her payment is double." According to the contracts Faustina signs she will possess the earth and the sky for just one moment. The signing of the documents is turned into a satire on bureaucratic formalism. Faustina drinks to the spirit of adventure. The scene ends with a thunderstorm during which the two men disappear. The storm subsides into a gently ringing rain.

The second scene takes place in the part around the Sofia Observatory. It is evening. Faustina comes along one of the walkways. She has changed beyond recognition: "*Younger looking, elegantly dressed. . . . She walks gracefully.*" She is talking to herself, and her voice reveals "*an intensive inner life.*" Her situation at that moment and the problems she has to cope with are exactly defined as they are in the first scene: "Am I really going to catch a variable double star? Blasted clouds! I could not photograph it! How trying it is to depend on chance clouds. They come and go, robbing you of your stars. . . . But there are worse clouds — my colleagues behind my back. The atmosphere is charged with electricity. (*She shrugs her shoulders and her face lights up.*) They who carry a charge in themselves attract the thunders. Beastly clouds! I'll have to snatch from their claws my shivering little star."

Walking across the park Faustina realizes she is being followed. It turns out to be her former husband. In the conversation which ensues it becomes clear that he has come to ask a favor of her. He has had a telegram that his friend from Brazil is coming on a visit. Faustina cannot believe her ears, but she manages to conceal her excitement. The husband admits that in answer to his friend's letters describing staggering architectural projects, he himself described his family life in glowing colors, portraying his wife "as a typical Bulgarian," a woman of a kind he was certain his friend missed and desired. The husband asks Faustina to pretend for one evening that nothing has happened . . . "Just for one evening. The following day I'll take him in the car to the new constructions along the Black Sea and all over the country." He wants this, he says, not for his own sake but for the sake of his friend: "Just think of what it will mean to him who lives in the darkness of alienation to know that there is a hearth burning somewhere in his motherland. . ."

Meanwhile the skies have cleared and Faustina rushes back to the Observatory, in spite of the attempts of her husband to tell her something else as well. After she has left we learn from him that he wanted to tell her about the troubles in store for her at her job.

The second part of the play takes us back to Faustina's apartment. For some time the heroine is the only person on the stage. She is expecting her ex-husband to bring his friend from the airport. Faustina is dressed up for the occasion. She is visibly excited. We know from one of the remarks of her husband in the previous scene that she is somewhat in love with the man about whom she has heard so much and whom she has never met.

Faustina inspects herself in a big mirror and, probably, the subconscious realization of vanity makes her see in the looking-glass her other self. She enters into a dialogue with her "double" and in this Blaga Dimitrova dramatizes the contradictory character of her heroine.

Faustina tries to explain and justify her divided personality: "What else am I" she asks herself rhetorically "but a variable double star? How can one divide a double star into two stars, separated from each other? They will die. My fire is kept by the rotation of the two of them! "

Her double in the mirror remarks: "And that is why your light is a flickering one! "

Faustina: "I must burn so that I could live! "

Her Reflection: "Divided."

Faustina: "A unity of two! "

Bringing into balance the two opposite principles of her nature seems to be Faustina's goal and, also, her ideal of human achievement.

The two men arrive and the friend is captivated by Faustina from the very beginning. She has idealized her husband's friend and he has formed an idealized picture of her too. So they are both somewhat agitated. This is reflected in the rapid and clever exchanges between the two of them and also in the obvious desire of each to find out more about the other. When asked what she values most in man, Faustina declares: ". . . his independent thinking." In answer to his question what her goal in life is, she says:

> From star to star,
> from hazard to hazard,
> from wound to wound,
> I gather the bitter honey of knowledge.

The friend who tries to establish points of contact with her observes: "I wander around the world, and you wander around the skies."

Speaking about the fragmentation in the life to which he belongs, the friend praises the cohesion in the family of his hosts — an idea suggested by the letters of his friend and nourished by his homesickness. This forces the husband to reveal the fact that Faustina and he are divorced. The guest's behavior changes immediately. According to the stage directions ". . . *he becomes imperious and elated, the businessman in him rears his head."* There follows a discussion about "man" and "woman" and in the course of it the two men acquire Mephistophelean features for a moment. The friend proposes to Faustina. He promises her love, the opportunities to see the wide world and to work in big, modern observatories.

One of the questions raised in the course of his proposal is that of one's relatedness to one's homeland. The friend asks Faustina a question which, he says, has been haunting him all his life. "Do you think," he queries, "that one can develop one's capacities to the full on this handful of earth?" She resorts to one of the laws of astronomy to convey her feelings about it: "Every point of the globe has its advantage in studying the sky . . . And everyone has to discover this advantage for himself. We don't know this fact and we often think that the stars elsewhere are bigger and closer. My life-long aim has been to discover the exact advantage of our small point on the globe, of my small human fate." Her husband remarks that this is the only thing about which there has been full agreement between the two of them. The importance of the idea is emphasized by the fact that Faustina suddenly feels drawn back to her husband, but he fails to see the expression in her face and misses the moment. In fact, he unwittingly repels her in a violent way. He tries once more to warn her about the campaign afoot against her in the Institute for which she works, but he bungles it up by making her think that he is one of the victims of what we call espionage-mania.

Faustina has implicitly rejected the proposal of the friend and has not returned to her husband. She goes to the Observatory leaving the two men on their own.

Speaking about Faustina and drinking, the two men gradually assume the appearance and the tone of voice of the devils from the first scene. The stage directions read: "*The lights slowly fade away. There are the shadows of two devils on the wall, their heads leaning toward each other conspiratorially."*

The last scene opens in the dusk of early dawn. "*The glowing tips of two cigarettes are conducting a Morse-like dialogue."* Again Faustina returns home and greets herself with, "Good morning, free bird." She sounds exhausted. Again she senses the smoke of cigarettes and she asks, this time without a trace of fear: "Who is it this time?" The answer is: "Us, the two grimymousy-grey ones! (*They flip their lapels to reveal their badges)."* In the conversation which ensues the two men remind one of police agents.

Faustina: I've been waiting for you. Where have you been all this time?
Friend: We have been collecting information about you.
Husband: Material against you.

The devils declare that the hour of reckoning has come. They make her read an article in one of the daily papers in which she is being attacked. It has turned out that someone else, "a man," her husband stresses, has discovered and described before her the double star which has been the object of her studies, and that his calculations are more accurate too. And now, as the friend observes, Faustina is "pale, worn out, looking older . . ." Both men pronounce that it is impossible to have both the earth and the sky, impossible "even for a man." But Faustina does not regret her choice. She has had her "starry moment," and she would again choose the earth and the sky if she were given the chance.

The two devils try to make her despair and take her own life, but they fail. Unlike Faustus, Dr. Faustina has managed to trick her Mephistopheles. She has been promised both the celestial and the terrestrial for just one moment. Faustina is a woman and, as she claims, "a bigger devil" than her adversaries. "The science of elementary particles," she says, "proves that there is no time in the micro-world. The moment can stretch to endlessness and repeat itself to eternity. It is infinite. I signed the contracts having such a moment in mind." She still has hopes. Husband and friend paint the consequences of her situation in the blackest possible colors but she has an optimistic answer to each of their prophecies of calamity.

Faustina tells the devils to go to hell, opens the windows wide and bright light floods the room.

* * *

Basically, *Dr. Faustina* is a feminist play. In a country where the equality of women has been legally guaranteed and where there are considerable achievements in its implementation, there are still remnants of former prejudices. This is one of Blaga Dimitrova's chief concerns in the play. The treatment of the problems of the relationship between men and women, and husbands and wives varies in its manner. One finds in *Dr. Faustina* some of the trite and tiresome accusations of women against men's attitude towards them, but on the whole, there is an obvious desire for fairness.

One of the major prejudices which the dramatist denounces is that women are inferior. Both husband and friend, the one representing the East, the other the West, state emphatically that what Faustina wants to achieve is difficult even for a man. Both say that "intellectual women" attract them "in the opposite direction," as one of them puts it. And once the friend asks the insulting question, "Has a woman got anything to think about?" Blaga Dimitrova also examines the concept that women are inherently weaker and need the support of men.

However, the central purpose of *Dr. Faustina* is not so much exposing as imposing attitudes. In a way, the play is an attempt to help women overcome inhibitions and fears in themselves and thus to obtain genuine equality. This is poignantly expressed in one of Blaga Dimitrova's well-known poems which she has incorporated into the play.

A WOMAN ALONE ON THE ROAD,
this is a risk, a discomfort
in our world, still made for men.
Insulting encounters
wait in ambush for you
round every corner.
Even the streets pierce you
with curious stares.
A woman alone on the road.
Your only defense
is your defenselessness.

You did not turn any man
into an artificial limb for your support,
or into a tree trunk to lean on it,
or into a wall, to huddle
under its shelter.
You did not step on any man
as if he were a bridge or a springboard.
You took to the road on your own
to meet him as an equal,
and really love him.

It does not matter how far you go.
Whether you will fall into the mud,
or be blinded by the vast expanse,
you do not know,
and yet you plod along.
Even if they crush you on your way,
the fact that you have set out
is an achievement in itself.
A woman alone on the road.
And still you move,
and still you do not stop.

No man
can be that alone
as a woman who is alone.
In front of you the darkness
locks a door.
A woman never starts a trip
on her own at night.
The sun like a doorkeeper
unlocks the world for you at dawn.

But you walk even in the dark,
not looking nervously over your shoulder.
And each step you take
is a token of trust
in that dark man
with whom they have frightened you for years.

Your steps ring out on the stones.
A woman alone on the road.
The quietest and bravest steps
along the injured earth,
which, too,
is a woman alone on the road.

And, of course, the heroine of the play is an embodiment of a woman who has achieved genuine equality with man.

When the friend tries to win Faustina for himself, he describes her as "a free woman." She corrects him saying, "a free person." This triggers off a discussion about man in general.

According to Faustina, the concept of "human being" has for centuries been identified with "the most pronounced features of man. The time has come," she says, "for woman to contribute her share to it." She claims that man has a serious weakness: he "is proud that he can divide himself — as a scientist, he is only a scientist forgetting his private life . . . Perhaps, it is because of this that he could create the atom bomb . . . it is precisely this division which woman will overcome. She will contribute to the content of 'human being' oneness, the unity of private and social life, of the earthly and the spiritual. . ." There is something ironic in this for Faustina herself is a divided character.

Blaga Dimitrova's pro-women bias dominates her approach even when she examines wider issues. That is why Faustina is the bearer of all the qualities which the dramatist values in a human being. Her ideal is a person of self-respect and stoicism. Early in the play her heroine declares:

All my life I have tried to live
with dignity — without fear,
with silence — without whimpering,
with pain — without painkillers,
with sleeplessness — without sleeping pills,
with a smile — without a partner.
There is only one thing
I cannot do without
and that is air . . .

Faustina's most pronounced quality, however, is her adventurous spirit. She is prepared to take risks. The word "risk" (which in Bulgarian has the additional connotations of "boldness," "spirit of adventure" and "hazard") is one of the key words in the play.

One of the reasons for Faustina's alienation from her husband which resulted in their divorce was that he, who had been a man of "daring and aspiration" in his younger years, had gradually become "careful, cautious and slow in his reactions." Twice the husband reproaches Faustina that she is "extreme." Her reaction to it the first time is: "It is not the extremes which are dangerous for they give rise to extreme measures, but the half-way tactics for they give rise to half-way measures." Repeatedly Faustina speaks against stagnation, resignation, formalism, complacency, philistinism and, above all, against uniformity and lack of personality which she identifies with "greyness." "Grey" is another word used as a leitmotif in the play. The two devils often comment or respond to Faustina in chorus. When they do it for the first time she tells them: "You are nothing but ordinary blackmailers. Clichés. . . You have none of the diabolical features! Your language is uniform, an editor has cut off your tails. Have the devils been engulfed by the grey stream too?" The phrase "the grey stream" was introduced in Bulgarian a number of years ago to describe a tendency in literature to write in a pale, unimaginative way, by-passing the serious problems of life. It gained currency and was applied to various spheres of activities and problems. Its mention here gives Blaga Dimitrova the opportunity to express her opinion on it: "The secret now is to be grey! It's the same as putting on an invisible cap. Nobody notices you. The important thing is . . . to be grey! Absolutely grey. You can sneak in everywhere, and no one will throw you out . . . Grey is the best protective coloring." Later on in the same scene Faustina tells the devils: "You teach people all kinds of devilish tricks: to avoid risk, to resort to playing it safe, to insurances, indulgences, hypocrisy, dogmas and clichés . . . ." She also tells them, "All devils are afraid of freedom."

The second time when the husband accuses Faustina of being "extreme," she retorts "better extreme than average."

Husband: You always push yourself too hard . . .

Faustina: I am true to myself!

Husband: (*with malice*) Those who cannot be true to someone else always say they are true to themselves.

Faustina: (*with conviction*) You know it is very easy and convenient to be true to someone else, but it is very difficult to be true to oneself.

In addition to self-respect, stoicism, daring and integrity, the author attributes to her ideal of human being also the qualities of vitality, loyalty to high principles, and the strength to uphold them.

In the course of the play Blaga Dimitrova manages to discuss or at least touch upon a host of problems of greater or lesser importance, such as the fate of divorced women, relationships between parents and children, one's duty to one's native country, the difficulties one has to cope with when transplanted onto foreign soil, the fragmentation of Western society and the causes of alienation in it, the fashionable interest in the subconscious, professional envy, loneliness, the meaning of freedom, the tendency to look upon things in a simplistic way, narrowmindedness, presumptuousness, and others. Occasionally Blaga Dimitrova sends shafts in the direction of real or alleged abuses and shortcomings of our social system. Thus, for example, at one point the husband asks: "Who is here in his right place today?" This clearly refers to the complaint of some people that because of political considerations individuals are often appointed to positions for which they are not qualified.

Blaga Dimitrova also directs attention to the practice of some people to turn every mistake or failure into a political issue. We learn that Faustina is a rugged character, an individualist who disregards "the collective" at her Institute for which she is disliked by her colleagues. When it turns out that she has failed in her research work, she becomes the object of persecution. In connection with this one of the devils tells her: "You will be accused of ideological sabotage and of having taken a hostile class position. That is no joke . . ." Faustina's comment is: "To err is human, to persecute is diabolical."

Before the two devils disclose their proposals to Faustina in the first scene, the friend tells her to disconnect the telephone for "there are," he says, "greater devils than us." The allusion to the possibility of bugging is more than obvious here.

* * *

The terms in which *Dr. Faustina* has been discussed so far may leave one with the impression that it is simply a play of ideas. A play of ideas it is, but it is also much more than that.

Even the two nameless men who, taken together or individually, stand for certain qualities or ideas — two types of male chauvinism, conservatism, selfishness, aggressiveness and the spirit of compromise, oppression and submissiveness — even they are brought to life. But what makes the play a fullblooded work of art is its heroine.

As already pointed out, Faustina is spirited, independent, intelligent and strong. She has principles and she is prepared to make sacrifices for them. She is also a woman of charm and wit. She succeeds in making not only the stranger fall in love with her, but also her former husband and that, in her own words, is quite an achievement.

Faustina comes across as alive in the play because she is represented as a complex person. Quite obviously, for Blaga Dimitrova a free modern woman does not mean a woman who has lost her femininity. As was mentioned earlier, the scene with the mirror at the beginning of the second part dramatizes Faustina's contradictory nature. She is a serious person, but at the same time she is vain and somewhat hardheaded. She is certain of herself, but at the same time she is honest enough to recognize her vulnerability.

Seeking independence, Faustina has divorced her husband, but the very first night after her divorce she feels lonely and she conjures up the images of two men — with the one she has lived for years, and she has been attracted to the other one by what she has heard about him. They appear as her temptors. They tell her: "We are the two types of men between whom you are torn." Faustina's comment is: "I detest the theory of types as I detest the racial theory . . ." But when all is said and done the two devils are creations of her mind, and in spite of her efforts to drive them away, they stay. In fact, when they disappear for a moment in the dark corners of the rooms, she says: "Where the devil have you gone." It does not matter that irony brings the two men to her, and that in reality they prove to be the devils she takes them to be.

Faustina's essential femininity finds an eloquent expression in the second scene when she hears footsteps following her. They occasion one of her verse soliloquies which reads in part:

> . . . . . .
> And when tired of pursuing me,
> the steps fade away in the night,
> a howling sorrow
> rears its head in my bosom
> like a starving she-wolf.
> Where are the male steps behind me?
> Have I stopped attracting them?
> Have I grown old?
> Or probably I am not . . .
>
> There is a mysterious
> earthly magnetism
> in the steps of a man
> following me,
> heavy with the darkness of night,
> strange and dangerous.
> An atavistic womanly yearn
> comes to life in my blood,
> the desire to run like mad,
> but be overtaken,
> to hide in a secret place,
> but be found.
>
> . . . . . .

However, Faustina's attraction as a character is chiefly due to the versatility, intelligence and liveliness suggested by the way she speaks. Her language is that of a well-educated person, it also sparkles with ingenuity and originality. The style of the whole play is colored by it.

The qualities of Faustina's mind become apparent in a number of ways. Sometimes she uses words of her own coinage, as for example: *negostoljubiv* (literally 'non-guest-loving'), *slovoborčestvo* ('word-fighting,' *borčestvo* alone does not exist as a noun, it is derived from the adjective *borčeski*), *zvezdočet* ('star-reading' or '-counting,' *čet* being a morpheme which occurs in words like *četa* 'read,' *otčet* 'account,' etc.), *prideben* ('close-stalking') and others.

Another characteristic feature of Faustina's speech, which has the same effect, is the unexpected turn she gives to words or set expressions. The play is saturated with examples of this kind, but most prominent is the use of the word *devil* and its cognates, and of expressions containing them. Here are two of them: *govorja po čoveški* means literally 'speak in a human way' i.e. 'to speak openly,' 'in plain language.' In the first scene Faustina says, *štom s xorata ne može po čoveški — s djavolite* ('If I cannot speak with men in a human way, I'll do it with the devils'); the second example is: *i za ednata djavolska čest* ('it's a matter of a devil's honor') which is a paraphrase of *za ednata čoveška čest* ('it's a matter of human honor').

Many of the expressions of this kind are paradoxical by nature, for example, *na nas djavolite angelŭt ni e slab* (literally 'the angel of us devils is weak'), *slab mi e angelŭt* ('my angel is weak') means 'to fall in love easily,' 'to be a lady's man'; speaking to the two devils Faustina says, *da ne čue djavolŭt* ('may the devil not hear of it') which is an idiomatic expression meaning 'touch wood,' 'God forbid.'

The witty use of words and expressions, often in the form of quick repartees, lends the dialogue the quality of scintillating dynamism.

The two devils often say things which sound like an echo of something Faustina has said. Thus, for example, when she declares that if one yields to "greyness," one becomes "grey" before one has realized it and then turns into *polučovek* (i.e. 'half a man,' 'semi-human being'), the two devils respond in chorus, *poluvek* (i.e. 'half a century'), followed by a string of words beginning with *polu-* ('half-,' 'semi-') all referring to the situation of a woman at fifty. One can quote more than a score of examples of this kind. In fact, the play ends with one of them. The last two lines of Faustina's final optimistic soliloquy read,

> . . . . . .
> Onova edva dokosvane
> na Zemjata i Nebeto.
> ('That gentle touch
> between the Earth and the Sky.')

The two devils rattle out,

> Veto! Veto!
> ('Veto! Veto!')

and the curtain falls.

These verbal tricks sound automatic and obvious and differ radically from the variety and imaginative inventiveness which characterize Faustina's diction. This difference is emphasized by the witty puns which one finds in Faustina's part, such as, *Vie djavolite se boite ot boite* ('You devils are afraid of colors,' when speaking about the "greyness" they teach), *izkustveno, makar i izkusno* (i.e. 'skillful though artificial'), *vmesto tvorenija — povtorenija* ('repetitions instead of creations'), *vmesto traktati — citati* ('instead of tracts — quotations'), etc. True, a couple of times the two men come up with clever puns too, but these are the exception rather than the rule.

What has been said about the language of *Dr. Faustina* so far may lead one to the conclusion that the play is highly mannered. Fortunately, this is not the case, for its idiom is also very close to that of spoken Bulgarian. Blaga Dimitrova uses many colloquial expressions, in fact, all of those with "devil," "devilish" and so on are distinctly colloquial.

Dr. Faustina is a well structured play. The first scene is the exposition. It gradually reveals the character of the heroine, her position and mental state at the beginning of the action. The signing of the contracts with the devils serves as a kind of inception of the action. The second scene informs us about Faustina's achievements in the sphere of the celestial — she has discovered a variable double star — and prepares us for the third, central scene of the play. The rapid upward movement in the third scene leads to a climax — the two men fall in love with Faustina. For a moment she is at the top of the world. But there is no downward movement after the climax. The last scene presents Faustina after her crash. It also indicates that with the help of her strong character and high ideals she has begun the process of overcoming the consequences of the catastrophe and the play ends on an optimistic note.

Structurally, the last scene is a kind of repetition of the first one (they begin in the same way, their endings are similar; certain elements related to the devils in the first scene reappear in the last scene). In this way the play is placed in a frame.

The stage directions at the beginning of *Dr. Faustina* are as follows:

Since the heroine is an astronomer she is accompanied by light effects in the full range of the spectrum, from dark violet to scarlet, the colors shading gradually into one another.

Electronic music is heard like an echo from space, its mood corresponding to the changing tonality of the colors of the spectrum . . .

This aspect of the play, the poems in it, the echo-like repetitions of the two devils and some of their stylized poses, introduce an element of formality in it. Quite obviously, the purpose of some of them is to create an atmosphere appropriate to the Faustian theme of the work. However, the play does not sound formal either from the page or from the stage. The main reason for this is the steady current of details about everyday life in it (housing, food, clothing, travelling, business problems, etc.). This and the circumstantial realism of the play keeps it firmly anchored in reality such as we know it.

* * *

In conclusion, I would like to say that *Dr. Faustina* is an interesting dramatic work, both from the point of view of theme and artistic realization. Its success on the stage of one of the Sofia theatres is perhaps the best proof of its qualities.

NOTES

1. See Vladimir Karakashev, *Revolyuciya i Drama* (*Revolution and Drama*), Nauka i Izkustvo, Sofia, 1973, p. 86.

2. V. Karakashev, *op. cit.*, p. 89.

3. Lyubomir Tenev, *Konflikti i vreme* (*Conflicts and Times*), Bŭlgarski Pisatel, Sofia, 1972, p. 26.

4. *Op. cit.*, p. 64.

5. L. Tenev, *op. cit.*, p. 153.

6. L. Tenev, *op. cit.*, p. 110.

7. See: John Updike, *The Music School,* New York, 1966, pp. 211–213; David Schneinert, "Une femme à Sofia," *Le Thyrs,* Belgique, 1968, No. 5, 6; "Journey to Oneself," *Times Literary Supplement,* London, April 3, 1969; William Cary, *New Man or No Man,* Bolton, USA, 1969, pp. 139–151; Mateja Matejić, "Impulsi, Poesija, Blaga Dimitrova," *Books Abroad,* New York, July 1973; André Stil, "Des yeux ouverts," *L'Humanité,* August 12, 1973, p. 6; Pierre Berthier, "La bulgare et l'enfant," *La Cité,* Bruxelles, August 15, 1973.

8. "Blaga Dimitrova" in "Bulgarian Poets of Our Day," *Literary Sketches,* Sofia Press, Sofia, n.d., pp. 122–23.

9. Z. Petrov, *op. cit.*, p. 124.

10. Z. Petrov, *op. cit.*, p. 123.

Krystyna Pomorska

THE OVERCODED WORLD OF SOLZHENITSYN

Solzhenitsyn is one of the most prominent analysts of the crisis of twentieth-century civilization. Like many other critics, he points at its two world wars, systems of tyranny, systems of regimentation as the means ultimately leading to an alienation and destruction of man. He also points at artificial codes of communication as both the source and the symptom of the disaster of our time.

Characteristically enough, in each case when the decay of civilization is in the focus of criticism, it is accompanied by the complaint about improper language inherent in the decay. The thinkers and critics of this phenomenon fall into two basic categories, according to the direction of improvement they propose. There are those who want to build an entirely new language discarding an old rotten stratum, and those who wish to return to an old model which they consider spoiled by redundant and false new layers. The avant-garde artists belong to the first type. Their vision of culture is eschatological and their verdict is final. One must recreate the world. The role of culture in it should be the leading one; it will be art that should change man himself. So the entire recreation of art becomes the task of the epoch. Only then, through it, will man be really free and happy. "The third revolution," the "revolution of the spirit," professed by the Russian Futurists is the most eloquent example of these concepts. The echo of it can still be found in such a remotely avant-garde work as *Doctor Zhivago*. The formative role of art for the history of mankind is proclaimed on the first pages of the novel. According to Zhivago's uncle, Vedeniapin, it is not "a stick" that "during centuries elevated people" but "music." In the years when Pasternak was close to Mayakovsky, Malevich created the system of visual signs relevant to a new, Cosmic world outlook. Matiushin developed a method that would teach people how to grasp the *fourth dimension* as a type of vision proper for the new era. The poets — Khlebnikov, Mayakovsky, Kruchonykh, Kamensky — were busy creating a new language. This language was meant to be used not only for poetry read by the chosen and selected connoisseurs, as the Symbolists tended to think; it was supposed to supply the new Man, the inhabitant of Cosmos, with a new kind of verbal communication. Not only were phonology, lexical repertory (neologisms), and syntax thoroughly revised, but other means of expression were introduced: a symbolic usage of sound system, numbers, as well as graphic representations, illustrations, and even paper texture entered into the new, extended means of expression. "Culture" was the most positive, the great idea. Creating the new culture and destroying the old one was the pathos of the generation.

The same idea had even earlier been questioned and ultimately rejected by Tolstoy. It was not called "culture," it was "civilization." Its products were wars, along with art, and a strictly coded behavior. Long before his late period when Tolstoy discarded art altogether (in "What is Art?") and claimed that it is we who should "learn from the peasant children," and not vice versa, he pointed at all the false codes created by civilized man. The arbitrariness and artificiality of these codes ultimately turn against man himself, make him ridiculous, unhappy, cruel. The behavioral code of love, instead of bringing two people closer to each other, makes them feel uncomfortable; in fact, it makes them realize their mutual distance and alienation. "Is this stranger to become my husband?" — Natasha asks herself after Andrei proposes to her in a manner obligatory in the contemporary salons. Pierre Bezukhov is pushed automatically toward Hélène by the language pattern that he knows by heart. He proposes to her as if reciting the table of multiplication. In order to avoid this petty and ridiculous code, Levin declares love to Kitty writing the first letters of his message on the little blackboard in the drawing room. Olenin loses Maryanka because his language sounds false against the primordiality of life with which she is connected. Natural, primordial, unspoiled language and its counterpart, behavior, should be restored. Tolstoy could not find it in his own art either, for all art is a man-man code.

Similar claims concerning language were made by various poets who were directly or indirectly opposed to the avant-garde:

No zabyli my, čto osijanno
Tol'ko slovo sred' zemnyx trevog,
I v Evangelii ot Ioanna
Skazano, čto slovo èto Bog.[1]

Gumilyov thinks of a word, in its classical primordiality, as holy and powerful. Tuwim, in his various periods, when talking about the political disaster before the Second World War, suggests that a good part of it was due to the falsification of language whose meaning was manipulated by crooks and charlatans. In *Kwiaty Polskie* (*Polish Flowers*), he prays to God:

A nade wszystko słowom naszym,
Zmienionym chytrze przez krętaczy,
Jedyność przywróć i prawdziwość:
Niech "prawo" zawsze "prawo" znaczy,
A "sprawiedliwość" — "sprawiedliwość."[2]

Similar ideas are to be found in his earlier poems, e.g. "Do prostego człowieka" ("To a Simple Man").

In the first short story of Solzhenitsyn published in his native land, "Incident at Krechetovka Station," one of the protagonists becomes an unintentional victim of the other because of the new language. The member of the old intelligentsia, Tveritinov, an actor sent to the front, is not sure of the new toponymy of his country: "Stalingrad" for him is still "Caricyn." In the eyes of his interrogator, Zotov, the product of a new society, this ignorance signifies an anti-Soviet attitude. In the "Right Hand" the dying man asks the passers-by for help addressing them in the terms of the new language: "comrades." Nobody responds to his call. The only man who tries to save his dying brother calls him by the old-fashioned, good popular name: "bratok" ('little brother'). The world presented by Solzhenitsyn suffers from having rejected the "natural" system of values inherent in man for the new, overbalanced, heavily coded pattern.

In every single work Solzhenitsyn deals with the problem of some specific code which has to be deciphered and/or carefully followed — if one wants to survive. How to live within the strictly coded world is the basic question in his novels, dramas, and memoirs. Often it is also the point of suspense, the very dramatic nerve, or the structural dominant of the work. Not only does the world of Solzhenitsyn's protagonists appear as strictly coded; but the code itself is evil since it is based on false values, and also because its narrow limits exclude any chance for man to act.

The narrowness of the code results in its strong palpability; in other words, the more attention paid to the system of communication, the stronger its semiotic character. Indeed, in almost all of Solzhenitsyn's writings one notices the metalanguage of communication. The main topic of discussion is how to overcome the destructive power of the system made by man for man. The signs of the system can be either verbal or material, but they work equally in the same direction.

The basic sign system in every place of confinement is that of numbers instead of proper names, in a concentration camp as well as in a hospital. The annihilating function of such a system is that it makes people faceless and indiscernible: the prediction of Zamiatin and Orwell. To act within this sort of code is only to revolve identically to the person next to you. Solzhenitsyn often mentions the fact of "going around stamped with a number" as the most abusive part of the system. In his first camp story, *One Day in the Life of Ivan Denisovich,* the problem of numbers and names is prominently developed. The very first misfortune in the protagonist's day comes when the Tatar chief warden approaches the plank bed of Shukhov and discovers that he did not get up for the bell. Taking the worn-out cover from Shukhov's head, the chief warden shouts his *number.* Later, at any unpleasant encounter of Ivan Denisovich with the camp supervisors, either his own number or the numbers of other *zeks* ('prisoners') are shouted; e.g. in the foremen's station where the protagonist washes the floor, or during each "razvod" ('task assignment') of the brigade, or during "shmon" ('frisking, search') when the guardsmen time and again shout ritual numbers: "the first, the second, the third, the fourth . . ." Thus the numbers belong to the language of those who oppress and who try to annihilate the personality of the oppressed. In abolishing a name they take away the living essence of a human being given to him by the act of naming. For this act equals that of predication — the nucleus of creative power of language. Predicating or naming, we create the reality anew. This process becomes obvious when one observes children learning their language. This is the reason behind the Christian tradition of giving a name to a newborn connected with a holy ceremony of baptism — the creation of a new man. By the same token, each proper name — like any common name, although statistically not unique — is unique for its bearer.[3]

People, even at the lowest point in their existence, resent the exchange of names for numbers; actually they ignore it. In the camp the members of the brigade 104, where Ivan Denisovich belongs, do not simply use each other's personal names, they also observe and respect the entire hierarchy of addressing according to people's age, former or present social position, and, above all, their moral prestige in the camp. For example, Ivan Denisovich is addressed solemnly by his first name and patronymic — as the title itself indicates — not only by those lower in hierarchy than himself; even the foremen's deputy, Pavlo, calls him in this very proper way.

The numbers in the camp serve as still another aspect of communication: to make each *zek* recognizable to the supervisors from a distance, so that the prisoner dare not make a forbidden move. Therefore the campers carry their numbers printed, or rather painted with a brush, on their clothes. Moreover, they are obliged themselves to take good care of this sign so that it does not fade and is well visible. Ivan Denisovich concludes from that: "The number for our man is nothing but evil: the supervisor will notice you from a good distance, the guard will take note and mark you down; and if you do not renew your number in due time — again you yourself go to the punishment cell." These words describe the system of communication *as a trap.*

In the drama "The Love Girl and the Innocent," still another form of an evil code is in focus. Nemov, a newcomer to the camp, brings with him the "old-fashioned," the regular hierarchy of values. Here, in the place of confinement, he finds this hierarchy turned upside down: all pluses become minuses, and vice versa. Nemov has to learn a virtually *new language* — including its new vocabulary that Solzhenitsyn supplies with a special glossary to enable the reader to penetrate into the code of the camp. The basic problem underlying the entire action of the drama is Nemov's gradual *decoding* of the new code. He does not accept it — and is crushed. The opposite example is Ivan Denisovich: he knows the code, knows how to live within it — and survives. His neighbor, Buinovsky, a newcomer like Nemov, uses a regular language rather than that of the camp — and is also crushed.

One Day in the Life of Ivan Denisovich is indicative for the narrowness of the code in the camp. The signs here are of a slightly different character. They belong rather to a behavioral code than to the strict signs of immediate communication. The behavioral pattern itself is peculiar: any active participation in it, any initiative is excluded. The protagonist's existence is placed between binary possibilities patterned by the whim of either man or nature:

to go to the cold cell / to be pardoned
to be sent to hard labor / to stay at the present one
to work in the freezing cold / to be spared
to work when ill / to be admitted to the infirmary

Ivan Denisovich's role is reduced to just awaiting what happens to him within this pattern. His passive awaiting, however, has yet another side: the knowledge of how to behave. Ivan Denisovich *knows* that begging the chief warden to pardon him will not help; he does it only "out of a routine." He cannot do anything about the new, threatening order for the brigade but just wait and pray. Similarly with his health situation: he does not try to enter the infirmary by force, disputing the doctor's verdict. He *knows* the rule that the doctor himself has to obey: only two men per day can be released from work. Neither does Shukhov try to stay in the zone "at his own risk," the possibility suggested to him by the infirmary man. He would not even think about protesting against the allegedly "illegal" order of the guards that all the *zeks* take off their shirts. Shukhov *knows* that in *osoblag* ('special camp') anything is "legal" that the authorities might fancy to order. Only the newcomer, Captain Buinovsky, *does not know it*; his protest sounds naive, even ridiculous in the given context.

In the light of the above illustrations, one can say that Shukhov's *zero activity* can be presented as a *careful behavior* of *non-resistance to necessities.* These two sides of his existence find two respectively appropriate formulae in the text. Summing up his day Ivan Denisovich sees it as a series of lucky avoidances: ". . . they *didn't* put me into a cold cell, *didn't* send the brigade to the *socbytgorodok* ('the hard labor zone') . . . *didn't* catch me with a blade. . . And I *didn't* get sick." This list pertains to the zero activity syndrome. Shukhov also has a formula relating to the syndrome of careful behavior: "Scream but bend, and if you straighten out by force — you'll break yourself."

Similar to the evil of the language of numbers is the evil of the behavioral code so narrow that it leaves no room for real activity. It annihilates the personality, or kills the person. One of the optimistic sides of the one day of a camp inmate is his struggle for some margin of *his own time*. To find it is his own ingenuity, and to use it for his own benefit permits Shukhov to maintain the remnants of human dignity.

The analogical behavioral pattern is presented in Solzhenitsyn's longest novel — *The First Circle*. Here the margin for people's activity is different:

they are given binary *choices*. All the foreground protagonists — Nerzhin, Sologdin, Rubin, Prianchikov, Bobynin — are free to choose: to collaborate with the oppressive system or to be immediately sent from the luxurious Mavrino *sharashka* back to the death camp, similar or worse than that of Ivan Denisovich. The similarity to the former binary pattern resides in the fact that the second choice leads immediately to threatening death. To give a man such a choice under normal circumstances would actually be not giving him any choice at all. Here, amazingly enough, people not only consider but choose the part of impending death.

In Solzhenitsyn's prose everything is peculiar: the size of the code, the signs of the code, and the operation of the code. The narrowness of the code is the most instrumental of all. Its purpose is to force human behavior to emulate either that of an animal or a machine. The danger of such a result was revealed by two Russian writers back in the 1920s: by Zamiatin in *We,* and as was recently shown in a very precise analysis of E. Semeka[4] — by Pilniak in his *Tale of an Unextinguished Moon.* Later, Orwell showed the same in his *Animal Farm* and *1984.* The question is still timely; it is an object of experimentation and research in recent cybernetic and semiotic endeavors — the question of the twentieth century. In Solzhenitsyn's prose all the prophecies, fears, and experimentations are shown as current, flesh and blood reality. The exceptional vividness and optimism of his writings comes from the fact that the protagonists of *The First Circle, The Cancer Ward* and *Ivan Denisovich,* although living within the system coded for animals or machines, have not become either. What makes it possible is that they are aware of the evil of the system, talk about it and analyze it, and also, in their own way, fight against it. This makes them heroes of our time.

The task of not collaborating with the system forms *the signatum,* the referent of the behavioral sign in the *The First Circle,* while in *One Day* such a referent consists of the idea of not resisting to necessities by force. The very behavior of each protagonist towards this task, his own way of doing it, forms *the signans.* The ingenuity of behavioral cases is enormous. It produces the richness and/or bulk of the text. It also provides the series of suspense moments. What will be the result of a behavioral case of Nerzhin, Bobynin, Prianchikov, Ivan Denisovich? It seems that all cases of Shukhov should be predictable from the very beginning; and yet it is not so. The reader waits impatiently for the outcome of Ivan Denisovich's illness. And so does he himself: who will conquer whom, Shukhov or his fever, not high enough for him to be admitted to the infirmary? The suspense is as vivid as if there were many possibilities, and not just one of the two. How will Abakumov treat Bobynin during their face to face talk? Or, how will Nerzhin react to the short moment of the meeting with his wife? Maybe he will change his decision? All the moments of suspense are included in the *signans* itself, since they corroborate the behavioral case. So, in spite of the narrow code pattern, the system of signs can be extremely contrived. In fact, in Solzhenitsyn's prose, like in Dostoevsky's, the narrower the span of possibilities, the more dramatic the behavioral case itself.

In addition to the quantitative patterning of choices for action — the "yes" or "no" pattern — one has to think about spatial and temporal limits: the quantitative character of *chronotopos,* as Bakhtin would call it. Both space and time are extremely narrow. The compulsory confinement provides the limited space, the author's choice of few days for action the extremely short temporal limits (one day and seven days).

Chronotopos forms a *context* for the system of signs. Signs are always context-sensitive, hence the importance of the latter. A behavioral performance towards the task must be done within a certain time, strictly limited, and in an equally limited space. The shorter the time, the more dramatic a decision. The more limited a space, the more difficult the performance. In *The First Circle* the space and time are particularly played out: their boundaries are felt by everyone in the most important moments of experience. Nerzhin and Simochka have to hide their love in the booth for voice instruments; the same Nerzhin meets his wife in the screened box; their words are counted, for the time is counted. Their important communication has to be quickly and carefully calculated while the emotions involved do not permit any calculation. Bobynin and Prianchikov are shown for a while an open space, the free world, as a background for their decision during the short talk with Abakumov. In the course of this talk they have to weigh every word and sentence in order not to fail.

Tossing in such a fashion both sides of the sign — its *signatum* (the task) and its *signans* (a behavioral case), in other terms, letting his protagonists act in various ways, within the binary choices, toward the heroic, superhuman, task, and showing those who behave in an average, human way, and finally those who are not human — Solzhenitsyn unmasks false signs (evil behavior) giving to the referents their real names. This procedure equals evaluation: the restoring of the proper and universal hierarchy of values.

It is not by chance that in the most important moments of the protagonists' life they have to deal with the technical means of communication and information. *The First Circle* is actually structured around two basic acts dependent on the channel of communication: the telephone and the vocoder. Innokenty Volodin tries to communicate to Professor Dobroumov an important message on which the life of the latter depends. He decides to use the telephone as the channel for this information. At the same time the people on the other side of the life barrier, the scientists in the Mavrino Institute, the famous *sharashka* confinement, work on the vocoder that is to become a trap for Volodin's life. Difficulties involved in the usage of the telephone itself are significant enough. Not only has Innokenty to calculate which telephone to use — private, office, or the public one in the booth on the street — but the very conversation, after the contact was formally established, turns out to be impossible to carry on. Neither the addresser nor the addressee trust each other, and therefore the real, psychological contact is blocked. So the instrument which was meant to make human communication easier and more efficient turns against a man. The channel is blocked with psychological distrust and fear. In the meantime people prepare another instrument of information that in fact plays the role of an "antimissile" vis-à-vis the telephone: it will further block the contact threatening both parties with their lives in case of any message that the authorities may consider suspicious. The vocoder is giving the oppressors the information that normally can remain encoded: the identity of both parties of the channel. So people break a contact between themselves by means of highly technical instruments, thus building a trap within the system of communication.

In *The Cancer Ward,* among all the myths that Kostoglotov discloses, there is one which he attacks in the most severe way. This is the myth of roentgenology. Not only does Kostoglotov prove to the doctors and to himself that the results of the x-ray treatment are as dangerous as the illness it is supposed to cure, but his concern goes further. He feels that the x-ray machine as the system of decoding man's organism is incomplete and therefore defective and dangerous. It is so because the machine excludes man's immediate role in the process of decoding. So many times Solzhenitsyn returns to the same scene: the doctor examining a patient. This immediate contact between the two pleases him because of the professional skill and intuition, and also simply as purely human rapport. He devotes a whole chapter to this last question, presenting the old-fashioned doctor Oreshchenkov as a medical ideal. Not only can he carefully and exactly feel the whole human body, but he can also solve the most important psychological problems: fears, doubts, and misconceptions of a patient, all that spiritual ballast that is so importantly tied with physiology. Solzhenitsyn belongs to those who believe that the psychological and spiritual aspects are actually the most important for therapy. The first analogy in this respect that comes to mind is Thomas Mann: Hans Castorp becomes ill due to improper psychological entourage and attitudes; the lectures of Doctor Krokowski prove this point scientifically. The successful therapy then has to include an immediate human contact to be complete. Once a machine replaces a man, the most crucial field slips from his hands and the process of alienation cannot be stopped. The doctor does not see the patient — only his pale, defective, and incomplete reproduction. Gradually, the doctor gets carried away from the real center of attention; the patient concerns him only as the point of experimentation, as material for statistics or dissertations. The evil machine has done it all by becoming a mediator between the two people: the ill person and his helper. The contact now is defective, the channel too narrow. The message — a diagnosis — is curtailed, the addresser and addressee mutually alienated. The context, or referent — the human body — actually ceases to exist. The doctor deals only with its one-dimensional representation.

Any mechanical object is evil for Solzhenitsyn, even if its actual role should be neutral. Let us recall the thermometer in *One Day of Ivan Denisovich.* The fact that it shows only 37.2° prevents Shukhov's being accepted to the infirmary and therefore subjects him to the danger of hard labor out in the freezing cold. If the scale of the thermometer reflects the real status of the human body, then people's decision of using its indication is quite arbitrary. In one way or another a machine serves as a mediator in evil. Even more indicative is the thermometer for air temperature. It appears in the text directly after Shukhov's visit in the infirmary and so the two mechanisms are immediately confronted. Their role is identical; this time the outside temperature is not low enough for the *zeks* to stay in the zone. "It's a defective thermometer!" exclaims one of its keen observers. His conviction makes the reader think likewise about the thermometer used in the infirmary.

The man-made mechanical encoding system becomes in the hands of the same man his own enemy. Or else the code of communication is limited to such an extent that it seems to close all possibilities for man to retain his identity by free action. The world is overloaded by artificial and artificially enforced codes. Due to that the world becomes narrow, provisional, a confinement for regimented masses. And yet within these limits man emerges again as elementary, primordial, "naked" — as Gorky used to say about some existential situations of people at the lower depths. In Solzhenitsyn's lower depths the very natural man is recreated. He has to think again about the elementary things: goodness, evil, life and death. He has to build himself anew. Such is a return to nature in the twentieth century. "Les extrèmes se touchent."

NOTES

1. 'We forget that just the word is haloed / Here where earthly cares leave us perplexed / In the Gospel of St. John is written / That the word is God: that is the text.' (Translation from V. Markov and M. Sparks, *Modern Russian Poetry,* Indianopolis and New York, 1966/7, p. 247.)

2. 'And, above all, to our words / Changed cunningly by twisters, / Return their oneness and their truth: / Let "right" always mean "right" / And "justice" — "justice".'

3. Cf. S. Bulgakov, *Filosofija Imeni,* YMCA Press, Paris.

4. E. Semeka, "On Boris Pilnjak's 'The Tale of an Unextinguished Moon'," to be published in the proceedings of the *Symposium on the Structural Analysis of the Narrative Text,* New York, NYU, November 1977.

Walter Schamschula

VÁCLAV HAVEL: BETWEEN THE THEATER OF
THE ABSURD AND ENGAGED THEATER

Writers whose work has become a political issue cannot escape the maelstrom
of inadequate criticism. Their evaluation has been turned over to the non-
professionals — political correspondents, high priests of ideological systems,
friends or foes who read everything in their work except the message of
literature: the aesthetic values. Today it seems as impossible to talk about
Havel's work without mentioning his involvement in the civil rights movement in his homeland, his share in the Charta 77, his several arrests and
releases, as it would appear inappropriate to talk about Solženicyn's work
without mentioning his involuntary exile. Such biographical data are, of
course, circumstances not only of the authors' lives but also of their works. Yet
even as a literary historian one is reluctant to talk about dramatic devices,
composition of the dialogue, etc. at a time when the mere survival of one of the
most talented contemporary Czech dramatists is at stake. On the other hand,
Havel expects us to do just this and to decode his work as dramatic art in the
first place, to be his critical audience, as it appears natural in a society that
needs neither public enemies nor champions of human rights.

Following the great success of Havel's *The Garden Party* at home and
abroad in 1963 and 1964, the author was labelled a representative of the
theater of the absurd. In his first scholarly analysis of the play, Miroslav Kačer
raised the question of whether there is such a phenomenon as a theater of the
absurd specific to Eastern Europe.[1] When Kačer wrote his article, the theater
of the absurd was already well established in Poland by plays of Sławomir
Mrożek, Zbigniew Herbert, Tadeusz Różewicz et al., and in Czechoslovakia
some of Ivan Vyskočil's and Miloš Macourek's plays had been staged.

The question raised by Kačer, however, cannot be answered without a close
look at the poetic universe, the techniques of the dialogue, and all the
recurrent devices in the works of its individual representatives. My contribution is aimed at determining Václav Havel's place within the theater of the
absurd by analyzing his accessible work. My sources are the following plays:

Zahradní slavnost (*The Garden Party*), first performed December 3, 1963
at the Theater at the Balustrade in Prague.

Vyrozumění (*The Memorandum*), first performed in 1965 at the same
theater.

Ztížená možnost soustředění (*The Increased Difficulty of Understanding*),
first performed 1968 at the same theater.

Spiklenci (*The Conspirators*), written 1970, first performed in German
translation in 1974 in Baden-Baden.

Žebrácká opera (*The Beggar's Opera*), Havel's version of John Gay's play, written in 1972, performed 1976 at the Teatro Stabile in Trieste and in 1975 by a non-professional ensemble in Horní Počernice, upon which Havel's driver's license was revoked.

Horský hotel (*The Mountain Hotel*), finished in 1976, to date not performed according to Havel's data.[2]

Audience (*The Audience*), a one-act play, written 1975, first performed at the Burgtheater in Vienna.

Vernisáž (*The Varnishing Day*), a one-act play, same as above.

Anděl strážný (*The Guardian Angel*), Havel's only radio play, broadcast in March 1969 by the South German Radio (Stuttgart).[3]

If we want to determine how much Havel owes to the model of the theater of the absurd, we should first try to outline the substantial facts underlying this model.[4] The theater of the absurd, in my view, has two genetic components which determine its life as long as it persists in the way we know it from Beckett and Ionesco. One is its innovative dynamism which opposes it to the theater of the naturalist tradition. The other component is its indebtedness to the philosophy of existentialism which itself is based upon the collective experience of World Wars I and II. Hence, there is a component inherent to the dynamism of the drama itself, and a component imported from outside literature into the world of art.

As to the first, there is evidence in Ionesco's theoretical writings that the drive for innovation is one of the major forces in the genesis of the theater of the absurd.[5] Our century has eradicated taboos and traditional concepts in the arts more thoroughly than have previous millennia. The visual arts have broken with the requirement that they should reproduce or reflect a visual experience. Music has departed from harmony and theme, poetry from coherent semantic structures that are capable of conveying "meaning" of any kind. As for drama, it has done away with motivated action, the element without which playing theater earlier would have appeared senseless. The motivation (be it psychological, ethical or sociological) has been destroyed either entirely or in part, so that the remaining fragments of a "meaningful" action have lost their logic. Ionesco and Beckett criticism have used the terms "non-action" or "anti-action," that is to say that the audience is no more involved in the *déroulement* of changing human interrelations, but that it is now increasingly fascinated by the way the familiar item called action is being torn apart. The process of destruction is now being focused upon. The defamiliarizing device has become fully autonomous, whereas in the traditional theater the device had merely a subsidiary function.[6]

Let us now return to the just mentioned way of destroying the action. Both types, the total destruction and the partial one, are represented in Havel's plays. In some of the plays the annihilation of anything that seemed vital to the theater is brought to perfection, and the very identity of the acting persons is at stake, e.g. in *The Mountain Hotel.* But he also offers examples of a partial destruction of the motivation with the result that the remaining fragments of an action have turned into nonsense. Such a partial abolition of logic may be found in *The Increased Difficulty of Concentration,* where in a dialogue between Mr. and Mrs. Huml, Huml's extramarital adventures are being discussed.

> Mrs. Huml: Maybe you feel it's silly, but do you know what worries me most in such moments?
> Mr. Huml: What?
> Mrs. Huml: The idea that you may be going to bed with her.
> Mr. Huml: But you know very well that I don't often sleep with her. Where should we, after all? For the most part it ends up with kissing, caressing the breasts at the most. May I have a roll?
> Mrs. Huml: I hope you're not lying to me to make me feel better! ... By the way, it's not only for my sake — you should do it for yourself! Don't you see how it's getting worse with you? Do you still read any books at all?[7]

This dialogue is arranged in a way as to destroy the psychological continuum of the action. The fact that Mrs. Huml speaks to her husband like a mother who is concerned with the physical and mental well-being of her son rather than talking to the point, shifts the whole affair of disloyalty to a different level, makes it appear superficial.

How Havel proceeds in destroying the traditional pattern will be our concern in the major part of this paper. Let me first briefly discuss the other component of the theater of the absurd: the impact of existentialist thought (it may be too pretentious to speak of existentialist philosophy). The symbolism of human abandonment in a hostile world, man's being unsheltered ("unbehaust") and left prey to the malice of this world, enters, in some plays of the French theater of the absurd, into the idea of some prison or cage, or of a trash can in which the acting persons find themselves trapped and from which there is no escape.[8] The existentialist background of this type of theater has turned all attention to questions of existence, such as physical survival, identity, physical desires, freedom versus captivity, etc. The moral issue has lost its significance where the individual is exposed to a system of madness which is beyond human control. This would make this model of drama unfit to serve as an educational tool or to fulfill certain didactic functions which used to be associated with the traditional theater. Ionesco has made it clear that in his theater the "social content" is incidental, secondary.[9]

Yet many dramatists have found it irresistible to fill the vacuum which was left after the abolition of logic. It must be tempting to include in a drama of the absurd fragments of actions that are taken from a real society and whose essential quality is absurd. In this context, criticism of a given society and satire are either an accompanying or the central phenomenon.

Satiric aspects are by no means restricted to Havel or to the theater of the absurd in Eastern Europe. First of all, didacticism has survived in some reduced measure even in the works of Beckett, Ionesco, or Max Frisch.[10] On the other hand, a didactic function is not indispensable in East European dramas of the absurd. The Beckett type of play, with a strong existentialist component, is reflected in Zbigniew Herbert's *Drugi pokój* or Mrożek's *Striptease,* and Havel's *Horský hotel* can hardly be called a social satire. Thus the distinction between a theater of the absurd in the West and in the East by the presence or absence of a satiric or didactic component of any kind is unjustified. The only statement we can make is that the satiric component is more prominent in the East European theater of the absurd than it is in the West European.

Since the world is conceived of as a huge madhouse, a system of defunctionalized interrelations, it is obvious that the easiest access which satire could find in this type of drama is in an area where not single phenomena but entire social systems or systems of communication are satirized. In Havel's work, the mentioned destruction of motivation of action undoubtedly also reflects a perversion of the social order. But this does not fully answer the question, which of the two components is more essential to his drama: the existentialist experience of the individual or the satiric defamiliarization of social structures with at least a glimmer of hope that some of these structures could be repaired.

Let us know analyze Havel's major techniques in order to provide a broader basis for answering the central question. While discussing *The Garden Party,* Kačer introduced the notion "absurdní ozvláštnění" (the absurd defamiliarization)[11] which seems workable. Taking this notion as point of departure, I will now discuss the most prominent types of "absurd defamiliarization" in Havel's work. As far as *The Garden Party* is concerned, some of them have already been described by Kačer.[12] The list, however, has to be completed in view of the more recent plays.

One of these devices is called the GAG by Havel himself.[13] The gag, in his definition, is a sequence of two phases which, taken by themselves, do not cause any particular effect. Only in their close succession do they become efficient as a comical device. The gag has the most immediate effect, being the most concise form of defamiliarization and resembling the joke as described by Freud. "The inauguration of a monument to prosperity is not a gag. A sleeping Chaplin is not a gag. When, however, the monument to prosperity is inaugurated and, while the cloth falls, it becomes apparent that the beggar Chaplin sleeps in the arms of the statue, then this is a gag."[14]

There are, according to Kačer, several type of gags in *The Garden Party,* such as the VERBAL GAG[15] with a great variety of possibilities. There is, e.g., the word game which adds a grotesque element to the language as a communication system that has lost all meaning:

> Doležal už odešel?
> Bohužel už odešel.[16]

Another type of gag is the sudden, seemingly unmotivated transition from one language to the other, a burlesque element widely utilized in a different context, in the medieval macaronic poetry of the vagrants. In *The Garden Party*, the alternating language is sometimes Slovak. This reflects a certain everyday experience in contemporary Czechoslovakia, where Slovak has been increasingly upgraded since the end of the war. In radio and TV, Czech and Slovak broadcasts alternate without being translated. The way this bilingualism is introduced in *The Garden Party*, however, is a particular effect which cannot be translated into any foreign language. In the first act, when Amálka brings in a cablegram sent by Franta Kalabis, and reads it aloud, she pronounces the text without the palatalizations, because there are no diacritic marks in Czech cablegrams: "Mily Oldrichu, nemuzu k tobe prijit, musim dnes vecer na zahradni slavnost likvidacniho uradu,"[17] upon which Pludek continues to speak: "Neprijde! To je nas konec! Bozka, nikdo nas nema rad!"[18] The missing ř is immediately associated with Slovak, and Mrs. Pludek goes on speaking Slovak: "Neprijde on za Hugem, prijde vraj Hugo za nim."[19] Similarly, Havel handles the dialogue in the fourth act, where there are three more cablegrams and some Slovak passages, without, however, being linked to the reading of the cablegrams.

One of the longest Slovak passages climaxes in two Russian words in a set of Slovak speech fragments: "Dosvidanija, mamá — naozaj negrusti,"[20] words that are familiar to a public whose first foreign language is Russian and who in all likelihood are also familiar with Sergej Esenin's sentimental poem written before his suicide. This Russian speech fragment is another device of defamiliarization which I call the ABSURD QUOTATION. Such quotations consist only of small but characteristic fragments which are taken out of the context and inserted into another one with the effect of a rupture of style and resulting in burlesque. Another example of such a montage is a quotation from Vítězslav Nezval's "Sbohem a šáteček" in *The Garden Party*. The two lines

> It has been wonderful alas all has its end
> A kiss a handkerchief a siren a ship bell[21]

are inserted into one of the climaxes in the system of emotionalized nonsense phrases.

In this connection, two more structural elements should be mentioned. One of them has been identified by Kačer as a parody of the proverb.[22] It could also be called a PSEUDOPROVERB. The other one is a PARODY OF THE RHETORICAL STYLE of official propaganda machineries, like: "Život je boj a ty jsi pes!

Vlastně Čech. Nezahyneš-li, nezahynu — zradíš-li, zradíš — budou-li, budem! jsi můj syn!"[23] It should be noted that the breach of syntactic parallelism intentionally mystifies the semantic structure of the reply. The pathetic phrase has become meaningless, and the nonsense is all the more obvious, the more the pretentious form of the phrase has raised high expectations.

The pseudoproverb keeps to the dualistic structure of the genuine popular proverb, e.g., "kdo se hádá o komáří řešeto, nemůže tančit s kozou u Podmokel."[24] This pseudoproverb not only reproduces the dual structure of the original proverb, but also a certain earthly concreteness of images and names that characterizes the Czech popular proverb, e.g., in the following: "Rač by s kozou tancoval, nežli co dal,"[25] to which Havel may be referring. The essence of Havel's pseudoproverbs is that while their structure promises profound wisdom, the promise, however, remains unfulfilled.

Word gags are sometimes a PLAY WITH SYNTACTIC STRUCTURES:

Hugo: Tak co, kocoure, jak se máme? Co děláme?
Director: Ale to víme! Žijeme — zahajujeme — kocoure —
Hugo: To je pravda, že žijeme, jen žijeme! (pause)
Director: Tak říkajíc — jak začneme?
Hugo: Notak to záleží — tak říkajíc — na nás, ne?[26]

The condescending address in the first person plural is carried on for about a page without the original condescending intention and is thus forming a defamiliarization of its own.[27]

Besides the verbal gag, the author also works with MIMETIC DEVICES. Wordless action, a traditional element of the burlesque, farcical theater, with a climax in the silent film and contemporary pantomime, has also been utilized in the theater of the absurd. Beckett's *Acte sans paroles* (1957) is a one-act play without any use of verbal language. In Havel's plays, pantomimic action is sometimes the continuation of the spoken theatrical dialogue. In Act III of *The Garden Party,* the secretary performs her act of liquidation first by registering, then by putting the registered documents into the wastepaper basket, thereafter by undressing the director and throwing his articles into the basket until he remains in his underwear.[28] In *The Audience,* drinking beer is an important means of characterizing the two *dramatis personae.* The brewer drinks beer at short intervals and urges the writer Vaněk to join him who, as an intellectual, does not like beer and only sips at the glass. Repeatedly — this is one of the recurrent elements — the brewer goes to the men's room and returns, buttoning his fly. At the time of his absence, Vaněk pours the contents of his glass into the glass of the brewer. Mimetic action has thus become a substantial part of the play and underlies the principles of defamiliarization.

The devices listed above are also procedures of the traditional burlesque theater and not necessarily an innovation of the theater of the absurd or of Václav Havel. What is new about them is that they are employed within the context of the absurd, adding to the overall idea of a world absorbed in senselessness. This context, however, is created by components of greater capacity than the listed burlesque devices: by the arrangements of larger units of the dialogue and the abolition of a semantic continuum. In this respect Havel appears to be very innovative and original.

Perhaps the most unmistakable trademark of the theater of the absurd is the abolition of those components that seemed to be essential to the theater: identity of characters, integrity and dramatism of action, and everything that comes with it.

Perhaps the most complex topic for an analyst of Havel's plays will be the question of identity of characters. There is no guarantee in his dramatic work that a person stays what he is throughout the entire play. Roles are interchangeable. A dialogue may be reversed in the sense that what had been said by person A and answered by person B is later said by person B and answered by person A. This already occurs in *The Garden Party* and becomes one of the prominent techniques in *The Mountain Hotel*. Havel himself refers to this procedure in his epilogue to the 1977 edition of his recent plays: "In all my former theatrical plays, I used more or less structural and time-dimensional tricks as there are refrains, modified, exchanged or contravening dialogues, muddled up replies, time cuts, etc., yet always only as auxiliary devices serving a particular subject; here [in *The Mountain Hotel*, W. S.] I have tried to give these procedures autonomy, make them themselves the subject, so to speak, and try out, how much they are capable — taken for themselves — to form meanings. (The theme of dissolution of the human identity and of existential schizophrenia naturally reappears here — but only inasmuch as these autonomized procedures can carry it: e.g., in the shape of unmotivated metamorphoses of one person into another.)"[29]

In *Horský hotel* which contains the most consistent use of this technique, a stereotyped set of absurd actions is passed on from one person to the other. It is, however, quite sizable in two other pieces also, *The Beggar's Opera* and *The Conspirators,* plays with a relatively traditional structure of action.

Besides the destruction of identity, there is another indicator of the loss of traditional action and its replacement by "how the destruction is done," namely the device called by Havel himself the RECURRENCE OF THE FRAGMENTS OF THE DIALOGUE, or REFRAINS; e.g., in *The Audience*:

Vaněk: Mister brewer —
Brewer: What's the matter?
Vaněk: I must go —
Brewer: Where should you go?
Vaněk: They will miss me in the cellar —
Brewer: They'll get along without you! There is, after all, Šerkézy![30]

Recurrence of fragments of the dialogue in either the same wording or in a slightly modified version is certainly not an element that can increase the drama of action. It can either retard the action or nullify its progress by always returning to the point of departure like in the myth of Sisyphus which has been correctly identified by Albert Camus as the myth of absurdity. Yet the recurrence of certain textual parts is not only a destructive tool. It may also help to bring into focus and thus to defamiliarize certain trivial or hollow phrases. A phrase which is repeated often enough in different situations does not need any further device of defamiliarization to become fully exposed.

Besides the recurrence of textual passages, Havel likes to make use of a CYCLICAL STRUCTURE of his theatrical pieces. In some of his plays, furthermore, a decisive breakthrough or solution is avoided by a reentry into the action from the very beginning. This is the case in *The Memorandum, The Conspirators, The Audience* and *The Varnishing Day* where the end marks a new start from the very beginning, which produces an impression of relativity and futility. Everything appears useless like the actions of Sisyphus who never reaches the top of the hill with his rock. The cyclical order of many of Havel's plays, of course, speaks much in favor of a more profound involvement of the philosophy of existentialism in his work.

There are, on the other hand, instances when Havel's plays result in a genuinely dramatic outcome, like in *The Guardian Angel,* where Machoň succeeds in cutting Vavák's ears. This type of a climaxing end of a drama is the alternative offered by some pieces of the theater of the absurd: a cruelty which is neither psychologically nor logically motivated and appears as senseless as the cyclical replay of the action. It therefore misses to produce the effect of the classical tragedy: identification of the audience with the heroes and shared grief. Examples in the French theater are Ionesco's *Le tableau,* where actors are shot with a pistol to make them change their identity, or Beckett's *Fin de partie,* where Nell and Nagg are caged in a trash can in order to rot and perish.

In connection with the recurrence of elements of the dialogue, we should also mention a particular effect which has been recognized and named by Jiří Voskovec in his preface to the 1977 edition of Havel's plays. He calls this device "havlovská spirála," the HAVEL SPIRAL: "It is a movement, a whirlpool of nonsense, a puzzled, accelerating, verbal and acted gallop of emptiness and futility by which, with certain modifications, the three mentioned plays [i.e., *Horský hotel, Audience* and *Vernisáž,* W. S.] end."[31] The best example of a Havel spiral may be found in *The Increased Difficulty of Concentration:* certain recurrent replicas tend to be repeated more often and at an increased pace until all of them, like an avalanche, burst upon the scene. Nonsense turns into madness, the nightmare has become a menacing reality, and the listener as the addressee of the performance has joined the author in this existential tarantella.

Let us now raise the question whether Havel has shown a development in the sense that, as a result of changes in the political situation in his country and in his personal life, some of his positions have been abandoned or modified. This is a legitimate question since the author himself has declared that the year

1968 marks a turning point in his career as a writer. After that year he found himself deprived of the possibility of being staged or printed in Czechoslovakia. Performances abroad could not be of any help since Havel was used to writing for a very specific public, the audience of the Theater at the Balustrade.[32] So he had to rethink and reconsider his way of writing plays, and he underwent a crisis of creativity to which, by the way, Věra and Michál in *The Varnishing Day* are referring when they talk about Bedřich's intention to take a job in a brewery:

Věra: Listen, did you not, by any chance, go there in order to have an excuse for yourself that you do not write?

Bedřich: Certainly not —

Michál: And why do you in fact write so little? Do you have some kind of trouble? Or are you perhaps in some sort of crisis?

Bedřich: It is difficult to say — these times, all that — one has such a feeling of uselessness.[33]

Havel tried to overcome the crisis by experimenting and searching for new means of expression. The question is, however, whether there is a fundamental shift from one position to another, from the critical period of his early plays to a more or less didactic or satiric drama. The first effect of the political changes was the creation of *The Conspirators,* where he translates the history of the communist road to power in Czechoslovakia into a permanent nonaction. The form is cyclical, there is a constant exchange of characters and roles, complete promiscuity of sexes (which is one of the expressions of the loss of action). At the end, the revolution stands where it stood at the beginning.

The Beggar's Opera is a unique piece in Havel's work insofar as it is the only paraphrase and remake of a well-established theatrical play, and as such it is limited by the structure of the original work in its possibilities of conveying a message to the audience. Nevertheless, there is a pessimistic view on the political forces acting within the state. Organized crime and the establishment are working together, the political institutions are corrupted by their affiliation with crime, and the criminals are upgraded and almost made honest citizens by police tolerance.

After *The Beggar's Opera* follows the least political of all of Havel's plays, *The Mountain Hotel.* It is the piece where the experiment has become the subject, where the exchange of characters and roles is made a system. Although there is an autobiographical type, Dr. Josef Kubík, and some reference to Havel's situation, his attributes, his character, and his situation are passed on to different persons, and the name Dr. Josef Kubík has become nothing more than the carrier of different stereotyped personalities. The mountain hotel where the play is located, is one of the "windowless cages," Thomas Mann's Magic Mountain turned into a madhouse with no escape.

After *The Mountain Hotel,* the two one-act plays *The Audience* and *The*

Varnishing Day, the most successful pieces of the second period of Havel's creativity, show a return to a reproduction of real circumstances, and this reproduction is more realistic than anything in Havel's work. There is no "exorcism of history" as in *The Mountain Hotel,* but the historical — for the most part autobiographical — details do not create a system of logical motivations of action. The cyclical structure of the plays prevents them from becoming semantically valid in an unequivocal way. On the surface, these plays are satires of certain aspects of contemporary Czech society. Underneath, however, the secret police in *The Audience* and the conformist couple in *The Varnishing Day* are becoming symbols of the uncontrollable menace of absurdity.

In terms of the employment of certain techniques and procedures, the second part of Havel's creative career shows more of an evolution than the first. He is indeed experimenting; his experiments, however, do not aim in one specific direction. But still, there is a common denominator: Havel has concentrated his devices, limited himself to a handful of tricks. While *The Garden Party* was a firework of gags and punch-lines, the reduction of devices in the later period has created a more somber and depressing atmosphere. *The Mountain Hotel* is no exception from this rule: there is an expression of anguish in the piece, of erosion of human values, a destructive force which is translucent through the entire mechanism of the experimental theater. It is not by accident that the most threatening image of anxiety, the Havel spiral, occurs in the last three pieces.

As to the intensity of disintegrating action, the plays of the second period show a variety of possibilities. *The Mountain Hotel* offers a maximum, the two one-act plays a minimum, of destructive techniques. Yet the destructive elements are there and forceful enough to short-circuit the fragments of an action which reflect the social reality around the author.

Since Havel's entire work shows consistency in its subordination under the principles of the theater of the absurd, the question remains to be answered whether this theater employs the model of the absurd in order to satirize the society in which the author lives or whether the defamiliarization of concrete circumstances of that social life serves to unveil something more profound and essential: the helplessness of a thinking individual in face of a mechanism of power which is universal. By formulating this question, I suppose I have already answered it: Havel's plays increasingly reflect a universal nightmare. An unfulfilled dream has turned into an evil one. If there is any indicator to prove this statement, it is the success of Havel's plays on the stages of the Western world. Could audiences in the West be touched and affected by a social satire of a civilization which is not their own? Certainly not — unless there were something more substantial to it, something that speaks to the heart of human beings in the East as well as the West.[34]

NOTES

1. "K významové výstavbě dramatické grotesky," *Struktura a smysl literárního díla*, ed. by M. Jankovič et al., Praha, 1966, pp. 215–228.

2. Václav Havel, *Hry 1970–1976*, Toronto, 1977, p. 309.

3. I am indebted to Radio Stuttgart for communicating to me the manuscript of the play. In the meantime another radio play, *Protest*, was broadcast by German radio stations (1979).

4. The most comprehensive study on the subject is Martin Esslin, *The Theatre of the Absurd*, rev. ed., Garden City, N.Y., 1969. Also in German, Martin Esslin, *Das Theater des Absurden*, Hamburg, 1965. In my outline I am not concerned with the antecedents of this model, e.g., Alfred Jarry or the theater of Dadaism, but with the fact that there has been a historical situation in which these antecedents have been revitalized and integrated into the context of the theater of the absurd. For further details on absurd fiction in the Slavic world, cf. William B. Edgerton, "Cosmic Farce or Transcendental Vision: Modern Manifestations of the Absurd in Slavic and Non-Slavic Literature," *American Contributions to the Seventh International Congress of Slavists, Warsaw, August 21–27, 1973*, vol. II, The Hague, 1973, pp. 119–146.

5. Eugène Ionesco, "Ai-je fait de l'anti-théatre?" *Express*, June 1, 1961.

6. I am well aware that this formula can be considered either over-simplified or overstated, yet my overstatement is intentional: I have tried to indicate and to define a process rather than an accomplished state.

7. *Ztížená možnost soustředění*, ed. Dilia, Praha, 1968, p. 15; translated by this writer.

8. Cf. Beckett's *Fin de partie*.

9. In his preface to *Le tableau*, which was first performed in 1955. Cf. also M. Benedikt and G. E. Wellwarth, *Modern French Theatre*, New York, 1964, p. 360.

10. In Max Frisch's *Biedermann und die Brandstifter* or in Edward Albee's most "absurd" play, *The American Dream*, social criticism has become quite prominent. *Biedermann* critically reflects on a particular historical event of the late 40s in Czechoslovakia: Beneš's inability to stop the seizure of power by the communists. It has also been related to the passiveness of German intellectuals in view of Hitler's road to power, or to the nuclear arms race as a constant threat to mankind. Cf. M. Esslin, *Das Theater des Absurden*, p. 213.

11. *Op. cit.*, pp. 219 ff.

12. *Ibid.* Devices listed by Kačer will be listed in the footnotes.

13. Kačer, *op. cit.*, pp. 219 ff. Cf. also Havel's article "Anatomie gagu," *Divadlo* 1963, No. 10, pp. 52 ff.

14. *Op. cit.*, p. 52.

15. Kačer, p. 224.

16. Havel, *Zahradní Slavnost*, Praha, 1964, p. 47. 'Is Doležal already gone? / Alas, he is already gone.'

17. *Op. cit.*, p. 13; 'Dear Oldřich, I cannot come, I have to go to a garden party at the Liquidation Office tonight.'

18. 'He doesn't come! Then we are finished! Božka, nobody loves us!'

19. 'He won't come for Hugo, but Hugo will come for him.'

20. *Op. cit.*, p. 47; 'Farewell, mother — do not be sad at all.'

21. *Op. cit.*, p. 14. Cf. Vítězslav Nezval, *Dílo V*, Praha, 1963, p. 190.

22. Kačer, *op. cit.*, p. 220.

23. *Zahradní slavnost*, p. 14. 'Life is a struggle, and you are a dog! actually a Czech. If you don't perish, I don't perish — if you are a traitor, you are a traitor — if they will be, we shall be! You are my son.'

24. *Ibid.*, p. 8. 'Who argues about a mosquito net cannot dance with a goat at Podmokly.'

25. Josef Dobrovský, *Českých přísloví sbírka (Spisy a projevy Josefa Dobrovského*, vol. XVII, Praha, 1963, p. 143). 'He would rather dance with a goat than give anything.'

26. *Zahradní slavnost*, p. 36. 'So what, buddy, how are we? What are we doing? — But we know that! We live — we inaugurate — buddy — That's true, that we live, just live! (pause) How shall we begin — so to speak? — Well, that depends — so to speak — on us, doesn't it?'

27. Kačer, *op. cit.*, p. 223.

28. *Ibid.*, p. 221f.

29. Havel, *Hry 1970–1976*, p. 309.

30. *Ibid.*, pp. 252, 257, 262.

31. *Ibid.*, p. 11.

32. *Ibid.*, pp. 306f.

33. *Ibid.*, p. 292.

34. Cf. Sergej Machonin's article "Hugo Pludek v západním Berlíně," *Literární noviny* 1964, No. 51–52, p. 9.

Mihai Spariosu

ORIENTALIST FICTIONS IN ELIADE'S *MAITREYI*

Mircea Eliade is widely known as an historian of religions and as an Orientalist, but his considerable literary output is virtually ignored in the West. Yet his reputation in Romania rests mainly on his fiction.

Before his self-exile in 1945, Eliade published several novels among which stand out *Isabel și Apele Diavolului* (*Isabel and the Devil's Waters*), *Maitreyi, Intoarcerea din Rai* (*Return from Eden*), *Nopți la Serampore* (*Nights at Serampore*), *Lumina ce se Stinge* (*Fading Light*), *Secretul Doctorului Honigberger* (*Doctor Honigberger's Secret*), and *Huliganii* (*The Hooligans*). He also published several remarkable shorter pieces such as "La Țigănci" ("The Gypsies"), "La Curtea lui Dionis" ("At Dionis' Court"), and "Ivan." Most of these works were well received by the Romanian public and critics.

In Paris, his home until 1957 when he came to America, Eliade found time, while engaged in his scholarly work, to write what many (including its author) consider his masterpiece, *Noaptea de Sînziene* (French title: *Forêt Interdite*, 1955). This is a two-volume sequel to *Huliganii* and is an impressive, unusual blend of socio-historical fiction and fairy tale.

Eliade's scholarly and literary pursuits are not mutually exclusive; on the contrary, they are compatible and complementary. In this he follows a long cultural tradition in Europe and, especially, Romania. In the preface to the English edition of his journal, *No Souvenirs,* he writes:

> Born in Romania near the turn of the century, I belong to a cultural tradition that does not accept the idea of any incompatibility between scientific investigation and artistic, especially literary, activity. As a matter of fact, some of the most original Romanian scholars have also been successful writers (Demetrius Cantemir, Hasdeu, Iorga), and the greatest of Romanian poets — Mihail Eminescu — was equally a philosopher and one of the most learned men of his time.[1]

And a little further Eliade discusses the relevance of his fiction to his scholarly work:

> For me, a historian of religions and an Orientalist, the writing of fiction became a fascinating experience in method. Indeed, in the same way as the writer of fiction, the historian of religions is confronted with different structures of sacred and mythical space, different qualities of time, and more specifically by a considerable number of strange, unfamiliar, and enigmatic worlds of meaning. (*N.S.* p. ix)

Indeed, it would be profitable to look at Eliade's scholarly work through his fiction and disclose the similar imaginative patterns underlying his creative and conceptual universe. Of course, there are those who would deny the "scientific" character of his work altogether, while praising its "poetic" quality.[2] And in a certain sense, these scholars are right, because there is no scientific work that will ultimately not lose its authority as practical construct, and be replaced by other such constructs. Some of these rejected scientific fictions, such as the Ptolemaic cosmos, Frazer's *The Golden Bough*, etc., are claimed by the realm of the aesthetic. In the same way, after losing its scientific authority, Eliade's work will certainly endure as a great imaginative source in Western culture.

I have chosen *Maitreyi* as the main focus of discussion in this paper for several reasons. First, this book is a good illustration of the subtle relationship between Eliade's scientific and literary work. Out of his Indian notebooks of 1928–1932 emerged several "Indian" novels including *Maitreyi* as well as his first scholarly works. Eliade himself notes this in his preface to *No Souvenirs*:

> For years my Indian notebooks and folders supplied not only the materials for two volumes consecrated to India, but they were also used in the preparation of many articles and essays and even some of my literary works. (p. ix)

Some of the same Orientalist fictions[3] have influenced both *Maitreyi* and a large section of Eliade's scholarly work.

Second, although it was first published in 1933, after Eliade's return from India, *Maitreyi* is very much part of the contemporary literary scene, because of its resurgence, with its republication in 1969, in the literary consciousness of post-war Romania. (Also, a French translation of the book, entitled *La Nuit Bengali* was published in the fifties.) It is true that, although he was on the index of banned authors until the late sixties, Eliade's novels and short fiction were circulated and read among Romanian intellectuals in pre-war or foreign editions. But for the younger "common" reader, the republication of *Maitreyi* and *Nuntă în Cer* (*Wedding in Heaven*) meant the first contact with Eliade's longer fiction. Finally, after twenty-five years of silence, Eliade's important place in modern Romanian literature was officially recognized. Thus *Maitreyi* has become a novel of the seventies, not unlike some Russian novels of the sixties (such as *The Master and Margarita*) which, although written in the twenties or the thirties, established themselves in Soviet literary consciousness only after the end of the Stalinist period. Eliade is already having an impact on contemporary Romanian literature as some recent fiction published in Romanian literary magazines clearly bear his mark.

Third, *Maitreyi* presents an interesting problem in the ontological status of literary fictions because its heroine, Maitreyi Devi, has recently published a novel entitled *It Does Not Die* (1976) in which she looks back, over a span of forty years, to the same events that are referred to in Eliade's book, and challenges their interpretation by Eliade's narrator and (according to her) *alter ego*. Indeed, on the surface *Maitreyi* is a thinly disguised "autobiographical" narrative referring to Eliade's forbidden liaison with Maitreyi Devi, the sixteen-year-old daughter of his guru, the philosopher Surendranath Das Gupta. But the "autobiographical" material is transfigured into a work of art which has little if anything to do with the "real" events that took place in Calcutta in 1930. Likewise, Maitreyi's book is an imaginative recreation of those events and has as little to do with them as Eliade's narrative does. Thus these two books which purport to "portray" the same historical "facts" but actually become independent and self-contained fictional worlds may offer good support against reflective or "mimetic" theories of literature.

On yet another level, *Maitreyi* can be seen as a neo-romantic extravaganza[4] abounding in *topoi* that have become familiar from Eliade's scholarly work: escape from "profane" into "sacred" time, "hierophanies" or the revelation of the sacred in everyday experience, nostalgia for origins or for "presence," *deus otiosus, coincidentia oppositorum,* etc.

However, in what follows I shall argue that today the book can best be read in terms of its critical presentation of its themes. All its neo-romantic *topoi* are actually undermined by the fictional form in which they are cast. This critical perspective is achieved specifically through the use of the "diary within diary" which attempts to reinforce the "confessional" form of the narrative but ends up creating the opposite effect: it exposes its fictional or illusionary character. By the end of his narrative Allan, the narrator, manages not so much to reveal as to conceal the meaning of his "confession." As in Gide's *The Immoralist* or in Ford's *The Good Soldier,* the narrator is unreliable and the reader learns the fictional "truth" not from him but *through* him.

At the beginning of his narrative, Allan starts a new notebook in which he plans to tell the story of his love for Maitreyi, the sixteen-year-old daughter of his boss and benefactor, the engineer Narendra Sen. For this purpose, he goes back to his old journal, kept during his Calcutta days, in which he had presumably recorded the day-by-day events which had led to his involvement with Maitreyi, their secret marriage, his banishment from Sen's house, his retreat to the Himalayas, his return to Calcutta and his final departure from India. But from the outset his old diary proves useless because it had failed to record events which, at the time of their occurrence, seemed insignificant but which now, at the time of their narration, appear of primary importance to the story. Indeed, the old diary failed to record the very beginning of Allan's involvement with Maitreyi, which makes it impossible for the narrator to begin his own story:

> I have hesitated for so long in front of this notebook because I haven't been able to find the precise date when I met Maitreyi. In my notes of that year I found nothing. Her name appears much later, after I had gotten out of the hospital and I had moved into Narendra Sen's house in Bhawanipore. But this took place in 1929, and I had met Maitreyi at least ten months before.

And if I somehow suffer in beginning this story, it is precisely because I do not know how to evoke her image of those days and cannot relive my wonder, the uncertainty and the confusion of the first encounters.[5]

Since Allan cannot find a beginning of his story in "recorded history" (his old diary) he *creates* this beginning and his new notebook becomes not only a commentary on his old one, but also an exercise in imagination. He in vain seeks meaning in his old diary and therefore sets out to create his own meaning. From now on he will frequently insert into his narrative excerpts from his old journal, which he will attack as falsifying "reality," i.e., the created reality of his story. But this imaginative reality itself is a falsification as it is in turn controlled by certain cultural beliefs of the narrator. Allan's narrative is built around certain Orientalist fictions operative in modern Western society and his Indian "experience" does not help him to discard these fictions but, on the contrary, to reinforce and consolidate them. His love for Maitreyi is determined by two apparently opposite attitudes, which, however, are based on the same Western cultural assumption: the "primitivism" of Oriental civilizations. One attitude, which Allan assumes in his old diary and exposes in his new one, is that of a "white father": he feels superior toward the childlike Oriental who is helpless, irrational, and irresponsible and therefore needs guidance and protection. Before getting involved with Maitreyi, Allan behaves Kipling-fashion, conscious of his "civilizing mission" in India. For instance, when he is transferred to Assam with the help of Sen, he writes:

a different India . . . was revealing itself to me then, among tribes, among people hitherto known only to ethnologists . . . I wanted to give life to these places . . . their people so cruel and so innocent. I wanted to discover their esthetics and their ethics, and I would collect stories, take pictures, sketch genealogies. The deeper I penetrated into the wilderness, the more there grew in me an unknown dignity and an unsuspected pride. I was good and righteous in the jungle, more correct and self-possessed than in the city. (p. 16)

At first Maitreyi repels Allan because of her "Indian" features. He finds her rather unattractive, "with her eyes too big and too black, with meaty, protruding lips, with her strong breasts of Bengali maiden, grown too full, like an over-ripe fruit." He likes the color of her skin, of an "uncommon brownness, as if of clay and of wax" but, predictably, he idealizes this feature rationalizing his attraction in mythological terms:

To this Harold I tried to describe — more to my elucidation than to his — Maitreyi's naked arm and the uncanniness of that dark yellow, so confusing, so unwomanlike, as if it belonged to a goddess or to an icon rather than to an Indian. (pp. 3–4)

Throughout the beginnings of this involvement racial difference controls the dialectic of attraction and repulsion in Allan's consciousness. For instance, he detects a certain kind of racial envy in Maitreyi's remarks about his white skin:

> She pronounced the word "white" with a certain envy and melancholy, with her eyes unconsciously glued to my arm, as it leaned against the table, half-naked in my work-shirt. I was both surprised and enchanted guessing her envy, but I tried in vain to continue our conversation. (p. 27)

He also relishes Maitreyi's protestations that she is less "black" than her sister, although he himself cannot "perceive any difference" between them. But his feeling of racial superiority goes beyond the color of their skin. Allan reads all kinds of anthropological signs into the games of Maitreyi and her sister. When Chabu mentions her beloved tree to which she offers her own food, Allan notes:

> I was happy and would repeat to myself: pantheism, pantheism. I thought what rare documents I had in front of me. (p. 32)

He sees Maitreyi as a primitive human being and this flatters his white male's ego:

> I did not understand her. She seemed to me like a child, a primitive. I was attracted by her words, by her incoherent thinking, by her naiveté — and for a long time, later on, I would flatter myself thinking that I was a whole man beside this barbarian. (p. 30)

The few comic scenes in the book rely on a racial type of comedy of errors, i.e., on misunderstandings which result from bringing together members of different cultures. A good example is the scene in which Allan brings Lucien, a French journalist, into Sen's house to enlighten his friend in regard to the life of upper-class women in Indian society. What follows is familiar to the English reader from Forster's *A Passage to India*:

> These three women, finding themselves before us, huddled together with the same panic-stricken eyes, and the engineer tried in vain to encourage them, to make them talk. . . . Some tea was spilt by mistake on the tray and on Lucien's trousers, and everybody hastened to his aid, the engineer lost his temper and started severely scolding his family in Bengali, while Lucien kept apologizing in French without succeeding in making himself understood. (p. 10)

After Allan falls in love with Maitreyi, he assumes the opposite Western attitude toward the Orient. Now he becomes anxious to convert to Hinduism, and to embrace what he believes are Oriental values. It is from the point of view of this "conversion" that he ridicules his "white father" postures from the old diary. When Harold, his Eurasian friend, comes to visit him at Sen's and tries to "save" him from the engineer's "clutches," Allan vehemently attacks his Eurasian prejudices, without being aware that he still shares them:

> It would be my greatest happiness to be received into their world. . . . A live
> world, with live people who suffer without complaining, who still abide by an
> ethic code, and whose women are saints, not whores like ours. . . . They are a
> dead world, our white continents. . . . If I were received into an Indian family,
> I would find the resources to rebuild my life hitherto founded on trifles,
> stupid interests, and abstractions. I would like to make a fresh start, to
> believe in something, to be happy. (p. 93)

If in the past Allan had a condescending view of Indian society, now he
idealizes it, placing within it his own Western moral utopia. He has the typical
attitude of a traveller who reads his own ideological biases into a foreign
culture. Now Maitreyi becomes for him a "passage to India" but also, by the
logic of the *coincidentia oppositorum*, an unreachable, inscrutable, and arbitrary Asian goddess. She is still a "primitive" but now this term becomes
valorized and is opposed to all that is pretense and superficiality in Western
civilization:

> I would listen to her as one listens to a fairy tale, but at the same time I felt her
> moving away from me. How complicated her soul! I understood once again
> that only we, the civilized, are simple, naive, and transparent. That these
> people whom I loved so much that I wanted to become one of them hide a
> history and a mythology impossible to penetrate, that they are rich and deep,
> complicated and incomprehensible. (p. 83)

Narendra Sen is rather suspicious of Allan's sudden "conversion" and does
not encourage him to change his religion. According to Maitreyi he has his
own plans, based on no less illusory cultural fictions: he would like to adopt
Allan as his own son and, after his retirement, live with his family in Allan's
country where "whites are good and hospitable, not like the British."

  That Allan's "new" attitude toward Maitreyi and her culture is really the old
one in its antithetical disguise becomes quite clear when, during his fits of
jealousy, Allan no longer idealizes Maitreyi's "primitivism" but on the contrary reverts to his racial distrust:

> If she had been a white woman, I wouldn't have believed all this, because
> although I knew their inconsistent substance and mad caprices, I still thought
> they were motivated by a certain pride, by a certain balance, which would
> prevent them from offering themselves to the first stranger. But I could not
> understand Maitreyi, I could not place her in a definite frame of predictable
> reactions, and it seems to me that, being so primitive and innocent, she could
> give herself to anyone, without pausing to consider the enormity of her act,
> without any sense of responsibility. (p. 108)

The progress that Allan persuades himself to have made from the old to
the new journal turns out to be a circular movement. For instance, his retreat

to the mountains and his encounter with Jenia reveal that he manages to emerge with all his Western preconceptions intact from the ordeal of his separation from Maitreyi. After Sen turns him out of his house and forbids him to contact his daughter, Allan decides to become a *Sannyasi* or a *Sadhu* (one who has renounced the world). But his retreat to the Himalayas proves to be a romantic pose, an abortive initiation rite. When he encounters Jenia, a South-African musician who has fled the Western world and has come to India "in search of the absolute," Allan despises and pities her Orientalist illusions, without fully recognizing in her his own image:

> In Jenia's head there was a muddle of inconsistent ideas, side by side with sentimental disillusions and female superstitions, (the cult of the "overman," of the "lone wolf," the isolation, the adventure, the renunciation). I was almost terrified listening to her, for since I had isolated myself I had come to follow a thought to its end, to consider an idea in all its implications and, in spite of myself, I was pained at the hybrid and incongruous substance of the mind of this young woman in search of the absolute. (p. 149)

In spite of Allan's claim that he had come a long way since his retreat, his description of Jenia's confused thinking is an accurate picture of his own ontological confusion. His "mauvaise foi" reveals itself when, for instance, he tries to rationalize his seduction of Jenia in terms of a "test": he supposedly wants to find out if his love for Maitreyi and his prolonged abstinence have dulled his senses, or, worse yet, have destroyed his "will to live" (note that he rationalizes his actions in the same pseudo-Nietzschean terms that he finds objectionable with Jenia). He pities Jenia's will to self-deception when she wants to be made love to as if she were Maitreyi, without questioning his own pitiful, "all too human" motives in performing his "experiment."

By criticizing his old journal, Allan attempts to give the illusion of having transcended not only his racial prejudices but also his fictionalization of experience which he always sees through his readings. For instance he exposes his description of the intensifying passion between Maitreyi and himself in his old diary as a fictionalization in terms of the Vaishnava mystical experience:

> (Note: In my diary of those days I was influenced by certain Vaishnava readings and I used the term "mystical" very often. In fact my comment on this event which I found in a stray notebook is pervaded throughout by "mystical experience." I was ridiculous.) (p. 68)

But this fictionalization permeates his new diary as well and it is based on the same Western cultural assumptions that were operative in his behavior toward Maitreyi and Jenia. Of course, Allan rationalizes his need to fictionalize in terms of art as recreation or reordering of events into an imaginative pattern which is more real than reality. On rereading his notes which record his stay in the mountains Allan is struck by their inability to convey his devastating grief and rejects them as irrevelant. He writes again parenthetically apropos of his old diary:

> (I am rereading today those notes written in blood and they seem to me cold and indifferent. . . . How incapable we are to render, at the time of their occurrence, the substance of an overwhelming joy or grief. I have come to believe that only memory, only distance can give them life. The diary is dry and irrelevant.) (p. 135)

Allan implies that this sort of recollection in tranquillity in which events are recreated and reordered into an ideal pattern is emancipated from history. But a second look at his narrative will reveal that his exotic love story set in India is very much historically determined by the narrator's cultural beliefs; in fact this narrative is nothing but the reenactment of a most common Christian myth: the story of the Fall of Man. Allan presents his story in such a way that we begin to see him repeating the events connected with the Fall: the sojourn in Eden (Sen's house), the temptation and fall through sex (his adventure with Maitreyi), the banishment from the garden of innocence (his forced departure from Sen's house), and the eternal misery that follows this banishment (his ordeal in the Himalayas and final departure from India). In this context, Narendra Sen becomes God the Father (Allan believes that the engineer wants him to marry his daughter when in fact he wants him to become his son and therefore Maitreyi's *brother*), Maitreyi becomes Eve or eternal temptation, while Allan himself becomes Adam who misuses God's trust and forfeits eternal bliss through sexual transgression (incest). Thus his cultural preconceptions are manifest not only at the immediate or surface level of his narrative, but also at its deep or symbolic level.

But why does Allan fictionalize events in terms of these myths? At least a partial answer may be found in his attempt to give his love story the dignity of tragedy, by implying that his separation from Maitreyi is demanded by the logic of the myth itself. But this also serves to conceal Allan's rather discreditable role in the denouement of his love affair. It is never very clear why Allan and Maitreyi cannot get married except for the arbitrary, godlike will of Narendra Sen. If, as the narrator claims, he and the girl did exchange hymenal garlands (the rite of *Gandharvavivaha*), together with other pledges, such as a wedding ring (laboriously described by the narrator), then according to Indian custom Allan could have successfully pressed his claim to Maitreyi's hand. Also, we are never told what became of Allan's plans to embrace Hinduism. The ending is a far cry from tragedy; in fact it turns into bourgeois melodrama when Allan once again reverts to his Orientalist phantasies to explain why he has given up any attempt to rejoin Maitreyi. Now in Singapore, he runs into an Indian friend who informs him that Maitreyi had caused a public scandal by giving herself to one of the servants. Allan remembers that Maitreyi had once suggested a desperate solution: if she were dishonored, then her father would be forced to turn her out of the house and she would be free to leave for Europe with Allan. At first Allan is flattered by this "barbarian" sacrifice to their love. But then he remembers a letter from one of Maitreyi's admirers which the girl for some obscure reason had given to him on her birthday and which he had only opened a few days before. From its contents Allan had inferred that Maitreyi had not been quite "faithful" to him. Allan's jealousy again takes a racial form: the girl is an unpredictable, cruel, sex-goddess who is beyond the Western moral code. The narrative ends, not unlike Gide's *The Immoralist,* on an ambiguous note. Torn between his reawakened love for Maitreyi and his cultural prejudices the narrator is thrown into a deep ontological confusion:

> I feel that she did it for me. . . .
> . . . And what if my love deceives me? Why should I believe?
> How do I know? I would like to look into Maitreyi's eyes. (p. 158)

The barrier between the two lovers is placed there not by an irate father or god, but by the narrator himself who builds it throughout his narrative out of his Orientalist fictions.

In 1976 Maitreyi Devi published her own version of this love story. Her book challenges the historical "accuracy" of many episodes in Eliade's *Maitreyi,* especially those dealing with sex. There is no secret marriage in *It Does Not Die,* nor is there any self-dishonoring sexual act, no matter how honorable its motives. Amrita, the narratrix, accuses Mircea Euclid, Maitreyi Devi's fictional character based on Eliade, of having given her up too easily and of having exaggerated the cruelty and willfulness of her father whom, however, she also judges severely. Amrita makes fun of Euclid's credulity and humorlessness: she constantly teases him about her guru, the famous poet Tagore, of whom Euclid is absurdly jealous. She laughs at his pedantry, at his habit of reading anthropological signs into her childish games. However, she acknowledges her deep emotional involvement, so deep that even after a lapse of forty years this youthful episode comes back to haunt her.

If *Maitreyi* revolves around certain Orientalist fictions, *It Does Not Die* predictably reveals certain preconceptions and simplistic generalization about the Western world. For instance, Euclid is presented as a cold-blooded, rational Westerner who spends his life (and passion) buried in books. At the end of the narrative Amrita must, both literally and symbolically, negotiate huge piles of books scattered all over Euclid's office in order to reach him. She also accuses him of "unfaithfulness," calls him a "European hunter," and charges that Westerners cannot understand pure — Platonic? — love, that for them "the fulfillment of love must be in bed." If anything, a comparison between *Maitreyi* and *It Does Not Die* will reveal an identity of human response manifested through the very wealth of economic, socio-political, or ideological difference.

One may argue that Maitreyi Devi confuses Mircea Eliade with the narrator of *Maitreyi,* or that she confuses a work of fiction with historical fact. But we must not forget that it is not Maitreyi Devi but Amrita who accuses Mircea Euclid (not Eliade) of not telling the truth or telling only "half-truths." Otherwise it would be impossible to decide who is telling the truth or even what "truth" means in this case. We have seen that Allan does not tell the "truth," but Eliade does. The latter is no more Allan or Mircea Euclid than Maitreyi Devi is Amrita or, for that matter, Allan's Maitreyi. And *It Does Not Die* is no more about the historical events (whatever they may have been) that concerned Devi and Eliade in Calcutta in 1929–30 than *Maitreyi* is. In fact, as its title indicates (it is an allusion to the śloka of the Gita which describes the immortality of the soul), *It Does Not Die* rejects these events as irrelevant to its themes. The book, which its author calls "a romance and a reminiscence" is built around the myth of the immortality of the soul and the confrontation between the atemporal and the historical results into a not uncommon fictional form. Paradoxically, *It Does Not Die* is of interest to the student of Eliade's fiction not so much because of *Maitreyi* as because of its startling structural resemblance to some of his other works, specifically to *Forêt Interdite.*[6] Just like the latter, Devi's book is built around what I shall, rather awkwardly, call a non-Aristotelian apocalyptic fictional structure.

In an Aristotelian apocalyptic fictional structure, present in tragedy, romance, and certain novels and described by Aristotle in his *Poetics,* the ending is the beginning revealed and recognized (hence the attribute of "apocalyptic").[7] Events form a causal chain and lead inexorably to an ending which has already been anticipated in the beginning (for instance, through a prophesy, vision, or dream). In a non-Aristotelian apocalyptic fictional structure the final revelation is not related to the events preceding it, but on the contrary it rejects these events as irrelevant. This kind of narrative consists of a succession of disconnected events which have no "meaning," i.e., they are not related to a whole. Its ending is calculated precisely to reveal this lack of meaning: it offers a revelation of a "reality" which is situated outside the succession of events and thus renders these events meaningless. Examples of such narratives include *Wuthering Heights, A Passage to India, The Master and Margarita.*

It is beyond the scope of this paper to look at the various narrative implications of this non-Aristotelian apocalyptic fictional structure, so I shall limit myself to signaling its presence both in *It Does Not Die* and in *Forêt Interdite.* When, in Maitreyi Devi's narrative, Amrita sees Euclid again after an interval of over forty years, although their reunion is disappointing at the "historical" level, she rejects the past and present events in favor of a mythical revelation of the future. The ending of the book is perhaps worth quoting at some length:

> Mircea raised his face. His eyes were glazed. Oh no, my worst fears are true — his eyes have turned into stone. He will never see me again. What shall I

do?... Fear changed me — I am no more Amrita. I turned into just a mortal and I thought like him — forty years, forty years! It is too late indeed.... I walked towards the door crossing over the little hillocks of books, when I heard Mircea's voice from the back, "Amrita, wait a little. Why are you breaking down now, when you were so brave for so many years. I promise you I shall come to you, and there on the shore of the Ganga, I will show you my real self."

I am not a pessimist. Inside my broken heart a tiny bird of hope was in its death throes but no sooner Mircea's words reached me, than the little bird revived and turned into a phoenix.... That huge bird flapped its great wings and then, picking me up, it rose higher and higher as the roof of Mircea's study opened like Pandora's box, and the walls disappeared — all the stony books turned into ripples — I heard the gurgle of flowing water.

That great bird, built with the illusion of hope, whispered to me, as we moved towards an unknown continent, crossing Lake Michigan, "Do not be disheartened, Amrita, you will put light in his eyes."

"When?" I asked eagerly.

"When you meet him in the Milky Way — that day is not very far now," it replied.[8]

There is in this ending a skillful interplay between the book's historical and mythical themes, with a gradual, subtle substitution of the former by the latter (even the comparison of a University office with Pandora's box has its merits in and out of this context).

The same kind of rejection of history takes place at the end of *Forêt Interdite,* where the protagonist Ştefan Viziru lives through a series of disconnected events (the rise of fascism in Romania, the war, the post-war period, the exile in France, etc.) without being able to give them any "meaning." But at the end of the book he experiences a revelation which also coincides with his physical death in a car accident. He had actually anticipated his death scene twelve years before to the day, during a walk with his life-long beloved, Ileana, in a forest outside Bucharest. Then, however, he had felt that there was a missing link in the scene: a car which was supposed, for some obscure reason, to pick them up. This car will of course be, in the completed scene, the agent of their "death-hierophany." Now, years later, Ştefan encounters Ileana again, in a forest near the Swiss border. Their reunion is at first unsuccessful because she is in love with someone else, but at the moment of the car accident they both recognize in a flash the long-forgotten scene in the Băneasa forest, and they come together again, in eternity. This "death-hierophany" or the revelation of the eternal through the repetition of a certain moment renders all the other moments in the book meaningless and irrelevant. As in *It Does Not Die,* we have a subtle manipulation of two opposed concepts of temporality, the mythical and the historical, or what Eliade calls "sacred" and "profane" time, with the latter being replaced by the former.

If, in his later fiction, Eliade resolves the conflict between history and myth in favor of the latter, the opposite may be said to be true in *Maitreyi.* Allan is caught in his Orientalist fictions which fail to yield any meaning. The technique of presentation, i.e., "the diary within a diary," allows the writer (not the narrator) to distance himself from his themes to the point where he can reject them as fictional illusion. *Maitreyi* holds a unique place in Eliade's work not because if *reflects* its main problematic, but precisely because it *refracts* it, through its self-critical perspective.

NOTES

1. Mircea Eliade, *No Souvenirs, Journal 1957–1969*, New York, 1977, p. ix.

2. See, among others, John A. Saliba, *"Homo religiosus" in Mircea Eliade*, Leiden, 1976.

3. By Orientalist fictions I understand the sum of linguistic constructs or the body of knowledge that the Western world has created about the Orient, whether these constructs are currently invested with scientific authority or not. I use the term fiction in its etymological sense of imaginative or linguistic construct (from the Latin *fingere* 'to make,' but also 'to construe').

4. This is more or less Dumitru Micu's view in his rather superficial introductory study to the 1969 Romanian edition of *Maitreyi* and *Nuntă în Cer.*

5. Mircea Eliade, *Maitreyi și Nuntă în Cer*, București, 1969. I shall use this edition for my own English translation which shall include the page numbers in the text.

6. The resemblance is all the more striking because Maitreyi Devi could not have read Eliade's major fiction which so far has not been available in English. *Maitreyi* was brought to her attention by friends who informed her of its contents. An English translation of *Forêt Interdite* is scheduled to come out in the spring of 1978 with Notre Dame University Press.

7. For a related discussion of apocalyptic fictions, see Frank Kermode, *The Sense of an Ending*, New York, 1967.

8. Maitreyi Devi, *It Does Not Die*, Calcutta, 1976, p. 269. The book first appeared in Bengali in 1974.

Halina Stephan

THE CHANGING PROTAGONIST IN
SOVIET SCIENCE FICTION

I. Science Fiction in Soviet Literature

Since the late 1950s, *naučnaja fantastika,* a Russian version of science fiction, has enjoyed a great resurgence of popularity.[1] Thematically, such literature has a natural connection to *naučno-texničeskaja revoljucija* (NTR) which is currently the most popular topic of cultural debates, and, at the same time, it is exempt from the realistic rules which confine the mainstream literature.[2]

Science fiction's interest in the future and in the New Man revives the tradition of revolutionary romanticism of the 1920s, its initial heyday.[3] At that time, the combination of a belief in the communist utopia, a constructivist fascination with technology, and a literary preoccupation with popular, plot-oriented prose accounted for the appeal of the genre. With the decline of the revolutionary pathos, the changing political climate, marked eventually by the turn to socialist realism, led to the demise of the fantastic and the development of *fantastika bližnego pricela,* a literature devoted to immediate socio-economic objectives. It was only in 1957, with the appearance of Ivan Efremov's utopian novel, *Tumannost' Andromedy,* that Soviet science fiction emerged from its decline. The revival coincided with the appearance of the Sputnik, the first great achievement of space exploration. The cosmos became an extension of everyday reality, and the scientist appeared as a high priest ushering in the utopian future. A romantic faith in the unlimited possibilities of science created a peculiar neo-technicism which manifested itself in the belief that all social problems were imminently solvable with the help of appropriate technological inventions. The communist utopia seemed within reach.

The proceedings of the XX Congress of the CPSU reinforced such expectations by opening the question of the communist future and the characteristics of the New Man. In this context, *naučnaja fantastika* found its mission in popularizing space exploits and introducing the reader to the scientific milieu. The notion of science as a panacea for all the ills of mankind led to an emphasis on the didactic potential of *naučnaja fantastika.* It opened to the reader a new world which held the promise of utopia and the possibility of modes of existence entirely different from the earthly pattern. Seen pragmatically, it also prepared the audience for the changes wrought by the ongoing *naučno-texničeskaja revoljucija* and even could help attract promising youth into the world of science.

The belief that scientific research is a supreme activity and that technological progress alone determines the development of mankind not only put pragmatic obligations on *naučnaja fantastika,* but also cast doubts on the function of the mainstream literature. In 1959, it finally led to the famous debate between the *fiziki* and *liriki* which began from the objections that literature had lost all meaning for modern man. The discussion then focused on the need to update both the form and content of literature in accordance with the modern experience. Some writers, like Vladimir Solouxin, entirely denied that progress in science and technology had any impact on art. In general, however, the question revolved around the kind and extent of such an impact. Obviously, science and technology could not replace the esthetic and ethical function of literature. In fact, they created new problems with moral dimensions to which literature could specifically address itself.[4] Despite the development in recent years of the so-called NTR style in literature,[5] fictional writing increasingly began to act as a counteragent to the technologization of life. It consciously stressed individual emotions, nature, and ethical authenticity. Correspondingly, NTR stopped being viewed as a determining agent, but began to be recognized as just one aspect of historical progress.[6]

It was only natural that while the mainstream literature was criticized for its inadequate response to modernization, *naučnaja fantastika* came to be regarded as a literary companion to NTR. Its proponents believed that by bringing together the essentially antagonistic realms of science and humanities, *naučnaja fantastika* could succeed in forming a paradoxical unity which was a quintessence of modern cultural experience.[7] The most interesting science fiction freed itself from direct subservience to science and found specific literary opportunities in "modeling," an approach borrowed from new research methods in the social sciences.[8] Since modern culture creates problems and opens speculations beyond the boundaries of the customary realistic setting, some issues can only be analyzed within hypothetical worlds. In these postulated settings, problems can be presented in a pure form, unobscured by realistic associations. Here, the protagonists can replay the essential theme of *naučnaja fantastika,* the confrontation of man with the unknown. This confrontation serves to enrich man's knowledge of himself and in that sense conforms to the broad concept of realism.

In recent years, Soviet science fiction has grown away from technologically oriented stories with semi-scientific adventure plots in favor of *social'naja fantastika* which creates hypothetical worlds in order to explore variations in the psychological and ethical aspects of human personality.[9] Within such fantastic settings recognizable elements from the present appear in an estranged form to produce a new, critical perspective.[10] While in earlier fiction the narrative focus was on the model itself, it is now increasingly directed to the figure of the protagonist. The initial positive figure of the hero-explorer is often replaced by an alienated individual whose inflexible emotional framework becomes a dissonant factor in the technologized and bureaucratized world.

This change is particularly visible in the work of the most popular Soviet science fiction writers, Arkadij and Boris Strugackij. The Strugackijs regard themselves as authors of *fantastika* rather than *naučnaja fantastika* and seek legitimization of their writing as part of the mainstream literature.[11] They insist on literary quality as a primary criterion equally applicable to science fiction. In this way they echo the position of Sinjavskij, who sets the same values for *naučnaja fantastika* as he does for traditional fictional writing.[12] Although the Strugackijs' early stories describe space exploits, they reject scientific authenticity as a necessary feature of science fiction. Science and technology supply them with plot devices, such as interplanetary communications and space flights, but these remain either extrinsic to the central conflicts, or serve to create a contrasting background for the emotional and ethical aspects of the hero's personality. This does not mean that such literature discards the illusion of scientific credibility. With the exception of explicitly satirical works which stress the fantastic, the illusion of the existence of hypothetical worlds is supported by the narrator's point of view which is consistently rationalistic. Additionally, in order to reinforce credibility, the narrator himself is often a scientist or a professional with an essentially scientific world view.

Although the Strugackijs sought recognition within the mainstream of literature as early as 1964, it has been only recently that critics in both the West and in the Soviet Union have begun to recognize the kinship of science fiction and the literary tradition of the fantastic. Increasingly, critical studies seek to create a poetics of science fiction, to submit such writing to literary criteria, and to classify it according to the categories of the fantastic.[13] To be sure, the stigma of trivial literature accounts for the fact that such studies are still in the embryonic stage. Yet in terms of its popular appeal, science fiction has begun to play the role of a modern myth — the folktale of the techno-electronic age.[14]

In the Soviet Union, a certain rapprochement between *naučnaja fantastika* and the mainstream literature became a possibility on the thematic level with the opening of the debates about the impact of technological progress on form and content in literature. Since NTR has remained a favorite subject of cultural discussions over the last two decades, this preoccupation has also put science fiction in the literary spotlight. *Naučnaja fantastika* may still appear in juvenile or educational publishing houses,[15] but it is also discussed in *Literaturnaja gazeta, Voprosy literatury,* and *Voprosy filosofii.* The number of critical studies published recently in the Soviet Union and the West testify to its growing prestige.[16]

Unlike Western science fiction, *naučnaja fantastika* has never been regarded as trivial literature,[17] but its seemingly scientific character, alleged educational purpose, and popular appeal have traditionally put it outside of belles-lettres.[18] At the same time, this peripheral status has evolved into a blessing. Together with the literary license of science fiction it could allow devices like the parable, the allegory, and the grotesque which were disfavored in the mainstream literature. Political and ethical issues which were otherwise taboo could be verbalized within the fantastic worlds of science fiction. Most recently, this literature has been specifically gaining recognition as a medium for reflecting the complex effects and perspectives of modernization.

II. The Protagonist

Science fiction can also succeed where Soviet mainstream literature traditionally failed: in developing the figure of the protagonist. In general, the vestiges of socialist realism in mainstream prose set limits to psychological authenticity and the type of experiences which a literary protagonist can undergo. Science fiction, which offers alternate visions of the existent world, expands the notion of reality and can confront the hero with hypothetical, highly charged situations which demand an unequivocal ethical response. Not without reason did a Soviet critic see in the protagonist of science fiction a resemblance to the Dostoevskian *geroj-ideja* who personifies a complex of moral issues and exists only in the dimensions of this complex.[19] On the one hand, it is a characteristic feature of science fiction that the characters are types rather than individuals. Yet, the same lack of individuality detrimental to realistic literature here becomes functional in terms of both content and structure. Within the content of a story, lack of individuality is motivated by the fact that the standardized, rational world of the future cannot accommodate colorful individualists. An adherence to individuality represents a regression — a rejection of the idea of progress. It has been pointed out that "science fiction as a genre actually deals with the disappearance of character in the same sense in which the 18th and 19th century bourgeois novel is about the emergence of character."[20] The demise of the autonomous individual, first presented in the modernist novel, has only been accelerated with the progress of technology and the development of mass culture. Science fiction simply projects the continuation of this evolution and magnifies the inevitable fact that the modernization of the world leads to conformity, homogeneity, and loss of identity.

Depending on whether modernization is viewed as helpful or detrimental to mankind, the protagonist becomes a positive or a negative character. A positive hero closely modeled on the socialist realist prototype has been successfully adapted by post-1957 Soviet science fiction. His personality is the wish fulfillment of the early interpretation of *naučno-texničeskaja revoljucija* which presented technological progress as a panacea for the ills of mankind. Structurally, this type of positive hero usually functions as a medium through which a new setting or a complex of moral issues is viewed. His idealistic value system can be clearly motivated by making him an inhabitant of utopia who explores a new world. Since his point of view determines the narrative perspective of the novel, he is often cast in the role of the narrator. His unfamiliarity with the setting and his utopian moral code produce an estranged vision which has a didactic effect.

With the deepening of the concept of NTR and the growing preoccupation with the detrimental effects of technological progress, Soviet science fiction has increasingly moved away from the utopian protagonist to focus on a hero whose traditional psychology and ethics stand in contrast to the level of scientific achievement around him. A new, explicitly negative hero develops as a result of the realization that modernization does not lead to the creation of a personality which fits the Soviet ideal. In science fiction, such a hero acts not just as a medium, but becomes a narrative focus in his own right. Although he first appeared as a satirical creation, his mediocrity, orientation toward consumption, and alienation from himself appear increasingly as unavoidable manifestations of a mass phenomenon which is a consequence of technological progress.

The appearance of the negative hero during the late 1960s and the 1970s is a surprising development, at odds with the political vision of the communist utopia. It marks a deviation from the pattern which was established in the 1920s and revived after 1957. As a type, this writing resembles the "warning" science fiction currently dominant in the West.

The reasons for this development are extra-literary. NTR created an expectation that scientific progress can lead to a whole new type of personality characterized by an unemotional attitude, an organized approach toward practical goals, and a sense of social responsibility. Yet it has become increasingly obvious that despite changing social conditions, human emotional life has not undergone any significant modifications.[21] In fact, technological advancement and the pace of modernization have tended to result in the emotional disorientation rather than the reorganization of man. Although the official political line has never discarded the notion of the communist utopia realizable in the not-too-distant future, it is increasingly evident that the current direction of humanity holds little promise for the appearance of the communist New Man.[22] Soviet science fiction can hardly disregard this fact, but it avoids direct controversy by placing its tales of warning in the interim between the present and the advent of the communist utopia, or by using an advanced bourgeois society as a setting.[23] In this context, the fantastic worlds of Franz Kafka have become a paradigm for science fiction and can also be seen in Soviet *fantastika*. Beyond the acknowledgement of an alienated, Kafkaesque individual, science fiction does indeed discover new types of human personality, but it sees them as a regression — a negation of the ideal.

In 1976, A. Strugackij, in a somewhat simplistic commentary on the occasion of the XXV Congress of the CPSU, stated that from a literary point of view the most interesting consequence of NTR is the appearance of new types of mass man, *massovyj naučnyj rabotnik* ('the scientific worker of the masses') and *massovyj sytyj nevospitannyj čelovek* ('the well-fed uneducated man of the masses').[24] The first represents a decline of the 1950s' ideal of the scientist. It acknowledges that normal human shortcomings are also present in the scientific milieu and grows out of the realization that the atmosphere of a research institute only marginally affects the inner personality. With the realization that the scientists' subculture closely resembles the outside world, Strugackij sees it as losing the narrative interest it offered in the initial days of space exploits.

Instead, he regards the second type, the *massovyj sytyj nevospitannyj čelovek,* as the most curious, if unexpected, outgrowth of NTR. Despite the early assumption that the satisfaction of material needs would result in the spiritual growth of man, it has become increasingly obvious that psychologically there is no stage at which an individual is willing to declare his material needs to be satisfied. Phenomenal material saturation, therefore, fails to translate into spiritual and intellectual expansion. It is this consumption for the sake of consumption, accompanied by a philistine outlook on life, that, in Strugackij's view, represents the most negative aspect of NTR. The *massovyj sytyj nevospitannyj čelovek* is essentially not a new phenomenon in the context of the Strugackijs' fiction, since their writing has regularly juxtaposed utopian ideals and philistine preoccupations. Yet recently this type of character has moved from a marginal position into the narrative focus. His *nevospitannost'* has multifaceted manifestations and often shows itself in a lack of resistance to the manipulations of his feelings and ethical code by the outside world. What may sound quite confining in A. Strugackij's theoretical pronouncement has, in their actual writing, the capacity to open a range of ethical conflicts and psychological experiences which form the essence of modern literature.

III. The Shift from Positive to Negative Hero in
the Writing of the Strugackij Brothers

The brothers Arkadij and Boris Strugackij have collaborated since the 1950s to produce some of the most popular and substantial works in Soviet science fiction. Their writing illustrates well the development of the science fiction protagonist from positive utopian hero to disoriented victim of scientific progress.

Almost since the beginning of their literary careers, the Strugackijs have stressed the psychological and ethical dimensions of their heroes with a view toward psychological credibility.[25] Their themes and their protagonists have evolved over the past two decades in a way which reflects changing attitudes toward NTR. The original admiration for the scientist, in their early writing, has since changed to an apprehension about scientific progress; the concern with ethics has shifted to psychology; the narrative focus has moved from the collective to the individual — from the positive to the negative hero. Between the polarities of the positive and the negative hero, the Strugackijs have created a gallery of protagonists who represent various patterns of man's behavior in confrontation with the unknown.

The very appearance of the individualized hero with a fully developed personality represents in itself the beginning of the Strugackijs' more sophisticated writing. In their earliest works, the characters belonged to an explorers' collective from a utopian society. Typically, they subjugated their private concerns to the progress of science, although some room was left for personal identity. Physically they were more varied than the Greek-like inhabitants of Efremev's utopia, uniformly harmonious in mind and body.[26] They readily expressed anger toward one another and used a youth vernacular which caused some raised eyebrows among the critics.

When the individualized protagonist does appear in the Strugackijs' writing, he is a positive hero who finds his individuality as a representative of utopian society in confrontation with a fantastic totalitarian setting that is really a veiled picture of contemporary society. It is not surprising that these novels, showing a totalitarian society, created the foundations of the Strugackijs' popularity among Soviet readers. For the reader, a confrontation of a utopian ideology with the dystopia became a confrontation with himself — with his own ideal imagined and fascist totalitarian reality remembered from the Stalinist purges, German occupation, or even the daily bureaucratic oppression. These topics appear however as side issues in a larger exploration of patterns of historical development. The Strugackijs devoted three of their novels to this theme: *Popytka k begstvu* (1962), *Trudno byt' bogom* (1964) and *Obitaemyj ostrov* (1971). In each case, the society described in the story represents a remote, inferior stage of mankind's development which shocks the utopian protagonist. The concentration camps, purges, aimless mass persecution, control of public opinion and supression of intellectuals pictured in these works are foreign to his mentality. It must be noted, however, that the actual picture of the utopia itself is never really presented; utopia is relevant only as an ultimate repository of moral standards. The action of the stories concentrates entirely on new planets where totalitarianism determines the political system and permeates the mentality of the inhabitants. The hero must undergo a painful process of comprehending such an unknown; he is forced to review his original utopian value system and face complex ethical choices. In spite of the dictates of his emotions, he learns that no amount of good will and technological help from the outside can change societal patterns or accelerate social and political evolution.

Although the recreation of a totalitarian pattern in a fictional society witnesses to the politically conscious use of science fiction devices, the actual message is less radical. Viewed positively, these novels discount the right or even the feasibility of a superior power intervening in the affairs of a society in a lower stage of development. Viewed negatively, they argue for the acceptance of totalitarianism with all its oppressive aspects. Totalitarianism appears as a historical necessity — an inevitable stage of development which cannot be tampered with from the outside if the historical evolution toward utopia is to proceed at its own natural pace.

The Strugackijs' first attempt at a construction of a fictional model of a totalitarian society, *Popytka k begstvu,* presents three heroes: two almost interchangeable young scientists and a rather mysterious older man who identifies himself as a historian. Together they land on a planet where they find a system of slavery obviously resembling the twentieth-century Stalinist and fascist labor camps. The suffering population apparently has no concept of freedom or personal dignity. Shocked by the insignificance of human lives in this society, the young scientists from the utopia feel impelled to help. Even if only to a minute degree, they wish to curtail this oppression, alleviate the physical suffering and share at least a token of the material achievements from their utopian society. The historian, apparently a stranger to the utopia, acts as a *raisonneur* explaining to the young men the intricacies of the system which they face. At the same time, he prevents them from having contact with the world they are visiting; he believes that any society must be left free to pass through its own stages of historical evolution. Any outside intervention would result in an imbalance; because of the moral and social immaturity of the inhabitants, any attempt at intervention would harm rather than benefit the oppressed. In the epilogue, the authors streamline this message by connecting the fictional labor camp setting with a fascist reality, not a Stalinist one. It is revealed that the mysterious historian is really a prisoner from a twentieth-century Nazi concentration camp who has escaped for a brief rest on another planet. He returns to the camp of his own free will, only to meet his death in accordance with his idea of the inevitability of the historical process.

In this, the Strugackijs' attempt at a totalitarian model, the authors appear to be understandably apprehensive about presenting too pointed a picture. Therefore, they deliberately stress the artificiality of the confrontation. Within the framework of an adventure novel, they set up the stock figures of Soviet literature: young scientists and a resistance fighter. In the exploration of the fictional planet, their moral codes reflect upon one another and create an ethical dimension independent from the immediate historical issues with which they are associated. Since the real identity of the historian as an anti-Nazi resistance fighter remains a mystery until the epilogue, his figure also adds tension to the story and delays the imposition of a single interpretation until the very end. Yet the moral codes of the protagonists are so clearly delineated from the outset that there is still little room for psychological authenticity or depth in the development of their characters. Real psychological interest appears only in the presentation of a minor figure, a guard from a labor camp who is interviewed by the protagonists. His simplicity and naiveté, shown along with an unrestrained and unashamed cruelty, create a more realistic picture of a fascist follower than the usual stock figure. Later, in the 1970s, the Strugackijs chose a similar character as their protagonist in order to explore the moral and psychological limitations of mass man.

The same confrontation of the utopian hero with a society in an inferior stage of historical development is repeated more successfully in the stylized medieval setting of *Trudno byt' bogom*. In this story there is no insecurity about the motivation of the plot and no attempt to restrict the interpretation of the totalitarian model. The narrative is permeated with a fantastic medieval atmosphere and succeeds in creating a multi-dimensional world — a realistic totality. The protagonist of *Trudno byt' bogom*, Anton, also a historian, is sent on a mission from utopia by the Earth Institute of Experimental History. He assumes a disguise as a medieval nobleman as he follows the socio-political changes in the life of the new planet. His earthly identity remains concealed from all around him, and he becomes involved in a network of personal bonds with the inhabitants of the planet. Unlike the protagonists of *Popytka k begstvu*, he becomes a member of the society he is visiting, with the sole restriction imposed by the institute that his activities be limited to bloodless intervention. The political system which he observes is directed against intellectuals, who allegedly bring an unhealthy ferment to an otherwise cohesive society. His intervention on behalf of the innocents is not successful. He also must experience suffering and terror as his personal life and the lives of those close to him are affected by a regression in historical development and the system becomes still more violent and rigid. Toward the end of the novel, a local opponent of the system explains to him that his efforts at intervention have no place in the historical process. At the end, the protagonist returns to the safety of the utopia, finally aware that his tampering with social evolution could not have been successful.

Beyond the interest in recognizable elements of the Stalinist system, the great popularity of *Trudno byt' bogom* derives from the richness and depth of the fantastic medieval world which the Strugackijs created. It has been observed that they succeeded in an interesting "domestication of the Scott-Dumas type of a historical novel" which has long enjoyed popularity in the Soviet Union.[27] The one-dimensional character of the hero is explained by the need for consistency in maintaining the utopian perspective on the totalitarian system. In a way reminiscent of traditional adventure stories, the narrative interest is created by the setting itself and the suspense of confrontations.

The latest novel to model the totalitarian world and to evaluate it through the eyes of a utopian character, *Obitaemyj ostrov*, appeared more recently, in 1971. In comparison to *Popytka k begstvu* and *Trudno byt' bogom*, the fictional setting of this novel has perhaps the greatest similarity to a negative picture of Soviet reality, including a semi-anonymous collective leadership, control of public media, and the suppression of dissent. In *Obitaemyj ostrov,* the stranger from the utopia visits a planet ruled by an anonymous council of *Neizvestnye otcy* who have succeeded through technical means in forcing the population into an absolute conformity of opinion which includes a belief in the leaders' own benevolence and infallibility. Although the conditions described are so close to contemporary Soviet reality, the protagonist is a stock character out of juvenile fiction. His connection to his own utopian society is so weak that his origins are of little consequence except to explain his superhuman physical qualities made possible by genetic engineering. Instead, the protagonist appears as a natural man, almost a child, who is adopted by the new society. He even manages to advance through the ranks of the local military system, and it is only in confrontation with the dissenters that he begins to understand the mechanics of oppression. When he finally turns against the system, the gesture reflects his natural instincts for right and wrong rather than his utopian background. As opposed to the other two works, here the authors do bring the protagonist into active struggle against the oppressive system. Yet the Strugackijs' rule of allowing historical development to proceed at a natural pace is also observed. The hero joins the already-existing local opposition, and so acts in character with the level of political consciousness around him. In such fictional confrontations with a totalitarian system, the Strugackijs illustrate their concern over the natural extension of NTR — ineffective change imposed from the outside, and the political misuse of technology.

In *Xiščnye vešči veka* (1965) the Strugackijs use the same pattern of the confrontation of a utopian protagonist with an inferior socio-political system. In this case, the inferior system is the model of a contemporary bourgeois society. In this meeting, the writers explore the perspective of a world that can satisfy all material needs. Such a world was, in fact, a goal of NTR. Although this world was initially seen as good, it has been gradually recognized that, instead of devoting his energy to higher goals, man finds his calling in consumerism.[28] Such is also the assumption in this book. *Xiščnye vešči veka* explores, then, this complete consumer society. The utopian protagonist, this time a Soviet cosmonaut, is sent on a United Nations mission to an allegorical *Strana Durakov* where the inhabitants, satiated with consumer goods, are addicted to an artificial stimulant which renders them completely passive. The Soviet cosmonaut, involved in a cloak-and-dagger search, succeeds in breaking up a gang which promotes this addiction and at least offers hope for the children of the corrupt population. The tale is prefaced by a moralizing introduction which offers a Marxist interpretation of the story. It is intended as a warning that a consumer mentality, with the accompanying intellectual emptiness already evident in the West, can also threaten Soviet citizens. In general, the book is not terribly successful. It suffers from a somewhat absurd plot, heavy moralizing, a failure to maintain a credible atmosphere and an obvious effort to equate the model setting with the United States. It is, however, noteworthy since it prefigures some of the issues voiced in the Strugackijs' works of the 1970s which focus on inhabitants of similar societies. In this early stage of the Strugackijs' writing, a somewhat featureless hero is defined by his role as an explorer in a strange setting and by his function as a narrator describing the modeled world. These model societies are used to bring out political and moral issues not allowable in the mainstream literature and to create hypothetical situations which reveal patterns of human response. Traditionally, the same kind of distilled view of reality is found in satirical literature, which has a similar didactic purpose.

The Strugackijs, in fact, have also used their modeling method to produce satire. In *Ponedel'nik načinaetsja v subbotu* (1965) and *Skazka o trojke* (1968) they abandon the space travel device, and instead base their models on the elements of a fairy tale. Again, a somewhat featureless positive protagonist-narrator, a *mladšij naučnyj rabotnik* ('junior scientific worker'), explores a new setting which this time combines Russian folklore and pseudo-scientific fiction. In these works utopia disappears as an ethical frame of reference as the · hero's point of view approximates that of the reader.

Ponedel'nik načinaetsja v subbotu and *Skazka o trojke* are most entertaining fantastic tales which parody the bureaucratic approach to research and authoritarian administration by pseudo-scientists. The two stories share the same protagonist-narrator, a young computer programmer, Privalov, who accidentally joins the *Naučno-issledovatel'skij Institut Čarodejstva i Volšebstva* ('Research Institute of Sorcery and Magic') known as AN SSR NIIČAVO. His introduction to the territory where the scientific pursuit of magic is practiced begins with an encounter with Baba Jaga and a whole gallery of familiar Russian fairy tale characters who happen to be connected with the institute. The fantastic creatures are noticeably attuned to the realities of modern life — only the essence of magic remains unchanged. The prosaic, de-glamorized attitude toward the fantastic also permeates the institute which has such divisions as *Otdel predskazanij i proročestv* ('Section of predictions and prophecies'), *Otdel linejnogo sčastja* ('Section of linear happiness') and *Otdel večnoj molodosti* ('Section of eternal youth'). In a parody of the workings of an actual research institute, magic is measured, analyzed, and experimented with according to a strict bureaucratic routine. *Skazka o trojke* further expands the grotesque and adds a political dimension. In this story, Privalov explores a distant floor of the same institute governed by a dictatorial trio of former plumbing inspectors who failed to return because of an elevator breakdown. The administrative meetings in which Privalov is forced to participate parody the bureaucratic mentality with its pompous self-righteousness and desire for unlimited power. In this fantastic setting, Privalov preserves a detached perspective which contrasts with the absurdity of the proceedings around him. From his viewpoint the laws of the fairy tale and the laws of bureaucracy seem to operate with the same lack of precision, and both require that the rules of daily logic be suspended.

Since the late 1960s the focus of the Strugackijs' stories has shifted from panoramic settings to the hero himself. He may still act as a medium, but he also becomes a personality in his own right. The exploration of the setting in which the hero finds himself has complex repercussions on his own ethics and psychology. The first of these stories, *Ulitka na sklone,* is probably the best of the Strugackijs' works for its imaginative power and stylistic quality. It contains two simultaneous, parallel tales with separate protagonists whose plot lines alternate in the text and contrast with each other. Both protagonists begin from the same point: they are connected with an Institute of Forest Research and Deforestation established in order to confront a mysterious forest, a giant living organism which defies all efforts at comprehension. One of the heroes, a biologist with the significant name of Kandid, separates himself from the institute, enters the forest, and there joins a peculiar native community which leads a dreamy, plant-like existence. The natives suffer periodic attacks by creatures whom Kandid discovers to be bio-robots controlled by a tribe of Amazons. When he tries to fight them, he realizes that he is involved in a hopeless struggle against a rational, merciless, and anonymous power. Kandid himelf is a very lonely hero who, in the depths of the forest, has no one with whom to share his concerns and efforts to comprehend the setting. Faced with his own inability to make sense out of the forest, he nevertheless decides to take a moral stand and defend the local inhabitants against the bio-robots. Here, for the first time in the Strugackijs' fiction, there is an intervention that is a conscious disturbance of historical progress. It is an anti-rationalistic gesture in which Kandid's private ethics are set against the inevitability of progress.

The hero of the parallel story is a low-ranking mathematician named Perec who is also intrigued by the forest. He is unable to penetrate the artificial facade, built up in the name of research, which totally hides the forest from view. Perec's attempts to reach the forest are reduced to a nightmarish struggle to free himself from the all-pervasive presence of an absurd institution. The conclusion is ironic: unable to escape, he finds himself set up as the director of the institute. Instead of realizing his dream of confronting the forest, he is forced to maintain bureaucratic pretenses in an illusion of rational activity which justifies the existence of the conglomerate.

Ulitka na sklone is a fine example of literary science fiction which suggests questions but leaves open a variety of answers. It focuses on man's confrontation with the unknown without spelling out the symbolic meaning of the forest. The setting no longer represents a socio-political model, but becomes a multi-dimensional construct which eludes a single interpretation. It is a partial projection of the hero's mind, an incarnation of his inner hopes and apprehensions. While in the Strugackijs' earlier works such a construct developed as a function of sociology, it is now a function of psychology. Reality no longer appears as an illusory totality, but as fragments reflected in the mind of the protagonist. Whether the central image in the story, the forest, stands for the world or functions "metaphorically as a kind of external unconscious,"[29] it is no better explained at the end of the story than at the beginning. What does emerge from the story are the patterns of responses to the unknown. Darko Suvin, in his perceptive analysis, views Kandid's and Perec's positions as the two extremes of conduct accessible to an intellectual in society — rejection or adjustment.[30] Kandid withdraws into the timeless organic past, and even there he remains an outsider. Perec regretfully accepts the present shaped by the modern bureaucratic institution which insists on rationalism, but produces the absurd and the grotesque. Critics have pointed out the Kafkaesque quality of both stories, with *The Castle* as the prototype for the Perec section. In a Kafkaesque way, both protagonists are passive, sensitive outsiders, over-whelmed by the maze which surrounds them and unable to realize their private dreams.[31]

Ulitka na sklone combines the thematic contrast between the protagonists with a careful stylistic balance between the slow-moving, folk-tale character of the Kandid story and the satirical, occasionally grotesque modern experience of Perec. Unfortunately, *Ulitka na sklone* not only had publishing difficulties at the time, but this direction is never developed in the Strugackijs' subsequent writing. Commentators note that outside factors might have influenced the reappearance of a more explicitly social direction in their stories with only marginal presentations of Kafkaesque alienation.[32]

Yet since the appearance of *Ulitka na sklone* the center of narrative gravity is no longer confined to the exploration of the fantastic setting but increasingly deals with the peculiar responses of the protagonists themselves as they confront the unknown. Many of the post-1968 stories describe such confrontations, showing the ingrained nature of the self-deceptions and protective reflexes which serve to defend the status quo of one's private world. In *Vtoroe našestvie marsian* (1968), subtitled "Notes of a reasonable man," the narrator describes the impact of a Martian invasion on society and his private life. His is a typical middle-class, *meščanstvo* response to the unknown which seeks the smoothest possible adjustment to calamity for the sake of preserving the private and public establishment. For the estrangement effect, the story is set in ancient Greece, but the details reflect contemporary life. This device illustrates the view of the authors that the middle-class mentality transgresses historical and political settings.

In the story *Gadkie lebedi* (1972) the hero is a well-known writer weighed down with problems which range from creative crises to alcohol, disagreements with his ex-wife, misunderstandings with his mistress, and a lack of communication with his teenage daughter. For him, the confrontation with the unknown consists of an encounter with a mysterious ostracized group, living literally and figuratively on the outskirts of town. It is this group which leads the children of the community in a search for moral and intellectual honesty and to a rejection of the compromises and illusions of the adult world. The children's naive but forceful intellectuality compels the writer to face both the reality of his middle age with all its self-justifications, and the superficiality of his writings. The theme of the perversion of intellectual responses to the world — of the submission of an intellectual to the immediate realities of life — is realized here in a semi-fantastic setting which entirely omits extraterrestrial phenomena in order to concentrate on the psychology of the hero's personal compromise and conformity.

In addition to middle-class and intellectual responses to the unknown, the Strugackijs have also presented a lower class mentality in similar confrontations. In *Paren' iz ispodnej* (1974) a narrator of a *skaz* reveals himself as a simpleminded soldier of peasant background who perceives the world in terms of a black-and-white code of honor instilled by the military. In a reverse of the situation typical for the Strugackijs' early tales in which a utopian protagonist confronts a dystopian society, this story presents an inhabitant of a planet with an inferior social system transferred to a utopian communist society on Earth. As in others of the Strugackijs' works, the image of the utopia itself is never made concrete. The hero is put in an isolated location and confronted mainly with technological achievements. Yet science and technology alone hold little interest for him. He perceives the world in terms of emotions and loyalties which are, to be sure, absurd, but also more human than the rational rigidity of the utopia. Like Prisypkin in Majakovskij's *Klop,* this man finds himself in a utopia and desires nothing more than to return to his own imperfect world. The experiment, in which the earthly mentor hopes to change the mentality of the protagonist, inevitably fails as the hero demands a return to his home planet.

We have seen that one problem opened by NTR concerns the rigidity of human response to change. A more recent concern revolves around the desirability of technological progress itself, and whether it should be limited. The Strugackijs address this issue in two recent stories, *Piknik na obočine* (1972) and *Za miliard let do konca sveta* (1976–77). The action of the first story takes place in a little town in the western hemisphere next to a zone in which extraterrestrial beings have left artifacts of their civilization. The nature of these remains is entirely incomprehensible to the population, but at the same time they hold the promise of money, power, and utopian fulfillment. The world which surrounds the zone operates according to the conventions of the Wild West. The protagonist is an adventurous type who explores the mysterious area for profit, survives the fantastic dangers and misfortunes of exploration, and, in the end, finds a symbolic golden ball which promises absolute wish fulfilment. Yet, at the moment when he finds the golden ball, he must also confront his own limitations: he realizes that his culture has failed to provide him with ideals beyond immediate concerns, and that in the process of exploration larger perspectives have been lost. In a somewhat forced political twist at the end of the story, he recalls his onetime friend, a Russian scientist, and repeats his formula of happiness, freedom and satisfaction of needs for everybody. The utopian note at the end of the story does not weaken the conclusion that the scientific exploration of the unknown has become a process which holds both dangers and such a powerful attraction that higher humanitarian ideals have been lost in its pursuit.[33]

In the story *Za miliard let do konca sveta* it is the natural laws of the universe which act to limit the excessive growth of knowledge. Several protagonists — an astronomer, a physicist, a chemist, and an engineer — all on the verge of breakthroughs in their respective fields, find their research frustrated by a chain of seemingly ordinary intrusions. As some of the events appear somewhat unusual, however, the scientists begin to suspect strange powers at work. Some critics see in this story an allegory of the fate of a scientist limited in his work by political factors. Still, the story has a broader meaning since it deals with the general limits to progress. One of the characters advances a "Theory of the Homeostatic Universe" which assumes that the universe itself cannot tolerate excessive intellectual growth because it disturbs the natural balance. The "Law of Conservation of Structure" protects the universe against the threat of humanity developing into a super-civilization.

Regardless of whether the technological and scientific progress leads to the golden ball which fulfills all wishes, or whether nature itself sets the limits to man's exploration of the universe, the protagonist in the Strugackijs' recent work is faced with questions far more complex than those arising from the earlier confrontations between the utopia and the dystopia. Whether the limits are set by the personality of the protagonist or by the Homeostatic Universe, man is increasingly faced with failures as the vision of the utopia initially associated with NTR continues to escape his grasp. The confrontation with the unknown, with the charmed zone or the threat of Martian invasion, evoke traditional patterns of negative response because the protagonists are unable to transcend their psychological limitations.

The best of Soviet *social'no-filosofskaja fantastika* reveals this disillusionment which grew out of the broadening of the concept of NTR. The Strugackijs' fiction, with its impressive sensitivity, creates imaginative visions with dimensions inaccessible to the mainstream literature. These estranged pictures of reality reflect the dilemmas of modern man subjected to the forces of modernization beyond his control.

NOTES

1. The critics usually make an attempt to differentiate between science fiction and *naučnaja fantastika*. The distinction is ambiguous because of the imprecise character of both terms. Darko Suvin suggests that the Russian trend is more value-oriented,

marked by a utopian perspective, and has never been entirely dominated by technology or adventure plots; cf. Darko Suvin, "Ein Abriss der sowjetischen Science Fiction," in *Science Fiction*, ed. Eike Barmeyer, Uni-Taschenbücher, 132 (Munich: Fink Verlag, 1972), p. 320. For a review of the use of the term *naučnaja fantastika*, see Bernd Rullkötter, *Die wissenschaftliche Phantastik der Sowjetunion. Eine vergleichende Untersuchung der spekulativen Literatur in Ost und West*, Europäische Hochschulschriften, XVIII, 5 (Berne: Herbert Lang, 1974), esp. pp. 4–6.

2. A general summary of the debates on NTR and the reaction to NTR in literature is presented in Anton Hiersche, *Sowjetliteratur und wissenschaftlich-technische Revolution* (Berlin: Akademie-Verlag, 1976). One of the more recent debates was published in *Voprosy literatury*, No. 11 (1976), pp. 3–92, under the title "XXV S'ezd KPSS i problemy literatury," and in *Voprosy filosofii*, nos. 10, 12 (1976).

3. Russian science fiction dates its beginnings from the utopian novel by Aleksandr Bogdanov, *Krasnaja zvezda* (1908), and its continuation, *Inžener Menni* (1912), which was written at the suggestion of Lenin. In the 1920s the development of science fiction was inaugurated by Aleksej Tolstoj's *Aelita* (1922). The anti-utopian *My* by Evgenij Zamjatin, written in 1920, has never been published in the Soviet Union. In the early 1920s, the members of the Left Front of the Arts — Šklovskij, Kušner, and Aseev — attempted to create models of popular utopian constructivist prose, but the samples published in *Lef* testify to their lack of success. In the late 1920s, a most successful writer with a strong scientific orientation was Aleksandr Beljaev, the author of *Golova professora Douélja* (1925), *Čelovek-amfibija* (1928), *Izobretenija professora Vagnera* (1928). He is often considered the founder of contemporary *naučnaja fantastika*. For the historical development of Russian science fiction, see A. F. Britikov, *Russkij sovetskij naučno-fantastičeskij roman* (Leningrad: Nauka, 1970) and his articles, "Zaroždenie sovetskoj naučnoj fantastiki," *Istorija russkogo sovetskogo romana*, kn. 1 (Moscow: Nauka, 1965) and "Évoljucija naučno-fantastičeskogo romana," *Istorija russkogo sovetskogo romana*, kn. 2 (Moscow: Nauka, 1965).

4. Anton Hiersche, *op. cit.*, pp. 18–19.

5. Jurij Osnos, "Literatura i NTR. Poiski. Obretenija. Zabluždenija." *Voprosy literatury*, no. 4 (1977), p. 9.

6. *Ibid.*

7. E. Tamarčenko, "Mir bez distancij (O xudožestvennom svoeobrazii naučnoj fantastiki)," *Voprosy literatury*, no. 11 (1968), p. 98. See also Jurij Smelkov, "Gumanizm texničeskoj ėry," *Voprosy literatury*, no. 11 (1973), pp. 42–71.

8. The modeling function of *naučnaja fantastika* is discussed by Rafail Nudel'man, "Razgovor v kupe," *Fantastika, 1964 god* (Moscow: Molodaja gvardija, 1964), pp. 347–67; by the same author, "Mysl' učenogo, obraz xudožnika," *Literaturnaja gazeta*, 4 March 1970; and by Evgenij Brandis, "Naučnaja fantastika i modelirovanie mira buduščego," *Neva*, no. 2 (1969), pp. 198–206.

9. Evgenij Brandis, "Naučnaja fantastika i čelovek v segodnjašnem mire," *Voprosy literatury*, no. 6 (1977), pp. 111–17.

10. Darko Suvin defines science fiction as "Literatur der erkenntnisbezogenen Verfremdung," in "Zur Poetik des literarischen Genres Science Fiction," in *Science Fiction*, ed. Barmeyer, pp. 86–105.

11. A. Strugackij, B. Strugackij, "Čerez nastojaščee — v buduščee," *Voprosy literatury*, no. 8 (1964), p. 74.

12. A. Sinjavskij, "Sovremennyj naučno-fantastičeskij roman," in *Puti razvitija*

sovremennogo russkogo romana, ed. V. M. Ozerov (Moscow: Akademija Nauk SSSR, 1961), pp. 333–50.

13. For a summary of recent critical perspectives on fantasy and the relation of fantasy literature to science fiction, see C. F. Frederics, "Problems of Fantasy," *Science Fiction Studies,* 5, no. 14 (1978), pp. 33–44. One of the most outstanding Soviet critics of science fiction, Jurij Kagarlickij, also interprets this genre in terms of the fantastic. See his articles "Fantastika iščet novye puti," *Voprosy literatury,* no. 10 (1974), pp. 159–78, and "Realizm i fantastika," *Voprosy literatury,* no. 1 (1977), pp. 101–17.

14. T. Černyševa, "O staroj skazke i novejšej fantastike," *Voprosy literatury,* no. 1 (1977), pp. 229–48.

15. *Naučnaja fantastika* (NF) is published mainly by "Molodaja gvardija," "Znanie," "Detgiz," and "Detskaja literatura." The journals in which it appears include *Texnika molodeži, Nauka i žizn', Znanie-sila,* in addition to the more literary *Neva, Aurora,* or *Zvezda.* For the periodic distribution showing the rapid growth of Soviet NF primary and secondary literature, see B. Ljapunov in: "Bibliografija (1917–1967)," in *Russkij sovetskij naučno-fantastičeskij roman,* pp. 363–436. Darko Suvin, *Russian Science Fiction 1956–1974: A Bibliography* (Elizabethtown, N.J.: Dragon Press, 1976) provides an alphabetical list of Russian NF books in the original as well as in translation and a selective, annotated yearly list of SF criticism between 1956 and 1970.

16. Jurij Kagarlickij, a Soviet expert on Western science fiction, has written a theoretical and historical monograph, *Čto takoe fantastika?* (Moscow: Xudožestvennaja literatura, 1974). Efemij Parnov, *Fantastika v vek NTR. Očerki sovremennoj naučnoj fantastiki* (Moscow: Znanie, 1974) and Jurij Smelkov, *Fantastika — o čem ona?* (Moscow: Znanie, 1974) are of a more popular character. Somewhat earlier appeared a book by Adol'f A. Urban, *Fantastika i naš mir* (Leningrad: Sovetskij pisatel', 1972). Abroad, several studies of Soviet science fiction were published in German as an outgrowth of recent interest in trivial literature. The first to appear was Hermann Büchner's occasionally opinionated study *Programmiertes Glück: Sozialkritik in der utopischen Sowjetliteratur* (Vienna: Europa-Verlag, 1970). It was followed by some very substantial publications: Bernd Rullkötter, *Die wissenschaftliche Phantastik der Sowjetunion*; Hans Földeak, *Neuere Tendenzen der sowjetischen Science Fiction,* Slavistische Beiträge, 88 (Munich: Otto Sagner Verlag, 1975); and Hartmut Lück, *Fantastik — Science Fiction — Utopie: Das Realismusproblem der utopisch-fantastischen Literatur* (Giessen: Focus-Verlag, 1977) which offers an impressive discussion of science fiction from a Marxist point of view and is largely based on Soviet materials. In a shorter version, Lück's work appeared in *Die deformierte Zukunft: Untersuchungen zur Science Fiction,* ed. Reimer Jehmlich and Hartmut Lück (Munich: Goldmann, 1974), pp. 149–88.

17. Darko Suvin, "The Utopian Tradition of Russian Science Fiction," *Modern Language Review,* 66, no. 1 (1971), pp. 139–59.

18. For a witty presentation of the spectrum of critical approaches to *naučnaja fantastika,* see G. Gurevič, *Karta strany fantazii* (Moscow: Iskusstvo, 1967).

19. E. Tamarčenko, "Mir bez distancij," p. 104.

20. Scott Sanders, "Invisible Men and Women: The Disappearance of Character in SF," *Science Fiction Studies,* 4, no. 11 (1977), p. 14.

21. Jurij Osnos, "Literatura i NTR," pp. 4–9.

22. Evg. Brandis and V. Dmitrevskij in "Die wissenschaftliche Phantastik lebt weiter," *Kunst und Literatur,* no. 8 (1976), pp. 792–807, discuss the reorientation of

science fiction which came as a result of a realization that the utopia would not materialize in the near future.

23. Patrick L. McGuire, "Understanding the Strugatzky Brothers," *Galileo,* no. 7 (1978), p. 12.

24. A. Strugackij, "Novye čelovečeskie tipy," *Voprosy literatury,* no. 11 (1976), pp. 16–18.

25. For a critical presentation of the Strugackijs' works until 1971 and for their reception in the Soviet Union, see Darko Suvin, "The Literary Opus of the Strugatskii Brothers," *Canadian-American Slavic Studies, 8, no. 3* (1974), pp. 454–63; and *id.,* "Criticism of the Strugatskii Brothers' Work," *Canadian-American Slavic Studies,* 6, no. 2 (1972), pp. 286–307.

26. For the exact references to the Strugackijs' works cited in this paper, see the most recent bibliography of their Russian editions and translations by Darko Suvin, "Nachwort," in: Arkadi und Boris Strugatzki, *Die Schnecke am Hang,* tr. by Hans Földeak, suhrkamp taschenbuch, p. 434 (Frankfurt: Suhrkamp, 1978), pp. 256–57.

27. Efremov's utopian visions and his characters are discussed in Leonid Geller, "Mirozdanie Ivana Efremova," *Vremja i my,* no. 24 (1977), pp. 134–51, and in an excellent recent study by Regula Heusser, "Die Darstellung von Mensch und Gesellschaft in den wissenschaftlich-phantastischen Zukunftsromanen von I. A. Efremov," Lizenziatsarbeit, Slavisches Seminar, Universität Zürich, n.d.

28. Darko Suvin, "The Literary Opus," p. 458. According to the results of a survey, A. Dumas' *The Count of Monte Christo* has been named as one of three books which exert the highest "spiritual" influence on the Soviet adolescent reader: see Maurice Friedberg, *A Decade of Euphoria: Western Literature in Post-Stalinist Russia, 1954–64* (Bloomington: Indiana University Press, 1977), p. 698.

29. A. Strugackij, "Novye čelovečeskie tipy," p. 17.

30. Darko Suvin, "Nachwort," p. 272; Ian Watson, "The Forest as a Metaphor for Mind: 'The Word for World is Forest' and 'Vaster than Empires and More Slow'," *Science Fiction Studies,* 2, no. 7 (1975), p. 231.

31. Darko Suvin, "Nachwort," p. 269.

32. Hans Földeak, *Neuere Tendenzen,* pp. 141–42.

33. Džon Gled [John Glad], "Vozroždenie antiutopii v proizvedenijax A. B. Strugackix," *Novyj žurnal,* no. 98 (1970), p. 152; and Patrick L. McGuire, "Understanding the Strugatzky Brothers," p. 14. Both authors mention publishing difficulties and attacks in the press against the Strugackijs around 1969. After some delay, the Strugackijs again seem to be in favor.

34. Cf. the review of the English translation of *Piknik na obočine* by Ursula K. LeGuin, "A New Book by the Strugackiis," *Science Fiction Studies,* 4, no. 11 (1977), pp. 157–59.

35. Patrick L. McGuire, "Understanding the Strugatzky Brothers," p. 14.

Rochelle Stone

ROMANTICISM AND POSTWAR POLISH DRAMA: CONTINUITY AND DEVIATION

Part I

Examining the development of Polish postwar drama, especially since 1956, we soon discover that it is rooted in a native tradition of 19th and early 20th century experimental drama which started with Romanticism and was always ahead of its age. Polish drama was from its inception too innovative in form, too provocative in ideas and, therefore, has always had to wait to become a part of a future theater repertory. And, though it had borrowed some foreign ideas during the Romantic and Neo-Romantic periods, the twenties, and the postwar period, it nonetheless preserved its own characteristics.

These become apparent when considered in the light of statements explaining how the Absurd idiom differs from traditional drama. According to Martin Esslin:

> The salient difference is that while traditional drama tried to give an objective representation of the external world, the Absurd endeavors to put onto the stage *metaphors for states of mind.* The traditional drama therefore tells a story; the Absurd develops a *pattern of metaphors and images* [emphasis mine, R. S.].[1]

The new dramatist has freed himself from subservience to the acceleration of science and knowledge. Contemporary drama probes into the many layers of our daydreams, as does poetry at its best. This distinction between traditional and contemporary, while applicable to Western and Russian drama, does not fit the Polish scene, since the characteristics attributed to the Drama of the Absurd correspond almost perfectly to the Polish Romantic plays which have been recognized as *the traditional drama* of Poland.

It is, therefore, natural that the Polish Romantic variant has served as a point of departure for postwar experimentations in this genre. Its provocative powers stem from anti-cultural rebellion, from its literary, socio-political and nationalistic polemics. The fusion of diverse elements, of contemporary history, of Shakespearean drama, of Greek tragedy, of the comic and the grotesque, of medieval morality plays and the naiveté of folk mythology with autobiographical elements (all of which we find in Mickiewicz), facilitates the open epico-lyric structure of the drama, which gives it an inexhaustible vitality. Patterns of metaphors and images alluding to the characters' states of mind demonstrate the Expressionistic tendencies of the Romantic drama *avant la lettre,* transcending the pattern of bourgeois theater (cf. the hero's change of identity in *Forefathers' Eve*).

Romantic drama can be accepted as a point of departure for postwar avant-garde drama not merely as a literary historical concept, but rather as a certain *topos*. It is "a creative catalyst, as living theater and most important of all as myth."[2] No other trend of Romantic drama in Europe can claim such a place in art and in national consciousness as does the Polish Romantic drama, because of its dual role, as a reflection of its Romantic ethos, and as a surrogate for the lost fatherland.

Ever since the time of the three bards, Adam Mickiewicz, Juliusz Słowacki and Zygmunt Krasiński, the main body of Romantic drama has been designed to have a direct political influence on the audience. Such a political aspect contrasts with the Romantic notion of the function of a work of art. This accounts for both the weakness and the strength of the Polish Romantic drama. On the one hand, attuned to the struggle for independence, it has been found by Jan Kłossowicz "obstinately monothematic, . . . specifically Polish and unintelligible to foreigners."[3] On the other hand, many features of the Romantic drama remain as topical for the postwar avant-garde dramatists as they were originally for the Romantic ones. However, their treatment differs. Presenting history in the making, the Romantic works deal with reality, ideology, and prophecy. Therefore, they are concerned with the most essential issues: (1) What to do with Poland? i.e., how to achieve its freedom?; (2) What to do with Poland's folk (*lud*)?; (3) The role of the poet and poetry; (4) The role of the common people in revolution;[4] (5) The fate of European civilization. The solution to these issues varies with each of the three bards. Consequently, we can characterize Polish Romanticism in terms of its major antinomies: (1) Mickiewicz sees Poland as the Messiah of nations while Słowacki sees her as their peacock and parrot. (2) Mickiewicz considers the poet a Priest and redeemer while Słowacki and Krasiński consider him a Jester[5] and a weakling (cf. *Kordian* and *The Undivine Comedy*). (3) All three poets view the folk as potential executioner, revolutionist, and boor (cf. Mickiewicz's *Forefathers' Eve*, part II — the scene with the landlord), while Mickiewicz and Słowacki envision them as harbingers of truth. (4) All three poets portray a nobility capable of bringing freedom to Poland but also guilty of selling her out. (5) While Mickiewicz considers poetry the ultimate truth, Słowacki and Krasiński denounce it as a false apparition. Hence, Gerould's accurate assessment of Polish postwar avant-garde drama as "pre-eminently a theater of revolt, historical crisis, social upheaval, conceived in metaphoric terms,"[6] may serve as a footnote to the Polish Romantic drama.

Polish modern literature inherited from Romanticism the ingredients for the theme "Kordian and the Boor," popular with writers from Stanisław Wyspiański and Leon Kruczkowski to Sławomir Mrożek. Hence, Kruczkowski's rebellion against Romanticism was belated, since rebellion against itself, self-irony and scepticism were part of the Romantic tradition, as were the antinomies which carried with them the seeds of the grotesque. Polish

Romanticism is more than just literature. It is the nation's guide from art and myth to reality. As has been observed in an excellent article by Marta Piwińska,

> . . . it is [also] a 'tyrant' who in Polish literature destroyed literature [itself], because it stole the soul of the individual and infused in its place Poland. . . . Having written for the Poles great roles — it [Romanticism] has transformed them into eternal actors and fitted them with a pose . . . a mug (*gęba*).[7]

This observation heralds the demythologization and indictment of Romanticism in the drama of the 20th century.

Part II

It took the genius of Stanisław Ignacy Witkiewicz to create a Polish avant-garde drama which, written mainly between 1918 and 1925, became *the dominant force* in the development of Polish contemporary drama. Hence, in the 1920s, despite the popularity of the Polish variant of the *pièce-bien-faite,* fashioned after Gabriela Zapolska, the Romantic, Expressionistic legacy continued to be the decisive one. It culminated in over thirty plays written by Witkiewicz, which exerted only a very limited immediate influence and brought him hardly any recognition in his lifetime. Therefore, since his works have become known and have initiated the *Sturm und Drang* period in drama after 1956 (especially with their publication by Konstanty Puzyna in 1962), Witkiewicz's plays ought to be included in the discussion of the Polish postwar avant-garde drama.

Written thirty years ahead of the Western and Polish Theater of the Absurd, of the Theater of Happenings, and some years ahead of Antonin Artaud's Theater of Cruelty, Witkiewicz's dramas represent the totality of avant-garde theatrical trends which became the vogue in the late 1950s and the 1960s. Curiously enough, though introduced to the Polish audience roughly at the same time as the plays of Ionesco, Beckett, Dürenmatt, Genet, and Albee, Witkiewicz's work retains an unimpaired vitality and exuberance. In fact, in many respects, as observed by Czesław Miłosz, these plays surpass in daring the Theater of the Absurd and are today still ahead of the times.[8] While his sources can be traced as far back as Shakespeare, the more immediate ones are found in Jarry's *Ubu Roi* (1896), Wedekind's grotesque tragedies, and in Strindberg's plays, especially his *Ghost Sonata,* to which Witkiewicz refers in his play *Mother* (1924).[9] However, by his own admission, along with the more recent native Expressionist plays by Wyspiański and Miciński,[10] the visual arts, especially the paintings by Picasso, by the Fauvists and by the Polish Formists were essential to the development of his Drama of Pure Form. There are also points in common with the Expressionist style of Pilnjak's *Naked Year,* with the early works of Ehrenburg, with the plays of Majakovskij and

with the theories of the Russian Constructivists.[11] Though Polish Romanticism does not seem to be a direct factor in the genealogy of Witkiewicz's drama,
it is easy to discern in it, as I shall point out, romantic themes and strains,
varying in intensity.

An iconoclast, whose extensive world travels enabled him to compare the
most primitive with the most advanced civilizations, Witkiewicz grew increasingly distrustful and rebellious against the traditions of Western civilization.
Having witnessed the revolution in art and participated actively in the political revolution in the Soviet Union, Witkiewicz became a serious explorer of
the new reality. Raised in the Neo-Romantic tradition of the cult of individuality, he feared the extinction of the creative, metaphysical individual in
an age where conformity, leveling tendencies of society, and the universal
greyness of mechanization threatened to become reality. Hence, Witkiewicz's
angst qualifies him to be considered a precursor of Existentialism. Though its
causes are rooted in Neo-Romantic tradition, the grotesque form of expressing it deviates from that tradition.

The sudden changes, the juxtaposition of various realities heightened the
feelings of insecurity in the individual and threatened his identity. Witkacy (as
he called himself) realized that the anxiety caused by the "metaphysical feeling
of strangeness of [man's] existence" can only be combatted by art, but by an
art stranger even than life itself. To achieve such an art, he considered the
Drama of Pure Form the most effective medium. For him drama was to be, as
it was in the Orient (cf. the theater of China, Japan, Bali), in Miciński's, as
well as in Leśmian's newly found plays,[12] a spectacle of ritual. It was to be a
unity of pluralities of forms, a synthesis of all the elements of the theater —
i.e., of setting, sound, gesture, mime, dance, and dialogue — for purely formal
ends since form, according to Witkiewicz, is all that can be judged in a play.[13]
However, every aspect of drama had to be based on a principle of 'defamiliarization' resembling Šklovskij's principle of *ostranenie,* whereby the spectator
would be liberated from images based on a reality familiar to him. This
technique attempts to make the familiar unfamiliar "as a means of intensification of perception" and render the known "as a vision of something not
recognizable."[14] The images are to be free of any vestige of logic. The goal of
the Drama of Pure Form was to shock the audience out of passivity so that
when "leaving the theater [it] would have the feeling that it had just awakened
from a strange dream, in which even the most ordinary things had a strange . . .
charm, characteristic of dream-reverie and unlike anything else in the world."[15]

In its deformation of life (i.e., its defamiliarization), Witkiewicz's Drama of
Pure Form resembles shifts of levels, found in Cubist paintings, which present
multiple states of psychology and action. Hence, often in a single play,
consisting of a plurality of realities, we find transitions from one reality to
another, and from one style to another "taking the spectator on a jolting ride
into new dimensions."[16] We witness this plurality of realities in *Mother.* Mrs.

Eely, the mother, dies in the second act. In the third act she lies in state, but at the same time she appears as a person younger by thirty years, and pregnant, expecting the birth of Leon, the hero of the play who is present in all the acts. Such is also the case in the play *The Madman and the Nun (There is No Bad Which Could Not Turn into Something Worse)*. Here even the subtitle alludes to shifts in perspective. The society in this drama represents a machine which is operated by no one. The mad poet Walpurg is confined to an insane asylum cell, which also represents the cell of his brain. The protagonist's attempt to free himself from the straitjacket symbolizes the state of an individual who will not conform. Walpurg attains ultimate freedom by hanging himself (cf. Miciński's *The Ballad of Seven Sleeping Brothers in China*[17]). However, he soon reenters the stage very much alive. Leaving the dummy of his corpse behind, he exists with his lover, Sister Anna, after having their jailors locked up. This revolt of the mad poet and the debauched nun, accompanied by a resurrection, topples the system, reversing all the existing values. The farcical, grotesque denouement is, as a rule, a consequence of the play's structure and of the character portrayal. In an attempt to confront the audience with 'strangeness of existence' Witkiewicz creates his theater as a parallel to the theater of life. The absurdity of his theater emphasizes *the absurdity of the practical, real life*. Jan Błoński brilliantly assessed the character of Witkiewicz's drama as "a metaphysical happening or a metaphysical comedia dell'arte,"[18] in which, as in life, characters play dual roles.

Moved by the same needs as the author, the characters consciously play a game in an attempt to experience "the mystery of true existence" either through art or in life. They assume an "artificial self."[19] In *The New Deliverance* (1920), Tatiana says: "It's a little comedy that I'm putting on."[20] As in life, the comedy they play is distorted by pretense and falsehood which prevent them from attaining their goal. The borderlines between the roles, between truth and comedy are erased. As a result we have on the stage, sometimes in the same scene, the hero, his dummy (the emblem of artifice and the comic), or his resurrected corpse coexisting as interchangeable parts of a comedy scheme (as seen in *The Madman and the Nun*). As conscious actors in a metaphysical buffoonery of a simulated life, Witkiewicz's characters lack the capacity to experience the true meaning of life: at best they can talk about it. "The only honest actor is the playwright himself."[21] Błoński characterizes them as gigantic "asocial, metaphysical ghosts without form who organize revolutions, . . . love five women at the same time, . . . murder best friends, . . . all in order to experience 'in pure manifestations of life' the shudder of the Mystery of Existence."[22] Degenerates, maniacs, misfits, and demonic women, who oscillate "between the 'she-animal' and the 'she-woman',"[23] and represent the power of the matriarchate (following Miciński's archetypal Basilissa Teofan), are best suited for a world gone mad, heading toward a "soulless bliss." Though the poet or artist appears in all but the last of Witkiewicz's tragicomedies projected into the future era of a triumphant technology and dehumanization, he is the last vestige of a metaphysical individual (cf. the Futurist plays *They*, 1920; *The Crazy Locomotive*, 1921; and others). In their desperate chase after the moments of metaphysical happiness and in their desire to taste mystery within the material reach of human life, the protagonists resort to perverse behavior, madness, and deceit. They hastily create situations in which sex orgies and murder become the quickest means of achieving a feeling of bliss and power. Hence, their game often ends in a massacre (cf. *Gyubal Wahazar*) or in a total loosening of man's basest instincts, where violent, animalistic feelings are expressed in a hyperbolic language. This is how the duchess Irina addresses Scurvy in *The Shoemakers*:

Dr. Scurvy, your utter helplessness excites me to perfect madness . . . Your doubts are a reservoir for me of the choicest, sexual, female, straight-from-the-guts-insect-style sensuality. I'd like to be like the female praying mantis — near the climax they devour their partners from the head down, who, despite that, keep on doing it — you know, hee, hee![24]

The orgiastic lust (the "perfect madness"), is recreated by a sultry language, saturated with detail, hyperbolic images, grotesque similes, and enumeration of modifiers of various language levels. The inflection, descriptions, visual quality, the sounds and rhythm of the above quotation give it a synaesthetic quality which seems to simulate the sexual act itself. This outpouring of aggressive verbiage is a good example of 'defamiliarization' which unveils the duchess' perverted psyche. Orgasm is attained by words, not deeds.

In general this quotation is a sample of the brutalized language used by Witkiewicz's characters, which consists of slang, dialect, puns and neologisms, mixed with highly poetic words. Even the proper names are strange neologisms, alluding to the personality of a character (cf. Plazmonick for the soft, indecisive artist, Tumor Brainowicz, Scurvy (cf. *skurwysyn* 'son-of-a-bitch'), Buffadero, Morbidetto, Tremendosa etc.). The Surrealist quality of the style is heightened by the excessive use of dialogue. Its tonality, high-keyed, mocking and sardonic, extremely emotional, is kept always on the same level, despite the drastic changes of events, ranking from murder to revolution. Uneducated characters express their opinions on philosophy, art, literature, and politics. The result is grotesque. It is as though the individual asserts his existence by a prolonged outcry of the human soul.

Most of Witkiewicz's dramas appear to be detached from the preoccupation with national Romantic trends. They seem unconcerned with: (1) the fate of Polish prophetic art; (2) the fate of the individual Pole; (3) Poland's catastrophe. They are concerned, on the other hand, with: (1) the fate of art in general; (2) the survival of the creative individual, the artist, in a future, mechanized, anthill civilization; (3) the world catastrophe in the face of Western Fascism and Eastern Communism. Therefore, Witkiewicz is rightly considered a universal playwright whose work, especially for Poles, became synonymous with an open window through which Europe in our times can be viewed and the art of a Sartre, of Ionesco's Theater of the Absurd, of Artaud's Theater of Cruelty can be properly perceived. According to Piwińska, Witkiewicz's universality helps some critics "to see, at last, Poland with its entire tradition in its true proportions."[25] Hence, Witkacy's renaissance "is a profound and threatening phenomenon since, in a way, it is a substitute for a literature which does not exist (in Poland)."[26] Piwińska's argument wishfully implies a literature liberated from the past by ignoring it, in order to create a new Polish psyche. However, even Wyspiański's serious attempt to negate the Romantic tradition has proven correct Stanisław Brzozowski's statement that "liberation through negation is a fiction."[27]

Yet, upon closer examination, it becomes apparent that even "the strangely un-Romantic . . . un-Polish"[28] Witkiewicz, perhaps the most European Polish dramatist of the twentieth century, could neither free himself nor totally escape the Polish Romantic tradition. Witkiewicz, though a highly original and universal writer, "manages to combine the elements of predecessors and those of an epigone."[29] Even the fate of his Romantic ancestors haunted him. As observed recently by Gerould:

> . . . he embodied the lonely Polish avant-garde, part of a movement . . . , but passing on a tradition of intense individuality . . . that would serve as a model for the lonely artist-hero for subsequent generations, much as the Romantic poet had for a previous century.[30]

The ideological and socio-political character of Witkiewicz's dramas follows Krasiński's universal and prophetic line concerning the fate of European civilization as expressed in *The Undivine Comedy*. He shares his Romantic predecessor's belief in the necessity and inevitability of social changes brought about by revolution. He also shares Krasiński's apocalyptic fears of the impending annihilation of man's individuality, and of the disintegration of a world of which he is a part. The themes of revolution and art are central to all of Witkiewicz's dramas, as they are in *The Undivine Comedy*. And although his vision of revolution is more prophetic, extensive, and explicit than Krasiński's (cf., e.g., *The Anonymous Work, The Shoemakers*), in both writers revolution fails to bring deliverance. It does, however, succeed in doing away with the old order of the beautiful but degenerate past, and in rendering art, or even craft, superfluous. Hence, it resolves the fate of the Hamlet-like poet or artist. This is exemplified in the self-imprisonment of Plazmonik, the painter in *The Anonymous Work*, and in his observation: "There are only two places for metaphysical individuals in our times: the prison and the insane asylum."[31] (Such statements apply to the reality of present-day dictatorships.) Suicide remains as the third alternative (cf. Walpurg). These disconcerting alternatives exemplify the incompatibility of art and the tyranny of the masses. Count

Henry in *The Undivine Comedy* chooses the last alternative — suicide. Creative art is replaced by the art of mass destruction and of violence in Witkiewicz's *The Anonymous Work* and *The Shoemakers*, as it is also in *The Undivine Comedy*. The leaders of this art are Leonard and Pancras in *The Undivine Comedy*, Lopak in *The Anonymous Work*: "There are no individuals! Down with the personality! Long live the uniform MASS, one and indivisible!!!! "[32] The baseness and cowardliness of the nobility are derided equally by both playwrights. Witkiewicz's heroes represent the old Romantic form; they present and represent ideas, hence, they often are not given proper names. As in Miciński, they are called Man or Wife in Krasiński, 'Doctor, Patient, or Mother in Witkiewicz.

In his four prophetic plays (*The Anonymous Work*, 1921; *They*, 1920; *Gyubal Wahazar*, 1921; and *The Shoemakers*, 1934), which only have become a part of the Polish drama and theater in the 1960s and 1970s, Witkiewicz has predicted future revolutions with astounding accuracy, reminiscent of Krasiński's *The Undivine Comedy*, but going beyond it. As Martin Esslin notes: "*The Anonymous Work*, . . . predicts the course of revolutions which, started on the basis of ideology, always tend to be taken over by brutal devotees of power for its own sake."[33] The horribly prophetic hero Gyubal Wahazar (of the play by the same name) and his cohorts foreshadow the genocide and other atrocities perpetrated by Fascist and Communist dictatorships.

In his earlier plays Witkiewicz tried to adhere to the tenets of his Pure Form. However, he soon realized its limitations. Drama, unlike music or painting, deals with people, not abstractions. Therefore, "the form may be pure but the materials (i.e. the people) are the impure facts of life,"[34] as illustrated in his last play *The Shoemakers*. The "explosive content and impure form,"[35] which represents a direct assault on the immediate world surrounding him, brings Witkiewicz's drama in closer touch with Polish traditional drama.

In *The Shoemakers* Witkiewicz abandoned Pure Form and created a thorough anatomy of the revolution. Its dialectics is a continuation of his *The Anonymous Work*, but especially of the archetypal *The Undivine Comedy*. The play, in which History is the hero, reflects the social and political reality of its time in a Polish setting. It presents the end of the corrupt capitalist system, the threat of a Fascist coup followed by a peasant-worker revolution, which leads to a third revolution carried out by mechanical men called 'Hyper-workoids.' In this frightful, grotesque vision of Europe at the time of Hitler, Witkiewicz is a prophet of doom. In his pessimistic view of human destiny he deviates from Krasiński, for in *The Shoemakers* "none of Witkacy's beautiful-but-damned individuals is present to oppose the law of History."[36] Yet, the play continues the line of Polish Romanticism, since, as noted by Jan Kott, "the essential and great tradition of Polish drama is its specific combination of poetry, history and politics."[37] It is a play of history in the making and a new form of social criticism. Obliquely, it also deals with the Polish issue. In these aspects it approximates Mickiewicz's and Słowacki's dramas, mentioned above. It is a heterogenous play which assaults all the senses of the audience by various means. Its dialogues, digressions, ridiculous allusions to philosophy and derision of Polish literature remind one of the Romantic poet-Jester, Słowacki, and especially of his *Beniowski*. For instance, the character Scurvy says, ". . . Witkacy, that slop-artist from Zakopane, tried to persuade me to take up philosophy."[38] Such self-mockery pokes fun at the hollowness of Romantic myths, of poetry's prophetic power, and of false pride in Polish culture. The rambling of the characters is a parody of the high rhetoric characteristic of Polish Romantic drama. But arguments reaching the boiling point explode into a rebellion, with which Witkacy substitutes action for the Romantic words. Neither do Wyspiański's Mulch and peasants escape his derision. The ineffectiveness of "Kordian and the Boor" persists, despite the change of historic events. The Mulch's tango with the duchess anticipates Mrożek. Yet, in affording the word a prime value above the other media of avant-garde drama, Witkiewicz shows a similarity to the poetics of all the Romantic bards. In this respect he remains an epigone of Polish Romanticism as well as of Neo-Romanticism.

The Shoemakers (A Theoretical Play with Songs) is exactly what the subtitle suggests. It is a verbal duel of contrasting theories, filled with self-destructive mockery, violence and frustration. The feverish, rhythmic beat of hammers, alluding to sexual lust, hides the fear of an inner void and of a meaningless existence. The characters wait endlessly for something to happen, to fill the emptiness created by bankrupt ideologies of the two successive revolutions. Instead, they are subjected to the brutal power of the new totalitarian forces, represented by comrades Abramovski and X. The sign 'Boredom' signals the fact that the individual has reached the end of the line, as did the author by creating an antiplay. In depicting "a metaphysical buffoonery and a supercabaret presenting the sadness, boredom, and despair of modern civilization with a spasmodic laugh,"[39] Witkiewicz leads toward the final spasm before the death of the drama. His prophecy was to be realized especially in the plays of Tadeusz Różewicz.

But the antiplay is only a part of Witkiewicz's contribution to the Polish postwar avant-garde drama. He created a grotesque idiom in which the burlesque verges on the tragic. His drama became both an expression of man's loneliness and confusion in a strangely incomprehensible universe, and of a totalitarian society's pressure upon the individual. Hence, Witkiewicz introduced into his plays a metaphysical and social aspect — in this respect following Polish tradition. Yet, his are the first dramas of ideas without ideology, since Pure Form has no place for logic. From the formal point of view, Witkacy's plays foreshadow a group experience — a happening. Thus, the farcical cruel endings are symptoms of the disintegration both of the individual into a formless, though heterogeneous, mass doomed to destruction, and of old forms being overtaken by time. With his denouements Witkiewicz sets a pattern for the avant-garde. His method of defamiliarization, applied to all the elements of these plays, leads to a grotesque process of deformation which produces his Pure Form.[40]

Part III

Romantic myths, presenting Poland as the sacred, absolute value, were unmasked in the twenties by the reality of an independent Poland. The demythologization of Polish Romanticism exploded in an orgy of perverse forms in Witkacy's plays. In the thirties, because of a considerable rise in nationalism, the Romantic 'sacred' and 'profane' myths became hopelessly entangled. They created an inflated pose which was often mythologized in literature and which resulted in a Poland resembling "a mystified nationalistic herd (*kupa*)."[41] This Romantic pose was reduced, especially in Gombrowicz's novel *Ferdydurke* (1937), to a duel of "mugs" (*gęby*). As a modern existentialist who believed that man exists because of others, i.e., that man's essence, his "form" is determined by them, Gombrowicz assaulted the absurdity of imposing an inflated, obsolescent, Romantic form upon a reality which negated this form. In *Ferdydurke* he indicted, by means of parody and a grotesque displacement of reality, the coveted institutions, the Church, and the social leaders for their attempt to impose a form of falsehood upon the individual. Together with Witkiewicz, Gombrowicz contributed to Polish Surrealist literature; the two are considered precursors of the Polish variant of the Theater of the Absurd.[42]

The Second World War nurtured Romantic myths. In fact, the poets-insurrectionists achieved a synthesis of word and deed, fulfilling the Romantic dream. However, in the new Messianism, the fighting Pole becomes the sacred myth. Man emerges sanctified in his tragic condition. Paradoxically, the war produced in these poets a kind of Romantic nihilism. Such a conscious and cruel nihilism is manifested in Andrzej Trzebiński's *To Raise a Rose* (1943), the only drama in Polish literature which continues Witkiewicz's legacy, enriched by some of Gombrowicz's techniques.

We can distinguish five main offshoots in the development of Polish avant-garde drama during the postwar period with regard to Romantic tradition. In the first place we will try to show how Witkacy's nihilism and the Ferdy-durkean strain were enriched by derision of all the great Romantic myths in the plays of Witold Gombrowicz, Sławomir Mrożek, and Tadeusz Różewicz. Although the derision of both the sacred and profane Romantic myths is ever-present in Gombrowicz's plays, they are not devoid of Romantic elements. While his ontological approach and idiom are novel, he shows a predilection for traditional themes and bourgeois genres (e.g. operetta) which, used as parodies, help him to create a new perception of reality. To borrow a phrase from Louis Iribarne, "Gombrowicz was apt to juxtapose the ugly-but-true with the beautiful-but-false."[43] This is exemplified by his prewar drama *Ivona, Princess of Burgundia,* published in 1935 in the journal *Skamander.* This tragi-farce, which takes place in some fairytale kingdom, is, like all three of Gombrowicz's plays, an extension of his theory of social behavior, posited in *Ferdydurke,* in which life is depicted as a carnival of changing masks. The mutual debasement, aggression and the duel of "mugs" and grimaces, depicted in it *contains his entire theater.* In all his plays Gombrowicz chooses the setting of a royal or aristocratic court, perhaps because it provides him with a rigidly stratified society whose often brutal behavior is governed exclusively by form.

The intrusion of a commoner, "the flower of the lowest social strata of . . . society,"[44] a real person, into the artifice of the court society, threatens to destroy the form and to cause a revolution from below. The court, longing to end the tyranny of nonsense and to restore the equilibrium, decrees that Ivona must be killed. The King informs the Chamberlain about the proper method of doing away with Ivona during her wedding to the Prince:

> King: Yes, yes, full regalia of course, plenty of light, lots of people and magnificent clothes. . . . Splendor, grandeur and glory. . . . We will do it in the grand manner, bear down on her from on high, not from below. Royalty will kill her. (55)

A pseudo-normalcy, i.e. falsehood, is restored when Ivona chokes to death on a fishbone. The play, which could be considered a social satire despite the author's protestations,[45] brings to mind Mickiewicz's satire on the nobility in his *Forefathers' Eve,* part III, and Krasiński's in *The Undivine Comedy.* The wedding, a Romantic *topos* of reconciliation, turns into a funeral, preventing a revolution at the court. Furthermore, the ending and the entire play are rooted in Romantic antinomies, as are also Gombrowicz's postwar dramas.

His second play, *The Marriage* (1946), written after his emigration to Argentina, ends similarly, but with a much more profound and complex meaning. It combines an autobiographical element with a strong derision of old and new Romantic myths, such as the cult of nationalism and of the tragic heroism of the war years. Gombrowicz holds the influence of Romantic myths responsible for the disintegration of individualism and of culture, and for the shattering of ideologies after the war. His longing to return to a Poland which no longer exists is manifested in the hero of his play *The Marriage.* Henry, a Polish soldier stationed in France, unable to return from the war, dreams of his homecoming. As Jan Kott has observed, "This *impossible* return to a *real* Poland is transformed in his dream into a *possible* return to an *unreal* Poland."[46]

The structure of the play is traditional, yet its form is based on the logic of a nightmarish dream, lending the play, according to the author "the character of a direct parody of Shakespeare." (18) The dream technique creates violent transitions in the mind of the protagonist who returns with his friend Johnny to a war-ravaged Poland. He finds there all the sacred Romantic myths horribly profaned. The fatherland-church is in ruins; the home is degraded to a pub. A shift of identity reveals his parents transformed into innkeepers, and his fiancée Maria degraded to a slut. Henry creates the characters, yet the external world imposes its form upon him. This results in a dual deformation, which approximates Witkiewicz's Pure Form.[47] Henry's father, symbolizing the Romantic myth of the past, cries out against the desecration of what is held sacred:

> If anybody touches me, something awful
> I repeat: something awful
> So awful that . . . that I don't know what.
> There'll be weeping and screaming and the gnashing of teeth,
> The rack and execution, hell and execration,
> A leveling, piercing, pulverizing squeal
> That'll blow this whole universe to kingdom come . . .
> Indeed! Indeed!
> Because no one, because no one may touch me
> Because no one, because no, be-be-because
> I'm untouchable, I'm untouchable, I'm untouchable
> Because I'll curse the lot of you! (51)

This quotation illustrates the parody of Shakespeare in depicting the father as a King Lear figure, whose language, approximating the original, verges on the absurd.

In order to restore the myths of the past, his own dignity, and a coherence to his shattered world, Henry resorts to the farce of imposing the form of King upon his father. He kneels before him and raises his Finger, the symbol of transformation. By elevating his father to an Untouchable King, i.e. restoring the sanctity to the myth, he can be granted a sanctified marriage. However, swayed by conspirator-Drunkards he dethrones his father and declares himself King. According to Gombrowicz, Man is his own Priest, Jester, and God. Thus Henry, as the author's spokesman, soon realizes that he can grant himself the wedding in which the innocence of his bride will be restored. As is customary in dreams, personal and national myth become intertwined. The peasant court-like masquerade of changing costumes (which may be considered the last masquerade of "the Polish folk") is a wedding which is transformed into a ritual. The pub is transformed into a cathedral of Polish honor, into a fatherland, a home in which the services of the archetypal Romantic *topos* for reconciliation (i.e. the wedding) is to be performed. But what actually follows is blasphemously contrary to the anticipated order. The Romantic amalgam of an apocalypse with an idyll turns into a nightmare. With the deposed King-Father, the sacred myth is shattered. At the Drunkard's instigation, Johnny and the bride, whom he embraces while presenting her with a flower, become symbolically "united." The enraged Henry shouts at the instigator: "You have bound them together / By a dreadful / And inferior bond. You have married them / you pig priest." (104) Thus, the intended wedding of the 'Virgin' Maria to King Henry is annulled. The model becomes distorted. The "human church," of which Henry is the Priest, also requires a sacrifice in order to become sacred. Johnny becomes its victim. He pays a price by killing himself, as ordered by the King. The wedding turns into a funeral. Henry orders himself imprisoned, yielding to the form of society's pressure. Brute power emerges victorious.

We find in the structure, themes, and ideas of this royal tragedy some similarities with the Polish Romantic dramas which were also rooted in Shakespeare. The dream sequence, as a structural device of dislocating reality, has been employed in the plays of Mickiewicz, Słowacki and Krasiński. The themes of marriage, revolution, art, the motifs of disguise, changed identity, and so forth, figure prominently in Krasiński's *The Undivine Comedy*. Its first part, a family drama, is also a *Heimkehrdrama* as is Gombrowicz's play. In the protagonist's — Count Henry's — marriage the power of form proves destructive, as it does for Gombrowicz's Henry. The hero's change of identity, i.e. of "form," from a husband-father to a poet-activist, results in the madness and death of the Wife. The change in Count Henry from a private Man to a Man-Leader, the Guardian of Romantic myths, can be compared to the elevation of the father to King in *The Marriage*. In both plays devastated churches symbolize the destruction of the old order. Count Henry's "royalty" is deposed by the revolutionary, brute power of the mob, as is the King-Father's by the power of the Drunkards.

Like Krasiński before him, Gombrowicz presents a vision of cataclysmic historical events viewed from an aristocratic and Christian point of view. In this parable of modern European history, Henry and Johnny have been equated, according to Lucien Goldmann's thorough analysis of the play, with the "intellectual and managerial levels of society" in the image of Trotsky and Stalin.[48] Though agreeing with the interpretation of other characters, I see rather a literary parallel with Pancras and Leonard of *The Undivine Comedy*. The comparison of two sets of literary figures helps us to focus on Gombrowicz's main idea in *The Marriage*. In it he postulates that the "interhuman sphere" can be enhanced only by "a creative force that goes beyond individual consciousness . . . the only divinity that is accessible to us."[49] In *The Undivine Comedy* Pancras realizes the importance of such a creative force in future interhuman relations when he comes to win over Count Henry, the poet, to the revolutionary side. However, in the Count's judgment, his creative force is false because, as an introvert, he was out of touch with people. As Gombrowicz would say, he lacked contact with the "interhuman sphere." Both King Henry and Pancras fail: Henry to "celebrate [his] marriage in the sacred human church"[50] (which symbolizes the real "marriage" he aspires to), and Pancras to enjoy the victory of the revolution. Both are unable to free themselves from the form imposed upon them by the social sphere to which they belonged.

In its structure *The Marriage* reveals some similarities to Krasiński's play by combining prose and verse with elements of stylization such as a chorus. In this, as well as in the transformation of time, place, and identity, it echoes Mickiewicz's *Forefathers' Eve*. Gustav's demented, dream-like monologue in part IV, about his desire to marry Maryla, who deceived him, reminds us of Henry's dream. In part III Gustav dreams about his home. Like Henry, he is confused by the strange power of dreams and changes into Konrad who in his "great improvisation" blasphemes against God, claiming his own creative power as the only divinity. This improvisation brings to mind Henry's monologue in *The Marriage* (cf. 136–137). However, here God is created "from below" among men, in a "human church," which is Gombrowicz's version of a revolutionary dream of equality. In its idealism it shows similarities to Marxism, and therefore differs from Krasiński's and Witkiewicz's view of revolution.

Language has an omnipotent function in *The Marriage*. It plays the role of a costume; it creates people and actions, deforms them and is deformed by them. It is a brutalized language, akin to that of Jarry's *Ubu Roi* and to that of Witkiewicz's plays. The style is a disjointed composite of contrasting levels of expression, grotesquely reflecting the characters' changing forms and moods. Following dream logic, it is based on the principle of defamiliarization (cf. fn. 14) and of parody.

In *Operetta* (1966), Gombrowicz's derision and parody of Romantic tradition reaches the peak of grotesqueness, based on the Romantic device of antinomy. The form — of a Viennese operetta — in "its divine idiocy and heavenly sclerosis . . . goes hand in hand with the monumental pathos of historical events."[51] We are introduced into a princely court of Himalaj (much as in *Ivona*) during *la belle époque* — 1910. The action progresses through two wars and two revolutions. The form of the operetta symbolizes the degenerate, empty existence of the overdressed, overstuffed aristocracy, devoid of ideology and unconcerned with the apocalyptic winds of history. Two aristocrats, Charm and Firulet, are enamored of a commoner Albertine to whom they are introduced by hired Pickpockets.

The protagonist of the play is History, and, to some extent, Albertine who dreams of nudity while her impotent suitors keep dressing her up. The fashion designer, Fior, an intellectual, tries to dress up History in new forms (ideologies), but realizes that he "can't divine" a form because ". . . an enigma/ History is without a face! "[52] Instead of continuing the cultural tradition, he is tired of it and allows the improvisation of the costumes to develop in an elemental way, which culminates in the masquerade ball suggested by Count Hufnagiel, the disguised revolutionary Joseph. During the ball and the puppet-like somnambulic dance of the aristocracy (cf. the Mulch dance),[53] followed by chaos and confusion caused by the stealing and raping Pickpockets, the horsetrader and terrorist Hugnagiel leads the lackeys in a revolution.

The final act takes place after two wars and a revolution in the ruins of the castle symbolizing Poland. The world has lost its old form, resulting in a strange confusion of matter. The aristocrats and the intelligentsia, changed into objects (cf. Prince-Lamp, etc.), hide from the onslaught of Hufnagiel who gallops mounted on the Professor-Horse. Their transformation from the previous puppet-like form into objects dehumanizes and reduces them to a state of dead matter. Gombrowicz exposes the bankruptcy of all political ideology[54] and derides the intellectuals for aiding the cause of the Bolshevik revolution. The Marxist Professor, suffering from incurable vomiting, expresses the futility of his utopian dream:

> I hate myself
> But I likewise hate this hatred of mine
> Because it's mine! A product of me!
> Who is it that hates?
> It is *I* who hate! I! I, a bourgeois!
> I am the pathological product of a sick system
> I, a morbid tumor, I, an ulcer, I, a disease
> Consumed to the core by a social sin
> And so I hate myself . . . but I also hate
> This hatred of mine . . . and again I hate
> The hatred of my hatred which also hates
> My hatred . . . and I'm puking, puking, puking! (69)

This pathetic self-hate of the intellectual echoes Słowacki's Kordian and Krasiński's Count Henry, as well as Witkiewicz's Sajetan in *The Shoemakers.* In Gombrowicz the bankrupt ideological revolution is replaced by a biological revolution led by Albertine and the Pickpockets. With her appeal for nudity she is an instigator of truth as well as an erotic symbol. Her youth and nudity are the incarnation of Gombrowicz's cosmogony; she is an antinomy of Form and, therefore, she manifests man's authentic existence. Albertine, believed dead, is reincarnated by a *deus ex machina* and rises from the coffin in all her youth and nudity, accompanied by a chant which could be considered a poetic summation of Gombrowicz's revolutionary ideas. Her nudity denies culture in its false forms:

> O youth, eternally youthful, hail!
> O nudity, eternally nude, hail!
> O youthful nudity, nudely youthful!
> O nudity of youth, youthfully nude! (107)

The function of language is of prime importance in Gombrowicz's plays. In this he follows the Romantic tradition. In *The Marriage* language plays essentially the role of a costume, a telegraphic message, or a dream-logic shorthand. In *Operetta* language likewise creates the characters' form but is intentionally musical. The style, consisting of repetitions, apostrophes, parody on Gallomania, onomatopoeia and alliteration, results in a farce and transforms the dialogue into operettic arias. The form accentuates the parody of "monumental" historical upheavals, ending on an optimistic note in an "Ode to Youth." Here, as in its Romantic archetype, youth replaces the fossilized old gray forms.

Gombrowicz created in exile and therefore was free to express his unorthodox views in his avant-garde plays. Such freedom became possible only after 1956 for the dramatists who were working in Poland. There was a rebirth of playwriting among poets, prose writers, and even philosophers, since drama offered an ideal release from frustration and an excellent means of communication with the public on every social level. Poland did not have to create an avant-garde drama. It simply revived the native Romantic traditional and twentieth-century avant-garde plays, based on poetry, metaphor, parody, and the grotesque. *The Green Goose,* called by its author Konstanty Ildefons Gałczyński "the smallest theater in the world," was published in the weekly *Przekrój* (*Profile*), between 1946 and 1950. It consisted of pure nonsense, mocking scenes, and prepared the audience for the Theater of the Absurd. It served as a link between Witkiewicz and the young generation of playwrights such as Mrożek and Różewicz who represent the mainstream of postwar Polish avant-garde drama.

In *Tango* (1964) Sławomir Mrożek (1930–) follows Gombrowicz's universality and his derision of Romantic myths. Like *The Marriage, Tango* illustrates the absurdity of imposing a form or ideology on reality which is anarchic and irrational in nature. *Tango (The Need for Order and Harmony)* is Mrożek's most incisive drama before the mid-1970s and a culmination of all his earlier plays. It deviates in structure from Romantic plays, approximating rather the bourgeois drama built on a precise plot, action, and denouement. Basically a family drama, it is a metaphor of the contemporary world. It extends in scope to an investigation of the social, cultural, historical, and political decline of a liberal Europe from the *fin de siècle* to the present time. The family consists of three generations each of which contributed progressively to the decline of cultural and moral values, which leads to total chaos. The hero, Arthur, is a contemporary version of the Romantic Konrad, a "priest" who wants to save the world singlehandedly, despite his artist-father's warning that his plan will end in a farce. A born pragmatist, he knows what he wants: "An orderly world . . . and the right to rebel."[55] He hopes to achieve this by reverting to tradition. In attempting to restore cohesion to a world reduced to a caricature, to bring order into the anarchic life of his family, and to give dignity to his sexual relationship with Ala, Arthur imposes the form of a ritual wedding (i.e. the sacred, Romantic *topos*) on the existing absurd reality. As in Gombrowicz's *The Marriage,* this experiment ends in a total disaster.

The preparation for the ceremony is a masquerade and an artifice. Arthur realizes that "there is no turning back to the old forms." (88) He is in "despair that form can never save the world" (89) and since God "[has] lost his appeal," what he is "after now is a living ideal." (91) He gets it watching his grandmother die. The new system requires sacrifices, since "death is . . . the supreme force." (94) Power is the only solution. Arthur, an intellectual weakling, is incapable of killing. He changes from a Konrad into a Kordian. He delegates this task to the brute Eddie. Here Mrożek, like Słowacki, becomes a Jester, deriding the hero's Romantic pose. Likewise, the wedding, as was the case in *The Marriage,* is only an empty, impaired myth which represents for Arthur the only form of rebellion against the immorality of his parents. It is also a means to achieve some order in the world, as Arthur admits:

> Nothing is important in itself. Things in themselves are meaningless. Unless we give them character, we drown in a sea of indifference. (42)

> I have to rebuild a world, and for that I must have a wedding. It's perfectly simple. (54)

As in Gombrowicz's play *The Marriage,* the bride deceives Arthur prior to the ceremony with Eddie, the servant. This parody wedding, a double deformation of a myth, ends in death. However, unlike in *The Marriage,* Arthur gets killed by the traitor. A minor family coup unleashes unexpectedly threatening, uncontrollable forces. *Tango* ends in a dance of the great-uncle Eugene, an intellectual, with Eddie — the Frankenstein. The tango continues the traditional Mulch dance (see fn. 53). Brute power takes over with frightening speed. Eddie, the obedient servant, becomes master, aided by the spineless intellectual. We have an ending as in *Operetta* where the vomiting Professor, an intellectual, fed up with culture, helps Hufnagiel in staging a Lopakian revolution. In both plays, *Tango* and *Operetta,* we have the authors' indictment against the ineffectiveness of the intelligentsia (cf. Słowacki) for their inability to counteract brute force (cf. also Krasiński), and a settling of accounts for aiding them.

Like most of the Polish contemporary dramas, *Tango* is, in many respects, a poetic lyrical play. It is written in prose with some interpolation of verse. The almost classical structure and predominantly simple style of *Tango* is transformed into the Absurd by the presentation of a heap of obsolescent ideologies, including Arthur's attempt to restore order. It abounds in grotesque elements, e.g., the juxtaposition of death and the wedding in the final act, and in absurdity; for example, the grandmother's dying is viewed as inappropriate behavior in society. Mrożek's plot composition is of remarkable precision. Like Chekhov, he gives hints of the denouement. The catafalque is ever-present, an omen of death. Eddie's casually uttered ditties, e.g., "Bring your bedding. Skip the wedding," (29) at the beginning of the play allude to the intrigue. Such elements show that Mrożek's techniques are not limited to those of the avant-garde.

Tadeusz Różewicz (1921–), the eminent poet, is another leading playwright in postwar avant-garde drama, i.e. the Polish variant of the Theater of the Absurd. Like Mrożek, he has been influenced by Gałczyński's miniature theater *The Green Goose*. But while Mrożek, in the manner of Gombrowicz, uses the traditional, bourgeois drama as the vehicle for his Absurd plays, Różewicz continues the line of Witkiewicz's anti-drama, filtered through Gałczyński's concise and laconic form. He emerges as the most original postwar Polish dramatist, having attained in his anti-plays a total departure from the norms of the twentieth-century, fifty-year-old Polish avant-garde drama.

Still, Różewicz shares Gombrowicz's and Mrożek's derision of Romanticism. He blames the past, nurtured on Romantic rhetoric, and the cult of heroism for the unbearable present. Having experienced the Holocaust, he is suspicious of the past. The theme of the bankruptcy of tradition, culture, religion, and ideologies during the Second World War, resulting in the disintegration of man's individuality, pervades Różewicz's plays. *The Old Woman Broods* (1968) presents a powerful metaphor of the contemporary world. The old woman, who can be viewed as an incarnation of present-day Poland, is covered by layers of old rags, representing the traditional values, which changed with the passing times. All the heritage left by the traditional past is reduced to suffocating "old decorations" and a heap of rubbish. The heap keeps growing, enlarged by modern civilization's refuse. The rubbish enfolds human beings who in turn become garbage themselves. The old woman, immobilized by the weight of her garb, sits on that heap, trying to give birth to a new life, to restore dignity to man's shattered individuality before it is too late. The powerlessness is the most dramatic situation in the play. The absence of drama constitutes the drama (cf. his earlier plays, and also plays by Beckett). The concern with the individual, Romantic in nature, indicates that even Różewicz, who among his generation in Poland went furthest in rejecting the stereotype "Polish" culture, tradition, and morality to create a new drama, cannot rid himself of tradition entirely. In his case Romanticism is used as a "mythological code of traditional signs"[56] to express problems topical for our times. Różewicz, as the conscience of contemporary Polish literature, indicts not only past tradition, but also the present. Therefore, this mythological code serves to deride both Romanticism and the present, since both the past and the present world of living automatons suffer from the same malaise. "They are without heart and without spirit, a throng of skeletons,"[57] to use Mickiewicz's indictment of the old world preceding Romanticism.

Paradoxically, in the very rejection and derision of tradition which led him to create a new form of drama, Różewicz continues in a way the tradition of the Polish avant-garde, started with the Romantic bards, which always reached for new, daring forms. His first, and one of Poland's most outstanding postwar dramas, *The Card Index* (1960),[58] deals with the problem of the disintegration of man's individuality. Among his plays it also exemplifies best the continuity and deviation from Romantic tradition. Even in the innovative structure of the play we can discern some continuity. Różewicz's "open form drama," as he calls it, is a composite of several elements such as prehistory (the Chorus of Elders which acts as the playwright's mouthpiece), dialogues, soliloquies, dreams, hallucinations, recollections, and flashbacks presented as a visual metaphor on the stage (cf. the prehistory and other elements in *Kordian, Forefathers' Eve, The Undivine Comedy*). As in *Forefathers' Eve,* part III, but carried to an extreme, the events in *The Card Index* are a collage-like conglomerate of nonsequential, accidental happenings and fragments from the life of the Hero who is the sole element unifying the open-structured drama (cf. all parts of *Forefathers' Eve*). The Chorus of Elders, commenting on the Hero's state, bring to mind choruses of angels and devils of the Romantic archetype, and of medieval morality plays. We find similarities in the Hero's change of identity, of names (cf. Gustav and Kordian) and in his transformation from a Romantic hero — an underground fighter (cf. Konrad) — to an anti-hero incapable of any action, a bored descendant of Kordian. This type of a drama does not describe the Hero's world; it merely synthesizes it by means of images.

In *The Card Index* language plays a dominant role. Though disjointed, it is realistic and simple. It is not a means of communication but rather of alienation. Therefore, language itself constitutes the drama. His is a Theater of Fact with socio-political overtones in its mocking of history and literature. These aspects are largely a continuation of the Romantic prototype, as is the Hero's cult of Napoleon and of nature. Różewicz, a scoffing Jester of tradition, does not, unlike Witkiewicz and Mrożek, build his drama on a parody of the old. Instead, as in a poem, he juxtaposes simple separate scenes, using the colloquial idiom stripped of ornamentation, and with simple people as heroes. *The Card Index* consists of "happenings" whose flexibility and mobility, precluding any beginning, middle, or end of action, Różewicz finds as a dramatic form best suited to reflect the *Zeitgeist* which is rooted in uncertainty and inconsistency. It is essentially a realistic play which takes place in the present, exposing the disintegration of the contemporary Hero, an Everyman who has passed the stage of the Ionesco heroes'"search for self,"[59] reaching total passivity. His desires are confined strictly to living matter, i.e. sexuality. He is preoccupied with his body, which in this first play foreshadows Różewicz's eventual escape into biologism. The drama consists of hastily juxtaposed accidental fragments of real life which do not differ in value or intensity. Hence, there are no points of culmination. The prehistory is the most essential part since it informs us about the Hero's childhood and his war experiences.

The setting consists of a windowless room dominated by a bed. Through the open doors various people pass by. We hear occasional snatches of their conversation. Some stop, look at the Hero, eavesdrop, read newspapers. "It appears as though there is a street passing through the Hero's room,"[60] says the author. The action is continuous. Lying in bed, the Hero is situated, literally and figuratively, as if on a crossing of various external and internal stimuli. Since there is no linear time progression, the Hero, confronted by various characters representing different facets of his past, is simultaneously a child, a grown man, a lover, a son, a former partisan fighter and presently an operetta director. His name changes with each new phase of his life, as though a different "self" were involved with every "happening." In a sense, this occurrence can also be viewed as a disintegration of one character into many. The Hero speaks, occasionally, in disjointed, grotesque monologues, soliloquies and dialogues which shed some light on his past, on his convictions, but which mostly reflect a stereotyped and automatized inner life.

The Hero is like a blank form in a file system, ready to be filled with fragments of information regarding reminiscences, associations, sentiments, duties and desires. This information is provided by a succession of "happenings" as various characters enter from the street. The parents arrive. There is an attempt at communication via a farcical quarrel, accompanied by the Chorus of Elders who recite a stanza from Mickiewicz's "Ode to Youth":

> He who in childhood cut off Hydra's head,
> Will in his youth the blood of Centaurs shed,
> Will rescue victims of the Demon,
> Will gather laurels up in Heaven. (40)

The Chorus, representing the old tradition, continually passes judgment, contrasting the anonymous Hero's inactivity with the great exploits of the heroes of the past, symbolized by Hercules. The high rhetoric detested by the author and intentionally juxtaposed here with the trivia of the parents' dialogue with the Hero (whom they treat as though he were still seven years old) renders the myth obsolescent and hollow. As is customary in Różewicz, quotations from Romantic works have an air of blasphemy and profanation. Furthermore, a number of parodic episodes display the author's detest for spineless intellectuals and servility of literature.

The formerly active Hero, seen now in a state of inertia, is a grotesque, sentimental, isolated, alienated figure who yearns for some stability even if it means staying in bed. His withdrawing into silence and turning his back toward the world is his only protest against dehumanization. He endures as the personification of the changeability of living matter into an object-like form. Here Różewicz carries to an extreme the theme of the ending in Gombrowicz's *Operetta*. The Hero's inactivity is too much for the Chorus to bear:

> Do something. . . . Push the action forward. At least scratch your ear. (60)

> But even in a Beckett play somebody talks, waits, suffers, dreams, somebody weeps, dies, falls, farts. If you don't move the theater is in ruins. (61)

The Hero, provoked to action, slaughters the Chorus with a knife, thereby silencing his conscience. In his soliloquy he admits, standing against the wall, that he is dead because he lacks belief in anything. The wall is the end of the line, as predicted by Witkacy. The times are suited neither for a dramatic hero, nor for a comedy.

The yearning for stability of the average, depersonalized hero, which we find in all of Różewicz's plays is the theme of *The Witnesses Or Our Small Stabilization* (1962). (The title, incidentally, has become a proverbial expression in Poland, just as Beckett's *Waiting for Godot* has in the West.) The puppet-like characters, who in our times are manipulated by big schemes, have the illusion of that stability which the strings allow them. The true progress and dynamism which would lead to that stabilization on a universal scale, yearned for by Różewicz, are ironically replaced by a small stabilization within the motion of a circle, such as going to bed and getting up. Różewicz notes the way in which the small stabilization provides security by supplying prefabricated possessions and ideas: "The trousers and poetics/the porcelain and aesthetics/and the wineglasses and ethics."[61]

Just as Robbe-Grillet has written a book, *The House of Encounters,* on how to write one, Różewicz has written a biography of how to write a play. The metaliterary theme was actually touched upon in all his plays but in *The Interrupted Act* and especially in *Birth Rate (A Biography of a Theatrical Play)* — discussed elsewhere[62] — it became the dominant feature. Drama does not consist of scenes with dialogues, but of descriptions of various situations. The scene directions explode the play from within, destroying its cohesiveness and substituting chaos. The commentaries and confessions become part of the internal drama while the pulsating human mass which bursts apart the train compartment becomes the first major manifestation of Różewicz's turn toward biologism.

At first, Różewicz's poetic world was possessed by death. The dead departed, replaced by people who only had the external appearance of people. They are puppets possessed by a passion for amassing material possessions — "the small stabilization." Hence, the world has become dominated by dead matter (i.e. things) and living matter (i.e. bodies and sex). The procreation of biological living matter full of lust and inhumanity has directed Różewicz toward obsessive sexual themes. But the biologism is a deceptive solution as we see in *Birth Rate* (1969–70) and especially in *White Marriage* (1974)[63] where bodily functions and sex are dramatized in a shocking manner. Różewicz, as Witkiewicz before him, tries to interpret life experiences along naturalistic lines. Besides existential anxiety, these experiences are somatically rooted in eroticism, an area in which the desire for transcendence of life's reality is united with an intensive experiencing of one's own uniqueness. (The same is evident in his long poem *Regio,* 1970.)

In Różewicz all big words are derided. The present is inhuman; therefore, it has no right to big words or tradition (cf. *The Card Index*). The noble vestments have turned to rags, which are used to cover the stinking sham of this world (cf. *The Old Woman Broods*). Romantic tradition appears in Różewicz's dramas as a ghost in a dream whose features are almost forgotten. It casts a shadow upon the emptiness of contemporaneity. Piwińska suggests that Różewicz could be considered "a crypto-Romantic" who learned to despise the potential victims of World War III, dressed luxuriously, enraptured with sex and leading their lives as in a dance macabre.[64] His attacks on the past, and especially on the present, are reminiscent of Słowacki's Byronic derision.

Różewicz, discarding all traditions and culture, especially the high variant of the human condition, battles with them on traditional grounds (as demonstrated earlier), but in a peculiar way. His loose collage-like drama, which forms a unity of principles higher than those used in traditional drama, is connected as much with Surrealism as it is with Mickiewicz's theory of Slavic drama, set forth in Lecture XVI. It is a Slavic mystery play, a panorama of powerlessness which Różewicz is transforming into a Polish funeral. One could join Dedecius in describing Różewicz's drama as "a progression of close-ups of a modern tragicomical hell [which] appears even more unnerving because it is without continuity and without alternative, without purgatory and without heaven."[65]

We can also find in some Polish postwar dramas a revisionist continuation of Romanticism. Its sacred myths are utilized in the form of either parody, anecdote, or reproach. Konstanty Ildefons Gałczyński's (1905–1953) *The Green Goose,* created immediately after World War II, is a mini-drama which consists of a series of such parodies and anecdotes. Gałczyński, considered the first Polish postwar creator of a purely native Surrealist drama and Theater of the Absurd, often derives his sense of humor from dramatizing Polish postwar realities. Anachronisms of the Romantic tradition colliding with the new Socialist order result in pure nonsense. In his dramas, varying from a few lines to a few pages, he parodies Romantic heroes, creating a whole gallery of caricatures and grotesque masks. Gałczyński's rationalism and common sense make him puncture the inflated grandeur of "Polishness." He ridicules the most holy Romantic themes, i.e. the Messianic martyrdom and the prophetic mission of the poet. In such plays as *A Mickiewicz Matinee* and *An Unknown*

Manuscript of Wyspiański, Gałczyński mocks the lofty tradition of Polish drama cults and the role of the poet-redeemer, and questions the value of art. Each Surrealistic joke and anecdote progressively cuts the ties with tradition, using the device of the curtain, which in Gałczyński's drama has a distinct personality and is perhaps its most important character. It thus literally draws a curtain on the end of Polish tradition. Gałczyński's jokes against Romanticism, filled with a gypsy-like abandon, make him a troubador of "a folk-like, fair-time spectacle."[66] His mini-plays, intended primarily to entertain and instruct the masses, entered the Polish stage after 1956. Because of their journalistic origin they provide, in addition, an unusual artistic chronicle of the intellectual and social life of the postwar period. Furthermore, the tiny, intentionally absurd scenes, published in the most popular weekly *Przekrój,* formed a taste for the unexpected in the Pole of the postwar period. The mini-drama prepared the way for the public's acceptance of the loosely structured avant-garde drama of the sixties, and influenced its playwrights.

Some of Mrożek's early plays are jokes, anecdotes based on Romantic themes. But unlike Gałczyński, in the case of Mrożek, as with Różewicz, the revision of Romanticism pervading the present becomes central in Polish literature. In his drama *The Turkey* (1960) Mrożek uses a peculiar literary pastiche to play a joke on Romantic themes. He transfers into the present a fairytale pub, replete with all the ludicrous stereotypes of Romantic works. In this play we can detect artistic traces of Słowacki's *Balladyna,* the platonic lovers from *In Switzerland* and the Kordian-like poet. The wedding of the pair does not materialize (cf. *Tango*) but is replaced by an institutionalized love in tune with our times. The Prince plans a Romantic war. The farce is heightened by a parable. Where the characters fail, the turkey succeeds in changing its routine. Its courtship of a chicken produces a new mysterious life — a pyramid-shaped egg.

The Death of a Lieutenant (1962) is an anecdote with a predominantly pedagogical message. Although Mrożek ridicules the Ordon case of Polish history here, more important is the portrayal of Romanticism taught in school as injurious to the Polish psyche, since each Polish child must memorize "Ordon's Redoubt" ("Reduta Ordona") by Mickiewicz. In this play Mrożek's technique of pastiche is even more pronounced than in *The Turkey.* Its very structure echoes *Forefathers' Eve.* Here Mrożek becomes the Jester joking about the poet-Priest ("44"), the falsehood of his myth, i.e. the heroic death of the much-eulogized Lieutenant whom Mrożek makes live till the present in order that he may expose the bard. The farce reaches its climax in the jail scene, a modern version of *Forefathers' Eve,* part III, where Orson shares the cell with guitar-strumming, jeans-clad beatniks. His dialogue with the Editor is a hilarious spoof of changing attitudes toward the Romantic notion of heroic death. To prove his identity, Orson resorts to exorcism. The scene from *Forefathers' Eve,* part II, is repeated. The Choir of the Derailed

Youth calls forth the ghost of the Poet, whom they accuse of having tortured them with his poetry. "Let's tear the classics to pieces, and when we are done with the classics, let's tear his plays and poems; let the bare bones shine! "[67] Orson decides to blow himself up so that this time there should not be any doubt; people will believe when they read about it in the press. But even this act becomes a debacle. The dynamite turns out to be a pile of books; the Poet's curse pursues him in the final farce: "I am dying unexploded! " (286) "At last, the national problem of the Lieutenants's death disappears," (286) says the Jailor, expressing the author's view of the hard-dying problem of Romanticism. Mrożek seems to share some of Orson's fate. In the pure nonsense of the Polish archive of the Absurd, he has again seen ghosts which came to haunt him. His constant return to Romantic themes, even in his parable of power, has developed into a complex and functions as autotherapy. The contemporary Pole suffers from the Kordian complex. This explains Mrożek's Surrealism. "Mrożek is a realist *above* the Polish Absurd [which is] natively Romantic."[68]

A similarity with Gałczyński's aims can also be found in the prominent poet Miron Białoszewski (1922–). A playwright and founder of the avant-garde Theater Apart, he has exerted a tremendous influence on The Student Theater, and The Theater of Pleonazmus. In his play *The Crusades* (1958) he shows an even greater inclination toward Surrealist metaphors than Gałczyński. *The Crusades* demonstrates Białoszewski's grotesque vision of history which follows Krasiński's derision of European tradition. The destructiveness, corruption, and perversion of the crusades are expressed by means of destruction of the traditional language into a linguistic grotesque. A mixture of contrived names of various origins such as 'burgrave Linde of Mount Lexicon' (a farcical reference to Linde's dictionary) or 'the cardinal Purée of Maggi-bouillon,' of neologisms, foreign words, nonsense words, repetition of morphemes, and transrational language create a linguistic tower of Babel and recreate the confusion, baseness, debauchery, and absurdity of the crusades. Humor and farce are maintained on a high level solely by means of an interchange of syntactic structures and morphological shifts: "Głos: Mohammed rasul Allah! / Baldwin: Deus sic veult! Do machin, . . . ! Deus ex machina! / Głos: Mohammed machina! .... Baldwin: Mohammed Ma-ha-ha-ha-hammed! .... Głos: Mohammed machen kaput! "[69]

Białoszewski's mistrust toward traditional language has been interpreted by Stanisław Barańczak as a form of Romantic rebellion, while the usage of a basically brutalized transformation of colloquial language was to signify a reconciliation between the artist and the simple people, separated by the high rhetoric of the Romantic bards, which he considers profane.[70]

There are also plays written in the mid-seventies which manifest an outright bitter attitude to Romantic tradition. They focus on themes of Romanticism, but are based on facts, not on their idealized version which is for school consumption. Tomasz Lubieński's dramas are representative of this trend.

His *Encampment* (1974) shows Mickiewicz visiting a Polish legion in Burgas, where the realities are far from heroic or beautiful. Although the play is written in a Romantic style, the intent is not to follow tradition, but rather to treat Romanticism as a national problem.

The plays of Ernest Bryll (1934–), a well-known poet and novelist, stand apart from the plays discussed earlier. He continues the Romantic tradition but in a way which is hard to categorize. *The November Affair* (1968), his first and most popular play which despite the critics' reservations was performed in every city in Poland, represents an eclectic mixture of tendencies (discussed above) regarding Romanticism: derision, revision, and submersion into Polish tradition. However, all these elements are haphazardly combined in such a way that the playwright's views are unclear. Written in a lively and facile verse, *The November Affair* is a loosely structured, collage-like play stylized mainly after Mickiewicz's *Forefathers' Eve,* parts II and III, with an admixture of Słowacki's *Kordian* and Wyspiański's *The Wedding* and *Deliverance.* The stylization of Romantic and Neo-Romantic *topoi* results in a "panoramic form"[71] which acts as a backdrop for the panorama of present-day Poland. Similarly, it is a poetics of allusions and quotations from the great Romantics through Norwid and other writers up to the very present. The form and language taken from the Romantic prototypes help Bryll to comment simultaneously on Poland, past and present. The title alludes to the Warsaw uprising of November 1830. Bryll rings changes on the present panorama by focusing upon an English journalist touring Poland. His two guides, who act as the playwright's spokesmen, try to show and explain the present by deriding and disputing the Romantic past. People play roles, ignoring the fact that under the pavement there is a cemetery.

The composition is based on two traditional antinomies: (1) nihilism and heroism — baseness and virtue, which constitute Polish national characteristics and (2) the contrast between the Polish and the Western experience. The latter is insinuated by The Old Poet:

> This is exactly the thing for you to see/ to write a story in England. Nowhere in the world/ — except perhaps in Mexico — will a man/ find the same love of the dead running through/ the peepshow of the living. Who else could/ stand these overcrowded graveyards and these/ corpses still waiting under the skin of/ Warsaw to be found?[72]

This schizophrenia is best understood by The Old Poet (who symbolizes Mickiewicz), but totally puzzling to the foreigner, who is oblivious of the fact that Warsaw is a cemetery filled with painful memories of traumatic war experiences.

All Souls' Day, opening the play, is followed by a wedding. The people do not communicate, scoff at Romantic love, dance like puppets to old tunes (cf. again the Mulch dance) unable to create new ones. Bryll apparently would like to get rid of the Romantic tradition, to get out of its vicious circle. But he is only capable of rousing emotions by means of an overdose of the Romantic *topoi,* failing to awaken any intellectual stimulation.

A self-questioning continuation of Romanticism is seen in dramas attempting to deal with the problems of the present-day Romantic hero. Helmut Kajzar's *With Three Crosses* (1973) is most representative of this type of play. Its loose form is inherited from the Romantic prototype, revealing Expressionist tendencies toward a "cry of the soul." The piece portrays an ill-adjusted contemporary Romantic hero-poet at odds with a world presented as evil, strange, alienated, forcing people to lie, to play parts, and to commit crimes. Yet, sincerity remains the highest value for the hero. He is childishly innocent and does not understand why his sincerity and his innocent smile provoke suspicion toward him. He is even incarcerated for it, interrogated for revolutionary activities against the totalitarian regime, beaten, sexually molested by the investigator, and forced to sign an admission of guilt. Having gotten rid of his identification papers and become an anonymous slave, he signs the fraudulent document with three crosses. The play contains a mixture of native, traditionally Romantic with foreign counter-cultural elements, which make it symptomatic of current trends in the fringe drama. It alludes to Artaud, Beckett, Hollywood stars, the American peace movement, among other things.

Outside the development of drama in the narrow sense, but continuing along similar lines, are such para-dramatic student performances as: *The Polish Dreambook* and *Exodus* by the STU Theater, *The Retrospective* and others by The Theater 77, and *Delerium Tremens* by The Theater Pleonazmus. These are not dramas, but "happenings" and collages of various fragments and ideas "written" on the stage. They also combine native Polish tradition with Western, as does to some extent The Laboratory Theater of Grotowski. Gombrowicz's idea of the Interhuman Church might have found a realization in The Poor Theater of Grotowski, who shares similar goals with the emigré playwright, especially in his *Apocalipsis cum figuris,* while French and Oriental mime can be considered a foreign influence. The Laboratory Theater seeks truth in man's inner being, believing that it is possible to attain truth, wisdom, authenticity, or holiness — the goal of an art whose highest achievements could be identified with the brotherhood of early Christianity.

Beside the main — reinterpreted — Romantic direction of the postwar drama the peasant drama deserves brief mention. While it has certain connections with Romanticism, dealing as it does with the question "What to do with the Polish peasants," it is nonetheless closely patterned on Wyspiański's *Curse.* Its predominant themes are: great passions leading to slaughter, elemental greed, feuds over soil for which one even pays with crimes (cf. the plays of Karol Hubert Roztworowski). Among the specimens of this genre are stylizations of Mickiewicz's *Forefathers's Eve,* parts I and II. We also find dramas about collectivization which from a literary point of view are negligible. Also, there are the poetic stylizations by Teresa Lubkiewicz-Urbanowicz — *Wijuny*; Ernest Bryll's *On the Mountains on the Clouds*..., a stylized nativity play, or his *Painted on Glass,* a musical based on themes of the Mountaineers. Both these texts go back to the pre-Romantic play by Wojciech Bogusławski — *A Supposed Miracle, or Cracovians and Mountaineers.*

The play *Quadrangle* (1976) by Edward Redliński is an attempt to present the migration of peasantry to the cities and to show the intelligentsia of peasant descent. However, the play by Ryszard Latko, *Daddy, Daddy, the Case Fell Through* (1976), deals strictly with the problem of the village. It shows the present-day village with its reaction to the changes in culture and civilization. Structurally the play is mediocre. It represents a series of sketches loosely tied together. But its value lies in its truthful observations, expressed in an authentic dialect of the Wadowice area on the borderline between the Cracow region and Silesia. It is interesting in its ideas but generally gloomy despite some humorous scenes. It is the Polish version of Franz Xaver Kroetz (the contemporary German playwright), and presently very popular. Its ties with the Romantic tradition are limited to its disdain for the cult of reason and civilization.

The dialect intensifies the realism of the play and is a device for the direct characterization of a person; it helps to penetrate the psyche of the protagonists. The important fact is that Latko has departed from the literary tradition and stereotyped plots, i.e. from the existing forms of peasant drama. Unlike *The Curse,* this play is not universal in its subject matter. Instead it deals with the idealized model of a contemporary Polish peasant as seen on television. Latko's play tells what results from this generalization. The protagonist Placek in his own way is very modern. He knows what norms to follow and is perfectly capable of adapting to them without hypocrisy. Who then is to be blamed for the hideous results? Placek's modern life consists of hoarding all kinds of appliances, all of which are locked up in an unused parlor, bought for the sake of prestige, so that all should be envious. He is expecting a visit of the Women's League and prepares an exemplary peasant speech, which is a sham. He constantly tells his son to study, yet interrupts him every minute. He keeps the old grandmother locked up and starved, only showing her off on festive occasions amid the amassed gadgetry. The peasant has lost his identity. He is left to his old shrewdness. "Play dumb if in need. Everyone will yield to a dumb peasant!"[73] His second trait is greediness and cruelty toward the grandmother and the half-witted son. The tragedy here turns into comedy. What is made fun of is not Placek but his expectations fueled by technology.

A Hegelian antithesis to Romanticism is a presentation of the simple folk (*lud*) not as a class which ought to be saved (i.e. in the intelligentsia's approach: "What to do with the folk?"), but as an independent subject of history and drama. The tendency in these dramas is to do away with the idealization of the subject, showing rather an inclination toward the opposite, i.e. to darken the picture.

It is not without significance that there is a chronological concurrence between Latko's play *Daddy, Daddy, the Case Fell Through* and Mrożek's *The Emigrants,* both of which appeared in the 1970s. The plays share the theme of an emancipated peasant or worker of peasant descent, i.e. of "the folk," as an autonomous subject. Up to this play most Polish playwrights, except Różewicz, were neither able to separate themselves from Romantic tradition, to speak seriously about the problems of the present, nor to find answers which would change the Polish mentality. Nurtured on Romantic rhetoric and stylization, they are unable to speak about big issues simply and sincerely; at best they can scoff and deride.

The Emigrants,[74] which I consider one of the best and most profound postwar Polish dramas, is Mrożek's first play written in a serious tone, his first to present *real people* and bare the dialectics of their soul in the manner of the great realistic tradition. Unlike his previous characters who were puppets manipulated by circumstances, these characters are concrete and able to rise above the situation. *The Emigrants* is a conventional, bourgeois play in which Mrożek uses the most ascetic form of dialogue to express complex contemporary issues, directly connected with the old and most essential problem: "What to do with Poland?" Hence, the new play can be considered a continuation of *Tango* with regard to this question, and a serious attempt at solving it. Formally "it rehabilitates all which is defined disdainfully as 'traditional'."[75]

In *The Emigrants* the two protagonists AA and XX, who share a room somewhere in present-day France, are diametrically opposed to each other "as though of different species and faiths" (18), they are direct descendants of *Tango's* Arthur and Eddie. AA, an intellectual and writer, and XX, a worker and a boor of peasant descent, brought together by emigration, carry on a vigorous, honest and simple dialogue in a language almost devoid of symbolism and allusion about issues concerning present-day Poland and its future destiny. Mrożek has pitted against each other intellectually unequal partners in a most important dialogue in order to find a solution for a better Poland. But the very process of the dialogue is just as important as the results it hopes to achieve. To begin with, the room which AA and XX share becomes a test tube in which we see what "an intellectual who wants *to be* [free] and a worker who wants *to have* can say to each other."[76] It becomes clear in the process of fraternization that they say to each other a lot revealing their innermost desires, secrets, and complexes. The "nudity" of the soul is a powerful equalizer and is truth-provoking (cf. *Operetta*).

Let us take a closer look at the heroes. AA at first puts on a whole mystery show for XX, parading as a political exile planning to write about an ideal slave whose prototype he has found in XX, a guilt-ridden savior of the simple people. AA is made to realize his limitation by the constant challenge of XX. When AA justifies his exile by saying "here one can spread one's wings," (11) an allusion to a soaring bird — a Romantic metaphor for a poet — XX cuts him down to size: "like a little fly . . . bzzz." (11) AA's comment "I only help you in the realization of your situation" (10) becomes the *key* to the new, serving role of an intellectual in a collective society. AA's gradually awakened awareness of the intellectual's new role is serious and sincere, but the burden of the Romantic heritage and of history makes his statements sound like a pose. AA realizes that "history is vengeful." (10)

But Mrożek achieves an additional effect by playing the role of a Jester, exposing through AA the absurdity of the Romantic mentality: (1) AA's belief in his superiority over XX and his flowery rhetoric, (2) his possessions, and, finally, (3) his lofty mission:

> I who considered myself always as a precious cell of the most highly developed brain substance . . . as a noble neuron, which is something higher and above matter . . . am in the company of a protozoan. (15) [A satire on Słowacki's metempsychosis of *Genesis from the Spirit*]

> Let's say that I have my dear, beloved words, words for all the letters of the alphabet. (22) [Cf. with the derision of Konrad]

> I will shake you and will scream at you until I make a man out of you. I will not rest until I achieve this. Because as long as you are an ox, I am a swine . . . Because it can't be that only one of us should be a man. Either both of us are people or neither of us. (25)

As we compare these quotations we notice a change in AA's language which descends from the Romantic bathos (cf. quotations 1 and 2), to a simpler language of self-deprecation (cf. 3), assuming in the last quotation, about his new role, a simplicity on the level of XX. However, even the final statement in its entirety (not cited here) has the tone of a Messianic vision, which infuriates XX and provokes him to threaten AA with his brute power. The quotations demonstrate at the same time the oscillation of AA from the Man-Head, the first among the human species (hence his name AA?), to the self-deprecation of a Jester (cf. Gustav and Kordian) and again to a visionary, an activist, a Priest (cf. Konrad). These oscillations are partly a residue of the Romantic burden, but mostly stem from inferiority feelings toward XX's strength and common sense: "You are the blood and [back]bone of our nation . . . the pride, a sacred substance for our patriots," (8) he says to XX while confiding: "You consider me a hero? . . . . I am an ordinary rag. An ordinary coward." (22) The primary oscillation, as insinuated by Mrożek, stems from his necessity for a compromise and his uncertainty of the new role demanded of him by the collective. Having tasted in emigration freedom and autonomy, which resulted in alienation, he longs for a home. AA is the first character in Mrożek's work whose desire for an affirmative life in Poland through collectivity is strong and sincere.

XX, representing until recently an unknown quantity in Polish history, has an advantage. Unlike AA he is burdened by neither tradition, culture, nor history. His basic peasant wholesomeness has not been impaired by culture; XX is stingy, egotistic, and suspicious, but not mean. He has pride and dignity as he proves on several occasions. He is strong like a rock, he is a nationalist, chauvinist, and like a rock deeply rooted in his native soil. Like his predecessor Eddie in *Tango,* XX hates "to think about thinking," (29) despises books, and believes that there are enough of "these abominations" without AA's contribution. Uninterested in politics, he does not think about regimes but material security. Therefore, a country which provides enough food and shelter is no prison to him. (21) Not having known freedom, he does not miss it. To him a day off from work means freedom. In contrast to AA, a political emigré without family whose sole possession is his vocabulary, XX has tangible possessions and a strong nucleus — his family and his country. His foremost goal in life is to earn money abroad and to acquire material possessions in order to show them off (cf. Latko's Placek). "Let them see that a lord returned home." (23)

XX's intellectual potentiality and logic impress AA, whose pretenses do not fool him. He proves the intellectual an anachronism, his old hypothesis obsolete. He exposes AA's reason for emigration — he realized that the power of a dictatorship equalized people and he considered himself superior. He also knows why AA lives with him: "Because you want to have someone to talk to." (31) When AA taunts him for being a slave in Poland and a slave to money in emigration, XX shows that he has not only "hands" but a "head" as well. He carries on a dialogue which leads from sociology to existentialism, to his awareness of himself as a man: "I think, therefore I am," without knowing Cartesian philosophy. He becomes skeptical about the wisdom of acquiring money, which has no end. Therefore, enraged by AA's insinuations, he tears up all the money which he saved by starving. He proves that he is not a slave, that he is even capable, without histrionics, of achieving supreme freedom, i.e. of committing suicide. This convinces AA that an ideal slave does not exist. Disgusted with AA's ineffectiveness, he decides against suicide since he can always start anew, as AA tells him.

In the end both have changed; XX has become more philosophical while AA has become simpler. This is evident in his final monologue where he uses XX's language: "If all of us have a common goal, if all of us want the same, then what prevents us from building such a good and wise collective life. You will return and you will never be a slave. Neither you nor your children." (38) The reaction to the concluded dialogue is symptomatic — XX turns to the wall and snores while AA sobs. The drama is based on the word. Everything said creates tension, builds a dramatic conflict, and constitutes the action of the play. In this dialogue, from that which is being said, *man* is being born.

Mrożek, who has always shown great intellectual independence, forces upon AA a condition. The only way out of the vicious circle of hypothesizing on mythical action is the will to develop self-discipline, a sense of seriousness and compromise, in order to resolve the Kordian and the Boor syndrome, in a full-fledged partnership toward a better collective life. XX, the peasant-worker, is a three-dimensional person, not a Messianic invention. He is an equal subject of action. In *Tango,* Uncle Eugene's dance with Eddie was a dance with Frankenstein. Here we have equal *partners.* Only through human interaction and dialogue can we reach the truth about ourselves, even if only a partial one. In this case the truth will create a new Poland. Mrożek seems to say through this play what AA says: that buffoonery does not entertain anybody anymore. It is time to face the truth. The partners of the dialogue, while attacking each other, define each other and confront each other with truths which history has provided in abundance. They argue with great obstinacy, behind which there stands an entire Polish literary tradition regarding the Kordians and the Boors. With *The Emigrants* Mrożek has achieved a resolution of one of the national Romantic issues, one that especially in present reality is of great importance. At last the theme of Kordian and the Boor has a chance for an optimistic resolution and of annulment.

Throughout the last twenty-five years Polish drama has continued the Romantic tradition by being above all politically oriented, concerned with reality while highly poetic, combining tradition with extravagantly grotesque humor and with techniques of the Absurd. Its experiments and explorations of new ways are greater in extent than in most other European drama.

The mid-1970s show a certain return toward tradition in form and toward realism in content. (Cf. the plays of Latko, Różewicz, and Mrożek which deal with issues confronting present-day Poland while still deriding Romanticism.) In this most recent period, Różewicz and Mrożek seem to have changed roles. Różewicz, usually serious, presents a startling parody on the traditional notion of sexuality in *White Marriage* (1974), while Mrożek, whose plays usually led from realism to parody, remains dead serious in *The Emigrants.*

In this cursory review of Polish avant-garde drama since 1956, which culminates in Mrożek and especially Różewicz's experimental plays, I have attempted to show its peculiar style, combining topicality and moral issues with the Theater of the Absurd and showing traces of Romantic tradition in works of nearly all the playwrights. The traces of tradition which have been discussed were mainly derided in a nihilistic way, but not for the sake of derision only. Postwar Polish drama presents an exposé of the lofty rhetoric of the Romantic bards, turning it into parody. But the parody of their words serves to expose the ills of the present. Hence, the Romantic tradition can be viewed as a code, an Aesopian device, and therefore, given the political realities of Poland, it will continue to exert its influence.

410 FICTION AND DRAMA IN EASTERN AND SOUTHEASTERN EUROPE

NOTES

1. Martin Esslin, "Commentary," *Comparative Drama*, 3 (Fall 1969), 219.
2. Harold B. Segel, Introduction to *Polish Romantic Drama: Three Plays in English Translation* (Ithaca, New York 1977), 71. The author presents a more detailed study of the dramas by the three Romantic bards.
3. Jan Kłossowicz, "From Romanticism to Avant-Garde," *Dialog*, Special Issue (1970), 116. The fact is that the works remained untranslated for over a century into the languages of the Western countries in which the poets lived and created them.
4. Alois Hermann, "Naród i rewolucja w polskiej literaturze romantycznej," *Pamiętnik Literacki*, LXIV (1973), z. 2, 57–66. This study has been of particular value to me.
5. See Leszek Kołakowski, "The Priest and the Jester"(Kapłan i Błazen), trans. by P. Majewski, ed. by Maria Kuncewicz, *The Modern Polish Mind* (New York 1963), 301–326. In this essay, whose title has become a coined expression, the author argues the necessity of a negative 'profane' vigilance of the Jester in the face of the absolute 'sacred' represented by the Priest.
6. Daniel Gerould, Introduction to *Twentieth-Century Polish Avant-Garde Drama*, ed. and trans. in collab. with Eleanor Gerould (Ithaca and London 1977), 13.
7. Marta Piwińska, "Przed 'Kartoteką' i 'Tangiem'," *Dialog*, 11 (1967), 97.
8. Czesław Miłosz, "Stanisław Ignacy Witkiewicz, A Polish Writer for Today," *Tri-Quarterly*, 9 (Spring 1967), 145.
9. Jan Kott, "Foreword" to Stanisław Ignacy Witkiewicz, *The Madman and the Nun and Other Plays*, ed. and trans. by Daniel Gerould and C. D. Durer (Seattle and London 1968), xii–xiii. The author cites a piece of dialogue from the play *Mother* in which the mother speaks of Strindberg's *The Ghost Sonata* as the work of a genius. In 1926 Witkiewicz gave this play its Polish premiere at the Formist Theater in Zakopane. For this information and Strindberg's influence on Witkiewicz, see Lech Sokół, *Groteska w teatrze Stanisława Ignacego Witkiewicz* (Wrocław, Warsaw, Cracow, Gdańsk 1973), 106–107.
10. Stanisław Ignacy Witkiewicz, "Czysta forma w teatrze Wyspiańskiego," *Studio*, 10–12 (1937), 2–7. Here he expresses his indebtedness to his friend T. Miciński for the ideas on magical theater presenting the mystery of existence in a direct way, and to Wyspiański whose "total theater" suited his idea of a "oneness of pluralities."
11. See Konstanty Puzyna, "Witkacy," Stanisław Ignacy Witkiewicz, *Dramaty*, Vol. I, ed. with an introd. by K. Puzyna (Warsaw 1962), 21.
12. Five new plays (all pantomimes) which I recently discovered will add immensely to our understanding of Bolesław Leśmian's innovative use of the Oriental theater, years ahead of other Western playwrights. The first three-act play/scenario will be published shortly by Państwowy Instytut Wydawniczy in Warsaw.
13. Here Witkiewicz's Pure Form closely follows theories of Polish Formism by Leon Chwistek whom he mentions in some of his plays.
14. Viktor Šklovskij's "Iskusstvo kak priem," *Sborniki po teorii poètičeskogo jazyka*, II (St. Petersburg 1917), 5; 7–9. The author presents various approaches to the deformation of reality by means of "ostranenie." He speaks about the basic function of the poetic image: "the poetic image is a means of intensifying the impression." (5)

However, the 'defamiliarization' of things, as a device used by Witkiewicz in his Pure Form plays, coincides especially with Šklovskij's following statements: "the aim of art is to convey a perception of a thing, as *vision* and *not as* cognition"; (7) "the device of art is the device of 'defamiliarization' of things and the device of the *impeded form,* which increases the *difficulty* and the *duration of perception,* since the process of perception in art is an aim in itself *and should be prolonged,* art is a way to relive the making of a thing, but the thing made is not important in art."[italics mine, R. S.], 7–8. This statement coincides with the idea of Pure Form devised by Witkiewicz, who used strange, difficult, and impeded forms of defamiliarization in order to shock the audience into new dimensions of perception, detached from reality. Likewise, Witkiewicz maintained, as pointed out in the present study, that form — the ultimate aim of which is to extend the creative process caused by the new perception — is all that can be judged in a play.

Just as Šklovskij cites L. N. Tolstoj's *Xolstomer* as an example of defamiliarization in which "the things are defamiliarized not by our perception of them but by that of a horse" (8–9) so, too, in Witkiewicz we see the world as perceived through madmen, dope addicts and perverts. See also Zbigniew Folejewski, "The Theatre of Ruthless Metaphor: Polish Theatre Between Marxism and Existentalism," *Comparative Drama,* III (Fall 1969), 178, who comments on 'estrangement' in the play *The Madman and the Nun*: "common, ordinary things seem unreal, the milieu of the insane asylum gives the whole scene a dream-like atmosphere." See especially Witold Gombrowicz, referred to in fn. 40 below, whose statement supports my idea that Pure Form is a form of 'defamiliarization' *par excellence.* It should be added that, according to Puzyna, Witkiewicz, who was in St. Petersburg at the time of the publication of Šklovskij's article, was in close contact with the Russian Constructivists, poets and dramatists, and therefore might possibly have been acquainted with Šklovskij's work.

15. Stanisław Ignacy Witkiewicz, "Bliższe wyjaśnienia w kwestii czystej formy na scenie," in *Nowe Formy w Malarstwie: Szkice Estetyczne: Teatr* (Warsaw 1974), 290. See also Puzyna, 29, for the same quotation [trans. mine].

16. Daniel Gerould, Introduction to *The Madman and the Nun and Other Plays* [see fn. 9 for complete reference], xliii.

17. See Teresa Wróblewska, "Post Scriptum do 'Romansu siedmiu braci śpiących w Chinach'," *Dialog,* 4 (1968), 151–152. This play foreshadows Witkiewicz's *The Madman and the Nun.*

18. Jan Błoński, "U źródeł teatru Witkacego," *Dialog,* 5 (1970), 82.

19. Błoński, 81.

20. Stanisław Ignacy Witkiewicz, "The New Deliverance," tr. by D. Gerould and J. Kosicka, *The Polish Review,* XVIII (1973), 99.

21. Lech Sokół, *Groteska w teatrze Stanisława Ignacego Witkiewicza* (Wrocław 1973), 84.

22. Jan Błoński, "Teatr Witkiewicza: Forma Formy," *Dialog,* 12 (1967), 69.

23. Krzysztof Pomian, "Witkacy: Philosophy and Art," *Polish Perspectives,* XIII (September 1970), 27.

24. *The Madman and the Nun and Other Plays,* 232–233. Except where otherwise noted, all quotations from Witkiewicz's plays refer to this English language edition.

25. Piwińska, 85 [trans. mine].

26. Piwińska, 85 [trans. mine].

27. Stanisław Brzozowski, *Legenda Młodej Polski* (Lwów 1910), 566–567.

28. Piwińska, 86 [trans. mine].

29. Andrzej Wirth, "Avant-Gardist as a Classical Author of the Period," *The Polish Review,* XVIII (1973), 17.

30. Gerould, Introduction to *Twentieth-Century Polish Avant-Garde Drama,* 27.

31. Stanisław Ignacy Witkiewicz, *The Anonymous Work,* in: *Twentieth-Century Polish Avant-Garde Drama,* 151.

32. Witkiewicz, *The Anonymous Work,* in: *Twentieth-Century Polish Avant-Garde Drama,* 149.

33. Martin Esslin, "The Search for the Metaphysical Dimension in Drama," an unpublished manuscript version of the Introduction to Witkiewicz, *Tropical Madness* (New York 1972). I am indebted for this information to Gerould. See his introduction to *Twentieth-Century Polish Avant-Garde Drama,* 36.

34. Gerould, Introduction to *The Madman and the Nun and Other Plays,* xliii.

35. Wiktor Weintraub, "Explosive Content and Impure Form," *The Polish Review,* XVIII (1973), 7.

36. See Louis Iribarne, "Revolution in the Theatre of Witkacy and Gombrowicz," *The Polish Review,* 3 (1973), 36.

37. Jan Kott, *Theatre Notebook: 1947-1967* (New York 1968), 22.

38. *The Madman and the Nun and Other Plays,* 252. For similar mocking remarks see also 538.

39. Tadeusz Boy-Żeleński, "Le Théâtre de Stanisław Ignacy Witkiewicz," *La Pologne Littéraire,* No. 18 (March 15, 1928), 1. Quotation trans. into English by Gerould. See his Introduction to *Twentieth-Century Polish Avant-Garde Drama,* 35.

40. Witold Gombrowicz, *Theatre* (Paris 1965), 88. Gombrowicz states that the process of deformation (i.e. 'defamiliarization') produces that which Witkacy calls Pure Form.

41. Piwińska, 99 [trans. mine].

42. Martin Esslin, *The Theatre of the Absurd* (New York 1969), 346. The author points out that "the younger generation of dramatists . . . in Poland in the nineteen-sixties clearly owes a great deal to, and continues the tradition of Surrealist drama created by Witkiewicz and Gombrowicz."

43. Iribarne, 69.

44. Witold Gombrowicz, *Princess Ivona,* trans. by Krystyna Griffith-Jones and Catherine Robbins (London 1969), 50. This title is a truncated version of the original, the full translation of which is given in the text. All quotations from this edition are marked by page numbers in parentheses.

45. Dominique de Roux, *Rozmowy z Gombrowiczem* (Paris 1969), 27. Gombrowicz insists that Ivona as a character "springs more from biology than from sociology."

46. Jan Kott, "Face and Grimace," Introduction to Witold Gombrowicz, *The Marriage,* trans. by Louis Iribarne (New York 1969), 13. All quotations from this edition are marked by page numbers in parentheses.

47. Witold Gombrowicz, "Idea of the Play," *The Marriage,* 17. According to the author, "this dual deformation produces that which Witkiewicz would have called Pure Form."

48. Lucien Goldmann, "The Theatre of Gombrowicz," *TDR* [*The Drama Review*] 3, No. 47 (1970), 102-115.

49. Witold Gombrowicz, *Dziennik, 1953-1956* (Paris 1957), 282-283.

50. Gombrowicz, *The Marriage* [see fn. 46], 137.

51. Witold Gombrowicz, "Komentarz," *Teatr* (Paris 1971), 153.

52. Witold Gombrowicz, *Operetta,* trans. by Louis Iribarne (London 1971), 69. All quotations from this edition are marked by page numbers in parentheses.

53. See Stefania Skwarczyńska, "'Chocholi taniec' jako obraz-symbol w literaturze ostatniego trzydziestolecia," *Dialog,* 8 (1969), 99–119, for an incisive study on the impact exerted by Wyspiański's Mulch dance on contemporary Polish literature.

54. Dominique de Roux, 127.

55. Sławomir Mrożek, *Tango,* trans. by Ralph Manheim and Teresa Dzieduszycka (New York 1968), 28. All quotations from this edition are marked by page numbers in parentheses.

56. Piwińska, 91 [trans. mine].

57. Adam Mickiewicz, "Oda do młodości," *Wybór pism* (Warsaw 1952), 8 [trans. mine].

58. Tadeusz Różewicz, *The Card Index and Other Plays,* trans. by Adam Czerniawski (London 1969). All quotations from this edition are marked by page numbers in parentheses. For a more detailed study of *The Card Index* and other plays by Różewicz, see Rochelle Stone, "The Use of Happenings in Tadeusz Różewicz's Drama," *Pacific Coast Philology,* XI (1976), 62–69. See also Henryk Vogler, *Tadeusz Różewicz* (Warsaw 1972), 105–106 and 118 for some observations on *The Card Index.*

59. Nevlin Vos, *Eugène Ionesco and Edward Albee (A Critical Essay)* (Grand Rapids 1968), 30.

60. Tadeusz Różewicz, "Notatki," *Teatr niekonsekwencji* (Warsaw 1970), 71 [trans. mine].

61. Tadeusz Różewicz, "Świadkowie albo nasza mała stabilizacja," *Sztuki teatralne* (Warsaw 1972), 101. See also Vogler [fn. 58], 111–118, for comments on this play.

62. See Stone [fn. 58], 62–63 and 67–69 on Różewicz's drama *Natural Growth,* referred to by Gerould as *Birth Rate* in his recent Introduction to *Twentieth-Century Polish Avant-Garde Drama,* 92–94, which also includes his translation of the play under the same title, 269–279.

63. Tadeusz Różewicz, "Białe małżeństwo," *Dialog,* 2 (1974), 5–33.

64. Piwińska, 93.

65. Karl Dedecius, "Formen der Unruhe, Tadeusz Różewicz in der Umarmung der Wirklichkeit," *Polnische Profile* (Frankfurt am Main 1975), 217 [trans. mine].

66. Jan Błoński, "Pozytywny ekscentryk, czyli o 'Zielonej Gęsi'," *Dialog,* 4 (1959), 104. See also Andrzej Wirth, "Teatr Gałczyńskiego," *Siedem prób: Szkice krytyczne* (Warsaw 1962), 198–209. For the most thorough discussion in English on *The Green Goose,* see Gerould's Introduction to *Twentieth-Century Polish Avant-Garde Drama,* 59–67.

67. Sławomir Mrożek, "Śmierć Porucznika," *Utwory sceniczne* (Cracow 1963), 283. All quotations from this edition are marked by page numbers in parentheses [trans. mine].

68. Jan Kott, "Rodzina Mrożka," *Dialog,* 5 (1965), 146.

69. Miron Białoszewski, "Wyprawy krzyżowe (Dramat historyczny)," *Dialog,* 4 (1958), 48.

70. Stanisław Barańczak, "Język poetycki Mirona Białoszewskiego," *Z Dziejów Form Artystycznych w Literaturze Polskiej,* Vol. XLI (Wrocław, Warsaw, Cracow, Gdańsk 1974), 136.

71. Jan Błoński, "Brylla obrachunki z Polską," *Dialog,* 5 (1968), 151.

72. Ernest Bryll, "Rzecz Listopadowa," *Dialog,* 2 (1968), 6 [trans. mine].

73. Ryszard Latko, "Tato, tato, sprawa się rypła," *Dialog,* 10 (1976), 38 [trans. mine].

74. Sławomir Mrożek, "Emigranci," *Dialog,* 8 (1974). All quotations from this text are marked by page numbers in parentheses [trans. mine].

75. Marta Fik, "Co znaczy Mrożek," *Twórczość,* 4 (1976), 115 [trans. mine].

76. Stanisław Gębala, "Mrożka 'Kordian i cham'," *Dialog,* 8 (1977), 120 [trans. mine].

Darko Suvin

BRECHT'S *CORIOLAN*,[1] OR STALINISM RETRACTED: THE CITY, THE HERO, THE CITY THAT DOES NOT NEED A HERO

I

There are two main oppositions in Brecht's *Coriolan,* the latest and, in some ways, the most intriguing version of that ancient historiographic and stage legend. The first and basic opposition in the play is the one between WAR AND PEACE; war or peace prevail either horizontally, between the ethnic units, the city-states of Rome and the Volsci, or vertically, between the two Roman classes — the direct producers, little people, or plebeians, and the rich power-wielders and political-military leaders, or patricians. The second and central opposition or conflict in the play is that between CAIUS MARCIUS (later called Coriolan) AND HIS CITY-STATE OF ROME. The two conflicts — the wars of classes and nations, and the war of the great individual against his society — are interwined and influence each other intimately within the dialectics of the play. However, for the purposes of initial analysis, they could be considered separately. For reasons explained later, I will call the wars of the classes and nations the DEMOCRATIC OR LENINIST CONFLICT, and the war of the great individual against society the INDIVIDUALIST OR SHAKESPEAREAN conflict; the peculiar strengths as well as problems of Brecht's play arise out of the fact that these two conflicts are not wholly compatible yet are mutually very illuminating. My analysis begins with the historical legend about the "great man" Coriolanus, in order to note how Brecht changed it in the era of High Stalinism.

That legend begins with Titus Livius. Now Livy was a staunch partisan of the official Roman State party-line in historiography which ascribed a special virtue to the behavior of Roman warriors and statesmen that ethically and almost cosmologically guaranteed their victories. What that virtue of *pietas* was exactly like is almost less important than the fact that it was correlative to winning — i.e., an ideological sublimation of the old sayings that might is right and the end sanctifies the means. Livy's "piety" rules Roman history, "res populi romani," and makes Rome great. Therefore, he is interested in Coriolanus only insofar as that little episode demonstrates that proper education in Roman *pietas* will overawe even a wayward warrior who was exiled for politico-economic clashes with the plebeians and took up arms against the Urbs, the City: when it comes to the crunch, his inner-directedness will out, and the imperial outcome of those struggles will roll on undisturbed. What Coriolanus does later is irrelevant, and Livy says that some rumors have him killed and others living to a ripe old age.

On the contrary, Plutarch is primarily interested not in the siege of Rome but in an individual split between the good and the bad. In fact, Plutarch is interested in history only as a gossipy backdrop to the trajectories of great men who are, as it were, supra-historical, abstracted from history into pseudo-eternal idealized regions of moralizing about freedom, patriotism, heroism, and the like. He is not interested in the statesman but in the man, and his subject-matter is not Livy's epically dynamic process of a political organism developing but an ahistorically organized series of static contrasts between great individuals, always opposed to their backgrounds in the manner of a Renaissance portrait, with the subject in the first plane and the florid landscape as backdrop.

Obviously, a Renaissance Individualistic dramatist such as Shakespeare had a great affinity for Plutarch's dramatically simplified clashes between the great individual and such a backdrop of petty bickerings around him. Shakespeare's Coriolanus is practically the whole play; furthermore, he is a hero not only WITH and IN SPITE OF his tragic flaw of pride and anger, but practically BECAUSE of it. In Plutarch, these flaws were explained as stemming from a deficient upbringing — an explanation not only contrary, but also complementary, to Livy's triumph of *pietas romana* in the final instance. In Shakespeare the flaws as well as the virtues stem from the mysterious, not to be questioned further, depths of a great man's individuality whose essence has nothing whatsoever to do with the formative influences of his environment — although the individuality can after all be shown only by the interaction with this environment turned into backdrop. The dramatic raison d'être of the whole scenic microcosm is to allow the hero to manifest himself, and many a Shakespearean tragic hero will do so most clearly when he is practically or literally alone on the stage, when the microcosm has been emptied of other necessary but cumbersome figures: in the great monologues, in the internal emigration or external exile of Hamlet, Macbeth, Lear — and of Coriolanus. As Brecht harshly noted in 1928:

> Shakespeare drives through four acts the great loner, a Lear, an Othello, a Macbeth, away from all his human ties of family and state and onto the heath, into total isolation, where he has to show greatness in his downfall. . . . It is passion which keeps this machinery going, and the purpose of the machinery is the great individual experience. Coming ages will call this drama a drama for cannibals. . . . (B15/149)

Clearly, a dramatist who concluded from modern urban and mass society that to define the stage microcosm exclusively through its central figure of the great individual was by now not only ethically dubious but — worse still — unbelievable, could not accept Shakespeare's way. Brecht thought of Shakespeare's plays as "being superseded not by what follows capitalism but by capitalism itself." To the objection that it is shallow to define Shakespeare's tragedy as dealing with the decline of great feudal men and concepts, Brecht replied: "But how could there be anything more complex, fascinating and important than the decline of great ruling classes?" (B16/587-88; MD 59). From that vantage point, Brecht strove to fashion a dialectical synthesis out of Livy's thesis that only social piety matters and Shakespeare's antithesis that only the individual law inside a great person's breast matters. Brecht's attempt at synthesis presents a new type of social piety being formed in collision with a character of genuinely great potentialities which become destructive when he uses them for class warfare against the plebeians and for national treason. As in the whole Coriolanus legend, the Hero and the City clash; as in Livy and contrary to Shakespeare, the City is right; as in Shakespeare and contrary to Livy, it is a pity that the Hero's qualities had not been used for better purposes.

Most importantly, however — and contrary to the politics of the whole Coriolanus legend — it is a new imaginary, wish-dream, or utopian City that is right in *Coriolan,* a City of popular unity and popular democracy guaranteed by the armed militia of the plebeians who have coalesced with the patriotic patricians. And contrary to the Individualistic psychology of the whole Coriolanus legend, the hero cannot be envisaged as either Livy's episodic maverick or Plutarch's great man; for these absolute and static either/or terms are not believable or realistic any more. Any Brechtian character is both/and: Coriolan is BOTH a supreme leader in the vital business of war, AND a supreme menace to civil peace. Brecht's is a radically new type of tragedy. First of all, it is a bipolar or double one: "the tragedy of the people that has a hero against it" (B16/877; BoT 258) AND the tragedy of the great personality which believes it is irreplaceable (B16/886). Secondly, the civic pole of this double-headed situation turns out not to be a tragedy because of the self-help of the Roman people; whereas the individual pole turns out to be a tragedy only because the great man is blind to the Antaean necessity to be in touch with the people, because he is simply an anachronism and his greatness an overspecialization, a professional disease. Brechtian tragedy is diametrically opposed to theories of an unchangeable Fate: it flows from the heroes' blindness to changed necessities of social existence. Mother Courage does not see that little people need a long spoon to sup with the demon of war, nor does Galileo see that scientists need the contact with the practical life and ethics of the little people if they are not to become a race of inventive dwarfs sellable to the highest bidder — who will again be the demon of war and destruction. Coriolan's tragedy is quite parallel: he does not see the necessity or the possibility of metamorphosis from antediluvian warrior-monster into a leader at a time of civic and international peace.

This complex of political motives, dealing with the ostensibly great leader versus the people, with pathetic personal heroism versus the workings of mass or statistical forces centered on economics, with the nature of true victory and defeat, had fascinated Brecht from his very youngest days. Subsequently, the experiences of the Germans in the First World War, the October Revolution in the Russian Empire, the various brief European revolts after it, the exacerbated class struggles in the Weimar Republic, the internal struggles in the Soviet Union, the rise of the Nazis and the Second World War, the Cold War between East and West and the formation of the two German states corresponding to the two power-blocs in Europe, Stalinism and the harsh last years of Stalin — all of these were fundamental factors in the existence of Brecht's generation, and thus in his life and work too. The cannibalic violence of war and civil war determining the most intimate reactions of people is perhaps his most persistent leitmotif, from *The Bible* and *Man is Man* to *Antigone* and *Days of the Commune.* In particular, his first major encounter with Shakespeare's *Coriolanus,* which made him a perennial advocate of the unorthodox view that it was "one of Shakespeare's grandest plays" (B15/181), was the 1925 Berlin staging by one of his favorite directors, Erich Engel — an event to which Brecht ascribed a "decisive importance" in the development of epic theatre (B15/133-34). Along with the formal stage devices, what must have appealed to him is that the story was played as a parallel or analogue to that same Spartacist revolt which he had skirted in *Drums in the Night*: according to contemporaries, one saw on Engel's stage the German paramilitary right-wingers, the Steel-helmets (*Stahlhelme*), fighting with grey proletarians with miserable flour-powdered faces in a décor more reminiscent of the working quarters of Berlin in 1919 than of consular Rome. From that point of view, Coriolanus's figure stands — as in T. S. Eliot's poem from the same years — for a would-be fascist dictator, and the plebeians for the failed communist revolutionaries of central Europe's interwar years.

A direct line leads from such a Coriolanus both to Brecht's parody of Hitler as Chicago gangster in *Arturo Ui,* and to the falsely great Romans of Brecht's exile years, the famous politician Caesar in the novel *The Business of Mr. Julius Caesar* and the famous general Lucullus in the radio-play *The Trial of Lucullus.* But in comparison to all these completely negated upper-class leaders, victors of destructive and therefore empty victories over their own people as much as over other peoples, Brecht's Coriolan — shaped six to nine years after the end of World War Two, when both reflection and new problems had intervened — is seen as a more complex figure. He is antisocial, to be sure, and therefore finally rejected, yet at the same time he has some genuine qualities of leadership and even of Shakespearean integrity. Indeed, pride, anger, and a disgust at electoral politicking were incipient virtues rather than sins in Brecht's materialist anthropology. The stage investigations into Coriolan's character are focused on this very fact of genuinely exceptional faculties being turned to destructive purposes. As a note of Brecht's — a capital document for understanding his play — puts it:

> In Plutarch as in Shakespeare, *Coriolanus* is the tragedy of a great and irreplaceable man. Even if Coriolanus goes too far in his demands, this is

only the excess of an in itself grand attitude, which then becomes the reason for his tragic fall.

In the adaptation, a tragedy of the individual shifts into a tragedy of the belief in irreplaceability. It turns out that the belief in irreplaceability does destroy the individual, but not necessarily the people. True, a great number of persons can be put into a tragic position — but then they have to liberate themselves from the individual who has risen up against them.

Our tendency: the individual blackmails society by means of his irreplaceability.

That is a tragedy for society. It loses (1) the individual; (2) it must expend vast means to defend itself. But most of all, it is a tragedy for the individual, who has wrongly thought of himself as irreplaceable.

The apparent irreplaceability of the individual is a gigantic theme for a long time to come, leading from Antiquity to our period. The solution has to be a positive one for society, i.e., it is not necessary that it allow itself to be blackmailed by the individual. The problem can in principle be solved, society can defend itself. In *Coriolan*: the way out for the plebs is self-defense.[2]

Thus, the theme at hand is structured around two closely intertwined basic conflicts: the wars of the classes and nations, and the war of the great individual against society. Both of these conflicts are clearly delineated in the historical legend of Coriolanus; though Shakespeare was interested in both, it was the second or Individualistic one which was not only quite central but also the sole tragically worthy conflict for him. Such a reduction of an originally bipolar situation could not satisfy Brecht, and he proposed to do full justice to both these poles and types of conflicts in a new way, by presenting a new view of the Hero as well as of the City. Brecht's Hero is a dialectical contradiction between his genuinely great potentialities of leadership and his petty, obtuse wrong-headedness in channelling them against the good of a new society. Brecht's City (about which more below) is in a dialectical process of transcending the class oppositions into a popular democracy, opposed to the Hero as justice to privilege and as creativity to destruction. (These two oppositions are manifested by the Popular-Front Senate deciding at the end of the play to restore the lands to the Volscians and to construct the aqueduct; the Senate disallows mourning for Coriolan in order to continue with such business.)

Yet even if it were agreed that all this has been demonstrated, I think some questions would remain. It is a curious fact that Brecht, choosing to adapt a play which shows his unquestionable deepest lifelong aversion, a warlike and slaughterhouse world, retained (say, in comparison to Livy) a relatively great role and even a dialectical respect for the destructive warrior-hero. How is it to be understood that, at the height of his playwriting career, he seemingly returned to focusing on the passion of a "living embodiment of war" (II. i), one one of those great lone leaders whose "running amuck," as he liked to say, makes "life and not death obscene" (B16/677) — instead of focusing on the little people? One has only to imagine a play centered on the generals of the

Thirty Years' War instead of on Mother Courage and her children, or on the Grand Duke and the Caucasian princes instead of on Grusha and Azdak, in order to see the force of such questions. In brief, how is it that Brecht found some elements in the Shakespearean "drama for cannibals" useful?

At one point of his famous discussion of how to adapt the first scene, Brecht almost blithely justifies war as a normal economic necessity for a class society such as ancient Rome (B16/881; BoT 260). In capitalist terms, just as, to quote a chairman of General Motors, the business of America is business, the business of Rome was war. In Marx's terms, as quoted from him by one of Brecht's closest collaborators in the *Coriolan* adaptation, at that stage of development of the productive forces "war is the great overall task, the required communal work." This quotation may have been — and the argument certainly was — known to Brecht, but its use is quite uncharacteristic for him, as can be seen if we compare his passionate position against war not only in his plays with a more "modern" localization but also in his *Antigone* whose story happens at a time of even greater primitivism and tribal barbarism than that of the Roman Republic. Thus, Coriolan, an incarnation of the passion for warfare just as Galileo was of the passion for science, becomes (also like Galileo) a dialectical tragic hero. True, in these Brechtian dialectics we are not supposed only to feel WITH but also AGAINST such a tragic hero, and we are finally led to distance ourselves from him (B17/1252-53); even so, Coriolan is vastly superior to Arturo Ui or Lucullus. Where Ui is a hyena and Lucullus a peacock, Coriolan is a tiger, dangerous and to be disposed of but undeniably fascinating. As Kenneth Tynan noted, the animus of the Brechtian play and production is not against Coriolan himself but against "the social role in which he is cast." [3] What, then, is Coriolan's "social role"?

II

The answer has to be approached through a consideration of the other pole of this play, the PLEBEIAN DEMOCRACY of Rome — the citizens and the tribunes. Brecht noted during the adaptation: "As far as the delight in the hero and the tragedy is concerned, we must go beyond the simple empathy into the hero Marcius in order to arrive at a richer delight; parallel to the tragedy of Coriolan, we must at least be capable to 'experience' also the tragedy of Rome, especially of the plebs" (B17/1252). Indeed, if Brecht kept much from Shakespeare's Coriolanus pole, he decisively stood on its head — or stood back on its feet — Shakespeare's view of the "citizens" or plebeians. The great Brechtian constellation of an at least balanced presentation of the rulers and the ruled, the social heights and depths, decisively enriches and widens the scope of the play from an Individualistic tragedy to a collective education for the spectators. As a Shakespearean scholar has remarked à propos of the first scene: "One is forced to believe, not only by political passages in *Coriolanus* but by such passages in Shakespeare's work generally, that the reason why Shakespeare does not provide these opponents of Menenius and Coriolanus with an effective argument in favor of democracy is simply that he does not think any can be offered."[4] Brecht supplies the missing arguments, not so much by any long speeches put into the citizens' mouths as by their behavior and action, especially by that of their most resolute or vanguard group led by the two tribunes. Where Coriolan begins as supremely good at war, the citizens begin as unwilling to fight, and are for that reviled by him:

> . . . Anyone who trusts you
> Finds hares when he wants lions, geese when he looks
> For foxes. You hate the great because they are great.
>
> (I. i)

But Coriolan could not have been more wrong, for Brecht. After the plebeians get a political and economical share in the common wealth of the commonwealth, they turn out to be not only foxes, slyly easing Coriolan out of his consulship, but also lions, prepared finally to defend the walls of a City "worth defending / Perhaps for the first time since it was founded" (V. iii). The citizens' share in the power of Rome amounts to a new founding of it upon the basis of social justice, which is at least as important as Romulus's drawing of the city walls in the blood of his brother Remus. The fratricidal City of false betters, the fathers or well-born called *patritii,* up in arms against false inferiors, the offspring-begetters called *proletarii,* turns in this utopian vision of Brecht's into a fraternal City of land distribution and irrigation — i.e., of justice and creativity.

Coriolan's own view of history as the deeds of great men lording it over other men in the Hobbean war of each against each, in the political bestiary or jungle of *homo homini lupus,* is in Brecht's play shattered by the (to Coriolan) totally unnatural sight of masons arming to "defend their walls," of hares turning into lions; it is when he realizes that even plebeians can be a new type of — a collective — lion or tiger that he collapses in the famous Volumnia scene. Brecht's bold substitution of the Adlerian king-of-the-beasts fixation of collective psychology for the Individualistic mother-fixation of Shakespeare's Coriolanus will, of course, work only for an audience that accepts the plebeians as invested with the strong affective charge of Brecht's Marxist utopianism — in this play not too dissimilar from the contemporary ideas of Ernst Bloch. Indeed, the Roman plebeians and their tribunes are the radically democratic, Leninist, or indeed Jeffersonian or Patrick-Henryan, pole of his play. They are the rabble in arms, as in the American and Russian revolutions, and their success is a Brechtian wish-dream or counter-project to the failed plebeian revolutions in Germany after both World Wars. *Coriolan* is therefore, richly but at times puzzlingly, not only a rewriting of Shakespeare and ancient Roman history, but also a rewriting of the Leninist theme of state and revolution and modern German-cum-Russian history.

The main object of Lenin's writings in the summer of 1917 was to draw conclusions from the various French and Russian revolutions as to the proper relation of revolution and state. An irreplaceable plank in his program of gaining power was the arming of plebeian masses. Even his vocabulary can be found in Brecht's play. Thus, Lenin's first major article on this theme is called "On Dual Sovereignty" ("O dvoevlastii"); at the height of the confrontation with the plebeians, Coriolan calls out:

> That's dual sovereignty (Das ist die Doppelherrschaft),
> . . . where greatness, power and wisdom
> Can't move a step without the yes or no
> Of the unreasoning mob. (II.iii)

Lenin's article defines the new type of power and state, on the model of the Paris Commune of 1871, as built on three pillars: first, the source of power is not parliament but the direct initiative of popular masses from below; second, the army and police are abolished and replaced by "direct arming of the whole people"; third, the bureaucracy or administrators are either abolished or put under special control with the possibility of instant recall by the people (L9-11). In a second long article, "The Tasks of the Proletariat in Our Revolution" ("Zadachi proletariata v nashei revoliutsii"), Lenin consecrates a chapter to "dual sovereignty." He finds that the main characteristic of the Russian situation between February and October 1917 is the existence of two governments: the main or executive one of the upper class, and the supplementary or "controlling" one of the Petrograd Soviet of Workers' and Soldiers' Deputies. The first government controls the state institutions, the second a great majority of the people, the armed workers and the soldiers. He also notes that one of the principal signs of each revolution is the sudden growth in the number of people actively participating in political life and the structure of the state (L14-15). Finally, in his book *The State and Revolution* (*Gosudarstvo i revoliutsiia*) Lenin sums up all his conclusions from the 19th-century revolutions, culminating in the Paris Commune, and from the Russian revolutions, culminating at that very moment, as the necessity of breaking up the bureaucracy and the standing army, which is replaced with the people in arms. He defines the essence of the whole problem of state and revolution as: "Does the oppressed class have arms?" and democracy as "a state organization that recognizes the subjection of the minority to the majority" (L176, 180).

In the 1950s Brecht was just fresh from studying this whole theme while writing his play *Days of the Commune,* itself stimulated by his returning to a divided postwar Germany where the question of revolutionary power and of competing armies and state authorities was a most crucial one. Immediately

AFTER his work on Coriolan he adapted Farquhar's *Recruiting Officer,* associating its sympathetic lower-class characters with the idea of "Franklin, Jefferson, and Washington," of the Declaration of Independence by a "rabble in arms," a militia of the oppressed. The position of Brecht's *Coriolan* between his Paris Commune and American Revolution plays characterizes its political locus too. For, heretically, Brecht does not follow Lenin's warning that "dual sovereignty" can only last a very brief time (L15). Instead, he fuses Livy's thesis that just such a civic cooperation between the upper and lower classes made for a strong Rome with the post-1930s' Marxist practice of a Popular Front of all patriots — ideally from both upper and lower classes — against militarism, right-wing dictatorship, and fascist aggression. This political practice led to the establishment of broad wartime coalitions in countries such as France and Italy and of "people's democracies" after the war, from China to Yugoslavia — and to East Germany. Whatever some of these popular fronts and democracies may or may not have turned into later on, under the impact of the Cold War and Stalinism, it is evident that Brecht had a great sympathy for their original warm impulse. The famous, and in the play's original demagogic context evidently false, parable about the belly and the members as "incorporate friends" (I.i) is taken seriously and literally by his plebeians. Where Menenius tries to convince them, against the evidence of their hunger, that when the senate-belly is full the citizen-members are also full, the tribunes demand — and enforce — a real distribution of the corn and olives among all members of the body politic. Quite logically in terms of the above parable, the citizen-members will not work or fight if they cannot eat. However, when evidence for the "incorporation" is obtained, when their delegates control the bureaucracy and the professional warlord is exiled, so that life, liberty, and the pursuit of happiness are open to them — then they are ready to enroll into a Jeffersonian or Leninist militia organized by electoral districts not too dissimilar from a Soviet. In this "democratic Rome . . . with the tribunes of the people" (B16/880-1) hare turns lion, or as Brutus the tribune says after the people's readiness has devastated Coriolan:

> The stone has moved. The people take
> Up arms, and the old earth shakes.
> (V.v; changed from Manheim's translation)

Such telescoping and foreshortening as well as distancing or estranging of urgent current historical issues into or between the lines of Shakespeare's play can, I would submit, also explain the contradictory nature of Brecht's Coriolan, so much more than simply a fascist-type general. In the famous discussion-essay on the first scene of this play, the East Berlin discussants in 1952–53 agree that the play comes to life for them only when it is centered around Coriolan's belief that he is irreplaceable. Thereupon, a pupil asks Brecht whether that feeling stems from the fact that "we find the same kind of thing here and feel the tragedy of the conflicts that result from it?" Brecht's answer, simply and starkly, is: "Undoubtedly" (B16/886–87; BoT 264). Now in that era of High Stalinism, the great leader running berserk and believing himself to be indispensable could not fail to be associated with Generalissimo Joseph Stalin (and possibly the lesser Stalins that Stalinism bred). Stalin was emphatically an individual who blackmailed his society "by means of his irreplaceability" as leader and organizer; this is why Brecht's long note quoted earlier discreetly alludes to the fact that such "seeming irreplaceability" is a gigantic theme in "our period" too. Stalin was officially proclaimed a strategist of genius, victor both in the Civil and the Second World War, both times in the city to which he was eponymous as Coriolan to Corioli — the city of Stalingrad. Furthermore, Trotsky perspicaciously compared his — and our — age to the bloody Italian Renaissance and Stalin to a *condottiere* (much like Coriolanus). But even apart from such direct parallels, Coriolan's expertise and usefulness in war is mainly a parable for Stalin's expertise and usefulness in organizing social productivity in the USSR, which Brecht always valued highly (see *Me-Ti,* B12/467, 491, 536, 538; I believe that this evaluation was rather too cheerful, though Brecht can largely, but not wholly, be excused by the fact that the full story of Stalin's immense anti-plebeian outrages was not yet documented at the time). Stalin's main failing was, to Brecht's mind, that his political capacities were not on the level of his organizational ones, so that he turned into a "workers' and peasants' emperor" rather than remaining the tribune of a Leninist people's democracy (B12/538–41). Analogously, all of Coriolan's wisdom is in warfare and none in politics. Furthermore, the precariousness of Stalin's political basis made it necessary for him, as Brecht noted, to be adulated as the greatest rather than the most useful one (B12/467, 491, 536). Much the same is said of Coriolan in the final explicit judgment on him, passed by Aufidius in words which are Brecht's addition to the legend:

> . . . He could not exchange
> The saddle for the seat of government
> Or war for peace. His deeds are great
> But he dwarfs them by extolling them. Our merit
> Depends upon the use our epoch makes of us. (IV.iv)

Coriolan, like Stalin, did not allow the epoch of the plebs to make full — or indeed any — use of him.

The confrontation of the tribunes and Coriolan is therefore, on one level of this complex dramatic parable, also a confrontation between the pristine and (as Brecht hoped) the resurgent democratic Leninism of the plebeian masses with the once — but now no longer — useful bloody stage of Stalinism. (It speaks for Brecht's perspicacity that the arming of the workers and the lifting of military threat is exactly what happened when Gomułka faced Stalin's successor Khrushchev in Warsaw 1956; and it is exactly what Dubček failed to do when faced with Khrushchev's successor in 1968 — he relied instead on a Volumnian pleading.) This very important constellation of forces is, I believe, the reason why Brecht returned in this play to the theme of the greatly talented *condottiere* or leader abusing his talents against a possible utopian step forward in history. Such a hero is no longer necessary to the self-governing City.

III

In conclusion, then, this play signifies an evolving and, in fact, radically changing world of modern politics based on popular power opposed to either upper-class usurpation or Individualist king-of-the-hill heroism. The direct participation of citizens in state affairs is identified with peace, unity, and creativity, and the oligarchic or monarchic irreplaceability with war, dissension, and destruction. The great but berserker — yet also berserker but great — Hero is tragic because he becomes useless and indeed dangerous to his City. The City of popular unity can avoid tragedy and dispense with the Hero by becoming a directly self-managing state, where (as the play shows in its balance of private and public scenes) all the quondam places of privilege have become as non-antagonistic as any family or private house. Even better, the distinction between a harmonious privacy (usually shown as an upper-class one) and a disharmonious public life of class strife is fading, parallel to the fading of ethnic usurpation through warfare.

Further, Brecht's version of the Coriolanus legend, though it has remained in a first-draft stage, must be acknowledged as one of considerable originality. Brecht wanted us to notice that the 2000 years since Livy or even the 350 years since Shakespeare are no mere trifle: history and the views on history evolve, and we cannot think of plebeians today as of Shakespeare's "rats," "dissentious rogues," "curs," "quarter'd slaves," "fragments," etc. (all of these lofty expressions from his first scene only). If "[the] plain fact is that [Shakespeare] is on the side of the patricians whenever they are to be taken as representing a theory of government," then the plain fact is that Brecht is on the opposite side — his is a plebeian theory of government. Quite formalistically, one can point to this as the most original twist to the Coriolanus legend in 2000 years. But more than formal matters are at issue: let us call them ethical and dramaturgic ones. Just as the monarchist playwright Shakespeare, so the Leninist playwright Brecht, though living in even bloodier times, "shows a singular detachment in his ability to find human faults on both sides and a singular breadth of sympathy in his ability to find human virtues on both sides."[5] On the one hand, the plebeians could fall under the spell of national victories and foolishly choose Coriolan for ruler — as the Soviets chose Stalin; the tribunes could foolishly refuse to believe the news of Coriolan's rising against them — as Ulbricht will have refused to believe in the workers' revolt of June 1953. On the other hand, I have argued how many virtues the Leninist playwright finds in the great leader Coriolan — almost, though not quite, as many as the monarchist playwright. But ultimately, no doubt, Brecht is here plumping for the second term of his permanent dilemma between the society's need for heroes and danger from them, most succinctly expressed in his *Galileo* as the famous replies:

A. Unhappy the land that breeds no hero.
G. No, Andrea: Unhappy the land that needs a hero.

(tr. C. Laughton)

Thus, Brecht is, of course, a playwright supremely interested in the interaction of the Hero and the City (Livy's *Urbs* or Aristotle's *polis*), and he can therefore be with Aristotle defined as a civic or political playwright. Even so, he is after all more playwright delighting in a good villain than politician eliminating his opponent: on the condition that the villain be finally defeated at the hands of the self-helping, self-governing, self-managing City which needs him no more.

The "raw material" of Shakespeare's beautiful barbaric play in its contradictory richness was indispensable to Brecht; he "merely" tried to reconduce it from Individualistic tragedy into bipolar dialectics. He is reported as saying that "He inclined to displacing contemporary problems into the past, as Shakespeare had done. The reason is simple: problems could be distanced, thereby more easily understood as well as presented in an unaccustomed, interest-rousing form."[6] In that perspective, Shakespeare is no more just raw material but an example of "great historical theatre" which is neither parodied nor simply reversed but "reintegrated into a dialectics of society."[7]

NOTES

1. For the sake of clarity, I am calling the Livy-to-Shakespeare hero and play Coriolanus, and the Brecht one Coriolan; the play is quoted in Ralph Manheim's translation from Brecht, *Collected Plays,* vol. 9 (New York: Vintage, 1973) by Act. scene in Roman numerals. Other abbreviations used in parenthesis in the text are: B = Bertolt Brecht, *Gesammelte Werke,* 1–20 (Frankfurt: Suhrkamp, 1973), cited by volume/page, translated by me unless otherwise indicated; MD = Bertolt Brecht, *The Messingkauf Dialogues,* tr. John Willett (London: Methuen, 1965); BoT = *Brecht on Theatre,* ed. and tr. John Willett (New York: Hill & Wang, 1966); L = V. I. Lenin, *Izbrannye proizvedeniia v dvukh tomakh,* II (Moskva: Ogiz, 1946). I wish to acknowledge, with gratitude, the support of a Social Sciences and Humanities Research Council of Canada leave fellowship in research on which this paper was based.

2. Quoted in Henning Rischbieter, *Brecht,* II (Velber: Friedrich, 1966), p. 75. I have been unable to trace this to B, but it is confirmed as authentic by Manfred Wekwerth, *Notate* (Frankfurt: Suhrkamp, 1967), pp. 130–31.

3. Kenneth Tynan, *Tynan Right and Left* (New York: Athenaeum, 1968), p. 161.

4. Willard Farnham, *Shakespeare's Tragic Frontier* (Berkeley: University of California Press, 1963), pp. 228–29.

5. Both quotations in this paragraph are from Farnham, p. 227.

6. Ernst Schumacher, "Er wird bleiben," in Hubert Witt, ed., *Erinnerungen an Brecht* (Leipzig: Reclam, 1964), p. 332.

7. Bernard Dort, "Brecht devant Shakespeare," *Revue d'histoire du théâtre,* 17 (1965), p. 83.

Tomas Venclova

ECHOES OF THE THEATER OF THE ABSURD AND OF THE "THEATER OF CRUELTY" IN MODERN LITHUANIA (K. SAJA, J. GLINSKIS)

"The position of the intelligentsia in present-day Lithuania is very different from the position of the intelligentsia in Moscow, Leningrad, and other cultural centers. This is because the intelligentsia was able to capitalize more effectively on the effects of de-Stalinization than their Russian or Ukrainian counterparts."[1] The quotation is from the author of a "samizdat" article who lives in Lithuania. The peripheral position of Lithuania, her traditional close ties with the West (specifically with Poland), and other factors which we cannot consider here, led to the fact that in the era of the Khrushchev reforms a special social microclimate, in part preserved until the present, took shape. In this climate cultural phenomena grew which, to all intents and purposes, were impossible in other areas of the Soviet Union. Specifically, plays were successfully staged which were very different from the models of ordinary 19th-century drama and from the standard models of socialist realism. In these avant-garde, grotesque, metaphorical dramas one can observe a curious parallel with the European Theater of the Absurd (S. Beckett, E. Ionesco), and also with the so-called Theater of Cruelty (A. Jarry, A. Artaud, J. Genet, P. Weiss).

In this paper we will analyze the plays of two Lithuanian playwrights of the middle generation — K. Saja (born 1932) and J. Glinskis (born 1933). K. Saja began with unpretentious situation comedies which he still writes; but four of his plays stand out against this background. Three of these (all one-act sketches: *The Maniac, The Orator* and *The Prophet Jonah*) were performed in 1967 and published together in book form in 1968.[2] The fourth (a play with a common format, *Hunt for Mammoths*) was presented in 1968 and published in 1969.[3] J. Glinskis, having begun as an interesting prose writer, drew attention with his play *The House of Terror* (a title perhaps also translatable as *The Straitjacket House*), produced in 1970 and published in a separate edition in 1971.[4] The productions of *Hunt for Mammoths* and *The House of Terror* by the talented director J. Jurašas, who later emigrated and now lives in New York, were the main theatrical events in postwar Lithuania. *The Maniac* and *The Orator* have been translated into English;[5] there is also an unpublished version of *The House of Terror*. However, we know of no extensive critical analyses of these plays.[6]

In the œuvre of Saja and Glinskis, the avant-garde dramas seem to have been a short episode only. Right now, along with situation comedies, Saja writes prose and leans toward dramatic composition with a folklore flavor. Glinskis published a biographical play about a well-known artist, M. K. Čiurlionis, incomparably more traditional than *The House of Terror*. However, it is precisely those avant-garde works which should be considered their main achievements.

The European Theater of the Absurd and Theater of Cruelty were known to the Lithuanian authors, although their influence on them apparently came about indirectly. Original texts of avant-garde dramas or corresponding theoretical writings are not easily accessible in Lithuania. Translations of plays appeared in insignificant numbers and only after the creation of the Lithuanian variant of the non-standard theater. Thus, in 1970, Beckett's *Happy Days* and Ionesco's *The Lesson* were published in Lithuanian; in 1972 Genet's *The Maids,* and in 1974 Jarry's *Ubu Roi*. Excerpts from Artaud's book *The Theatre and Its Double* were prepared for publication but were held back by the censor. Somewhat earlier than the Lithuanian translations, absurdist plays were accessible in Russian translations (*Rhinoceros* by Ionesco, published in 1965; *Waiting for Godot* by Beckett, 1966; and a "samizdat" translation of *The Lesson* was circulating in Moscow and Lithuania as early as 1960). Probably, an even more important role was played by numerous Polish translations of avant-garde plays usually published in the journal *Dialog*; this journal was very popular among the Lithuanian intelligentsia which as a rule knows Polish rather well. Western influence in general penetrated, to a significant degree, via Poland where the Theatre of the Absurd (S. Mrożek) at times assumed a satirical and allegorical character, reflecting criticism of the concrete totalitarian society and the stereotyped thought that goes with it.[7] It is also possible that the Russian tradition of the grotesque and metaphoric drama (from A. Suxovo-Kobylin right up to E. Shvarts) made some impact. The dramatic output of the "Oberiuts," however, had not, in general, penetrated into Lithuania.[8]

The five plays we will discuss are interesting not only from a purely literary point of view, but also from a broader semiotic and cultural-anthropological perspective. Theater is, as we know, a semiotic double: on the one hand, in it are interwoven many sign systems (verbal language, the language of pantomime, music, color, form, etc.) and, on the other, the verbal text itself possesses a certain secondary symbolism constructed on the ordinary meaning of the words. On both these planes the plays mentioned present a wealth of material for investigation. In addition, as was noted by some scholars, avant-garde plays frequently present *specific* semiotic problems by artistic means.[9] In our necessarily general and summary overview, we can only briefly indicate this specific character of those plays, noting that the plays of Saja are to a certain degree metalinguistic (they are about language and communication, about the role of clichés and rhetorical figures in contemporary society), whereas the play of Glinskis is a kind of translation of a ritual connected with the structure of carnival[10] into the language of contemporary theater.

The content of Saja's one-act plays is simple. *The Maniac* takes place in a railroad car. An everyday conversation and harmless misunderstandings among the passengers are interrupted by an official who reveals that a maniac has managed to get on the train with the intention of hijacking it. For the sake of general safety, the maniac should be apprehended and held in custody. A "game of vigilance" begins: one passenger informs on another and then himself soon becomes the object of suspicion — each in turn is thought to be the maniac. After the majority have been singled out, the train ominously begins to pick up speed.

The Orator takes place in a room which falls apart before the viewer's eyes: the home is run by a certain Commandant, who conducts himself "as if he were the owner of the house instead of its manager,"[11] only worrying about his own needs, never about the well-being of his tenants. The orator — an occupant of the room — tries to compose and present a speech about this problem, but is paralyzed with fear. The Commandant hears only the orator's occasional outburst, directed at someone else, and the ending remains unclear (but apparently catastrophic).

The Prophet Jonah develops a well-known biblical motif. A ship carrying the prophet begins to sink in a storm: the terrified passengers start to throw their goods overboard and then, trying to hold on to what remains, they throw the Scribe Paschor and the prophet Jonah himself overboard. Paschor, having been in the mouth of the whale, makes it back to the deck (almost out of his wits and speechless). Everyone turns out to be a butcher and at the same time a sacrifice, losing all human qualities. The logic of their behavior is extremely peculiar. There is no choice — whoever values himself higher than the ship deserves to be thrown in the sea, and he who does not is automatically among those to go down. "There are no slaves anymore because there are no free people."[12] The evil captain, obviously, leads them all to destruction.

The plays can easily be read as transparent allegories à la Mrożek: dealing with a police state run by a madman but also made up of madmen (*The Maniac*); with the interrelations between the cowardly and powerless intelligentsia and the all-powerful ruler (*The Orator*); with the sacrifice of the individual to the future which will destroy that future, creating instead a total concentration camp (*The Prophet Jonah*). Still, they are more than simple allegories. "The Absurdists have attempted to make their stage a universal metaphor — it stands directly for all the world."[13] In the plays of Saja, this very principle of the global metaphor is preserved: here we have a conventional and at the same time extreme situation that molds the existential condition of man, his total alienation within a strictly determined and, by the same token, "mad," unpredictable world (irrespective of concrete historical and social circumstances).

The plays are quite disparate in style but similar in structure. *The Maniac* is reminiscent of the typical comedy with many allusions to contemporary life; *The Orator* is distinctive for its significantly greater abstractness; *The Prophet*

Jonah appears externally to be something like a stylized historical sketch. However, in all three plays we see the same spatial opposition: the characters are locked in the stifling world of "here" (the train, a room, the deck of the ship) beyond which, i.e., "there," is found danger (the maniac, the Commandant, a whale which swallows Paschor and Jonah); and the danger appears to be a projection of their individual — including verbal — behavior. In all three plays the characters are "reduced" figures: they act out set roles which turn them into puppets and lead them to destruction. The characters in *The Maniac* amount to social roles (an official, an activist, a bureaucrat, a madame, a physician, etc.), to stereotyped professional patterns, to "instructions." In *The Prophet Jonah* the travelers are interchangeable and practically indistinguishable (toward the end they are dressed in identical prison garb). The situation in *The Orator* is somewhat different — the hero represents all the characters: the dramatis personae are his various components, the personified "passions" of the classical theater, as it were (intelligence, ambition, feeling), very stereotypically realizing their "roles." One way or another, the leveling of character and its simultaneous disintegration is emphasized throughout. True, in all three plays we have a raisonneur — distinct from the others, not fulfilling a stereotyped role (like Ionesco's Béranger). In *The Maniac* it is the professor, in *The Orator* it is the hunchback (irony), and in *The Prophet Jonah* the raisonneur speaks with two voices, Paschor's and Jonah's. Paschor, inside the whale, is prepared to give up his identity, to be "digested"; his words call to mind the ending of Orwell's *1984*:

> And I began thinking that for a tiny creature — an insect — it's a great happiness to merge with an enormous fish. "A great happiness, a great happiness" — but it will squeeze me, then let go, squeeze me, then let go ... [14]

Saja does not go as far as the classical Theater of the Absurd in criticizing thought and language (he comes closest to this only in *Hunt for Mammoths*). In the one-act plays the principles of causality, of the common memory of the characters, and of semantic cohesion are not violated. [15] The author limits himself to playing around with and exposing linguistic stereotypes and mechanical phrases, and above all to the stereotypes which characterize a modern Fascist-like society. In *The Maniac* he presents a whole parade of stereotypes to the reader or viewer. "Characters don't speak; rather, 'through them is spoken' the universal phrase." [16] Media clichés, known to everyone, are spoken, for example, by the activist: "I wanted to say ... I ask to be appointed to the most difficult phase! For You I will truly ... Word of honor! Any duty at all!" [17] "Preserve your talent. Remember—it belongs to the people." [18] "We are not afraid of dirty work!" [19] Her phrases are put in a context which imbues them with an extremely parodistic nature (thus, "dirty work" can be interpreted as "denouncing," and other expressions take on sexual overtones). In the lines and monologues of the official are parodized orders, slogans, and standard descriptions of the situation in the tone of optimistic officialese:

> Everything is in order. All is as it should be. We are increasing our speed and all stations are giving us green light. We will smash everything that gets in our way on the track or disrupts the order within the train! [20]

> As you can see, the train is rushing forward, not backward. So, more courageously, more happily! Give it all you've got. [21]

Similar clichés in the style of *lingua Tertiae Imperiae* lead to a loss of information, to the alienation and depersonalization of man, are demagogically utilized for the purpose of irresponsible power. Right in line with the Theater of the Absurd are, for example, the verbal portrait of the maniac: it is expressly senseless and without informative value. But this senselessness has a function — the portrait could be of practically anyone:

> Longish-faced male, medium height, according to our information fifty years of age, but looking younger. Although he sports a mustache, he might have shaved it off. The eyes are of uncertain color — more hazel than blue in the dark, and the reverse in the light. He had a haircut a little while ago, but may have had time for his hair to regrow. [22]

We see a collection of stereotypes in *The Orator,* too: the mechanical praise of the Commandant, empty and bombastic hymns to man, which clearly parody the poetic output of the Fascist-like countries, and ultimately the standard formulae of "worldly wisdom." In *The Prophet Jonah,* besides everything else, there are plays on biblical phrases which tend to become stereotypes: Paschor re-interprets them and, in addition, they are put in "defamiliarizing" contexts — the phrases "circumcise your heart"and "an eye for an eye and a tooth for a tooth" are uttered during a nightmarish fight. [23] One way or another, the author consistently demonstrates to us words which have lost their meaning; symbols no longer functioning as symbols but as stimuli provoking conditioned behavior. [24] Power grows from controlling language, from the authority of the printed word, which consists of nothing but external textuality; the masses are controlled by existential "das Man"; and "das Man" finds its place in a demagogically used language. The disruption of the act of communication in all three plays leads to a complete loss of language, turning it into a non-language and — predictably — also to the physical annihilation of the communicators. *The Maniac* ends with a round dance and senseless chorus by people who have lost any resemblance to individuals, externally united but in fact totally separated. In *The Orator* the planned speech never takes place, being replaced by the same kind of conventional round dance and chorus. In *The Prophet Jonah,* language, given the same value as things, symbolically "is thrown overboard": the travelers in their striped garb quietly withdraw from the scene in which Paschor, stripped of reason, remains in total silence.

Hunt for Mammoths is a more complex play in which the author, as mentioned earlier, comes closer to the pure structure of the Theater of the Absurd. It undoubtedly has something in common with *Waiting for Godot.* The text of the play is distinguished by a degree of disorder, absence of uniformity. However, the background of the text is unknown to us — it is entirely possible that it has been distorted by external or the author's internal censorship. To an even greater degree, this applies to *The House of Terror.* It is interesting that in both *Hunt for Mammoths* and *The House of Terror* there are "meta-scenes" where the censor is brought on stage in person.

The basic plot of *Hunt for Mammoths* consists of the following: A group of characters is assembled, dressed in masquerade costumes; they have come to a large city for a celebration (a carnival or fiesta). However, wandering through the labyrinth of streets, they cannot find the place of celebration. A guide appears — a balloon vendor — but he only adds to the confusion. The group meets another "mirror-image" group led by an umbrella vendor. Both leaders, acting like farcical barkers, quarrel among themselves and are generous with promises to their groups. After various troubles the characters fall into a trap — there is a sticky river of "universal tar" on their way in which they all get stuck. The second half of the play is their fruitless efforts to escape; after all their efforts fail, the characters, gradually sinking into the tar, begin to lead a "normal life" in it — repeating everyday gestures. The play's end is reminiscent of *Happy Days*: the last major stage direction is devoted to a description of gestures which seem to have lost all sense:

> The fat man rustles his newspaper. The drunkard is drinking. The woman sews on a torn-off button. The nun tries to scratch the hump on her back. The man in the checkered suit does gymnastic exercises. The man in the striped suit phlegmatically smokes. The chimney-sweep fools with the balloon seller's wheezy clarinet. He and She, standing face to face, play a game with their hands. Miss "You-saw-me-then-die" preens before a tiny mirror. Dogs bark. The organ-grinder plays his organ.[25]

The symbolism of *Hunt for Mammoths* is also complex. Here, too, of course, is suggested a direct allegorical interpretation: presumptuous, mercenary demagogues and charlatans, playing on people's faith in a social utopia, lead them into a blind alley. The Lithuanian audience and also the authorities took precisely this "level" of the play's meaning (they prohibited its performance in the capital and soon, in spite of its tremendous success, took it off the repertoire in the second largest Lithuanian city, Kaunas). However, a more abstract interpretation is also absolutely possible (the unattainability of man's fundamental metaphysical goals, the meaningless existence "by inertia" in the face of time and death). The festival-carnival is easily interpreted in the sense of Bakhtin as an ideal condition which leads to a renewal of the "world body," but which is inaccessible to modern man.

The carnival cannot take place; thus, instead of the carnival uproar and the renewal of the whole personality, we observe its gradual annihilation, its being swallowed up by hackneyed official "culture." The play is constructed as an elimination of a series of oppositions, leading to entropy, grayness, and numbness. At first glance, the characters are extremely varied and colorful, and the play in general sparkles with a bright theatricality. But, paradoxically, the truth is that there is no variety on the stage. In particular the "mask vs. personality" opposition is to be eliminated. The carnival costume does not change anything, it turns out to be, so to speak, doubly deceptive (thus, a woman playing a hunchback is hunchbacked in reality). Almost every character totally merges with his stereotyped role which consists of the repetition of hackneyed, mechanical words and gestures. Next, the contrasts between characters are dissolved: it is obvious that the characters are completely interchangeable, only their external features distinguish them. One extreme example: the man in the checkered suit and the man in the striped suit copy each other's words and even each other's impressions exactly. Groups of people, too, are distinguished only externally: they present a dichotomy (a group of "balloons" and a group of "umbrellas"), but this dichotomy — based, by the way, on Freudian symbols — is false and does not allow the possibility of any true choice. The groups reflect each other like mirrors, and their fates are identical. It is true that here, too, the author introduces a hero-raisonneur who is, in principle, separated from the others. The organ-grinder probably symbolizes art (though weak, second-rate, and clownish). His folk-theater monologues are almost the only truly significant and informative texts in the play. The organ-grinder (who later gains a double — the watchman who unmasks/accuses the characters trapped in "universal tar") tries to restore values to a world of empty signs, but this attempt is fruitless. Men become objects; they are identified with the balloons, manipulated by clever demagogues:

> Nun—Give us a lashing too. Give us a lashing, tear us to pieces, don't spare us. Dupe us, and tie us up, well.
>
> Balloon Vendor—Remember, the balloon has a string. But in good hands the balloon should float like a little cloud in the sky. So from a distance, it looks like it's not attached to anything. That's where great art comes in.[26]

Finally, man is not only reduced to his social role, not only becomes a mere object, but is ultimately reduced to a sequence of alienated bureaucratic signs. An exhaustive description of one of the characters trapped in the tar is rendered in the following manner:

> Money, checks, money and papers, papers, papers. . . A school diploma. A
> certificate of your whereabouts. A statement of your achievements . . . A
> permit to enter — a permit to leave. A document that gives you the right . . .
> The right to possess, the right to direct, the right to judge. A certificate of
> ownership. A receipt. A payment receipt. Photographs. Your wife. A naked
> child. A naked lover. Notes. Telephone numbers. A list of victories. A
> reminder to appear at the VD clinic. Tickets for Stravinsky. Another certifi-
> cate. Another receipt. Tables. Cigarettes. A letter (. . .) A lottery ticket (. . .) It
> entitles you to receive another ticket free. (. . .) A birth certificate. A death
> announcement. And some more money. . .[27]

The "reduction" of man is expressed in the reduction of language; the theme
of violence to individuality and its ultimate destruction (as in *The Lesson*), is
shown largely through an investigation of the act of communication.[28] *Hunt
for Mammoths* is significantly more metalinguistic than Saja's one-act plays.
If newspaper jargon was parodied in the one-act plays (at times in a somewhat
feuilleton-like and primitive manner), then here many more cases of meaning-
lessness are examined: a whole spectrum of petrified, emasculated, dead
language forms. Language itself is suspect. Situations are laid bare in which
language is deprived of its informative quality and ceases to be a system of
signs.[29] At the same time, the play's characters repeatedly enter into linguistic
"games," distort words, resort to clumsy neologisms and compound words,
stupidly attempting to understand the functioning of language and speech.

> *The organ-grinder*—Let's shout, all together: "Eh, people!"
>
> *The Man in the Striped Suit* — Wait a minute, just wait a minute. What does
>   "Eh" mean, and who are these "people?"[30]

The author employs a number of typical devices of the Theater of the
Absurd: repetitions, echoes, non sequiturs, intentional distaxis.[31] Phatic clichés are extremely common: the characters are in constant verbal contact, but
tell each other nothing.[32] A conversation between the marionette lovers is
based on the device of "deaf chatter."[33] The nun's stories are totally senseless,
vaguely reminding one of Ionesco's absurd anecdotes, e.g., the circumstantial
story about catching carp and their tenaciousness — carp, it seems, are
capable of existing "without a head, without a tail, without a belly, without
anything."[34] Stichomythia (line by line exchange of brief cues) occurs during
the rapid sequence of which any logical order and semantic coherence is lost.[35]
These are also the empty pseudo-folklore songs which at times consist only of
interjections;[36] flat "Armenian-riddle" jokes,[37] double entendres; genital imagery which has lost all relation to the carnival mentality;[38] and word play
with terms which have become part of the mass consciousness, but have lost
their informative quality: "Radiation . . . Organization . . . Inflation. (. . .)

Cybernetics. Genetics. . .Dumping. Camping. (. . .) Erotica, exotica. . . I buy, I sell. (. . .) Try your luck in the lottery. . ."[39] The balloon and umbrella vendors' absurd tirades play a slightly different role: their demagogical clichés and "persuasive rhetoric"[40] lead to the direct enslavement of man. Here the author cleverly parodies propaganda and advertising jargon, mingling "eastern" and "western" forms. In the patter of the vendors, impressiveness is dominant: every possible rhetorical figure is used — metonymy, metaphor, rhyme. By the same token, tautologies are presented as a special wisdom.[41] Occasionally and not without some nerve, official ideological formulae are parodied in keen "popular" wit: "In your country, one man rides piggyback on another. In our country it's the other way around! "[42] "We have nothing to lose but . . . tar."[43] "We have to trample, and trample, and yet again trample . . . the tar."[44]

In this world everything is replaced by false designations, and the solution to real problems is replaced by sterile symbolic rituals (hence, the curious scene of sign therapy, self-hypnosis — "tooth-exorcism"[45]). Meanwhile, however, the signs themselves, deprived of their functionality and application to reality, gradually disappear. Like the one-act plays, *Hunt for Mammoths* ends with the loss of language — only the language of hackneyed gestures remains. The ultimate sense of the work is a void: the crisis of the code signifies the crisis of an ideology which presents itself as a false consciousness.[46]

In comparison with Saja's plays, Glinskis' play *The House of Terror* seems to be closer to traditional models. Externally, it is based on historical events — the fate of the Lithuanian poet A. Strazdas (1760–1833). Strazdas was one of the first to write secular poetry in Lithuanian and published the first small book of such poems (1814). He was a priest, but a priest of the Rabelaisian type who broke many of the rules that had been established for Catholic clergy and became a hero of folk legends and anecdotes. Spiritual hymns are interspersed with impious profane elements in his compositions. In 1828 Strazdas was sent to a monastery to do penance. He escaped and returned to his parish, but apparently never made peace with the official Church. His biography was repeatedly used by writers, but only *The House of Terror* became an event worthy of Strazdas' role in the history of Lithuanian letters.

The dramatis personae in *The House of Terror* are by no means interchangeable, stereotyped figures: they are true characters (many of them are real historical persons, as testified by archival documents). The play's language is partly stylized in the early-19th-century manner and is full of biblical and folkloric allusions and barbarisms, tending both towards naturalism and the baroque. It is a far cry from the stereotypes of our times. The originality of *The House of Terror* lies in something else: in the startling boldness and ritualistic-mythical framework which shows through quite clearly. The play's construction is complex, in many ways recalling the dramas of Genet and Weiss' *Marat-Sade*: real events are mixed with hallucinations which are "on the same level" with reality; and "theater within theater" and similar devices are used. The setting is a monastery, where sinful clergy repent — highly contemporized and transformed into a unique psychiatric hospital, slightly reminiscent of the Napoleonic Charenton. The play begins with a formula opening: the stylized secret message. An institution must be established for locking up people

> . . . diseased by thoughts, manias and other evident or latent mental derangements, who are becoming well-known as libertines and writers of incendiary songs or else have joined with the rebels as robbers and honor them publicly or secretly as martyrs while true servants of God and state are dishonored and ridiculed; causing by their actions the worst kind of disobedience among the citizens and affecting the greatness of this mighty Empire and the well-being of its people. . . . so that the willfulness, depravity, and the free-thinking of those errants might be curbed.[47]

In the psychiatric hospital, besides Strazdas, are the debauched and mad bishop Orlovskis and the diocese archivist Ryla. Their relationship is complex and is not cleared up until the end. Certain events have linked them in the past; however, these events, played anew in the hallucination scenes, cannot be completely reconstructed. Orlovskis, apparently, is guilty of seducing and murdering Maria, Ryla's daughter. The scenes with Maria in the convent recall the corresponding scenes in *Justine,* although, of course, in a very toned-down way: the convent reminds one of the closed world of Sade in which rules are deliberately violated and values overturned. It must be noted that the harsh and dangerous conjunction of religious and sexual experience, and the blasphemous and sacrilegious motifs in the play paradoxically aided its official acceptance, although the author was clearly striving for something quite different.

In *The House of Terror* the characters are in individual cells, similar to the garbage cans of Beckett or the prison cells of Genet. The environment permits many shocking moments: scenes of sado-masochistic delirium, flagellation, and nightmares (even burning a rat in a candle flame) pass before the audience. The play is extremely sinister and intricate if one tries to interpret it "realistically," but it lends itself in part to a semiotic interpretation, in M. Bakhtin's terms. Apparently, the most important of the play's languages is *body language.*

> Into the corporeal category are drawn a mass of the most varied objects and phenomena. Here they are absorbed into the atmosphere of the body and its physical activity; these objects and phenomena enter into new and unexpected relationships with the organs and processes of the body. They are devaluated and materialized in this corporeal category.[48]

This can be seen on the word and phraseological level, and also on the level of plot and composition. A solemn, rhythmized speech is constantly mixed with very naturalistic expressions, with the "low" forms of folklore, with the "unprintable speech" strata, and with carnival praise and abuse. One's attention is constantly directed to bodily excretions (an extreme case is the wild scene of "vomiting the archivist"), to the sexual sphere of life, and to the genitals and their functions. Of course, this carnival spirit is to a great extent on the decline and has more in common with baroque literature than it has with the literature of ridicule of the Middle Ages: the carnival mentality disintegrates and basically all that remains are the negative moments — blood, decay and death. The dramatis personae see the body as evil — both when they choose negative values (Orlovskis) and when they ecstatically try to revive positive values to the point of heresy and blasphemy (Ryla). Strazdas himself is the only exception: for him — and only him — corporeal life is not a source of evil, but rather (in accordance with the true spirit of carnival) a source of renewal.

> Introducing religious ideas and symbols into food, drink, defecation and sexual intercourse ... is, of course, nothing new. Various forms of parodistic-blasphemous literature from the late Middle Ages are known, such as parodistic Gospels, parodistic liturgies (The *Missa Gulonis* from the 13th century), and parodistic holidays and rituals.[49]

Compositionally, *The House of Terror* is just such a parodistic, distorted ritual. In it we find hymns (interspersed, as in Strazdas' work, with foul ditties), a sermon (Strazdas' monologue which takes a central position in the play imitates a sermon precisely), a sacrilegious offering-substitution and a blasphemous "eucharist" (fat and vodka). This cruel parodying of sacred rituals is linked not only with the traditions of the Goliards, but also, probably, with the nihilist tradition of the "Black Mass."[50] In the final analysis, the converted ritual leads to myth. It is easy to see that the world of decay, overturned values, and the all-encompassing and sterile body, in a word, the world of the asylum, is a world of the *dead*. There are also real corpses in it, for example Strazdas' enemies, his persecutors Petraševskis and Emalinavičius, who to the viewer (according to the author's stage direction) disintegrate and become dust. The poet turns out to be the mediator who appears in this world preserving the language of the living, and who undergoes complex trials. In complete accord with his legendary image, he performs as a jester ("a fool and a joker — the metamorphosis of a king and a god, presiding in the nether world, in death").[51]

This interpretation is confirmed by the play's topology and also by the complex onomastic symbolism: Strazdas is found at first *above* — here there is a play on his name, 'thrush', and on certain biographical legends linked to him. Thus, the poet's lover is called Marija Pikulienė, her husband is Adomas Pikulis, and her son by the poet is Pranciškus Pikulis. Pikulis was the Lithuanian heathen god of the earth and the underworld. Consequently, in Marija the earth and the Mother of God are joined, as it were (in one scene she is directly identified with the earth), her husband is the first man and a man of the earth, and her son is simultaneously a Saint Francis and a God-fighter and rebel. As is peculiar to the myth, the dramatis personae on some abstract level are identical (thus, Ryla in certain respects replaces Strazdas), and meanings spill over into one another and cannot be interpreted in full. However, the main idea is clear: undergoing his trials, encountering love, lies, power and death, the poet (or any man) is resurrected to a new life in his work, overcoming insurmountable limits.

The rise of the Lithuanian theater at the end of the sixties is unique. For the first time during the Soviet period, and indeed in all of its own history, the Lithuanian theater created original models related to some of the important trends in the culture of the modern world. Today this page of East European literature has been turned, but that, in my opinion, does not make it less important.

NOTES

1. E. Finkelshtein, *Old Hopes and New Currents in Present-Day Lithuania,* in: *Lituanus,* v. 23, 3 (1977), 52.

2. K. Saja, *Mažosios pjesės,* Vilnius, 1968.

3. K. Saja, *Mamutų medžioklė,* Vilnius, 1969.

4. J. Glinskis, *Grasos namai,* Vilnius, 1971.

5. K. Saja, *The Orator,* in: *Lituanus,* v. 13, 3 (1967), 29–46. *The Maniac,* in: *Lituanus,* v. 14, 4 (1968), 73–94.

6. Some valuable remarks can be found in M. Valgemäe, *Death of a Sea Gull: The Absurd in Finno-Baltic Drama,* in: *Books Abroad,* v. 46, 3 (1972), 374–9. See also the short but competent reviews by A. Landsbergis in: *Books Abroad,* v. 44, 1 (1970), 167; v. 44, 4 (1970), 702–3; v. 47, 2 (1973), 401–2. For observations on *The House of Terror,* in part analogous to ours, see A. Landsbergis, *Faces of Evil in Three Lithuanian Plays,* in: *Baltic Literature and Linguistics,* Columbus, Ohio, 1973, pp. 63–68.

7. M. Valgemäe compares *The Maniac* with S. I. Witkiewicz's play *The Crazy Locomotive, The Orator* with Ionesco's *The Chairs* and *Hunt for Mammoths* with *Rhinoceros.* In our view, these comparisons are somewhat superficial. *The Maniac* is rather close to Mrożek's *Charlie* (and *The Prophet Jonah* to his play *Out at Sea*).

8. Even closer to the Theater of the Absurd than the plays we have examined was an unpublished dramatic trilogy by the prematurely deceased A. Ambrasas, which was performed posthumously at the beginning of the seventies.

9. O. G. Revzina, I. I. Revzin, *Semiotičeskij èksperiment na scene (Narušenie postulata normal'nogo obščenija kak dramaturgičeskij priem),* in: *Učenye zapiski Tartuskogo Gosudarstvennogo Universiteta, Trudy po znakovym sistemam,* 5 (Tartu, 1971), 232–54.

10. See M. Baxtin, *Tvorčestvo Fransua Rable i narodnaja kul'tura Srednevekov'ja i Renessansa,* Moscow, 1965.

11. K. Saja, *Mažosios pjesės,* 165.

12. *Ibid.,* 226.

13. Roderich Robertson, *A Theatre for the Absurd*, in: *Drama Survey*, v. 2, 1 (1962), 37.
14. K. Saja, *Mažosios pjesės*, 238.
15. Cf. O. G. Revzina, I. I. Revzin, *op. cit.*, 243.
16. J. Błoński, *Ionesco: genealogia stereotypu*, in: *Dialog*, 1 (1967), 70.
17. K. Saja, *Mažosios pjesės*, 142.
18. *Ibid.*, 150.
19. *Ibid.*, 154.
20. *Ibid.*, 156.
21. *Ibid.*, 158.
22. *Ibid.*, 139-40.
23. *Ibid.*, 220.
24. Cf. U. Eco, *La struttura assente*, Milano, 1968, 90.
25. K. Saja, *Mamutų medžioklė*, 93.
26. *Ibid.*, 30-1.
27. *Ibid.*, 71-2.
28. O. G. Revzina, I. I. Revzin, *op. cit.*, 247.
29. In this sense it is possible to draw an interesting parallel between *Hunt for Mammoths* and such a phenomenon as contemporary Polish "linguistic poetry."
30. K. Saja, *Mamutų medžioklė*, 61.
31. Cf. J. Eliopulos, *Samuel Beckett's Dramatic Language*, The Hague-Paris, 1975.
32. *Ibid.*, 82-6.
33. K. Saja, *Mamutų medžioklė*, 9-10.
34. *Ibid.*, 11.
35. *Ibid.*, 42-6. Cf. J. Eliopulos, *op. cit.*, 78-82.
36. K. Saja, *Mamutų medžioklė*, 34, 60.
37. *Ibid.*, 6, 23.
38. *Ibid.*, 15, etc.
39. *Ibid.*, 7.
40. U. Eco, *op. cit.*, 83-92.
41. *Ibid.*
42. K. Saja, *Mamutų medžioklė*, 41.
43. *Ibid.*, 61.
44. *Ibid.*, 69.
45. *Ibid.*, 48-50.
46. Cf. U. Eco, *op. cit.*, 97, J. Błoński, *op. cit.*, 71.
47. J. Glinskis, *Grasos namai*, 5-6.
48. M. Baxtin, *Voprosy literatury i èstetiki*, Moscow, 1975, 323.
49. *Ibid.*, 334.
50 Cf. a similar construction in James Joyce's *Ulysses*.
51. M. Baxtin, *op. cit.*, 311.

Thomas G. Winner

MYTHIC AND MODERN ELEMENTS IN THE
ART OF LADISLAV FUKS:
NATALIA MOOSHABER'S MICE[1]

> Time present and time past
> are both perhaps present in time future
> And time future contained in time past . . .
> What might have been is an abstraction
> Remaining a perpetual possibility
> Only in a World of speculation.
> What might have been and what has been
> Point to one end, which is always present.
> T. S. Eliot, "Burnt Norton"

Introduction

Prague, in the interwar years, was one of the principal centers of the European avant-garde, where dadaism, cubism, futurism, poetism and surrealism competed in their efforts to reverse traditionalism in the arts. Surrealism altered, as did all avant-garde forms, the relation between the artistic sign and its denotatum, since the traditional denotatum, that is conscious life and the objective world governed by nineteenth-century rules of time and space, was replaced by the imaginative unconscious freed from these constraints. For cubism in the visual arts, the principle of mimesis became irrelevant in the search for new ways to relate sign and signification, and in a new emphasis on the signifier. The verbal arts also weakened the bond between the sign and its denotatum. The concept of the "self-valuable word" implied a rejection of the principle of an iconic relation of sign to external reality. Rather, iconicities, or equivalences, were to be sought primarily within the boundaries of the work itself. Hence the new, and often radical, experimentation with language not only in poetry but also in prose (for instance the "poetic" prose of Vančura), and the poetization of the language of the street and of journalism (Čapek).

One of the sources for new models and themes was the art of the primitive, both native and exotic folk art. Consequently, we find the mixing of high and low genres, the increased interest in mythic themes and forms, and the return to syncretism in all the arts. In the visual arts, collages introduced verbal material into the visual object (for example, by projecting snatches of verbal texts upon the visual canvas) and paintings depicted music (e.g. Bracque's "L'hommage à Bach"). The verbal arts also turned to more syncretic forms, to the experimentation with the pure music of language and the introduction of heightened visual perception into the verbal. Thus the Czech poetists talked about "poetry of optical forms" and poets and visual artists created "optical poems." (Cf. Chvatík and Pešat, eds. 1967: 112–17, discussed in Grygar 1972: 88.) On a more philosophical level, the Czech visual and verbal arts of the 20s and 30s shared with all European art the altered sense of time and space. In the visual arts, this meant the defiance of traditional spatial orderings and relationships and of the temporal relationships that are implied by space. Influenced by the discoveries in the sciences, the visual arts (pre-cubism and cubism) abandoned post-Renaissance perspective with its single and unified point of view, for a multi-perspectival approach which placed the viewer both inside and outside of the canvas, and which also provided several perspectival attitudes within the canvas itself, thus showing all units of space from various perspectives, and hence all figures in motion. In the verbal art of the surrealists, futurists, and poetists this attitude to time and space led to the abandonment of linear time, and thus of traditional plot structures, and to a blurring of the traditional dichotomy of narrator's discourse/character's discourse by the device of reported discourse.

In the political atmosphere of postwar Czechoslovakia, the avant-garde tradition of the 1930s was attacked. But during the brief freer climate in the 1960s, experimentation was begun again. A surrealist movement, led by Vratislav Effenberger, the closest associate of the late Karel Teige, re-emerged, and even published one issue of a new periodical, *Analogon*. In a brief, but brilliant burst of energy, Czech art created new forms, building on the rich heterogeneity of the art of the interwar years. The first break with the strictures of official ideology was heralded by the publication of Josef Škvorecký's novel *The Cowards* (*Zbalělci*) cast, in the fashion of Salinger's *Catcher in the Rye*, in the idiom of a teen-age narrator. Slang and jazz language form a *skaz* which render the potentially heroic, the Russian liberation of a small town, grotesque. In short, many of the prewar avant-garde traditions were not only revived, but utilized for further artistic experimentation. The art of the 1960s expressed the new views of time and space, further developed syncretic forms by synthesizing the verbal and the visual inherited from cubist painting and futurist poetry, and experimented with non-rational motivation and the gothic aspect of narration inherited primarily from surrealism. The aesthetics of Czech poetism of the 1930s, its emphasis on the grotesque, the absurd, the clownish and the carnival spirit, which was so strongly exemplified in the theaters of Voskovec and Werich, now found its renewal in the style of a new theater, the theater "Na Zábradlí." (Cf. Winner 1973.)

One of the most significant writers of the 1960s, Ladislav Fuks (b. 1923), demonstrates all these trends: thus we find in his works elements of cubofuturist poetics, based on relativization of time and space, as well as surrealist poetics in his grotesque and absurd scenes which overlook the boundary between the real and the dream world. In his carnivalesque scenes, we may also detect the aesthetics of the poetists. Fuks' first novel, which is the only one translated into English, *Pan Theodor Mundstock* (1963), set in a Jewish milieu in occupied Prague, is a grotesque mixture of horror and the ridiculous, the elevated and the low, despair and hope, expressed through a semantic ambivalence and paradox which blurs the boundary between physical reality and imagination, and which turns all goals into their opposite. Fuks' next novel, *Variations for a Dark String* (*Variace pro temnou strunu,* 1966), for which he received a prize, is again a novel of paradox and the absurd, and again is infused with strong surrealist and cubo-futurist elements. Multiple temporal perspectives co-exist in a complex system in which linearity is forever juxtaposed to simultaneity (for a detailed discussion of this novel, cf. Winner 1970–1972, 1973). Fuks' third novel, *Spalovač mrtvol* (*The Burner of Corpses*), which appeared in 1967 and was subsequently made into a film, is cast as a modern horror story whose anti-hero is the crematorium official Kopferkringl who professes kindliness and harmlessness, but is in fact a murderer. Again, the novel focuses upon a paradox: the protagonist does not appear to be an evil man; rather he is perfectly normal and quite human; he upholds the normal platitudes of decency, believes that man should not suffer, and is obedient to law and order. And yet he commits ghastly murders, not out of hate but because the circumstances of his time lead him to crime. He begins by killing his part-Jewish wife and children, and ends up putting his crematorium experience to work in the concentration camp gas chambers. His violent acts, he explains, will save his victims from an even worse fate. The many repetitions and variations of key episodes and phrases achieve both a fragmentation of traditional reality and an intensification of the internal structure of the work.

These novels are all united by such contemporary themes as that of alienation, and perspectives contributed by cubism and surrealism. But Fuks adds to this synthesis a fundamental element, also not alien to contemporary art forms, namely that of myth. For, as we shall see, mythic structures may be seen as the strongest organizing force, casting Fuks' novels into a circular form and into a text with resonances of meanings which are reunited in a new composite.

Traditions Contributing to *Natalia Mooshaber's Mice*

In Fuks' most significant novel, *Myši Natalie Mooshabrové* (*Natalia Mooshaber's Mice*), published in 1970, we perceive a striking culmination of these trends.

The remainder of this paper will be concerned with an analysis of this novel and its place in the semiotic system of Czech art and culture of the 1960s.

In *Natalia Mooshaber's Mice,* Fuks continues the tradition of his earlier works. The novel is a brilliant synthesis of various elements of modern art: of the grotesque, gothic horror story set in a Kafkaesque dream-world, of science fiction, of the *nouveau roman* of the absurd; and these are, in turn, juxtaposed to the fairytale and to archetypal myths. In this work, Fuks defines entirely new attitudes to genre, by amalgamating the most variegated traditional genres into a new stylistic whole, freed from the conventions of both the realistic and the surrealistic text.

The following is a brief synopsis of the text. The novel is set in an anonymous place and in an indefinite time, in a fairytale-like capital of a principality which is both ancient and modern, in which people drive in horse carts and have their weddings in rural inns, but the capital of which has elements of modern technology: a subway and a satellite airport from which shuttle satellites depart daily for the principality's colony on the moon. The names of the streets and people are reminiscent of German-speaking Switzerland, or perhaps of Liechtenstein. The principality's president, Albín Rappelschlund, officially rules together with the monarch, Princess Augusta. Their two portraits hang everywhere. The "widowed monarch, Princess Augusta," as she is always referred to, has, however, not been seen for many years, giving rise to suspicions among the populace that she has been murdered or imprisoned by Rappelschlund, or that she is in hiding from him. Against this background, and in this medieval/modern fairytale/science fiction setting, Fuks relates the story of Natalia Mooshaber, an unhappy widowed mother, deserted and mocked by two whom she believes to be her daughter and son, the prostitute Nabule and the criminal Wezr who has robbed her of her savings. Natalia Mooshaber has several occupations: she is employed by the state agency, Child and Family Care, and she works as a volunteer caretaker at the capital's cemetery. In the capacity of her first position, she is repeatedly charged with the investigation of the cases of disobedient children. She pities their parents because, as an unhappy mother, she identifies with the unhappy parents of disobedient children. She also occupies herself with catching mice in traps baited with poisoned bacon, and there is much talk of the various types of white-powdered mouse poison throughout the novel. But Natalia Mooshaber also bakes cakes and pies and covers them with powered sugar and almonds. Some of the children she "investigates" die mysteriously immediately after having eaten sweets covered with a white powder presented to them by Mrs. Mooshaber, or after just having looked at the sweets. However, several of the children reappear later alive. The novel ends on the birthday of the lost Princess: Mrs. Mooshaber has prepared a feast at the house of her latest "charge." The people revolt because they fear that Rappelschlund has hurt the Princess. Rappelschlund is overthrown and Natalia Mooshaber is revealed to be the Princess who had been driven into hiding by the dictator Rappelschlund. The dignitaries of the principality appear and kneel before her, a golden coach is waiting outside. But at this moment Mrs. Mooshaber kills herself by eating a piece of cake poisoned with her own mouse poison.

This novel is highly complex, and must be understood on many intersecting planes. It is clearly an allegory of modern man lost in an alienated and totalitarian society. It is also a fantastic and surrealist mythic story which combines pictures of the modern political state and modern technology with primitive formulae of evil, mysticism, magic and mythic themes. Its general atmosphere recalls that of the carnival, which is the poetics of poetism.

On the deepest level the novel partakes of mythic structures and is informed by archetypal myths which have shaped much of its formal and thematic construction.

However, Fuks' novel is not a direct translation of mythic themes, but an entirely new reordering of mythic units within the context of methods and themes of the modern verbal and visual arts, especially those of cubism and surrealism, and within the context of the cultural world view of the present.

Recently, V. V. Ivanov has presented some penetrating analyses of the relation of myth to literature. Basing himself on Belyj's study of Gogol (Belyj 1934), Ivanov (1971: 141–2) suggests that the grotesque depictions of some physical characteristics in Gogol's *Dead Souls* recall myth and anticipate the art of the twentieth century. Gogol, he says (142), has used mythological archetypes for the creation of his peculiar "fantastic realism." In a later work (1973b), Ivanov also examines the ritual and mythological sources for the opposition seeing/unseeing in Gogol's short story *Vij*.

Fuks' story of Natalia Mooshaber, who is at the same time a persecuted princess and an old down-at-the-heels woman, or a burlesque of the female principle, presents both mythological forms and contents. We shall see that Fuks takes typical mythical texts and joins them in a Lévi-Straussian *bricolage*. We know from Mukařovský (1942) that in myth details (individual signs) have a certain independence, and can be arranged in a somewhat arbitrary fashion. As Mukařovský has pointed out, it is the specific characteristic of folk art that it consists of complexes of relatively independent sign units which may be conjoined relatively freely. Hence, folklore in its concatenation of signs is freer from thematic motivation than is "high" art (1942: 221).

According to Lévi-Strauss, a characteristic feature of mythic thought is that it is a kind of *bricolage* of elements which are finite and heterogeneous and which, by themselves, bear no relation to the concrete project at hand. The elements "each represent a set of actual possible relations; they are 'operators' but they can be used for any operations of the same type" (1966: 18). The elements which the *bricoleur* collects are both free and constrained. They are constrained by the fact that they are drawn from a mythic code in which they already are endowed with meaning which imposes a limitation upon their maneuverability. But they are free in the sense that the mythic text operates solely on the transformation of a finite set of elements. Myth, according to Lévi-Strauss, is both diachronic and timeless. While it refers to events, the specific pattern described is a timeless one and explains not only the past, but also the present and the future. Myth is built up of units which are bundles of relations, and relations belonging to the same bundle may be combined in such a way that they appear diachronically at remote intervals (Lévi-Strauss 1966: 211). Mythic thought, Lévi-Strauss holds, is based on an awareness of irreconcilable contradictions and oppositions, and all myth progresses from the awareness of these oppositions towards their resolution and reconciliation through a third term, the mediator, which partakes of features from both opposing terms and thus mediates between them. Thus relatively arbitrary elements that remain quite concrete, and are combined into various units, can be used in diverse ways to reconcile abstract oppositions by introducing extended metaphors. This approach, to a certain extent, describes some aspects of the method and meaning of Fuks' novel, where elements, on the whole, operate like percepts rather than concepts. That is, the interrelation of concrete details, such as sugared cakes associated with little children, signifies in a particular way abstract concepts, in this case, maternity and fertility.

Certain concrete details are replayed repeatedly and appear in combination with a multitude of other elements, so that, in Lotman's terms (1974), we might see the novel as a gigantic kaleidoscope which operates only by the rearrangement of its inner elements into ever new combinations. But myths are also diachronic, and so the novel moves simultaneously along two axes: the linear and the permutational. The latter is like Lotman's "primary text" which proceeds not in linear fashion, but by inner permutation alone. But the novel operates also along the lines of a regular plot structure (Lotman's "secondary text") which operates by the addition of new elements. However, the mythological dimension is probably the strongest in this work, which is characterized by constant reverberation of mythic meanings, and by a mythic circular time. Indeed, the novel is a complex montage of such mythic elements, a structure which is foregrounded by the projections of these elements upon an every-day prosaic framework, and by the infusion into the novel of all the devices of modern art.

Thus among the traditions which partake in this work are the following:

(1) First of all, surrealism, for clearly the fantasy, irreality, dreamlikeness, the conjoining of dreamlike sequences with every-day signs, are surrealistic forms of foregrounding, recalling Dali's *Melting Watch* or Kafka's Gregor Samsa the insect and the realia of a Prague bourgeois household. Other dreamlike sequences are the many absurd and illogical scenes, exemplified by the statement of a pharmacist to Mrs. Mooshaber about the varying quality of different mouse poisons:

> . . . Rattenol is such a strong powder. It is a white powder, just like Marokan, and it is more dangerous. And it can also be confused with sugar, but it is three times stronger. Which can be seen if you put it on these scales here . . . (208)[2]

(2) The aesthetics of cubism, which breaks up space and time, and fragments point of view, is closely related to the organization of myth, based as it is on a dual time perspective. This relation was already noted by Belyj (1934: 210), and by Ivanov (1971: 141) who wrote

> The prototypes of the grotesque depiction of the body (in the work of Gogol) . . . are reminiscent of cubist portraits (and are found in) mythological transformations. Gogol in this is closest to the archaic tradition of the construction of mythological models of the world . . .

(3) The relativization of time and space and the transformation use of details is also clearly a part of the aesthetics of the *nouveau roman* and can be clearly observed in the novels of Robbe-Grillet.

The Inner Structure of the Novel

Let us now examine the unique structure of this novel, and ask how it creatively synthesizes these many traditions, meanings and systems. The first task is the identification of the mythological elements in the novel. How are they organized on the level of character, space and time?

Mythic elements

The main character of the novel, Natalia Mooshaber, is both an every-day person and a mythic character who exists outside of time and space, and who is constantly being transformed into her own opposite. Thus she is simultaneously

(1) Life-giver and food provider/death dealer and poisoner. She bakes cakes for the wedding party of her daughter, and she feeds her friends; she works for the state agency, Care of Child and Family. But she poisons mice (and perhaps also children). She is both a mother-protector and a figure closely related to death through her constant association not only with the cemetery but with the color black.

(2) She is the poor old Natalia Mooshaber/she is the ruling monarch Princess Augusta.

(3) She is both herself/she is not herself. She burlesques herself. She often appears in disguise and wears a mask. Whenever she goes out to "investigate," she is disguised. For instance, "with a hat with a long colored feather, with her face rouged and powdered white, with painted lips and eyebrows, with a chain of bamboo balls, and in white gloves . . ." (64). One page later she is described in exactly the same way: "with a long green and red feather, with her face rouged and powdered white, with painted lips and eyebrows, with a chain of bamboo balls, and white gloves . . ." (66).

(4) She is a witch/she is a goddess. She has the magic of poison, but she can also cure, as she cures the eye of the first victim, the little boy Faber, who dies shortly after she bandages his eye.

There is still another element of myth in the novel, and that is the entire life story of Natalia Mooshaber as the widowed monarch, Princess Augusta, who is persecuted by the male dictator Rappelschlund. The relation of the two sexes portrayed in the various myths of early female dominance and male assertion of dominance in later myths are well known. Campbell (1959: 315–16) posits a paleolithic cult of the woman, of a mother-goddess who was to become conspicuous in the later early agricultural civilizations of the Middle East. He cites various primitive myths around the world which show the rule of women being overthrown by the rebellion of men.

Natalia Mooshaber's life and death "and rebirth" are related to a transformation of such early myths, that of Persephone captured and hidden away by Hades. Persephone's disappearance is linked to a lack of food, and she can return to the living only part-time because of the forbidden fruit she has eaten while she was with Hades. Natalia Mooshaber returns to life only as a part-princess and constantly is related to death images. Like Persephone, she is depicted as constantly related to feasts. The festival of Persephone and Demeter are accompanied by feasting on suckling pigs. One of the repeated epithets of Natalia Mooshaber is food for feasting. In her case it is, of course, lowered to every-day food — ham, meat salad and lemon soda. And her very death is tied to a banquet-like feast. At that feast, just as she is "discovered" as the Princess, she eats a cake with raisins and poisons herself, just as Persephone eats a pomengranate.

We can thus see that the novel, in mythic fashion, is based on some fundamental oppositions, and that Natalia Mooshaber, in her various transformations, is the mediating agent between them. Indeed, a unifying theme at a deep level is that of Natalia as both a life and death symbol which is successively transformed. This basic opposition is transformed into fertility/ barrenness (she is a dead tree and a substitute or a real mother offering food). Fertility is then transformed into the positive or free community, as opposed to the repressive one, in a weak evocation of the Persephone myth, when upon Natalia's death she is regenerated into the happy community, which happens at the occasion of her birthday and funeral just after the fall of the dictator.

As Ivanov and Toporov have shown in their documenting of conservative mechanisms in myth that preserve form and content, a common mythic device is the classification of all personages according to a common set of such parameters "within which they may be described either in a similar or directly contrasting fashion — one trait being replaced by its polar opposite" (1976: 267). Such parameters are often composed of binary oppositions, which may be exchanged, singly or in groups, from personage to personage at various points in the myth. This structure may be emphasized by repetition of sound images as it is in this story, but space does not permit me to document this here.

Furthermore, Ivanov and Toporov note that mythic content is generally coded at a deep level, thus being only decipherable by those having the key to the decoding. Thus such content is least subject to change (1976: 268). However, it is necessary to add that certainly partial decoding is carried out by those who share a common cultural tradition, even if at a subliminal level, and clearly the whole mythic tradition which elaborates upon the exchanging of life and death principles between male and female is expressed in many complex ways in Fuks' novel, and is communicated in some way to the receivers, whether or not they are sophisticated in the themes and methods of mythic reconstruction.

The various oppositions in the novel can be ranged in a series of transformations which reverberate throughout the text in a circular manner. Of these we list below only the most pronounced. The fundamental opposition is life/death, in various transformations. Mrs. Mooshaber is the mediating agent.

Life	Mediator	Death
1. The live Princess	NM is the "dead" Princess who is really alive. She dies when the Princess is alive again.	The "dead" Princess
2. Fertility	NM has children, Wezr and Nabule, but in the end it is shown that they are adopted.	Barrenness
3. Female	NM symbolizes Woman persecuted by man. But she is also a ruler.	Male
4. The free community	NM is a victim of repression and restores the free community by her "rebirth."	Repression
5. Live children	NM saves children in her capacity as worker for Care of Child and Family, but she is also involved in their deaths.	Dead children
6. Food	NM provides both food and poison.	Poison
7. Wedding	NM participates in both.	Funerals
8. Birthday celebration	NM participates in both, and they are equated.	Death banquet
9. Care of Child and Family	NM's two jobs.	Care of graves
10. Lullaby	NM sings the lullaby to children. The requiem, rehearsed throughout the novel, is sung for her as the dead Princess.	Requiem

| 11. Mice | She is overrun with mice; dreams of a giant mouse the size of a lion. She poisons mice in traps. | Mouse poison and traps |
| 12. Bright colors | NM's multi-colored masks, rouged face, white gloves and her colored jewelry, white poison and sugar/ NM's black jacket, shirt and hand-bag, the black flag for which she is the self-appointed caretaker. | Black |

As Ivanov and Toporov have commented, not only is the mythic structure characterized by binary oppositions, but also by opposition of functions (Ivanov and Toporov 1976: 267). Here we note the opposed functions of:

persecution / concealment
passivity / rebellion
feeding / murder

Relativization of Character

We have seen that everything in the novel may be changed into its opposite, time and space are relativized, and people are what they are not.

We have already spoken of Natalia Mooshaber who is always transformed into her own opposite, and who mediates between opposites. On the level of character, she has a double, Mrs. Kralcová the superintendent of her apartment house, who always repeats what Natalia Mooshaber has said and tells what she has seen. But Natalia can also be "another" woman. Not only does she frequently appear in mask-like disguises, but sometimes she is "not she." Thus, after she has returned one of her "charges," a little boy, to his house, the boy denies that it was she who had taken him:

"This lady," he smiled and shook his head, "did not take me home. That was quite a different lady" (91).

People are always themselves and at the same time someone else. Thus, talking about a thief:

"that is not the Mrs. Klaudinger in whose house your son-in-law lives," Mrs. Knorring shook her head. "That is only a coincidence of name. That Klaudinger, as I already said, looks very much like you, which is a coincidence." (94)

A variant of this type of character splitting is the appearance of a person with equal description in different roles. For example, at the funeral of one of the children, a man is robbed. He is described as the man "in the bowler hat with a watch chain on his waistcoat." A person with the same appearance shows up in several sections of the novel as a tour guide:

> Some old guide was ... explaining to a group of foreigners about the statue of Anna Marie the Blessed ... and kept touching his waistcoat on which hung a golden chain (98).

He also appears in Mrs. Mooshaber's reflections.

> Mrs. Mooshaber saw how an elderly man shook his head on which he wore a bowler hat, and that his overcoat was unbuttoned, and under it his jacket was unbuttoned so that one could see the waistcoat with a watch and a gold chain (204).

The relativization of personages is also carried onto the level of discourse. There is, thoughout the novel, a blurring of the identities of the speakers, an adumbration of the distinction between information provided by the characters and information presented by the narrator. Individual utterances are constantly being shifted and projected upon other utterances. This is done in a variety of ways:

(1) By having the same statement in direct discourse repeated by different persons, e.g.:

> "So I am here," she said, and her head was spinning. "She is here," Nabule burst out . . . (60).
>
> "Not in church," Mrs. Mooshaber shook her head, "I do not believe in God." "Mrs. Mooshaber does not believe in God," the janitor's wife was saying smilingly, "Mrs. Mooshaber believes in fate" (109).
>
> "This is Marokan," (said Mrs. Mooshaber), "a mouse poison. I shake it on pieces of food in these traps."
> "Marokan," the black dog[3] said smilingly, "a mouse poison. You shake it on pieces of food, Madam" (131).

(2) By repeating the same, or similar, sentences in first person direct speech, and in third person narrator's discourse, in direct sequence, e.g.:

> In the evening Mrs. Mooshaber wanted to go to the park to the water fountain . . . "In the evening I'll go to the park to the water fountain," she said to herself (54).
>
> . . . she said to herself, "I look like an actress or a footman's wife. Or like a merchant's wife from the Papuan Islands . . ." Only now it seemed to Mrs. Mooshaber that some of the mothers or governesses even nodded to her . . . Mrs. Mooshaber did not know if she saw correctly, but it was possible, she looked like an actress or a merchant's wife from the Papuan Islands (68).

It was surprisingly empty here.
"It is quite empty here," said the janitor's wife . . . (100)

(3) By shifts between direct, indirect, and reported discourse.[4]

It was really already fall — it was in the second half of October, and the leaves on the trees had dried, turned yellow and fallen down even more than *those three days ago,* and it was damper and more penetrating. Now it was no longer necessary to water the graves, nor to cut the grass, now it was necessary only to dust the gravestones and the inscriptions, so that Mrs. Mooshaber no longer carried garden shears and a watering can in her black bag, but only rags and a dust brush. Mrs. Mooshaber wanted to fix her graves for All Souls Day today, so that next week *when it will be time to get hold of the bunting, she would have less* work. A few days before All Souls, she usually went to the cemetery administration *to get* decorative pine branches *for* her graves and one or two artificial flowers with which she then decorated the graves. This is what people were insured for and had paid for (197).

. . . and Mrs. Mooshaber in the square said to herself: I wonder what Mrs. Linpeck is doing right now? Perhaps she's sitting in her booth selling beer and soft drinks, it was afternoon, right after lunch, *so she probably doesn't have that many customers.* "I'm sure she's getting alimony," said Mrs. Mooshaber in the square, "I'm sure she doesn't want to throw herself under the train anymore, but if the boy doesn't improve, he'll destroy her before she goes back to the theater. If she has bought him a winter coat and hat, it's winter, maybe he really isn't wearing the green sweater anymore, for Christmas he'll get skis" (198).

(4) Still another syntactic aspect contributes to the fragmentation of character. This is the obliteration of the boundary between the inner world and the external world, achieved by the frequent use of aposiopesis, the sudden interruption of an utterance, usually graphically indicated by dots, as though the speaker were unable or unwilling to complete the statement. This allows the text to sound into a void, to express forlornness, indefiniteness, uncertainty, and to make it unclear whether the sentences are actually spoken or exist only in the internal world of the narrator.

"You there," she said to the manager's wife, a woman in a short summer skirt, "you come, too . . ." Mrs. Mooshaber nodded quickly and entered the passageway (17).

"Whenever he goes to get beer, he drinks some of it," the manager's wife laughed, "You know Mrs. Mooshaber, he never has to bring home more than half a pitcher. But sometimes I get the feeling . . ." The manager's wife suddenly stopped and adjusted her blouse, "Sometimes I get the feeling that maybe the only reason he drinks that beer on the way home is that they don't give him enough to eat" (23).

"So in the morning I got ready for the wedding," she said to herself, "and in the evening I went to hang out the black flag. What a lot of things have happened today," she said to herself. "What am I to make of it all? Maybe it's been kind of a holiday too . . ." (33).

Relativization of Space and Time

The writings of Husserl and Bergson in philosophy, the new discoveries in physics, and the invention of the camera have created a new perception of space and time in the twentieth century, and this perception is reflected both in the visual arts (cubism and surrealism) and in the verbal arts of our century. This is especially marked in Fuks' writing, and particularly in *Natalia Moos-haber's Mice,* and is also obviously closely related to the mythological base of the novel. Time and space are no longer linear and seen from a single perspective but, as in cubist painting, time and space literally surround us. Spatial boundaries are blurred and space seems to be circular with the same markers reoccurring at frequent intervals.

Space

We have already observed the anonymity of the place (as well as the time) of the novel's action. The names given to people and to localities are geographically confusing, consisting of an admixture of names of various national provenance. Germanic names predominate (Mooshaber, Rappelschlund, Eichen-kranz, Knorring, Blauthal), but a few are Italian (Count Scarcola) and Slavic (Czech — Kralcová, Kradrupský, Drozdov). The story's action jumps from place to place and spatial boundaries are not preserved. Mrs. Mooshaber is both inside and outside the cemetery without having passed through the gate. There is the cemetery itself and a subway station "Cemetery." Sometimes spatial objects are presented in split-image fashion. Thus a pharmacy looks like a funeral home and is thus spatially related to the cemetery:

> The pharmacy was faced with black marble and looked more like a funeral home than a pharmacy. In the window were little boxes [are they related to children's coffins? TGW]. And over the entrance hung a cross. A black and yellow cross, for the pharmacy was called something like that . . . But also that black and yellow cross looked threatening and terrible. So threatening and terrible that the blood thickened in the veins of many who passed here, blood could thicken in the veins and the heart stop (207).

Time

> The elimination of the static, the exclusion of the absolute: this is the essential tendency of modern times, the most burning question of the day . . .
>   The new doctrine denies the absolute nature of time and, concomitantly, the existence of a universal time. Each speed of the flow of time was not the same (Manifesto of Futurist Painters, in Jakobson 1919: 28).

In Fuks' novels, exclusive linearity of time does not exist. Against the background of the plot, which evolves in linear fashion, the protagonists do not exist in evolving time, but in a time which moves, then stands still again, and then may begin anew in circular fashion. This is not only the time of modern science, but also the time of memory. Thus story time moves back and forth, as the plane of reality moves from "thingness" to the visions of the unconscious. Fuks departs from linearity and renders each moment as a dimensionless "now" in which we move from space to space and from time unit to time unit without anchoring these units in traditional dimension. All this is of course, as we have already said, also closely related to the novel's mythological plane.

The plot of the novel, just as myth, is essentially circular. It begins at a feast, the wedding for Mrs. Mooshaber's "daughter" Nabule. In the country inn, under the portraits of the ruler Rappelschlund and the Princess, sits the wedding party which includes Mrs. Mooshaber, who is later forced to leave the party, ejected by her daughter; two students sit with Mrs. Mooshaber and she confides in them. Mrs. Mooshaber has baked cakes for the party. The students tell her that they room with a rich merchant, and she tells them of her old school friend Maria who is now a housekeeper in a rich family. The food on the table is ham and meat salad. The daughter takes one of the cakes and throws it to the ceiling so that the raisins drop out, and then throws the whole bowl of cakes out of the open window for the horses to eat. The old tree suggests Mrs. Mooshaber.

The novel ends with another banquet in the very house of the rich merchant of whom the students have spoken. The students are present again. So is Maria, the old-time friend, for it is in this house, we now learn, that she has been housekeeper all these years. Again they eat ham and meat salad. Again Mrs. Mooshaber has baked cakes, this time two bowls of cakes, one with almonds and one with raisins. But this time it is not a wedding, but a party at the occasion of the national holiday, the birthday of the Princess Augusta who turns out to be Natalia Mooshaber. But it is also Natalia's funeral dinner (and therefore Augusta's): the table is set on the tablecloth created by Natalia's black flag and a cemetery candle is burning on top of the black flag. In the end, as Natalia Mooshaber is discovered to be the Princess, she poisons herself with the cake with the raisins which she has baked herself. The beginning scene had been filled with death images which are repeated in the final scene. As, in the opening, Mrs. Mooshaber is ejected from the wedding by her daughter, and goes toward the cemetery, the street is empty, only "on the opposite sidewalk there stood an old dried-out tree" (15). Then, as the novel ends, and Natalia Mooshaber poisons herself, we read:

> Then she fell on the rug, as an old, dried-out tree that had been cut down, and those who knelt near her heard her last quiet words: "All that was my fate. God have mercy on my poor soul." (291)

Thus birth and wedding are equated with death. The dictator who was her nemesis is now dead and the people rejoice. But her death is also equated with rebirth (although it is only suggested by the celebration of the people) and the final circularity is reached.

Mukařovský, in working out Mathésius's functional sentence perspective of Rheme and Theme for aesthetic texts, pointed out that the way in which a text's reception proceeds is not linear but advances by an accumulation of meaning, in which the horizontal axis of the objective time sequence is projected upon the vertical axis of subjective simultaneity (Holenstein's formulation; see Holenstein 1976: 31). According to Mukařovský, there is a simultaneous perception of the linear progress of time. Every linear element, following upon earlier elements already perceived, is seen against the background of all the other elements which have already passed before the receiver's consciousness. So that, instead of a horizontal time line, time is represented in a prism:

A—B—C—D—E—F
 | | | | |
 A   B   C   D   E
 | | | |
 A   B   C   D
 | | |
 A   B   C
 | |
 A   B
 |
 A   (Mukařovský 1940: 117)

In Fuks' novel, linear time is constantly marked by the indication of exact clock time or calendar time, which is indicated more than forty times throughout the novel, mercilessly ticking to Mrs. Mooshaber's death. But against this exact time, there are marked certain time equivalences, similar to Mukařovský's vertical progression, in the form of pervasive themes, motifs, details, and even phrases which occur independently of linear time, until these details become repetitively obsessive. At each occurrence, they are illuminated from a different angle, reflecting the shifting contexts. Fuks uses the term "resonances" to describe his technique. He says that resonances

> function both independently and in their mutual interrelations; thus they are provided with a context, and the book contains a second and third level . . .

The detail resounds in different fashions and repeatedly throughout the work, and thus it is raised to a higher power. (Opelík 1964: 6)

On the level of the semantic episode, we note such recurrent themes as the mice, the mousetraps and the poison, the constant complaints about bad children voiced almost always in the same phrase: "'You know what may await him?' 'I know,' nodded Mrs. Mooshaber . . . 'I know it well. Reform school, house of correction, unqualified labor, day laborer'" (184). Other recurrent themes are the question of the whereabouts of the Princess, and the visits of the police to Mrs. Mooshaber's house, always with the same remarks ("We have come to see how you live"), as well as the requiem mass, rehearsed throughout the novel and sung at Natalia Mooshaber's funeral.

On the level of motifs we single out three of many: the ever-repeated remarks about food (ham and meat salad), the life of Rappelschlund, recited by heart by the children, and the black flag of which Mrs. Mooshaber is the caretaker, and which in the end of the novel she uses to cover the table for her birthday/funeral banquet. Sometimes certain motifs are repeated almost verbatim: Thus in Chapter 9, the action is interrupted rhythmically by the description of people buying lemonade.

> At that moment some middle-aged man stepped up to the kiosk and asked for a lemon soda, he was quite bald. Suddenly, as though struck by a whip, Mrs. Linpeck's face lit up behind her window. She reached somewhere and opened a bottle with an opener. Then she poured the soda into a glass, which she had behind the counter, and the bald man gave her a fiver, took the glass, stepped aside and drank. Mrs. Mooshaber followed him with her eyes, saw how he held the glass and drank, but then she turned and looked again at Mrs. Linpeck (106).
>
> In the meantime, the bald man had finished, threw the glass into the ash can and left. Mrs. Mooshaber looked at him and at the ash can and then she looked again at Mrs. Linpeck. She was as though changed (107).
>
> A customer appeared. It was an elderly woman in a flowered dress. "A lemon soda, please," the woman said and paid a fiver.
>
> Mrs. Mooshaber and the janitor's wife stepped aside a little and Mrs. Linpeck behind her window suddenly brightened and a smile appeared on her red lips. "A lemon soda," she smiled behind her window, reached somewhere and opened a bottle with an opener. She poured the soda into a glass, the woman in the flowered dress took the glass, stepped aside and drank. Mrs. Mooshaber followed her with her eyes, saw that she drank, and then turned again to Mrs. Linpeck.
>
> The flowered lady over there drank up and put her glass in the ash can and left (108-9).
>
> Again a customer appeared, a youngish man and woman, both in glasses and old beige clothes, and the man opened his mouth, raised two fingers, turned his hand around and raised it to his lips, with his head slightly bent. Mrs. Linpeck's face behind the window again began to shine and a smile

appeared on her lips. She took a bottle of soda, raised it and the man nodded. She opened two bottles, poured them into glasses, raked in the two fivers and the man and woman took the glasses, stepped back and drank. "They are deaf-mutes," Mrs. Linpeck said (112).

The man and woman in the eye glasses and the old beige clothes finished their drink, moved their fingers before their eyes and put the glasses into the ash can (113).

Then a customer approached the kiosk again, a well-dressed man with a little girl. "One beer, please, and a lemon soda," he said and laid two fivers on the counter. Mrs. Mooshaber and the janitor's wife again stepped aside a little, Mrs. Linpeck behind her window again had a shine on her face and a smile appeared on her lips. She reached somewhere, opened the beer with an opener, and then the soda, and poured them into glasses. The man and the little girl stepped back and Mrs. Mooshaber followed them with her eyes. She saw how they drank . . . (119).

The well-dressed man and the girl who stood aside drank up and put their glasses into the ash can and left . . . Mrs. Mooshaber looked at the ash can and the glasses in it. It was full of glasses, and then she looked after the man and the little girl . . . (117).

Finally, on the semantic level, there are the *epitheta constantia,* attached to the various protagonists of the novel. Thus Mrs. Mooshaber is always described in the same way as being dressed in a black jacket, a long shiny black skirt, and in shoes without heels, and with a black handbag which she shakes most every time she speaks.

On the level of the sentence, time is relativized by a constant repetition of the same sentences in different contexts.

Conclusions

Thus we see that in Fuks' world view which is both mythological and informed by modern art, a conventional plot is only weakly suggested and serves to emphasize the absurd, nonrational world in which time moves forward and backward, individuals merge into each other and into the outside world; the living and the dead merge, the dead interact with the living.

Fuks' debt thus is not only to the archetypal myths of world culture but to art, visual and verbal, of the twentieth century, which become elements in his system of resonances and refractions.

NOTES

1. I am indebted to Irene Portis Winner for anthropological insights which contributed to the mythological analysis in this paper.

2. All references to the novel will be to its only edition (Prague, Československý spisovatel, 1970). Citation will be by the page number only.

3. A criminal who is perceived by Natalia as looking like a black dog and who is always referred to by this epithet.
4. Reported discourse italicized.

REFERENCES CITED

Belyj, Andrej
1934

Masterstvo Gogolja. Moscow.

Campbell, Joseph
1959

The Masks of God. Primitive Mythology. New York.

Chvatík, K. and Z. Pešat, eds.
1967

Poetismus. Praha.

Grygar, Mojmír
1973

Kubizm i poèzija russkogo i češskogo avangarda. In Van der Eng and Grygar, eds., 1973: 59-101.

Holenstein, Elmar
1976

Roman Jakobson's Approach to Language: Phenomenological Structuralism. Bloomington.

Ivanov, V. V.
1971

Ob odnoj paralleli k gogolevskomu "Viju," Trudy po znakovym sistemam, V. Tartu: 133-142.

1973a

Kategorija vremeni v iskusstve i kul'ture XX veka. In Van der Eng and Grygar, eds. 1973: 103-150.

1973b

Kategorija "vidimogo" i "nevidimogo" v tekste: ešče raz o vostočnoslavjanskix fol'klornyx paralleljax k gogolevskomu "Viju." In Van der Eng and Grygar, eds., 1973: 151-176.

Ivanov, V. V. and V. N. Toporov
1976

The Invariant and Transformations in Folklore Texts. In L. Matejka, ed., Soviet Semiotics of Culture. Dispositio, Special Issue: 263-70.

Jakobson, Roman
1919

Futurism. Iskusstvo 7. August 2, 1919. Cited R. Jakobson 1973: 25-30.

1973

Questions de poétique. Paris.

Lévi-Strauss, C.
1963

Structural Anthropology. I. New York.

1966

The Savage Mind. Chicago.

Lotman, Jurij
1970

K probleme tipologii kul'tury. Trudy po znakovym sistemam III. Tartu: 30-38.

Mukařovský, Jan
1938

Sémantický rozbor básnického díla: Nezvalův Absolutní hrobář. Slovo a slovesnost IV. Cited from Mukařovský 1966: 272-85.

1940

O jazyce básnickém. Slovo a slovesnost VI. Cited from Mukařovský, Kapitoly z české poetiky I: 78-128.

1942

Detail jako základní sémantická jednotka v lidovém umění. Printed from ms. in Mukařovský 1966: 209-22.

1966

Studie z estetiky. Praha.

Opelík, J.
1964

O zdrojích a smyslu literatury. Hovoříme s Ladislavem Fuksem. Kulturní tvorba, II, 38: 6.

Van der Eng, Jan and M. Grygar, eds.
1973

Structure of Texts and Semiotics of Culture. Paris-The Hague.

Winner, T. G.
1970-72

Some Remarks on the Art of Ladislav Fuks. Ricerche Slavistiche. XVII-XIX: 587-99.

1973

Czech Avantgarde Prose of the Sixties. Mosaic VI/4 (The Eastern European Imagination in Literature): 107-19.

COPYRIGHTS

OTHER BOOKS FROM SLAVICA PUBLISHERS

American Contributions to the Eighth International Congress of Slavists, Zagreb and Ljubljana, Sept. 3–9, 1978. Vol. 1: Linguistics and Poetics, ed. by Henrik Birnbaum, 818 p., 1978; *Vol. 2: Literature,* ed. by Victor Terras, 799 p., 1978.

Henrik Birnbaum: *Common Slavic Progress and Problems in Its Reconstruction,* xii + 436 p., 1975.

Malcolm H. Brown, ed.: *Papers of the Yugoslav-American Seminar on Music,* 208 p., 1970.

Ellen B. Chances: *Conformity's Children: An Approach to the Superfluous Man in Russian Literature,* iv + 210 p., 1978.

Catherine V. Chvany: *On the Syntax of Be-Sentences in Russian,* viii + 311 p., 1975.

Frederick Columbus: *Introductory Workbook in Historical Phonology,* 39 p., 1974.

Dina B. Crockett: *Agreement in Contemporary Standard Russian,* iv + 456 p., 1976.

Paul Debreczeny and Thomas Eekman, eds.: *Chekhov's Art of Writing A Collection of Critical Essays,* 199 p., 1977.

Bruce L. Derwing and Tom M. S. Priestly: *Reading Rules for Russian A Systematic Approach to Russian Spelling and Pronunciation With Notes on Dialectical and Stylistic Variation,* vi + 247 p., 1980.

Ralph Carter Elwood, ed.: *Reconsiderations on the Russian Revolution,* x + 278 p., 1976.

Folia Slavica, a journal of Slavic and East European Linguistics. Vol. 1: 1977–78; Vol. 2: 1978; Vol. 3: 1979; Vol. 4: 1980.

Richard Freeborn & others, eds.: *Russian and Slavic Literature,* xii + 466 p., 1976.

Victor A. Friedman: *The Grammatical Categories of the Macedonian Indicative,* 210 p., 1977.

Charles E. Gribble, ed.: *Medieval Slavic Texts, Vol. 1, Old and Middle Russian Texts,* 320 p., 1973.

Charles E. Gribble, *Словарик русского языка 18-го века/A Short Dictionary of 18th-Century Russian,* 103 p., 1976.

Charles E. Gribble, ed.: *Studies Presented to Professor Roman Jakobson by His Students*, 333 p., 1968.

William S. Hamilton: *Introduction to Russian Phonology and Word Structure*, 187 p., 1980.

Pierre R. Hart: *G. R. Derzhavin: A Poet's Progress*, iv + 164 p., 1978.

Raina Katzarova-Kukudova & Kiril Djenev: *Bulgarian Folk Dances*, 174 p., 1976.

Andrej Kodjak: *Pushkin's I. P. Belkin*, 112 p., 1979.

Demetrius J. Koubourlis, ed.: *Topics in Slavic Phonology*, viii + 270 p., 1974.

Michael K. Launer: *Elementary Russian Syntax*, xi + 140 p., 1974.

Jules F. Levin & others: *Reading Modern Russian*, vi + 321 p., 1979.

Maurice I. Levin: *Russian Declension and Conjugation: a structural sketch with exercises*, x + 160 p., 1978.

Alexander Lipson: *A Russian Course*, xiv + 612 p., 1977.

Thomas F. Magner, ed.: *Slavic Linguistics and Language Teaching*, x + 309 p., 1976.

Mateja Matejic & Dragan Milivojevic: *An Anthology of Medieval Serbian Literature in English*, 205 p., 1978.

Alexander D. Nakhimovsky and Richard L. Leed: *Advanced Russian*, xvi + 380 p., 1980.

Kenneth E. Naylor, ed.: *Balkanistica: Occasional Papers in Southeast European Studies, I (1974)*, 189 p., 1975; *II (1975)*, 153 p., 1976; *III (1976)*, 154 p., 1978.

Felix J. Oinas, ed.: *Folklore Nationalism & Politics*, 190 p., 1977.

Hongor Oulanoff: *The Prose Fiction of Veniamin A. Kaverin*, v + 203 p., 1976.

Jan L. Perkowski: *Vampires of the Slavs* (a collection of readings), 294 p., 1976.

Lester A. Rice: *Hungarian Morphological Irregularities*, 80 p., 1970.

Midhat Ridjanovic: *A Synchronic Study of Verbal Aspect in English and Serbo-Croatian*, ix + 147 p., 1976.

David F. Robinson: *Lithuanian Reverse Dictionary*, ix + 209 p., 1976.

Don K. Rowney & G. Edward Orchard, eds.: *Russian and Slavic History*, viii + 311 p., 1977.

William R. Schmalstieg: *Introduction to Old Church Slavic*, 290 p., 1976.

Michael Shapiro: *Aspects of Russian Morphology, A Semiotic Investigation,* 62 p., 1969.

Rudolph M. Susel, ed.: *Papers in Slovene Studies, 1977,* 127 p., 1978.

Charles E. Townsend: *Russian Word-Formation, corrected reprint,* xviii + 272 p., 1975 (1980).

Charles E. Townsend: *The Memoirs of Princess Natal'ja Borisovna Dolgorukaja,* viii + 146 p., 1977.

Daniel C. Waugh: *The Great Turkes Defiance On the History of the Apocryphal Correspondence of the Ottoman Sultan in its Muscovite and Russian Variants,* ix + 354 p., 1978.

Susan Wobst: *Russian Readings & Grammar Terminology,* 88 p., 1978.

Dean S. Worth: *A Bibliography of Russian Word-Formation,* xliv + 317 p., 1977.